أَلَآ إِنَّ

أَوْلِيَآءَ ٱللَّهِ

لَا خَوْفٌ عَلَيْهِمْ وَلَا هُمْ يَحْزَنُونَ

اَلْمُؤْمِنُ اَلْمُهَيْمِنُ اَلْعَزِيْزُ اَلْجَبَّارُ اَلْمُتَكَبِّرُ

ب اَلرَّزَّاقُ اَلْفَتَّاحُ اَلْعَلِيْمُ اَلْقَابِضُ اَلْبَاسِطُ

حَكَمُ اَلْعَدْلُ اَللَّطِيْفُ اَلْخَبِيْرُ اَلْحَلِيْمُ اَلْعَظِيْمُ

اَلْحَفِيْظُ اَلْمُقِيْتُ اَلْحَسِيْبُ اَلْجَلِيْلُ

فَادْعُوْهُ بِهَا

الْحُسْنٰى جَلَّ جَلَالُهٗ

اِلٰهَ اِلَّا هُوَ

اَلْوَاسِعُ اَلْحَكِيْمُ اَلْوَدُوْدُ

اَلْحَقُّ اَلْوَكِيْلُ اَلْقَوِيُّ

اَلْمُحْصِيْ اَلْمُبْدِئُ اَلْمُعِيْدُ

اَلْوَاجِدُ اَلْمَاجِدُ اَلْوَاحِدُ اَلْاَحَدُ

اَلْاٰخِرُ اَلظَّاهِرُ اَلْبَاطِنُ اَلْوَالِيْ اَلْمُتَعَالِيْ اَلْبَرُّ

اَلْمُقْسِطُ اَلْجَامِعُ اَلْغَنِيُّ اَلْمُغْنِيْ اَلْمَانِعُ

اَلْبَاقِيْ اَلْوَارِثُ اَلرَّشِيْدُ اَلصَّبُوْرُ صَدَقَ اللّٰهُ الْعَظِيْمُ

اَلرَّحۡمٰنُ اَلرَّحِيۡمُ اَلۡمَلِكُ اَلۡقُدُّوۡسُ اَلسَّلَا

اَلۡخَالِقُ اَلۡبَارِئُ اَلۡمُصَوِّرُ اَلۡغَفَّارُ اَلۡقَهَّارُ اَلۡ

اَلۡخَافِضُ اَلرَّافِعُ اَلۡمُعِزُّ اَلۡمُذِلُّ اَلسَّمِيۡعُ اَلۡبَصِيۡ

اَلۡغَفُوۡرُ اَلشَّكُوۡرُ اَلۡعَلِيُّ اَلۡكَبِيۡرُ

وَلِلّٰهِ الۡاَسۡمَآءُ الۡحُسۡنٰ

اَلۡاَسۡمَآءُ

هُوَ اللّٰهُ اَلَّذِ

اَلۡكَرِيۡمُ اَلرَّقِيۡبُ اَلۡمُجِيۡبُ

اَلۡمَجِيۡدُ اَلۡبَاعِثُ اَلشَّهِيۡدُ

اَلۡمَتِيۡنُ اَلۡوَلِيُّ اَلۡحَمِيۡدُ

اَلۡمُحۡيِيۡ اَلۡمُمِيۡتُ اَلۡحَيُّ اَلۡقَيُّوۡمُ

اَلصَّمَدُ اَلۡقَادِرُ اَلۡمُقۡتَدِرُ اَلۡمُقَدِّمُ اَلۡمُؤَخِّرُ اَلۡاَوَّلُ

اَلتَّوَّابُ اَلۡمُنۡتَقِمُ اَلۡعَفُوُّ اَلرَّءُوۡفُ مَالِكُ الۡمُلۡكِ

اَلضَّآرُّ اَلنَّافِعُ اَلنُّوۡرُ اَلۡهَادِيۡ اَلۡبَدِ

بِسۡمِ ٱللَّهِ ٱلرَّحۡمَٰنِ ٱلرَّحِيمِ

بہجت اس سر کی ہے جو بہجۃ الاسرار میں ہے
کہ فلک وار مریدوں پہ ہے سایا تیرا

Grace is that secret which is in Bahjat al-Asrār
That your shade is as the sky is a canopy above your murīds.

[Aʿlā-Ḥaḍrat Imām Aḥmad Riḍā al-Qādirī Muḥaqqiq Bareillwī ﷺ]

Volume One

بهجة الأسرار ومعدن الأنوار

Sublime Secrets and Treasures of Lights

بسم الله الرحمن الرحيم

إِنَّ يَدِيْ عَلٰى مُرِيْدِيْ كَسَمَآءٍ عَلَى الْأَرْضِ

My hand is on my murīd like the sky above the earth.

[Sayyiduna Ghawth al-Aʿzam ﷺ]

وعبد القادر المشهور اسمي

وجدي صاحب العين الكمال

بسم الله الرحمن الرحيم

زينوا مجالسكم بذكر الله

Beautify your gatherings with the Remembrance of *Allāh* ﷻ

Bahjat al-Asrār is the most authentic and prolific biography of Sayyiduna Ghawth al-Aʿzam Shaykh ʿAbd al-Qādir al-Jilānī ﷺ
[470/1078 – 561/1166]

بهجة الاسرار ومعدن الانوار

Sublime Secrets and Treasures of Lights

by
ʿĀrif-Billāh Imām al-Awḥad Imām al-Ajal Muḥaddith al-Muqrī Shaykh ʿAlī b.Yūsuf b. Jarīr b. Faḍal b. Maʿḍād Abu al-Ḥasan Nūr al-Dīn al-Lakhmī al-Shatnūfī al-Shafāʿī
[713/1314]

English Translation, Notes & Reference by
Qādiri Faqīr Khādim al-Awliya wa al-Sāliḥīn
Shaykh Abu-Muḥammad ʿAbd al-Hādī
al-Qādirī Raḍawī Nūrī

Prepared by
Imām Aḥmad Raza Academy

Published by
SUFI PAGES
Knowledge is Light

Name of original book: Bahjat al-Asrār wa Maʿād al-Anwār
English Title: Sublime Secrets and Treasures of Lights
Author: ʿĀrif-Billāh Imām al-Awḥad Shaykh Nūr al-Dīn ʿAlī b. Yūsuf b. Jarīr al-Lakhmī al-Shatnūfī Shafāʿī رضي الله عنه
English Translation & Notes by: Shaykh Abu-Muḥammad ʿAbdul-Hadī al-Qādirī Raḍawī

First Edition: Ramaḍān al-Mubārak 1439 Hijri May 2018 2100 copies

Prepared in South Africa by
IMAM AHMED RAZA ACADEMY
incorporating
BARKAATUR-RAZA PUBLICATION
1st Floor, 92 Bertha Mkhize Street [Victoria Street]
Durban 4001 South Africa
Phone: +27 [31] 3016-786
Telefax: +27 [31] 3017-638
E-mail: info@raza.org.za
Website: www.raza.org.za

Printed by
Al-Baghdād Printers
Faisalabad, Pakistan
E-mail: ab_printers007@yahoo.com

Book design and Typography by Raza Graphics - SA
Cover Design by Raza Graphics - SA
Available online from: sufipages.com

ISBN NO: **978-0-620-73324-3**

Contents

Volume One

Transliteration Keys xxxi
Dedication xxxii
Acknowledgement xxxiii
Foreword xxxv
Answers to Objections on Bahjat al-Asrār and its noble author xxxvii
Poetical description of the stunning features and Ḥaḍrate Ghawth ﷺ Li
About the author and his book Lix
Some Important Family information of the Great Ghawth ﷺ
& His Notable Sons Lxxiii
Preface by the author, *Khutbah* 1
Narrations of the *Mashā'ikh* 5
Narration One 5
Narration Two 6
Narration Three 6
Narration Four: Concerning Shaykh Tāj al-Dīn Abul Wafa ﷺ 7
Narration Five 8
Narration Six 8
Narration Seven: Concerning Shaykh ʿAqīl al-Mambajī ﷺ 9
Narration Eight: Concerning Shaykh ʿAli b. Wahb ﷺ 10
Narration Nine: Concerning Shaykh Ḥammād b. Muslim al-Dabbās ﷺ 10
The *Mashā'ikh* who personally heard the words of Sayyiduna
Ghawth al-Aʿzam ﷺ 14
Those *Mashā'ikh* who heard the command of Sayyiduna
Ghawth al-Aʿzam ﷺ through *Kashf* 18
Sayyid Sharīf Shaykh Abu-Sāʿad al-Qaylawī ﷺ 18
Shaykh Baqa b. Bat'tū ﷺ 19
Shaykh ʿAdī b. Musāfir ﷺ and Shaykh Aḥmad b. Rifāʿī ﷺ 20
Shaykh Mājid Kurdī ﷺ and Shaykh Mutir ﷺ 20
Shaykh Makārim ﷺ 21
Shaykh Khalīfa Akbar ﷺ 23
Shaykh Lulu Armīnī ﷺ 24
Names of *Mashā'ikh* who testified that Sayyiduna Ghawth al-Aʿzam ﷺ
made this declaration by the command of *Allāh* ﷻ 27
Shaykh ʿAdī b. Musāfir ﷺ 27

Shaykh Sharīf Abu-Saʿīd al-Qaylawī 27
Shaykh ʿAlī b. al-Hītī 28
Shaykh Aḥmad al-Rifāʿī 28
Shaykh Ḥayāt b. Qays al-Ḥarrānī 29
Those *Mashā'ikh* who bent their heads on the command of the Ghawth 30
Shaykh Baqa b. Bat'tū 30
Sayyid Sharīf Abu-Saʿīd al-Qaylawī 31
Shaykh Sayyidī ʿAlī b. al-Hītī 31
Shaykh Sayyid Aḥmad al-Rifāʿī 32
Shaykh ʿAbd al-Raḥmān al-Tafsunjī 33
Shaykh Abu-Najīb ʿAbd al-Qāhir al-Sohrowardī 34
Shaykh Mūsā al-Zūlī 34
Shaykh Muḥammad Mūsā b. ʿAbdullāh al-Basrī 35
Shaykh Ḥayāt b. Qays al-Ḥarrānī 35
Shaykh Abu ʿAmar ʿUthmān b. Marzūq and Shaykh Abu al-Karam 36
Shaykh Mājid al-Kurdī 37
Shaykh Suwayd al-Sanjārī 37
Shaykh Raslān al-Damishqī 38
Shaykh Sayyidī Shoʿaib Abu-Madyan al-Maghribī 39
Shaykh Sharīf ʿAbd al-Raḥīm al-Qanāwī 39
Shaykh ʿAmar ʿUthmān b. Marzūq al-Bathḥāiḥī 40
Shaykh Makārim Nahar Malikī 41
Shaykh Khalīfah al-Nahr Malikī 41
Shaykh ʿAdī b. Musāfir al-Amawī 42
Concerning the reverence of the great Ghawth 45
Sayyiduna Shaykh ʿAbd al-Qādir al-Jilānī attributes all favours and blessing to *Allāh* 49
Concerning the youth of Sayyiduna Ghawth al-Aʿzam 53
The attendance of the months in the presence of the Ghawth 56
Sayyiduna Ghawth al-Aʿzam deliberating with predestination 59
Glad-tidings for those who saw Sayyiduna Shaykh ʿAbd al-Qādir 60
Shaykh Maʿrūf Karkhī replies from his grave 60
The entire era has been entrusted to Sayyiduna Ghawth al-Aʿzam 61
Using the *wasīlah* of Sayyiduna Ghawth al-Aʿzam to seek desires from *Allāh* 61

The reins of the era were entrusted to Sayyiduna Ghawth al-Aʿzam 63
The words of Sayyiduna Ghawth decorated with amazing conditions 64
Seventy doors of ʿIlme-Ladunni opens for Ḥaḍrat Ghawth al-Aʿzam 65
The sequence of priceless gems 66
The Beloved Prophet and Sayyiduna ʿAlī place their sacred Saliva in the sacrosanct mouth of the Great Ghawth 67
Shaykh ʿAlī b. al-Hītī dreams of the Holy Prophet 68
Discussion on Sayyiduna Nabī Ādam 69
Shaykh ʿAbd al-Raḥmān al-Tafsunjī claims superiority 72
Discussing Sayyiduna Nabī Mūsā 74
A trader is saved from a murderer 78
The majesty of Sayyiduna Rasūlullāh 80
The status of Sayyiduna Rasūlullāh above other Prophets 81
Ḥaḍrat Ghawth fulfils the requests of people 84
Sayyiduna Ghawth erased *ʿIlm al-Kalām* from the heart of Shaykh Shahāb al-Dīn al-Sohrowardī 90
A discourse with reference to Sayyiduna Nabī Ibrāhīm 91
Eternal love manifested in the existence of Sayyiduna Nabī Ibrāhīm 94
Rule over water 97
The creation of Sayyiduna Nabī Ādam 98
Discussing Sayyiduna Nabī Mūsā 100
Meʿrāj al-Nabī 102
Allāh focuses special favours on His *Awliya* 110
Nubuwwah and *Wilāyah* [Prophethood and Sainthood] 113
The definition of *karāmat* 114
Intellect, *Sharaḥ* and Prophethood 119
Intellect 119
Prophethood [*Nubuwwah*] 120
Waḥī – Revelation 120
Alcohol becomes vinegar 122
The verses of acquittal of Sayyidah ʿĀ'īeshah Siddiqah 122
Maʿārifah and inebriation 125
Wisāl – Divine Communion 128
Take what you desire 130
Firāq – separation or absence of the Beloved 131
The dried date tree comes to life 133

The Secrets of the Divine Names of Allāh ﷻ	134
Principals of the stations of the *ʿĀrifīn*	138
The book of philosophy changes to the excellence of the Holy *Qur'ān*	145
A person's foolish claim that he is greater than Nabī Yūnus ﷺ and the anger of the Ghawth ﷺ	147
Concerning the *dhikr* of *Allāh* ﷻ	147
Obedience to the sacred *Sharīʿah* affords the favours of both worlds	147
The Love of *Allāh* ﷻ	151
Disobedience of a servant and its consciences	154
Regarding *Tanziyah* – purity and all praises are for Almighty *Allāh* ﷻ	155
Amazing incident of a trader	160
Comments of Ḥaḍrat Ghawth al-Aʿzam ﷺ concerning Shaykh Mansūr al-Ḥallāj ﷺ	162
The Holy *Kāʿabah* in front of his eyes	163
The hand of Shaykh Ḥammād ﷺ is rectified	165
Advices for the *Faqīr* [spiritual pauper]	168
The reason of being named Muḥiyy al-Dīn	169
The reasons of gaining the closeness of *Allāh* ﷻ	170
Adhān called at mid-night	171
Abstain from this *duniya* and focus to the *Ākhirah*	172
The first *Ḥajj* of Sayyiduna Ghawth al-Aʿzam ﷺ	173
Advices of the Ghawth ﷺ on *zuhd* [Asceticism]	175
The saliva of Shaykh Aḥmad ﷺ stops by the command of Sayyiduna Ghawth ﷺ	178
Ḥaḍrate Ghawth ﷺ comments about *kashf* [spiritual unveiling]	179
Creation of the sky and earth	183
The night is a garden of the *ʿĀrifīn*	189
The intense devotions of Sayyiduna Ghawth al-Aʿzam ﷺ	186
Advices of Sayyiduna Ghawth ﷺ for the *ʿĀrifīn*	189
Blood flows from the bags	192
The mysterious apple	192
The *murīd* [disciple] and *murād* [desired]	193
Excessive performance of *nafil* takes one close to *Allāh* ﷻ	195
The difference between *murīd* and *murād*	196
Sayyiduna Ghawth al-Aʿzam ﷺ cured the blind and raised the dead	197

To function in the graves like the living	199
The *Mutasawwif* and the *Sũfi*	200
Reason for the name *Sufi*	201
The difference between *Wilãyah* and *Nubuwwah*	205
The cooked chicken becomes alive	206
The dead vulture is resurrected	207
The signs of *taqwa* [piety]	208
Method of acquiring piety	209
The excellence of Sayyiduna Ghawth al-Aʿzam	210
What is piety and religiousness [*waraʿh*]	211
Sayyiduna Ghawth al-Aʿzam offers Assistance to a distant place	213
Concerning the dangers of the heart	214
The devil is a liar	219
Allãh is the Manifestor of wonders	219
The Commands of Sultãn al-Awliya Sayyiduna Ghawth al-Aʿzam regarding the ʿÃrifin	222
The appointment of an *Abdãl*	224
Incident of a girl kidnapped by the Jinn	228
Cured from epilepsy	230
The Status of Sayyiduna Rasũlullãh	230
Wilãyah and *Nubuwwah*	231
The *Walĩ* who flies in the air	232
The greetings of the *Rijãl al-Ghayb* in court of the great Ghawth	232
The roof collapses	233
The comments of Sayyiduna Ghawth about Shaykh Mansũr al-Ḥallãj	233
It happened as the great Ghawth predicted	234
The three conditions of the path of *sulũk*	236
The treasurer of destiny	238
O Israelite, listen to Muḥammadĩ words	239
The creation of the human being	229
Sultãn *ʿAql* and Sultãn *Hawa* [ego]	240
Obedience to the intellect	240
No rain on the *majlis*, but rain elsewhere	241
The power of the *ʿAsã* [staff] of the Ghawth	242
The rain stopped	242

The rain clouds moved away from the *majlis* of Sayyiduna Ghawth ﷺ	243
Truth and cleanliness	243
Descent of misfortune due to the anger of the Ghawth ﷺ	245
The hearts of the people are in my hands	246
The reality of *fana* [extinction]	246
A brilliant light	249
A tranquil discourse	250
The *Ḥanafī Walī*	252
Regal glory and excellence	253
The miracle of the hand of Sayyiduna Ghawth ﷺ	254
Deliverance from sickness	255
The speed of a weak camel	255
The dove recites the *tasbīḥ* of *Allāh* ﷻ and the powerful *Kashf* of Sayyiduna Ghawth ﷺ	256
The stations of *Ma ̔ārifah*	257
The meaning of *Qutb*	263
Instructions of Sayyiduna Ghawth al-Aʿzam ﷺ	269
Stripped of status and spiritual conditions	270
Allāh ﷻ is pleased with Shaykh Abu-Bakr al-Ḥamāmī ﷺ	271
The method of Sayyiduna Ghawth al-Aʿzam's ﷺ *dhikr*	275
For forty years he performed *fajr salāh* with his *'Esha wuḍū*	277
Spiritual seclusion	278
Twenty five years in the jungles	279
His condition of *mujāhidah*	280
People regarded Sayyiduna Ghawth ﷺ as insane	280
Challenging the cursed devil	281
Being informed of the hidden things	282
Triumph over conditions	283
I am a beggar of my lord ﷻ	284
The speech of a bull and blessings of truth	285
The snake spoke to Ḥaḍrate Ghawth ﷺ	286
Sayyiduna Ghawth ﷺ was steadfast both, externally and internally	287
He is one who will die	288
The Ghawth ﷺ would sweat in extreme winter	289
Life and death	289
The progeny and attributes of Sayyiduna Ghawth al-Aʿzam ﷺ	290

Some information about his grandfather, Sayyiduna ʿAbdullāh Somaʿī رضی اللہ عنہ 291
His pious mother 293
It rained by the *duʿā* of his pious aunt 294
Physical description of Sayyiduna Ghawth al-Aʿzam رضی اللہ عنہ 296
The discourses of Sayyiduna Ghawth al-Aʿzam رضی اللہ عنہ 296
The secret of the heart is exposed 300
Removal of darkness with a single flame 301
Advice to those who came to repent and become *murīds* 302
Mischief upon mischief 302
Seventy thousand people in the *majlis* of the Ghawth رضی اللہ عنہ 303
His valuable advices 303
The *khutbah* of his *majlis* and discourse 304
The address of Sayyiduna Ghawth رضی اللہ عنہ to those with imperfect *Imān* and *Taubah* 305
The rain of mercy on the *majlis* of the Ghawth رضی اللہ عنہ 306
The *duʿā* of the Ghawth رضی اللہ عنہ in his *majlis* 306
The *majālis* of Sayyiduna Ghawth al-Aʿzam رضی اللہ عنہ 308
The *Jinns* listened to his discourses 308
Garbs of honour descends in the *majlis* of the Ghawth رضی اللہ عنہ 308
The opening of the knots 309
Spiritual rapture [*ḥaal*] in his *majlis* 310
The audience heard him equally from near and far 310
Being aware of the condition of the hearts 311
Everyone used be present in the *Majlis* of the Ghawth رضی اللہ عنہ 311
The garbs burn 313
Order to be obedient 314
The presence of angels and prophets علیہم السلام in the *majlis* 315
Four hundred *ʿUlama* record the lectures of the Ghawth رضی اللہ عنہ 315
The Ghawth رضی اللہ عنہ would weep when listening to the Holy *Qurʾān* 316
The door of *Jannah* opens 316
One hundred thousand sinners and vagabonds repent 317
The *rafḍī* [*shiʿā*] repent 317
The monk of Yemen embraces *Islām* 317
A voice from the unseen 318
Pandemonium in the *majlis* 318
The state of engrossment [*istghrāq*] on his seat 319

The *'Ulama* and *Mashā'ikh* attended the *majlis*	320
Green birds in the lecture	321
A bird falls in pieces	321
The audience began screaming	322
The manifestation of lordly lustres	323
An iron spike sinks in the foot	324
Answer to his sneeze	325
The awe of the great Ghawth ﷺ	326
The excellence of his companions and their glad-tidings	327
Jannah for up till seven generations	329
Concealing the faults of the *murīd*	330
Representation in the Divine Court of *Allāh* ﷻ	330
The blessings of his *du'ā* and garb	331
Contact with the Ghawth ﷺ is a reason for salvation	332
Diving in the Ocean of Mercy	332
Love and affiliation to the Ghawth ﷺ is a Reason for forgiveness	333
Taking a bath seventy times	334
The promise of my Lord ﷻ	334
The status of those attributed to the Ghawth ﷺ	335
Punishment reduced due to the Ghawth ﷺ	335
Every world has a powerful representative of the great Ghawth ﷺ	336
Ḥaḍarte Ghawth ﷺ has the most companions and *murīds*	337
A sacred light	339
I am a guarantee for all my *murīds* till *Qiyāmah*	339
Sayyiduna Ghawth al-A'zam ﷺ assists all who call on him	340
Salāt al-Ghawthiyah	341
Method of performance	341
His excellent conduct	343
Sand falls from the ceiling	343
A bird dies and falls to the ground	344
Ya Allāh ﷻ everything belongs to You	344
A pauper becomes wealthy	345
All the gold pieces were distributed to seventy *Awliya-Allāh*	345
Serving the *Foqaha* and guests	346
He took off his *qamīs* and gave it to a *faqīr*	347
Great restlessness in the audience	348

His stunning qualities	349
Names of some of his *Mashã'ikh*	352
Sayyiduna Ghawth ﷺ studied under these illustrious *'Ulama*	353
Acquiring *'Ilm al-Tarĩqah*	355
Taking his seat on the Station of *Qutbiyat*	356
Forty meanings of one verse of the *Qur'ãn*	394
The Ghawth ﷺ spoke in 13 sciences	395
He issued *Fatwa* in accordance to the *Shafa'ĩ* and *Ḥanbalĩ* Schools	395
An amazing question and answer	397
The Ghawth ﷺ visits the grave of Imãm Aḥmad b. Ḥanbal ﷺ, he meets and speaks to him	397
Sayyiduna Ghawth al-A'zam ﷺ and the *Awliya-Allãh*	398
Steadfast on the Science of esoteric Spiritual Reality	398
Seeing the Divine Light of Beauty	399
O cursed! Go away	400
The Difference between the presence of the Divine Being and presence of Divine Attributes	401
The meaning of Love	403
The meaning of *Tawḥĩd*	405
The meaning of *Tajrĩd*	406
The meaning of *Ma'ãrifah*	407
The difference between the statements of Shaykh Manthũr al-Ḥallãj ﷺ and Shaykh Abu-Yazĩd Bustãmĩ ﷺ	407
The meaning of *Himmah* [High Spirits]	410
The meaning of *Haqĩqah* [Reality]	410
The meaning of *Dhikr*	410
The meaning of *Shouq* [zeal]	411
The meaning of *Tawakkul* [reliance]	411
The meaning of *Inãbat* [repentance]	412
The difference between the '*Ana*' of Shaykh Manthũr ﷺ and the cursed devil	412
The meaning of *Taubah*	413
The meaning of *Ikhlãs* [sincerity in faith]	413
Weeping	413
Duniya [this mundane world]	414
The meaning of *Tasawwuf*	414

Ta'azzaz and *Takabbur* [Reinforcement and Pride] 414
The meaning of *Shukar* [Thankfulness] 414
The Meaning of *Sabar* [patience] 417
The meaning of *Fana* [annihilation] 417
The meaning of *Baqa* [permanence] 418
The meaning of *Wafa* [fidelity] 418
The meaning of *Riḍã* [pleasure] 418
The meaning of *Irãdah* [will - intention] 419
The meaning of *'Inãyah* [favour] 419
The meaning of *Wajd* [spiritual ecstasy] 420
The meaning of *Khawf* [fear] 420
The meaning of *Raja* [hope] 420
'Ilm al-Yaqĩn [knowledge of certainty] 421
The meaning of *Muwãfiqat* [conformity] 422
Du'ã [supplication] 422
Ḥaya [modesty] 423
Mushãhidah [observance] 423
Qurb [Divine Proximity] 424
Sukar [inebriation] 424
Chains of narrations concerning *dhikr* 426
The excellence of *sawm* [Fasts] 428
The status of the *Saḥãbah* 429
To sit on burning fire 430
The fasts of the beloved Prophet ﷺ in *Ramaḍãn* 431
Shaking hands with the Angels and the structure of *Jannah* 432
The day of *'Eid* 434
The miracle of the splitting of the moon 435
The recompense of good deeds 437
The vision of *Allãh* ﷻ in *Jannah* 438
When will *Qiyãmah* come? 442
The fresh dates - and fall into the well and come out 443

End of Vol One

Volume Two

The *Mashā'ikh* who honour and praise Sayyiduna Ghawth ﷺ 1
The disposition and events of Shaykh Abu-Bakr b. Hawār al-Batā'īḥī ﷺ 3
The exclusivity of his *Mazār al-Sharīf* 4
The sayings of Shaykh Abu-Bakr al-Hawārī ﷺ 5
Tawḥīd [monotheism] 5
Tasawwuf [spiritual culture] 5
Zuhd [asceticism] 5
Khouf [fear] 6
Khushū' [submissiveness] 6
Tawāḍa'h [humility] 6
Nafs Ammāra bis soo 6
The incident of Shaykh Abu-Bakr's ﷺ *taubah* 7
The *karāmat* of Shaykh Abu-Bakr al-Hawārī ﷺ 9
Lions assembled around him 9
Raising the dead 10
Supplications for *barakah* 11
Earthquakes stopped 12
Fragrance at time of his demise 13
The *Awtād* of Irāq 13
The disposition and events of Shaykh Abu-Muḥammad al-Shabnakī ﷺ 15
The anecdotes of Shaykh Shabnakī ﷺ 17
The *taubah* of Shaykh Abu-Muḥammad al-Shabnakī ﷺ 19
The *Karamat* of Shaykh al-Shabnakī ﷺ – the dead became alive 20
Alcohol becomes water 21
The goat becomes alive 21
Shaykh 'Azāz ﷺ loses consciousness 21
Greetings of the angels 22
The house collapses 23
Removal of poverty 23
The sacred *ziyarah* of Sayyiduna Rasūlullāh ﷺ 24
The prediction of the coming of Sayyiduna Ghawth al-A'zam ﷺ 25
The disposition and events of Shaykh 'Azāz b. Mustauda'āh al-Batā'ihī ﷺ 27
The anecdotes of Shaykh 'Azāz ﷺ 27
Types of unconsciousness 29
The gentle heart 30

Intension [*irādah*]	30
Tasawwuf	30
Wajd [spiritual rapture]	30
Perfect knowledge	31
The charismatic talents of Shaykh ʿAzāz ﷺ	31
The love of wild animals and Jinns	32
His love for *Allāh* ﷻ	32
The stones addressed the Shaykh ﷺ	32
The lion falls dead	32
An astonishing *karāmat*	33
Stones turned to dust in his hands	34
Forty days in deep spiritual engrossment	34
The prediction of the arrival of Sayyiduna Ghawth al-Aʿzam ﷺ	35
The disposition and events of Shaykh Mansūr al-Batā'ihī ﷺ	37
The anecdotes of Shaykh Mansūr ﷺ	39
The characteristics of the *Awliya*	39
An amazing *karāmat* of Shaykh Mansūr ﷺ	41
The injured arm was cured	42
Kashf of the elevated angelic realm	42
Punishment changes to mercy	43
What is love	43
Examples of love	44
The Date reads the Tasbiḥ of Allāh ﷻ	44
The Status of Sayyiduna Ghawth al-Aʿzam ؓ	45
The disposition and events of Tāj al-ʿĀrifīn Abul-Wafa ؓ	47
How to recognize a true Shaykh	48
The anecdotes of Shaykh Abu al-Wafī ﷺ	48
Dhikr	48
The *karāmat* of Shaykh Abu al-Wafī ﷺ to see *Hāwiyah*	49
Every part of the body in *dhikr*	50
His excellent demise	50
Reason for the name Abu al-Wafā	51
The dignified status of Sayyiduna Ghawth al-Aʿzam ﷺ	51
The beads of the *tasbīḥ* would spin	52
The hand would tremble holding the bowl	53
The status of Sayyiduna Shaykh ʿAbd al-Qādir al-Jilānī ؓ	53

The disposition and events of Shaykh Ḥammād b. Muslim al-Dabbās ﷺ	55
The anecdotes of Shaykh Ḥammād ﷺ	56
The *karamāt* of Shaykh Ḥammād ﷺ	57
The spread of leprosy on the body	57
The blessings of his vision	59
The horse flies away with the minister	60
The *Mazār al-Sharīf* of Shaykh Ḥammād ﷺ	61
The two signs of *wilāyah*	61
Sayyid al-ʿĀrifīn Ghawth al-Aʿzam ﷺ	61
The disposition and events of Shaykh Abu-Yaʿqūb Yūsuf b. Ayyūb al-Hamdānī ﷺ	63
The reality of *simāʿ* and the teachings of Shaykh Abu-Yaʿqūb ﷺ	64
The *Sūfīs* of the sky	64
The miracles of Shaykh Abu-Yaʿqūb ﷺ	65
The death of an insolent	65
Freeing a captured youth from Istanbul	65
All difficulties solved	66
The disposition and events of Shaykh ʿAqīl al-Mambajī ﷺ	67
To fly in the air	67
The excellence of four *Mashā'ikh*	68
The anecdotes of Shaykh ʿAqīl ﷺ	68
The status of Shaykh ʿAqīl al-Mambajī ﷺ	69
A miracle of Shaykh ʿAqīl ﷺ	70
The sign of a faithful and the shaking of the mountain	70
Assembly of wild beasts	71
A fountain began flowing	71
Who is *Bāz al-Ash'hab*?	71
The disposition and events of Shaykh Abu-Yaʿzī al-Maghribī ﷺ	73
The anecdotes of Shaykh al-Maghribī ﷺ	74
The miracles of Shaykh al-Maghribī ﷺ	74
Control over wild beasts	74
The complains of wild animals and birds	76
The land would bloom	76
Prostrating while raining	77
His Excellence over the people of the east and west	77
The disposition and events of Shaykh ʿAdī b. Musāfir al-Amawī ﷺ	79

The anecdotes of Shaykh ʿAdī	80
The *Shaykh* and *Murīd*	81
Excellent conduct	81
Abstention from the transgressors [*bidʿatī*]	82
The miracles of Shaykh ʿAdī	83
A fountain springs up	83
Memorizing the holy *Qur'ān* in a second	85
Reach *Baḥar al-Muḥīt* in a split of a second	86
Observing the deeds of creation	86
The sound of the rooster	87
An amazing mirror	87
The *Khalīfa* invites the *Mashā'ikh* and *ʿUlama* of Irāq	88
The walls and pathways became lit up	89
To leave the ocean and come to a stream	90
The disposition and events of Shaykh ʿAlī b. al-Hītī	91
The state of four *Mashā'ikh*	91
Curing the deaf	92
The disappearance of the *khirqah* [*Sūfī* Garb]	92
The status of Shaykh ʿAlī b. al-Hītī	92
Gifts in every city	93
The anecdotes of Shaykh ʿAlī	94
Sharīʿāh and *Ḥaqīqah*	94
Miracles of Shaykh ʿAlī b. al-Hītī	96
A black ant in a dark night	96
Gold beads from the stomach of a hen	97
The murdered person becomes alive	97
Knowledge returns back to the chest	98
The date trees bends	98
Gold, fruits and water from a well	99
Acquiring ripe dates	99
The Shaykh of Irāq	101
Sayyiduna Khiḍar brings a message	101
I am a Muḥammadī	102
The army returned walking backwards	103
The disposition and events of Shaykh ʿAbd al-Raḥmān al-Tafsunjī	105
The anecdotes of Shaykh ʿAbd al-Raḥmān	106

Murāqabah 106
Audition 108
The *karamāt* of Shaykh ʿAbd al-Raḥmān 108
The excellence of his hands 108
His spiritual authority 109
Barkat in Dates by his Duʿā 109
The speaker becomes dumb 110
His vision from the earth to the *ʿArsh* 110
Things of the unseen [*ghayb*] 110
The winds glorified *Allāh* 111
The glorification of the mountains 112
His respect for Sayyiduna Ghawth al-Aʿzam 112
His Advice to his Son before his Demise 113
The sound of a Lion 113
The anecdotes of Shaykh Baqa b. Bat'tū 115
What is Faqr? 116
Who is a sincere *faqīr* 117
The *karamāt* of Shaykh Baqa b. Bat'tū 118
The impact of his *haybah* [awe] 118
That which had passed does not return 119
The Jurists [*Foqaha*] seek forgiveness 119
The raging fire extinguished 120
The clouds nourished the ground 120
The army repents from futile play and rebellion 120
The awe of Sayyiduna Ghawth al-Aʿzam 121
Kissing the threshold [*chokat*] 122
The disposition and events of Shaykh Abu-Saʿīd al-Qaylawī 123
The miracles of Shaykh Abu-Saʿīd 124
The meaning of *Tasawwuf* 124
Tawḥīd 125
The Signs of the Truthful and Untruthful 125
He cured the sick and made the healthy sick 126
The Rock split into pieces 127

A sour pomegranate becomes sweet 127
Another miracle 128

Two apples sufficient for travel 128
The visitation of Sayyiduna Khiḍar ﷺ 128
The status of Sayyiduna Ghawth al-Aʿzam ﷺ in the sight of the *Mashā'ikh* 129
The disposition and events of Shaykh Mutir al-Bāzrānī ﷺ 133
The anecdotes of Shaykh Mutir ﷺ 134
The *karamāt* of Shaykh Mutir ﷺ 137
Riding on a spider 137
The power of the vision of a *Walī* 137
Barkat in the harvest 138
The milk increased 138
The appearance of lustres 138
Compliance and obedience to Sayyiduna Ghawth al-Aʿzam ﷺ 139
The King of the *Awliya* 140
The disposition and events of Shaykh Mājid al-Kurdī ﷺ 143
The anecdotes of Shaykh Mājid ﷺ 144
Splendid disposition 145
The miracles of Shaykh Mājid ﷺ 146
Different things in one boat 146
Containers filled with food 147
Grapes, apples and pomegranate growing on one tree 148
The Imām of the dwellers on the earth 149
The disposition and events of Shaykh Jagīr ﷺ 151
The anecdotes of Shaykh Jagīr ﷺ 152
The miracles of Shaykh Jagīr ﷺ 154
Whatever he said happened 154
He saved the boat from drowning 155
The status of Sayyiduna Ghawth al-Aʿzam ﷺ 157
The disposition and events of Shaykh 159
Abu-Muḥammad Qāsim b. ʿAbd al-Basrī ﷺ 159
The anecdotes of Shaykh Abu-Muḥammad Qāsim ﷺ 160
The miracles of Shaykh Abu-Muḥammad Qāsim ﷺ 163
To be aware of the intentions of the heart 163
Figs and sand becomes a sweet dish [*Ḥalwa*] 164
An amazing journey 165
A group of Jews and Christians see the *janāza* of the Shaykh

and embrace *Islām* 168
Sayyiduna Khiḍar ﷺ is alive and Sayyiduna ʿAbd al-Qādir Al-Jilānī ؓ is *Qutb al-Awliya* 169
The disposition and events of Shaykh Abu-ʿAmar ʿUthmān b. Marzūq al-Qurashī ؓ 173
The anecdotes of Shaykh ʿAmar ʿUthmān ؓ 174
The miracles of Shaykh Abu-ʿAmar ؓ 177
The ground folded 177
The Sultān of the jungle 178
Sattu and water came out of the sand 180
A Persian learns Arabic and an Arab learns Persian in one night 180
The friend of *Allāh* ﷻ 181
Sayyiduna Ghawth al-Aʿzam ؓ is the master of all *Awliya* 184
The disposition and events of Shaykh Suwayd al-Sanjārī ؓ 187
The principles of the *ʿĀrifīn* [Gnostics] 188
The types of eyes 189
The miracles of Shaykh Suwayd ؓ 192
Slandering the predecessor *Sāliḥīn* 193
The punishment of slander 193
Become blind and then to be cured 194
Miraculous healing of a cut nose 195
The leper gets cured 195
Water and *sattū* comes out of a rock 196
The body becomes like a block of ice 196
The Mujāhidah of the Nafs 196
The pain Disappeared 197
The *Qāḍī* and audience checked with fever 197
Sayyiduna Ghawth al-Aʿzam ؓ is the chief of the *ʿĀrifīn* of the Glorious Chamber 198
The disposition and events of Shaykh Ḥayāt b. Qays al-Ḥarrānī ؓ 199
The anecdotes of Shaykh Ḥayāt ؓ 201
Ḥalāl sustenance 201
Ghaflat [negligence] 201
The Performance of the *sunnah* and *farḍ* 202
Love 203
The miracles of Shaykh Ḥayāt ؓ 204

The *Ka'ābah* appears in front of him 205
The wooden boat broke 205
Dates from a acacia tree 207
A house of hairs 208
Sayyiduna Ghawth al-A'zam ﷺ is *Sultān al-'Ārifīn* 210
Sayyiduna Ghawth al-A'zam ﷺ is *Sayyid al-Awliya* 210
Disposition and events of Shaykh Raslān al-Damishqī ﷺ 211
The anecdotes of Shaykh Raslān ﷺ 212
The union of the *'Ārif* 212
Sadness 214
The miracles of Shaykh Raslān ﷺ 214
Blessings in the bread 215
A lion rolls on his feet 216
Throwing pebbles 217
Listening to *Simā'* 217
The integrity of his *Janaza* 218
Sayyiduna Ghawth al-A'zam ﷺ is the deputy of the Holy Prophet ﷺ 219
The disposition and events of Shaykh Abu-Madyan Shu'āib al-Maghribī ﷺ 221
The anecdotes of Shaykh Abu-Madyan ﷺ 221
Communion 223
Honour 223
Faqīr 223
The heart 224
Mushāhidah and *faqar* 224
Ikhlās 224
The miracles of Shaykh Abu-Madyan ﷺ 226
Attendance in the Divine Court of *Allāh* ﷻ 226
Shaykh Abu-Madyan ﷺ fights off the swine and drives them off 227
An amazing incident with the lion 228
The Boat stopped 229
Grapes out of Season 229
The Fish returned the Ring 230

The container falls from the hand 230
The Tree lights up 231

How should a discourse be	231
The bird dies	232
An *Abdāl* and an *ʿĀrif*	233
The status of *Maʿārifah* and *Tawḥīd*	234
The deceit of the devil	235
An ocean of light	236
Achievement of *Maʿārif*	237
Sayyiduna Ghawth al-Aʿzam is the proof of the *ʿĀrifīn*	242
The disposition and events of Shaykh Abu-Muḥammad ʿAbd al-Raḥīm al-Maghribī	243
The Anecdotes of Shaykh Abu-Muḥammad	244
Tajrīd	245
Riḍā – Raza	245
Tamkīn	245
Hunger	246
Asrār – secrets	247
Taqwa – piety	247
Kashf – unveiling	248
Dhikr	249
The miracles of Abu-Muḥammad Shaykh ʿAbd al-Raḥīm	249
His access to the *Louḥe-Maḥfūz*	251
Blessings in his *wuḍū* water	252
The low water level of River Nile	252
Abundance in the wheat harvest	253
Light [*nūr*] appeared from his grave	254
The *Awtād* of existence is Sayyiduna Ghawth al-Aʿzam	255
The disposition and events of Shaykh Abu-ʿAmar ʿUthmān al-Batāʾiḥī	257
Anecdotes of Shaykh Abu-ʿAmar	258
Love is an ocean	258
The *mujāhidah* of Shaykh al-Batāʾiḥī	259
The miracles of Shaykh al-Batāʾiḥī	261
Sitting in the company of lions	261
He raised the dead animals	262
The incident of the leper and blind man	263
The best Ghawth of the people of the earth	264
The disposition and events of Shaykh Qaḍīb al-Baan al-Mosulī	265

The anecdotes of Shaykh Qaḍīb al-Baan ﷺ	266
The miracles of Shaykh Qaḍīb al-Baan ﷺ	267
Abstain from exposing secrets	268
Changes in the image of Shaykh Qaḍīb al-Baan ﷺ	270
His state of absorption [*Istighrãq*]	270
He breaks his *salãh*	271
Cover great distances in few moments	271
Unconsciousness	272
Sajdah at the door of the *Ka ʿãbah*	273
Sayyiduna Ghawth al-Aʿzam ﷺ is the leader of the caravan of the lovers	273
The disposition and events of Shaykh Makãrim al-Nahar Khãlisī ﷺ	275
The anecdotes and Shaykh Makãrim ﷺ	277
Understanding grief	277
Wilãyah – sainthood	277
Wasal – union	277
Qurb – Divine Proximity	277
Faqar – spiritual poverty	277
Zãhid – ascetic	278
Taqwa – piety	278
Mujãhidah – spiritual struggle	278
Mukhlis – sincere devotee	279
Shãkir – thankful	279
Mutawakkil – one who relies on *Allãh* ﷻ	279
Ãshiq – lover	280
The miracles of Shaykh Makãrim ﷺ	281
The rejecter of Hell is shown the condition of Hell	281
The condition of five guests	283
The eyes have not seen anyone like him	285
The disposition and events of Shaykh Khalīfa b. Mũsã Nahar Malikī ﷺ	287
Anecdotes of Shaykh Khalīfa ﷺ	288
The miraculous mantle	291
Making *ziyãrah* seventy times of the beloved Prophet of *Allãh* ﷺ in one Night	292
Seeing the caravan en route to *Ḥijãz*	292
Desire fulfilled	294
Ziyãrah of the Beloved Prophet ﷺ at the time of demise	295

Flying in the air 296
The blessings of Sayyiduna Ghawth al-Aʿzam ﷺ 297
The disposition and events of Shaykh Abu-Ḥasan al-Jowsiqī ﷺ 299
Anecdotes of Shaykh Abu al-Ḥasan al-Jowsiqī ﷺ 300
Perfect *ikhlās* 301
Tawakkul - reliance on *Allah* ﷻ 301
Wisāl – Communion 302
The reason of discord of the *ʿUlama* 302
An accepted *duʿā* 303
The master of all the *Mashā'ikh* 303
The miracles of Shaykh Abu al-Ḥasan al-Jowsiqī ﷺ 304
The knowledge of the unseen 305
Cure the hunch-backed 305
The dates spoke 308
The disposition and events of Shaykh Abu-ʿAbdullah
Muḥammad al-Qurashī ﷺ 309
Observation of Qiyāmah 310
Meeting with six hundred *Mashā'ikh* 311
Anecdotes of Shaykh Sayyid Muḥammad al-Qurashī ﷺ 313
Ahle-Ḥaqīqah – people of reality 314
The signs of a *walī* 315
Sālik – traveller of the path 317
The miracles of Shaykh al-Qurashī ﷺ 319
A solid pact with the *nafs* 319
Acquiring sweet water 320
Crying sounds from an apple 322
The crying of the child stops 324
Benefits and blessings 324
Steadfast on spiritual state 325
Fire and blood 326
A stone under his side 328
Effects of a *Jinn* on a girl 329
The settlement of the *Jinns* 329
Body white like silver 330
The containers of alcohol breaks 331
Chasing away the *Jinn* 332

Blessings of his company 333
Finding the Night of *Qadar* 333
Most exalted and perfect amongst the *Awliya* 334
The disposition and events of Shaykh Abu al-Barkãt b. Sakhar Amawĩ ﷺ 335
The anecdotes of Shaykh Abu al-Barkãt ﷺ 337
What is love 337
The miracles of Shaykh Abu al-Barkãt ﷺ 342
The desire for roasted meat 342
All the trees in the jungle were filled with pomegranates 345
The *Abdãl* of era 345
Floating in the air 345
An amazing incident 346
Easy to memorize the Holy *Qur'ãn* 348
Hand like a stick 349
Exercising authority from the grave 350
The disposition and events of Shaykh Abĩ-Isḥãq Ibrãhĩm b. ʿAlĩ Aʿzab ﷺ 351
The anecdotes of Shaykh Abu-Isḥãq ﷺ 352
What is adab – discipline 355
The miracles of Shaykh Abu-Isḥãq ﷺ 356
The effect of his vision 357
To stand in a fire 357
Riding on a lion 358
Claims of authority and the condition of the rejecter 358
Whoever the Shaykh wished for, he came to him 359
The heart sort assistance in the absence of the Shaykh ﷺ
and He offered his Assistance 360
Answer from the Grave 361
Thirty thousand *khatams* of the Holy *Qur'ãn* 362
Rash is cured from the body 362
A stately gathering of *simã*ʿ 363
The sick gets consolation from the Shaykh 364
The *wajd* of the Shaykh ﷺ 364
The Sun of the Earth 367
The Imãm of the *Siddiqĩn* 367
The disposition and events of Shaykh Abu al-Ḥasan ʿAlĩ b. Aḥmad ﷺ 369
The anecdotes of Shaykh Abu al-Ḥasan al-Sabbãgh ﷺ 371

The miracles of Shaykh Abu al-Ḥasan al-Sabbāgh ﷺ	374
Everything made Sajdah	375
The power of the Shaykh's ﷺ hand	376
He Reached Egypt in a moment	377
Removing a person from the mouth of a python	378
Everything spoke to the Shaykh ﷺ	379
Rijāl al-Ghayb	379
His vision melts a rock into water	380
Return one's Spiritual Condition	380
One hundred people ate the food of seven people	381
A call from the unseen	381
Fixing a popped out Eye	382
Spiritual rapture when hearing the voice of a pigeon	383
Comprehensive exclusivity	388
The disposition and events of Shaykh Abu al-Ḥasan ʿAlī b. Idrīs ﷺ	389
The status of Shaykh Abu al-Ḥasan ʿAlī b. Idrīs ﷺ	390
His condition	393
Tasawwuf is the name of all *Islāmic* Disciplines	394
The time of lectures	397
Mujāhidah – spiritual struggle	399
The Miracles of Shaykh Abu al-Ḥasan ʿAlī b. Idrīs ﷺ	399
An unknown arrow	400
The tree filled with fruits	401
The disposition and events of Shaykh ʿAlī b. Wahb al-Sanjārī ﷺ	403
The *ziyārah* of elite personalities	404
The anecdotes of Shaykh ʿAlī b. Wahb al-Sanjārī ﷺ	406
The miracles of Shaykh ʿAlī al-Sanjārī ﷺ	407
A stone splits in two by the word *Allāh* ﷻ	407
The perfection of Shaykh's ﷺ seeker	408
Fifty days performing *salāh* with one *wuḍū*	409
Some of the copper dishes become silver and some gold.	410
Resurrection of a dead bull	411
Shaykh ʿAbd al-Qādir al-Jilānī ﷺ is the King of the world	411
The disposition and events of Shaykh Mūsā b. Mahīn al-Zūlī ﷺ	412
The sun of Baghdād	413
The anecdotes of Shaykh Mūsā al-Zūlī ﷺ	414

The miracles of Shaykh Mūsā al-Zūlī	415
Iron became soft in his hands	415
The fire extinguished with his staff [*ʿAsa*]	416
Words of the unseen [*Ghayb*]	416
A four year old child	416
The Shaykh's *duʿās* were always accepted	416
Performing *salāh* in the grave	417
The Angels of the sky revered him	417
The disposition and events of Shaykh Abu-Najīb ʿAbd al-Qāhir al-Sohrowardī	419
A lecturer at *Madrassa Nizāmiyah* and its *Muftī*	419
The anecdotes of Shaykh ʿAbd al-Qāhir	420
The stages of *Tasawwuf*	421
The miracles of Shaykh ʿAbd al-Qāhir	423
Christians and Jews embrace *Islām*	424
The carcass of a lamb spoke	424
The fruits spoke	424
Alcohol becomes water	425
Ghawthiyat al-Kubra – highest stage of a Ghawth	426
The disposition and events of Shaykh Sayyid Aḥmad b. Abu al-Ḥasan Rifāʿī	427
An amazing incident	428
The definition of a strong man	428
The Shaykh ate after six months	428
The anecdotes of Shaykh Sayyid Aḥmad al-Rifāʿī	430
The fishes assembled	431
Bones of fishes became alive	432
Roasted birds became alive	432
Another miracle of the Shaykh	433
The lofty status of Sayyiduna Shaykh ʿAbd al-Qādir al-Jilānī	435
The consequence of the rejecter of Sayyiduna Ghawth al-Aʿzam	436
Epilogue	437
Translators concluding note	438
List of our Publications	441

الله
نور السموات والأرض
نور على نور

Transliteration Keys

Sp. Symbol	*Arabic letter*	*English equiv.*	*Arabic e.g.*	*English e.g.*
ã - Ã	ا - أ - ء	aa	اَللّٰهُ	Allãh
ĩ - Ĩ	ی	ee	دِیْنٌ	Dĩn
ũ	و	oo	رَسُوْلٌ	Rasũl
ˁ	ع	Deep ˁAin from the throat	عَلِیٌّ	ˁAlĩ
ḥ - Ḥ	ح	Deep Ḥaa from the throat	حَبِیْبٌ	Ḥabĩb
ḍ - Ḍ	ض	Daaḍ - mouth rounded when pronounced	وُضُوْء	wuḍu
dh	ذ	Za – with the tip of the tongue pressed on upper incisors	ذِكْرٌ	dhikr
ﷻ	جل جلاله	Glorified is He [used only for Allãh ﷻ]	اَللّٰهُ ﷻ	Allãh ﷻ
ﷺ	صلی اللہ علیہ و سلم	Peace and Blessings upon him [used only for Sayyiduna Muḥammad ﷺ]	سَیِّدُنَا مُحَمَّدٌ ﷺ	Sayyiduna Muḥammad ﷺ
عليه السلام	علیہ السلام	Peace be upon him [used only for Prophets عليه السلام]	سَیِّدُنَا مُوْسیٰ عليه السلام	Sayyiduna Mũsã عليه السلام
رضي الله عنه	رضی اللہ عنہ	May Allãh be pleased with him [used for the Saḥãbah]	سیدنا ابوبکر رضي الله عنه	Sayyiduna Abũ-Bakr رضي الله عنه
قدس الله سره	قدس اللہ سرہ	May Allãh sanctify his secrets [used for the Awliya]	سیدنا غوث الاعظم قدس الله سره	Sayyiduna Ghawth al-Aˁzam قدس الله سره

بسم الله الرحمن الرحيم

Dedication

I
dedicate this
book to the beloved
parents of Ḥaḍrat Sayyiduna
Ghawth al-Aʿzam ﷺ, Sayyiduna Abu-
Sāliḥ Mūsā Jangi Dost Ḥasanī ﷺ and
Sayyidah Umm al-Khayr Amat al-Jabbār Fātima
who raised their beloved son to the pinnical of
Perfection. Their dignified son was a beacon of
guidance for the beloved Ummah of their
Glorious Grandfather, Sayyid al-Mursalīn Raḥmat
lil-ʿĀlamīn Sayyid al-Ḥāmidīn ash-Shākirīn Imām al-
Maḥbūbīn Sayyiduna wa Mawlāna Muḥammad ﷺ

Acknowledgement

Firstly, I glorify Almighty *Allāh* ﷻ and express my deep gratification *shukar* [thanks]; His ﷻ *Tawfiq* and source of inspiration, the courage in affording me the opportunity and bestowing upon me the moral and intellectual strength in undertaking this monumental task of translating this intrinsic classical book, *Bahjat al-Asrār fī Maʿādin al-Anwār*. Choicest *Salāms* and Salutations upon our compassionate Master, the most beloved Messenger of *Allāh* ﷺ whose tender grace and blessings guided and inspired me throughout this arduous venture. I am indebted to my succour and strength, the appointed senior representative in the Dominion of *Allāh*, *Sultān al-ʿĀrifīn* Sayyiduna wa Mawlāna Ghawth al-Aʿzam Shaykh ʿAbd al-Qādir al-Jilānī رضي الله عنه who assisted and guided my weak hand to embellish this literal awe-inspiring garland with selected and appropriate pearls. My *Murshid al-Kāmil* and Spiritual Master, the Ghawth of his era, *Murshid al-Kāmil Pīr Dastagīr* Muftī Aʿzam Qutb al-ʿĀlam Imām Mustafa Riḍā al-Qādirī Barkātī Nūrī رحمه الله was a pillar of twofold reinforcing support, physically and spiritually to nurture me in order to sow the seed and ensure it to transform into a lush fruitful tree of rich virtuous literature. May the Sublime Lord of Power ﷻ sanctify their pure souls in the lofty abodes of *Jannah*.

I express my sincere gratitude to many individuals who made valuable suggestions and provided altruistic support throughout this prolific book. My special appreciation is extended to the following individuals in bringing this inspirational task to fruition:

- ✓ The renowned *ʿĀlim* of *Dīn*, Muftī Nasīm Ashraf al-Qādirī Raḍawī Ḥabībī [South Africa] for reading through the Arabic poetic text, correcting and translating them.
- ✓ Moulana Ḥāfiz Muḥammad Rayḥān Qādirī [M. Phil] Fiqah & Principles of Fiqah Jamia al-Aḥqāf, Ḥaḍratmout Yemen; Muftī Abu-Bakr Shāzalī [Pakistan] and Muftī Aʿjāz Qādirī Raḍawī Owaisī [Karachi] for suggestions and translating some of the Arabic poetry.
- ✓ Special gratitude and deep appreciation to Professor Dr. ʿAbd al-Raḥīm Qādirī Chishtī Nizāmī [South Africa] who despite his ill health, and other commitments, sacrificed his valuable time for diligently

editing and proofreading the English texts. He indeed did a thorough editing of the English language.

- ✓ I also thank Brother Muḥammad Imtiyāz Qādirī Raḍawī of UK for reading through the final edition before print for omitted errors.
- ✓ I thank my beloved wife and children who supported and encouraged me during my long hours of engrossment at the expense of their family time. It was a long and difficult journey for them in sacrificing their prime time for allowing me to dedicate undivided attention for over 16 months to complete this monumental work.
- ✓ Not forgetting Janab Khalīl Aḥmad Rana of Pakistan who provided the information of the objections on *'Bahjat al-Asrār'* and its answers to be included in this edition.
- ✓ Finally, I beseech the most Compassionate *Allāh* ﷻ to bless the souls of my beloved late parents.

May the Merciful *Allāh* ﷻ with the blessings of Sayyiduna Rasūlullāh ﷺ; Sayyiduna Ghawth al-Aʿzam ؓ, my *Murshid al-Kāmil* Ḥaḍrat Muftī al-Āʿzam ؓ, the *Awliya* and *Sāliḥīn* ؓ shower all with blessings and Divine Providence and grant us *Tawfiq* to sincerely serve the religion of *Islām*. I beg *Allāh* ﷻ to accept my humble service and make this dedication a reason for Him ﷻ to open the doors of my heart to the transcendental world and the mysteries of His ﷻ *Maʿārifah* to illuminate my heart and soul. My fervent desire is that this book be of benefit to the readers in particularly to the present day youth and generations to follow and to guide them tranquillity and lead them to the world of success within the Divine Proximity of the Real Absolute Lord of Power ﷻ.

Qādirī Faqīr ʿAbd al-Hādī Raḍawī Nūrī
President: Imām Aḥmad Raza Academy
Director: Barkātur Raza Publication
Chairperson: Sufipages.com

Foreword

All Praises are for *Allāh* ﷻ the Cherisher and Sustainer of the universe. Peace and blessings upon the most exalted creation, our master, Sayyiduna wa Mawlana Muḥammad Mustafa ﷺ, the unique beloved of the Sublime Lord ﷻ. I am grateful to *Allāh* ﷻ Who facilitated my undertaking in editing the first ever English translated version of the original manuscript of this monumental publication.

Indeed! I express my sincere gratitude to Shaykh ʿAbd al-Hādī al-Qādirī Raḍawī Nūrī, for placing confidence in me and entrusting me with a challenging task of editing the English translated version of this classical literary publication which deals with the occult spiritual sciences of *Islām*.

The translator must be commended in undertaking a difficult task which is beyond the potential, and as well beyond the intellect of an ordinary scholar. The translator admits to the fact that he has not accomplished this magnanimous undertaking on his own accord, but had received an inspiration from *Sultān al-Awliya* Sayyiduna Ghawth al-Aʿzam Shaykh ʿAbd al-Qādir al-Jilānī ؓ and his *Murshid al-Kāmil*, Ḥaḍrat Muftī al-Aʿzam Qutb al-ʿĀlam al-Ghawth Imām Mustafa Riḍā al-Qādirī Nūrī ؒ. It took the translator more than 16 months of absolute dedication and commitment, working for a duration of approximately 14 to 16 hours per day in bringing this noble task to fruition. He further stresses upon the fact that his role in this endeavour was not more than a pen, which is unproductive without a creative hand to move it. The translator glorifies *Allāh* ﷻ Who has appointed His beloved *Walī*, Ḥaḍrat Ghawth al-Aʿzam, Sayyiduna Shaykh ʿAbd al-Qādir Ḥasanī al-Ḥusainī al-Jilānī ؓ to intervene in acting as the hand to move the useless pen. Henceforward, the translator was the pen and the Great Ghawth ؓ was the driving force. This intervention lead to this awe-inspiring prolific publication in your hands.
This publication encompasses the following:

- Love for the Divine Being, *Allāh* ﷻ.
- Status and obedience to the final and glorious Messenger of *Allāh* ﷻ.

- The institution of *Wilayah* with particular reference to *Muhjāhadah* [Spiritual Struggle] and *Mukāshifah* [Divine Observance]
- Sufism – the Laws of Tasawwuf.
- Ethics pertaining to Human rights and Divine Rights.
- Morals and Ethics from an Islāmic perspective.
- Consciousness of the Divine Being.
- Piety.
- Cleansing of the inner self.
- Multi-faceted Sciences of Sacred Knowledge.

This book is a welcome addition to the dearth of Islāmic literature in particular to the esoteric dimensions of *Islām*, with particular reference to the comprehensive and authentic biography of the Grand Master of Spiritualism and the Chieftain of the Gnostics, *Sultān al-ʿĀrifīn* Ghawth al-Aʿzam Sayyiduna Shaykh ʿAbd-al Qādir al-Jilānī ﷺ.

I strongly confess that the editing of this book greatly enhanced my knowledge of the spiritual world of *Islām*. Subsequent to this publication, I intend to keep this informative *Sūfī* Manual as a part of my daily litany [*wazīfa*] in order to enhance my spirit to attain the ultimate Proximity of the Sublime Lord ﷻ.

The translator must be commended for his altruistic endeavours. To date nobody in the *Muslim* world has undertaken a challenge of translating this magnum opus into the English language. May *Allāh* ﷻ crown the efforts of the translator. I compliment the translator for his efforts in accomplishing this momentous task. It is my fervent supplication to *Allāh* ﷻ to bestow the translator with a lengthy lifespan, sound health and an increased knowledge of gnosis with *Taufiq*.

Dr. ʿAbd al-Raḥīm Ebrāhīm (D. Phil.)
Graduate UKZN (UDW Campus)
Ex-educator. Department of Education.
Ex- Research Assistant (NRF FUND) – University of Durban Westville.

Answers to Objections on Bahjat al-Asrãr and its noble author

Objection:

The research scholars have a contradictory view on the book, entitled *'Bahjat al-Asrãr'*. It is ipso-facto that they have vehemently criticized the book, and simultaneously have strongly condemned its author, Imãm Shatnũfī ﷺ. The opponents allege that anyone who reads this book shall identify that there are many fabrications found therein. [Reference: Three monthly *Nida al-Jamī ͨāh* editions, Lahore, March 2012.) Some of their pessimistic criticisms are as follows:

Citations of their objections:

1) ͨAllama Dhahabī vociferously declared:

لقد اتی بمصائب فی کتاب بہجۃ الاسرار یشھد القلب ببطلانہ

Indeed in the book, Bahjat al-Asrãr, I faced many difficulties and the heart testifies to its invalidity.[1]

2) Ḥãfiz Ibn Ḥajar ﷺ quotes Shaykh Kamãl al-Dīn Ja ͨãfar who remarked about *'Bahjat al-Asrãr'*:

ذکر فیہ غرائب و عجائب و طعن الناس فی کثیر من حکایات و اسانید فیہ

There are strange and astonishing narrations reported in it [Bahjat al-Asrãr], and people have criticized many of its narrations and chains of narrators. [2]

3) Ibn al-Wardī states:

انّ فی البہجۃ امورا لا تصح و مبالغات فی شان الشیخ عبد القادر لا تلیق الّا بالربوبیّۃ

Indeed in Bahjat al-Asrãr there are invalidities, and exaggerations pertinent to the status of Shaykh

---

[1] *Lisãn al-Mīzãn* Vol. 4, p. 238

[2] *Al-Durar al-Kãmina* Vol. 3, p. 142

ʿAbd al-Qādir ﷺ which cannot be equated to the Divinity and Lordship of Almighty Allāh ﷻ.[3]

4) Ḥāfiz Ibn Ḥajar ﷺ had documented that Ibn al-Wardī has condemned the author of *'Bahjat al-Asrār'* [Imām Shatnūfī ﷺ] and has classified him as a fabricator of *Ḥadith*.[4]

5) ʿAllāma Zayn al-Dīn ibn Rajab writes:
Abu al-Ḥasan Shatnūfī has compiled 3 volumes on the works and excellence of Shaykh ʿAbd al-Qādir Jīlānī ﷺ comprising of correct and incorrect narrations. This, by itself, is sufficient for anyone to regard it as falsehood as he [the author] recorded every word that he heard [from people].

He further deliberates:
'I have seen some parts of this book and my heart did not grant me the permission to trust narrations taken from untrustworthy people. This book contains unclear utterances, disastrous and futile words that cannot be summed up. It is not correct to attribute such words to Shaykh ʿAbd al-Qādir ﷺ.'[5]

Moreover he propounds:
'Due to reporting such words by Shatnūfī in this book [Bahjat al-Asrār]; it will make Shatnūfī guilty of fabrication.'[6]

Answer:

The references used by the antagonists to condemn the book *'Bahjat al-Asrār'* and to brand its author Imām Shatnūfī ﷺ as a liar, are inappropriate. When we reverted to these references, we were astonished to ascertain that the references used by the antagonists to condemn the book *'Bahjat al-Asrār'* and to implicate its author Imām Shatnūfī ﷺ as a liar, is in reality, not the very same

[3] *Kashf al-Zunūn* Vol. 1 p. 657

[4] *Lisān al-Mīzān* Vol. 4, p. 338

[5] *Tabqāt al-Ḥanābalah,* Vol. 3, p. 293, Dār al-Maʿārifah, Beirut.

[6] *Tabqāt al-Ḥanābalah,* Vol. 3, p. 293, Dār al-Maʿārifah, Beirut.

book, i.e. *'Bahjat al-Asrār'* of Imām Shatnūfi ﷺ. In fact this *'Bahjat al-Asrār'* is the book of ʿAlī b. ʿAbdullāh b. Jah'dam.

Whilst quoting the scholars of *Islām,* the anti-forces acted deceptively, and enthralled in mutual evil intentions to confuse the *Muslim Ummah.* We shall scrutinize the citations which are listed hereunder and thereby provide an exposition of the mischief of the *salafi* perpetrators:

The rivals cited *'Lisān al-Mizān'* to quote the words of ʿAllāma Dhahabī as follows;

لقد اتی بمصائب فی کتاب بہجة الاسرار یشهد القلب ببطلانه

I came across many discrepancies in the book, 'Bahjat al-Asrār' and my heart testifies to its invalidity.[7]

When we thoroughly examined the above quotation, we discovered the following statements:

علی بن عبد الله بن جهضم الزاهد ابو الحسن شیخ الصوفیة بحرم مکة و
مصنف کتاب بہجة الاسرار متهم بوضع الحدیث قال ابن خیرون تکلم فیه
قال و قیل انه کان یکذب و قال غیره اتهموه بوضع صلوة الرغائب توفی 414
هجری......

ʿAlī b. ʿAbdullāh b. Jah'dam was the Shaykh of the Sūfis in the Ḥaram of Makkah and the author of the book 'Bahjat al-Asrār'. He was reproached for the fabrication of Ḥadith. Ibn Khayrūn states that he was Mutakallim Fihi[8] *and it has been said that he used to lie. Others accused him of adding the Salāt al-Raghā'ib into the text of his book. He passed away in 414 hijrī.*[9]

It further enunciates:

---

[7] *Lisān al-Mīzān,* Vol. 4, p. 238

[8] NB: there is a scholarly debate pertaining the authenticity of his narrations

[9] *Lisān al-Mīzān,* Vol. 5, p. 554

و قال المصنف فی تاریخ الاسلام "لقد اتی بمصائب فی کتابه بهجة الاسرار یشهد القلب ببطلانه". و روی عن ابی بکر النجاد عن ابن ابی العوام عن ابی بکر المروذی محنة احمد. فاتی فیها بعجائب و قصص لا یشك من له ادنی ممارسة ببطلانها، وهی شبیهة بما وضعه البلوی فی محنة الشافعي

Imãm Dhahabĩ in his 'Tãrĩkh al-Islãm' said: 'I have come across many discrepancies in the book 'Bahjat al-Asrãr', my heart testifies to its invalidity'. He has narrated from Abu Bakr an-Najjad who narrates from Ibn Abu al-Awwãm and he narrates from Abĩ-Bakr al-Marrũzi (trials of Imam Aḥmad). I have thus found many strange narrations within it (al-Bahja), and such stories whose invalidity can be recognised by the one who has the slightest amount of understanding. It resembles that which has been mentioned by al-Balwĩ of the trial that befell Imãm ash-Shafa'ĩ.'

A thorough examination and a diligent study of the following citation from the book *'Tãrĩkh al-Islãm'* by Imãm Dhahabĩ astonished us to discover the use of the expressions which are contained therein and which are quoted below:

علی بن عبد الله بن الحسن بن جهضم بن سعید بن ابو الحسن البورانی الصوفی نزیل مکة و مصنف کتاب بهجة الاسرار فی اخبار القوم .... لقد اتی بمصائب فی کتاب بهجة الاسرار یشهد القلب ببطلانه

'Alĩ b. 'Abdullãh b. al-Ḥasan b. Jah'dam b. Sa'ĩd b. Abu al-Ḥasan al-Bũrãnĩ al-Sũfĩ living in Makkah and is the author of the book 'Bahjat al-Asrãr' regarding the information of the nation ..... I have come across discrepancies in the book 'Bahjat al-Asrãr' of which my heart testifies to its invalidity...

Furthermore, 'Allãma Dhahabĩ in his *'Siyar A'lãm al-Nubalã'* asserts in reference to the book, *'Bahjat al-Asrãr'* of 'Alĩ b. 'Abdullãh b. Jah'dam as follows:

علی بن عبد الله بن الحسن بن جهضم الهمدانی المجاور مصنف کتاب بهجة

الاسرار ......ليس بثقة بل متهم ياتى بمصائب قال ابن خيرون قيل انه يكذب

ʿAlī b. ʿAbdullāh b. al-Ḥasan b. Jah'dam Hamdānī al-Mujāwir, the caretaker, the author of 'Bahjat al-Asrār'... is not trustworthy, rather he has been accused [of fabrication] and has recorded discrepancies. Ibn Khayrūn states: 'It has been said that he lies.' [10]

It is apparent and clear from our references of *'Lisān al-Mizān'* of Imām Ibn Ḥajar; *'Tarīkh al-Islām'* and *'Siyar Aʿhlām al-Nubalā'* of Imām Dhahabī that the book Imām Dhahabī condemned, was the *'Bahjat al-Asrār'* of Alī b. ʿAbdullāh b. al-Ḥasan b. Jah'dam and NOT the *'Bahjat al-Asrār'* of Imām Abu al-Ḥasan Shatnūfī ﷺ.

Moreover, the opponents have further quoted Ḥāfiz Ibn Ḥajar ﷺ who referred to the criticism of Shaykh Kamāl al-Dīn Jaʿāfar on the book *'Bahjat al-Asrār'* and affirmed:

ذكر فيه غرائب و عجائب و طعن الناس فى كثير من حكايات و اسانيد فيه

Strange and amazing narrations are mentioned in it [Bahjat al-Asrār] and people have criticized many of its stories and chains of narrators. [11]

The answer to this objection is to be found in the book, *'Al-Aʿhlām Liz-Zarkalī'*. Whilst discussing Imām Shatnūfī ﷺ, the words of Ḥāfiz Ibn Ḥajar are mentioned and refuted in its marginal notes. The excerpt by *'Al-Aʿlām'* is as follows:

على بن يوسف جرير بن معضاد اللخمى ابو الحسن الشطنوفى عالم

بالقرأات كان الشيخ الديار المصرية فى عصره من فقهاء الشافعية......

قال ابن حجر ذكر فيه غرائب و عجائب و طعن الناس فى كثير من حكايات

---

[10] *Sayr Aʿhlām al-Nubalā*, Imām Dhahbī, Vol. 33 p. 265

[11] *Al-Durar al-Kāmina*, Vol. 3, p. 142

و اسانید فیہ

ʿAlī b. Yūsuf Shatnūfī was an Imām of qirʾāt, the Shafaʿī Jurist and Shaykh of Egypt. Ibn Ḥajar has said that Shatnūfī in 'Bahjat al-Asrār' has written phenomenal things and people have criticized many of its narrations and chains.

Very Important Note:

In different periods there are two books produced by two different scholars with the similar title *'Bahjat al-Asrār'*. One was written by Alī b. ʿAbdullāh b. al-Ḥasan b. Jah'dam who lived in Makka al-Mukarrama and passed away there in 414 *hijrī* and the other was written by Imām Abu al-Ḥasan Shatnūfī ﷺ who lived in Egypt and passed away there in 713 *hijrī*. There is an interval of 3 centuries between these two authors.

Hereunder is documented proof of the confusion that the author and book *'Bahjat al-Asrār'* which was condemned by some scholars is the first author; Alī b. ʿAbdullāh b. al-Ḥasan b. Jah'dam and his *'Bahjat al-Asrār'* and not the second author, Imām Abu al-Ḥasan Shatnūfī ﷺ and his *'Bahjat al-Asrār'*.

Henceforth, in the marginal notes of *'Aʿlām'*, the following information has been furnished by Shaykh Khayr al-Dīn Zarkalī:

قلت هذا خلط بین ترجمة الشطنوفی الذی عاش و مات بمصر و
ترجمة ابن جهضم علی بن عبد الله الهمدانی المجاور بالحرم المکی
المتوفی قبله بثلاثة قرون

This is a mix-up between the translation of Shatnūfī who lived and passed away in Egypt and that of Ibn Jah'dam ʿAlī b. ʿAbdullāh al-Hamdānī, the Mujāwir [caretaker] of the Ḥaram of Makkah who passed away 3 centuries before him (Shatnūfī).[12]

[12] *Al-Aʿlām Li-Zarkalī* Vol. 5, p. 34

Moreover, the comment of Shaykh Kamāl al-Dīn which was quoted, has two points for observation. Firstly, he alludes to the fact that there are brilliant factors contained therein, to which we also conform and are in agreement with. This is relevant because *karamāt* [miracles] invariably fall into the mystical and awe-inspiring category. Secondly, it is alleged that many individuals had objected on numerous narrations and certifications of *'Bahjat al-Asrār'*. Thus, the allegations of Shaykh Kamāl al-Dīn are unauthentic and invalid that Imām Shatnūfī ﷺ is blameworthy of fabrication, because nor did the Shaykh mention those indictments of fabrications and its categories or names and details of the antagonists. On the contrary, there are numerous illustrious scholars who commended Imām Shatnūfī's ﷺ *'Bahjat al-Asrār'*. They have also prescribed and have highly recommended it as authentic and a profound book for reference in comparison to the few peculiar ones who vociferously raised objections to it. The objection of a few individuals has no credibility and legitimacy in comparison to the majority of scholars who acclaimed and recommended Imām Shatnūfīs' ﷺ *'Bahjat al-Asrār'*. Henceforth, the unwarranted allegations or objections of Shaykh Kamāl al-Dīns' shall not be considered and nor endorsed in the presence of the praises, recommendations and acknowledgements of the majority of the senior *'Ulama* and *Mashā'ikh* of *Islām*.

Furthermore, the point is to be taken into consideration that before the above-mentioned citation of Ḥāfiz Ibn Ḥajar ﷺ, whilst discussing Imām Shatnūfī ﷺ, and pertaining to the above citation of Shaykh Kamāl al-Dīn's comment, he wrote:

كان الناس يكرمونه و يعظمونه وينسبونه الى الصلاح

The people used to praise and honour him and
counted him amongst those with good character. [13]

In addition, he also records:

كَانَ عَالِمًا تَقِيًّا مَشْكُورُ السِّيْرَة

[13] *Al-Durar al-Kāminah,* Vol. 3, p. 142

He [Imām Shatnūfi] was a pious
scholar with a notable biography.

These statements explicitly prove that according to him, Imām Abu al-Ḥasan Shatnūfi ﷺ is not a liar, and nor is he deceitful. If this is the case then the opinion of Shaykh Kamāl al-Dīn is certainly not credible because he declares that scholars have condemned certain narrations in *Bahjat al-Asrār.* If some narrations were condemned on grounds of fabrications in *'Bahjat al-Asrār',* certainly, then its author [Imām Shatnūfi ﷺ] would be found guilty of lies and fabrication. On the contrary, it is not so because both the above quoted comments of Ḥāfiz Ibn Ḥajar ﷺ bear testimony which are contrary to the objections of Shaykh Kamāl al-Dīn.

Apart from these facts, it seems that the *salafi* author of this objection did no read the informative book of Ḥāfiz Ibn Ḥajar ﷺ; *'Ghab'tata al-Nāzir fi Tarjumah al-Shaykh 'Abd al-Qādir* ﷺ*'.* If he did, he would not have been a victim of misconception concerning Ḥāfiz Ibn Ḥajar ﷺ. This is so because in this book, Ḥāfiz Ibn Ḥajar ﷺ has recorded the events and narrations of Sayyiduna Shaykh 'Abd al-Qādir ﷺ which he quoted from the very same *Bahjat al-Asrār* of Imām Shatnūfi ﷺ. There are many places where he recorded: قال الشيخ نور الدين شطنوفی.... - *Al-Shaykh Nūr al-Dīn Shatnūfi* pronounced this... This in itself provides clear evidence that Ḥāfiz Ibn Ḥajar ﷺ had great regards for Imām Nūr al-Dīn Shatnūfi ﷺ and greatly trusted his renowned *'Bahjat al-Asrār'.* If it was not so, why would he then quote and refer to the *'Bahjat al-Asrār'* of Imām Shatnūfi ﷺ?

The *salafi* author of *'Nida al- Jamī'āh'* who reported the objections against Imām Shatnūfi ﷺ and his *Bahjat al-Asrār* also quoted the condemnation of Ibn al-Wardī in *'Kashf al-Zunūn';* but however he deliberately or ignorantly did not quote the appropriate answer noted in refutation to the comments of Ibn al-Wardī. It seemed as though lightning had struck the pen of the *salafi* author who completely omitted this refutation. At this juncture we would like to quote the refutation of the comment of Ibn al-Wardī by Shaykh Ḥājī Khālifah ﷺ, author of *'Kashf al-Zunūn'*:

> ذکر ابن الوردی فی تاریخه "انّ فی البهجة امورا لا تصح و مبالغات فی شان الشیخ عبد القادر لا یلیق الا بالربوبیة انتهی.....و مثل هذه المقالة, قیل عن الشهاب ابن حجر العسقلانی و اقول ما المبالغات التی عزیت الیه مما لا یجوز علی مثل و قد تتبعت فلم اجد فیها نقلا الا و له فیه متابعون و غالب ما اورده فیها نقله الیافعی فی اسنی المفاخر و نشر المحاسن و روض الریاحین, و شمس الدین بن الزکی الحلبی ایضا فی کتاب الاشراف و اعظم شئی نقل عنه انه احی الموتی کاحیاته الدجاجة و لعمری ان هذه القصة نقلها تاج الدین السبکی و نقل ایضا عن ابن الرفاعی و غیره و انی لغبی جاهل حاسد ضیع عمره فی فهم ما فی السطور...
>
> *Ibn al-Wardī has mentioned in his 'Tarīkh' 'there are such narrations in Bahjat al-Asrār that are not correct and exaggerations attributed to Shaykh ʿAbd al-Qādir ﷺ which are of Divine Lordship, and other similar issues. ..... I question: 'Which are such undesirable exaggerations that are attributed to Shaykh ʿAbd al-Qādir? I have searched and have not found them to be transmitted except that they have been followed. And most of its narrations are transmitted by Imām Yāfaʿī ﷺ in his 'Asna al-Mafākhir', 'Nashar al-Muhāsin' and 'Rowḍah al-Riyaḥīn', as well as Shaykh Shams al-Dīn Zakī al-Ḥalabī, in his 'Kitāb al-Ashrāf'. The greatest thing that has been transmitted from him (Shaykh ʿAbd al-Qādir ﷺ) is the resurrection of the dead, like his resurrection of the chicken. And I take an oath on my life, that this incident has been transmitted from Imām ʿAllāma Tāj al-Dīn Subkī ﷺ as well as from Ibn Rifāʿī and others. It is only the uncouth, ignorant and envious, who have wasted their entire life trying to understand what are in these lines.....*

The *salafī* antagonistic and bias author of *'Nida al- Jamīʿah'* since its inception, highlights the condemnation of the book *Bahjat al-Asrār* as a fabrication by presenting the following statement: *'Ḥāfiz Ibn Ḥajar has written that Ibn al-Wardī has accused Abu al-Ḥasan Shatnūfi as a fabricator of narrations.'*

When the *salafi* author of *'Nida al- Jamī'āh'* presented the above comment of Ḥāfiz Ibn Ḥajar, we henceforth searched for this comment in the *'Lisān al-Mizān'* of Ḥāfiz Ibn Ḥajar, but failed to detect any such comment in the entire book. According to our thorough examination of *'Lisān al-Mizān'*, all that we located is that ʿAlī b. ʿAbdullāh b. Jah'dam is mentioned as a weak narrator; liar and condemned his book *'Bahjat al-Asrār'* as being futile. In the entire book [*Lisān al-Mizān*] we have not discovered anywhere that Imām Shatnūfi ﷺ is condemned as a liar or of being untrustworthy; and nor is his book *'Bahjat al-Asrār'* ranked as unreliable.

The *salafi* author of *'Nida al- Jamī'āh'* has quoted a statement of ʿAllāma Ibn Rajab Ḥanbalī who alleged that Imām Shatnūfi ﷺ is a liar and that his book *'Bahjat al-Asrār'* is unreliable. When we examined the original text of ʿAllāma Ibn Rajab Ḥanbalī, we did find that this was indeed his viewpoint, as quoted by the *salafi* author of *'Nida al-Jamī'āh'*. This certainly did not surprise us because his condemnation of Imām Shatnūfi ﷺ and his book *'Bahjat al-Asrār'* is directly the influence of his association and teachings of Ibn Taymiya, Ibn Qayyim and Ibn Kathīr. The belief code of these three are in contradiction to the mainstream *Ahle Sunnah wa Jamā'at*. Let alone *'Bahjat al-Asrār'*, the beliefs documented in all the books of *Tasawwuf* are in contradiction to the beliefs of the father of *salafism*, Ibn Taymiya and his associates. By the virtue of the association and influence of the *salafi* teachings, it did have a great impact on Ibn Rajab and thus, he released such a statement. Amazingly, this intimidation of influence was not embedded into his heart permanently, because the people who have studied his book, are fully aware of the fact that owing to the influence of his teachers, he made such a statement, but he could not remain steadfast onto it. Eventually he cited narration from the very same *'Bahjat al-Asrār'* of Imām Shatnūfi ﷺ and disclosed:

من احسن ما فی هذا الکتاب

'(this is) the best of what is in this book.'

He quoted 27 verses of the *Marsiya*[14] from this book. ʿAllāma Ibn Rajab's comment: *'that most of the narrations of 'Bahjat al-Asrār' was taken from unknown sources'*, hence, there is no evidence to nullify the credibility of an author or his book. According to the majority of the scholars, the narration of unknown persons are accepted and it is possible that the narrations which ʿAllāma Ibn Rajab regards as unknown could be authentic in the view of Imām Shatnūfī ﷺ.

Apart from this issue, set aside all the interpretations and explanations and whilst we accept the quotes of the *salafī* author of *'Nida al- Jamīʿah';* then too the assumed inauthentic contents of *Bahjat al-Asrār* and the unreliability of Imām Shatnūfī ﷺ shall never be endorsed and deemed as valid. This is because ʿAllāma Ibn Rajab stands alone in this matter. This relevant fact ought to be well understood by the *salafī* author of *'Nida al- Jamīʿah'* that if one *Muḥaddith* objects to a book or author; this objection does not totally condemn the book or its author. If this was the case, then the *'Siḥā Sittā'*[15] will also be outside the limits of trustworthiness and authenticity. Although, it is not the case in this instance. Similarly, on the one hand there is the objection about the weakness of Imām Shatnūfī ﷺ and his *'Bahjat al-Asrār'* by ʿAllāma Ibn Rajab Ḥanbalī; whilst on the other hand the acknowledgements and praises of numerous *Muḥaddithīn ʿUlama, Sūfiyyah* and *Mashāʾikh* are prevalent The foolish and bias *salafī* author of *'Nida al-Jamīʿah'* could see a single statement

---

[14] A poem written to commemorate the exploits of great men of *Islām*; usually to describe the battle fought on the Plains of *Karbala* in Iraq by Ḥaḍrat Sayyiduna Imān Ḥusain ﷺ and his supporters against the unscrupulous army of the corrupt Yazīd. It is usually a poem of mourning.

[15] The six books containing collections of *Ḥadith* [sayings or traditions of the Beloved Messenger of *Allāh* ﷺ] compiled by six *Sunni Muslim Ḥadith* Masters in the ninth century CE. 'Saḥiḥ Bukhārī', collected by *Imām Bukhārī* (d. 870), includes 7000+ *Āḥādith*; 'Saḥiḥ Muslim', collected by Imām Muslim b. al-Ḥajjaj (d. 875), includes 9000+ *Āḥādith*, 'Sunan al-Nasaʿī', collected by Imām al-Nasaʿi (d. 915), Sunan Abu-Dāʿūd, collected by Imām Abu Dāʿūd (d. 888), 'Jāmiʿ al-Tirmidhī', collected by Imām al-Tirmidhī (d. 892), 'Sunan ibn Mājah', collected by Imām Ibn Mājah (d. 887)

of ʿAllāma Ibn Rajab Ḥanbalī; but however, his squint eye could not, or I would rather deliberate that the prejudiced *salafi* orientated eye did not aspire to view the recommendations and praises of the senior *Muḥaddithīn, ʿUlama* and *Mashā'ikh* attributed to Imām Abu al-Ḥasan Nūr al-Dīn Shatnūfī ﷺ. Here I would list a few praises attributed to Imām Shatnūfī ﷺ, in anticipation of eradicating the vengeance and ignorance of the *wahābī salafī* antagonists.

Imān ʿAllāma Ibn Ḥajar ʿAsqalānī ﷺ states:

كان الناس يكرمونه و يعظمونه و ينسبونه الى الصلاح

The people used to praise and honour him and counted him amongst those with good character. [16]

كَانَ عَالِمًا تَقِيًّا مَشْكُورُ السِّيْرَة

He [Imām Shatnūfī] was a pious scholar with a notable biography.. [17]

ʿAllāma Imām Jalāl al-Dīn Suyūtī ﷺ in his book, *'Ḥusn al-Muḥāḍarah'* states:

الامام الاوحد

The matchless Imām. [18]

Likewise ʿAllāma Imām Jalāl al-Dīn Suyūtī ﷺ in his other book, *'Ghayt al-Wiʿāt'* reports:

كان كثير من الناس يعتقده و القضاة تكرمه

Numerous people believed in him and the jurists honoured him. [19]

Shaykh al-Muḥaqqiq Imām ʿAbd al-Ḥaqq Muḥaddith Dehlawī ﷺ in his *'Zubdat al-Āthār'* states:

الشيخ الامام الاجل الفقيه العالم المقرى الاوحد البارع

The Master, the illustrious leader, The Jurist, the

---

[16] *Al-Durar al-Kāminah* Vol. 3, p. 142

[17] Ibid

[18] *Husn al-Muḥāḍrah* Vol. 1, p. 506 Cairo

[19] *Ghayt al-Waʿāt* Vol. 2 p. 213, Cairo

erudite scholar, the Master reciter of the Holy Qur'ãn, the unique, the skilful. [20]

ᶜAllãma Shams al-Dĩn Dhahabĩ in his *'Tabqãt al-Qurrã'* writes:

الامام البارع شيخ القراء

The brilliant leader, the Master of the Qur'ãnic Reciters. [21]

Imãm ᶜAbdullãh al-Yãfaᶜĩ al-Yemenĩ ﷺ in his *'Mir'at al-Jinãn'* states:

الشيخ الامام الفقيه العالم المقرى

The Chief; the leader, the Jurist, the Scholar, the Master reciter of the Holy Qur'ãn. [22]

Imãm Muḥammad b. al-Jazri ﷺ in *'Ghayat al-Nihãyah'* states:

الاستاذ المحقق البارع

The teacher, the skilful research scholar. [23]

Why did the *salafĩ* author of *'Nida al-Jamĩ'ãh'* not perceive the above statements of the senior honourable Imãms of *Islãm*; or are these illustrious personalities not credible to him? Are the above citations not meritorious enough to prove the excellence and elevated status of Imãm Shatnũfĩ's ﷺ knowledge?

Subsequently, in rectifying the misconception and establishing the truth with solid evidence, is it not now sheer ignorance to discard the above citations and persist in giving preference to a single view of Shaykh Ibn Rajab Ḥanbalĩ? The decision now rests on the reader. May *Allãh* ﷻ grant us the *Tawfiq* of insight,

[20] *Zubdat al-Ãthãr* p. 5, Bombay
[21] *Tabqãt al-Qurrã* Vol. 1, p. 1262
[22] *Mir'at al-Jinãn* Vol. 2 p. 561 Beirut
[23] *Ghayat al-Nihãyah* Vol. 1 p. 516, Beirut

understanding and the unconditional acceptance of the Truth and to be steadfast on the pristine Path of the *Ahle Sunnah wa Jamāʿat.*

English translation by
Qādirī Faqīr,
ʿAbd al-Hādī al-Qādirī Raḍawī Nūrī

Compiled by;
Khalīl Aḥmad Rana
Pakistan

Synopsis from *'Fatāwa Otrakhand'* pgs. 200 to 210 by:
Moulana Muḥammad Zulfiqār Khan
Naʿīmī Kakralwī,
India

وَقُلْ جَاءَ الْحَقُّ وَزَهَقَ الْبَاطِلُ إِنَّ الْبَاطِلَ كَانَ زَهُوقًا

Poetic Description of the Stunning Features and Splendid Disposition of Sayyiduna Ghawth al-Aᶜzam ﷺ.

In 1322 *hijrī* / 1904, Ḥaḍrat Moulana Maḥmūd Jān Qādirī Raḍawī ﷺ had requested his *Murshid al-Kāmil*; the great *Mujaddid* and *ᶜĀrif Billāh, al-Qutb al-Irshād* Aᶜlā-Ḥaḍrat Imām Aḥmad Riḍā al-Qādirī Barkātī Muḥaqqiq Bareillwī ﷺ for a poetic description of Sayyiduna Ghawth al-Aᶜzam Shaykh ᶜAbd al-Qādir Ḥasanī al-Ḥusainī al-Jilānī ﷺ. He did this because his *Murshid al-Kāmil* ﷺ was the *Nā'ib* [chief representative] of the great Ghawth ﷺ who sat in his consecrated *majlis* and regularly consulted with him in matters of *Dīn*. Who else will be the best person to give a physical description of the Cardinal Pole and succour of the ardent lovers, our Master and Guide, Muḥiyy al-Dīn Sultān al-ᶜĀrifīn Sayyiduna wa Mawlāna Shaykh ᶜAbd al-Qādir al-Jīlanī ﷺ? Thus, Imām Aḥmad Riḍā ﷺ compiled the following verses that explicitly describes the stunning features and splendid disposition of Sayyiduna Ghawth al-Aᶜzam ﷺ. The great *Mujaddid* ﷺ named this description according to the *Abjad* Formula as listed below:

سراپائے نورانی شاہ جیلانی محبوب ربّانی

۱۳۲۲ ہجری

The Embodiment of Light, the King of Jīlān,
the Beloved of Allāh ﷻ.

1322 *hijrī*

اَلْحَمْدُ لِلّٰہِ وَ الصَّلٰوۃُ وَ التَّسْلِیْم عَلٰی حَبِیْبِہِ الْکَرِیْمِ وَ اٰلِہٖ

All Praise to Allāh ﷻ; Blessings and Salutations upon Allāh's Beloved, The Noble Prophet ﷺ, & upon the Prophet's progeny ﷺ.

حمد حق، نعت نبی، توصیف غوث بعد ازاں سن طالب تعریف غوث

Allāh's ﷻ Praise, the Prophet's ﷺ eulogy and a tribute of the Ghawth ﷺ; after these, O seeker, hear the attributes of the Ghawth ﷺ!

غوث اعظم کے فدائی، کان لا ذکر شہ ہے، نذر شہ کو جان لا

O the devotee of the Ghawth, be attentive, come closer; this is the King's remembrance, for him bring your life as an offer!

حلیہ اقدس کہ عین نور ہے بہجت الاسرار میں مذکور ہے

A manifestation of light, his holy appearance is such; in "Bahjat al Asrãr", it is recorded as such!

ترجمہ ترتیب دار اس کا لکھوں گوہر منثور کو لڑیوں میں لوں

So I pen its translation in its proper order; and string the precious gems into proper order.

وہ مبارک نثر ہو نثرہ نثار یہ ثریّا نظم ہو شعری شعار

May prose be sacrificed upon that holy scroll; may this lofty poem (Pleiades star) become a resemblance of the Sirius star.

كان شيخنا شيخ الاسلام محي الدين أبو محمد عبد القادر الجيلي

رضی اللہ تعالی عنہ

He is our Shaykh, Shaykh al-Islãm, Muḥiy al-Dĩn Abu-Muḥammad, ʿAbd al-Qãdir al-Jeelĩ ﷺ- May Allãh ﷻ be pleased with him

نحيف البدن

Slender Bodied

وہ اکہرا جسم نازک خوش نما وہ نحافت میں نزاکت کی ادا

The angular body, thin, and beautiful; the slender body, with a conduct so graceful.

جس پہ وارین خلد میں اپنی پھبن یاسمیں، نسریں، سمن گل نسترن

Upon which sacrifice in heaven, their beauty; the flowers of Jasmine, Jonquil, Orchid and Lilly.

ربع قامہ عریض صدر

Of Moderate Height, Wide Chested

قد میانہ سرو باغ مصطفیٰ سینہ چوڑہ صحن باغ اصفیا

Of moderate height, a cypress in the garden of Mustafa ﷺ; the wide chest, a courtyard of the gardens of Asfiya.

کیوں نہ ہو سینہ کشادہ دلکشا حاشیہ ہے شرح صدر شاہ کا

Why would not the chest be wide, pleasing to see? On the exegesis of the King's heart, it is a commentary!

عریض اللحیۃ طویلھا

Having Wide and Long Beard

ہے عریض ان کی محاسن اور طویل ہیں جزیل ان کے محاسن اور طویل

His beard is wide and long; his hairs are strong, and long.

عرض و طول ریش وافر باوقار طول عرض سائلاں کے ذمہ دار

The width and length of beard, thick and stately; responsible for lengthy applications of the needy.

أسمر اللون

Light Brown, Wheat Coloured Skin

اسمر اللون ان کی رنگت گندمی خوبی حسن وملاحت سے بھری

His complexion is light brown, wheat like; filled with beauty and enduringly attractive.

گندمی رنگت سہانی دل کشا وہ سنہرا پھول باغ نور کا

A light-wheat complexion, beautiful, a spectacle of delight; such is the golden flower of the garden of light.

مقرون الحاجبین

With Joint Eye-Brows

ابروئے پیوستہ کی دل کش بہار سو ہلال عید ہوں جس پر نثار

The joint eyebrows are a spring blossom, so nice; upon it a hundred ʿEid crescents I would sacrifice!

دونوں ماہ عید کی یکجا ہے دید لو مبارک قادریو عید عید

Combined is the spectacle of the two crescents of ʿEid; O Qādirīs! Congratulations of ʿEid upon ʿEid.

شاد شاداں جان و دل قرباں کرو جان کہنہ دے کے جان تازہ لو

O the happy ones, sacrifice your hearts and lives; give up the tired ones, and gain fresh lives

شام تک عید مہ نو ہے تمام یہ مہ جاوید ہے عید دوام

The Eid of the new moon lasts only until the evening; this new moon is lasting, the ʿEid is everlasting.

أدعج ألعينين

Having Captivating Eyes

اجعد العینین ہے وصف مبیں یعنی آنکھیں ہیں بڑی اور سرمگیں

The captivating eyes is an attribute distinct; which means the eyes are large, with black tint.

کیا بڑائی ان بڑی آنکھوں کی ہو جو عیاں دیکھیں رسول اللہ کو

How can one praise those great eyes? For clearly seen is the Messenger of Allah ﷺ by those eyes!

کیا بڑی اللہ اکبر آنکھ ہے دید اکبر سے مکبّر آنکھ ہے.

Allāhu Akbar! How great is the eye! Blessed with the great spectacle is the eye!

وہ خدا ہیں بندہ پرور آنکھ واہ مصطفیٰ ہیں فیض گستر آنکھ واہ

It beholds the Lord ﷻ and compassionate for the slave is the eye! It beholds Mustafa ﷺ, reflecting the beneficence is the eye!

قدرتی بے سرمہ آنکھیں سرمگیں باغ مازاغ البصر سے خوشہ چیں

Without antimony, naturally dark are the eyes; from the garden of "the sight did not waver" benefit the eyes.

ذا صوت جھوری

Having Resonant Voice

جھوری الصوت خوش اندازہ ہے وہ بلند آوا بلند آوازہ ہے

Resonant and pleasing to hear is his voice; high ranking, with words of high import is the voice.

و سمت بھی و قدر علی و علم وفی

With Majestic Head, of High Esteem and Firm Knowledge

ہے عجب روشن روش رتبہ رفیع علم والا کامل و پاک ووسیع

Amazing is his high stature, radiant is his stride; his crown is large, complete, pure and erudite.

رضی اللہ تعالی عنہ

May Allah Be Pleased With Him

بعد جد اس جود پر صبح وشام سو دردیں سو تحیت سو سلام

After his ancestor, upon this generosity all mornings and evenings; hundreds of blessings, and salutations and peace greetings.

اس سراپا نور پر بعد رسول سر سے پا تک ہو درودوں کا نزول

After the Messenger ﷺ, upon this light's embodiment; from

head to toe may blessings descend.

بے عدد بے انتہا بے حد مدام　　　تا ابد ہر آن ہر لحظہ دوام

Without count, without end, infinite, lasting forever; until eternity, at every moment, at all times forever.

دعا

Supplication

یا الٰہی اس سراپا کے لئے　　　قادریوں پر تری رحمت رہے

O Allāh! For the sake of his entity; may Your mercy be upon every Qādirī [disciple].

تیری رافت حفظ ہر آفت سے ہو　　　ان سے جو کچھ کام ہو رافت سے ہو

From every calamity, may Your compassion be their protection; may all the works they do, be with compassion.

زندگی بھر ناز و نعمت میں پلیں　　　بعد مردن ظل عزت میں چلیں

May they be blessed with prosperity and favours all life; and walk in the shade of respect, in the after-life.

جب گروہوں کی پکار اس جا پڑے　　　یہ پکارے جائیں ان کے نام سے

When the groups are summoned on the day of resurrection; may the Qādirīs be called with his designation.

ان کی دعوت میں ہو شامل ان کا نام　　　یوم ندعو کل ناس بامامام

When he is called upon, may they be with their leader; "On the day when We shall summon every group along with the leader"!

یہ رضا اور اس کے احباب اقربا　　　سب انہیں میں پائیں رضوان و رضا

May Raza, his friends and every family member; being among the Qādirīs, find paradise and Your good pleasure.

ان میں ہوں ان میں رہیں ان میں مریں　　　ان میں اٹھیں عیش خلد ان میں کریں

May we be Qādirīs, remain such, and die as Qādirīs; rise up as Qādirīs, and enjoy Paradise amongst the Qādirīs.

جیتے جی بندہ غلام شاہ ہو   بعد مردن ان کی خاک راہ ہو

May the bondman whilst alive be a slave of the King; after death be the dust on path of the King

وہ محرک نظم کے محمود جاں   سید والا حسب صالح جواں.

The initiator of this poem is Maḥmūd Jān; the leader of pious descent, the virtuous young man.

وہ بھی ہوں مسعود تن، محمود جاں   میں بھی ہوں محمود تن مسعود جاں

May he be fortunate, with a praiseworthy life; may I also become praiseworthy, with a fortunate life.

یا إلہ الحق اجب قولی اجب   استجب اللہ اکبر استجب

O the Truthful Lord, accept my plea, please accept! Accept my prayer, O Allah the Greatest, accept!

Original Work in *Urdu* by Aʿla Ḥaḍrat Imām Aḥmād Riḍā al-Qādiri Barkātī ﷺ and rendered into English by ʿĀqib Farīd al-Qādirī, at the request of Ḥaḍrat Maulana ʿAbdul Hādi al-Qādirī Raḍawī,
Shaʿbān 1437 Hijri / May, 2016.

It is easier for me to raise the dead than making an idiot understand

Sayyiduna Nabi Sulayman عليه السلام

About the Author and this book:

The erudite author and Sūfī Master, Imām Abu al-Ḥasan Nūr al-Dīn Shatnūfī al-Shafāʿī ﷺ was born in 644/1247 in Cairo and passed away there in 713 h. / 1314. He hailed from a pious family who originally lived in *Shām* [Syria]. His illustrious father ﷺ settled in Cairo and Imām al-Shatnūfī ﷺ was born there. He received all his education in Cairo and grew up to be a legend of his time. He was appointed a senior lecturer in *Ḥadith* and *Qir'at* at the world renowned Al-Azhar University. Many great scholars and authorities of *Dīn* attended his classes and they extolled him. This will be documented later in the book.

Imām Nūr al-Dīn al-Shatnūfī ﷺ was an ardent *Qādirī* disciple and greatly revered Sayyiduna Ghawth al-Āʿzam Shaykh ʿAbd al-Qādir al-Jilānī ﷺ. Imām al-Shatnūfī ﷺ met and narrated from some of those illustrious personalities who met and narrated directly from Sayyiduna Ghawth al-Aʿzam ﷺ. The uniqueness and authenticity of the narrations of Imām al-Shatnūfī ﷺ in this book is that all the authorities he narrates from are *Awliya-Allāh*. Such narrations are rarely found in *Islāmic* literature.

I document here the words of the great Mujaddid and ʿĀrif Billāh, Aʿlā-Ḥaḍrat Imām Aḥmad Riḍā al-Qādirī ﷺ that wrote about Imām Nūr al-Dīn al-Shatnūfī ﷺ in his book, *Tard al-Afā'ī*.[24] This will give the reader a wider spectrum of the scholastic attributes of Imām al-Shatnūfī ﷺ and the authenticity of his narrations. Here is what the great Mujaddid and Qutb ﷺ records:

At random, some traced narrations recorded by authentic *Asnād* [chain of narrators] viz, Imām al-Ajal Shaykh Abu al-Ḥasan ʿAlī b. Yūsuf Lakhmī Shatnūfī al-Shafāʿī ﷺ in his celebrated work, *Bahjat al-Asrār wa Maʿdan al-Anwār – Sublime Secret and Treasures of Light*, shall be documented. It is important to initially elucidate that this noble *Imām* lived two generations after the demise

[24] This book of Aʿlā-Ḥaḍrat Imām Aḥmad Riḍā ﷺ was translated into English by Shaykh ʿAbd al-Hādī al-Qādirī and is available at the Imām Aḥmad Raza Academy SA and online from sufipages.com

of Sayyiduna Ghawth al-Ā'zam Shaykh ʿAbd al-Qādir al-Jīlānī ﷺ [470/1078 – 561/1166]. Imām al-Shatnūfī ﷺ is invariably a beloved devotee of Sayyiduna Ghawth al-Aʿzam Shaykh ʿAbd al-Qādir al-Jīlānī ﷺ. Listed below are his chains of transmissions:

- ✓ Imām Abu al-Ḥasan al-Shatnūfī ﷺ is a student of the great Muḥaddith, Sayyidī Abu-Bakr b. Imām al-Ḥāfiz Taqī al-Dīn al-Anmātī ﷺ
- ✓ Muḥaddith Abu-Bakr ﷺ is a student of Imām al-Ajal ʿAllāma Muwaffiq al-Dīn ibn Qūdāma al-Maqdisī ﷺ who is the student and *Khalīfa* of Sayyiduna Sayyid al-Sadāt Shaykh ʿ Abd al-Qādir al-Jīlānī ﷺ.

The 2nd chain of transmission is traced as follows:

- ❖ Imām Shatnūfī ﷺ narrates from the Qāḍī al-Quḍāt Imām Muḥammad b. Imām Ibrāhīm b. ʿAbd al-Wāhid al-Maqdisī ﷺ
- ❖ He narrates from Imām ʿArif-Billāh Abu al-Qāsim Haybatullāh b. Imām Mansūr Naqīb al-Sadāt ﷺ who is a disciple of Ghawth al-Āʿzam Sayyiduna Sayyid al-Sadāt Shaykh ʿAbd al-Qādir al-Jīlānī ﷺ.

The 3rd chain of transmission encompasses the following:

- ❖ Imām Shatnūfī ﷺ reports from Shaykh Junaid Abu-Muḥammad Ḥasan b. ʿAlī Laḥmī ﷺ.
- ❖ He narrates from Sayyidi Shaykh Abu al-ʿAbbās Aḥmad b. ʿAlī al-Damishqī ﷺ and he narrates from Sayyidunā al-Shaykh ʿAbd al-Qādir al-Jīlānī ﷺ.

The 4th chain recorded stipulates:

- ❖ Imām Abu al-Ḥasan al-Shatnūfī ﷺ narrates from Imām Safī al-Dīn Khalīl b. Abī-Bakr al-Murāʿī ﷺ and Imām ʿAbd al-Wāhid b. ʿAlī b. Aḥmad al-Qurashī ﷺ.
- ❖ Both of them report from the eminent Sayyid Imām al-Ajal Sayyidi Shaykh Abu-Nasar Mūsa al-Jīlānī ﷺ who narrates from his illustrious father the *Qutb al-Aqtāb*, Sayyidunā Shaykh ʿAbd al-Qādir al-Jīlānī ﷺ.

In addition to the above mentioned four sequences of transmission, there are many more chains which link Sayyidī Imām Abu al-Ḥasan Shatnūfī ﷺ directly to the great Ghawth ﷺ, leading to two generations. Imām Shatnūfī al-Shafāʿī

ﷺ was born in 644/1247 and passed away in 713/1314.[25] The illustrious *Āimmah* of *Dīn* recognized him as a great *Imām* and *Sūfi* Master. Imām Dhahbī [d. 748/1347] ranks him as a master in the field of *Asmā al-Rijāl*[26]. It is astonishing that a scholar like Imām Dhahbī attributes to him an exceptional and elevated status, and substantiates his comments for reasons as follows:

- Firstly, Imām Shatnūfī ﷺ must have possessed an extraordinary expertise in this field.
- Secondly, Imām Dhahabī had very little regard for the illustrious *Sūfi* fraternity and their Transcendental Knowledge of *Allāh* ﷻ. His perspective for the noble *Sūfis* at times reached a level of zilch.
- Thirdly, in view of his negative attitude[27] towards the *Ash ͑arī* Scholars, which was exposed by his student Imām Tāj al-Dīn Subkī ibn Imām al-Ajal Barkat al-Anām Sayyidi ͑Ārif-Billāh Taqī al-Dīn ͑Alī b. ͑Abd al-Kāfī

[25] Amongst his contemporaries, some of the scholastic and saintly giants in the *Islāmic* World were: Imām Shaykh ‘Abdullāh Yafa‘ī Makki ﷺ [d.750/1349], Imām Abu-Zakariyya Muḥiyy al-Dīn Yaḥ’ya b. Sharf al-Nawawī ﷺ [d.676/1278], Imām Nāsir al-Dīn Abī-Sa͑īd ͑Abdullāh b. ͑Umar Bayḍāwī ﷺ [d.685/1286], Shaykh Sa͑adī Shirāzī ﷺ [d.688/1291], Shaykh Abu al-Ḥasan al-Shazalī ﷺ [d.656/1258], Khawaja Sultān Nizām al-Dīn Awliya Meḥ’būb-e-Ilahī ﷺ [d.725/1325], Mawlanā Jalāl al-Dīn Rūmī ﷺ [d.672/1273], Sayyidī al-Qutb Ibrahīm Dasūqī ﷺ [d.676/1278], Sayyidī al-Qutb Aḥmad al-Badawī ﷺ [d.675/1276], Shaykh ͑Ataullāh Askandarī ﷺ [d.709/1310], Imām Aḥmad b. Aḥmad Awzā͑ī ﷺ [d.733/1333], Imām Qāḍī al-Quḍāt Kamāludīn Abu al-Ma͑ālī Muḥammad b. ͑Alī b. ͑Abd al-Wāḥid b. Zamalkānī al-Ansārī al-Damishqī al-Shāfa͑ī ﷺ [727/1327], Imām Muḥammad Sharf al-Dīn Bū’sayrī ﷺ [d.696/1296], Shaykh Sharf al-Dīn Yaḥ’yah Manīrī ﷺ [d.756/1355], Imām Abu al-Barkāt Nasafī ﷺ [d.710/1310], Imām Abu al-Fida ͑Imād al-Dīn Ismā͑īl b. ͑Alī b. Meḥmūd al-Ayyūbī [672/1273—732/1338] etc.

[26] This is the science of knowledge of the details, names and biographies of all, or most, of the *Ḥadith* narrators found in *Ḥadith* Manuals such as *Saḥīḥ al-Bukhāri* and *Saḥīḥ Muslim* and the four *Sunan* books by *Al-Nasā’ī, al-Tirmidhī, Abu-Dā ͑ūd* and *Ibn-Mājah*. The biographies relate to the standing of each narrator relating to his narrating ability which is referred to in Arabic as *͑Ilm al-Rijāl*.

[27] This was so because Imām Dhahabī was a student of Ibn-Taymiya and his attitude was apparent towards the *Ash ͑arī* Scholars. Refer to *Fatawa Ibn Taymiyya fī al-Mizān* by Muḥammad b. Aḥmad Maskat b. al-͑Atīq al-Ya͑qūbī and *‘Akhtā Ibn Taymiyya fī Ḥaqqe Rasūlillāh* ﷺ *wa Ahle Baytihī’* by Dr. Sayyid Meḥmūd Sayyid Sabīḥ for details of his wavering beliefs.

ﷺ [d.771/1370]. He reveals that when his teacher encountered any *Ash ʿarī* [28] scholar, he ignored them with aversion.

- Fourthly, their presence provides evidence which nullifies the concept of contradiction or rejection. This is perceptible because Imām Dhahabī personally attended the classes of Imām Shatnūfī ﷺ in Cairo and was certainly impressed with his deep extraordinary knowledge. Although Imām Shatnūfī ﷺ was a follower of the *Ash ʿarī* school, he undoubtedly made a great impact on Imām Dhahabī, so that he would

[28] Ashʿarī theology is an early theological school of *Sunni Islām* based on clerical authority and rejection of cause and effect reasoning, it was founded by Imam Abu al-Ḥasan al-Ashʿarī ﷺ (d. 324 AH / 936 AD). The disciples of the school are known as Ashʿarites, and the school is also referred to as the Ashʿarite school. It is considered one of the orthodox theologies in *Sunnī Islām* alongside the *Maturīdī*. Amongst some of the most famous Ashʿarites authorities are:

Imām al-Juwaynī ﷺ, Imām Abu Ishaq ﷺ, Imām al-Shirazi ﷺ, Imām al-Tabaranī ﷺ, *Ḥadith* scholar, Major Collector of *Hadith*, Imām Ibn Ḥibban ﷺ, *Hadith* scholar, Master of *Ḥadith*, Imām al-Bayhaqī ﷺ, *Ḥadith, Fiqh* scholar, Imām Qāḍī ʿAyāḍ ﷺ, Imām al-Khatib al-Baghdadī ﷺ, Imām Abu al-Walid al-Bajī ﷺ, Imām al-Qushayri ﷺ, Imām al-Ghazalī ﷺ, *Hujjat al-Islām* (Authority of *Islām*), Jurist, Philosopher, Theologian, Imām Dhun-Nūn al-Misrī ﷺ, Shaykh Sayyid Aḥmad Al-Rifāʿī ﷺ, Ghawth Abu Madyan Shuʿayb al-Maghribī ﷺ, Imām Fakhr al-Din al-Rāzī ﷺ, Imām al-Bayḍāwī ﷺ, Imām Sayf al-Din al-Amīdī ﷺ, Imām Badr al-Dīn Ibn Jamaʿā ﷺ, Sultān Salāh al-Dīn al-Ayyūbī ﷺ, Founder of Ayyūbid Dynasty, Sultān of Egypt and Syria, Imām ʿIzz Al-Dīn ibn ʿAbd Al-Salām ﷺ, Imām Ibn ʿAsākir ﷺ, Imām Sharf al-Dīn al-Nawawī ﷺ, *Ḥadith* scholar, *Shafaʿī Sunnī* Jurist, Theologian, Biographer, Imām Ibn Ḥajar al-ʿAsqalānī ﷺ, Shaykh al-Islām (Outstanding scholars of the *Islāmic* sciences), *Ḥadith* scholar, Shafāʿī *Sunni* scholar, *Tafsīr* scholar, Imām Abu Bakr al-Aydarus ﷺ, Imām Jalāl al-Dīn Davānī ﷺ, Imām Ibn ʿArafa ﷺ, Imām Maḥmūd al-Nasafī ﷺ, Imām Nizām al-Dīn Nishapūrī ﷺ, Imām Abu Ḥayyān al-Gharnātī ﷺ, Imām Ibn Daqīq al-ʿEid ﷺ, Imām Jalāl al-Dīn al-Maḥallī ﷺ, Imām Jalāl al-Dīn al-Suyūtī ﷺ, Theologian, Shafāʿī scholar, Scholar on *Ijtihād, Ḥadith, Qur'ānic* Exegesis (*Tafsīr*), *ʿAqidah* (*Tawḥīd*), Imām Zakariyya al-Ansarī ﷺ, Imām Taqī al-Dīn An-Nabhanī ﷺ, Taqī al-Dīn al-Subkī ﷺ, Imām Tāj al-Dīn al-Subki ﷺ, Imām Ibn Hajar al-Haytamī ﷺ, Imām Sirāj al-Dīn al-Bulqinī ﷺ, Imām Jalāl al-Dīn al-Bulqinī ﷺ, Imām Saʿād al-Dīn Taftazānī ﷺ, Imām Ibn al-Jazarī ﷺ, Imām al-Mazirī ﷺ, Imām Abu al-Qāsim al-Rafāʿī ﷺ, Shaykh Ibn ʿAtā Allāh al-Iskandarī ﷺ, Imām Shams al-Dīn al-Ramlī ﷺ, Imām Shihāb al-Dīn al-Ramlī ﷺ, Imām ʿAla al-Dīn al-Bukhārī ﷺ, Imām Shams al-Dīn al-Sakhāwī ﷺ, Shaykh ʿĀrif Billāh Aḥmad Zarrūq ﷺ and host of other senior authorities and *Awliya* of *Islām*.

acknowledge his extensive and profound knowledge in the field of *Ḥadith*. Hence, Imãm Dhahabĩ in his book, entitled *Tabqãt al-Muqar'rĩn,* addresses Imãm Shatnũfĩ ﷺ as *Al-Imãm al-Awḥad [The Unique Imãm]*.

Apart from this, there are statements recorded by Imãm Dhahabi [d.748/1347] that are indicative of the praises, superiority and excellence about the status of Imãm Shatnũfĩ ﷺ. To this effect, he pens down the following:

'Alĩ b. Yũsuf Lakhmĩ al-Shatnũfĩ is a par-excellence Imãm in the entire country of *Qãhira* [Egypt] and is also a proficient master in the subject matter of the Holy *Qur'ãn*. He is a *Shaykh* of *Qir'ãt*. His surname is Abu al-Ḥasan and his family was originally from *Shãm* [Syria]. He was born in 644 *Hijri* in Cairo and at a later stage, he held the designation of a senior lecturer at the world renowned al-Azhar University. I attended his classes and experienced immense tranquillity, both in his speech and in his silence.'

The exalted Imãm, Sayyidi ʿAbdullãh b. Asad Yafaʿĩ ﷺ [d.750/1349] elucidates in his *Mir'at al-Jinãn*:

'Our Master Shaykh Sayyid ʿAbd a-Qãdir al-Jilãnĩ ؓ was bestowed with innumerable Divinely Ordained Charisms [*karãmãt*][29] which could not be counted. Some of them have been mentioned in my book, named *Nashar al-Muḥãsin.* Amongst all the celebrated senior *Imãms* with whom I met, all of them were unanimous about the fact that the magnitude of the *karãmãt* of Sayyidunã Ghawth al-Ãʿzam ؓ had reached the state of *Tawãtur* [30] or close to it, and all these *karãmãt* were authentic and left no

[29] Any miracle performed by a *Walĩ* of *Allãh* is termed as *Karamat*. True miracles or *Karamãt* will radiate from a saintly person who is bonded with *Allãh* ﷻ. Such a person is consistently obedient to the *Sharĩ'ãh* at any given moment and place. His personality will be illuminated to such a degree that just a view of him, will immediately transform one in beginning to contemplate on *Allãh* ﷻ and hence one's love and attachment for the *Duniyah* [this mundane world] will also disappear from one's mind and heart.

[30] Continuous. This is a tradition reported by a large number of people in different reliable

scope for a shadow of doubt. It is also an accepted fact that, except Sayyidunā ʿAbd al-Qādir al-Jilānī ﷺ there was no other *Walī* of *Allāh* in the entire world that executed voluminous *karāmāt* as he did.'

The great Mujaddid, Imām Aḥmad Riḍā al-Qādirī ﷺ alludes to one *karāmat* from this book which is recorded by Imām Abu al-Ḥasan Shatnūfī ﷺ in this celebrated *Bahjat al-Asrar*. This *karāmat* is narrated by six distinguished *ʿĀrifīn*[31] who were the leaders of the *Mashā'ikh* of their time. They were:

1) ʿĀrif-Billāh Sayyidī ʿUmar al-Kamīmānī ﷺ,
2) Sayyidī Imām ʿUmar b. Masʿūd Baz'zār ﷺ,
3) Sayyidī Shaykh Abu-Saʿūd Mudallal ﷺ,
4) Sayyidī Abu al-ʿAbbās Aḥmad al-Sar'sarī ﷺ,
5) Sayyid al-Sadāt Imām al-Ajal Sayyidunā Tāj al-Millat wa al-Dīn Abu-Bakr ʿAbd al-Razzāq b. Sayyidunā Ghawth al-Āʿzam ﷺ, and
6) Sayyidī Imām Abu-ʿAbdullāh Muḥammad b. Abī al-Maʿālī b. Qāidwānī ﷺ.

All of the above mentioned *Mashā'ikh* report as follows:

'A woman brought her young son to Sayyidunā Qutb al-Wūjūd Ghawth al-Aʿzam Shaykh ʿAbd al-Qādir al-Ḥasanī al-Ḥusainī al-Jilānī ﷺ and entrusted him to take her son under his consecrated care, because of the son's fervent reverence for the Great Ghawth ﷺ. She appealed to the Ghawth: *"O Master! I have forsaken my rights over my son, and do hereby place him in your capable hands. Please accept him and train him in the Spiritual Path."*

She left her son with the *Ghawth* ﷺ and departed. After a certain period of time, she returned to visit him, and was perturbed to find him in a deteriorating health condition, pale-faced, whilst he was eating pieces of

times which makes it is impossible for any falsehood to creep into it.

[31] The Aware one - Gnostics, People with the realization of *Allāh* ﷻ. Whomsoever the Lord ﷻ causes to witness his own self, so that the states are manifested to him. *Maʿārifah*, realization, is his condition.

dry barley bread. Being very concerned about her child, the lady proceeded to the private chamber of the *Ghawth* ﷺ. The door was open and she caught sight of a plate of chicken bones, which was in front of the Sayyidunā Ghawth al-Aʿzam ﷺ who had just taken his meal. She exclaimed: *"O my Master! You eat chicken and my son eats dry barley bread."* The Master listened to her comment and placed his sanctified hand on the plate containing the bones of the chicken and stipulated:

قُوْمِی بِاِذْنِ اللهِ الَّذِی یُحْیِ الْعِظَامَ وَ هِیَ رَمِیْم

Yes! Get up by the command of Allāh ﷻ
Who will give life to decayed bones.

In response to his command, the chicken was immediately resurrected and began to make noises. Thereafter, the Grand Ghawth ﷺ informed the lady: *"When your son reaches this state, then he too can eat whatever he desires."*

The same group of *ʿĀrifīn* [Gnostics] report another incident which took place in the gathering of the Great Ghawth ﷺ. Once, while the Master was addressing a gathering, a vulture flew above the audience making loud noises. Such disturbance diverted the attention of the audience. The Ghawth ﷺ noticed this, and commanded the air to grab the neck of the vulture. As soon as he decreed this command, the body of the vulture fell to the ground and its head fell in the opposite direction. When the discourse concluded, Sayyiduna Ghawth al-Aʿzam ﷺ descended from his chair and proceeded to the vulture. He placed his sacrosanct hand on it; and thereafter, he recited: بسم الله الرحمن الرحیم. Everyone witnessed that the vulture instantly rose to life and flew away into the atmosphere.

قادرا قدرت تو داری ہر چہ خواہی آں کنی
مردہ را جانے دہی و زندہ را بیجاں کنی

O Powerful! Your [Divinely Blessed] power
allows you to do as you please,
You give life to the dead and take the life of the living

[by the Permission of Allāh ﷻ]. [32]

Imām Muḥaddith Shaykh al-Qurrā Shams al-Millat al-Dīn Abu al-Khayr Muḥammad Muḥammad Muḥammad b. al-Jazrī ؒ [d.833/1430] in his book, *Nihāyat al-Darāyāt fi Asma Rijāl al-Qirā'āt* inscribed the following comments:

> ʿAlī b. Yūsuf b. Jarīr b. Faḍal b. Maʿḍād Nūr al-Dīn Abu al-Ḥasan Lakhmī Shatnūfī al-Shafāʿī is a proficient and brilliant educator. He has such an impressive personality that whosoever sees him gets astounded. He was born in 644 *hijrī* [1247] in Cairo. At the Al-Azhar University, he held the position of a professor, and owing to his profound knowledge, scholars flocked to him. I am also given to understand that he penned a commentary of *Shātabiyya Mubārakah.* If this particular commentary can be retrieved, then it would be classified as the best amongst all the commentaries. His marginal notes are of tremendous benefit. Imām Dhahabī affirms that Imām Shatnūfī ؒ had intense affection for Sayyiduna Shaykh ʿAbd al-Qādir al-Jilānī ؓ. He has compiled three volumes on the life and works of Sayyidunā Ghawth al-Aʿzam ؓ. I [Shams Jazrī ؒ] declare that these compilations are preserved in the *Zāwiya* [*Khanqah*] of Ḥaḍrat Sultān Salāḥudīn Ayyūbī [d.589/1193] [33]

[32] Poetry of Imām Aḥmad Riḍā ؒ see *Aksīr al-Aʿzam.*

[33] It is incredible to note that the driving force and influence on the life of Sultan Salāḥ al-Dīn Ayyūbī ؒ was that of Sayyiduna Shaykh ʿAbd al-ʿAzīz Jilānī ؓ s/o Sayyiduna Ghawth al-Āʿzam ؓ [d.602/1205]. The Sultān was a fervid *Qādiri* disciple of the great Sūfī Master who left his home town in Baghdad and settled in the North Kurdistan. It is here that Sayyiduna Shaykh ʿAbd al-ʿAzīz Jilānī ؓ perceived that, although the Kurds were sincere *Muslims,* they lacked education. He embarked on educating the Kurds and commissioned them to recapture the sacred *Ḥaram* of *Al-Quds* [*Masjid al-Aqsa*]. After perfecting the sciences of knowledge from his illustrious Father ؓ, Sayyiduna Shaykh ʿAbd al-ʿAzīz Jilānī ؓ, spent most of his time in the north of Iraq [Kurdistan] imparting knowledge and inculcating Divine Love within the Kurds. Eventually he settled in the north and passed away there on 18th Rabīʿ al-Thānī 602 *hijrī.* His *Mazār al-Sharīf* is situated in a town called Aqrah in the locality 85 miles away from Mosul. Sayyiduna Ghawth al-Aʿzam ؓ used to visit him in this remote northern area of the country. Here, a *Khalwa* [place of *Murāqibah*] is also attributed to the Great Ghawth ؓ. It is unfortunate that historians disregard this important chapter in history for they are not informed of its reality. The existing proof of the *Sultān* being a devout *Qādirī Murīd* is his sword which

[May *Allāh* ﷻ illuminate his eminence]. My teacher, the Master of *Ḥadith*, Muḥiyy al-Dīn ʿAbd al-Qādir Ḥanafī ﷺ and other *Shuyūkh* have granted me permission to transmit the narrations of this book. The author of this book [Imām Shatnūfī] passed away on Saturday 19th *Zil-Ḥajj* 713 [5th April 1314] at the time of *Zuhr* and was buried on Sunday 20th *Zil-Ḥajj* 713 [6th April 1314]. May *Allāh* ﷻ shower His Mercy upon him.

Imām ʿUmar b. ʿAbd al-Wah'hāb Farḍī al-Ḥalabī ﷺ records the following marginal notes on his copy of *Bahjat al-Asrār:*

'Verily, I have read this book from the beginning to the end and have thoroughly scrutinised each narration. I have not discovered a single narration which has not been endorsed by a vast majority of other narrators. These narrations were recorded by Imām Yafaʿī ﷺ [d.750/1349] in *As'na al-Mafākhir, Nashr al-Muḥāsin* and *Rowḍah al-Riyaḥīn.* Similarly, Imām Shams al-Dīn Zakī Ḥalabī ﷺ also records the same in his *Kitāb al-Ashrāf.*

The most significant aspect recorded in *Bahjat al-Asrār* reveals the resurrection of the dead, similar to the miraculous case of the resurrected chicken. I swear

he used in all his victorious conquers and also in the liberation of *Al-Quds*. It is preserved in the Topkapi Museum in Istanbul. This sword is engraved with Arabic inscriptions on both sides of the blade. On the one side is engraved the *Kalimah* لاالٰہ الا اللہ محمد رسول اللہ and on the other side is the name of Shaykh ʿAbd al-Qādir al-Jilānī ﷺ یاشیخ عبد القادر جیلانی شیأً للہ. Indeed this relic provides an existing proof that he was a devout *Qādirī Murīd* and sought spiritual assistance from Sayyiduna Ghawth al-Āʿzam ﷺ in all his conquers. History bears testimony to the fact that owing to his link and unwavering allegiance to Sayyiduna ash-Shaykh ﷺ, he was not defeated in war by an enemy force. He was always victorious because he was altruistically supported by Almighty Allāh's ﷻ appointed Supreme Ruler of his time. Sultan Salāḥ al-Dīn Ayyūbī ﷺ and also Sultān Sayyid Nūrudīn Maḥmūd Zangī Shahīd ﷺ had meetings with the Great Ghawth ﷺ and derived substantive *Barakāt* from him. In fact, it was the motivation of Sayyidi ʿAbd al-Qādir al-Jilānī ﷺ that was the driving force in the life and success of both the *Sultāns*. The symbolic proof of Sultān Salāḥudīn's ﷺ Love and allegiance to the great Ghawth ﷺ is the engraved name of the Ghawth ﷺ on the blade of his sword. # refer Ramaḍān Annual of Makkī Publications Durban South Africa *[Translator]* by my life that Imām Tāj al-Dīn Subkī ﷺ [d.771/1370] also quoted this incident. This *karāmat* was also narrated by Ibn Rifāʿī ﷺ and other distinguished *Awliya*. How absurd is it for the ignorant, as well as the mentality of a biased individual to ever understand the connotation of recorded words, pertinent to the lofty status of *Awliya?* Individuals of this category have wasted their entire lives by engaging in idleness, thus discarding inner purification and concentration in *Allāh* ﷻ. Whilst claiming to be travellers on the mystical path, they still have the audacity to impede into Divine Dictates. It is for this reason the Cardinal Pole of noble Saints [*Qutb*], Sayyidī Shaykh Junayd Baghdādī ﷺ articulated:

اَلتَّصْدِيْقُ بِطَرِيْقَتِنَا وِلَايَةٌ

The confirmation of our [Awliya] path
is also Wilāyah [Sainthood].[34]

[اَقُوْلُ][35] رحمه الله تعالى The author of *Bahjat al-Asrār* validates in the *Khutbah* of his book as follows:

لَخَّصْتُهُ كِتَابًا مُفْرَداً مَرْفُوْعَ الْاَسَانِيْدِ مُعْتَمَدًا فِيْهَا عَلَى الصِّحَّةِ دُوْنَ الشُّذُوْذِ

I have compiled this book and ratified it with authenticity by terminating each chain of transmission to its original and

---

[34]Cited in *Kashf al-Zunūn,* Vol.1, pg.245, Dār al-Fikr ed.

[35]Whenever the great *Mujaddid,* Imām Aḥmad Riḍā ﷺ notes the word اَقُوْلُ *Aqūlu* [meaning, *I say*] in his books, his Divinely Blessed Knowledge unfolds which overwhelms the scholars of *Dīn*. It was due to his profound and diverse branches of knowledge that the illustrious *ʿUlama* of *Ḥaramayn al-Sharīfayn* and the Arab world greeted him with great dignity and conferred upon him the honorific title of *"Imām Ahlus Sunnah"*, *"The Great Jurist of Islām"* and *"The Interpreter of Science and Learning"*. Owing to his supremacy in knowledge, Arab scholars like Shaykh Sayyid Ismaʿīl b. Khalīl ﷺ and Shaykh Mūsā 'Alī Shāmī ﷺ commended him as a Revivalist [*Mujaddid*] of the 14th century A.H. Refer to the books *Al-Dowlat al-Makkiyah bi al-Maddat al-Ghaybiyyah* [translated in English by Shaykh ʿAbd al-Hādī al-Qādirī and available online from sufipages.com and *The Neglected Genius of the East,* etc.

authentic source. Great precaution was taken in the genuineness of every narration to avoid any room for fault and doubt.[36]

Hence, the above mentioned information from the *Khutbah* confirms that the author had carefully evaluated every single narration recorded in *Bahjat al-Asrār* to be absolutely authentic, and free from all defects. Hence, it is ipso-facto [the fact in itself] that no narration in this book can be rated as *Ḍa ʿīf,*[37] *Gharīb*[38] or *Shāz.*[39]

الحمد لله رب العالمين

N.B.

One of the unique fact in the narrations found in this monumental book is that every narrator cited herein is an erudite authority of *Islāmic* Law [*Dīn*] and a *Walī* of *Allāh*. [Translator].

Imām Khātim al-Ḥuffāz Sayyidī Jalāl al-Millat wa al-Dīn al-Suyūtī ﷺ [d.911/1505] in his book *Ḥusn al-Muḥāḍara fi Akhbār al-Misr wa al-Qāhira* documents the following comments on Imām al-Shatnūfī ﷺ:

> ʿAlī b. Yūsuf b. Jarīr Lakhmī al-Shatnūfī was an unparalleled *Imām*. Imām Nūr al-Dīn Abu al-Ḥasan was the *Shaykh al-Qurra*[40] of Egypt. He was born in 644 *Hijri* and was also a lecturer at *Jāme ʿh al-Azhar*. Students always rallied around him. He passed away in *Zil-Ḥajj* 713.

---

[36] Refer to the *Khutbah* of *Bahjat al-Asrār*.

[37] *A Weak Narration:* It means that there is some doubt either in the chain of transmission, or in the proper understanding of the transmitter, or its contents are not in conformity with *Islamic* beliefs and practices. In fact it is a weak tradition or is extracted from a source that is less reliable.

[38] *A Poor Narration:* The narration in the chain of transmission in which the narrators are reduced to one at any stage is known as *Gharīb.*

[39] *An Isolated Narration - Shāz:* A narration which is comparatively less authentic and the narrator opposes the view of the one whose account is more authentic than his.

[40] A Master of all the methods [*Tajwīd*] in the recitation of the Holy *Qur'ān*. *Imām* of the seven *Qir'ats*. A leader of the *Qurra'*.

Shaykh al-Muḥaqqiq Mawlanā ʿAbd al-Ḥaqq Muḥaddith Dehlawī ﷺ [d.1052/1642] states in his *Zubdat al-Āthār*:

> There was only an interim of two generations between the author of *Bhajat al-Asrār*, the *Shaykh*, the *Imām*, the Jurist, the *ʿĀlim*, the Master Reciter, the unparalleled Scholar, the genius, Nūr al-Dīn Abu al-Ḥasan ʿAlī b. Yūsuf al-Shafāʿī al-Lakh'mī and Sayyiduna Ghawth al-Āʿzam Shaykh ʿAbd al-Qādir al-Jilānī ﷺ.

Furthermore, Shaykh-e-Muḥaqqiq ﷺ writes in his other publications, *Risāla Salāt al-Asrār*:

> The esteemed book *Bahjat al-Asrār wa Maʿdan al-Anwār* is an authentic and famed book for reference and its author is from amongst the celebrated *ʿUlama*. There are only two chains [generations] between him and Ḥaḍrat Sayyiduna Shaykh ʿAbd al-Qādir al-Jilānī ﷺ. He lived before Imām ʿAbdullāh Yafaʿī ﷺ and was amongst the sincere lovers of the great Ghawth ﷺ.

He further elaborates:

> In *Makkah al-Mukarramah*, this *Faqīr* was in the company of the illustrious Shaykh, the exalted Master Shaykh ʿAbd al-Wah'hāb Muttaqī [41] ﷺ who was the *murīd* of Ḥaḍrat Shaykh Imām ʿAlī Muttaqī [42] ﷺ. He stated that as far as he was concerned, the book *Bahjat al-Asrār* is an authentic book in this time and period and he had thoroughly examined it. It was his unique characteristic that if he discovered a book that was prolific and beneficial, he always compared it with other books and corrected it. When I met him, he was busy in studying *Bahjat al-Asrār*.

[41] Shaykh ʿAbd al-Wah'hāb al-Muttaqī al-Qādirī ﷺ was a beloved disciple of Shaykh ʿAlī al-Muttaqī ﷺ and succeeded him after his demise in Makkah al-Mukarramah. Refer *Akhbār al-Akhyār* for details.

[42] Shaykh ʿAla al-Dīn ʿAlī b. ʿAbd al-Malik Ḥusām al-Dīn al-Muttaqī al-Hindī al-Qādirī ﷺ (1472 - 1567 CE/888 - 975 AH) was a great *Imām, Ḥadith* scholar and *Sūfī* Master of his era who is renowned for writing the world famous *Kanz al-ʿUmmāl*.

Alḥamdulillāh! It is clear from the verbatim words of these illustrious *Imāms* of *Dīn* that the author of *Bahjat al-Asrār*, Imām Abu al-Ḥasan ʿAlī Nūr al-Dīn al-Shatnūfī ﷺ is a profuse *Imām*, inimitable Scholar, impeccable Jurist and a Master of *Qirāt*. He was also rated as a leader of the high-ranking *ʿUlama* and *Mashā'ikh* of his time. Furthermore, his book *Bahjat al-Asrār*, is classified as bona fide by distinguished *Imāms* who have quoted from its source in view of the fact of its reliability as a reference book. Similar to the books of *Ḥadith*, they also acquired accreditation for narrations contained in it. Amongst the books of biography of Sayyiduna Ghawth al-Aʿzam ﷺ, the legitimacy of narrators of this book is similar to the *Mu'atta* of Imām Mālik ﷺ in the books of *Ḥadith*. In so far as the authenticity of narrators in all the books, concerning praises and virtues [*Faḍā'il*] of *Awliya*, it holds a similar equation to that of *Saḥiḥ al-Bukhārī*. In fact, there are *Shāz*[43] *Ḥadith* in the *Siḥā*, but there is absolutely no *Shāz Ḥadith* narrated in *Bahjat al-Asrār*.

Imām al-Bukhārī ﷺ had only taken into account the sturdy nature and validity [*Siḥat*] of the narration. On the contrary, the narrations found in *Bahjat al-Asrār*, Imām Shatnūfī ﷺ not only took great care in sound validity [*Siḥat*], but he also ensured that no false or fabricated narrations were recorded.[44] Imām ʿAllama ʿUmar al-Ḥalabī ﷺ provides an exposition that Imām Shatnūfī ﷺ has fully complied with all the correct rules and regulations that are relevant to the transmission of narrations in his book. Hence, all of his narrations are impeccable and are unquestionable, because they can be confirmed by various other narrations.

والحمد لله رب العالمين

Certainly! A dignified and unique *Imām* has compiled a remarkable and exceptional book, wherein every *Ḥadith* is *Saḥiḥ*. We supplicate that the Sublime Lord ﷻ shall bless us with the *Barkāt* of both the Worlds!

---

[43] *An Isolated Narration - Shāz:* A narration which is comparatively less authentic, and the narrator opposes one whose account is more authentic than his.

[44] Refer to page 52, the *Khutbah* of Imām Shatnūfī ﷺ.

وباللہ التوفیق

By:
Qutb al-Irshād ʿĀrif Billāh Mujaddid
Imām Aḥmad Riḍā al-Qādirī
Muḥaqqiq Bareillwī رضي الله عنه
Extracted from his book
Tard al-Afāʿī

یا شیخ عبد القادر جیلانی شیئاً للہ

Some Important Family information of the Great Ghawth ﷺ & His Notable Sons

Ibn Najjār ﷺ narrates in his *Tārīkh* that Sayyiduna Shaykh ʿAbd al-Razzāq al-Jilānī ﷺ said that *Allāh* ﷻ blessed his father with 49 children, 27 sons and 22 daughters.

On the contrary, Imām Nūr al-Dīn al-Shatnūfī ﷺ in his famous and most authentic *Bahjat al-Asrār* states that the great Ghawth ﷺ had twelve sons. Since *Bahjat al-Asrār* is the highest and most authentic authority on the life and works of the Ghawth ﷺ, hence we will quote from it. The twelve sons are as follows:

1) Shaykh Imām Sayyid Abu-ʿAbdullāh Sayyiduna ʿAbd al-Raḥmān al-Jilānī ﷺ (b.508/1115). He was an astonishing *Ḥadith* Master of his age. He passed away in Baghdad in 587/1191 and was buried there.
2) Shaykh Sayyid Imām Sayf al-Dīn Abu-ʿAbdullāh ʿAbd al-Wah'hāb al-Jilānī ﷺ (b. 522/1128). He held the highest status amongst all the brothers and he was a senior *Faqhī* (Jurist). He was also a great orator and very eloquent in conducting discourses in the presence of his illustrious father. He passed away in Baghdad in 593/1197 and was laid to rest in the *Madressa* of his father. The great *ʿĀrif* and *Sūfī* Master; Ḥaḍrat Sayyid ʿAlā al-Dīn ʿAlī Aḥmad Sābir Kalyarī ﷺ was his grandson; who was the senior *Khalīfah* of Ḥaḍrat Khawaja Farīd al-Dīn Musʿūd Ganje Shakar ﷺ.[45]
3) Shaykh Sayyid Imām Sharf al-Dīn Abu-Muḥammad al-Jilānī ﷺ (d.573/1178). His *Kunniyah* is Abu-ʿAbd al-Raḥmān ʿIsā. He was an accomplished *Ḥadith* Master and *Faqhī* imparting these sciences to the people of Baghdad and Egypt. He passed away in Cairo 12 years after the demise of his father and 20 years after his elder brother, Sayyiduna ʿAbd al-Wah'hāb ﷺ. He lies buried in Cairo where he is known as Shaykh ʿĪsā Abu-Rum'māna Jilānī ﷺ.

[45] The geonology of Ḥaḍrat Sābir Paak ﷺ is as follows; Sayyiduna Khawaja ʿAlā al-Dīn Sābir Paak Kalyarī ﷺ s/o Sayyid ʿAbd al-Raḥīm al-Jilānī ﷺ s/o Sayyid ʿAbd al-Wah'hāb al-Jilānī ﷺ s/o Sayyiduna Ghawth al-Aʿzam Shaykh ʿAbd al-Qādir al-Jilānī ﷺ

4) Shaykh Sayyid Imām ʿAbd al-Jabbār Jamāl al-Dīn Abu-ʿAbd al-Raḥmān al-Jilānī ﷺ (d. 575/1180). His *Kunniyah* is Abu al-Faraḥ. He mastered the art of calligraphy. He was a devout *Sūfī* Master. He always sat in the company of the *Mashā'ikh* and absorbed spiritual grace from them. He also taught people *Ḥadith* and a host of other sciences. He passed away in Baghdad at a young age of 28 years before his brother, Sayyiduna ʿAbd al-Razzāq ﷺ, and lies buried in the *Khanqah* of his father.
5) Shaykh Sayyid Imām Tāj al-Dīn Abu-Bakr ʿAbd al-Razzāq al-Jilānī ﷺ (d. 623-1226). He was the most prominent son of the great Ghawth ﷺ. It was through him that the *Qādirī Silsila* flourished and spread out throughout the world. He was a prolific scholar and a great *Sūfī* Master reaching out to far parts of the *Islāmic* world. He mastered all sciences of knowledge by the tutorship of his illustrious father. He passed away in Baghdad and was laid to rest next to Imām Aḥmad b. Ḥanbal ﷺ on the banks of the Tigris River. This *Mazār al-Sharīf* is now submerged in the Tigris River due to the widening of the river banks over a long period of time. At times when the water level drops, the tip of the dome can be seen in the river. It is also said that he passed away in Ḥalab – Syria and is buried there. *Allah* ﷻ Knows best.
6) Shaykh Sayyid Imām Shams al-Dīn Abu-Muḥammad ʿAbd al-Azīz al-Jilānī ﷺ (d.602/1206). His *Kunniyah* is Abu-Bakr. He was an accomplished scholar and great *Sūfī* Master. In 580/1184 his father, Sayyiduna Ghawth al-Aʿzam ﷺ, sent him to promote *Islām* in the north western regions of Iraq - Jiyāl[46] now known as Kurdistan. Though the Kurds were sincere *Muslims* but they lacked *Islāmic* knowledge. He began his educational mission in Jiyāl where Sultān Salāḥ al-Dīn Ayyūbī ﷺ sat in his company studying Spiritual Culture and perfecting himself in spirituality. It was Sayyid ʿAbd al-ʿAzīz al-Jilānī ﷺ who was responsible in initiating and

[46] This is a small village of the Jodi Mountain range. This locality was a 7 day journey from Baghdad where the great Ghawth ﷺ initially settled and built a home for his family before relocating to Baghdad. He built this home with his hard-earned money. It was here that Ḥaḍrat Khawaja Gharīb Nawāz ﷺ first met Sayyiduna Ghawth al-Aʿzam ﷺ and derived spiritual blessings from him. The Khawaja ﷺ was then 20 years of age. Cited in *Iqtibās al-Anwār'*, refer to it for details.

advising Sultãn Salãḥ al-Dĩn al-Ayyũbĩ ﷺ to liberate *Masjid al-Aqsa* from the occupation of the Christian Crusaders. Unfortunately, the majority of historians don't mention this great service of this *Sũfĩ* Master. The world is totally unaware of the fact that Sultãn Salãḥ al-Dĩn al-Ayyũbĩ ﷺ and Sultan Sayyid Nũr al-Dĩn Maḥmũd Zangĩ ﷺ were *Qãdirĩ* disciples. I have briefly mentioned this in the chapter where the four sequences of transmission of the book *Bahjat al-Asrãr* was discussed. Sayyiduna ʿAbd al-ʿAzĩz al-Jilãnĩ ﷺ settled here with his family and eventually passed away here in 602/1206. He was buried in the locality of ʿAqrah about 85 kilometers from Mosul. There is also a *Khalwa* [private room of worship - retreat] of Sayyiduna Ghawth al-Aʿzam ﷺ wherein he prayed whenever he visited his beloved son.

7) Shaykh Sayyid Imãm Abu-Isḥãq Ibrãhĩm al-Jilãnĩ ﷺ (527/1133). He was an embodiment of the most wonderful qualities, each being a reflection of his pure progeny [*Ahle-Bayth*]. He too was a great *Ḥadith* Master and narrated *Ḥadith* from his august father, the great Ghawth ﷺ. He left Baghdad for *Islãmic* propagation purposes and settled in Wãsit, a city 160 km from Baghdad. He passed away in this town in 592/1196 and lies buried there.
8) Shaykh Sayyid Imãm Abu al-Faḍal Muḥammad al-Jilãnĩ ﷺ (d. 600/1204). He achieved the status of a master of *Ḥadith* from his eminent father, Ḥaḍrate Ghawth al-Aʿzam ﷺ and other notable *Ḥãdith* Masters. He then taught the Science of *Ḥadith* to the people. He was rated as an incredible Master of *Ḥadith* of his age. He passed away in Baghdad and was laid to rest in *Maqbara Ḥalba.*
9) Shaykh Sayyid Imãm Ḍiya al-Dĩn Abu-Nasar Mũsã al-Jilãnĩ ﷺ (b. 535/1141 - d.618/1221). He too was a great *Faqhĩ* [Jurist] and a *Ḥadith* Master [*Ḥafiz al-Ḥadith*]. He was rated amongst the senior teachers of Baghdad due to his mastery in various sciences of knowledge. He also imparted knowledge in Egypt and Syria where thousands of students attended his classes. He eventually settled in Damascus and passed away there. He was laid to rest in the famous *Bãb al-Saghĩr* cemetery of

Damascus. Some scholars opine that he passed away in the city of Hama – Syria; *Allāh* ﷻ Knows best.

10) Shaykh Sayyid Imām Abu-Zakariyyah Yaḥyah al-Jilānī ﵁ (b. 550/1155 d.600/1204). Once Sayyiduna Ghawth al-Aʿzam ﵁ fell very ill and people thought that his illness will terminate his physical life on earth. The great Ghawth ﵁ intercepted their feelings and said, *"I will not die now because I have in my back a sperm of a son who will be called Yaḥyah. He will be born in the future."* People did not take this comment seriously and regarded it as a result of his serious illness. However, as the Ghawth ﵁ predicted, he recovered from his sickness. Thereafter, after some time, Sayyiduna Yaḥyah ﵁ was born. He completed his studies under his distinguished father and left for Egypt at a very young age. Later, he returned to Baghdad with his son. He served as a lecturer in his father's *Madressa* and eventually passed away in Baghdad. His *Janāza Salāh* was performed in the *Madressa* of his father and he was laid to rest besides his elder brother, Sayyiduna ʿAbd al-Wah'hāb al-Jilānī ﵁.

11) Sayyiduna ʿAbd al-Jabbār al-Jilānī ﵁. I could not trace any information in books of history about the dates of his birth and demise. He was an erudite and prolific scholar decorated with perfect spiritual qualities by his illustrious father ﵁. He states that whenever his pious mother entered a dark room, it would illuminate with light. One day when this happened in the presence of his honourable father ﵁ and he uttered some words. A loud and scary shriek was heard. He then said: *'That light was of the cursed devil and I have chased it away.'* He then pointed his consecrated finger to the wall and the room lit up. My illustrious father ﵁ then said to my chaste mother ﵂; *'I have eradicated the satanic light and replaced it with a Divinely Blessed Light which will illuminate darkness from you.'* Sayyiduna ʿAbd al-Jabbār al-Jilānī ﵁ passed away in Baghdād and was laid to rest in the sacred *Khanqah* of his illustrious father ﵁. His *Mazār al-Sharīf* is in the precincts of the *Qādirī Darbār* Compound [*Zāwiyah*] and a great source of *Barakāt* and solace for the millions that pay homage to him.

12) Sayyiduna Sãliḥ al-Jilãnĩ ﷺ. Unfortunately, I could not trace any information in books of history about the dates of his birth and demise. Similarly, information about him is very scattered. He too was a great *Sũfi* Master and an erudite *ʿÃlim* of *Dĩn*. He passed away in Baghdãd and was laid to rest next to his pious brother, Sayyiduna ʿAbd al-Jabbãr Jilãnĩ ﷺ in the *Qãdirĩ Zãwiyah* of his illustrious father ﷺ. Millions of devotees visit him and derive his spiritual tender grace. His *Mazãr al-Sharĩf* is certainly a great heaven for spiritual blessings.

The Pious Wives of the Ghawth

It is said that Sayyiduna Ghawth al-Aʿzam ﷺ was not interested in marriage untill the ripe age of 50 years. He avoided marriage because he was deeply engrossed in spiritual devotion until once he dreamt of the beloved Prophet of *Allãh*, Sayyiduna wa Mawlãna Rasũlullãh ﷺ who said to him; *'You are my beloved son and you are avoiding my Sunnah of marriage,'* The great Ghawth ﷺ regarded this as a direct Prophetic Command and then decided to marry. He married 4 wives and he states that Almighty *Allãh* ﷻ has blessed him with 4 pious wives according to his choice and desire i.e. extremely devout and pious. They were mothers of 27 (and according to some books 26) sons and 22 daughters. The names of 22 daughters will be mentioned below. Some books mention the names of the 4 pious wives as follows without any source of reference;

1) Sayyidah Madĩna ﷺ d/o Mĩr Muḥammad al-Masjidĩ
2) Sayyidah Sãdiqah ﷺ d/o Muḥammad al-Shãfaʿĩ
3) Sayyidah Moʿminah ﷺ
4) Sayyidah Meʿḥbũbah ﷺ

The Pious Daughters of the Ghawth

Bahjat al-Asrãr does not report detail names of all the daughters of Sayyiduna Ghawth al-Aʿzam ﷺ. However, some information is found about their marriages to certain *Shuyũkh*. A brief record is found in *Bhajat al-Asrãr* and

Qalãid wa al-Jawãhir as follows:

1) Sayyidah Khadījah was married to Shaykh ʿAbd al-Razzãq s/o Shaykh ʿAbdur-Raḥman al-Tafsunji
2) Sayyidah Fãtimah al-Sãmiyyah was married to Sayyiduna Shaykh Qaḍīb al-Baan al-Mosulī and after her demise, the great Ghawth married another daughter to him, whose name is not known. Both these pious daughters are buried next to their illustrious husband in Mosul, north-western Iraq.
3) Sayyidah Tãj ,
4) Sayyidah Zãhidah ,
5) Sayyidah Zãkirah
6) Sayyidah Umm al-Faḍal
7) Sayyidah Sharīfah
8) Sayyidah ʿÃbidah
9) Sayyidah Rijī
10) Sayyidah Umm al-Fãteḥ
11) Sayyidah Zah'ra
12) Sayyidah Jamãl
13) Sayyidah Khayr an-Nisa
14) Sayyidah Shah Khãtim
15) Sayyidah Shah Bibī
16) Sayyidah Faqīrah
17) Sayyidah Umm-e-Salma
18) Sayyidah Faḍal an-Nisa
19) Sayyidah Tãj an-Nisa
20) Sayyidah ʿÃfia
21) Sayyidah Yasīn
22) Sayyidah ʿÃlīmah

It reported in *Bhajat al-Asrãr* and *Qalãid wa al-Jawãhir* that a daughter was also married to Shaykh Muslimah al-Samãwī but her name is unknown. There was another daughter by the name of Sayyidah Ãʿīeshah and nothing either is known about her or her marriage.

N.B. I could not find an authentic reference for the names of numbers; 3 to 22 from any authentic source. I found these names in an article without any reference so I included it here - *Allāh* ﷻ Knows best. Furthermore, some sources state that many of Sayyiduna Ghawth al-Aʿzam's ؓ blessed children passed away in infancy therefore, not much is known about them in authentic books. *#Translator – Faqīr ʿAbd al-Hādī*

Some of His Illustrious Khulafah

The great Ghawth ؓ had numerous *Khulafah*. A detailed list of their names is not recorded. We have accumulated some of them from various books and present them here for the benefit of the reader. They are:

1) Shaykh Sayyid Abu-ʿAbdullāh Sayyiduna ʿAbd al-Raḥmān al-Jilānī ؓ
2) Shaykh Sayyid Imām Sayf al-Dīn Abu-ʿAbdullāh ʿAbd al-Wah'hāb al-Jilānī ؓ.
3) Shaykh Sayyid Imām Sharf al-Dīn Abu-Muḥammad ʿIsā al-Jilānī ؓ.
4) Shaykh Sayyid Imām ʿAbd al-Jabbār Jamāl al-Dīn Abu-ʿAbd al-Raḥmān al-Jilānī ؓ.
5) Sayyiduna Imām Tāj al-Dīn Abu-Bakr ʿAbd al-Razzāq al-Jilānī ؓ.
6) Shaykh Sayyid Shams al-Dīn Abu-Muḥammad ʿAbd al-ʿAzīz al-Jilānī ؓ.
7) Shaykh Sayyid Imām Abu-Isḥāq Ibrāhīm al-Jilānī ؓ.
8) Shaykh Sayyid Imām Abu al-Faḍal Muḥammad al-Jilānī ؓ.
9) Shaykh Sayyid Imām Ḍiya al-Dīn Abu-Nasar Mūsā al-Jilānī ؓ.
10) Shaykh Sayyid Imām Abu-Zakariyyah Yaḥyah al-Jilānī ؓ.
11) Qutb Shaykh Abul-Ḥasan ʿAlī b. Aḥmad al-Hītī ؓ.
12) Ḥaḍrat Shaykh Ḍiya al-Dīn Abu-Najīb ʿAbd al-Qāhir al-Sohrowardī ؓ – paternal uncle of *Shaykh ash-Shuyūkh* Shahāb al-Dīn ʿUmar al-Sohrowardī ؓ.
13) Ḥaḍrat Shaykh Shahāb al-Dīn ʿUmar al-Sohrowardī ؓ.
14) Ghawth Abu-Madyan Shoʿayb b. Ḥusain al-Ansārī al-Maghribī ؓ.
15) Ḥaḍrat Shaykh Abu-ʿUmar ʿUthmān b. Marzūq al-Batā'iḥī ؓ.
16) Ḥaḍrat Shaykh Abu-Muḥammad ʿAbdullāh al-Jabā'ī ؓ.

17) Ḥaḍrat Shaykh Abu al-Ḥasan ʿAlī b. Idrīs al-Yaʿqūbī رضي الله عنه.
18) Ḥaḍrat Shaykh Abu-ʿUmar ʿUthmãn al-Sarīfīnī رضي الله عنه.
19) Ḥaḍrat Shaykh Qaḍīb al-Bãn al-Mousilī رضي الله عنه.
20) Ḥaḍrat Shaykh Aḥmad b. Mubãrak al-Baghdãdī رضي الله عنه.
21) Ḥaḍrat Shaykh Abu al-Faraḥ Sadaqah b. Ḥusain al-Baghdãdī رضي الله عنه.
22) Ḥaḍrat Shaykh Muḥammad al-Awãfī famous as Ibn al-Qalã'īd رضي الله عنه.
23) Ḥaḍrat Shaykh Abu-Saʿūd b. Shibal رضي الله عنه.
24) Ḥaḍrat Shaykh Muwaffaq ad-Dīn Abu-Muḥammad ʿAbdullãh b. Qudãmah al-Maqdisī رضي الله عنه.
25) Ḥaḍrat Shaykh ʿAbd al-Ghanī al-Maqsadī رضي الله عنه.
26) Ḥaḍrat Shaykh Ibrãhim b. ʿAbd al-Wãhīd al-Maqsadī رضي الله عنه.
27) Ḥaḍrat Shaykh Jamãl al-Dīn Yūnus Qasãr al-Hãshimī رضي الله عنه.
28) Ḥaḍrat Shaykh Abu al-Baqã ʿAbdullãh b. Ḥusain b. ʿAbdullãh al-Akbarī رضي الله عنه.
29) Ḥaḍrat Shaykh Ḥasan b. Muslim b. Ḥasan al-Jowzī رضي الله عنه.
30) Ḥaḍrat Shaykh Abu al-ʿAbbãs b. ʿÃrif Sanjãrī al-Andlūsī رضي الله عنه.
31) Ḥaḍrat Shaykh Isḥãq b. Aḥmad b. Muḥammad Ghãnim al-ʿAlsī رضي الله عنه.
32) Ḥaḍrat Shaykh Yaʿqūb al-Maristãnī رضي الله عنه.
33) Ḥaḍrat Shaykh Shams al-Dīn al-Ḥaddãd رضي الله عنه.
34) Ḥaḍrat Shaykh Abu al-Ḥasan b. ʿAlī al-Jãmʿeh رضي الله عنه.
35) Ḥaḍrat Shaykh Abu-Muḥammad ʿAbdullãh ʿAlī al-Asadī رضي الله عنه.
36) Ḥaḍrat Shaykh Abu-Muḥammad Ḥasan b. ʿAbd al-Karīm al-Fãrsī رضي الله عنه.
37) Ḥaḍrat Shaykh Aḥmad b. Sãliḥ al-Jīlī al-Shafaʿī رضي الله عنه.
38) Ḥaḍrat Shaykh Raslãn b. ʿAbdullãh al-Kanīrãnī رضي الله عنه.
39) Ḥaḍrat Shaykh Aḥmad b. Asad b. Wahb al-Baghdãdī رضي الله عنه.
40) Ḥaḍrat Shaykh Abu-Bakr al-Tamīmī رضي الله عنه.
41) Ḥaḍrat Shaykh Abu al-Ḥasan ʿAlī Mashhūr bī ibn Naja al-Ansãrī رضي الله عنه
42) Ḥaḍrat Shaykh Abu-ʿUmar ʿUthmãn b. Ismãʿīl b. Ibrãhim Saʿãdī Muqallab bī al-Shãfaʿī رضي الله عنه.
43) Ḥaḍrat Shaykh Abu-ʿAbdullãh al-Kanīrãnī رضي الله عنه.
44) Ḥaḍrat Shaykh Abu-Isḥãq Ibrãhīm b. Marbīl b. Nasar al-Makhrūmī رضي الله عنه.
45) Ḥaḍrat Shaykh Abu-ʿAbdullãh b. Muḥammad b. Shaykh Raslãn b. ʿAbdullãh رضي الله عنه.

46) Ḥaḍrat Shaykh Abu al-Qāsim ʿAbd al-Raḥmān ﷺ.
47) Ḥaḍrat Shaykh Abu-Barr ʿAbdullāh b. Nasar b. Ḥamza al-Tamīmī al-Baghdādī ﷺ.
48) Ḥaḍrat Shaykh Abu al-Qāsim Khalaf b. Ayyāsh b. ʿAbdul ʿAzīz al-Misrī ﷺ.
49) Ḥaḍrat Shaykh Abu al-Ḥafḍ ʿUmar b. Aḥmad al-Yemenī ﷺ.
50) Ḥaḍrat Shaykh Abu-Muḥammad Madāfiʿh b. Aḥmad ﷺ.
51) Ḥaḍrat Shaykh Abu-Isḥāq b. Ibrāhim b. Bishārat b. Yaʿqūb al-ʿAdnī ﷺ.
52) Ḥaḍrat Shaykh Abu-ʿAbdullāh Muḥammad al-Batā'īḥī ﷺ
53) Ḥaḍrat Shaykh Abu al-Ḥaram b. Makkī ﷺ
54) Ḥaḍrat Shaykh Mawaffiq al-Dīn Abu al-Qāsim ʿAbd al-Raḥmān ﷺ
55) Ḥaḍrat Shaykh Abu al-Baqa Sāliḥ Bahā al-Dīn ﷺ
56) Ḥaḍrat Shaykh ʿAbd al-Razzāq b. Shaykh ʿAbd al-Raḥman al-Tafsunjī ﷺ
57) Ḥaḍrat Shaykh ʿAlī b. Muḥammad b. Aḥmad al-Baghdādī Maʿrūf bī Ibn al-Ḥumāmī ﷺ
58) Ḥaḍrat Shaykh Muḥammad b. Aḥmad al-Baghdādī ﷺ
59) Ḥaḍrat Shaykh Abu al-Qāsim Haybatullāh b. ʿAbd al-Qādir b. Ḥusain Mashūr b. Manthūr ﷺ
60) Ḥaḍrat Shaykh Isḥāq b. Ibrāhīm b. Saʿīd Wārī al-ʿAslī ﷺ
61) Ḥaḍrat Shaykh Abu al-ʿAbbās Aḥmad b. ʿAlī b. Khalīl al-Jowsiqī ﷺ
62) Ḥaḍrat Shaykh Abu-Bakr Muḥammad b. al-Khāl ﷺ
63) Ḥaḍrat Shaykh Muḥammad b. Aḥmad b. Muḥammad b. Qudāma al-Maqdasī ﷺ etc......

The Chain of the Four Salāsil of the Ghawth
The Siddiqī Silsilah Chain

Sayyiduna Ghawth al-Aʿzam Shaykh ʿAbd al-Qādir al-Jilānī ﷺ received the *Khilāfah* of the *Siddīqī Silsila* which originates from Amīr al-Muʿminīn Sayyiduna Abu-Bakr as-Siddīq ﷺ. The sequence of the Chain is as follows:-

1) Sayyiduna Shaykh ʿAbd al-Qādīr al-Jilānī ﷺ
2) Shaykh Aḥmad Aswad al-Dīnawarī ﷺ
3) Shaykh Mamshād ʿAlī al-Dīnawarī ﷺ

4) Shaykh Abu al-ʿAbbās al-Nihāwandī ﷺ
5) Shaykh Abu-ʿAbdullāh Muḥammad b. Khafīf ﷺ
6) Shaykh Abu-Muḥammad b. Ḥusain al-Jazrī ﷺ
7) Shaykh Sayyid at-Tā'ifah Qutb al-Madār Qāsim Junayd al-Baghdādī ﷺ
8) Shaykh Abu-Saʿīd al-Khizār ﷺ
9) Shaykh Bishar al-Ḥāfī ﷺ
10) Shaykh Abu-Raja al-ʿAtaradī ﷺ
11) Shaykh Khawaja Fuḍayl ibn ʿAyāḍ ﷺ
12) Shaykh Manthūr al-Salmī ﷺ
13) Shaykh Muḥammad b. Muslim al-Zāhidī ﷺ
14) Shaykh Muḥammad b. Jayr al-Nu'falī ﷺ
15) Shaykh Abu-Muḥammad al-Mutʿām ﷺ
16) Amīr al-Muʿminīn Sayyiduna Abu-Bakr as-Siddique ﷺ [47]

The Farūqī Silsilah Chain

This is the Chain of *Khilāfah* that the great Ghawth ﷺ received from Amīr al-Muʿminīn Sayyiduna ʿUmar al-Fārūq ﷺ. The Chain is as follows:-

1) Sayyiduna Shaykh ʿAbd al-Qādir al-Jilānī ﷺ
2) Shaykh Abu al-Khayr Ḥammād b. Muslim al-Dabbās ﷺ
3) Shaykh Yūsuf ﷺ
4) Shaykh Abu al-Ḥasan ʿAlī ﷺ
5) Shaykh Aḥmad b. ʿAbd al-ʿAzīz ﷺ
6) Shaykh Abu-Makarim Jaʿafar Abu-Bakr ʿAbdullāh al-Shiblī ﷺ
7) Shaykh Sayyid at-Tā'ifah Qutb al-Madār Qāsim Junayd al-Baghdādī ﷺ
8) Shaykh Abu-Saʿīd al-Khizār ﷺ
9) Shaykh Abu-ʿAbdullāh al-Masmūʿī ﷺ
10) Shaykh Abu-Turāb al-Nakhshabī ﷺ
11) Sultān al-ʿĀrifīn Ḥaḍrat Shaykh Ba-Yazīd al-Bustāmī ﷺ
12) Shaykh Amīn al-Dīn al-Shāmī ﷺ
13) Shaykh ʿAbdullāh Alamdār ﷺ

[47] See *Tadkirah Mashā'ikh Qādirīyyah* by Moulana ʿAbd al-Mujtabah Qādirī (Alayhir-Raḥmah)

14) Amīr al-Muʿminīn Sayyiduna ʿUmar al-Fārūq ﷺ[48]

The ʿUthmānī Silsilah Chain

The sequence of the *ʿUthmānī* Chain from Amīr al-Muʿmīnīn Sayyiduna ʿUthmān al-Ghanī ﷺ is as follows:-

1) Sayyiduna Shaykh ʿAbd al-Qādir al-Jīlānī ﷺ
2) Qutb al-Ghawth Shaykh Abu al-Khayr Ḥammād b. Muslim Dabbās ﷺ
3) Shaykh Saʿīd Muḥammad al-Maghribī ﷺ
4) Shaykh Abu-Bakr Aḥmad b. ʿUthmān al-Maghribī ﷺ
5) Shaykh Abu-Faḍal ʿAbd al-Wāḥīd al-Yemenī ﷺ
6) Shaykh Aḥmad b. Ismāʿīl al-Makkī ﷺ
7) Shaykh Abu-Makārim Jaʿafar Abu-Bakr ʿAbdullāh al-Shiblī ﷺ
8) Shaykh Sayyid at-Tāifah Qutbe-Madār Junayd al-Baghdādī ﷺ
9) Shaykh Khawaja Abu-Saʿīd al-Khizār ﷺ
10) Shaykh Abu-ʿUbayd Ḥasan al-Masūḥī ﷺ
11) Shaykh Abu-Turāb al-Nakhshabī ﷺ
12) Shaykh Abu-ʿAbd al-Raḥmān Ḥātim al-Asam ﷺ
13) Shaykh ʿAbdullāh al-Khawās ﷺ
14) Shaykh Shafīq[49] al-Balkhī ﷺ
15) Shaykh Ibrāhim b. Adham al-Balkhī ﷺ
16) Shaykh Fuḍayl ibn ʿAyāḍ ﷺ
17) Shaykh ʿAbd al-Wāḥid ibn Zayd ﷺ
18) Shaykh Kumayl ibn Ziyād al-Yemenī ﷺ
19) Amīr al-Muʿminīn Sayyiduna ʿUthmān al-Ghanī ﷺ[50]

The ʿAlawī Silsilah Chain

The following is Shaykh ʿAbd al-Qādir Jīlānī's ﷺ *Ḥasanī* Family sequence of the *ʿAlawī* Chain from Amīr al-Muʿmīnīn Sayyiduna ʿAlī al-Murtuḍah ﷺ:-

---

48 Ibid

49 Some authorities opine that his name was Shaqīq Balkhī. *Allāh* ﷻ and His *Rasūl* ﷺ knows best.

50 Ibid

1) Sayyiduna Shaykh ʿAbd al-Qādir al-Jilānī ﷜ s/o
2) Sayyiduna Shaykh Abu-Sāliḥ Mūsā Jangi-Dost ﷜ s/o
3) Sayyiduna Shaykh ʿAbdullāh al-Jilī ﷜ s/o
4) Sayyiduna Shaykh Yaḥyah al-Zāhid ﷜ s/o
5) Sayyiduna Shaykh Muḥammad ﷜ s/o
6) Sayyiduna Shaykh Dāʿūd ﷜ s/o
7) Sayyiduna Shaykh Mūsā al-Thānī ﷜ s/o
8) Sayyiduna Shaykh Mūsā al-Joon ﷜ s/o
9) Sayyiduna Imām ʿAbdullāh al-Mahaz ﷜ s/o
10) Sayyiduna Imām Ḥasan al-Muthan'nah ﷜ s/o
11) Sayyiduna Imām al-Ḥasan ﷜ s/o
12) Amīr al-Moʿminīn Sayyiduna ʿAlī al-Murtuḍah ﷜.

The Qādiriyyah Mashāi'kh Silsilah Chain

This golden Chain is of the *Mashā'kh* of the Sacred *Qādiriyyah Silsilah* which is found in the *Shajrah al-Sharīf* of all the *Mashā'ikh* who follow the *Qādiriyyah Sūfī* Order.

1) Sayyiduna Shaykh ʿAbd al-Qādir al-Jilānī ﷜, [*murīd* of - m/o]
2) Shaykh Abu-Saʿīd Mubārak al-Makhzūmī ﷜ m/o
3) Shaykh Abu al-Ḥasan ʿAlī al-Hankārī ﷜ m/o
4) Shaykh Abu al-Faraḥ Yūsuf al-Tartūsī ﷜ m/o
5) Shaykh Abu al-Faḍal ʿAbd al-Wāḥid al-Tamīmī ﷜ m/o
6) Shaykh Abu-Makārim Abu-Bakr ʿAbdullāh al-Shiblī ﷜ m/o
7) Sayyid at-Tāīfah Qutb al-Kabīr Qāsim Junayd al-Baghdādī ﷜ m/o
8) Shaykh Sirrī al-Saqatī ﷜ m/o
9) Shaykh Maʿrūf al-Karkhī ﷜ m/o
10) Sayyiduna Imām ʿAlī al-Riḍa ﷜ m/o
11) Sayyiduna Imām Mūsā al-Kāzim ﷜ m/o
12) Sayyiduna Imām Jaʿāfar as-Sādiq ﷜ m/o
13) Sayyiduna Imām Muḥammad al-Bāqir ﷜ m/o
14) Sayyiduna Imām Zayn al-ʿĀbidīn ﷜ m/o
15) Sayyid ash-Shuhadāh Imām al-Ḥusain Shahīd-e-Karbala ﷜ m/o
16) Amīr al-Muʿminīn Sayyiduna ʿAlī al-Murtuḍah ﷜ m/o

17) Sayyid al ᶜĀlamīn Sayyiduna wa Mawlana Muḥammad Rasūlullāh ﷺ [51]

His Sad Demise

In the last moments of his life his illustrious sons were seated at his bedside when suddenly the Ghawth said, *"Move away from me, because though I may be near you in body but spiritually I am with others. Besides, here are other creations gathered in my presence therefore, make place for them."* The assembly of the spiritual gathering consisted of Elite Souls [Confidants] of the Divine Presence [*Qurb*] and the Angels of Mercy. They came in troops and greeted the Ghawth. Just then he began saying:

وَعَلَيْكُمُ السَّلَامُ وَرَحْمَةُ اللهِ وَبَرَكَاتُهُ غَفَرَ اللهُ لِيْ وَلَكُمْ وَتَابَ اللهُ عَلَيَّ وَعَلَيْكُمْ

Peace and Blessings be upon you. May Allāh forgive me and you and focus His Mercy on me and you.

His illustrious sons state that their honourable father continued repeating these words of salutation for the entire day and night. The Ghawth then said that the Blessings of Almighty *Allāh* ﷻ will not cease and he recited the following verse of the Holy *Qur'ān*,

﴿نَحْنُ أَوْلِيَاؤُكُمْ فِي الْحَيَاةِ الدُّنْيَا وَفِي الْآخِرَةِ ۖ وَلَكُمْ فِيهَا مَا تَشْتَهِي أَنفُسُكُمْ

وَلَكُمْ فِيهَا مَا تَدَّعُونَ ﴿٣١﴾﴾

We are your friends in the life of this world and in the Hereafter; in it for you is all that you may wish for, and for you is all what you ask. [52]

The Ghawth said: *"I have pity on you on that which you assume about me because I don't care about anyone, not the Angel of Death nor any Angel. O Angel of Death! He Who has blessed me with power and authority loves me and He can fulfil my work*

[51] Ibid

[52] *Al-Qur'ān al-Karīm, Surah Fussilāt*, verse 31

without you."

Sayyiduna Shaykh ʿAbd al-Razzāq al-Jilānī ﷺ and Sayyiduna Shaykh Mūsa al-Jilānī ﷺ state that the day before their beloved father passed away, he raised his hands and made this *Duʿā*,

وَعَلَيْكُمُ السَّلَامُ وَرَحْمَةُ اللّٰهِ وَبَرَكَاتُهُ تُوْبُوْا وَادْخُلُوْا فِي الصَّفِّ هُوَ ذَا اٰجِئُ اِلَيْكُمْ

Peace and Blessings be upon you. Repent and join the queue.
I am coming towards you at this moment.

The Ghawth ﷺ said, *"Exercise gentleness and do not compare me to others nor compare others to me."* Just then his son, Sayyiduna Shaykh ʿAbd al-ʿAzīz al-Jilānī ﷺ, asked him, *"What is your condition now?"* He replied, *"Do not question me about anything because I am moving from one state to another, of which Allāh ﷻ is aware."* He asked his father again, *"What sickness do you have?" "No one knows my sickness and no one is privileged with it, no human, nor any Angel or any fairy,"* replied the Ghawth ﷺ. He then mentioned some intrinsic words of the Secrets of Reality [*Ḥaqīqah*]. Just then his other son, Sayyiduna Shaykh ʿAbd al-Jabbār al-Jilānī ﷺ inquired, *"What parts of your body ache?"* He replied, *"Every part of my body aches besides my heart. My heart is healthy and strong in the Divine Presence of my Lord ﷻ."* As the moment of his *Wiṣāl* [demise] drew close, he uttered the following words:

﴿اَسْتَعِنْتُ بِلَا اِلٰهَ اِلَّا اللّٰهُ سُبْحَانَهُ وَتَعَالٰى الْحَيِّ الَّذِيْ لَا يَخْشٰى الْفَوْتَ سُبْحَانَهُ

مَنْ تَعَزَّزَ بِالْقُدْرَةِ وَقَهَرَ الْعِبَادَ بِالْمَوْتِ لَا اِلٰهَ اِلَّا اللّٰهُ مُحَمَّدٌ رَّسُوْلُ اللّٰهِ﴾

I seek assistance with the Kalimah of Tawḥīd, there is none worthy of worship but Allāh. He is Pure and Exalted. His Existence is such that He has no fear. He is Pure of death and His Divine Being is Dominant with Power and overpowers His servants with Death. And there is none worthy of Worship besides Allāh, Sayyiduna Muḥammad ﷺ is Allāh's

ﷻ beloved Messenger.

His son, Sayyiduna Shaykh Mũsa al-Jilãnĩ ﵁ states: *"My beloved father uttered the word 'Ta'azzazu' [praiseworthy are You (O Allãh ﷻ)] but he could not pronounce it correctly. Then he made an effort to pronounce it correctly by raising his voice and succeeded. Thereafter, he recited the Isme Jalãlah 'Allãh! Allãh! Allãh!' three times and his voice receded with his tongue drawn back into his consecrated mouth. In the same instant, his sacrosanct soul departed from his consecrated body towards his Real Absolute Lord of Power ﷻ. May Allãh ﷻ sanctify his soul and raise his status in to high levels in Jannah, Ãmĩn".*

﴿إِنَّا لِلَّهِ وَإِنَّا إِلَيْهِ رَاجِعُونَ﴾

Verily we belong to Allãh and indeed it
is to Him we are to return.[53]

Sayyiduna Ghawth al-Aᶜzam ﵁ passed away on the 11th of *Rabbĩ ᶜ al-Ãkhir* 561 / 14th February 1166 in Baghdad on a Sunday night after the *'Esha Salãh* at the age of 91 years. His *Janãza Salãh* was led by his eldest son, Sayyiduna Sayf al-Dĩn ᶜAbd al-Wah'hãb al-Jilãnĩ ﵁. The congregation of his *Janãza Salãh* was so huge that there was not a single person in Baghdad who did not attend it. He was laid to rest in his *Madressa* in the locality of *Bãb al-Azj* [now called *Bãb ash-Shaykh*]. Till this day, millions pay homage to his sacred *Mazãr al-Sharĩf* and derive in abundance, their hearts desire. His *Rowḍah al-Mubãrak* is a source of spiritual succour, a beacon of hope and tender grace for the Seeker of the Path of Truth. May the Compassionate *Allãh* ﷻ bless us with the *Fuyũḍ* and *Barakãt* of Sayyiduna Ghawth al-Aᶜzam Shaykh ᶜAbd al-Qãdir Jilãnĩ ﵁.

Qãdirĩ Faqĩr ᶜAbd al-Hãdĩ Qãdirĩ Raḍawĩ Nũrĩ
Imãm Aḥmad Raza Academy
Durban, South Africa

[53] *Al-Qur'ãn al-Karĩm* Chapter Baqarah verse 156

To sit in the company of the Pious is better than doing Good and to sit in the company of the evil [immoral] people is worse than doing evil

Khawaja Ghareeb Nawaaz رضی اللہ عنہ

Volume One

بهجة الاسرار ومعدن الانوار

Preface by the Author:

Khutbah

بِسْمِ اللّٰهِ الرَّحْمٰنِ الرَّحِيْمِ

وَصَلَّى اللهُ عَلٰى سَيِّدِنَا مُحَمَّدٍ وَّعَلٰى آلِهٖ وَصَحْبِهٖ وَسَلَّمْ ' أَسْتَفْتِحُ بَابَ الْعَوْنِ بِأَيْدِيْ مَحَامِدِ اللهِ كُلِّهَا ' وَأَسْتَنْجِحُ سَعْيَ الْقَصْدِ بِأَيَادِيْهِ الْغُرِّ وَبَلِّهَا وَطَلِّهَا ' وَأَسْتَلْمِحُ بُرُوْقَ الْحَقِّ لِعَيْنِ سَرِيْرَتِيْ فِيْ مَقْعَدِ ظِلِّهَا ' فَأَسْتَقِيْهِ لِمَصَادِرِ أَفْعَالِيْ مِنْ مَوَارِدِ أَفْضَالِهٖ نَهْلِهَا وَعَلِّهَا ' وَأَسْتَشْفِيْهِ مِنْ أَدْوَاءِ نَفْسِيْ فِيْ حَالَةِ صَفْوِهَا وَغِلِّهَا ' وَأَسْأَلُهُ أَنْ يَّلْحَقَهَا بِأَنْفُسِ جَرِّهَا وَنَاصِبِ سَعْدِهَا إِلٰى رَفْعِهَا فِيْ وَصْلِهَا ' وَأَضَافَهَا عَامِلُ فِعْلِهَا فِيْ تَمْيِيْزِهَا إِلٰى حَلِّ عَقْلِهَا فِيْ عَقْلِهَا ' وَأُصَلِّيْ عَلٰى سَيِّدِ الْخَلِيْقَةِ طُرًّا وَأَجَلِّهَا وَمُخْرِجِهَا بِنُوْرِ رِسَالَتِهٖ مِنْ ظُلْمَةِ جَهْلِهَا ' وَبَانِيْ أَرْكَانِ قُبَّةِ الْإِسْلَامِ حَتّٰى عَلَتْ فِيْ صَدْرِ مَحَلِّهَا ' وَرَافِعِ دَرَجَاتِ الْأَوْلِيَاءِ عَلٰى قَوَاعِدِ أَصْلِهَا ' وَمَالِكِ أَزِمَّةِ أَمْرِهَا فِيْ عَقْدِهَا وَحَلِّهَا ' وَعَلٰى آلِهٖ وَصَحَابَتِهٖ خَيْرِ صَحَابَةٍ كَانَتْ مِنْ قَبْلِهَا.

May Allāh ﷻ send peace and blessings on our Master, Sayyiduna Muḥammad ﷺ, his family and companions. I intend to open the doors of succour with the majestic hands of all the praises of Allāh ﷻ. His Divine Hands[103] that are Rain and Dew of Mercy. I seek success in these narrations from the flashes of truth for the eyes of my heart under

[103] 'Hands' in this context refers to the Divine *Qudrat* [Power] of Almighty *Allāh* ﷻ. It is the pristine belief of the *Ahle Sunnah wa Jamā'at* that *Allah* ﷻ is absolutely free and pure of all

the shade of His Mercy.

Then for the sources of my actions, I seek multiple drinks of water from the lakes of His ﷻ excellence. I seek cure from the Sublime Lord ﷻ for all the sicknesses of my soul in the state of cleanliness or otherwise. I seek that from Him ﷻ that enjoins elegance and fortune that elevates me to the stable lofty Station of Proximity so that His working servants are compelled to diligently strive for excellence. May Allāh ﷻ grant me discernment to revert to the intellect at times of spiritual contraction [qabḍ].

I send salutation on such a master of the entire creation who is superior to all. He removes creations from the darkness of ignorance of their souls with the light of his Messengership [Risālah]. He is the founder of the sacred Law of Islām. He rules from the higher seat of the Palace of Administration. He informed us of the correct methods to determine the stations of the Awliya. He owns and controls the reins of the Awliya. Also peace and blessings on his noble family and illustrious companions, who are by the virtue of companionship and assembly, the best of companions.

Thereafter, note that I was indeed solicited about the vociferous command: *'My foot is on the necks of all the Awliya'* of our Shaykh, the Shaykh of *Islām*, leader of the *Awliya*, the gateway to guidance, the reviver of Religion, Abu-Muḥammad ʿAbd al-Qādir b. Abī-Sāliḥ Jilī, [may *Allāh* ﷻ sanctify his soul and illuminate his grave]. I intend to accumulate all the narrations, that I know in this regard because Sayyiduna Ghawth al-Aʿzam ؓ is a unique pearl in the necklace of this era. He is the priceless gem in the sequence of speech, the garb of nobility, and occupies the station of honour in which he dwells alone. I then consulted with Almighty *Allāh* ﷻ regarding this question posed to me, and I received a positive answer.

A specific book on this subject has been written by me which encapsulates

forms and shapes which is beyond the comprehension of the human mind. Therefore, the term *'Divine Hands'* are used as a metaphorical expression for human understanding. Readers are therefore cautioned not to be confused regarding this reality and to adhere to the explanation provided in the text.

trustworthy and distinctive certificates of narration. All weak and unauthentic narrations have been omitted, and duly supported by the sentiments, statements and actions of high profile authorities that reached out to me. These sentiments support their excellence and status.

After recording this, I have noted the venerated words of the great Ghawth ﷺ. He unveils such a lofty station that cannot be achieved by personal efforts, nor can they be assembled by one's desires. It is solely the blessings of the Sublime Lord ﷻ that affords one this opportunity. Good fortune opened its doors; abundance drew its ropes; consideration gathered its boundaries, and grace solidified it. *Tawfīq* held its reins, research opened its lips and Divine Command brought forth his statement. Pronouncements exposed the lustres of Divine Proximity, and the gardens of sanctity declared the magnificence of information, and that, these words were reinforced by guidance, for the purpose of which this book was written. Its bridle was lifted and raised, so that one does not assume that this was a fleeing camel or a thirsty animal that has returned to quench its thirst.

Thereafter, I have written chapters on the words of superiority on an exquisite rosary whose veracity removed the veils of all doubts. The eyes of sanctified narrations lifted the veils of thirst and expanded the treasures of Direct Knowledge [*ʿIlm al-Tawḥīd*]. In it are exclusive treasures of wisdom coupled with eloquent poetry, similar to a sacred drink. This is compared to the rain from the rain clouds. Hence, there is a heart in every chapter, glowing with the eagerness of union with the beloved. With every breath, there is a flame of light for the soul, and a line of reality with every sector. The observer views its meanings with pearls and rubies, and thereby, receives medication through the pearls and sustenance through the rubies. I have enhanced the contents of this book with such an astonishing and charismatic legacy from [Sayyiduna Ghawth al-Aʿzam's ﷺ] early days of youth, so that its prelude adorned the blossoms of spring, and moreover, engulfed in a stunning garb. It is through this radiance that the flowers on the branches reached heights and flourished and its subtlety made the heart of the morning breeze cry. Its excellency became the owner of an exquisitely decorated necklace consisting of precious gems. All this occurred to ascertain news of the past. Such knots were made in its necklaces that it became impossible to undo them. Its proof portrayed sheets, and hence, its authenticity sealed the paths and spirits of the antagonists.

Thereafter, I have recorded the benefits of his obedience and the excellence of his disciples. Mention is made of numerous narrations, bearing the glad tidings for his companions and friends. In doing so, his beloved ones shall become aware of what they shall reap through his love and reverence, and as well as the treasures they shall receive in their blessed life.

Thereafter, I have mentioned the brilliance of his lustres, his noble progeny, his perfect disposition, his actions, propagation and discourses on religion. In addition, mention is made of the reverence that the *Awliya* had for him, thus providing confirmation of his lofty status. Information of his sad demise and his final advices and testimonies are also recorded.

I, then reveal apt citations that will increase one's excellence in the vision of the pious. Thereafter, I have also discussed the eminence of some of the senior companions of Ḥaḍrate Ghawth ﷺ and terminated this book with their meritorious virtues. This is so because the appreciation and virtue of obedience can only be ascertained and attained from the virtues of the followed. The velocity of the flow of water of a stream depends on the massive dimension of the spring. There are those who become disillusioned with lengthy details and abstain thereof, because anything that exceeds the prescribed limit causes discontentment. Anything that is insufficient to explain the specific point, is however incomplete, as well as misleading. The best notion is to be less excessive; and to provide more than that which would suffice. In this there is ample proof, satisfaction and an all-encompassing facet of the subject in question. This is a lesson for the perceptive individuals:

I have named this book '*Bahjat al-Asrār wa Ma'ādin al-Anwār*' - *Sublime Secrets and Treasures of Lights*. May *Allāh* ﷻ guide all those with the former mentioned discourses and those that will be included at a later stage. May *Allāh* ﷻ grant me *Tawfiq* to be protected from any deficiency.

NARRATIONS OF THE MASHĀ'IKH

Narration One:

Shaykh Abu-Bakr b. Sawār رحمه الله narrates that two *Shuyūkh* informed him; Shaykh, the erudite scholar Zayn al-Dīn Abu al-Ḥasan ʿAlī b. Abī-Muḥammad ʿAbdullāh b. Abī al-Tayyib al-Maghribī al-Jazāirī al-Mālikī al-Muqarrirī رحمه الله prominent as Ibn Qalāl in 664 *hijrī* in Cairo and Shaykh Sāliḥ Abu-Zayd ʿAbd al-Raḥmān b. Abī an-Najāt Sālim b. Aḥmad b. Abī Ḥamīd b. Sāliḥ b. ʿAlī al-Qurashī al-Muḥaddith رحمه الله narrated to me in Cairo: both of them stated to me, that they were informed by the Shaykh and leader, Abu al-Fataḥ b. Abī al-Ghanā'im al-Wāsatī رحمه الله in 623 *hijrī,* presently in Alexander, Egypt. He asserted that he had heard from his Shaykh, Sayyid Aḥmad b. Abī al-Ḥasan رحمه الله, attributed as a Rifāʿī in Umm ʿUbaydah, as he was informed by the Judge, Shaykh Abu al-Faraḥ ʿAbd al-Malik b. Muḥammad b. ʿAbd al-Majūdīn Aḥmad b. ʿAlī al-Wāstī Abī al-Shāfāʿī رحمه الله in 670 *hijrī* in Cairo affirmed that he was informed by Shaykh the blessed, Baqiyat al-Salf Abu al-ʿAzāim Miqdām b. Sāliḥ b. ʿAbd al-Raḥmān b. Yūsuf Irāqī al-Rifāʿī رحمه الله, who was visiting Ḥadāwiya in 623 *hijrī* stated that he was informed by his Shaykh, Aḥmad b. Rifʿaī رحمه الله who declared that when his maternal uncle passed away, he was just over 50 days old.

He was informed by his maternal uncle Shaykh Mansūr al-Batā'iḥī رحمه الله who was informed by his Shaykh, Abu-Muḥammad al-Shabnakī رحمه الله, and as well as by the trustworthy Shaykh, Abu al-ʿĀfāf Mūsā b. Shaykh ʿĀrif Abī al-Maʿālī ʿUthmān b. Mūsā b. ʿAbd al-Karīm b. ʿAlī al-Baqāʿī رحمه الله originally, Damishqī, born and lived in ʿĀqībī in 673 *hijrī* in Damascus confirmed that his father informed him in 614 *hijrī* that three *Shuyūkh*, Shaykh Abu al-Khayr Saʿīd b. Sayyidī Sharīf Imām Abu-Saʿīd al-Qaylawī رحمه الله, Shaykh Abu-ʿAbdullāh Muḥammad b. Aḥmad b. Madayīnī رحمه الله and Shaykh Abu-ʿAbdullāh Muḥammad b. ʿAlī al-Fidī رحمه الله who frequently visited Qaylawa concurred that they were informed by their Shaykh Abu-Saʿīd al-Qaylawī ﷺ and also the Shaykh of noble origin, Abu-ʿAbdullāh Ḥasan b. Badrān b. ʿAlī b. Muḥammad b. Sāliḥ al-Baghdādī al-Ḥanbalī ﷺ in 670 *hijrī* stated that they were informed by the Jurist [*Faqīh*] Abu-Muḥammad ʿAbd al-Qādir b. ʿUthmān b. Abī al-Barkāt b. ʿAlī b. Rizqullāh b. ʿAbd al-Wah'hāb al-Tamīmī al-Bardānī al-Ḥanbalī ﷺ in 635 *Hijrī* in Baghdād; professed that he was informed by Shaykh Abu-Muḥammad ʿAbd al-Latīf b. Abī-Zāhir Aḥmad b. Muḥammad b. Haybatullāh al-Qurashī al-Baghdādī Faqī al-Ḥanbalī Sūfī ﷺ in 635 *hijrī* in Baghdād proclaimed that he had heard from Sayyid Sharīf Shaykh Abu-Saʿīd al-Qaylawī ﷺ in Qaylawa; stating that he was informed by his Shaykh Abu-Sāʿad b. Tāj al-Batāʾīḥī al-Ḥāmidī ﷺ who pronounced that he was informed by his Shaykh Abu-Muḥammad al-Shabnakī ﷺ said......:

Narration Two:

We were informed by Shaykh Abu al-Ḥasan ʿAlī b. Abī-Bakr b. ʿAmar b. Isḥāq b. Naʿīm al-Baghdādī al-Azjī al-Ḥanbalī al-Muḥaddith ﷺ in 661 *hijrī* in Cairo who enunciated that he was informed by Shaykh ʿĀrif Abu-Tāhir al-Jalīlī b. Shaykh, the leader, Abu al-ʿAbbās Aḥmad b. ʿAlī b. Khalīl al-Sarsarī al-Jowsiqī ﷺ in 631 *hijrī* in Sarsar; stating that he was informed by his father who had been informed by Shaykh Ghazāz b. Istowdaʿh Batā'īḥī al-Ghālī ﷺ who pronounced in Ḥadāwiyah that he had heard from his Shaykh Abu-Bakr b. Hawār ﷺ in his gathering one day; expressing the spiritual condition of his associates and the *Awliya*. He then affirmed:

> 'Shortly there will be in Irāq an *ʿAjamī* man [*Walī*] of *Allāh* ﷻ who will be greatly revered amongst the people. His name will be ʿAbd al-Qādir. He will settle in Baghdād and will declare that his foot is on the necks of all the *Awliya*. The *Awliya* of his era will submit to his command and he will be the Unique One [*Fard*] of his era.'

Narration Three:

Shaykh ʿAbdullāh Jūnī ﷺ states that he had heard from the Shaykh of noble origin, Abu-ʿAbdullāh Muḥammad b. Shaykh Abu al-ʿAbbās Aḥmad b. ʿAbd al-

Wāsiʿh b. Amīr Kāh b. Shāfeʿh b. Sālih b. Ḥātim al-Jilī ﷺ originally from Baghdād who enunciated in 668 *hijrī* in Cairo that he had heard from his father in 635 *hijrī* in Baghdād who had heard from Shaykh Imām ʿĀlim-e-Rabbānī ʿAzīz al-Dīn Abu-Rushd ʿUmar b. ʿAbd al-Malik al-Dīnwarī ﷺ who stated that he had heard from his Shaykh ʿAllāma Burhān al-Dīn Abu-Jāʿafar Muḥammad b. Abī Zayd b. ʿAbd al-Raḥmān al-Asfahānī ﷺ who confirmed that he had heard from his Shaykh the master of any two languages, Akmal al-Dīn Abu-Faḍal Muḥammad b. Jāʿafar al-Nowḥī ﷺ who states that he had heard from his Shaykh Abu-Sālih ʿAbdullāh b. Tabqī al-Rūmī ﷺ who enunciated that he had heard from his Shaykh Imām Abu-Yāʿqūb Yūsuf b. Ayyūb b. Yūsuf b. al-Ḥusain b. Shouʿayb Hamdānī Nūr al-Bajardī ﷺ, revealed in 493 *hijrī* in Hamd Āin, that he had heard his Shaykh Abu-Aḥmad ʿAbdullāh b. Aḥmad b. Mūsā Jūnī ʿAqab bihi Ḥaqqī ﷺ; acclaimed in his seclusion in 468 *hijrī* on the Mount of Jarad:

> 'I testify that shortly in the land of *ʿAjam* [Persia] a child will be born whose *Karāmāt* [miracles] will greatly manifest and all the *Awliya* will honour and respect him. He will declare that his foot is on the necks of all the *Awliya* and all the *Awliya* of that time will be under his foot. The people of his time will be blessed due to him and whoever will see him will benefit from him.'

Narration Four:

[Concerning Shaykh Taj al-ʿĀrifīn Abu al-Wafa ﷺ] Shaykh Abu-ʿAbdullāh Muḥammad b. Abu al-ʿAbbās Aḥmad b. Manzūr Kinānī al-ʿAsqalānī al-Shafaʿī ﷺ in 671 *hijrī* in the grounds of Maqsam in Cairo stated that he had heard from Shaykh ʿĀrif Abu-ʿAbdullāh b. Abī al-Fataḥ al-Hirwī ﷺ born in Baghdād, who came to us in 623 *hijrī* and said that he heard Shaykh, the leader ʿAlī b. al-Hitī ﷺ who in 557 *hijrī* had said in Baghdād and we were also informed by Shaykh Thaqqa Abu-Ḥafs ʿUmar b. Muḥammad b. ʿUmar b. Ibrāhīm al-Wīzī famous as Ibn Mazāḥim ﷺ in 665 *hijrī* in his grounds when he said that he had heard Shaykh Abu-Muḥammad ʿAlī b. Abī Bakr b. Idrīs Raḥāwī al-Yaʿqūbī ﷺ

who stated then in 616 *hijrī* that he had heard from their Shaykh ʿAlī b. al-Hītī Irāqī al-Darbānī ﷺ who said it there in 560 *hijrī*...

Narration Five:

We were informed by Faqī al-Maʿālī ʿAbd al-Raḥīm b. Muzaffar b. Mahzab b. Abī ʿAlī al-Qurashī Bahar al-Baghdādī ﷺ in 670 *hijrī* in Cairo that he had heard from Qāḍī al-Quḍāt Abu-Sāliḥ Nasar b. Ḥāfiz Abu-Bakr ʿAbd al-Razzāq b. Shaykh al-Islām Abu-Muḥammad ʿAbd al-Qādir al-Jīlī ﷺ and Shaykh Abu al-Ḥasan ʿAlī b. Sulaymān b. Abī al-Mazz ﷺ popularly known as as the Baker in 629 *hijrī* in Baghdād. Both verify that they had heard in 690 *hijrī* from the honourable Shaykh Abu-Ḥafs ʿUmar al-Kimyānī ﷺ in Baghdād when he had said the he had heard Shaykh Baqā b. Bat'tū al-Irāqī ﷺ state....

Narration Six:

Shaykh Abu-Muzaffar Ibrāhīm b. ʿAbdullāh Muḥammad b. Abī-Bakr b. Nasar b. Nisār b. Mansūr al-Baghdādī al-Qarwī ﷺ informed us in 669 *hijrī* in Cairo by stating that he had heard from his grandfather, the honourable Shaykh Abu-ʿAmar ʿUthmān b. Nasar b. Mansūr al-Baghdādī ﷺ [who passed away in Baghdād] in 607 *hijrī* that he was informed by his Shaykh Abu-Muḥammad b. ʿAbdullāh ﷺ who said that Shaykh ʿAbd al-Raḥmān al-Tafsunjī ﷺ had said to Shaykh ʿAlī al-Karkhī ﷺ [who acquired knowledge from him and lived for a long period in his company] that all these personalities deliberate that Shaykh ʿAbd al-Qādir al-Jīlī ﷺ in his youth visited our Shaykh Tāj al-ʿĀrifīn Abu al-Wafa Kakees ﷺ in Baghdād in the locality of Qalmūniya. When Shaykh Abu al-Wafa ﷺ used to see him, he stood up and ordered the people present to stand up for the *Walī* of *Allāh*. There were many occasions on which Shaykh Abu al-Wafa ﷺ walked a few steps towards Shaykh ʿAbd al-Qādir ﷺ to meet him. He often exclaimed:

> *'The person who does not stand up for this youth, he will not stand up for any Walī of Allāh.'* This comment was heard many times and some of the *murīds* of Shaykh Tāj al-ʿĀrifīn ﷺ commented and the Shaykh ﷺ said:

'A time will dawn on the youth that the commoner and elite will be dependent on him and I see that he will announce in a massive public gathering and he will be truthful when he will declare: 'My foot is on the necks of all the Awliya.' Thus, all the Awliya will hear this command and bend their heads in submission because he will be their Qutb. Therefore, if any one of you lives till that period, then it will be compulsory to obey and serve him.'

Narration Seven:

[Concerning Shaykh ʿAqīl al-Mambajī ﷺ] The Shaykh of augmented origin Abu al-Muḥāsin Yūsuf b. Shaykh Abu-Bakr b. Shaykh Barkat b. Aḥmad Ḥumsī al-Irāqī originally Arīlī ﷺ informed us in 667 *hijrī* in Cairo that he had heard from his paternal grandfather, Shaykh Barkat Ḥumsī al-Irāqī and Shaykh Sāliḥ Baqiyat al-Salf Abu-Aḥmad Maḥmūd b. Muḥammad Kurdī al-Jiblāwī al-Shaybānī al-Arīlī ﷺ who informed us in 611 *hijrī* in Arīl when both stated that they had heard from Shaykh ʿAdī b. Musāfir ﷺ and both the *Shuyūkh* proclaim that they had met with him and had lived in his company for several years....

We were informed by the trustworthy [*Thaqqa*] Shaykh Abu-Muḥammad Rajab b. Abī-Mansūr b. Nasrullāh b. Abī-Khālī al-Irāqī ﷺ originally from Dārī, born and settled in Nasīban, who informed us in Cairo in 665 *hijrī* that he had heard in 623 *hijrī* from Shaykh, the leader, Abu-ʿAbd al-Raḥīm b. ʿAskar b. ʿAbd al-Raḥīm b. ʿAskar b. Usāma al-ʿAdawī al-Nasībanī ﷺ in Nasīban when he said that he had heard from Shaykh ʿAbd al-Malik Dayān b. al-Maʿālī b. Rasad b. Nabhān al-Irāqī al-Shaybānī ﷺ in 595 *hijrī* when he said that he was informed by Shaykh Abu-ʿImrān b. Barmahīn al-Zūlī ﷺ who had said in Mardīn, that one day someone questioned his Shaykh ʿAqīl al-Mambajī ﷺ: who is the present *Qutb*? He replied:

'At this moment he is hidden in Makkah al-Mukarramah. Besides the Awliya, no one knows him. Shortly, here [pointing towards Iraq] will emerge a young man and he will be from ʿAjam Sharīf and he will address the populace in Baghdād. His charismatic traits will be recognized by the common and elite and he will be the Qutb of the era. He will announce that his foot is on the necks of all the Awliya and all the Awliya will bend their necks in submission. If I had

been present in that time, I would have bent my neck for him. This person will be vested with such authority that whosoever conceives his karãmãt, Allãh ﷻ shall grant him benediction.

Narration Eight:

[Concerning Shaykh ʿAlĩ b. Wahb] Shaykh Abu-Muḥammad ʿImrãn b. Abĩ ʿAlĩ b. ʿUthmãn b. Muḥammad b. Aḥmad b. ʿAlĩ al-Sanjãrĩ al-Shafaʿĩ Muwaddab stated in 699 *hijrĩ* in Cairo that he was informed by Shaykh Sãliḥ Jawãb b. Shaykh Kãmil b. Shaykh Jawãb al-Sanjãrĩ who said that he had heard from Shaykh Sãliḥ Muʿammar Abu-Bakr b. Ḥamĩd Shaybãĩ al-Sanjãrĩ prominently known as Ḥabãrĩ, the Imãm of our Shaykh ʿAlĩ b. Wa'hab said that he had heard from Shaykh Abu al-Fara Ismãʿĩl b. al-Faqĩh Abĩ-Isḥãq Ibrãhĩm b. Waraʿ b. ʿIsã b. Abĩ al-Ḥasan Munzarĩ al-Maghribĩ al-Asl Misrĩ, in 656 *hijrĩ* in Cairo that he had heard from his father in 599 *hijrĩ* who heard from Shaykh Qays b. Yũnus al-Shãmĩ, the companion of Shaykh the leader, Abĩ al-Ḥasan ʿAlĩ b. Wa'hab al-Sanjãrĩ said that one day a group of *Fuqara* [spiritual paupers] visited our Shaykh ʿAlĩ b. Wa'hab who asked where they had come from. '*ʿAjam*' they replied. '*Which ʿAjam?*' asked the Shaykh. '*Jilãn*' they said. The Shaykh then said:

'Verily Allah ﷻ has Ordained to illuminate existence with such a person who will shortly emerge from amongst you. He will be very close to Allãh ﷻ and his name will be ʿAbd al-Qãdir. He will appear in Iraq and will announce in Baghdãd that his foot is on the necks of all the Awliya. All the Awliya of that era will submit and confirm his authority. May Allãh ﷻ sanctify their souls.

Narration Nine:

[Concerning Shaykh Ḥammãd b. Muslim al-Dabbãs] Our Shaykh, Shaykh al-ʿÃlam Ḍiya al-Dĩn Abu-Baqa Sãliḥ b. Shaykh Abĩ-Isḥãq Ibrãhĩm b. Aḥmad b. Ibrãhĩm b. Nasar b. al-Qurayshĩ al-Asʿardĩ originally from Zarãtĩ, born in Damascus and now living in Cairo had said to me in 661 *hijrĩ* in Cairo that he had heard from Shaykh, the leader Shãhãb al-Dĩn Abu-Ḥafs ʿUmar b.

Muḥammad b. ʿAbdullāh al-Sohrowardī ﷺ who narrated in 620 *hijrī* in Damascus that he had heard from his uncle Shaykh Najīb al-Dīn Abu-Najīb ʿAbd al-Qāhir b. ʿAbdullāh al-Sohrowardī ﷺ who said in 559 *hijrī* in Baghdād that he heard from Shaykh Abu al-Ḥafs ʿUmar b. Muḥammad b. ʿAbdullāh b. ʿAbd al-Samīʿh b. ʿAbd al-Jabbār b. Sāliḥ al-Mihājī ﷺ born in Sharaʿī living in Shafāʿī said that in 673 *hijrī* that he had heard from Shaykh Abu-Muḥammad Sāliḥ b. Masʿūd b. Mutir al-Sūfī renowned as Rūmī ﷺ said in 630 *hijrī* that in his retreat in the outskirts of Cairo, he had heard from his Shaykh Abu-Najīb ʿAbdul Qāhīr al-Sohrowardī ﷺ who said that in 560 *hijrī* in Baghdād that he was present with Shaykh Ḥammād b. Muslim al-Dabbās ﷺ, in 503 *hijrī* in Baghdād, the day on which Shaykh ʿAbd al-Qādir al-Jilānī ﷺ visited him and respectfully sat in front of him. After some time Shaykh ʿAbd al-Qādir ﷺ got up to leave when Shaykh Ḥammād ﷺ commented:

> The foot of this *ʿAjamī* is such that in his time, it will be high above the necks of the *Awliya*. He will certainly be ordered to declare: *'My foot is on the necks of all the Awliya Allāh'*. He will indeed make this declaration and all the *Awliya* will definitely bow in submission. Some say that, that person's name shall be ʿOun while others say his name will be Abu-Yāʿqūb Yūsuf b. Ayyūb Hamdānī. [104]

I was informed by Faqih Abu-Aḥmad ʿAbd al-Malik b. Abī al-Fataḥ b. Mansūr b. Muqallid Munjī al-Muḥaddith al-Shafāʿī ﷺ by birth Aʿzāzī now living in Cairo, said in 666 *hijrī* that he had heard from the exalted Faqih Abu-ʿAmar ʿUthmān b. Jawwād b. al-Qawī al-Malālī al-Aʿzāzī ﷺ who said in 626 *hijrī* in Cairo, that he was informed by Shaykh Abu-Faraḥ ʿAbd al-Raḥmān b. Shaykh Abu al-ʿAlī Baḥar b. Sharf al-Islām Abu al-Barkāt ʿAbd al-Wah'hāb b. Abī al-Faraḥ ʿAbd al-Wāḥid al-Ansārī Fazrajī Saʿādī al-ʿIbādī al-Shirāzī ﷺ originally Lowshqī and popularly known as Ibn Ḥanbalī who in 601 *hijrī* said in Damascus

[104] Since there is a consensus of the *Mashā'ikh* that has reached *Hadd-e-Tawātur* – stage of recurrence, that numerous *Awliya* were personally present when Sayyiduna Ghawth al-Aʿzam Shaykh ʿAbd al-Qādir al-Jilānī ﷺ made this declaration. This has been dealt in detail by the noble author in this book. Therefore, the view of a few individuals will be ruled out. # *Faqīr ʿAbdul Hādī*

that he was informed by Shaykh Abu al-ʿAlī ʿAbd al-Wah'hāb ﷺ and also the dignified Shaykh Sāliḥ Zāhid Abu al-Muḥāsin Yūsuf b. Iyās b. Marjān b. Munīʿh Baʿalbakī Muqrī al-Ḥanbalī ﷺ who informed us in 669 *hijrī* in Cairo that he had heard in 633 *hijrī* from Shaykh Muʿāmmar Abu al-Fataḥ Nasar b. Riḍwān b. Tharwān Darānī al-Firdousī al-Ḥanbalī al-Muqrī ﷺ in the *Jāmʿeh Masjid* of Damascus [*Jāmeʿh Omawī*], when he was informed in 580 *hijrī* in Damascus by Shaykh Abu Saʿīd ʿAbdullāh Muḥammad b. Haybatullāh b. ʿAlī b. al-Muzhar b. Abī-ʿAsrūn al-Tamīmī al-Shafaʿī ﷺ who said that in his youth he went to Baghdād in the quest for knowledge. In those days, Ibn Saqqa was my friend as well as my class colleague and an associate in spiritual devotion at the *Madrasa Nizāmiyah*. We also visited the *Mashā'ikh* together. In those days there was a Shaykh who was recognized as the *Ghawth* and it was confirmed that whenever he wished to, he appeared and when he desired to, he remained concealed. Then, Ibn Saqqa and Shaykh ʿAbd al-Qādir al-Jilānī ﷺ, who was then young and I, decided to meet this *Ghawth* ﷺ. On the way, Ibn Saqqa said that he will ask the *Ghawth* such a difficult question that he will not be able to answer. I [Shaykh Abu Saʿīd] said that I shall pose a question and note what answer he gives. Then Shaykh ʿAbd al-Qādir al-Jilānī ﷺ said; *'Allāh ﷻ forbid! That I ask him any question! In fact, I will be in his presence in anticipation of the Barakāt of his tender grace.'* When we went to his home, we did not find him on his seat, hence we waited there. After some time, we suddenly saw him, seated on his seat. The *Ghawth* ﷺ then stared with anger at Ibn Saqqa and cautioned him:

> *'O Ibn Saqqa! May you be doomed. You intend asking me such a difficult question and think that I will not be able to answer? Now listen, this is your question and this is the answer to it. Indeed I see the fire of kufr ablaze in yourself.'* Then the *Ghawth* ﷺ looked at me and said; *'O ʿAbdullāh! Do you desire to ask a question and see what I will answer? This is your question and this is my answer, Due to your disrespect, the world will drown you till your ear lobes.'*

Thereafter, he looked at Shaykh ʿAbd al-Qādir al-Jilānī ﷺ and called him close to him with respect and articulated:

'O ʿAbd al-Qādir! Due to your adab [respect], you have pleased Allāh ﷻ and His Rasūl ﷺ. I see you in Baghdād sitting on a chair and addressing the people that your foot is on the necks of all the Awliya, and I see all the Awliya of that time bend their heads in submission owing to your veneration.'

The *Ghawth* ﵀ affirmed the above documented testimony and instantly disappeared. Thereafter we did not see him. Shaykh ʿAbdullāh ﵀ revealed thereafter that the state of Shaykh ʿAbd al-Qādir al-Jilānī ﵀ had reached its zenith, that his close proximity to *Allāh* ﷻ manifested. The common folks and elite were all attracted and began visiting him. Eventually, by the Will of *Allāh* ﷻ at the appropriate time, he announced that his foot is on the necks of all the *Awliya*. The condition of Ibn Saqqa was that he was engrossed in seeking the knowledge of *Sharīʿah,* so much so that he became a legend of his time and excelled in knowledge. He was exceptionally articulate. Moreover, it is to be noted that whomsoever entered into a debate with him had no option, but to remain silent. The present *Khalīfah* was impressed with him and secured him as his confidant and sent him to the Roman Empire to debate with the Christians. The Roman King realised the potential of Ibn Saqqa and was further amazed at his versatility. However, a debate was arranged between him and the Christian Monks and Ibn Saqqa defeated them. This impressed the Roman King and he showed great respect for him. Just then he saw the daughter of the King and became enthralled by her beauty. He requested the King to marry his daughter. The King agreed with conviction on condition that Ibn Saqqa convert to Christianity. Thereupon Ibn Saqqa agreed to renounce *Islām*, and converted to Christianity and married the princess.

Ibn Saqqa later remembered the words of the *Ghawth* ﵀ and realized that all the adversity that ensued, was the serious consequences of his words. Shaykh ʿAbdullāh's condition became critical and he left for Damascus and Sultān Nūr al-Dīn Zangī Shahīd ﵀ summoned him and coerced him to take up an official governmental post. Thereafter, the worldly commodities flocked towards him. Hence, every word predicted by the Ghawth ﵀ began to unfold absolutely and precisely.

The Mashā'ikh who personally heard the words of Sayyiduna Ghawth al-Aᶜzam ﷺ

I was informed by Shaykh Al-Faraḥ ᶜAbd al-Wah'hāb b. Abī al-Mafākhir Ḥasan b. Faytiyān Muḥammad b. Aḥmad al-Kūnī ﷺ originally Azīlī born in Baghdād and narrated this in 665 *hijrī* in Cairo: He said that he had heard from Shaykh Sāliḥ Muᶜammar Baqiyat al-Salf Abu al-Thanā Maḥmūd b. Aḥmad al-Kurdī al-Ḥamīdī al-Jilānī ﷺ and later Baghdādī al-Shafaᶜī also stated in 620 *hijrī* in Baghdād; that at this time, his age was over 120 years. I had the privilege of seeing and meeting Shaykh ᶜAbd al-Qādir al-Jilānī ﷺ, Shaykh Baqa b. Bat'tū ﷺ, Shaykh Sharīf Abu-Saᶜīd al-Qaylawī ﷺ, Shaykh ᶜAdī b. Musāfir ﷺ, Shaykh ᶜAlī b. al-Hītī ﷺ and Shaykh Aḥmad al-Rifāᶜī ﷺ. I was informed by the Honourable Jurist, Abu-Aḥmad ᶜAbd al-Malik b. Abī al-Fataḥ b. Mansūr Musqah Manjī Aᶜzāzī al-Shafāᶜī al-Muḥaddith ﷺ who proclaimed in 636 *hijrī* in Cairo, that he was informed by Shaykh Muᶜammar Baqiyat al-Salf Sharaf Abu ᶜAbdullāh Muḥammad b. ᶜAlī al-Subkī al-Shafaᶜī ﷺ who came to him in Aᶜzāz in 621 *hijrī* and declared that he had passed a 100 years of age, when Shaykh ᶜAbd al-Qādir al-Jilānī ﷺ passed away, I was 61 years old. I spent many years in his company in Baghdād. I was informed by the *Faqih* of pure origin, Abu-Muḥammad Ḥasan b. Shaykh Abu-Muḥammad ᶜAbd al-Raḥmān b. Ibrāhīm b. ᶜAlī Zardār al-Baghdādī ﷺ who said that in 634 *hijrī* in Baghdād; that he was informed by Imām ᶜAllāma ibn Abu al-Baqā ᶜAbdullāh b. al-Ḥusain b. Abī al-Baqa b. al-Ḥusainī ﷺ, a visually impaired celebrated grammarian who originally hailed from ᶜAkbarī and was born in Baghdād, stressed, that in 611 *hijrī*, in Baghdād that he had heard from Shaykh Abu-Muḥammad ᶜAbdullāh b. Aḥmad Khishāb al-Baghdādī al-Ḥanbalī al-Naḥwī ﷺ and Shaykh Imām Abu-Bakr ᶜAbdullāh b. Nasar b. Ḥamza Tamīmī al-Bakrī al-Baghdādī al-Ḥanbalī ﷺ when both of them accentuated in 564 *hijrī* in Baghdād, that they had heard from Shaykh Khalīl Muḥiyy al-Dīn Abu-Muḥammad b. Yūsuf b. Imām Abu al-Faraḥ ᶜAbdur-Raḥman b. ᶜAlī Jowzī Faqih al-Ḥanbalī ﷺ who verified in 639 *hijrī* in Baghdād that he had heard from Shaykh Abu-Hurayrah b. Muḥammad b. Abī al-Futūḥ Layth b. Sujāᶜh b. Masᶜūd b. Abu al-Faḍal al-Baghdādī Azjī al-Dunyārī ﷺ who, although visually impaired, was well renowned by the name of Ibn Abu-Sultānī expressed in 613 *hijrī* in Baghdād that he was informed by Ḥāfiz Abu al-Khayr ʿAbd al-Mughīth b. Abī Ḥarb Zuhayr b. Zuhayr al-ʿAlawī al-Baghdādī Jūbī al-Ḥanbalī ﷺ who stated in 573 *hijrī* in Baghdād: that we were present in the *majlis* of Shaykh ʿAbd al-Qādir al-Jilānī ﷺ at his *rubāt* [guesthouse]. In this assembly, most of the senior *Shuyūkh* of Iraq were present. Amongst them were:

1) Shaykh ʿAlī b. al-Hītī al-Zarirāmī ﷺ,
2) Shaykh Baqā b. Bat'tū al-Nahr Mulkī ﷺ,
3) Shaykh Sharīf Abu-Saʿīd al-Qaylawī ﷺ
4) Shaykh Mūsā b. Mahīn al-Zūlī ﷺ who had just returned from *Ḥajj* on that day,
5) Shaykh Abu al-Najīb ʿAbd al-Qāhir b. ʿAbdullāh al-Sohrowardī ﷺ,
6) Shaykh Abu al-Kirām Muʿammar b. Shaykh Abu al-ʿAbbās Aḥmad b. ʿAlī Jowsiqī al-Sarsarī ﷺ,
7) Shaykh Mājid al-Kurdī ﷺ
8) Shaykh Abu-Ḥakīm b. Ibrāhīm b. Dinār al-Neharwānī ﷺ
9) Shaykh Abu-ʿAmar ʿUthmān b. Marzūq al-Qurashī ﷺ who had just arrived in Baghdād on this day to visit Sayyiduna Ghawth ﷺ
10) Shaykh Makārim Akbar ﷺ
11) Shaykh Mutir al-Bādrānī ﷺ
12) Shaykh Jāgīr ﷺ
13) Shaykh Khalīfah b. Mūsā Akbar ﷺ
14) Shaykh Sadaqah b. Muḥammad al-Baghdādī ﷺ
15) Shaykh Yaḥyah b. Muḥammad al-Dūrī Murta'ish ﷺ
16) Shaykh Ḍiya al-Dīn Ibrāhīm b. Abī ʿAbdillāh b. ʿAlī al-Jūbī ﷺ
17) Shaykh Abu-ʿAbdullāh Muḥammad b. Daryāmī al-Qurashī ﷺ who had also just arrived in Baghdād on that day.
18) Shaykh Abu ʿAmar ʿUthmān b. Mardah al-Batā'iḥī ﷺ
19) Shaykh Qaḍīb al-Baan al-Mosulī ﷺ
20) Shaykh Abu al-ʿAbbās al-Baqlī famous as Rayḥānī ﷺ
21) Shaykh Abu al-ʿAbbās Aḥmad al-Qurashī ﷺ the one with external authority, and his student,

22) Shaykh Dā'ūd ﷺ who was young at that time and it is said that he performed his 5 daily *salāh* at the *Ka'ābah* in Makkah al-Mukarramah.
23) Shaykh Abu-'Abdullāh b. Muḥammad 'Abdullāh al-Irāqī famous as Khās ﷺ
24) Shaykh Abu-'Amar 'Uthmān b. Aḥmad al-Irāqī famous as Shoukī ﷺ, it was said that he was from the *Saylānī Rijāl al-Ghayb*
25) Shaykh Sultān b. Aḥmad al-Mazīn ﷺ
26) Shaykh Abu-Bakr b. 'Abd al-Ḥamīd al-Shaybānī famous as Ḥayyārī ﷺ
27) Shaykh Abu al-'Abbās Aḥmad b. Ustād ﷺ
28) Shaykh Abu-Muḥammad Aḥmad b. 'Īsā ma'rūf al-Kūsjī ﷺ
29) Shaykh Mubarak b. 'Alī al-Jamīlī ﷺ
30) Shaykh Abu al-Barkāt b. Ma'dān al-Irāqī ﷺ
31) Shaykh 'Abd al-Qādir b. Ḥasan al-Baghdādī ﷺ
32) Shaykh Abu al-Mas'ūd Aḥmad b. Abī-Bakr al-Ḥazīmī 'Attār ﷺ
33) Shaykh Abu-'Abdullāh Muḥammad Abī Ma'ālī b. Qā'id al-Adnī ﷺ
34) Shaykh Abu al-Qāsim 'Umar b. Mas'ūd Baz'zār ﷺ who was very young
35) Shaykh Shahāb al-Dīn 'Umar b. Muḥammad al-Sohrowardī ﷺ who was young
36) Shaykh Abu al-Thanā Maḥmūd b. 'Uthmān Na'al-band ﷺ
37) Shaykh Abu al-Ḥafs 'Umar b. Nasar al-Ghazāl ﷺ
38) Shaykh Abu Muḥammad al-Farsī, later Baghdādī ﷺ
39) Shaykh Abu Muḥammad 'Alī b. Idrīs al-Ya'qūbī ﷺ who was young
40) Shaykh 'Ibād Darbān ﷺ
41) Shaykh Muzaffar Jamāl ﷺ
42) Shaykh Abu-Bakr al-Ḥamāmī ﷺ famous as Mazīn
43) Shaykh Khalīl Sāḥib Qadam Warza ﷺ
44) Shaykh Abu-'Amar 'Uthmān al-Tarīfī ﷺ
45) Shaykh Abu al-Ḥasan al-Jowsiqī ﷺ famous as Abī-'Awāja
46) Shaykh Abu-Muḥammad 'Abd al-Ḥaqq al-Ḥazīmī ﷺ
47) Shaykh Abu-Ya'lā Muḥammad b. Muḥammad Fara ﷺ etc....

Shaykh Muḥiyy al-Dīn 'Abd al-Qādir al-Jilānī ﷺ was addressing them and they were attentive. The Ghawth ﷺ declared; *'My foot is on the necks of all the Awliya*

Allāh.'

Thereafter, Shaykh ʿAlī b. al-Hītī ﷺ stood up and ascended the pulpit [*mimbar*], took thc consecrated foot of Ḥaḍrate Ghawth ﷺ and placed it on his neck and covered himself with the Shaykh's cloak. Subsequently, the entire gathering presented their necks.

I was informed in 635 *hijrī* by Shaykh Abu al-Ḥasan ʿAlī b. Muḥammad b. ʿAbdullāh b. Abī-Bakr b. ʿAlī b. Aḥmad al-Abharī Asl al-Baghdādī ﷺ living in Cairo, that he was present in the gathering [*majlis*] which was filled with the *Mashā'ikh* of Baghdād. The proclamation of Haḍrat Shaykh ʿAbd al-Qādir al-Jilānī ﷺ; *My foot is on the necks of all the Awliya Allāh'* was discussed. Shaykh Khalīl b. Shaykh Abu al-ʿAbbās Aḥmad al-Sarsarī ﷺ then said:

> 'I visited Shaykh Abu al-Masʿūd ﷺ in 579 *hijrī* and I inquired from him about this proclamation of Sayyiduna Shaykh ʿAbd al-Qādir al-Jilānī ﷺ. He said that he was present in that gathering and personally heard this command from the magnanimous lips of the Ghawth ﷺ. In that gathering, an estimate of 50 illustrious senior *Mashā'ikh* of that era were present. I noticed that when he effected this declaration, then all the *Mashā'ikh* bent their heads, hence signifying their humility and submission. I also saw Shaykh ʿAlī b. al-Hītī ﷺ ascending the pulpit, moved towards the great Ghawth ﷺ and took his head and placed it on his neck. Shaykh Abu al-Khifāf al-Baghdādī ﷺ then fully endorsed that he heard the very same words from Shaykh Abu-Masʿūd ﷺ several times.

Shaykh Abu ʿAmar ʿUthmān b. Sulaymān, popular as al-Qas'sīr ﷺ affirmed:

> I also visited Shaykh Abu-ʿAbdullāh Muḥammad Abī Maʿālī b. Qā'id al-Adnī ﷺ on 10th *Muḥarram* 584 *hijrī* and inquired from him concerning the same statement of Sayyiduna Shaykh ʿAbd al-Qādir al-Jilānī ﷺ. His reply was in the affirmative and it was also unanimous to that of Shaykh Abu-Masʿūd ﷺ.

I was informed by Shaykh Abu-Yūsuf Yaʿqūb b. Badrān al-Ansārī al-Muqrī al-Qāhirī ﷺ in Qāhirah in 667 *hijrī* that he had arrived in 661 *hijrī* in Baghdād to visit and attend the classes of Qāḍī al-Quḍāt Abu-Sāliḥ Nasar al-Jilānī ﷺ. I saw an assembly around him. One person questioned Shaykh Abu-Sāliḥ Nasar ﷺ; *'What have you heard about that statement of Shaykh ʿAbd al-Qādir al-Jilānī ﷺ?'* In response, the Shaykh ﷺ replied:

> 'I heard on several occasions from [his father] Shaykh Abu-Bakr ʿAbd al-Razzāq al-Jilānī ﷺ and my uncles; Shaykh Abu-ʿAbd al-Raḥmān ʿAbdullāh al-Jilānī ﷺ, Shaykh Abu ʿAbdullāh ʿAbd al-Wah'hāb al-Jilānī ﷺ, Shaykh Abu-Isḥāq Ibrāhīm, the *awlād* [progeny] of Shaykh ʿAbd al-Qādir al-Jilānī ﷺ'. All of them asserted that they were present in that *majlis* when their father ﷺ decreed that his foot is on the necks of all the *Awliya Allāh*. There were approximately 50 senior *Mashā'ikh* of Baghdād present in this *majlis*. All of them bent their necks in submission and Shaykh ʿAlī b. al-Hītī ﷺ took the foot [of our father] and placed it on his neck. We later received information from several *Mashā'ikh* from different towns who were present there that indeed, they put forward their necks in submission. They all confirmed this and nobody informed us about any person who defied this command.'

Those Mashā'ikh who heard the command of Sayyiduna Ghawth al-Aʿzam ﷺ through kashf

1) Sayyid Sharīf Shaykh Abu-Sāʿad al-Qaylawī ﷺ.

I was informed by the exalted Jurist [*Faqih*] Abu-Ghālib Rizqullāh b. Abī-ʿAbdullāh Muḥammad b. Yūsuf al-Raqqī al-Shafaʿī ﷺ in 629 *hijrī* in Cairo that he had heard from Shaykh Sāliḥ Abu-Isḥāq Ibrāhīm b. Shaykh, the leader, Abu al-Fataḥ Mansūr b. al-Aqdām al-Raqqī ﷺ in 623 *hijrī* in Qayy, who related that he had heard from Shaykh Mansūr ﷺ in 586 *hijrī* and that he was informed by Shaykh, the leader, Abu-ʿAbdullāh Muḥammad b. Mājid al-Raqqī ﷺ who stated that in 560 *hijrī*.....

It was narrated to me by Shaykh Abu al-Futūḥ Nasarullāh b. Abī Muḥāsin Yūsuf b. Khalīl b. ʿAlī b. Mafraj al-Baghdādī Azjī al-Ḥanbalī al-Muḥaddith ﷺ who also narrated in 667 *hijrī* in Cairo that he had narrated from Shaykh Abu al-ʿAbbās Aḥmad b. Ismāʿīl b. Ḥamza b. Abī al-Barkāt Mubārak b. Ḥamza b.

ʿUthmān b. Ḥasan al-Baghdādī al-Azjī, popular as Ibn al-Tabāl in 627 *hijrī* in Baghdād, remarked that he narrates from two *Shuyūkh*; Shaykh Muʿammar Abu al-Muzaffar Mansūr b. Mubarak b. Fuḍayl b. Abī-Naʿīm al-Wāsitī al-Wāʿiz and Shaykh Imām Abu-Muḥammad ʿAbdullāh ibn Abī al-Ḥasan b. Abī al-Faḍal al-Shāmī al-Jabbārī originally from Baghdād, who then settled in Ashān; narrated in 601 *hijrī* in Baghdād; that he narrates from Sayyid Sharīf Shaykh, the leader, Abu-Sāʿad al-Qaylawī whom I had heard stating in Qaylawa that when Shaykh ʿAbd al-Qādir al-Jilānī pronounced that his foot is on the necks of all the *Awliya*, *Allāh* ﷻ sparkled a lustre [*tajallī*] on his heart and Sayyiduna Rasūlullāh ﷺ gave the Intimate Angels a special garb to adorn him. This congregation was attended by: the existing *Awliya* in their personal capacities, the souls of the *Awliya* who had physically transcended this transitory world, the angels and the entire *Rijāl al-Ghayb.*[105] They encircled the ambience of the *majlis,* which was suspended in the air, and stood with folded hands in lines in a befitting deportment, hence covering the horizons. There was no *Walī* on earth that did not bend his neck in submission to the directive of the Ghawth.

2) Shaykh Baqa b. Bat'tū

I was informed by Shaykh ʿAllāma Shams al-Dīn Abu ʿAbdullāh Muḥammad b. Al-Shaykh Imām ʿĀlim ʿImād al-Dīn Abu-Isḥāq Ibrāhīm b. ʿAbd al-Wāḥid b. ʿAlī al-Maqdisī al-Ḥanbalī who had narrated in 665 *hijrī* in Cairo, that he narrates from the Shaykh of the sacred *Sharīʿāh*, Abu al-Qāsim Haybatullāh b. Aḥmad al-Khatīb distinguished as Ibn Manthūrī narrated in 631 *hijrī* in Baghdād: and he narrates from the Shaykh and leader, Abu al-Qāsim ʿUmar b. Masʿūd prominently known as Baz'zār in 592 *hijrī* in Baghdād that he had heard Shaykh Baqa b. But'tū disclosing: *'When Shaykh ʿAbd al-Qādir al-Jilānī decreed that his foot is on the necks of all the Awliya Allāh, then the angels said,*

[105] These exclusive *Awliya* are Men of the Unseen who are the statesmen of the Spiritual Parliament. They are unknown to people and if and when they desire; they become imperceptible.

'O servant of Allāh! You have spoken the truth.'

3) Shaykh ʿAdī b. Musāfir and Shaykh Aḥmad b. Rifāʿī.
I was informed by the Shaykh of noble origin, Faqih Abu al-Faḍal Manthūr b. Aḥmad b. Abī al-Faraḥ al-Irāqī al-Dorī later al-Baghdādī al-Ḥanbalī in 674 *hijrī* in Cairo, who narrates from Shaykh ʿAllāma Kamāl al-Dīn Abu al ʿAbbās Aḥmad b. Muḥammad b. Samdawī al-Ḥarīqīnī Faqih al-Ḥanbalī who exclaimed in 641 *hijrī* in Cairo, that he had heard from Shaykh Sāliḥ Abu-Muḥammad Yūsuf Muzaffar b. Shujāʿh al-ʿĀqūlī originally al-Baghdādī who came from Asjī Asfār and reported in 622 *hijrī* in Baghdād that he had visited Shaykh ʿAdī b. Musāfir in early 656 *hijrī*, and he enquired from me about where I had come from. I responded: *'I am from the companions [Aṣḥāb] of Shaykh ʿAbd al-Qādir and came from Baghdād.'* The Shaykh said;

> '*Subhānallāh*! He is the *Qutb* of the earth and when he announced that his foot is on the necks of all the *Awliya Allāh*, then 300 Awliya and 700 *Rijāl al-Ghayb*, all those that were flying in the air including all those that were stationed on earth, bent their heads in submission to his command.'

Shaykh ʿĀqūlī comments that according to him, he felt Shaykh ʿAdī had made a fundamental statement. However, after some time he went to Umm ʿUbaydah [106] to visit Shaykh Aḥmad Rifāʿī. He inquired about the statement of Shaykh ʿAdī b. Musāfir and Sayyidī Aḥmad Rīfāʿī thereby reinforced that Shaykh ʿAdī had spoken the truth.

4) Shaykh Mājid al-Kurdī and Shaykh Mutir
I was informed by Shaykh Abu-Muḥammad b. Khālid b. Abī-Bakr b. Sīma b. Ghānim al-Iraqī Ḥalwānī al-Baghdādī in 671 *hijrī* in Cairo. He narrates from Shaykh Sāliḥ Abu-Bakr Muḥammad b. Shaykh ʿIwaḍ b. Salāmat Gharād al-

[106] Present day Nasriyyah in South Iraq. Approximately 180 klm from Basra

Baghdādī al-Sūfī ﷺ in 630 *hijrī* in Baghdād, and reports that his father, Shaykh ʿIwaḍ ﷺ who was a companion of Shaykh ʿAbd al-Qādir al-Jilānī ﷺ informed him that Shaykh Muḥammad Shabnakī ﷺ, Shaykh Abu-Aḥmad ʿAbd al-Bāqī b. ʿAbd al-Jabbār al-Hirwī al-Baghdādī Sūfī al-Ḥirḍī ﷺ and Shaykh Abu-ʿAbdullāh Ustāz Mahr b. Muḥammad al-Khaylānī ﷺ embarked on to meet Shaykh Mājid al-Kurdī ﷺ at the Ḥumrayn Mountain. When we reached there, Shaykh Mājid ﷺ accorded us a cordial welcome. We spent a few days with him and when we sort his permission to leave, the Shaykh ﷺ then revealed:

> 'I want to give a provision, which I would like you to take back with you. When Shaykh ʿAbd al-Qādir al-Jilānī ﷺ announced that his foot is on the necks of all the *Awliya Allāh*, then there was no *Walī* on the earth who did not bend his head in submission and as well as in acknowledgement of the status of this *Walī* of *Allāh*. Furthermore, there is no assembly [*majlis*] of the pious Jinns where this was not discussed. I visited them and the most pious Jinns repented at the hands of Shaykh ʿAbd al-Qādir al-Jilānī ﷺ and embraced *Islām*.'

We then assembled at the door of the Shaykh ﷺ where he bid us farewell. We departed with the intention of meeting Shaykh Mutir ﷺ. Within our hearts, we perceived that Shaykh Mājid ﷺ had put forth an immense statement. When we reached Shaykh Mutir ﷺ, he welcomed us and affirmed: '*What my brother Shaykh Mājid ﷺ said concerning Shaykh ʿAbd al-Qādir al-Jilānī ﷺ is the truth.*'

5) Shaykh Makārim ﷺ

I was informed by Shaykh Abu-Muḥammad ʿAbd al-Wāḥid b. Sāliḥ Yaḥyah b. Muḥammad al-Qurashī al-Baghdādī ﷺ in 673 *hijrī* in Cairo, who narrates from Shaykh ʿAllāma Muḥiyy al-Dīn Abu ʿAbdullāh Muḥammad b. Ḥāmid b. Āmidī al-Jilānī, originally Mutir al-Baghdādī Ḥanbalī prominently known as Tawḥīdī ﷺ, the grandson of Ḥāfiz Abu-Bakr ʿAbd al-Razzāq al-Jilānī ﷺ who

enunciated in 639 *hijrĩ* in Baghdãd, that he narrates from Shaykh Abu-Muḥammad ʿAbdur Raḥman b. Shaykh Abu-Ḥafs ʿUmar b. Nasar b. ʿAlĩ b. ʿAbd al-Dã'im al-Baghdãdĩ Wãʿiz ﷺ renowned as Ibn al-Azãl in *Jãme'h Mansũr* in early *Rajab* 614 *hijrĩ* in Baghdãd, stipulated that he met Shaykh Abu-ʿAbd al-Raḥmãn ʿAbdullãh b. Shaykh Muḥiyy al-Dĩn Abĩ-Muḥammad ʿAbd al-Q̱ãdir al-Jilãnĩ ﷺ in the *Madrassa* of his father in 539 *hijrĩ* in *Bãb al-Azj* and asked him if he was present in the *majlis* when his father made the declaration: *'My foot is on the necks of all the Awliya Allãh.'*? He replied in the affirmative and confirmed: *'There were approximately 50 such Mashã'ikh present who were luminaries. I saw all of them bend their necks. When my father ﷺ left for his home and the people dispersed, Shaykh Makãrim ﷺ, Shaykh Muḥammad Khãs ﷺ and Shaykh Aḥmad b. ʿArbĩ ﷺ and his student Dãʾũd remained behind. My two brothers, Shaykh ʿAbd al-ʿAzĩz al-Jilãnĩ ﷺ and Shaykh ʿAbd al-Jabbãr al-Jilãnĩ ﷺ and I went and sat with them.'*
Shaykh Makãrĩm ﷺ then expounded:

> 'I regard Almighty *Allãh* ﷻ omnipresent and testify that this day amongst all these people who were blessed with sainthood [*wilãyah*] in the entire country, be they close or far; there was no *Walĩ* who did not see that the flag of *Q̱utbiyat* was raised for Shaykh ʿAbd al-Q̱ãdir al-Jilãnĩ ﷺ and the Crown of Superiority was placed on his head. They have all witnessed that he was bestowed with the general authority on everything in this world to grant Sainthood [*wilãyah*] to whom he desires and to denigrate whomsoever he desired.
>
> He is moulded in both: the sacred *Sharĩʿah* and *Ḥaqĩqah*. They must have heard him declaring that his foot is on the necks of all the *Awliya Allãh*. It is for that reason that every *Walĩ* at once bent his head, in so much so, that the 10 *Abdãls* were the special emperors of the world. I questioned who they were and he replied:
>
> 1) Shaykh Baqa b. But'tũ ﷺ

2) Shaykh Abu-Sa'īd al-Qaylawī ﵁
3) Shaykh ʿAlī b. al-Hītī ﵁
4) Shaykh ʿAdī b. Musāfir ﵁
5) Shaykh Mūsā al-Zūlī ﵁
6) Shaykh Aḥmad b. Zouʿī ﵁
7) Shaykh ʿAbd al-Raḥmān al-Tafsunjī ﵁
8) Shaykh Abu-Muḥammad ʿAbdullāh al-Basrī ﵁
9) Shaykh Ḥayāt b. Qais al-Ḥarrānī ﵁
10) Shaykh Abu-Madyan al-Maghribī ﵁

Thereafter, Shaykh Abu-Muḥammad Khās ﵀ and Shaykh Aḥmad b. al-ʿUrbī ﵀ assured him: '*You have spoken the truth.*' Shaykh Abu ʿAbd al-Raḥmān al-Jilānī ﵀ then specified that his brothers and himself memorised this particular incident and had it locked in their memories.

Ibn Ghazāl ﵀ exposes that he had returned from him and came to his two brothers, Shaykh ʿAbd al-ʿAzīz al-Jilānī ﵀ and Shaykh ʿAbd al-Jabbār al-Jilānī ﵀ and asked them about the same incident. Both of them reiterated precisely the same facts without any differences to what their brother Shaykh Abu-ʿAbd al-Raḥmān al-Jilānī ﵀ had declared.

6) Shaykh Khalīfa Akbar ﵁

I was informed by Shaykh Abu Muḥammad Ḥasan b. Abu al-Qāsim Aḥmad b. Muḥammad b. Abī al-Qāsim ﵀ and Shaykh Khalaf b. Aḥmad n. Muḥammad al-Baghdādī al-Ḥarīmī eminently known as Jadda ibn Qouqah ﵀ reverberated in 666 *hijrī* in Cairo, that he was informed by Shaykh Muḥammad b. Alif ﵀ in 625 *hijrī* in Baghdād, when he heard from Shaykh Abu al-Qāsim b. Abī-Bakr b. Aḥmad b. Abī Saʿādāt Ḥamd b. Mukarram al-Bandliḥī, originally al-Baghdādī al-Azjī ﵀ who resonated in 593 *hijrī* in Baghdād, that he had heard Shaykh Khalīfah ﵀ verbalize in Baghdād that he was the one who frequently saw Sayyiduna Rasūlullāh ﷺ in his *kashf*, and confirmed that: '*I had made the ziyārah of the beloved Messenger of Allāh ﷺ and thus respectfully inquired from him: 'Indeed Shaykh ʿAbd al-Qādir al-Jilānī elucidated that his foot is on the neck of every Walī of Allāh.'* The beloved Prophet of *Allāh* ﷺ replied: '*Shaykh ʿAbd al-Qādir spoke the truth and why should he not say this when he is the Qutb and I am his protector.'*

7) Shaykh Lulu al-Armīnī ﷺ

The author ﷺ professes that he was informed by Shaykh Sāliḥ Abu-ʿAlī ʿAbbās b. Shaykh Abu-Mūsā ʿImrān b. Ibrāhīm b. Ismāʿīl b. Ibrāhīm al-Qarārī al-Shāfaʿī ﷺ in 636 *hijrī* in the protected city of Cairo; that he narrates from his father Shaykh ʿImrān ﷺ and his uncle Shaykh Abu-Muḥammad ʿAbdullāh b. Muḥammad b. Ibrāhīm b. Ismāʿīl ﷺ popular by the name of Sādiq Fazārī in 622 *hijrī*: both said they had heard from their leader Abu al-Khayr ʿAta b. ʿAbd al-ʿAzīz b. Naʿīm b. Nāzūka b. Kaymān b. Razīn b. Misrī ﷺ in 590 *hijrī* in the vicinity of Cairo; who clarified that in 500 *hijrī* he was a *Mujāwir* [cleaner] in *Makkah al-Mukarramah* [may *Allāh* ﷻ sanctify its precincts] and Shaykh Lulu al-Armīnī ﷺ whom people knew as a *Qutb* and Shaykh Mārdīnī ﷺ were present with him. One day I visited him and found my Shaykh Abu ʿAbdullāh Muḥammad b. Samīrī ﷺ, Shaykh Abu-ʿAbdullāh Muḥammad al-Daysanī ﷺ, Shaykh Salāḥ al-Dīn ﷺ conspicuously known as *Imām al-Ḥaram*, Shaykh Abu-Ḥafs ʿUmar b. Muḥammad al-Maghribī al-ʿAdadī ﷺ and Shaykh Abu-Muḥammad ʿAbdullāh b. Ayah-Ghash al-Mārdīnī ﷺ were present with him.

I witnessed Shaykh Lulu Armīnī's ﷺ communion with *Allāh* ﷻ that no one else had noticed. I then contemplated in my heart: *'I wonder which Shaykh he links himself to?'* At that juncture, he intercepted my thoughts and proclaimed: *'O ʿAtā! My Shaykh is Shaykh ʿAbd al-Qādir ﷺ who had explicitly decreed: my foot is on the neck of every Walī of Allāh and at that time 313 Awliya around the world bent their heads in submission. Included amongst them were the following:*

- 17 in Ḥaramayn Sharīfayn
- 60 in Iraq
- 40 in ʿAjam [Persia]
- 30 in Shām [Syria]
- 20 in Egypt
- 27 in al-Maghrib [North Africa]
- 23 in Yemen
- 11 in Habsha [Abyssinia, now Ethiopia]
- 7 in Sadd Yajūj Majūj

- 7 in Sarindīb [Sri Lanka]
- 47 in Kohe Qāf [107]

---

[107] The Mountain of *Qāf* is a central point where most of the *Awliya* assemble. This mysterious mountain is inhabited by senior *Awliya* at any given time. The Cardinal Pole of noble Saints [*al-Qutb*], *Shaykh al-Islām wal-Muslimīn* Aʿla-Ḥaḍrat Mujaddid Imām Ahmad Rīḍā al-Qādiri ﷺ in his classic *Al-ʿAtā an-Nabawiyyah fī Fatāwa ar-Raḍawiyyah,* Vol. 12, pg.191 Raza Foundation Edition Lahore, states that Almighty *Allāh* ﷻ has encircled the entire earth by a mountain called *Qāf*. There is no piece of earth that the roots of this mountain have not reached. This is similar to a massive tree whose partial roots are exposed, but below the earth. Its roots spread out to many places which makes the tree very stable and strong. Therefore, this mountain survives in the most inclement weather and gale force winds. The bigger the tree, the bigger its roots will be and the further they will spread. Similarly, the Mountain of *Qāf* has infiltrated the entire earth, with a network of its roots and there is no place that is void of them. This web or network of roots sometimes seen above the ground which are called "mountains" and at some other places called "rocky terrains" or "canyons." The root of this mountain is below water level and very deep at places. In such places the surface soil of this area is relatively softer than other places which is called '*Sahl*' in Arabic. The neighbouring vicinity of our area [Bareilly, UP, India] is an example of this soft soil surface region. However, the roots of *Qāf* Mountain incorporate every portion of the earth. Wherever Almighty *Allāh* ﷻ Ordains to initiate a tremor or earthquake [may the Mercy of Almighty *Allāh* ﷻ and the Mercy of His beloved Rasūl ﷺ protect us from this devastation], He orders the *Qāf* Mountain to vibrate that specific part of its roots and hence, tremors or earthquakes are only felt on those portions of the earth. The intensity of the earthquake is determined by the intensity of the Divine Command. If the Command is mild, the Mountain will vibrate the thinner roots and *Allāh* forbid, if the Command is violent, then the bigger roots will vibrate that portion of the earth, causing catastrophic damage on the surface of the earth. Sometimes the vibration of a tremor or earthquake is felt in the neighbouring cities depending on the underground location of that specific root. In some places the ground opens up and water gushes out and at other places where the earthquake is very volatile, the split throws out fire [volcanoes] and gives off loud scary explosions. This is due to the buildup of gases created by the heat of the radiation of the sun that is spread out under various places of the earth. Some quakes or eruptions of volcanoes spit out smoke and gases [ashes] that engulf the atmosphere. Scientists who study the earth say that the eruption or quake occur when gases under the earth build up and this pressure build up blows up the earth to release itself. But according to *Islām* the reasoning of scientists is limited on the basis of assumption or superficial knowledge. The knowledge of *Islām* is direct and factual, hence where frontiers of human intellect ends, the direct and true knowledge of the sacred *Sharīʿah* begins. Science is of the view that when the earth 'intends'

❖ 24 in the Island of *Bahr Muḥīt* [a mystical Atlantic Ocean Island].

---

to release this pressure buildup then an eruption takes place but the *Sharīʿah* states the entire universe was created by *Allāh* ﷻ and is under His Divine Control. Thus, the 'intent' of the earth is controlled by the Divine Intent of the Supreme Lord of Power ﷻ. Hence, creation only 'intends' when the Divine Power of its Creator ﷻ orders it to do so. Imām Ibn Abī-Duniya رضي الله عنه in his *Kitāb al-Oqūbāt* reports on the authority of Sayyiduna ʿAbdullāh ibn ʿAbbās رضي الله عنه as follows:

وَابْنُ أَبِي الدُّنْيَا فِي كِتَابِ الْعُقُوبَاتِ عَنِ ابْنِ عَبَّاسٍ رَضِيَ اللّٰهُ عَنْهُمَا قَالَ: خَلَقَ اللّٰهُ جَبَلًا يُقَالُ لَهُ ق مُحِيطٌ بِالْعَالَمِ وَعُرُوقُهُ إِلَى الصَّخْرَةِ الَّتِي عَلَيْهَا الْأَرْضُ فَإِذَا أَرَادَ اللّٰهُ أَنْ يُزَلْزِلَ قَرْيَةً أَمَرَ ذَلِكَ الْجَبَلَ فَحَرَّكَ الْعِرْقَ الَّذِي يَلِي تِلْكَ الْقَرْيَةَ فَيُزَلْزِلُهَا وَيُحَرِّكُهَا فَمِنْ ثَمَّ تُحَرَّكُ الْقَرْيَةُ دُونَ الْقَرْيَةِ

Allāh created a Mountain called Qāf which encompasses the entire earth. Its rocky roots are spread out under the ground on which this mountain stands. Whenever Allāh ﷻ Ordains a quake in a specific place He Orders this mountain to vibrate its roots situated under that specific area which causes a tremor in that selected town. It is for this reason that only a selected area experiences a quake while the neighbouring areas are not damaged. [Also cited in Tafsīr Ad-Durr al-Manthūr li al-Suyūtī vol. 13 page 140]

Unfortunately, the restricted knowledge of the scientists fail to comprehend the process of writing with a pen. The pen is operated by the fingers and the fingers are operated by the power of the hand which in turn gets its power from the soul. Hence, in reality the design made by the pen is actually the manifestation of creativity of the soul. But the oblivious scientists confine the procedure writing only to the pen, fingers and arm. Scientific intellect is bereft at this limit and ceases to see further. Similarly, the *Qāf* Mountain functions on the same principles. As the intellect of scientists and experiments conducted by science ceases at the arm, similarly does it cease at the junction of gaseous energy build-up before an eruption. The Dictates of the sanctified *Sharīʿah* goes beyond the devices of science and leads one to the actual and real cause of the eruption. This focal point is under the supervision of senior *Awliya* who are directly under the command and supervision of the great Ghawth, Sayyiduna Shaykh ʿAbd al-Qādir al-Jilānī رضي الله عنه. This strategic locality is far beyond the accessibility and comprehension of the ordinary human mind. *[Faqīr ʿAbdul-Hādī al-Qādirī]*

Names of those Mashā'ikh who testified that Sayyiduna Ghawth al-Aᶜzam ﷺ promulgated this declaration by the Command of Allāh ﷻ.

1) Shaykh ᶜAdī b. Musāfir ﷺ

It was related to us by Shaykh Abu-ᶜAbdullāh Muḥammad b. Abī al-Ḥasan ᶜAlī b. Ḥusain b. Aḥmad b. ᶜAbd al-Raḥmān al-Damishqī ﷺ living in Mosul; who declared in 633 *hijrī* in Cairo, that he had heard Shaykh, the leader, Abu al-Mafākhir ᶜAdī b. Shaykh Abī al-Barkāt Sakhar ﷺ state that he heard that his uncle, Shaykh ᶜAdī b. Musāfir ﷺ specify:

> 'Did you hear any former *Mashā'ikh* submit the statement that Shaykh Abd al-Qādir al-Jilānī ﷺ reverberate that his foot is on the neck of every single *Walī* of *Allāh?*' I replied in the negative and questioned as to what the meaning of this was? The Shaykh responded: *'This proves that he is a distinctive individual [Fard] of his time.'* I queried: *'Is there a Fard in every period?'* He replied: *'Yes but none of them besides Shaykh ᶜAbd al-Qādir al-Jilānī ﷺ was instructed to make this statement.'* I then questioned: *'Was he instructed to make this statement?'* He remarked: *'Why not? He was instructed to make this statement. The reason as to why all the Awliya bent their heads was because he was instructed to advocate this declaration. Do you not know that the angels did not make sajdah to Nabī Ādam ﷺ at any time, except upon the Command of Allāh ﷻ?'*

2) Shaykh Sharīf Abu-Saᶜīd al-Qaylawī ﷺ

It was related to us by Shaykh Faqih Abu al-Qāsim Muḥammad b. ᶜUbādah b. Muḥammad b. ᶜUbādah b. ᶜAbdul Ḥasan b. Munzarī al-Ansārī al-Ḥillī ﷺ in 674 *hijrī* in Cairo that he had heard from Shaykh ᶜĀrif Abu al-Ḥasan ᶜAlī al-Ghaznī ﷺ in 612 *hijrī* in Damascus saying that their Shaykh Abu-Saᶜīḍ al-Qaylawī ﷺ was asked if *Allāh* ﷻ had ordered Shaykh ᶜAbd al-Qādir al-Jilānī ﷺ to resonate the statement that his foot is on the neck of every *Walī* of *Allāh*? I heard this conversation in a sound state. The Shaykh ﷺ advocated as follows:

> 'Why not? He proclaimed this by Divine Command and there is no doubt about it. This statement was from the tongue of *Qutbiyat*, and in

every era, some *Qutbs*[108] are ordered to observe silence, without any option. There are some *Qutb*s who are ordered to speak and hence, they have no option but to speak. Such *Qutbs* are more senior than others because they are endowed with the tongue of intercession [*Shafā ʿat*].'

3) Shaykh ʿAlī b. al-Hītī ﷺ

It was narrated to me in 671 *hijrī* in Cairo by Shaykh Abu-Muḥammad ʿAbdus Salām b. Ibrāhīm b. ʿAbdullāh al-Basrī ﷺ, born and lived in Baghdād: that he narrates from Shaykh Sharīf Abu al-Qāsim Haybatullāh b. ʿAbdullāh b. Aḥmad ﷺ prominent by the name Ibn al-Mansūrī who related in 631 *hijrī* in Baghdād: that he narrates from Shaykh ʿĀrif Abu-Muḥammad ʿAlī b. Abu-Bakr b. Idrīs al-Yaʿqūbī ﷺ who had declared there, in 611 *hijrī,* that when Shaykh ʿAbd al-Qādir al-Jilānī ﷺ decreed: *'My foot is on the neck of every Walī of Allāh,'* Shaykh ʿAlī b. al-Hītī ﷺ then moved forward towards him, ascended the mimbar and grabbed the feet of Ḥaḍrate Ghawth ﷺ. He then placed his sacred feet on his neck and screened himself under the Shaykh's ﷺ cloak. His companions later requested his reason for doing this and he answered:

> 'The reason I did this was because the Ghawth ﷺ was ordered to make this statement. He was further ordered that if any *Walī* rejects his command, he will be relegated of his status. Therefore, I intended to be the first one to obey this command.'

4) Shaykh Aḥmad al-Rifāʿī ﷺ

It was narrated to me in 670 *hijrī* in Cairo by Shaykh Abu al-Ḥasan ʿAlī b. Shaykh Abī al-Majja Mubārak b. Yūsuf b. Ghassān al-Qurashī al-Batāiḥī al-Shafāʿī ﷺ who conceded that he narrates in 621 *hijrī* from the Shaykh and leader Abu-Isḥāq Ibrāhīm b. Shaykh ʿĀrif Abu al-Ḥasan Rifāʿī al-Batāiḥī ﷺ well-

[108] The Pillar or the Help. [The hidden centre of the hierarchy of saints or the summit of spiritual evolution.] He is, by his essential nature, unique and alone in his time, except when the moment has led [others] to seek the protection of his loving concern [*ʿInayah*]. The Cardinal Pole of noble Saints [*Qutb*], the one person who forms the focus of *Allāh*'s ﷻ supervision of the world in every age. He belongs to the heart of Isrāfīl ﷺ [the angel of the Resurrection and of form].

known by the name Aʿrāb, divulged in his home in Umm ʿUbaydah that his father had relayed to Sayyidī Aḥmad Rifāʿī ﷺ: *'Did Shaykh ʿAbd al-Qādir al-Jilānī ﷺ say the words, my foot is on the neck of every Wali of Allāh – by command or not by command?'* Sayyidī Aḥmad ﷺ confirmed: *'He said it by command.'*

I was informed by Shaykh Abu al-Muḥāsin Yūsuf b. Abī al-ʿAbbās Aḥmad b. Nasīb b. Ḥusain al-Basrī al-Mālikī ﷺ in 679 *hijrī* in Cairo that he had heard Shaykh Abu al-Faraḥ Ḥusain b. Muḥammad b. Aḥmad b. Dowirah al-Basrī Muqrī al-Ḥanbalī ﷺ state in 638 *hijrī* in Basra, that he was informed by Shaykh Abu al-ʿAbbās Aḥmad b. Mutīʿh Bā-Sabrī ﷺ who had affirmed in 617 *hijrī* in Basra, that he had heard Shaykh, the leader, Abu al-Qāsim b. ʿAbdullāh al-Basrī ﷺ spell out in Basra;

> 'When Shaykh ʿAbd al-Qādir al-Jilānī ﷺ was ordered to assert that: My foot is on the neck of every *Wali* of *Allāh*, then I saw all the *Awliya* of the east and west respectfully bend their heads. There was a person from one of the countries in *ʿAjam* who did not bend his head so his condition had deteriorated.'

5) Shaykh Ḥayāt b. Qays al-Ḥarrānī ﷺ

It was narrated to me in 672 *hijrī* in Cairo by Faqih Abu-Muḥammad ʿAbd al-Raḥmān Aḥmad b. Muḥammad b. ʿAbd al-Dā'im b. ʿAlī al-Qurashī al-Maqdisī al-Ḥambalī ﷺ who narrates from Shaykh Abu-Muḥammad ʿAbd al-Malik b. Shaykh ʿĀrif Abī ʿAbd al-Malik Zayāl b. Shaykh Abī-Muḥammad ʿAbdullāh b. Shaykh ʿArif Abu al-Maʿālī b. Arsha b. Nabhan ﷺ originally an Irāqī, but settled in Maqdas. He stated that in 631 *hijrī*, his father had narrated to him that in 613 *hijrī* he visited Shaykh, the leader Ḥayāt b. Qays al-Ḥarrānī ﷺ on Friday 3rd *Ramaḍān* 579 *hijrī* in *Jām ʿeh Ḥarrān* [Damascus]. At that moment, a person arrived and requested the Shaykh ﷺ to initiate him as his *murīd*. The Shaykh responded: *'There is a sign on you besides me.'* He declared: *'Indeed I am linked to Shaykh ʿAbd al-Qādir al-Jilānī ﷺ but I did not take his Sūfī Garb [khirqah] from anyone.'* The Shaykh ﷺ confessed:

> 'For a long time I have lived under the shade of Shaykh ʿAbd al-Qādir al-Jilānī ﷺ and drank cups of sweet and tasty water from his Fountain of

'Irfān [spiritual knowledge] which returned my truthful soul to him. His light spread throughout the earth similar to the flames of fire. Thereafter, the undisclosed lofty conditions of his companions inherited the light from him. When the Ordinance came to him, to pronounce that: my foot is on the neck of every *Wali* of *Allāh*, then Almighty *Allāh* ﷻ increased the *barkāt* of light and knowledge in the hearts of the *Awliya-Allāh*. It was due to this *Barkāt* that they bent their heads. They were elevated in the garb of the previous [*Awliya*] which led them to the Divine Presence of *Allāh* ﷻ. Reference here is made to the syndicate of the Prophets, *Siddiqīn*, *Shuhadah* and *Sāliḥīn*.'

Those Mashā'ikh who bent their heads on the Command of the Ghawth رضي الله عنه

1) Shaykh Baqa b. But'tū رضي الله عنه

I was informed in 673 *hijrī* in Cairo by Shaykh Abu al-Ḥasan ʿAlī b. Azūmar al-Baghdādī al-Muḥammadī رحمه الله that he had heard from Faqih Abu-ʿAbdullāh Muḥammad b. ʿAlī b. ʿAbd al-Raḥmān Yūsuf al-ʿIrāqī Bā-sarī al-Ḥanbalī later al-Baghdādī رحمه الله in 633 *hijrī* in Baghdād, pronounce that he had heard from Shaykh Sāliḥ Abu-Bakr b. Shaykh Abu al-Ghanā'im Isḥāq b. Bat'tūr Nahar Mulkī رحمه الله in 589 *hijrī* in Baghdād that he was present with his uncle Shaykh Baqa b. But'tū رضي الله عنه in the *Masjid* of Shaykh ʿAbd al-Qādir al-Jilānī رضي الله عنه in Baghdād. At that time Shaykh ʿAbd al-Qādir رضي الله عنه heralded: *'My foot is on the neck of every Walī of Allāh. Then my uncle bent his head.'*

I was informed in 670 *hijrī* in Cairo by Shaykh Abu al-Maʿālī Sāliḥ b. Yūsuf b. ʿAjlān b. Nasar ʿAsqalānī al-Baghdādī Qutnī al-Shafaʿī رحمه الله that he had heard from Shaykh Abu-Muḥammad b. ʿAbd al-Latīf al-Baghdādī رحمه الله generally known as Mutriz who stated in 628 *hijrī* in Baghdād, that he had heard from Shaykh Abu Muḥammad b. Abī-Bakr b. Shujāʿh al-Baghdādī al-Ḥanbalī رحمه الله commonly known as Ibn Nuqta who voiced in the corner of his room in 559 *hijrī* in Baghdād, expressed that he was sitting beside Shaykh Baqa b. But'tū رضي الله عنه in the *majlis* of Shaykh ʿAbd al-Qādir al-Jilānī ﷺ when he articulated: *'My foot is on the neck of every Walī of Allāh. Then Shaykh Baqa ﷺ bent his head.'*

2) Sayyid Sharīf Abu-Saʿīd al-Qaylawī ﷺ

I was informed in 668 *hijrī* in Cairo by Shaykh Abu al-Faraḥ ʿAbdul Ḥamīd b. Maʿālī b. ʿAbdullāh b. ʿAlī al-Sarsarī al-Ḥanbalī ﷺ and later Baghdādī stated that he had heard from Shaykh Abu-Ḥafs ʿUmar b. Shaykh Khayr Saʿīd b. Shaykh Sharīf Abu-Saʿīd al-Qaylawī ﷺ in 570 *hijrī* in Qaylawa, that he was in the *majlis* of Shaykh ʿAbd al-Qādir al-Jilānī ﷺ with Sayyid Abī-Saʿīd ﷺ in 560 *hijrī* in Baghdād. At that time he decreed: *'My foot is on the neck of every Walī of Allāh.'* My father then bent his head.'

I was informed in 674 *hijrī* in Cairo by Shaykh Abu al-Faḍal Mansūr b. Aḥmad b. Abī Faraḥ al-Irāqī al-Dourī then al-Baghdādī al-Ḥanbalī ﷺ that he had heard from Shaykh ʿĀrif Abu al-Faḍal Isḥāq b. Aḥmad b. Ghānim al-ʿAlthī ﷺ in 583 *hijrī* in a section of ʿAlath, revealed that he was present in the *majlis* of Shaykh ʿAbd al-Qādir ﷺ in his guest house and Shaykh Saʿīd ﷺ was sitting in front of him. When Shaykh ʿAbd al-Qādir al-Jilānī ﷺ asserted: *'My foot is on the neck of every Walī of Allāh.'* Thereafter, Shaykh Sharīf Abu-Saʿīd al-Qaylawī ﷺ bent his head.'

3) Shaykh Sayyidī ʿAlī b. al-Hītī ﷺ

I was informed in 625 *hijrī* in Cairo by Shaykh Abu-Muḥammad Rajab b. al-Mansūr b. Nasrullāh ʿAwnī Wādī al-Nasībanī ﷺ that he and Shaykh Masʿūd al-Ḥārithī ﷺ in 617 *hijrī* went to Yaʿqūbah to meet Shaykh ʿAlī b. Idrīs ﷺ. When they reached him, someone questioned him if Shaykh ʿAlī b. al-Hītī ﷺ grabbed the foot of Shaykh ʿAbd al-Qādir al-Jilānī ﷺ when he testified that his foot is on the neck of every *Walī* of *Allāh*? He replied:

> 'When Shaykh ʿAbd al-Qādir al-Jilānī ﷺ issued this statement, I was a young man and was present there. Our Shaykh ʿAlī b. al-Hītī ﷺ stood up and ascended the pulpit and placed Shaykh ʿAbd al-Qādir's ﷺ foot on his neck, covered himself with the Shaykh's garb and professed: *'This is an all-embracing and absolute form of obedience.'*

I was informed in 673 *hijrī* in Cairo by Shaykh Abu al-Ḥasan ʿAlī b. Ādam b. ʿAbdullāh al-Baghdādī al-Muḥammadī ﷺ and he had heard from Shaykh Muʿāmmar Baqiyat al-Salf Abu al-Ḥasan ʿAlī b. Muḥammad b. Muḥammad b. Aḥmad b. Ḥasan al-Baghdādī Sūfī al-Ḥanbalī ﷺ who was well known by the name Siqa who in 629 *hijrī* stated in Baghdād in the *Jāmeʿh al-Khalīfah Masjid*:

> 'My age at that time was 107 years and I spent a considerable amount of time in the company of Shaykh ʿAbd al-Qādir al-Jilānī ﷺ and served him. I was present in that gathering when Shaykh ʿAbd al-Qādir ﷺ declared that his foot is on the neck of every *Walī* of *Allāh*. I heard the words from his lips and at that time I was more than 20 years old. I saw Shaykh ʿAlī b. al-Hītī ﷺ stand up at the pulpit and place Shaykh ʿAbd al-Qādir's ﷺ foot on his neck.' When the people left, then his *murīds* questioned him about the reason for doing what he did; to which the Shaykh exclaimed: *'Alas! Had you known the reason, then you would have not asked!'*

I was informed in 669 *hijrī* in Cairo by Shaykh Abu al-Muzaffar Ibrāhīm b. Abī ʿAbdullāh b. Abī Bakr b. Nasar al-Baghdādī al-Muqrī ﷺ who narrates from Shaykh Imām Sāliḥ Muʿammar Abu al-Ḥasan ʿAlī b. Niya b. Sāliḥ b. Nasar b. Yūsuf Kurdī al-Ḥamīdī al-Baghdādī Qatīʿī al-Ḥanbalī ﷺ in 611 *hijrī* in Baghdād, stating that:

> I was just over 30 years old and present in the *majlis* the day Shaykh ʿAbd al-Qādir al-Jilānī ﷺ pronounced: *'My foot is on the neck of every Walī of Allāh.'* I personally heard the words of this declaration and saw Shaykh ʿAlī b. al-Hītī ﷺ stand up at the pulpit and place Shaykh ʿAbd al-Qādir's ﷺ foot on his neck and declared: *'I was at his service for the past seven years.'* The rest of the *Awliya* present in the *majilis* also bent their heads.'

4) Shaykh Sayyid Aḥmad b. Rifāʿī ﷺ

I was informed in 677 *hijrī* in Cairo by Shaykh Abu-Muḥammad Sālim b. ʿAlī b. ʿAbdullāh b. Sinān Sūfī al-Damyātī ﷺ who narrates from the senior pious *Mashā'ikh* who were the leaders of Iraq viz. Shaykh Abu-Tāhir Khalīl b. Shaykh Abu al-ʿAbbās Aḥmad al-Sarsarī al-Jowsiqī ﷺ, Shaykh Abu al-Ḥasan Khafāf al-

Baghdādī ﷺ, Shaykh Abu-Ḥafs ʿUmar al-Barīdī ﷺ, Shaykh Abu al-Qāsim ʿUmar al-Darwānī ﷺ, Shaykh Abu al-Walīd Zayd b. Saʿīd ﷺ, Shaykh Abu-ʿAmar ʿUthmān b. Sulaymān al-Baghdādī ﷺ prominently known as Qas'sīr; all narrated in 624 *hijrī* in *Jameʿh Mansūr* that they narrate from Shaykh Abu al-Faraḥ ʿAbd al-Raḥīm ﷺ and Shaykh Abu al-Ḥasan ʿAlī ﷺ who was the nephew of Shaykh, the leader, Abu al-ʿAbbās Aḥmad b. Abī al-Ḥasan Rifāʿī ﷺ, he came to us sometime in 580 *hijrī* in Baghdād and both of them accented:

> 'We visited our Shaykh Aḥmad b. Rifāʿī ﷺ who was on one side of Umm-ʿUbaydah [present day Nasriya]. He moved his head forward and stressed: '*On my neck too.*' We asked him the reason as to why he had voiced this, and he replied: '*At this moment in Baghdād, Shaykh ʿAbd al-Qādir al-Jilānī ﷺ decrees that his foot is on the neck of every Walī of Allāh.*'

I was informed in 677 *hijrī* in Cairo by Shaykh Abu-ʿAbdah Muḥammad b. Abī al-ʿAbbās Khiḍar b. ʿAbdullāh b. Yaḥyah b. Muḥammad al-Ḥusainī al-Mosulī ﷺ who narrates from Shaykh Abu al-Faraj ʿAbdul Ḥasan ﷺ whose name was Ḥasnah b. Muḥammad Aḥmad b. Dowayrah Muqrī al-Ḥanbalī al-Basrī, in 637 *hijrī* in Basra, narrates from Shaykh Abu-Bakr ʿAtīq b. Abī al-Faḍal Muḥammad b. ʿUthmān b. Abī al-Faḍal al-Bandaljī originally al-Baghdādī ﷺ eminently known as Maʿtūq in 601 *hijrī* in Baghdād states that in 576 *hijrī*, he met Shaykh Sayyidī Aḥmad b. Abī al-Ḥasan Rifāʿī ﷺ in Umm ʿUbaydah:

> There I heard from his senior companions and old *murīds* who specified that their Shaykh was sitting at that spot [pointing out to a specific spot in the tent] and bent his head and appealed: '*Also on my neck.*' We then queried from him, his reason for implementing and articulating this, and thus he replied: '*Verily at this moment in Baghdād, Shaykh ʿAbd al-Qādir al-Jilānī ﷺ certifies that his foot is on the neck of every Walī of Allāh.*' We then noted the time and date, and after investigation, we precisely discovered its veracity.'

5) Shaykh ʿAbd al-Raḥmān al-Tafsunjī ﷺ

I was informed in 667 *hijrī* in Cairo by Shaykh Sāliḥ Abu-Ḥafḍ ʿUmar b. Abī al-Maʿālī Nasar b. Muḥammad b. Aḥmad al-Qurashī Hātimī al-Tafsunjī al-

Shafaʿī ﷺ who narrates from the Shaykh of noble origin, Sālih Abu-ʿAbdullāh Muḥammad b. Abī al-Shaykh Sāliḥ Abu-Ḥafs ʿUmar b. Shaykh, the leader, Abu-Muḥammad ʿAbd al-Raḥmān al-Tafsunjī ﷺ in 623 *hijrī* in Tafsunj, narrates from Shaykh Abu-ʿUmar ﷺ in 573 *hijrī* as follows:

> He reports that one day in Tafsunj, his father was sitting with his companions, bent his head and stated: '*Also on my neck.*' We then questioned him about his reason for effecting and saying this; and thereby he replied: '*Verily at this moment in Baghdād, Shaykh ʿAbd al-Qādir al-Jilānī ﷺ announced that his foot is on the neck of every Walī of Allāh.*' We then noted that particular time and date, and after our inquiry, we established that it was at the exact time and date that Shaykh ʿAbd al-Qādir ﷺ had forwarded this declaration.'

6) Shaykh Abu-Najīb ʿAbd al-Qāhir Sohrowardī ﷺ

I was informed in Cairo by Faqih Abu-ʿAlī Isḥāq b. ʿAlī b. ʿAbdullāh b. ʿAbd al-Dā'im b. Sāliḥ al-Hamdānī Sūfī al-Shafāʿī Muḥaddith ﷺ who narrates from Shaykh Khalīl al-Asl Abu-Muḥammad ʿAbd al-Latīf b. al-Shaykh Abī-Najīb ʿAbd al-Qāhir b. ʿAbdullāh b. Muḥammad b. ʿAbdullāh al-Sohrowardī Faqih Shafaʿī Sūfī al-Baghdādī ﷺ in 608 *hijrī* in Irbil, as documented below:

> He discloses that he was present with his father Shaykh Abu-Najīb ﷺ in Baghdād in the *majlis* of Shaykh ʿAbd al-Qādir al-Jilānī ﷺ who then confirmed that his foot is on the neck of every *Walī* of *Allāh*.' My Father bent his head to the lowest degree that it almost touched the floor and then he insisted: '*On my head, on my head, on my head.*'

7) Shaykh Mūsā al-Zūlī ﷺ

I was informed in 663 *hijrī* in Cairo by Faqih Abu-ʿAlī Ḥasan b. Najam al-Dīn b. ʿĪsā b. Muḥammad al-Ḥawarnī al-Ḥanbalī ﷺ who narrates from Shaykh Abu al-Futūḥ Yaḥyah b. Shaykh Abu as-Saʿādat Saʿādullāh b. Abī ʿAbdullāh b. Majd al-Tikrītī ﷺ. He expressed in Tikrīt:

> 'Once in 517 *hijrī*, together with a delegation I went with my father to Baghdād to visit Shaykh ʿAbd al-Qādir al-Jilānī ﷺ. We then set out to Mārdīn to visit Shaykh Mūsā al-Zūlī ﷺ. Thereafter, once, we

accompanied Shaykh Mūsā al-Zūlī ﷺ to Baghdād with the intention of proceeding for *Ḥajj*. We attended the *majlis* of Sayyiduna Shaykh ʿAbd al-Qādir al-Jilānī ﷺ and he proclaimed that his foot is on the neck of every *Walī* of *Allāh*' and Shaykh Mūsā al-Zūlī ﷺ bent his head.'

8) Shaykh Muḥammad Mūsā b. ʿAbdullāh Basrī ﷺ

I was informed in 663 *hijrī* in Cairo by Shaykh Abu al-Muḥāsin Yūsuf b. Abī al-Maʿālī Aḥmad b. Shabīb b. Ḥusain al-Basrī al-Mālikī ﷺ. He narrates from Shaykh Faqih Muqrī ʿĀdil Abu-Tālib ʿAbd al-Raḥmān b. al-Fataḥ Muḥammad b. Abī al-Muzaffar ʿAbd al-Samīʿh b. ʿAbdullāh al-Qurashī al-Hāshimī al-Wāsitī ﷺ in Wāsit in 640 *hijrī*, and states:

> In those days, when I was a child, I accompanied my father, Shaykh Abu al-Fataḥ ﷺ to Basra to visit Shaykh, the leader, Abu-Muḥammad b. ʿAbdullāh al-Basrī ﷺ. The Shaykh ﷺ was speaking to his companions and suddenly stopped speaking and observed silence in a state of amazement. Owing to his esteem, the entire gathering became silent and subsequently the Shaykh ﷺ placed his head on the ground and resonated: '*On my head.*' Thereafter, the Shaykh ﷺ entered his room, and my father and I followed him into his room. My father then built up courage and asked the Shaykh: '*O my master! I pledge to you the allegiance of Allāh* ﷻ *to please inform me what has happened to you today and what did you say that we have witnessed?*' The Shaykh ﷺ replied: '*Indeed! Shaykh ʿAbd al-Qādir has revealed today in Baghdād that his foot is on the neck of every Walī of Allāh and there was no Walī on earth that did not place his head on the ground as I did, and as you have witnessed.*' My father, at that moment wrote the date and time and left for Baghdād. I also accompanied him. It was then revealed to us that Sayyiduna Shaykh ʿAbd al-Qādir ﷺ had made the same proclamation on the very same day on which my father had noted down in Basra.

9) Shaykh Ḥayāt b. Qays al-Ḥarrānī ﷺ

I was informed in 671 *hijrī* in Cairo by the illustrious Faqih, Abu al-Makārim Khalīfah b. Muḥammad b. ʿAlī b. Aḥmad b. Muḥammad al-Ḥarrānī al-Ḥanbalī ﷺ, and later Baghdādī who narrates in 631 *hijrī* from Shaykh Abu-Tālib ʿAbd al-Latīf b. Shaykh Abu al-Faraḥ Muḥammad b. al-Shaykh Abu al-Ḥasan b. ʿAlī

b. Ḥamza b. Fāris b. Muḥammad al-Ḥarrānī originally al-Baghdādī ﷺ, the trader popularly known as Ibn al-Qutbī in Baghdād, as follows:

My father Shaykh Abu al-Faraj Muḥammad ﷺ who always attended the *majlis* of Shaykh Ḥayāt b. Qays al-Ḥarrānī ﷺ, informed me that one day in Ḥarrān, he was visited by the Shaykh ﷺ and he put forward his head and requested: *'On my head.'* My father and the Shaykh's son, Shaykh Abu-Ḥafs ʿUmar ﷺ enquired from Shaykh Ḥayāt ﷺ as to why he did this and he thereby replied: *'At this moment Shaykh ʿAbd al-Qādir has resounded in Baghdād that his foot is on the neck of every Walī of Allāh.'*

I was informed in 671 *hijrī* in Cairo by the reliable Shaykh, Najīb al-Dīn Abu al-Faraj ʿAbd al-Latīf b. Shaykh ʿAllāma Najam al-Dīn b. ʿAbd al-Munʿim b. ʿAlī b. Nasar b. Mansūr b. al-Fuḍayl al-Ḥarrānī ﷺ who conveyed:

I heard several times from my father, Aḥmadullāh ﷺ revealing that he saw Shaykh Ḥayāt b. Qays ﷺ in Ḥarrān at the moment when Shaykh ʿAbd al-Qādir al-Jilānī ﷺ disclosed: *'My foot is on the neck of every Walī of Allāh'*, hence he also bent his head and appealed: *'On my head too.'*

10) Shaykh Abu ʿAmar ʿUthmān b. Marzūq ﷺ and Shaykh Abu al-Karam ﷺ

I was informed in 666 *hijrī* in Cairo by Shaykh Sāliḥ b. Abu al-Ḥasan ʿAlī b. Shaykh Abī-Zakariyyah Yaḥyah b. Abī al-Qāsim Aḥmad b. ʿAbd al-Raḥmān al-Baghdādī ﷺ narrates in 631 *hijrī* from Shaykh Abu-Muḥammad ʿAbd al-Karīm b. Mansūr b. Abī-Bakr b. ʿAlī al-Mosulī al-Baghdādī Muḥaddith al-Shafaʿī ﷺ renowned known as Atharī al-Baghdādī, narrates from the Shaykh of pure origin; Imām Abu al-Khayr Sāʿad b. al-Shaykh the leader ʿAllāma Abu-ʿAmar ʿUthmān b. Marzūq b. Ḥamīd b. Salāmah al-Qurashī al-Ḥanbalī al-Misrī ﷺ born in 590 *hijrī* in Baghdād converse:

I heard from my father, who notified that he had left Cairo with the intention of performing *Ḥajj*. He then proceeded to meet the *Mashā'ikh* [in Baghdād]. May *Allāh* ﷻ bless us through them. He then attended the *majlis* of his Shaykh, Muḥiyy al-Dīn ʿAbd al-Qādir al-Jilānī ﷺ. On that day, the senior *Mashā'ikh* of Irāq were in the congregation and I saw

Shaykh Abu al-Karam Muʿammar ﷺ and Shaykh Abu-ʿAbdullāh Muḥammad Darbānī al-Qazwīnī ﷺ sitting in one corner of the *majlis*. Shaykh ʿAbd al-Qādir al-Jilānī ﷺ subsequently heralded: *'My foot is on the neck of every Walī of Allāh.'* At that moment every one present bent their heads and I also bent my head to the lowest extent, that it almost touched the ground. Shaykh Abu al-Karam ﷺ also did the same. When the people left, Shaykh Abu al-Karam ﷺ divulged to me that there was no *Walī* on earth that did not bend his head like everyone did in the *majlis,* besides one person in Asbān who did not bend his head and as a result, his was disparaged [of his *Wilāyah*]. Thereafter, Shaykh al-Darbānī ﷺ testified to this fact.

11) Shaykh Mājid al-Kurdī ﷺ

I was informed in 678 *hijrī* in Cairo by Shaykh Abu-ʿAbdah Muḥammad b. Muḥammad b. ʿĪsā b. ʿAbdullāh b. Qaymāz b. Alī Ourlī Rūmī al-Baghdādī ﷺ who narrates from the Shaykh of noble origin Abu-Muḥammad ʿAbbās b. Shaykh Khalīl Abī-Najāt Sulaymān b. Shaykh the leader, Abu-Muḥammad Mājid al-Kurdī ﷺ in Baghdād. He says;

My father informed me that he accompanied his father to visit Sayyiduna Shaykh ʿAbd al-Qādir al-Jilānī ﷺ at his guesthouse. Then Shaykh ʿAbd al-Qādir al-Jilānī ﷺ ordained: *'My foot is on the neck of every Walī of Allāh.'*

12) Shaykh Suwayd Sanjārī ﷺ

I was informed in 663 *hijrī* in Cairo by Shaykh Aʿyoulī Ḥasan b. al-Najam b. ʿĪsā b. Muḥammad al-Ḥowrānī al-Ḥanbalī ﷺ and he narrates from Shaykh Abu-ʿAmar ʿUthmān b. ʿĀshūra al-Sanjārī ﷺ in 616 *hijrī* in Sanjār who stated that:

One day Shaykh Suwayd ﷺ bent his head in his guesthouse situated in Sanjār, and thereafter Shaykh Ḥusain al-Talʿafrī ﷺ questioned him about the reason for bending his head, thus to which the Shaykh responded: *'At this moment Shaykh ʿAbd al-Qādir al-Jilānī ﷺ has commanded in Baghdād that his foot is on the neck of every Walī of Allāh.'* We recorded that date and found out later, that it was on the very same day when Shaykh Suwayd ﷺ had revealed this.

13) Shaykh Arsalān al-Damishqī ﷺ

I was informed in 670 *hijrī* in Cairo by Shaykh ʿĀlim Abu-Yūsuf Yaʿqūb b. Badrān b. Mansūr al-Ansārī al-Muqrī ﷺ who narrates from ʿĀrif Abu-Muḥammad Raghīb al-Raḥbī ﷺ in the month of *Rajab* 621 *hijrī,* and he indicates that:

> In Damascus Shaykh Arsalān al-Damishqī ﷺ bent his head at the time when Shaykh ʿAbd al-Qādir al-Jilānī ﷺ pronounced in Baghdād that his foot is on the neck of every *Walī* of *Allāh*. Shaykh Arsalān ﷺ alludes to the fact that the pronouncement [of Shaykh ʿAbd al-Qādir ﷺ] provides information that benediction from *Allāh* ﷻ is for that person who drinks from the Celestial Oceans and sits on the rostrum of Gnosis and Love. His inner self perceives the magnificence of the Lordship and reverence of the Absolute Being ﷻ. His encomium evidence then becomes extinct in comparison to the stateliness of the Sublime Lord ﷻ. During the introspection of the Station of Tranquillity, his state of existence proceeds to the state of non-existence. The breeze of eternity gently brushes over the soul without any reservation or fear. Henceforward, one will speak with wisdom from the Treasures of Lights. The tone of one's heart will be embodied by concealed secrets which will lead one to the Divine Proximity of *Allāh* ﷻ, in an acute state of being engrossed in Divine Perception. He stands with existence; with open and clean ears; speaks with humility; ascertains submissiveness in need; is selected for intimacy; addressed with honour and excellence; bestowed with blessings and salutations from his Lord ﷻ. It will be then defined to him: *'Is there anyone present today with such honour and dignity?'* He will testify: '*Yes! Shaykh Muḥiyy al-Dīn ʿAbd al-Qādir* ﷺ *is his Master.*'

Shaykh Abu-Yūsuf al-Ansārī ﷺ states that he heard from Shaykh Rāghib al-Raḥbī ﷺ that after hearing this command he affirmed:

> Shaykh ʿAbd al-Qādir ﷺ is a *Qutb* of par excellence and an incredibly dignified person of this time. Direct Knowledge [*ʿIlm al-ʿIrfān*] ends with him. The reins of the Realities of the Worlds were handed over to him. He is the luminous [high flying] falcon amongst the Gnostics, the

beloved amongst the *Awliya* and the leader of the Caravan of the Truthful. It is his distinctive characteristic, that when he speaks; he speaks with an authority of supremacy and an aura of devotion. His speech is inspirational and his silence engulfs the heart with the garb that illumines exaltation.

14) Shaykh Shoʿayb Abu-Madyan al-Maghribī ﷺ
I was informed in 659 *hijrī* in Cairo by Faqih Sālih Abu-ʿAbdullāh Muḥammad b. Masʿūd ʿUmar b. ʿAbd al-Dā'im b. Ghāzī al-Maghribī al-Sajlamāsī al-Mālikī ﷺ who narrates from prolific ʿĀlim, Shaykh Abu-Zakariyyah Yaḥyah b. Muḥammad b. ʿAlī b. Faqih al-Muḥaddith ﷺ alias Maʿāri, who narrates from Shaykh, the leader, Abu-Muḥammad Sālih b. Der'jān al-Maghribī al-Bar'barī al-Wakālī ﷺ and I was informed by Faqīh Zāhid Abu-Muḥāsin Muḥammad b. Shaykh Abī al-ʿAbbās Aḥmad b. Abī al-Makārim Isḥāq b. Yūsuf al-Qurashī al-Hāshimī al-Maghribī al-ʿUthmānī al-Mālikī ﷺ in 667 *hijrī* in Cairo, when he narrates from Shaykh ʿĀrif Abu-ʿAbdullāh Muḥammad b. Shaykh, the leader, Abu-Sālih b. Der'jān al-Maghribī al-Bar'barī al-Wakālī ﷺ in 656 *hijri*; who narrates from his father Shaykh Abu-Muḥammad Sālih ﷺ who pointed out that Shaykh Abu-Madyan Shoʿayb ﷺ whilst sitting amongst his companions, during the time of *Maghrib*; bent his head and stated: *'I am also amongst them. O Allāh! I make You and all Your angels witness that I heard and exercised obedience.'*

His companions then enquired and the Shaykh replied: *'Verily, at this time in Baghdād Shaykh ʿAbd al-Qādir asserted that his foot is on the necks of all the Awliya Allāh.'* We took note of this time and date. Later our traveller friend arrived from Baghdād and informed us that Shaykh ʿAbdul Qādir ﷺ on a certain day and time declared that his foot is on the neck of every *Walī* of *Allāh*. May *Allāh* ﷻ be pleased with all of them.

15) Shaykh Sharīf ʿAbd al-Raḥīm al-Qanāwī ﷺ
I narrate in 676 *hijrī* in Cairo from Shaykh Jalīl al-ʿAbbās Aḥmad b. Abī ʿAbdullāh Muḥammad b. Abī al-Ghanā'im Muḥammad b. Abī al-Mafākhir Muḥammad al-Ḥusainī al-Damishqī ﷺ who narrates from the Shaykh of noble

origin, the leader Abu-ʿAbdullāh Ḥusain b. Shaykh, the leader Abu-Muḥammad ʿAbd al-Raḥīm b. Aḥmad Ḥajūn b. Aḥmad b. Jāʿafar Zakī b. Muḥammad b. Māmūn b. ʿAlī Ḥārisī b. Ḥusain Joon b. Muḥammad b. Jāʿafar al-Sādiq b. Muḥammad al-Bāqir b. Zayn al-ʿĀbidīn b. Imām al-Ḥusain b. ʿAlī b. Abī Tālib ﷺ, al-Maghrībī, originally from Sāʿidī, proclaimed in Qanah which is a plateau of greater Cairo, that in 643 *hijrī,* when Shaykh ʿAbd al-Qādir ﷺ pronounced that his foot is on the neck of every *Walī* of *Allāh*ﷻ; then his father Shaykh ʿAbd al-Raḥīm ﷺ in Qanah stretched out his neck and declared: *'The one who speaks the truth and believes in the truth and spoke the truth.'* When questioned as to who that was, he affirmed: *'Shaykh ʿAbd al-Qādir ﷺ decreed that his foot is on the neck of every Walī of Allāh and indeed, all the Awliya of the East and West expressed humility.'* We noted the precise time and date. Subsequently, we were informed that the time and date Sayyiduna Shaykh ʿAbd al-Qādir ﷺ confirmed, corresponded with the time and date we had noted.

16) Shaykh ʿAmar ʿUthmān b. Marūzūq al-Batḥā'iḥī ﷺ

I was informed in 670 *hijrī* in Cairo by Shaykh Abu al-Faraj ʿAbd al-Malik b. ʿAbdul Maḥmūd b. Aḥmad b. ʿAlī al-Wāstī al-Rabʿī al-Shafaʿī ﷺ and he narrates from Shaykh Abu-ʿAbdullāh Muḥammad b. ʿAlī b. Aḥmad al-Hamāmī Faqhī Shafaʿī ﷺ who stated in 629 *hijrī* in Wāsta; who narrates from Shaykh Abu-Ḥafs ʿUmar b. Musaddiq b. Muḥammad b. Ḥusain al-Wāstī al-Rabʿī ﷺ stated in 588 *hijrī* in Wāsta, that in Batā'iḥa, he spent many years in the service of Shaykh Abu-ʿAmar ʿUthmān b. Marūza ﷺ. Once I was present with him continuously for three days and in the morning of the fourth day he informed me; *'O ʿUmar! I have the intention to go to Baghdād.'* I conversed with him: *'O my Master! I will also accompany you.'* The Shaykh recited: *'Bismillāh! You follow me by placing your foot on my footsteps.'* I stated that I will do as instructed. We then left Batāiḥ and I followed him as he ordered me. After a short while, we reached Baghdād. Thereafter, he proceeded to the guesthouse of Sayyiduna Shaykh ʿAbd al-Qādir al-Jilānī ﷺ and joined his *majlis.* I confessed that I recognized all the *Mashā'ikh* of Baghdād that were present in the gathering. Shaykh ʿAbd al-Qādir al-Jilānī ﷺ attested: *'My foot is on the neck of every Walī of Allāh.'* The entire gathering bent their heads in submission. Upon termination of the assembly, everyone left. Shaykh ʿUthmān ﷺ then got up and accosted Sayyiduna Shaykh ʿAbd al-Qādir ﷺ and kissed his hands. The Ghawth ﷺ instructed him: *'Hurry and return to your home.'* We then left and I did exactly the same as when we had left from home for Baghdād.

Shortly, we reached a jungle. I queried from the Shaykh about his reason for coming to Baghdād, and moreover, in returning the same day. To this effect, he replied: *'I was ordered to attend the majlis of Shaykh ʿAbd al-Qādir al-Jilānī ﷺ and I had no other intention besides this for coming to Baghdād.'*

17) Shaykh Makārim Nahar Mulkī ﷺ

I was informed in 669 *hijrī,* in Cairo by Shaykh Abu al-Futūḥ Dāʿūd b. Shaykh Abu al-Maʿālī Nasar b. Shaykh Abī al-Ḥasan ʿAlī b. Shaykh Majd Mubārak b. Aḥmad b. Muḥammad al-Zāhirī al-Baghdādī al-Ḥarīmī al-Jīlī ﷺ. He narrates from his father Shaykh Abu-Majd ﷺ in 577 *hijrī* in Baghdād who states that he made the *ziyārah* of Shaykh Makārim ﷺ in the city of Sawād. They then went to Baghdād and entered the guesthouse of Sayyiduna Shaykh ʿAbd al-Qādir al-Jilānī ﷺ. I was with Shaykh Makārim ﷺ and observed the presence of most of the *Mashā'ikh* of Iraq whilst Sayyiduna Ghawth ﷺ was addressing them. We were seated between Shaykh Abī-Najīb Sohrowardī ﷺ and Shaykh Sultān Muzayyan ﷺ. Sayyiduna Shaykh ʿAbd al-Qādir al-Jilānī ﷺ then declared: *'My foot is on the neck of every Walī of Allāh.'* Shaykh Mukārim ﷺ bent his head and all those that were present, bent their heads in submission.

18) Shaykh Khalīfah al-Nahr Mulkī ﷺ

I was informed in 660 *hijrī* in Cairo by Shaykh Abu-Muḥammad Hasan b. al-Qāsim Aḥmad b. Muḥammad b. Abī al-Qāsim Dilaf b. Aḥmad b. Muḥammad al-Baghdādī al-Ḥarīmī ﷺ whose grandfather is well known as Ibn Qūqah. He narrates from Shaykh Abu al-ʿAbbās Aḥmad b. Yaḥyah b. Barkat b. Maḥfūz Baz'zār al-Baghdādī ﷺ who is eminently known as Ibn al-Zayqī in 605 *hijrī,* narrates from Shaykh Abu-Yaḥyah ﷺ who exclaims that he had visited Sayyiduna Shaykh ʿAbd al-Qādir al-Jilānī ﷺ in his guesthouse in Ḥalba. It was full with *Mashā'ikh* and I was seated beside Shaykh Khalīfah ﷺ. Shaykh ʿAbd al-Qādir al-Jilānī ﷺ then heralded: *'My foot is on the neck of every Walī of Allāh.'* Shaykh Khalīfah ﷺ bent his head and I heard him confirm: *'It is not surprising that he declared this because he is the unique individual [fard] of this era.'*

1) Shaykh ʿAdī b. Musāfir al-Amawī ﷺ

I was informed in 668 *hijrī* in Cairo by Shaykh ʿĀlim Abu-Muḥammad Ḥasan b. Dāʿūd b. Muḥammad al-Qurashī al-Mahzūmī al-Khālidī al-Shafaʿī ﷺ. He narrates from Shaykh ʿĀrif Abu-Isḥāq Ibrāhīm b. Maḥmūd b. Jowhar al-Baʿālbakī al-Damishqī ʿUqbī Muqrī al-Ḥanbalī ﷺ alais al-Batāi'ḥī in 627 *hijrī* in Damascus. He states that Shaykh, the leader, Abu-Muḥammad Sāliḥ al-Batāi'ḥī ﷺ in Baghdād conversed with me on numerous occasions, that Shaykh ʿAdī b. Musāfir ﷺ requested Sayyiduna Shaykh ʿAbd al-Qādir al-Jilānī ﷺ for me to be given to him in order to perform *Salāh* with him. Sayyiduna Ghawth ﷺ ordered me to go with him; to which I conceded. I remained in his company for 5 years and performed *Salāh* with Shaykh ʿAdī ﷺ.

During this period, he remained in seclusion and did not come out of his sanctuary. He always held a staff [*ʿAsa*] from a fruit tree in his hand, which he used to mark out circles on the mountainous regions, wherein he used to sit and simultaneously proclaim: *'He who intends to listen to the words of Sayyiduna Shaykh ʿAbd al-Qādir ﷺ in Baghdād, should come and sit inside the circle.'* Thereafter, the senior *murīds* would come and sit in the circle and listen to the words of Ḥaḍrate Ghawth ﷺ. During that time Sayyiduna Ghawth ﷺ was conveying to the people that: *'The eye of Shaykh ʿAdī b. Musāfir is present with you.'* The narrator reports that one day Shaykh ʿAdī ﷺ entered the circle and bent his head to the lowest extent, that it almost touched the ground. He was enraptured into a deep state of ecstasy. Henceforth, he entered his room and began speaking about the exquisite conditions of the *Awliya Allāh*. When we approached him about the reason for his dictums, he relayed: *'Verily, today Sayyiduna Shaykh ʿAbd al-Qādir al-Jilānī ﷺ declared in Baghdād: 'My foot is on the neck of every Walī of Allāh."* Immediately, we placed on record the date and time. After a certain duration, a traveller arrived from Baghdād and informed us that indeed, Sayyiduna Ghawth ﷺ vociferously enunciated in Baghdād that his foot is on the neck or every *Walī* of *Allāh*. It was exactly on that very day that we had recorded this occurrence.

I was informed in 691 *hijrī* in Cairo by Shaykh Jalīl Abu al-Barkāt Yūnus b. Abī al-Najāt Muslim b. Abī al-Ḥasan ʿAlī b. Muḥammad b. Aḥmad b. ʿAlī al-Tamīmī al-Bakrī al-Irbilī Muqrī al-Shafaʿī al-ʿAdawī ﷺ originally Mosulī, who narrates from Shaykh, the leader Abu al-Mafākhir ʿAdī b. Shaykh Abī al-Barkāt b. Shaykh Abī al-Qawī Sighar b. Musāfir ﷺ in 618 *hijrī* on Jabal Hakkār; who narrates from Shaykh Abu al-Barkāt ﷺ who verified that his uncle, Shaykh ʿAdī b. Musāfir ﷺ had bent his head on an open section of Lālish.[109] When he was questioned about this incident, he replied: *'Verily, at this moment in Baghdād Sayyiduna Shaykh ʿAbd al-Qādir ﷺ had declared that his foot is on the necks of all the Awliya Allāh. He disseminated praiseworthy statements that elevated the name of Shaykh ʿAbd al-Qādir ﷺ.'* We then noted the following factual information of Shaykh ʿAdī ﷺ:

> Shortly the arrows of fear will be fired on the souls; the result of which, shall either be injury or benefit. If one is saved by it, then one is free, but if one is struck by it, then one's soul shall perish. O man! If you accept this advice then you are enlisted in our army, but if you reject this advice, then you shall be doomed. If you stay alive, live like the pious and if you die, die like the martyrs. Place your *nafs* in the Station of Destitution and drown it in the Ocean of Despair. Subject the self to the Army of Purity and attack it with the Men of Sincerity. Erect the tent of surrender and submission; and thus hoist the flag with meditation and chastity. Mount the horse of reliance and fix it with the bridle of certainty. Adorn yourself with the garb of patience, draw out the sword of fear and endure the pangs of war with hope. Protect yourself with the shield of sincerity, enter the battlefield with fervour; and advance with

[109] The original manuscript used the name 'Lākish', and after research, I could not find this name in Iraq. It is possible that in those years it was known by that name, but presently the location of the *Mazār al-Sharif* of Sayyiduna Shaykh ʿAdī b. Musāfir ﷺ is in the town of 'Lālish' in Northern Iraq. *Allāh* ﷻ Knows best. Faqīr ʿAbd al-Hādī.

truth and virtue with a fixed Flag of Reverence. Go to war with a secretive devoutness and attributes of deliberation and progression, hence reaching out ahead, with the ladder of knowledge and forbearance.

Thereafter, instil the Bow of Contentment and connect it effectively to the string of contemplation. Furthermore, arm it with the arrow of observation and absorb it with the hands of gnosis. Fire it, and target for Divine Proximity with the hope of attaining the rope of communion. When you infuse these traits within the self, then denounce greed, abandon your authority and eradicate your desires. Consistently, look forward zealously towards your Lord ﷻ. Take two steps towards Him ﷻ and you will be assured: *'Look! Here is your Lord.'* This is comparable to both palms, which become close together. Be mindful of the fact that the nation has fasted from Fasts, slept in slumber and have become extinct with extinction. They have been invoked by the tongue of eternity with its secrets. Their souls have fled from the stages of fabrication and distortion, and they are on a serene flight in the angelic realm; through the Divinely Ordained blessings. They were embellished with the garb of inspirational knowledge from the infinite secret treasures, to a degree that they tore up their perishable veils and reached the eternal Station of Divine Proximity. They are relaxed on the carpet of friendship. They then witnessed the castles of sanctity and were served by designated angels. They experienced modesty which took them into the Realm of Wonderment, where they lost their senses. In this spiritual domain, life continued where they were seated and spoken to by the Divine Being. They expressed their love and drew closer and their experiences grew. Eventually, they were blessed with Eternal Bliss and Communion. The devotees then forgot themselves and had become oblivious of their existence. Here they witnessed and recognized the Truth, hence they sat with contentment. Then the Omnipotent and Omniscient Lord ﷻ gave them a cup of Drink of Divine Love in the Divine Presence. They lost their mental dimension after drinking the

Drink of Divine Love and entered the Station of Truth in the Proximity of their Sovereign; Omnipotent Lord ﷻ. At this point Almighty *Allāh* ﷻ calls out to them and explicitly spells out: *'O My servants! You do not have and fear or sorrow.'*

Concerning the Reverence of the great Ghawth رضي الله عنه

I was informed in 671 *hijrī* in Cairo by Shaykh Saqqa Abu-Zayd ʿAbdur Raḥman b. Abī al-Najāt Sālim b. Aḥmad Ḥamīd b. Sāliḥ b. ʿAlī al-Qurashī al-Muḥaddith رحمه الله who narrates from Shaykh ʿĀrif Abu al-Khayr Neʿmatullāh b. Shaykh Abu al-Maʿālī Zarīf b. Aḥmad b. Muḥammad al-Jazīlī ʿAsqalānī al-Shafaʿī رحمه الله who states that in the beginning of 629 *hijrī,* he narrates from Shaykh Abu al-Maʿālī Baqā al-Jazīlī رحمه الله and Shaykh Abu-Yaḥyah Maḥmūd b. Qāsim al-Qāsimī رحمه الله originally Shāmī, in 613 *hijrī,* that they both narrate from their Shaykh Aḥmad b. Abī al-Qāsim al-Batā'ihī al-Ḥaddādī رحمه الله who was visiting *Shām* [Syria]. He narrates in 581 *hijrī* in Syria: that he had arrived on Mount Lebanon in 579 *hijrī* with the intention to visit the *Sāliḥīn* [*Awliya*] there. In those days there was a pious person living there from Asbahān known as Shaykh Ḥabal رحمه الله. He had lived for a long time on Mount Lebanon. I sat in his company and inquired: *'O my master! How long are you living on this mountain?' 'For sixty years:'* he replied. I then questioned him pertaining to the amazing things that he had seen during this period. He declared:

'One moonlit night in 559 *hijrī,* I saw the men [*Awliya*] of the mountains assemble; and line after line they flew in the air towards the direction of Iraq. I approached a friend amongst them as to where were they going. He stated that Sayyiduna Khiḍar عليه السلام ordered them to go to Baghdād and present themselves in front of the *Qutb.* I questioned: who that was, and thereby he informed me that it was Shaykh ʿAbd al-Qādir رضي الله عنه. I suggested to him that I shall accompany him, and to this, he consented. We then flew to Baghdād and after a short journey, we reached there and found the high ranking *Awliya* and *Mashā'ikh* assembled and were chanting: *'O our Master.'* When they were ordered, they hastened to fulfil the command [of the Ghawth رضي الله عنه]. Later they were ordered to return and they flew back and I also returned with my friend.'

When we returned to our mountain, I expressed to my friend that he had not experienced anything like that before; that all of you depicted great reverence in his presence and hastened to execute his commands. My friend replied: *'My dear brother! Why should we not obey his commands when he revealed that his foot is on the neck of every Walĩ of Allãh and we were ordered to obey his commands and respect him.'*

I was informed in 666 *hijrĩ* in Cairo by Shaykh Sãliḥ Abu al-Fida Ismã'ĩl b. al-Faqih Abu-Isḥãq Ibrãhĩm b. Wara b. ʿĪsã b. Abĩ al-Ḥasan al-Munzirĩ, then al-Maghribĩ, and then Mah'marĩ al-Shafaʿĩ رحمه الله. He narrates from Shaykh ʿĀrif Abu al-Muḥãsin Yũsuf b. Shaykh Abĩ al-Ḥasan al-Barĩjãnĩ رحمه الله, holding the title of '*the dumb lion Asadĩ*' who narrates in Barĩjãn from Shaykh ʿÃa'lĩ Abu al-Ḥasan ʿAlĩ b. ʿAbdullãh b. Abĩ-Bakr ʿAlĩ b. Aḥmad al-Abharĩ رحمه الله originally born in Baghdãd and Shaykh Abu-Muḥammad Sãlĩm b. ʿAlĩ b. ʿAbdullãh b. Sanãnũ Miyãtĩ Qãhirĩ al-Shafaʿĩ رحمه الله in 669 *hijrĩ* in Cairo; both narrate from Shaykh Imãm Muʿammar رحمه الله, the remembrance of their predecessors Abu al-Thana Maḥmũd b. Aḥmad al-Kurdĩ Ḥamĩdĩ Ḥanbalĩ al-Baghdãdĩ al-Shafaʿĩ رحمه الله in 620 *hijrĩ* in Baghdãd who confess that when Sayyiduna Shaykh ʿAbd al-Qãdir al-Jilãnĩ رضي الله عنه proclaimed that his foot is on the neck of every *Walĩ* of *Allãh*, thus after this proclamation whichever *Walĩ*, *Abdãl* and *Awtãd* visited his illustrious personality, expressed their greetings in the following words:

اَلسَّلَامُ عَلَيْكَ يَامَلِكَ الزَّمَانِ وَيَااِمَامَ الْمَكَانِ وَ يَاقَائِمًا بِأَمْرِ الرَّحْمٰنِ وَيَاوَارِثَ
الْكِتَابِ وَ يَانَائِبَ رَسُوْلِ اللهِ صَلَّى اللهُ عَلَيْهِ وَسَلَّمْ يَامَنْ مِنَ السَّمَآءِ وَ الْاَرْضِ
عَائِدَتُهُ يَامَنْ اَهْلُ وَقْتِهٖ كُلُّهُمْ عَائِلَتُهٗ يَامَنْ يَّنْزِلُ الْغَيْثُ بِدَعْوَتِهٖ وَ يَدِرُّ
الضَّرْعُ بِبَرْكَتِهٖ وَرَحْمَةُ اللهِ وَبَرَكَاتُهٗ

Peace be upon you O King of the era; O Leader of the House, O Distributer [bounties] by the Command of Allãh جل جلاله, O inheritor of the Book [al-Qur'ãn], O Deputy of the Messenger of Allãh ﷺ, O you whose table spread of food is in the skies and on the earth, O You whose children are all the Awliya, O You with whose du'ãs it rains, O You by your blessings, milk is found in the breasts. May the Mercy and blessings of Allāh ﷻ be upon you.

I was informed in 668 *hijrī* in Cairo by Shaykh Abu-Muḥammad Ḥasan b. Abī-ʿImrān Mūsā b. Aḥmad b. Ḥasan b. Dāʿūd al-Qurashī Makhzūmī al-Khālidī al-Shafaʿī ﷺ who reports:

In *Rajab* 613 *hijrī* in Damascus I visited Shaykh Faqih Taqī al-Dīn Abī ʿAbdullāh b. Muḥammad b. Abī al-Ḥusain b. ʿAbdullāh b. ʿĪsā al-Yunīnī Taʿalbakī Faqih al-Ḥanbalī al-Muḥaddith ﷺ. I spend many days with the Shaykh ﷺ. Shaykh Abu al-Ḥasan ʿAlī al-Qurashī ﷺ thereafter disappeared from Iraq and emerged in a *Zāwiya* [retreat] on Mount Qāsiyūn [Damascus]. Shaykh Faqih Taqī al-Dīn al-Yunīnī ﷺ came to visit him and I also accompanied him. When we met him, before us Shaykh Abu-Yūnus ʿAbdullāh b. Yūnus al-Arminī ﷺ, Shaykh Abu-ʿAmar ʿUthmān al-Rūmī ﷺ and Shaykh Abu-Ibrāhīm b. Ismā'īl b. ʿAlī al-Kurānī ﷺ were already present there.

Shaykh ʿAlī al-Qurashī ﷺ began talking and we listened attentively. He stated that he questioned Shaykh Qāḍīb al-Baan Mosulī ﷺ: *'Did you ever see anyone similar to Shaykh ʿAbd al-Qādir al-Jilānī ﷺ?'* He replied in the negative and thereafter expressed: *'After Shaykh ʿAbd al-Qādir's ﷺ reverberated of 'his foot', when the Awliya from abroad visited him, I saw their heads bent owing to the reverential esteem of the Shaykh ﷺ.'*

I was informed in 669 *hijrī* in Cairo by Shaykh Sāliḥ Abu al-Muḥāsin Yūsuf b. Ayās b. Marḥān b. Manīʿh al-Baʿalbakī Muqrī al-Ḥanbalī ﷺ that he narrates from two *Shuyūkh*, Shaykh Abu-Yūnus ʿAbdullāh b. Yūnus ﷺ well known as al-Armīnī. He narrates in *Rajab* 629 in the *Jāʿmeh* [*Amawī*] of Damascus [110] and Shaykh Abu-ʿAbdullāh Muḥammad b. Abu al-Ḥusain b. Muḥammad ʿĪsā al-Yūnīnī al-Baʿalbakī al-Damishqī ʿUqbī Muqrī al-Ḥanbalī ﷺ well known as al-

[110] The *Jāʿmeh* of Damascus generally refers to the celebrated *Jāʿmeh al-Amawī* as this is the biggest and oldest *Masjid* in Damascus. In it is also the *Mazār al-Sharīf* of Sayyiduna Nabī Yaḥyah ﷺ [John the Baptist]

Batā'iḥī in *Ramaḍān* 609 *hijrī* narrates from two persons, Shaykh Abu-Yūnus ʿAbdullāh b. Yūnus ﷺ well known as al-Armīnī narrates in *Rajab* 629 in the *Jāʿmeh* [*Amawī*] of Damascus and Shaykh Abu-ʿAbdullāh Muḥammad b. Abu al-Ḥusain b. Muḥammad ʿĪsā al-Yūnīnī al-Baʿalbakī al-Damishqī ʿUqbī Muqrī al-Ḥanbalī ﷺ well known as al-Batā'iḥī narrates in Baʿalbak in 603 *hijrī* and Shaykh ʿĀrif Abu-Muḥammad Ibrāhim b. Muḥammad b. Jowhar al-Baʿalbakī al-Damishqī ʿUqbī Muqrī al-Ḥanbalī ﷺ well known as al-Batā'iḥī narrates in *Ramaḍān* 609 *hijrī* in ʿUqaybah. Both say that they heard several times from Shaykh Abu-Muḥammad al-Batā'iḥī ﷺ saying;

> I visited my Shaykh, Shaykh ʿAbd al-Qādir al-Jilānī ﷺ at his home, where I discovered four people with him, whom I had never seen before. I took my seat and when they got up to leave, Shaykh ʿAbd al-Qādir ﷺ stated to me: *'Go and meet with them; and request them to make Duʿā for you.'* I met them in the veranda of the *Madressa* and before they could leave, I requested them for *Duʿās*. One of them beseeched: *'Glad tidings to you, You are a servant of such a dignitary that owing to him, Almighty Allāh ﷻ protects the earth, be it soft, rocky, jungle or watery and through his supplications Allāh ﷻ is merciful to creation, be they pious or sinners. We, and all the Awliya humble ourselves in his [august] presence and remain under the shade of his [sacred] feet and remain within his circle.'* Thereafter, they walked out through the door of the *Madressa* and disappeared. I then returned to Ḥaḍrate Shaykh ʿAbd al-Qādir ﷺ, and before I could say anything to him, he instructed: *'O servant of Allāh ﷻ and my brother! Whatever they said to you, do not reveal it to anyone.'* I respectfully replied; *'O my Master! Who are these people?' 'They are senior Awliya of Kohe-Qāf and they have now reached their stations in Kohe-Qāf,'* replied the Ghawth ﷺ.

I narrate in 695 *hijrī,* in Cairo from Shaykh Faqih [the Jurist] Abu al-Maʿālī ʿAbd al-Raḥīm b. Muzaffar ʿAlī al-Qurashī al-Baghdādī al-Ḥanbalī ﷺ and he narrates in 635 *hijrī,* in Baghdād from Shaykh Abu al-Muḥāsin Faḍalullāh b. Ḥāfiz Abu-Bakr ʿAbd al-Razzāq b. Shaykh Muḥiyy al-Dīn ʿAbd al-Qādir al-Jilānī ﷺ who narrates from Shaykh ʿĀrif Abu-Muḥammad b. ʿAlī b. Abī-Bakr b. Muḥammad b. ʿAbdullāh b. Idrīs al-Yaʿqūbī ﷺ in 610 *hijrī* in Baghdād who disclosed that he had heard from his Shaykh ʿAlī b. al-Hītī in Zudwirān in 560 *hijrī,* revealing:

> 'Once I visited Sayyiduna Shaykh ʿAbd al-Qādir al-Jilānī and located him on the roof of the *Madressa* performing the *Ḍuḥā salāh*[111]. When I looked towards the field, I saw 40 *saffs* [lines] of *Rijāl al-Ghayb* [112] with 70 men in each line. I questioned them: *'Why do you not sit down?'* They replied: *'When the Qutb completes his salāh and orders us to sit, then only will we sit, because his hand is above our heads and his foot is on our shoulders. His command rules over us.'* When Sayyiduna Shaykh terminated his *salāh* with *salām*, the group of *Rijāl al-Ghayb* hastened towards him, greeted him and kissed his hands. Shaykh ʿAlī b. Hītī affirms that whenever we looked at Sayyiduna Shaykh ʿAbd al-Qādir, we saw virtuousness.

Sayyiduna Shaykh ʿAbd al-Qādir al-Jilānī attributes all favours and blessing to Allāh

The great Ghawth states; Remember! May *Allāh* bless you in being a beneficiary of excellent Sainthood [*wilāyah*] and protect you with exclusive clemency. Verily, when one seeks the path of truth, one achieves it. When the hand of enthusiasm is absorbed, then one becomes the owner; and when the gratefulness of love imprisons one, it then kills oneself. When nobility becomes extinct, then everything becomes abandoned through mystification. When the tree of communion becomes solid, it then grows; and when the principles of its proximity are strong, it is thereby sanctified. When the gardens of sanctity are exposed, they are luscious and fresh and when the breeze of love blows, it spreads. When the eyes of the intelligent see, they become inebriated; and when the hearts of friends observe, they fall in love. The ears of the souls are then close by, thus they hear, and when the eyes of secrets are present, they thus see. When the tongue of the nation issue orders, it speaks. Thus, the excellence of the servant, in entirety belongs to *Allāh*, Who in

[111] This virtuous forenoon prayer is a *Sunnah* and performed 20 minutes after sunrise.

[112] *Rijāl al-Ghayb* are the Men of the Unseen. They are Statesmen [*Awliya*], under the command of the *Qutb* who supervises them and their duties. # [*Qādirī Faqīr ʿAbd al-Hādī*]

the first stage; addresses with the verbatim Speech of generosity, which heralds excellence, hence calling towards the assembly of communion.

Thereafter, this is disclosed to the people of reality of love and leads the neighbours towards the Station of Proximity. These individuals then, with the experience of eternity, observe the sanctity of beauty and they are able to eventually observe the honour of the quintessence of the Easts. Their vision is raised in requisition to the general unseen [*'Āwām al-Ghayb*], as well as to the milestone of *Tawḥīd*. Their inner eyes [vision] perceives the phases of purity and destiny. Their eyes are locked towards the signs of victory, which is the manifestation of the veils of the Royal Court of the Sublime Lord ﷻ. Their hearts are propped on the boards of love which are in the celestial palaces, and are situated in between its reception. They are seated on the secrets of the sheet of prosperity and fortune.

Their souls are ecstatic with the address of flowers and if any of them are silent, it is owing to *Ḥaqq al-Yaqīn* [113] and if anyone is talking, then it is owing to *'Amar al-Yaqīn* [114]. If there is fear in the hearts of their *murīds* of the revelation of the Divine Injunction: *'They are fearless of Allāh's ﷻ Ordainment'*, or they have despair in their hearts about this that *Allāh* ﷻ is putting His fear the hearts of His servants, then a messenger calls out to them: *'You both don't fear because verily, I am with you.'* The testifiers of virtues comment: *'Today you are given glad tidings.'* The ambassadors of munificence declare: *'Announce the affluence and blessings of your Lord. If there is any award for their intentions, then bring them to Me so that I make him exclusive for Me. Only he is admitted to the Royal Court who is blessed with special Mercies. He ﷻ draws close those whom He ﷻ loves.'* O *Allāh*! You have sanctified Your servants. Peace is by Your Speech upon those who move towards that assembly. Their Cherisher and Sustainer ﷻ has given them pure drink and exposes his glorious Self for their reception. Thus, *Allāh* ﷻ stipulates: *'Take what I give you.'* As a result the servant stretches out his hands

[113] The Spiritual State of True Certainty
[114] The Spiritual State of Ordained Certainty

and pleads: *'O my Lord! Open my chest [for Your Love].'* His Compassionate Lord ﷻ then calls out to him: *'Inform my servant.'* The tongue of Truth then informs the servant: *'I have informed that which You have commanded me to say.'*

If the servant is steadfast in the obedience of the directives of the Messenger ﷺ, he then becomes firm on that path. What the Messenger ﷺ gives, accept it, and thus, one shall be fortified in this circle. If you are the friend of *Allāh* ﷻ, then you will align yourself to Him. The Messenger of *Allāh* ﷺ advised: *'One who is obedient to me, then he is from me.'* His roots will be watered by *Sāḥibe Qāba Qousayn*[115] ﷺ and assisted with the Ocean of Abundance. The Messenger of *Allāh* ﷺ does not speak on his own accord and if you read his virtuous message to the letter, and love it, then he too will love you.

If you ponder over their[116] nobility, then you will find *Allāh* ﷻ pleased with them and if you probe into their status, perceive then: that Knowledge is with the Lord of Power ﷻ. If you intend to praise them, then bring to your realization that they are people of far superior stations. The words that emanate from them are elevated and that which is in their bosoms are also gracious. There are some who understand the bounties that are prepared for them by Divine Ordinance, and there are some who do not understand the blessings that are kept concealed for them.

Why should this be so when it is narrated in the *Ḥadith* that *Allāh* ﷻ had sent revelation to one of the Prophets عليه السلام of *Bani Isrā'īl* that there are some servants that love me and I love them. They are eager for Me and I am eager for them. They remember Me and I cause them to be remembered. They look towards Me and I look at them. That Prophet عليه السلام enquired:

> *'O Allāh! What are their signs to recognize them?'* Almighty *Allāh* ﷻ replies: 'Firstly, they love the sunset similar to the animals who rush to return to their habitats. When night falls, they lay their mats on the floor, and prepare to Worship Me. A friend goes into seclusion to meet with a

[115] This is an exclusive title of the beloved Messenger of *Allāh* ﷺ

[116] Refers to *Awliya-Allāh* رحمهم الله

friend. The lovers [*Awliya*] then stand upright in devotion, and make the floor their faces for prostration [*sajdah*]. They have a secret conversation with Me, whilst some remain standing and others seated. I take an oath on My Divine Eye! They do not have a burden to worship Me. I take an oath on my Divine Ear! They do not complain in My love. The first thing I instil in their hearts is My Light [*nũr*] and they [*Awliya*] give information about Me as I do about them. Secondly, if the seven skies and earths are placed on a scale, then I shall make it light for them. Thirdly, I focus my Gracious Face [Divine Vision] towards them. No one ever knows, what Mercy I ordain in order to bless them, when I focus my Vision of Grandeur on them.

Hence, O brother! It is compulsory for you to be obedient to them [*Awliya*] and become their followers. Hand over to them, all that you see and hear and; you shall then achieve excellence in all facets; and shall be a recipient of lofty stations.

I implore *Allãh* ﷻ to adorn our eyes with the kohl [117] of the light of salvation and strengthen the pillars of our beliefs [*aqãid*] with His Favour and Grace.

I was informed in 674 *hijrĩ,* in Cairo by Shaykh, the erudite scholar, Shams al-Dĩn Abu-ʿAbdullãh Muḥammad al-Shaykh ʿAllãma ʿImãd al-Dĩn Abu-Isḥãq Ibrãhĩm b. ʿAbd al-Wãḥid b. ʿAlĩ al-Maqdisĩ al-Ḥanbalĩ ﵀ who narrates in 663 *hijrĩ* from two *Shuyũkh*, Shaykh Abu al-Qãsim ʿUmar b. Masʿũd Baz'zãr al-Baghdãdĩ ﵀ in Baghdãd who narrates in 564 *hijrĩ* from Shaykh ʿÃlim-e-Rabbãnĩ Najĩb al-Dĩn ʿAbd al-Qãhir b. ʿAbdullãh Sohrowardĩ ﵀ in Baghdãd whom I heard stating:

> I was in the company of Shaykh Ḥammãd b. Muslim al-Dabbãs, the juice merchant ﵀ in 563 *hijrĩ,* whilst Shaykh ʿAbd al-Qãdir ﵁ was voicing sublime words. Shaykh Ḥammãd ﵀ commented: *'O ʿAbd al-Qãdir! You have spoken astonishing words. Do you not fear that Allãh ﷻ is testing you?'*

---

[117] Kohl is an ancient eye liner which is also known as *surma* in the sub-continent

Shaykh ʿAbd al-Qādir ﷺ henceforth placed his palms on the chest of Shaykh Ḥammād ﷺ and commanded: *'Look with the eye of your heart what is written on my palms.'* Concurrently, Shaykh Ḥammād ﷺ was overpowered by a state of unconsciousness and Shaykh ʿAbd al-Qādir al-Jīlānī ﷺ removed his palm from his chest. Shaykh Ḥammād ﷺ confessed: *'I saw his palm that took a guarantee from Allāh ﷻ seventy times not to test him.'* He further conceded to Sayyiduna Shaykh ʿAbd al-Qādir ﷺ: *'Fear not [say what you please] this is the blessings of Allāh ﷻ Who gives anyone whatever He Ordains.'*

I was informed in 675 *hijrī* in Cairo by Shaykh Sharīf Abu al-ʿAbbās Aḥmad b. al-Shaykh Abu-ʿAbdullāh Muḥammad b. Abu al-Ghanā'im Muḥammad b. Azharī b. Abī al-Mafākhir Muḥammad al-Ḥasanī al-Damishqī al-Baghdādī ﷺ who narrates from his father Shaykh Abu al-Faraj ﷺ who served Sayyiduna Ghawth ﷺ for fifteen years. I narrate from Shaykh Abu al-Faraj ʿAbd al-Wah'hāb b. Abu al-Mafākhir Ḥasan b. Qatbān b. Muḥammad b. Aḥmad al-Kūfī al-Irbilī al-Baghdādī ﷺ in Cairo in 665 *hijrī* who narrates from Qāḍī al-Quḍāt Abu-Sāliḥ Nasar b. al-Ḥāfiz Abu-Bakr ʿAbd al-Razzāq b. Shaykh al-Islām Muḥiyy al-Dīn ʿAbd al-Qādir al-Jīlī al-Baghdādī ﷺ in 631 *hijrī* who proclaims that he narrates from Shaykh ʿAbd al-Razzāq al-Jīlānī ﷺ in 600 *hijrī*. [Concerning the above incident of Shaykh Ḥammād ﷺ]

Concerning the youth of Sayyiduna Ghawth al-Aʿzam ﷺ

People inquired from Sayyiduna Ghawth al-Aʿzam ﷺ as to when did he come to know that he was a *Walī* of *Allāh*? He replied: *'When I was ten years old and attended the Madressa, the teacher would instruct the students to make place for the Walī of Allāh in order that he may sit.'*

Sayyiduna Shaykh ﷺ then revealed:

In reference to another incident, a person came to me whom at that time I did not recognize. He admitted that he heard on that day from the angels, who communicated with each other: *'Who is this boy?'* The other angel replied: *'Shortly, his status will very exalted. He will be given in abundance and not restricted. He will be granted power and authority which will not be concealed from him.'*

After forty years, I recognized that person. He was from the *Abdāls*. During my youth, I joined the children with the intention of playing with them. I used to hear an unknown voice to me: *'O blessed boy! Where are you going?* I became fearful and ran to the lap of my mother. It is now, that I realize and understand these words.

Once during my youth, I was on a journey and I heard an unknown voice addressing me: *'O ʿAbd al-Qādir! I have chosen you for Myself.'* I used to hear the voice by could not see anyone. In the days of my Spiritual Services [*mujāhidah*] when I used to slumber, I used to hear an unknown voice calling out to me: *'O ʿAbd al-Qādir! I have not created you to sleep. Verily, I was your friend when you were non-existent. Now that you are existent [created], do not be neglectful of Me.'*

I narrate in 675 *hijrī* in Cairo from Shaykh Abu-Muḥammad ʿAlī b. Azūmar Muḥammadī ﷺ and Shaykh Abu-Muḥammad ʿAbd al-Wāḥid b. Sāliḥ b. Yaḥyah b. Muḥammad al-Qurashī al-Baghdādī al-Ḥanbalī ﷺ, that both narrate from Shaykh Muḥiyy al-Dīn Abu-ʿAbdullāh Muḥammad b. ʿAlī b. Muḥammad b. Khālid al-Baghdādī ﷺ prominently known as Tawḥīdī who in 641 *hijrī* in Baghdād narrates from Shaykh Sharīf Abu al-Qāsim Ḥaybatullāh b. ʿAbdullāh b. Aḥmad al-Khatīb ﷺ popularly known as Ibn Mansūrī, in 623 *hijrī* in Baghdād narrates from two *Shuyūkh*, the leader, Shaykh Abu-Masʿūd Aḥmad b. Abī-Bakr al-Ḥarīmī ʿAttār ﷺ and the leader, Shaykh Abu-ʿAbdullāh Muḥammad b. Qā'id al-Awānī ﷺ in 581 *hijrī,* when both state that they narrate from Shaykh Sadaqah al-Baghdādī ﷺ who had issued such a statement; that is rejected within the parameters of the sacred *Sharīʿah*. This reached the present ruling *Khalīfah,* who summoned the Shaykh ﷺ and ordered the executioner to punish him. When the Shaykh ﷺ was brought blindfolded to the court, his servant [*khādim*] turned away in disgust. When the executioner intended to behead the Shaykh ﷺ, his hands got paralyzed and *Allāh* ﷻ introspected his heart through Divine Awe. The minister informed the *Khalīfah* whose heart *Allāh* ﷻ also introspected through Divine Awe. The *Khalīfah* immediately ordered the Shaykh to be released. Shaykh Sadaqah ﷺ then proceeded to the guest house of Sayyiduna Ghawth al-Aʿzam ﷺ and found *Mashā'ikh* assembled there; and awaiting the arrival of Sayyiduna Ghawth ﷺ to address them. Then the Ghawth ﷺ arrived and sat on his chair and remained silent, nor did he order the *Qārī* to recite the Holy *Qur'ān*. Everyone were submerged into a state of spiritual ecstasy and were overwhelmed by a strange feeling. Shaykh Sadaqah ﷺ contemplated in his heart that; neither did the Ghawth ﷺ speak, nor did he order the *Qārī* to recite the Holy *Qur'ān*, then how did this state of spiritual ecstasy engulf the people. Sayyiduna Ghawth ﷺ then turned to him and expounded: *'O Sadaqah! A murīd of mine came from Baith al-Muqaddas in a single step to repent at my hands. Today he is the guest of all of you.'*

Shaykh Sadaqah ﷺ interpreted within his heart: *'For what sin will a person repent who is capable of taking one step from Baith al-Muqaddas to Baghdād and what dependency does he have on a Shaykh?'* Sayyiduna Ghawth ﷺ then turned to me and elaborated:

> *'O Shaykh Sadaqah! He came to make tawbah for flying in the air and not turning to me. He is dependent on me to show him the path of the Divine Love of Allāh* ﷻ*.'* The Ghawth ﷺ further stipulated: *'My sword is famous and my bow is drawn and loaded with an arrow to fire. My arrow is accurate on target and my spear is precise. My horse is saddled and ready. I am a flaming fire of Allāh* ﷻ *and authoritative in diminishing ranks. I am a shoreless ocean and the proof of time. I am one who addresses the gathering of adversaries. I am protected, observed and fortunate. O fasting ones! O standing ones! O residents of the mountains! Your mountains have crushed. O people of the churches! Your churches have crumbled. Come towards the Command of Allāh* ﷻ*. I am one of the Commands of Allāh* ﷻ*. O guides of roads! O men! O brave ones! O children! Come and take from that ocean which has no shores. O beloved! You are alone in the skies and I am alone [matchless] on earth. I am communicated to seventy times every day and night that I was selected as a beloved so that I*

may flourish in the Vision of Allāh ﷻ. I am told; 'O ʿAbd al-Qādir! I give the oath of My Rights, eat, I give you the oath of My Rights, drink, I give you the oath of My Rights, speak. I ﷻ have made you carefree from destruction.'

I narrate in 671 *hijrī* in Cairo from Shaykh Abu-Muḥammad ʿAbdus Salām b. Abī-ʿAbdullāh b. ʿAbdus Salām b. Ibrāhīm b. ʿAbdus Salām al-Basrī رحمه الله originally al-Baghdādī, and he narrates from Shaykh Abu al-Ḥasan ʿAlī b. Sulaymān al-Baghdādī the baker رحمه الله who narrates in 633 *hijrī* in Baghdād from two *Shuyūkh*, Shaykh Abu al-Qāsim ʿUmar b. Masʿūd Baz'zār رحمه الله and Shaykh Abu-Ḥafs ʿUmar Kamyamānī رحمه الله in 591 *hijrī* in Baghdād; both say that their Shaykh, Shaykh ʿAbd al-Qādir رضي الله عنه used to fly in the air in the presence of the people in the *majlis* [gathering] and he used to declare:

'When the sun rises, it greets me. The year comes to me and greets me and informs me of all the happenings that are to take place in that year. The day greets me and informs me of all the occurrences of that day. I take the oath of the Honour of Allāh ﷻ, the pious and wicked are presented to me on the sacred Tablet of Records [Louḥe-Maḥfūz]. I dive into the Ocean of Allāh's ﷻ Knowledge and Observation. I am a proof of Allāh ﷻ upon all of you and the heir of Sayyiduna Rasūlullāh ﷺ on this earth.'

The Attendance of the Months in the presence of the Ghawth رضي الله عنه

I narrate in 666 *hijrī* in Cairo from Shaykh Abu-Muḥammad b. Abī al-Qāsim Aḥmad b. Muḥammad b. Shaykh Abu al-Qāsim Walif b. Aḥmad b. Muḥammad al-Baghdādī al-Ḥarīmī رحمه الله and he narrates from his grandfather in Baghdād in 625 *hijrī* who narrates from Shaykh Abu al-Qāsim Walif رحمه الله in 691 *hijrī* who narrates from Shaykh Abu-Saʿūd Abu-Bakr Ḥouḍ رحمه الله, Shaykh Abu al-Khayr Bishr b. Maḥfūz b. Ghanīmah رحمه الله, Shaykh Abu-Ḥafs ʿUmar al-Kamyamānī رحمه الله, Shaykh Abu al-ʿAbbās Aḥmad Askā رحمه الله and Shaykh Sayf al-Dīn ʿAbd al-Wah'hāb al-Jilānī b. Shaykh ʿAbd al-Qādir al-Jilānī رضي الله عنه that: we all were present with our Shaykh, Sayyiduna Shaykh ʿAbd al-Qādir al-Jilānī رضي الله عنه on the last *Jumʿah* of the month on 30th Jamādi al-Ākhir 560 *hijrī*. Sayyiduna Ghawth al-

Aʿzam ﷺ was delivering his sermon and they were all seated and listening. Consequently, a young handsome man came and sat beside the great Ghawth ﷺ and resonated: *'O Walī of Allāh! May there be peace upon you. I am the month of Rajab. The reason I come to you is to give you glad tidings and inform you about the things that will transpire in me so that this month is better for the people.'*

The narrator conveys:

> In this month of *Rajab*, people did not experience anything besides graciousness. When Sunday dawned and this month expired, thereafter a very ugly person came and at that time we were also present. He asserted: *'O Walī of Allāh! May there be peace upon you. I am the month of Shaʿbān, the reason I come to you is to give you glad tidings and inform you about the things that will happen in me. Many people will die in Baghdād in this month; there will be scarcity in Ḥijāz and wars in Khurasān.'* As informed, all these predictions were precise. In Baghdād, severe sicknesses [epidemics] were experienced. News reached us that the *Hijāz* experienced a grave recession and there was bloodshed in Khurasān. Sayyiduna Shaykh ʿAbd al-Qādir al-Jīlānī ﷺ fell sick for a few days in *Shaʿbān* and when Monday, the 29th of *Shaʿbān* arrived, we were still present with Sayyiduna Ghawth al-Aʿzam ﷺ. On this day, Shaykh ʿAlī b. al- al-Hītī ﷺ, Shaykh Najīb al-Dīn ʿAbd al-Qāhir Sohrowardī ﷺ, Shaykh Abu al-Ḥasan al-Jowsiqī ﷺ Qāḍī Abu-Yaʿla ﷺ and Muḥammad b. Bara ﷺ were present with him. A handsome and stately person arrived and pronounced: *'As Salāmu ʿalaykum ya Walī Allāh! I am the blessed month of Ramaḍān. I have come to apologise to you that all that is to happen in me is pre-destined. I now bid you farewell as this is my last meeting with you. I shall not meet with you again and he left.'* Sayyiduna Shaykh ʿAbd al-Qādir ﷺ passed on in the following month of *Rabīʿ al-Thānī* and did not live to physically see the next *Ramaḍān*.
>
> The narrator further confirms that he had heard Sayyiduna Shaykh ﷺ sitting on the chair and pronouncing several times: *'There some servants of*

Allāh ﷻ who are visited by Ramaḍān with an apology. The month informs them if they are to fall sick or experience hunger and inquires about their welfare.'

The narrator further elaborates that the two sons of Sayyiduna Shaykh ؓ, Sayyiduna Shaykh ʿAbd al-Wah'hāb al-Jīlānī ؓ and Sayyiduna Shaykh ʿAbd al-Razzāq al-Jīlānī ؓ states that whenever anyone visited him, he used to see them from a distance and elucidate: *'He does not hear this. Glad tidings to the friends of Allāh ﷻ.'* We will thereby perceive integrity in that person, and the signs of turning his focus to Almighty *Allāh* ﷻ [engaging in worship], as validated by the approval of the comment of the great Ghawth ؓ.

Amongst the people, there were some who visited Sayyiduna Shaykh ؓ and looked at him from a distance; and remarked about him: *''He does not hear this. May he not be given Glad tidings as he is rejected.'* We would then notice the signs of rejection by *Allāh* ﷻ in those persons; which confirmed the comment of Sayyiduna Shaykh ؓ.

I narrate in 671 *hijrī* in Cairo from Shaykh Abu-Muḥammad Sālim b. ʿAlī b. ʿAbdullāh b. Sinān al-Damyātī al-Misrī ؒ who narrates from Shaykh, the leader Shahāb al-Dīn ʿUmar b. ʿAbdullāh al-Sohrowardī ؒ in 624 *hijrī* in Baghdād who affirms that he had heard Sayyiduna Shaykh ʿAbd al-Qādir ؓ dictate in his *Madressa* whilst seated on his pulpit: *'Every Walī is on the footstep of a Prophet and I am on the footstep of my Grandfather*[118] ﷺ*. Wherever Sayyiduna Mustafa* ﷺ *placed his sacred foot, I also placed my foot. The only difference is that his footstep is of Prophethood and no one besides a Prophet is privileged to step there.'*

I narrate in 673 *hijrī* in Cairo from Shaykh Abu-ʿAlī Ḥasan b. Najmudīn b. ʿĪsā b. Muḥammad al-Ḥawrānī ؒ who narrates from Shaykh ʿĀrif Abu-Muḥammad ʿAlī b. Idrīs al-Yaʿqūbī ؒ in 617 *hijrī* in Cairo that he had heard from Sayyiduna

[118] Sayyiduna Rasūlullāh ﷺ

Shaykh ʿAbd al-Qādir ﷺ who declared: *'There are Shuyūk*[119] *of the humans and I am the Shaykh of the Jinns, the angels and everyone.'*

The narrator says that he had heard Sayyiduna Shaykh ﷺ testify to his sons on his bed of demise: *'There is a distance between me, you and the entire creation, similar to that of the skies and the earth. Do not compare me with others and don't give similarity to others over me.'* I had heard Sayyiduna Ghawth ﷺ instructing his son, Shaykh ʿAbd al-Jabbār ﷺ: *'You sleep and stay awake, sacrifice yourself on me and you will always stay awake.'*

Sayyiduna Ghawth al-Aʿzam ﷺ Deliberating with Predestination

I narrate in 670 *hijrī* in Cairo from Shaykh Faqih Abu-ʿAbdullāh Muḥammad b. ʿAbd al-Malik b. ʿAlī b. Jaʿāfar b. Darāzah al-Qurashī ﷺ who narrates from Shaykh Abu al-ʿAbbās Aḥmad b. Sulaymān b. Ḥamīd b. Ibrāhīm b, Mahlahal al-Qurashī al-Makhzūmī Bulbulī al-Shafaʿī ﷺ, generally known as Kaysā, narrates in 631 *hijrī* in Cairo from Ḥāfiz Abu-Muḥammad ʿAbd al-Ghanī b. ʿAbd al-Wāḥid b. ʿAlī al-Maqdisī al-Ḥanbalī ﷺ, he narrates in Cairo in 599 *hijrī* from Faqih Abu al-Maʿālī ʿAbd al-Raḥīm b. Muzaffar Madhab b. ʿAlī al-Qurashī al-Baghdādī ﷺ who narrates in 671 *hijrī* in Cairo from Shaykh Ḥāfiz Abu-Muḥammad ʿAbd al-ʿAzīz b. Abī-Nasar b. Maḥmūd b. Abī al-Qāsim Mubarak b. Maḥmūd al-Waḥnābazī ﷺ originally from Baghdād and commonly known as Ibn al-Akhḍar who in 616 *hijrī* stated in Baghdād that he had heard Sayyiduna Shaykh ʿAbd al-Qādir Jilī ﷺ verifying: *'My condition is separate from others, my intellect is separate from the intellect of others. When all the men of Allāh ﷻ [Awliya] reach the door of Pre-destination, they stop, but when I reach there a window opens for me and I enter it. There I deliberate with the Pre-destination of Allāh ﷻ with Truth [Ḥaqq]. Thus, the perfect man is he who deliberates on Pre-destination, and not in contradiction to it.'*

[119] Shaykh - pl. Suyūkh.

Glad-tidings for those who saw Sayyiduna Shaykh ʿAbd al-Qādir ﷺ

I narrate in 660 *hijrī* in Cairo from Shaykh Abu al-Futūḥ Muḥammad b. Shaykh Abu al-Muḥāsin Yūsuf b. Ismāʿīl b. Aḥmad b. ʿAlī al-Qurashī al-Tamīmī Bakrī al-Baghdādī al-Qatqanī ﷺ who narrates in 615 *hijrī* from two *Shuyūkh*, Shaykh Shaykh Abu al-Ḥasan ʿAlī b. Abu al-Majd Mubarak Muḥammad b. al-Tāhirī ﷺ in Ḥarīmī and Shaykh Abu al-Ḥasan Khafāf al-Baghdādī ﷺ in in 620 *hijrī* Baghdād; both narrate in 580 *hijrī* from Shaykh Abu al-Saʿūd Aḥmad b. Abu-Bakr Ḥarīmī ʿAttār ﷺ in Baghdād, stating that they had heard from their Shaykh, Shaykh ʿAbd al-Qādir Jīlī ﷺ: *'That person should rejoice who has seen me and he should also rejoice who saw those who saw me or saw those ones that saw me. I have regret for those who did not see me.'*

Shaykh Maʿrūf Karkhī ﷺ replies from his Grave

I narrate in 673 *hijrī* in Cairo from Shaykh Abu-Muḥammad ʿAbd al-Wāḥid b. Sāliḥ b. Yaḥyah b. Muḥammad al-Qurashī al-Baghdādī ﷺ who narrates from Shaykh Abu al-Ḥasan ʿAlī b. Muḥammad b. Sulaymān al-Baghdādī the baker ﷺ, and Shaykh ʿAbd al-Wāḥīd b. Saʿād al-Baghdādī ﷺ in 630 *hijrī* in Baghdād; both narrate from Shaykh Qāsim ʿUmar b. Masʿūd Baz'zār ﷺ who narrates in 605 *hijrī* in his guesthouse in Cairo. He narrates from his Shaykh, Shaykh ʿAlī b. al-Hītī Zayrānī ﷺ in 563 *hijrī* in Baghdād; who stated that: I accompanied Sayyiduna Shaykh ʿAbd al-Qādir al-Jīlānī ﷺ to visit the grave of Shaykh Maʿrūf al-Karkhī ﷺ. Sayyiduna Shaykh ﷺ then professed: *'As Salāmu ʿalaykum Ya Shaykh Maʿrūf! You have progressed two stations above me.'*

The next time we visited the grave of Shaykh Maʿrūf ﷺ and Sayyiduna Shaykh ʿAbd al-Qādir ﷺ reinforced: *'As Salāmu ʿalaykum Ya Shaykh Maʿrūf! I have progressed two stations above you.'* Then we heard Shaykh Maʿrūf ﷺ answer from his grave; *'Wa ʿalaykum salām O Master of the era.'*

The Entire Era has been entrusted to Sayyiduna Ghawth al-Aᶜzam ﷺ

The above-mentioned narrator further endorses that Sayyiduna Ghawth al-Aᶜzam ﷺ pronounced to his *murĩds*: *'Irãq has been entrusted to me.'* After some time, he then re-affirmed: *'At first I said to you that Irãq was entrusted to me, but now the entire earth, east to west including its entire plains, its inhabitants, the jungles, oceans, soft earth and mountainous terrains have all been entirely entrusted to me.'*

The narrator further states that there was not a single *Walĩ* that did not present himself to the great Ghawth ﷺ and greet him owing to his lofty station of *Qutbiyat*.

Using the Wasĩlah [medium] of Sayyiduna Ghawth al-Aᶜzam ﷺ to seek desires from Allãh ﷻ

I narrate from Shaykh Abu al-Ḥasan ᶜAlĩ b. Zakariyyah al-Baghdãdĩ ﷺ who narrates from Qãḍĩ al-Quḍãt Abu-Sãliḥ Nasar b. Ḥãfiz Abu-Bakr ᶜAbd al-Razzãq b. Shaykh al-Islãm Muḥiyy al-Dĩn Abu-Muḥammad Sayyid ᶜAbd al-Qãdir al-Jilãnĩ ﷺ in 629 *hijrĩ* in Baghdãd; who narrates from Shaykh ᶜAbd al-Razzãq ﷺ and he narrates from Shaykh Abu al-Ḥasan Faqih Abĩ-ᶜImrãn Mũsã b. Aḥmad b. al-Ḥusain al-Qurashĩ al-Shafaᶜĩ ﷺ in 690 *hijrĩ* in Cairo; both narrate from Shaykh, the leader Abu al-Ḥasan al-Qurashĩ ﷺ in 613 *hijrĩ* in Damascus who states that he had heard from Sayyiduna Shaykh ᶜAbd al-Qãdir al-Jilãnĩ ﷺ as follows: *'When you seek any desire from Allãh ﷻ, seek it with my wasĩlah [through my medium].'*

I narrate in 667 *hijrĩ* in Cairo from Shaykh Abu al-ᶜÃaf Mũsã b. Shaykh Abu al-Maᶜãlĩ ᶜUthmãn b. Mũsã b. ᶜAbdullãh b. ᶜAbd al-Dã'im b. Majlĩ Baqaᶜĩ ᶜUqbĩ al-Damishqĩ ﷺ and he narrates from his father in 614 *hijrĩ* in Damascus who narrates from two *Shuyũkh*, Shaykh ᶜÃrif Abu-ᶜAmar ᶜUthmãn Sarĩfinĩ ﷺ and Shaykh Abu-Muḥammad ᶜAbd al-Ḥaqq Ḥarĩmĩ ﷺ in 567 *hijrĩ* in Baghdãd; who stated that we had heard from Sayyiduna Shaykh ʿAbd al-Qādir ﷺ who was seated on the chair, and addressed as follows:

> 'O dwellers of the earth! Be you in the east or west. O dwellers of the skies! Almighty *Allāh* ﷻ states that He creates such things that you do not know. I am amongst those things that you do not know. O dwellers of the east and west! Come, learn from me. O people of Irāq! You are like the clothing that hangs in my home. I can wear any garb as I desire. Protect yourself from me because I can bring such an army that you cannot face. O servant! You may travel for a thousand years, but come and listen to me. O servant! Listen to a single word from me. Sainthood is with me and status is with me. I distribute the Robe of Honour in my *majlis*. There is no Prophet ﷺ that has been sent who does not grace [bless] my *majlis*[120], and there is no *Walī,* that does not attend my *majlis*. The living *Awliya* attend in person whilst the *Awliya* that have transcended this mundane world, attend with their souls. O servant! Ask the angels *Munkar Nakīr* about my condition when they come to you in your graves.'

I narrate in 670 *hijrī* in Cairo from Shaykh Faqih al-Ḥasan ʿAlī b. Shaykh Abu al-ʿAbbās Aḥmad b. Mubārak b. Asbāt b. Muḥammad al-Baghdādī Ḥarīmī al-Shafaʿī ﷺ, and he narrates from Faqih ʿAbd al-Qādir b. ʿUthmān b. Abu al-Barkāt b. ʿAlī b. Rizqullāh b. ʿAbd al-Wah'hāb Tamīmī al-Bardānī al-Ḥanbalī ﷺ in 630 *hijrī* in Baghdād; he narrates from Shaykh Muḥammad ʿAbd al-Latīf b. Abī Tāhir Ahmad b. Muḥammad b. Haybatullāh Tarsī al-Baghdādī al-Ḥanbalī Sūfī ﷺ in 571 *hijrī* in Baghdād; stated that his Shaykh, Sayyiduna Shaykh

[120] Dear Reader! Please do not be confused with this statement of the great Ghawth ﷺ. He uses the word grace which is apparent that the Prophets ﷺ bless his *majlis* with their Prophetic support. It is not otherwise as misconstrued by the ill-informed individuals that Sayyiduna Ghawth ﷺ - *Allāh* ﷻ Forbid, is claiming superiority to the noble Prophets ﷺ. This is certainly not the case. The appearance of the noble Prophets ﷺ in his *majlis* is to muster support for the great Ghawth of *Allāh* ﷺ as he was appointed by the Sublime Lord ﷻ as a senior representative in His ﷻ Kingdom. This is similar to a father who supports his son to reach his goal of victory. # Qādirī Faqīr ʿAbd al-Hādī.

Muḥiyy al-Dīn ʿAbd al-Qādir ﵁ articulated distinguished words, that he was ordered to present:

'The oath of *Allāh* ﷻ on you, say this as you speak the truth. This is apt because I speak words of certainty. There is no doubt in as to what I am ordered to speak. When I am bestowed, I distribute; and when I am commanded, I then respond. The responsibility is on him who orders; and the compensation is for the intelligent. Falsifying me is an instantaneous fatal poison, which can make you lose both: your religion, and the world [*deen-o-duniya*].

I have a sword in my hand, as I am a warrior, and therefore *Allāh* ﷻ cautions you. If my lips were not restricted by the sacred *Sharīʿah*, I would have informed you of what you eat and store in your homes. You are like a transparent bottle in my presence. I see what is within your bellies, as well as that of your external selves. Had there be no lock on my tongue, I would have informed you of the measurement of Prophet Yūsuf ﵇, but it is a secret, which is not to be disclosed.

The Reins of the Era has been entrusted in the Hands of Sayyiduna Ghawth al-Aʿzam ﵁

I narrate in 671 *hijrī* in Cairo from Shaykh Abu-Muḥammad Mājid b. Khālid b. Abī-Bakr b. Sīmā b. Khānam al-Irāqī Khalwatī al-Baghdādī ﵀ who narrates from Shaykh Sāliḥ Abu-Bakr Muḥammad b. Shaykh ʿIwaḍ b. Salāmata ʿIrād al-Baghdādī Sūfī ﵀ in 630 *hijrī* in Baghdād, and he narrates from Shaykh Abu al-Qāsim b. Abī-Bakr Aḥmad b. Abī al-Saʿādāt Aḥmad b. Karam b. Ghālib al-Bandalījī al-Baghdādī ﵀, residing in Azj in Baghdād in 575 *hijrī,* that he used to note down those words of Sayyiduna Shaykh ʿAbd al-Qādir al-Jilānī ﵁, whist he sat on his chair and communicated. Thus, the words he expressed in the month of *Safar* in 561 *hijrī* are as follows:

My heart is hidden from creation in a Realm of the Knowledge of *Allāh* ﷻ and that is an angel. At the Door of *Allāh* ﷻ, the *qibla* of everyone that visits me is exposed and I take my seat on the Seat of Love and Divine

Proximity, far away from the closed doors. I am an [a unique] individual [*fard*];[121] a King that has one associate who is aware of the secrets of people and looks at the hearts of people. *Allāh* ﷻ has keeps this individual focused on Him ﷻ, so that he not contaminated by the vision of the defiled people. In so much so, that he becomes a pure slate in which the chart of the Sacred Tablet of Records [*Louḥe-Maḥfūz*] descends. The reins of the people of that era is given in his hands and he is granted the authority to give or not to give [bounties whatever it maybe] to whomever he wishes. He is addressed by the Tongue of the Unseen, 'Currently in Our Presence, you are exalted and trustworthy. He is seated on the veranda of the Souls of the People of Certainty in this world and including those in the Hereafter. He will comprise four faces: between the Creator ﷻ and Creation; between external and internal; between the known and unknown. With one, he sees at the world; with the other he sees creation; and with one he sees his Creator ﷻ.

He is made a *Khalīfah* of his land and worlds. When he intends to do anything, then turns from one face to another and transforms from one image to another. The Treasures of Secrets are subsequently exposed to him, because he is matchless, alone in the kingdom and a representative of the Prophets عليهم السلام. He is the trustee in the kingdom and every night 360 Bounties of *Allāh* ﷻ are entrust upon him.

The Words of Sayyiduna Ghawth رضي الله عنه which are decorated with Amazing Conditions

Anyone, who makes a firm intention to ascertain the meaning of the ultimate or intends to reach the boundaries of limits, courage will indeed then draw him with fervent desires that are farfetched. He will ascend to such a peak whose path is exceedingly difficult, because the imminence of his goals is

[121] *Fard* is a unique and lofty Spiritual Station above the Station of the *Ghawth*. This *Walī* is incomparable and second to none.

extremely far from the endeavours. Apart from this, there is sturdy help of grace and favour, because this is so immense, that the extent of its Master cannot be estimated. The extent of this essence is such; where the assistance of the book cannot reach; and it is a jungle, as such, which the light of the fire extinguishers. Such is this jungle; that if, the horses gallop towards it, they will fall to the ground.

Such is this place of accomplishment, that if the seekers of Ultimate Goal temporarily cease or default, they are at that juncture, returned. This region is such that, if the arrow of victory reaches it, it begets astonishment and gives up its pursuit.

Seventy Doors of ᶜIlme Ladunnī opens for Ḥaḍrat Ghawth al-Aᶜzam ﷺ

I narrate in 671 *hijrī* in Cairo from Faqih al-Asl ᶜAbdul Aḥad b. Shaykh ᶜĀrif Abu al-Majd ᶜAbd al-Samad ᶜAbd al-Karīm b. Ḥasan b. Muḥammad al-Qarshī Tamīmī al-Baghdādī Azjī al-Shafaᶜī Qāhirī ﷺ who narrates from Qāḍī al-Quḍāt Abu Sālih Nasar al-Jilānī b. Imām ᶜAbd al-Razzāq al-Jilānī ﷺ and Shaykh Abu al-Ḥasan ᶜAlī b. Sulaymān, the Baker ﷺ in 630 *hijrī* in Baghdād, narrates in 600 *hijrī* from Shaykh Ḥāfiz Tāj al-Dīn ᶜAbd al-Razzāq b. Shaykh al-Islām Muḥiyy al-Dīn ᶜAbd al-Qādir Jīlī ﷺ in the Madressa in Baghdād at the Door of Azj, and Shaykh Abu al-Baqa ᶜAbdullāh b. Ḥusain al-Malkabrī Faqih al-Naḥwī [visually impaired] ﷺ in 603 *hijrī* in Baghdād, and Shaykh Abu-Sālih ﷺ narrates from his father Shaykh Sayyid ᶜAbd al-Razzāq al-Jilānī ﷺ and his two uncles; Shaykh Sayyid ᶜAbd al-Wah'hāb al-Jilānī ﷺ and Shaykh Sayyid Ibrāhīm al-Jilānī ﷺ in 588 *hijrī* in Baghdād, and Shaykh Abu al-Hasan al-Kamyamānī ﷺ and Shaykh Baz'zār ﷺ in 591 *hijrī* in Baghdād, when I professed to all of them that in 557 *hijrī* we were present in the Madressa of Sayyiduna Ghawth al-Aᶜzam ﷺ who was eating figs, in Bāb al-Azj. Suddenly, Sayyiduna Shaykh ﷺ stopped eating, and entered into a state of unconsciousness for long period. After he had gained consciousness, he then apprised: *'At this moment*

70 doors of ʿIlme Ladunnī [122] *was opened on my heart and every door was so wide, similar to the extent of the sky and earth.'*

Thereafter, the Ghawth ﷺ conversed about the elite for a long period of time; so much so, that people plunged into a state of unconscious. I presumed that, after Sayyiduna Ghawth ﷺ, there will be no one that will ever speak in this manner of such intrinsic phenomena [*Maʿārifah*].

I narrate in 672 *hijrī* in Cairo from Faqih Abu-Aḥmad ʿAbd al-Mālik b. ʿAbd al-Mahmūd b. Yūsuf b. ʿUthmān al-Sarsarī al-ʿIrāqī ﷺ who narrates from two *Shuyūkh*, Shaykh Abu-Zakariyyah Yaḥyah b. Yūsuf b. Zakariyyah b. Yaḥyah al-Ansārī al-Sarsarī ﷺ and Shaykh Kamāludīn Abu al-Ḥasan b. Muḥammad b. Muḥammad b. Wasāḥ Sherabān ﷺ in 638 *hijrī* in Baghdād, when both narrate from Shaykh, the leader Abu al-Ḥasan ʿAlī b. Abī-Bakr b. Idrīs al-Yaʿqūbī ﷺ in 612 *hijrī* in Baghdād, who narrates from Shaykh, the leader Abu al-Ḥasan ʿAlī b. al-Hītī ﷺ in 562 *hijrī*, who stated that in this era I have not seen anyone vested with more *karāmāt* than Sayyiduna Shaykh Muḥiyy al-Dīn ʿAbd al-Qādir ﷺ. Anyone could witness a *karāmat* from him immediately, whenever he desired. Sometimes these miracles emanated from him; and at times within him.

The astonishing sequence of priceless Gems

I narrate in 671 *hijrī* in Cairo from Shaykh Abu al-Maʿālī Sāliḥ b. Aḥmad b. ʿAlī b. Abī al-Qāsim b. ʿAbdullāh Lakhmī al-Baghdādī Qarwī al-Mālikī ﷺ who narrates from two *Shuyūkh*, Shaykh Abu-Muḥammad Ḥasan al-Baghdādī Qarwī Mutriz ﷺ in 625 *hijrī* in Baghdād. Shaykh Abu-Ḥasan ﷺ narrates from his Shaykh, Shaykh Abu al-Saʿūd Aḥmad b. Abī-Bakr al-Ḥarīmī ﷺ in 580 *hijrī* in

[122] Non-Acquired: Divinely Inspired Knowledge. Communicated in most cases by the Unique Mystic, Sayyiduna Khiḍar ﷺ, who is the ocean of this Secret Knowledge, entrusted to him by the Almighty *Allāh* ﷻ. It was for this science that the noble Prophet Sayyiduna Mūsā ﷺ undertook the journey to the mysterious shores to meet with Sayyiduna Khiḍar ﷺ and acquire this knowledge. Refer *Sura Khaf* in the Holy *Qur'ān* for details.

Baghdād; who narrates from his Shaykh, Shaykh Abu-ᶜUmar ᶜUthmān al-Sarīfīnī ﷺ, who swears an oath on *Allāh* ﷻ, that the Sublime Lord ﷻ has not exposed to creation any person like Sayyiduna Shaykh Muḥiyy al-Dīn ᶜAbd al-Qādir al-Jilānī ﷺ; nor will *Allāh* ﷻ expose another like him. His miracles were categorized to the sequence of gems; one following the other. If anyone intended to count them, they would then, not be in a position to present an account of them.

Shaykh Abu al-Ḥasan ﷺ and Shaykh Abu-Muḥammad ﷺ state that the *Masha'ikh* of ᶜIrāq regarded the words of these *Shuyūkh*[123] as being exceptionally honourable and never exposed them. This is so because, if they did not inform one another about the future, then both would have not reported it. If a fast flying bird emerges from a deep ocean or dust and dissipates into a bright star, then that does not matter. Can a swift camel reach the closeness of the sun; or can one determine the blooming of the petals of flowers in the gardens?

Thus, O Luminous Masters! Fear, because there is no one who can comprehend the pearls of the oceans, and shortly we shall discuss this allusion, which is sufficient enough for the intellectual mind. It is *Allāh* ﷻ who is the owner of *Tawfīq* and Guidance.

The Beloved Prophet ﷺ and Sayyiduna ᶜAlī ﷺ place their sacred Saliva in the sacrosanct Mouth of the Great Ghawth ﷺ

I narrate in 670 *hijrī* in Cairo from Shaykh Faqih Abu al-Fataḥ Nasrullāh b. al-Qāsim Yūsuf b. Ḥanbal b. Aḥmad al-Hashimī al-Baghdādī al-Karkhī ﷺ, and he narrates in Baghdād from his father Sayyiduna Shaykh ᶜAbdur Razzāq al-Jilānī ﷺ; Sayyiduna Shaykh ᶜAbd al-Wah'hāb al-Jilānī ﷺ, Shaykh ᶜImrān Kamyānī ﷺ and Shaykh Baz'zār ﷺ; all of them concur that in 521 *hijrī* Sayyiduna Shaykh ᶜAbd al-Qādir ﷺ was seated on his chair and confessed:

[123] Shaykh Abu al-Saᶜūd Aḥmad b. Abi-Bakr al-Ḥarīmī ﷺ and Shaykh Abu-ᶜUmar ᶜUthmān al-Sarīfīnī ﷺ

'I saw Sayyiduna Rasūlullāh ﷺ on Tuesday 16th *Shawwāl* 521 *hijrī*; who said to me: *'O my Son! Why do you not lecture?'* I replied; *'O my Father! I am a non-Arab person in Baghdād and how can I lecture in the presence of the eloquent Arabs?'* The Prophet of *Allāh* ﷺ instructed me to open my mouth, to which I adhered, and he placed his sacred saliva seven times in my mouth. After which he ﷺ commanded: *'Lecture to the people and invite them with superb wisdom and advice.'* Thereafter, I performed the *Zuhr salāh* and sat on the pulpit. Many people came to me and began screaming. Simultaneously, I saw Sayyiduna ʿAlī al-Murtuḍah ﷺ standing in front of me in the *majlis*, pronouncing: *'O my Son! Why do you not lecture to the people?'* I replied: *'O my Father! People are screaming at me.'* Sayyiduna ʿAlī ﷺ thereby directed me to open my mouth which I did, and thus he placed his sacred saliva six times in my mouth. I asked him why did he not place his saliva seven times to which he replied: *'It is because of the respect for Sayyiduna Rasūlullāh ﷺ.'* He then disappeared. I then affirmed: *'The divers of contemplation in the Ocean of the Heart harvest the Pearls of Wisdom. Then only do they surface at the shores of their chests. Their tongue becomes an agent to interpret his words and Allāh ﷻ issues the Divine Decree to elevate their gatherings. They purchase Exceptional Obedience for a praiseworthy price.'*

The narrator states that these were the first words expressed by Sayyiduna Ghawth al-Aʿzam ﷺ from his seat.

Shaykh ʿAlī b. al-Hītī ﷺ dreams of the Holy Prophet ﷺ

I narrate in 670 *hijrī* in Cairo from Shaykh Sharīf Jalīl Abu al-ʿAbbās Aḥmad b. Shaykh Abu-ʿAbdullāh Muḥammad b. Abī al-Ghanāim Muḥammad Azharī b. Mafākhir Muḥammad Mukhtārī al-Ḥusainī al-Baghdādī ﷺ who narrates from his father in 629 *hijrī* in Damascus; who voiced that he was present in the assembly of Sayyiduna Shaykh ʿAbd al-Qādir al-Jilānī ﷺ in 605 *hijrī*, when there were about 10,000 people present. Shaykh ʿAlī b. al-Hītī ﷺ was seated in front of Sayyiduna Shaykh ﷺ at the bottom of the platform of the *Qārī*. He slumbered, and Sayyiduna Shaykh ﷺ commanded the people to observe silence and hence, there was pin drop silence; so much so, that people could not hear their breathing. Sayyiduna Ghawth al-Aʿzam, thereafter got off his seat and stood respectfully in front of Shaykh ʿAlī b. al-Hītī. When Shaykh ʿAlī woke up, Sayyiduna Shaykh questioned him: *'Did you dream of the Messenger of Allāh ﷺ?'* He replied in the affirmative; and Sayyiduna Shaykh promulgated: *'This is the reason I have exercised adab. What did the Holy Prophet ﷺ advice you?' 'He enjoined upon me to serve you'* replied Shaykh ʿAlī.

The narrator states that Shaykh ʿAlī b. al-Hītī was questioned about the reason as to why Sayyiduna Shaykh ʿAbd al-Qādir asserted: *'Therefore I exercised adab.'* He replied: *'Whatever I see in a dream, the Ghawth sees it in wakefulness.'*

The narrator further states that on that day seven men passed away in this *majlis,* and there were others who were carried to their homes in a state of unconsciousness and passed away the same day.

Discussion on Sayyiduna Nabī Ādam

Sayyiduna Ghawth, when speaking about Sayyiduna Nabī Ādam declared: 'When the angels heard with the intellect of their ears, the Command of *Allāh*: *'I am to create a Khalīfah and for him, there will be created flashes of lightning of the Shore of Compassion which will flash. When I arranged [Nabī Ādam] and blew the soul in him, then the angels inquired: 'O Lord! Where will this Khalīfah be?' Allāh* replied: *'In the central point of earth.'* The angels, with the tongue of objection, then inquired: *'Are You to place him on earth? How will this lightning flash from a Cloud of Sand? Is sand not a place of darkness? Is not a small portion of sand the centre of defects and not a centre of the unseen [ghayb]? O Allāh! We are dervishes of high towers and the Shaykhs of refinement and purity. We are dwellers of the Station of Affinity and engaged in Your glorification day and night without tiring.'*

The Respondent of their pre-destination, cautioned: *'Your erroneous views has faltered in your reflection. Do you not know that in the earth there are mines of rubies and jewels are found in the oceans of the earth? The creation of Prophets ﷺ were from the same soil? Indeed, the treasury of the marvels of the Secrets of Eternity are buried in it. The body of Ādam, Safiullah ﷺ was created from the soil of the earth. When pre-destination fashioned the image, the sperm was placed in it [soil] verily, I ﷻ am to create a human and on the pages of the slate of existence, it was expanded with the Divine Hands*[124] *of creation. When I arranged it, and according to My Ordinance, by the virtue of the elevated knowledge, man came into existence. His baby was placed in his lap and exalted Ādam ﷺ; and was raised in the period of Sadd* [صد],[125] *and Ādam ﷺ was taught the names of things.*

The angels saw a person who was in the form of sand and these secrets were shining on him. *Allāh* ﷻ infused the soul in him; and for them [angels], the morning dawned from the east. Hence, *Allāh* ﷻ instructed the angels: '*You all prostrate to Ādam ﷺ and observe his Robe of Honour. I ﷻ said to Ādam ﷺ to wait and he inferred: O Ādam! Inform them.*' The angels then relayed: '*Sit on the throne of the Kingdom as the beloved; as it will lead you to the city of elation. He is a lover on whom the breeze of communion of the beloved has blown; he is dear, who has reached the kneaded sand from the image of the angels.*' Sayyiduna Nabī Ādam ﷺ intended to remain permanently in the Divine Presence but his focus separated from his beloved, without any reason, and wandered to other words that: indeed! You will not remain hungry. His enemy slipped into his mind and lured him: '*Must I not show you the tree of permanence?' These vulgar words of the devil betrayed him that your Lord has not forbidden you [to eat from this tree].*[126]

---

[124] Here 'Hands' does not refer to the physical hands. Almighty *Allāh* ﷻ is free and pure from any form or shape. Hands is used in a metaphorical sense for explanatory purposes and refers to the *Qudrat* or Power of *Allāh* ﷻ.

[125] Unfortunately the word '*Sadd*' used by the great Ghawth ﷺ could not be understood, therefore no translation of this word is done. We assume it refers to a specific period of time more likely a hundred years. *Allāhu* ﷻ *wa Rasūlihi* ﷺ *A'hlam..... #Qādirī Faqīr 'Abd al-Hādī*

[126] Readers are cautioned that this act of noncompliance of the noble Prophet ﷺ is not to be believed as a sin as assumed by misinformed individuals. [Similar to the concocted Christian

This tree was a lamp which was exposed to his wife [Sayyidah Ḥawwah ﷺ], which encircled her with wings. Both, then ate from it and were burnt in the flame of fire. *Allāh* ﷻ elucidated: *'Did I not caution you about it?'*

The darkness of the earth had absorbed the unconsciousness, which led to forgetfulness. Since the Prophet ﷺ has celestial light imbued in him, he understood his shortcoming and pleaded: *'O my Creator! I have oppressed my soul in the disunion of the initial abode.'* The noble Prophet ﷺ then cried: *'I do not have the courage to bear the burden of the absence of the beloved.'* It was revealed to him; *'O Ādam! There is a veil of wisdom between you and your Lord. You were in a state of purity with Him and you did not take any step with impurity towards Him. It was firmly established that noncompliance to the beloved will separate the lover from the beloved. How can you live in the home of the beloved when you are noncompliant to him?'*[127]

The noble Prophet ﷺ replied: *'O my Lord! Your determined pre-destination cannot be averted by endeavour. The arrows of your ultimate Decision cannot be rejected by the insignificant particles of excuses. I did not daringly disobey you, nor intentionally, but in an unconsciousness state and I did not oppose your Command because it was Your decision, which pre-destined for me.'* The Prophet ﷺ heard this reply; *'O Ādam! The cry of the disobedient is more beloved to Me than the sound of a worshipper's Tasbīḥ. Confession and regret of sins is in itself, an atonement and I am most forgiving to those who repent. I have per-written your forgiveness and before you were created, I have accepted your apology and have erased it. I was certain that you will be steadfast*

---

belief or doctrine of the original sin] This is in fact the Wisdom of *Allāh* ﷻ that made the beloved Prophet ﷺ and his pious wife forget so that they be removed from *Jannah* and send them to earth to start and procreate the human race. This was indeed an act of the wisdom of *Allāh* ﷻ. It is not correct to attribute a sin to a Prophet of *Allāh* ﷺ because they are *Ma'sūm* [sinless] creations of *Allāh* ﷻ.

[127] This Command of Almighty *Allāh* ﷻ to His beloved Prophet ﷺ is a lesson for the Prophet's ﷺ progeny of the future reminding them that: *'Disobedience to the Allāh ﷻ will separate one from the closeness of the Sublime Lord ﷻ.'* The following Command of *Allāh* ﷻ clarifies all doubt and misconceptions.

in not doing this again.'

I narrate [the above narration] in 673 *hijrī* in Cairo from Shaykh Abu al-Ḥasan ʿAlī b Najīm b. ʿĪsā al-Howrānī ﷺ and Shaykh ʿAlī b. ʿĪsā al-Jowsiqī ﷺ and Shaykh Abu-Muḥammad Rajab b. Abī-Mansūr b. Nasrullāh al-Dārī ﷺ; all of them narrate from Shaykh Abu al-Ḥasan ʿAlī b. Idrīs al-Yaʿqūbī ﷺ in 617 *hijrī in Cairo*, who narrates from Qāḍī al-Quḍāt Abu-Sāliḥ Nasar al-Jilānī b. al-Ḥāfiz Abu-Bakr ʿAbd al-Razzāq al-Jilānī ﷺ b. Shaykh al-Islām Muḥiyy al-Dīn ʿAbd al-Qādir ﷺ who stated that he had heard this from his illustrious father ﷺ in 594 *hijrī.*

Shaykh ʿAbd al-Raḥmān Tafsunjī's ﷺ Claim Superiority

I narrate in 636 *hijrī* in Cairo from Shaykh Abu-Muḥammad Abu al-Ḥasan b. Aḥmad b. Muḥammad b. Dilaf ﷺ whose grandfather was well-known as Ibn Touq who narrates from three *Shuyūkh*, Shaykh Abu al-Qāsim Haybatullāh b. ʿAbdullāh b. Aḥmad ﷺ, distinguished as Ibn al-Mansūr in 636 *hijrī* in Baghdād; narrates from Shaykh Abu-ʿAmar ʿUthmān ﷺ, recognized as Qas'sīr and Shaykh Abu al-Ḥasan ʿAlī b. Sulaymān ﷺ, well-known as Ibn-Anjāz in 639 *hijrī* in Baghdād; state that Shaykh Abu al-Qāsim ﷺ narrates from Shaykh Abu al-Saʿūd Aḥmad b. Abī-Bakr al-Ḥarīmī ﷺ, familiarly known as Mudāl in 576 *hijrī* in Baghdād, Shaykh Abu-ʿAmar Abu al-Ḥasan ﷺ relates that he narrates in 576 *hijrī* in Baghdād. Shaykh Abu-ʿAmar Abu al-Ḥasan ﷺ declares that he was informed in 591 *hijrī* in Baghdād by Shaykh ʿImrān Kamyānī ﷺ and Shaykh Baz'zār ﷺ. All of them agree that Shaykh ʿAbd al-Raḥmān Tafsunjī ﷺ sat on his chair and resonated: *'I am like a long necked heron*[128] *[bird] amongst the Awliya.'*

On hearing this proclamation, a *Walī* with outstanding spiritual disposition, Shaykh Abu al-Ḥasan ʿAlī b. Aḥmad Ḥibbī ﷺ stood up, threw his mantle on the floor and expressed to the Shaykh: *'Come wrestle with me.'* Shaykh ʿAbd al-

[128] A heron is a bird that has the longest neck.

Raḥmān ﷺ witnessed this and he remained silent. He then asked Shaykh Abu al-Ḥasan ﷺ to pick up his mantle and wear it. Thereupon he replied: *'I do not wear that which I had removed and thrown away.'* He then pointed towards Ḥibbā [his home town] and called out to his wife: *'O Fātimah! Give me some clothing that I may wear.'* His chaste wife heard his call from her distant home and threw her husband's garb towards the road. Shaykh Abu al-Ḥasan ﷺ stretched out his hand, took his garb and wore it. Shaykh ʿAbd al-Raḥmān ﷺ questioned him as to who his *Murshid* was, and hence he replied: *'My Murshid is Shaykh ʿAbd al-Qādir al-Jilānī ﷺ.'* Shaykh ʿAbd al-Raḥmān ﷺ professed: *'I have heard the name of Shaykh ʿAbd al-Qādir on the earth and I have spent 40 years at the Door of Destiny, but I have not seen him there.'* He then issued directives to a group of his *murīds*: *'Go to Baghdād and visit Shaykh ʿAbd al-Qādir ﷺ. Tell him ʿAbd al-Raḥmān conveys his salāms and states that he has spent 40 years at the Doorstep of Destiny, but has not seen him going in there, nor coming out.?"*

At the same moment in Baghdād, the great *Ghawth,* Shaykh ʿAbd al-Qādir ﷺ accentuated to ʿAbbād al-Baw'wāb ﷺ [the doorkeeper], Muzaffar al-Jam'māl ﷺ [the camel driver], ʿAbd al-Ḥaqq al-Ḥarīmī ﷺ and ʿUthmān al-Sirīfīnī ﷺ: *"Get ready to go towards Tafsunj. On the way you will meet a group of murīds of Shaykh ʿAbdul Raḥmān with such and such message for me. Take them back with you to Tafsunj and convey this message to their Shaykh; ʿAbd al-Qādir sends his greetings of peace and says: one who is on the steps cannot see those present in the veranda - those in the veranda cannot see those present in the room - the ones in the room cannot see those in the inner room [secret chamber]. I [ʿAbd al-Qādir] am present in the Secret Room. I enter and exit through the Door of Secrets which you cannot see. The first proof of this is that when you received your first Garb of Riḍā [Approval], it was my hand that bestowed it upon you. The second proof is that on a certain night you received the Garb of Fataḥ [Victory] and it was my hand that presented it to you. The third proof is when I put forward my hand to you on a certain night in the presence of 12 Awliya to award you the wide Sacred Garb, which was green in colour with Surah al-Ikhlās being embroidered on it. It was my hand that conferred it upon you. "*

The emissaries of Sayyiduna Ghawth ﷺ reached half their destination and met with the envoy of Shaykh ʿAbd al-Raḥmān ﷺ. They were turned around and went back to Tafsunj to relay the message of the Ghawth ﷺ. When this message was relayed to the Shaykh ʿAbd al-Raḥmān ﷺ, he immediately bent his head in submission and declared: '*Shaykh ʿAbd al-Qādir has spoken the truth and he is indeed the authoritative King of this time and age.*

Discussion on Sayyiduna Nabī Mūsā ﷺ

Sayyiduna Ghawth al-Aʿzam ﷺ asserted about Sayyiduna Nabī Mūsā ﷺ and declared: The Prophet ﷺ was a child and had been raised in his cradle. *Allāh* ﷻ had destined for him to be raised and nurtured in His Presence, as well as to be fed with milk; for He ﷻ had reserved the Prophet ﷺ for Himself. His mother feared that he will be killed; and henceforth, positioned the unattended infant, into a basket; like a dead person and placed him into the River Nile. The Ordinance of Destiny brought him to safety at the hands of his enemy, [Pharaoh] where he was like the coolness of their eyes. He was then returned safely into the arms of his mother with the guarantee that he will not be killed. They did this with an opinion that they will benefit from him. Thereafter, his infant intellect prompted him to observe the marvels of creation. He recognised *Allāh* ﷻ by the light of: 'open my chest'. He was aware of the proofs of the Laws of the All-Powerful because Prophets are created from the Light of Gnosis [*Maʿrifah*]. Their souls are created on the level of the proof of *Tawḥīd* of *Wājib al-Wujūd*[129] of the Creator ﷻ. Their knowledge of the future captures the images of creation and eventually, the imperfect eyes are lit up and for them, a messenger heralds: '*We have ordered them and destiny mobilizes their dormant intentions. Their sleeping thoughts are alerted by decisive laws and then, the clouds of their floods, flowed to the valleys of Sayyiduna Shoʿayb* ﷺ *and*

[129] *Allāh* ﷻ exists by His Divine Being [*zāt*]; His existence is of Himself. As He exists now, He has always been existing and will continue to exist. [From Eternity to Eternity] There cannot be non-existence before or after His Being. His existence is indispensable, i.e. He is *Wājib al-Wujūd* [the Indispensable Being]. There cannot be non-existence at that rank. *Allāh* ﷻ is One, i.e. He does not have a partner nor a likeness.

irrigated the land of the valleys of Madyan and I intended to marry the solid fruits.' When Sayyiduna Nabī Mūsā ﷺ completed his duration, he then set out with his wife. Her pregnancy and the night manifested like the eye ball of the Virgins of Paradise. The eyes of the clouds rained tears; swords of lightning were drawn out from their sheaths and the roaring of the lions of thunder were echoing in the jungles.

Thereafter, a hole or pond was sought for some water supply in order that the darkness of the night could be lit up with sparks of the rock to search for fire in the sacred valley. The breeze and enthusiasm encompassed love, with its head and burning desire for the beloved; seated with its soul. Zeal was indicative of communication with the heart; whilst ego was boiling in the chest.

Only then did the light manifest from the point of the fire. The hunter spread out his net to hunt for the bird of his soul; and that indeed! *'I am Almighty Allāh* ﷻ*.'* A line of words was seen on the pages of destiny; the lantern of Mount Tūr was exposed for the intellect of his soul, the feet of his intellect got entrapped in the sympathetic lover's net and a cup of pure drink was poured in his ear that: *'I am Allāh and there no deity besides Me.'* The Pure Drink of Divine Speech intoxicated him; and in the ardour of inebriation, he began walking. The waves of the Oceans of Affection began scaring him and the excitement of ardent love overwhelmed his heart and the sweetness of Divine Speech tore the openings of his ears to such an extent that they reached his eyes.

The eyes then sort its share of vision, whilst the fervour of the heart ratified this. He then insisted: *'O my Lord! Manifest Yourself so that I may see You.'* Thereby came the reply: *'O Mūsā! First look at the mirrors of the mountain and test the stability of your sleep on this scale. If it is stable, then consider your peacefulness at the time of the intensity of Divine Radiation.'* At the timeous flashing of Divine Light, the Mount of Tūr burst into smouldering ruins and the Breeze of Proximity perfumed the trees of the Sacred Valley. At the juncture of Divine Communion, the gardens bloomed with a reddish colour and the lustre transformed the mountains of Tũr into a lush garden. Owing to this exalted experience of seeing *Allãh* ﷻ, the vicinity flocked with angels.

The souls of the Prophets ﷺ stood in anticipation to observe what will happen next. They heard such words which were dissimilar to human speech. Such an Existence addressed them; that was certainly not a genre of creation. Every direction of creation reported this and everything became eyes and ears. The eye of the heart then looked at the Mount of Tũr and the rays of the light of the eye of intellect, flashed on the radiation of light, on the mirror of the mountain.

Sayyiduna Nabĩ Mũsã ؑ lost his eyesight when the refection of these rays fell on the flashes of the cloud of the beauty of vision. The Tongue of Disposition hung out in veneration; and the sources of the senses ceased; and, so did the speech of Sayyiduna Mũsã ؑ. The tone of voice, glorifying his Lord ﷻ became faint. A messenger relayed information of his true quest and Sayyiduna Mũsã ؑ fell unconscious on the ground.

It was revealed to him; *'O Mũsã! Your belly is weak to digest the splendour of excellent drink. Your poor vision could not withstand the intensity of powerful radiation, which you had requested to be shown to you, so that you may look at it. In the rays of the sun of the feet, the finite eye cannot open, on the tree of the Laws of Existence. You certainly cannot see your Lord ﷻ before death. The vision cannot exceed this limit. In this world, the honourable robe of vision is a Treasury of the Unseen that has been made exclusive to Sãḥibe-Qãba Qousayn Sayyiduna Muḥammad ﷺ. This exclusivity in this world is specific to the Master of Humanity and the guide of Orphans ﷺ and no one can attain this privilege. Divine Decree expostulates: 'Do not go near the wealth of the orphans [do not usurp it] until he reaches maturity.'*

Sayyiduna Mũsã ؑ succumbed to the blow of this sword; that you will never be able to see *Allãh* ﷻ. He was then resurrected by the Soul of Will; stood up on his feet and confessed: *'O Allãh! I repent to You.'* Only then, was his justification gracefully accepted and *Allãh* ﷻ exalted him. Thereafter,

Sayyiduna Mūsā ﷺ wore a veil of humiliation and returned to his wife [Sayyidah Safūrah ﷺ] so that no one could see the effects of the light on his face. The chaste daughter of Sayyiduna Nabī Shoʿayb ﷺ exclaimed: *'O Kalīmullāh! I am longing to see your blessed face, therefore remove your veil so that I may see it.'* The Prophet ﷺ replied: *'Why should I expose such a face for you that was blessed by the splendours of Divine Lustres on Mount Tūr? How can I show such a splendid exquisite fragrant garden? But what you can look at: are the remnants of that Divine Drink with the veneration in the cheeks of the cups that were reduced to pieces. Look at the brilliance of the secrets of my face to which the Mighty Lord ﷻ spoke to.'*

She replied: *'I am happy to look at it and then die because in lieu of a single glance of the freshness of the beauty of your face, it is easier for me to surrender my life.'*

O servant of *Allāh*! If your quest is sincere, be like the daughter of Sayyiduna Nabī Shoʿayb ﷺ. She was prepared to trade her life for a single vision of the face of the beloved. Hasten to the sanctified precincts with love to achieve one's goal; and the zeal to see the face of the beloved with unyielding intentions. Stand on the station of servitude; and strive for the love and pains of nobleness; and henceforward, you will stand next to the sanctified souls.

You will then see the heart of Nabī Yaʿqūb ﷺ and the city of Nabī Yūsuf ﷺ. If such a fragrance comes from them that elevate the light of beauty and the breath of the soul, then its strong fragrance will make you ecstatic and enthralled. Surrender your life in return for His communion; and for the return of the flashes of His light; and as well as for His love. I take an oath that a person is never at a loss who surrenders the self for a single glace of the beloved. The goal of the eye is vision and besides *Sāḥib al-Maqām al-Maḥmūd* Sayyiduna Rasūlullāh ﷺ, no one in the entire creation can achieve this goal in this world. The reference to *mushāhidah* [vision] in this context refers to seeing [*Allāh* ﷻ] with the eye of the heart [not the physical eye; as this is unattainable].The stations of its mandate is vision from the Supreme Court. It is *Allāh* ﷻ, through His Infinite Mercy, Who specifies whomsoever He shall ordain for the experience of this exclusivity.

O sincere *murīd*! Express the spirit of enthusiasm. In the secrecy of your inner dimensions if you are successful in achieving the honorary Garb of Observance: Congratulations to you! But if you have not reached there, then be steadfast on the Path of Truth until you reach certainty i.e. death, *in-sha-Allāh!* You will enter the abode of the *Sādiqīn* [truthful]. There you shall unearth your desired goal; and take the share of the vision of the beloved. Bravery is a moment of patience!

O servant! Imbibe high spirits like Sayyiduna Mūsā ﷺ who firmly pronounced: *'I relayed that to them which You enjoined upon me to do,* i.e. worship Almighty *Allāh* ﷻ. Be a man of Aḥmadī Firmness[130], whose eye did not blink nor exceeded the limits. The initial condition of the Prophets ﷺ [*Anbiya*] is the last step of the feet of the *Awliya;* and the beginning of the felicity of the Messengers [*Rusul*] is the last step of the *'Ārifīn* [Gnostics].

O beggar of *Allāh*! May that night be of happiness to you; that the Mūsā of your intellect be at the blessed proximity; at the edges of the jungle of your *Ma'ārifah*. If you intend to recognize this; seek then those varieties in the pages of signs of the proof of actions. Say that you will act; and shortly, Almighty *Allāh* ﷻ, His beloved Messenger ﷺ and the believers will observe your actions.

O flies of the intellect! Graze on the flowers of the garden and accumulate the honey of *Ma'ārifah* from these gardens. If any *Walī* from amongst the *Awliya;* without the disposition of love, falls sick, we will report it to the physicians of the *'Ārifīn;* and chief doctor of the *Sharī'ah* of this *Ummah*. He will be instructed to read with such an eloquent tongue that, which I have ordained: *'O people! Indeed, from Allāh ﷻ has come the shifa [cure] and advice for sicknesses*

130 To adopt the virtuous conduct of the glorious Messenger of *Allāh* ﷺ.

of the chest and the mercy of guidance for the believers.'

A Trader is saved from a Murderer

I narrate in 669 *hijrī* in Cairo from Shaykh Abu al-Ḥasan ʿAlī b. Abī-Bakr b. Isḥāq b. Naʿīm al-Baghdādī al-Muḥaddith ﷺ who narrates from Shaykh ʿĀrif Abu-Tāhir Jalīl b. Shaykh Abu al-ʿAbbās Aḥmad b. ʿAlī Khalīl al-Sarsarī ﷺ in 630 *hijrī* in Cairo.

I narrate in 670 *hijrī* in Cairo from Shaykh Abu-Bakr Muḥammad b. Abī al-Qāsim Aḥmad b. ʿAlī b. Yūsuf b. Sālih al-Baghdādī al-Ḥarīmī ﷺ and he narrates from Shaykh Abu al-Ḥasan Khifāf al-Baghdādī in 624 *hijrī* in Baghdād; who narrates from Shaykh Abu-Saʿūd Aḥmad b. Abī-Bakr al-Ḥarīmī al-Baghdādī ﷺ in 580 *hijrī* in Baghdād. He states that Shaykh Abu-Muzaffar Ḥasan b. Najam b. Aḥmad al-Baghdādī ﷺ, the trader visited Shaykh Ḥammād b. Muslim al-Dabbās ﷺ, the juice trader in 521 *hijrī*. He related to the Shaykh; *'O my Master! I have made preparations to go to Shām [Syria] for trade and I will be carrying goods worth 700 dinārs.'* The Shaykh ﷺ professed: *'If you travel in this year, then you will be killed and your good will be stolen.'*

I heard this, and thus, returned in a state of dejection. I then visited Sayyiduna Shaykh ʿAbd al-Qādir al-Jilānī ﷺ who in those years, was young.[131] I repeated the same occurrence that I revealed to Shaykh Ḥammād ﷺ. Sayyiduna Ghawth al-Aʿzam ﷺ replied: *'You will leave in the morning and return with goods. I am your guarantee for this.'* He then left for Syria and sold his goods for one thousand dinars. One day in Ḥalab, he went to the toilet to relieve himself and placed the bag of money in a recess in the wall. He forgot this money and left. He decided to rest, and thereby slept away. He dreamt that the robbers had

[131] It seems to be amazing that the narrator documents that Sayyiduna Ghawth ﷺ was young in those days. He was born in 471 *hijrī,* whilst this incident took place in 521 *hijrī,* which denotes that he was 50 years of age. An assumption is made that, in their culture and tradition in those years, an unmarried man was regarded as young or for some other unknown reasons. *Allāh* ﷻ and His *Rasūl* ﷺ know best. [Faqīr ʿAbul Hādī]

attacked the caravan, killed everyone and had looted everything. One robber came to him and also stabbed him to death with a spear. He got up with a fright, found traces of blood on him and felt the pain of the wound. He stood up quickly and looked for his money; and when he did not find it, he remembered that he had left it in the toilet. He went there and found the money as he had left it. When he returned to Baghdād, he thought as to whom he should he first visit. Shaykh Ḥammād who was old, forbade him, whilst Shaykh ʿAbd al-Qādir approved his trip which turned out to be as he had predicted. Consequently, he decided to visit Sayyiduna Ghawth . coincidentally, on his way, he met Shaykh Ḥammād in the Sultānī Bazār who saw him and advised: *'O Abu-Muzaffar! Go and meet Shaykh ʿAbd al-Qādir first because he is a beloved of Allāh . He has made du ʿās to Allāh seventeen times and it was accepted. Allāh changed your fate and your physical killing was changed into a dream and the looting of your wealth to forgetfulness.'* I then visited Sayyiduna Shaykh ʿAbd al-Qādir al-Jilānī ; and before I could say anything, he proclaimed: *'Shaykh Ḥammād informed you that I made du ʿās seventeen times for you. I take an oath on the Honour of my Lord! I had made du ʿās, 17 multiple times and thereafter, pleaded to Allāh 70 times on your behalf until my Lord transformed your murder into a dream and the theft of your wealth into forgetfulness.'*

A discourse pertaining to Sayyiduna Rasūlullāh

The renowned Ghawth, Shaykh ʿAbd al-Qādir al-Jilānī discoursed pertaining to Sayyiduna Rasūlullāh : When the intellect of the possessor of Light [*nūr*] was scented with perfume [*ʿittar*], *Allāh* Ordained: 'I destined to create a human from sand and appoint a *Khalīfah* on earth; the upper Angelic Realm was then filled with light. It was affirmed to the worshippers of the elevated Sanctified Sanctuary that; when I arranged him [Nabī Ādam] and infused the spirit in him, all the angels fell in prostration to him. As for those angels who were engaged in glorification [*tasbīḥ*]; the sand converted into musk in their brain and they discovered that Prophet Ādam was gloriously garbed in a stunning robe; which signified that Almighty *Allāh* is pleased and loves him. The angels prostrated to Nabī Ādam owing to the luminosity of this light.

Sayyiduna Mūsā ﷺ heard the nightingale singing in a melodious voice: *'Verily, I am Allāh and I place the Pure Drink of Love of Eternity in the cups that: "I have chosen for you."* It was for this reason that Mount Tūr was attracted; and at the bottom, the surrounding area of the mountain folded, and stood under the tree of the Sacred Valley enthusiastically of having a vision of the cupbearer. Its state of inebriation shook its sides and as a result, the state of excessive ardour inscribed the following words on the paper of love with its hand: *'O my Lord! Let me look at you.'* The pen in hand, then summersaulted and it wrote: *'You will never be able to see Me.'* At that moment, a light was flashed upon the eye of his intellect and the entire vicinity of the mountain became a garden of Paradise. Upon regaining his consciousness, he articulated: *'Glorified are You and I turn to You.'* Subsequent to the distribution of this bounty, it was commanded to hand over the pen and inkpot of Messengership to Nabī Mūsā ﷺ and instructed him to write: *'He will talk to people in his cradle. Write in the Book of My Tawḥīd, Verily, I am a servant of Allāh ﷻ. Now write these lines in Book of Messengership, I give glad tidings of such a Messenger who will come after me, whose name shall be Aḥmad.'*

The status of Sayyiduna Rasūlullāh ﷺ above other Prophets ﷺ

The consecrated crown of Sayyiduna Rasūlullāh ﷺ is: *'Purity is to Him Who took His servant in a [short] part of the night for a journey.'* He was then introduced to the dwellers [angels] of the skies. When the sacrosanctity of his Messengership was enhanced, it was sanctified with: *'I have revealed a book on My servant.'* On the night when Sayyiduna Aḥmad ﷺ was decorated as a bridegroom, the lustres in the upper heavens tripled in brilliance; and the light of the garden of his personality was adorned. The overwhelming light of the Sayyiduna Rasūlullāh ﷺ, overpowered the eyes of the angels.

It was declared to the angels; 'O residents of heights; who are the ones of the lights of the sacred sanctuary! Absorb light from the brilliant Lamp; as you are now under the security of the *Imām* of the Prophets ﷺ. The Sun of the skies has now hid itself, because of the rising of the Sun of the Earth. The stars of the skies have hid themselves in modesty, owing to the rising of the Madinite Star. The meteor of the skies was extinguished because of the rise of the Mekkan Meteor. Other lights [*Anwār*] have joined the light of Sayyiduna Aḥmad ﷺ and the pious worshippers of the heavenly sanctuaries [angels] have come out to view such exquisiteness, which is referred to as: *'He does not speak on his own accord.'* It was conversed to him [holy Prophet ﷺ]: *'O Reason of Existence! Your Tūr is the carpet [Rafraf] of the Light of Me'rāj and your Sacred Valley [Sinai] is Qāba Qousayn. The nightingale that will revert to you, is very melodious.'* He then turned to his servant; and that Nabī Mūsā ﷺ did, was exposed to you. He received the command; *'The eyes did not swerve nor exceeded limits.'* You are the last alphabet written on the Sacred Realm of the Prophets. You are the lofty sentence, penned by Divine Command: *'This is the Messenger who was given excellence [above others] and your assembly has been decorated in the dignified Transcendental Realm.'*

One of his garb of excellence is that he had seen the great signs of *Allāh* ﷻ. A spectacular crown was made for your head that was never made before. No Prophet ﷺ was blessed with such honour as you have been bestowed with on that night [*me'rāj*]. His special servant [Sayyiduna Rasūlullāh ﷺ] was taken on a journey to the gardens of *Qāba Qousayn;* which other Prophets were not even privileged to smell the fragrance of its air; nor did any one of them were esteemed with the greeting: '*As Salāmu 'alayka ya ayyuhan Nabī – Peace be upon you O Prophet!*' and no other Prophet ﷺ got close to the status of '*Aw-adna – or even less*' [132] All of them remained behind veils. The beloved Ḥabīb ﷺ proceeded closer to the region of – *'Then the Spectacle became closer, and came down in full view, and even closer,'* where the brides of existence appeared to

[132] This is the Ultimate Realm that was destined and blessed for Sayyiduna Rasūlullāh ﷺ on the Night of *Me'rāj. Allāh* ﷻ confirms: *So the distance between the Spectacle and the beloved was only two arms' length, or even less. [The Heavenly Journey of Prophet Muḥammad ﷺ – was with body and soul.]*

him; attired in Reverential Garments. Verily, he did see [his Lord ﷻ] and he did not prolong his concentration, in consideration for the respect of: *'Do not exceed the vision of your eye.'* That was the Sacred Valley; and where was Prophet Mūsā ﷺ? This is the Sacred Presence; and where is Nabī ʿĪsā ﷺ? This is the cold water of the bathroom; and where is Nabī Ayyūb ﷺ?[133] How much did the intellect travel in the fields of the Unseen [*ghayb*]; and how high did the birds of contemplation fly to the lofty gardens for the fulfilment of their desires; and to seek the sanctified, most distinguished and excellent atmosphere? They yearned for the fragrance of the illuminant gardens and tried to enter the currents of the oceans. Whatever attempt they made, they failed to achieve their goal.

The Tongue of *Maʿārifah* then revealed: 'O seal of Messengers! You are the Sanctified Soul; you are the soul of the body of existence; you graced the garden of creation, and you are the eye of the life of both the worlds. Revealed unto you are the rare pearls of *Waḥī,* threaded; and the breeze of eternal fragrance blew on the footsteps of your soul. Attributed to you, is a Garland of Honour as your flag; and shortly, *Allāh* ﷻ will grant you that, with which you shall be pleased. The elevated Angelic Realm was perfumed owing to the intensity of praises of the light of your knowledge; the lanterns of *Sharīʿāh* were lit by the lanterns of your speech and the firmament of command was illuminated.'

The Prophets ﷺ stood behind you in rows so that they would follow you in the assembly with Reverential Esteem, because you are second to none. Then the messenger of Destiny thereby verbalized: 'O residents of the homes of fortune, and Oh! Proofs over people! This is the Crown of Stature; this is the Sun of Brightness and the Pearl of the Crown of Prophets. Thus, look at the splendour of its glory with your eyes; and remove the veils from those eyes; and open them with its radiant light; you will then find him to be invariably a rare pearl, which is the elegant glory of the elite pearls of Messengership

[133] This a comparative analysis of the *meʿrāj* of the beloved Ḥabīb ﷺ; to and from the heavens, extending to the experiences of the respected Prophets ﷺ on earth.

[*Risālah*]. It is for this reason that the frills of the Garb of Revelation were adorned. Recite this verse then, with the tongue of confession that: *'There is none amongst us whose station is not known.'*

Ḥaḍrat Ghawth ﷺ acceded to the requests of people:

I narrate in 668 *hijrī* in Cairo from Shaykh Abu al-Futūḥ Muḥammad b. Shaykh Abu al-Muḥāsin Yūsuf b. Ismāʿīl b. Aḥmad b. ʿAlī al-Qurashī Tamīmī Bakrī al-Baghdādī Qatfanī al-Ḥanbalī ﷺ who narrates from Shaykh Sharīf Abu-Jaʿāfar Muḥammad b. Abī al-Qāsim Labīb b. Abī al-Karam Yaḥyah al-ʿAlawī al-Ḥasanī ﷺ in 630 *hijrī* in Baghdād, and he narrates from Shaykh ʿĀrif Abu al-Khayr Muḥammad b. Maḥfūz b. Utayma ﷺ whose home was in the locality of *Bāb al-Azj* in Baghdād. He stated on 3rd *Rajab* 593 *hijrī,* that he and Shaykh Abu al-Saʿūd b. Abī-Bakr al-Ḥarīmī ﷺ; Shaykh Muḥammad b. Qā'id al-Adānī ﷺ, Shaykh Abu-Muḥammad Ḥasan al-Farsī ﷺ, Shaykh Jamīl ﷺ, the person with the footprint and spear[134], Shaykh Abu al-Qāsim ʿUmar b. Masʿūd Baz'zār ﷺ, Shaykh Abu-Ḥafs ʿUmarī Abī-Nasar Ghazāl ﷺ, Shaykh Khalīl b. Shaykh Aḥmad al-Sarsarī ﷺ, Shaykh Abu al-Barkāt ʿAlī b. Ghanā'im b. Fatḥ ʿAdawī ʿUmrī al-Batā'iḥī al-Humāmī ﷺ, Shaykh Abu al-Futūḥ Nasar b. Abī a-Faraj Muḥammad b. ʿAlī al-Baghdādī al-Muqrī ﷺ, distinguished as Ibn al-Ḥaḍramī and Shaykh Abu-ʿAbdullāh Muḥammad b. Wazīr ʿAwn al-Dīn Abī al-Muzaffar b. Hubayra Abu al-Futūḥ ʿAbdullāh b. Haybatullāh Abu al-Qāsim ʿAlī b. Muḥammad b. Sāḥib ﷺ; that these *Mashā'ikh* were present with Sayyiduna Shaykh ʿAbd al-Qādir al-Jilānī ﷺ in his *Madrassa*. Sayyiduna Ghawth ﷺ expressed to them; *'Each one of you mention your desire so that I may give it to you.'* Shaykh Abu al-Saʿūd ﷺ declared that he had intended to abandon his desires; Shaykh Ibn Qā'id ﷺ pronounced that he requests strength in *Mujāhidah* [spiritual struggle], Shaykh Baz'zār ﷺ asserted that he desired the fear of *Allāh* ﷻ, Shaykh Abu al-Ḥasan al-Fārsī ﷺ confessed that he had a special condition with *Allāh* ﷻ, which he had lost, and requested it to be reinstated. Shaykh Jamīl ﷺ requested for the preservation of time; whilst Shaykh ʿUmar Ghazāl ﷺ desired

134 It is presumed that this was the sacred footprint and spear of Sayyiduna Rasūlullāh ﷺ

for increase in knowledge. Shaykh Khalīl al-Sarsarī ﷺ indicated that he desires the station of *Qutbiyat* before his death. Shaykh Abu al-Barakāt al-Ḥamāmī ﷺ requested for the extinction in the love of *Allāh* ﷻ. Shaykh Abu al-Futūḥ b. Ḥaḍramī ﷺ desired to memorize the Holy *Qur' ān* and *Ḥadith*, I requested for the attributes of differentiating between matters of truth and falsehood; whilst Shaykh Abu-ʿAbdullāh Hubayrah ﷺ intended to be the deputy of a minister. Shaykh Abu al-Futūḥ b. Haybatullāh ﷺ desired to be an *Ustāz* of the home; and Shaykh Abu al-Qāsim b. Sāḥib ﷺ determined that he desired to be a servant of the door Sayyiduna Shaykh ﷺ.

Sayyiduna Ghawth al-Aʿzam ﷺ replied: *'I offer my assistance in every one of your desires; and all these are the gifts from your Lord* ﷻ*, and your Lord's* ﷻ *gifts are not forbidden.'*

Shaykh Abu-Khayr ﷺ swears an oath on *Allāh* ﷻ; that whatever each one desired, they received; and each one was noticed in accordance to the condition of his desire; besides Shaykh Khalīl Sarsarī ﷺ in view of the fact that the time had still not come for the fulfilment of his desire.

The condition of Shaykh Abu-Saʿūd ﷺ was such that, he had reached lofty stations of reliance and surpassed the status of many former *Mashā'ikh*. I heard him confess: *'There was not a time that my heart left the confines of my prayer mat.'* His condition was indeed the same and this was very rarely found in others.

The *Mujāhidah* of Shaykh Ibn Qā'id ﷺ intensified to the extent, that there was none like him in his era. He sat on the ground only after 28 years. In 560 *hijrī* I heard him declare: *'I encountered severe hunger and thirst. I slept a lot; I stayed awake a lot and I feared a lot. Bala [misfortune] fled from me for Allāh* ﷻ *is victorious in His Command.'*

Shaykh Baz'zār ﷺ attained elevated stations for the fear of *Allāh* ﷻ. His condition became so intense that at times, owing to the fear of *Allāh* ﷻ, his brain would melt and flow out through his throat.

Shaykh Abu al-Ḥasan al-Fārsī ﷺ states that Sayyiduna Ghawth al-Aʿzam ﷺ once, caste a remarkable glance at him; which terrified him and he stood up. The next day I beseeched him as to what had happened and he replied: *'The spiritual condition that I lost, Sayyiduna Shaykh ﷺ not only returned it to me in a single glance, but he also increased it.'*

The condition of Shaykh Jamīl ﷺ reached such a state, that he preserved every moment; and to our knowledge, he reached such a spiritual stage that no one had achieved; so much so that when he went to the toilet, he hung his *tasbīḥ* outside, on a hook and we would see each bead moving on its own, in a sequence. This continued until he held them. We saw this several times.

Sayyiduna Shaykh ʿAbd al-Qādir al-Jilānī ﷺ proclaimed to Shaykh Khalīl Sarsarī ﷺ; *'O Khalīl! You will not die before becoming a Qutb.'* I have heard several times Sayyiduna Shaykh ﷺ articulating that until Khalīl Sarsarī does not become a *Qutb*, he will not die.

Shaykh ʿUmar Ghazāl ﷺ accumulated numerous sciences and memorized the majority of it. He has sold over one thousand books from his collection and people admonished him for this; to which he replied: *'I have memorized all the books that I had sold.'*

In the same meeting, Sayyiduna Ghawth a-Aʿzam ﷺ caste such a glance at Shaykh Abu al-Barakāt al-Ḥamāmī ﷺ, that he fell unconscious onto the ground. Then, He was then carried away from the presence of the Ghawth ﷺ. I located him after a long period in the grounds of Karakh, staring at the sky. I greeted him, but he did not respond; and so I returned. After many years, I went to Basra and discovered that he was sitting in the same condition as before. I greeted him, and yet he did not respond. Thereby I sat down on one side and implored: *'O Allāh! For the sake of Shaykh ʿAbd al-Qādir ﷺ, return his senses so that he may talk to me.'* As soon as I made this *duʿā*, he stood up, came to me and greeted me. I questioned him as to why he was in this condition, and hence he replied: *'My brother! That single vision of Sayyiduna Shaykh ʿAbd al-Qādir ﷺ caste on me, infused such love of Allāh ﷻ in me that my soul and existence disappeared and made me as you had found me.'* He then returned to his spot and went back to his extinct state as before. I left him and returned crying. Later, I was informed that he had sacrificed his life [passed on] in this state for the love of *Allāh* ﷻ in 573 *hijrī*.

Shaykh Abu al-Futūḥ b. Ḥaḍramī ﷺ memorized the Holy *Qur'ān* in six months with ease, which he previously found to be very difficult. He also memorised the seven *Qirāts* and many books of *Ḥadith*. Regularly he recited them to the people and they benefitted immensely from him, until his demise.

My condition was such that when I was sitting in the presence of Sayyiduna Shaykh ﷺ, I found a light [*nūr*] in my chest; and to date, I can differentiate between matters of truth and falsehood; salvation and damnation. In the past, I was extremely confused and worried about these matters.

Shaykh Abu-ʿAbdullāh Hubayrah ﷺ was inaugurated as a deputy minister, and served in this designation for many years.

I was informed by Shaykh Abu al-Futūḥ Muḥammad b. Yūsuf al-Qatfanī ﷺ who stated that he had heard from two *Shuyūkh*, Shaykh Abu-ʿAmar ʿUthmān b. Yūsuf Sulaymān ﷺ, prominent as Qas'sīr in *Muḥarram* 635 *hijrī* in Baghdād and Shaykh Abu al-Ḥasan ʿUliyah b. Sulaymān ﷺ, distinguished as the Baker in 643 *hijrī* in Baghdād; both stated that Shaykh Khalīl al-Sarsarī ﷺ became a *Qutb* seven days before his demise.

I was informed by Shaykh Abu al-Ḥasan b. Haybatullāh b. Saʿīd b. Muḥammad Aḥmad Yemenī al-Zubaydī al-Shafaʿī in 670 *hijrī* in Cairo who asserts that he had heard from Shaykh, the leader Abu al-Layth ʿAbd al-Raḥmān b. Jamīl al-Yemenī ﷺ in *Rajab* 624 *hijrī*, pronouncing that there was a person in Baghdād by the name of Shaykh Khalīl Sarsarī ﷺ who became a *Qutb*, within seven days, before his demise.

Sayyiduna Ghawth al-Aʿzam ﷺ explains the following verse in a prolific mode:

يُحِبُّهُمْ وَيُحِبُّوْنَهُ

Allāh ﷻ *loves them and they love Allāh* ﷻ[135]

Sayyiduna Ghawth ﷺ heralds: 'They have seen Him with the eyes of the heart. They removed the veils of negligence from the faces of Secrets; and in the

[135] *Al-Qur'ān al-Karīm* Surah al-Māidah, Verse no. 54

presence of the people of the hidden world, they saw with the mirror of purity. They graze in the meadows in spring at the streams of the secrets of wisdom, where the garlands of intrinsic meanings of the jewels of revelation are sacrificed. The brides with eternal character are embellished; and enlightened with the symbols of reflection. They were presented to such hearts that were not affiliated to the physical bodies; and were introduced with such sanctified souls, that loved the images of the homes. They brought forward images of clay homes from the surroundings of consecrated stations for the intellect. They used the help of the honourable carriers of their courage to seek the gardens of the glory of Divine Unity and; to smell the fragrance of the garden of the *Qur'ān*, they diverted their attention to the minds of their souls. It was disclosed: *'The lovers are the souls and the beloved are the hearts.'* This refers to the sanctity of creation, which is the ultimate goal of the seekers. Thus, soon *Allāh* ﷻ will create such a nation; who will love *Allāh* ﷻ and He will love them.

They lay, asleep in the hidden sanctuaries on the Beddings of Eternity. They were young; in the caves of forgiveness, destiny then cleansed their dirt with the fire of purity, before the particles of their bodies became grains of sand. On the mint of infinity, the beneficent mint-master moulded the Injunction: 'يُحِبُّهُمْ *- they love Allāh* ﷻ' in gold. When they were in the veils of non-existence, it was promulgated: 'يُحِبُّوْنَهٗ *- Allāh* ﷻ *loves them.'* The language of the animals can only be understood by the Sulaymān of his time and the signs of the eyes of a lover can never be understood by anyone, except by the extinct lover himself.

When the Scribe of Eternity wrote with a sanctified pen; and with the ink of love on the scrolls of the souls; in the Eternal Court of Antiquity: 'يُحِبُّهُمْ وَيُحِبُّوْنَهٗ - *Allāh* ﷻ *loves them and they love Allāh* ﷻ, the dervishes of the Sanctuaries of Existence were non-existent. Their Pearls of Existence was hidden in the shells of oysters; concealed in the Veils of the Unseen; they lay asleep behind the veils under the shade of the trees of '*Kun*'[136] alongside their souls. Then the Messenger of Destiny woke them up, and with the gentle fragrant breeze [zephyr]; and they came into existence. The darkness of this mundane world lit up; with the light from the lanterns of their existence. Their souls took up residence in the Palaces of Images. Their purity merged with turbidity; their light merged with elementary darkness; and their souls ended up like travellers in distant cities. When they noticed the Light of Eternity, they became fervent for it; hence, whatever they were familiar with in the Realm of Sanctity, they expressed their desires for them. They spent a considerable amount of time in this state; and the elements of their existence, transmuted into flying fragments. Henceforth, they moved towards the Station of Divine Proximity; generosity held their hands; and took them to the pre-destined lofty stations and embellished them with the garb of love. The elite were handed the flag, declaring that: '*Allāh* ﷻ *loves them and they love Allāh* ﷻ' in the Assembly of Love. For them, the principled rope of 'سَارِعُوٓا - *hurry*' was hung on the shores of the Ocean of Love. The scribe of the Court of Eternity was commanded to record the Divine Decree, and the official seal was appended to it, encompassing the command: 'وَاللّٰهُ يَدْعُوٓا إِلٰى دَارِ السَّلَامِ -*And Allāh calls to the abode of peace*. The preface of this address was entitled: فَاتَّبِعُونِي يُحْبِبْكُمُ اللّٰهُ - *follow me [the beloved Prophet* ﷺ*] – Allāh will love you.* The messenger of this declaration was sent, riding on the carrier of: 'قَدْ جَآءَكُم مِّنَ اللّٰهِ نُورٌ وَكِتَابٌ مُّبِينٌ – *Indeed, towards you has come a light* from Allāh, and a clear Book. [* The Holy Prophet* ﷺ *is a light from Allāh* ﷻ*].* O Addressed! Verily, this Throne of Secrets is placed in the tent of a sandy nature. A dot was noticed with the Eye of Certainty in this Letter of *Tawḥīd*. The Law of the foundation of existence is encapsulated in the following verse:

﴿هُوَ الْأَوَّلُ وَالْآخِرُ وَالظَّاهِرُ وَالْبَاطِنُ.....﴾

He only is the First and He only the Last, and He

[136] The Divine Command: 'Be!' and creation comes into existence.

only is the Evident and He only, the Concealed;.... [137]

Sayyiduna Ghawth ﷺ erases ʿIlm al-Kalām from the heart of Shaykh Shahāb al-Dīn Sohrowardī ﷺ

I narrate in 671 *hijrī* in Cairo from Shaykh Abu-Muḥammad Ḥasan b. Abī-ʿImrān Mūsā b. Aḥmas al-Qurashī al-Khālidī ﷺ and Shaykh Abu-Muḥammad Sālim b. ʿAlī b. ʿAbdullāh al-Damyātī ﷺ. Both narrate from Shaykh ʿĀlim-Rabbānī Shahāb al-Dīn Abu-Ḥafs ʿUmar b. Muḥammad b. ʿAbdullāh al-Sohrowardī ﷺ in 618 *hijrī* in Ḥalab who narrates from Shaykh Sālim ﷺ in 614 *hijrī* in Baghdād; who had conveyed that Shaykh Shahāb al-Dīn Sohrowardī ﷺ conceded that: I was a young man, when I was engaged in studying *ʿIlm al-Kalām*[138]. I had memorized numerous books in these sciences; and had become a *Faqih* [authority] in this field. My uncle [Shaykh ʿAbd al-Qāhir ﷺ] forbade me, in respect of this practice, but I paid no heed to him. One day he took me along with him to visit Sayyiduna Shaykh ʿAbd al-Qādir al-Jilānī ﷺ and on the way, he accentuated to me: '*O ʿUmar! Allāh ﷻ states, O believers! When you visit Sayyiduna Rasūlullāh ﷺ to discuss anything in privacy with him, you must first give charity. We are going to visit such a personality whose heart is focused on Allāh ﷻ; in communication. Think carefully! About the condition of your heart with which we are undertaking to visit him in order to derive blessings?*' At that juncture, we sat in the presence of the honourable Ghawth ﷺ and his uncle related to him: '*O my Master! This is ʿUmar, my nephew. He is engaged in ʿIlm al-Kalām and I forbid him, but he does not listen to me.*' Sayyiduna Shaykh ﷺ posed a question: '*O ʿUmar! Which are the books of ʿIlm al-Kalām have you memorized?*' I made reference to certain books. Sayyiduna Ghawth ﷺ rubbed his blessed hands on my chest and by the dictates of *Allāh* ﷻ! That knowledge was erased from my heart in a modus operandi, such that I could not remember a single word of it. *Allāh* ﷻ had obliged me to forget every single letter of it; but simultaneously Sayyiduna Ghawth ﷺ imbued my heart with *ʿIlme Ladunnī*. I progressed in his august

[137] *Al-Qur'ān al-Karīm* Sura Ḥadīd, Verse no. 3

[138] *ʿIlm al-Kalām* - Knowledge of Theological Rhetoric – Scholasticism

presence in such a state; that I began communicating words of wisdom. The great Ghawth ﷺ declared to me: *'O 'Umar! You have become the last of the famous of 'Irãq.'* Shaykh Shahãb al-Dĩn ﷺ stated with conviction: that Ḥaḍrate Shaykh ﷺ is a King of Reality, who is an authority in exercising his powers in matters, pertinent to the reality of existence.

I was informed in 671 *hijrĩ* in Cairo by Shaykh Ḥasan b. Mũsã al-Khãlidĩ ﷺ and Shaykh Abu al-Ḥasan b. Abu-Bakr Abu al-Thana Aḥmad b. Sãliḥ al-Qurashĩ Hãshimĩ al-Taqlĩsĩ ﷺ. Both narrate from Shaykh Najam al-Dĩn al-Taqlĩsĩ ﷺ who was a *murĩd* and companion of Shaykh, the leader Shahãb al-Dĩn ʿUmar Sohrowardĩ ﷺ in 631 *hijrĩ* in Baghdãd who confessed that: he was for 40 days in spiritual solitude [*khalwa*], under the guidance of his Shaykh, Shaykh Shahãb al-Dĩn ʿUmar ﷺ in Baghdãd. On the 40th day of my meditation, I saw Shaykh Shahãb al-Dĩn ﷺ on a high mountain with heaps of jewellery. There are many people at the bottom of the mountain; and Shaykh ﷺ has a container in his hand with which he fills the jewellery, and throws it to the people, who grab them. When the jewellery decreases by the Shaykh, it refills as a spring fills up with water.

After the completion of my 40 days in solitude, I came to my Shaykh to report my experience to him. Before I could say anything to him, he affirmed to me: *'It is the truth that you saw; and there are more things to this effect, which Sayyiduna Shaykh Muḥiyy al-Dĩn 'Abd al-Qãdir ﷺ blessed me in lieu of 'Ilm al-Kalãm. This is so because his hands are spread out towards Almighty Allãh ﷻ with full authority. His actions are always a manifestation of charisma [karamãt].'*

A discourse with reference to Sayyiduna Nabĩ Ibrãhĩm ﷺ

Sayyiduna Ghawth al-Aʿzam ﷺ discoursed with reference to Sayyiduna Nabĩ Ibrãhĩm ﷺ as follows:

> The Prophet ﷺ was raised in the cradle of Eternal Favours under the Tree of Reverence. He was fanned by the Excellence of Goodwill whose fragrant breeze stroked him with the verse: وَلَقَدْ آتَيْنَا إِبْرَاهِيمَ رُشْدَهُ مِن قَبْلُ - *And*

indeed We bestowed Ibrahim with guidance from the beginning.[139] This was when Destiny assembled the elements of the existence of beings; and the souls of animals in the Assembly of Vows. When the vow of the necks was taken from them by the Divine Question of: ' أَلَسْتُ بِرَبِّكُمْ - *Am I not your Lord?*,[140] The pious and fortunate ones of friendship, henceforth replied: *'Yes'*. Thereafter, the ears of secrets experienced the pleasure of: ' سَلَامٌ عَلَىٰ إِبْرَاهِيمَ - *Peace be upon Ibrāhīm!*[141] The Cupbearers of Eternity distributed the cups of Pure Drink when it was proclaimed: 'وَاتَّخَذَ اللَّهُ إِبْرَاهِيمَ خَلِيلًا - *And Allāh ﷻ made Ibrāhīm His close friend.*[142] They all whirled in the elation of love, and in deep inebriation fell on the bedding of excitement. Their hearts pounded in enthusiasm and the pastures of their intellect were seized by the King of Love. They lay in the pure assembly in the fragrant breeze as witnesses; until the time of their appearance arrived in the era of Nimrod b. Kinān.

He [Sayyiduna Ibrāhīm ﷺ] then woke up, and began smelling the fragrance of the life of the breeze in the jungle of love. While seeking solitude, he entered astonished, in the Assembly of *'Bala – Yes.'*[143] He experienced the pleasure and sweetness of love, together with its concealment. Eagerness refreshed his love; when it resurfaced, and supressed his zeal. The great Khalīl [Nabī Ibrāhīm ﷺ] emerged from the cave in a state; that the fire of love was erupting in his heart. The eyes of his heart; including his contemplation, was staring at the faces of the brides of the heavens, and its companion soul heard the themes of beauty in the following words: *'The coolness of my and your eye.'* The rays of vision flashed like lightening; and this lightning was flashed for him,

---

[139] *Al-Qur'ān al-Karīm* Sura Anbiya verse 51
[140] *Al-Qur'ān al-Karīm* Sura Maryam verse 3
[141] *Al-Qur'ān al-Karīm* Sura Anbiya verse 69
[142] *Al-Qur'ān al-Karīm* Sura Nisā verse 125
[143] *Al-Qur'ān al-Karīm* Sura Aʿrāf verse 172

with the assertment: وَكَذَٰلِكَ نُرِي إِبْرَاهِيمَ مَلَكُوتَ السَّمَاوَاتِ وَالْأَرْضِ *'We will show Ibrāhīm ﷺ the Kingdom of the sky and earth.'*[144] The vision of contemplation, for him then; in the elevated gardens of the fields of the world, announced glad tidings for him. Two flashes of lightning distracted the oblivion of love. Every eye of the heart saw such flashes that complimented their desires; and whatever emerged in the secret eye, reflected as the vision of the beloved. When any image appeared to him, its figure was regarded as a cupbearer holding a cup in its hand; inviting him to drink. The night shaded the clothing of existence with its darkness; and laid the spacious bedding on the floor of the tents. The gardens of the heavens were illuminated; and all the lights were spread in all directions. The teeth of destiny laughed; and faces of existence reduced the zephyr to a state of unconsciousness. The lustres of splendour veiled the clouds; and the purifier of the eyes removed its veils from its doors. The flamboyant wedding tents were meticulously adorned. Ecstatically, the elevated dome patrolled from right to left.

Decorated were the skies with the flowers; comprising stars. The exalted ocean danced along with bright pearls of the shooting star; whilst the attributive stations of stars, marched along the stages of the east and west. Jupiter was deeply intoxicated; similar to a devout lover. Mars was ablaze in the fire of love; just as the condition of an ardent lover. *Surayyah* [the furthest star] resembled an emaciated, weak lover who, apart from having vision in his eyes, was physically disabled. Orion was comparable to the tent of the King of Love; and it entered into the locality of the soul of the lover; thereby possessing his heart. The zephyr was like the messenger of the beloved who conveyed the proceeding message to the souls of friends: *'Is there anyone who supplicates and is there anyone who repents? Come to the door and remember, Love will make the heart of a friend a lover and the fire of love will burn the soul of the seeker. Enthusiasm is similar to the contemplation of the beloved and love is victorious over the heart of a*

[144] *Al-Qur'ān al-Karīm* Sura Anʿām verse 75

dejected person.'

Eternal love manifested in the existence of Sayyiduna Nabī Ibrāhīm عليه السلام

Eternal love was exposed to the existence of Sayyiduna Ibrāhīm عليه السلام; the picturesque flowers, comparable to cupbearers was exposed to him; and its rays of light was glittering on them. In its astounding condition, a military of flowers gracefully walked as though they were on an official patrol. The speech of his vision thereby said, with the reflection of its intellect; if in its travel, it personally possesses the ability in equation to the power of those in authority, he will then move in the stations of the sky in comparison to them. He will then say with the dialect of love in his heart: هَٰذَا رَبِّي -*'This is my Lord.'* On the contrary, if he has no control over his reins, which are in conflict with destiny; opposition to graciousness will conceal him; and he will not be in a position to avoid the injury to his *nafs*.

In addition to this, there is another desire which is accepted by my caller. Thereafter, the descending army intervened between the two lines; and both armies which were in descent, drowned in the ocean of darkness. They hid behind the flanking veils and disappeared. Reality was then exposed to his eye of meditation, and he spoke with the tongue of certainty and clarity: قَالَ لَا أُحِبُّ الْآفِلِينَ -*'I do not have affinity with those who dwindle.'*[145] The moon then rose, and lit up the palaces of the sky with the beauty and radiance of its light. He sent the resplendent army to his presence and he pronounced: *'This is a something of great honour and dignity.'* In the event of if its brilliance and glory being void of changes; rising and setting, and transcendence of the soul; then in accordance to my understanding, I would confirm with my tongue and heart: *'This is my Lord.'* However, the brilliant face of the moon was hidden, in

[145] *Al-Qur'ān al-Karīm* Sura Anʿām verse 76

concealment; and time grasped its light and conquered its splendour. Destiny destroyed the signs of its existence with the sword of absence; it took a dive resembling one, fleeing from the sinking sand of the earth; and the voice of its guide ceased in the prison of acquisition. Nabī Ibrāhīm ﷺ henceforth, proclaimed with the tongue of Prophetic Authenticity: قَالَ لَئِن لَّمْ يَهْدِنِي رَبِّي لَأَكُونَنَّ مِنَ الْقَوْمِ الضَّالِّينَ- *'If my Lord ﷻ did not guide me, I would certainly be amongst the stray nation.'* [146]

Thereafter, the king of the light of the sun emerged in the east, and replaced the fear of the people with love. The restrictions of the heart were opened, whilst the restrictions of the vision of the eye were extended. Tents of lights were erected in their palaces onto the sky. Sheets of Light were broadened by the army of light in the edges of all the plains. Its light spread in the Paradise of the sky in a manner, such that it appeared like a golden border on a black and white Paradise. Owing to modesty for the honour and glory of the Sublime Lord ﷻ, the stars prostrated to those rays. The faces of the rising and setting entities humbled owing to the stateliness and reverence for the Lord of Power ﷻ. The army of glittering stars fled, because of the irresistible grandeur of the sun. The exquisiteness of its brilliance overpowered the bright full moon; and the Prophet ﷺ thereby confessed: *'This is very venerated; brilliant, glorious and extremely valuable.'* If this depicts from the fury of emotions of the stations of movement; and is in dispute with the heart on the path of command, it shall be then voice with my tongue and heart: هَٰذَا رَبِّي -*'This is my Lord.'* When its reign changed and verified its departure; and hid its face behind the veils of the horizon, the hands of dust plundered it. The contemplation of destiny attacked it; and the neighbouring palaces fell in darkness by its setting. The area of the horizon encircled the edges of the sky. By the virtue of the testimony of authority, the Ruler of Admonition declared: *'I do not consider the authority of a kingdom whose conditions fluctuates, hence a supreme Ruler, free*

[146] *Al-Qur'ān al-Karīm* Sura Anʿām verse 77

of changes is more appropriate and a King with solid skills deserves to be more prudent in governing.' A palace comprising emeralds does not change its colour. The Hand of Divine Power at that juncture, exposed the jewels of the stars on the black and white bedding; and the Hand of Wisdom, under the air arranged the layers of the clouds. The dark night was parallel with the storm of the ocean and moreover, it was arranged relatively to the bright day; similar to the face of the full moon on the floor of wisdom; which gave the absolute surety of the trust of expertise. Eternity is not that, which suffices disposition, and cannot be included in *Johar* [147] and *ʿArḍ* [148].

Then, the tongue of *Tawḥīd* spoke with the intellect of justice: *'O Khalīl* عليه السلام*! The colour of existence made movement and peace, apparent and hidden. Two things, loved and lover, rising and shining and the quality of new things after coming into existence, are all in the hands of determination. So, do not suppose eternal actions on your actions and do not equate the properties of Unitarianism with other things which your eye of your intellect sees.'* Then, the Herald of Eternity with the tongue of compassion and favour announced; *'O Ibrāhīm! Travel towards the Sanctity of Honour and request the frills of the veils of Divine Power, concentrating in the meadows of Divine Glory of Unity. Stand at the door of Eternal Quintessence of such a Creator who is matchless in the Kingdom of Destiny. He* عزوجل *is pure of similarity with His creation. Make the intention to revert to your Lord* عزوجل *with placing on your head, the purity from polytheism and declare; 'Verily, I turn to that Being who has created the skies and earth.'* Then, to achieve your goal, the tongue of His happiness said; *'How long will you sidestep those things which are not objectionable? This avoidance is for such a person who has absolute proof of Nafil and Farḍ and whose love is manifest everywhere.'* Why should it not be so, when he declares;

[147] Origin or reality of matter.

[148] That which cannot exist on its own, and which is always dependent on its origin [*Johar*].

﴿إِنِّي وَجَّهْتُ وَجْهِيَ لِلَّذِي فَطَرَ السَّمَاوَاتِ وَالْأَرْضَ حَنِيفًا ۖ وَمَا أَنَا مِنَ الْمُشْرِكِينَ﴾

I have directed my attention towards Him Who has created the heavens and the earth, am devoted solely to Him, and I am not of the polytheists.[149]

Rule over Water

I narrate from Shaykh ʿĀrif Sālih Abu-ʿAbdullāh Muḥammad b. Kāmil b. Abu-Maʿālī b. Muḥammad al-Nisānī ﷺ who narrates from Shaykh ʿĀrif Abu-Muḥammad Mafraj b. Nabhān b. Barkāt Shaybānī al-Nisānī ﷺ who said that Shaykh ʿAtā ʿOunī ﷺ in the morning travelled with *Sharīʿah* [on water] to Nisān on every Friday. His *murīds* accompanied him. He was a *Walī* with excellent disposition and spiritual culture. There were some amongst them that travelled on a lion.

I was a bit confused and henceforward, I travelled to Baghdād and visited Sayyiduna Shaykh ʿAbd al-Qādir ﷺ. I related the condition of Shaykh ʿAtā ﷺ to him, but for a few days, he did not respond with a reply to me. When I sought permission from Sayyiduna Ghawth ﷺ to take leave, he thereby assigned to me a directive at the time of my departure, as follows: *'When you reach Sharīʿah [Makhāsa -the water or river], then you must stand near it and clarify: 'ʿAbd al-Qādir orders you not to allow Shaykh ʿAtā and his companions to pass.'*

Upon my return, I stopped at Makhāsa and conveyed the message there of Sayyiduna Ghawth ﷺ. When Friday dawned, Shaykh ʿAtā ﷺ and his *murīds* as customary, intended to enter the water. There was a massive valley and it was full with water; and as a result they could not get across. Shaykh ʿAtā ﷺ then instructed his *murīds*: *'Return! This is something new and extremely unusual. Remove your head gear; and expose your head bare; in order that we may go to Baghdād and seek forgiveness from Shaykh ʿAbd al-Qādir ﷺ.'* Simultaneously, his

[149] *Al-Qur'ān al-Karīm* Sura Anʿām verse 79

son Shaykh Ibrāhīm ﷺ suggested: *'No, we should go to Shaykh Mafraj and apologize to him.'* When they finally intended, the water in the valley receded to its normal state. They proceeded to Nisān in the presence of Shaykh Mafraj ﷺ. With absolute humility, they pleaded for forgiveness from him. Indeed! This forgiveness, brought to their realization, that it was a great day for them.

The creation of Sayyiduna Nabī Ādam ﷺ

Sayyiduna Ghawth al-Aʿzam ﷺ expounds that; when the drums sounded in *ʿĀlame-Malakūt*[150] that; *I* ﷻ *am the Creator*, a splendour of lights [*nūr*], lit up the upper regions that; *I* ﷻ *have instilled my soul into it.* The flag spread out in the skies and the angels fell in prostration. The rays of this light manifested in the Unseen World, that *Allāh* ﷻ chose for Sayyiduna Ādam ﷺ. The Hands of Divine Power fashioned the body of Sayyiduna Ādam ﷺ with the Divine Command of '*Kun;*' and placed the Crown of Excellence on his head. He was blessed with the Station of *Khilāfah*, dressed in the garb of love and communion; and was seated upright. An emblem of honour and status was placed on his head; the eyes of the inhabitants of the upper heavens looked at him with the vision of veneration. The hands of the residents of the elevated shelters pointed to him in amazement. The recorded secrets of his consecrated face were exposed to them. They could not decipher the lines of the letters of his creation, and could not understand the concealed realities of his physicality. Thereafter, the eloquence of the structure was removed in order to understand the treasures of secrets in the Unseen World. Destiny reverted the claim of their status i.e.: *We glorify Your praises*. By the proof of this decree, the angels confessed: *'We do not have knowledge.'* The Tongue of Honour thereby announced from the Transcendental Realm:

> 'O worshippers of illuminant sanctuaries! This is the first dot that was recorded by the secrets of the Pen of Divine Power on the scroll of the creation of the Human World. It was written with the assistance of the ink of the Ordinance of Destiny. This was the first arrow dismissed

[150] The Angelic Realm.

towards the plains of existence, by the power of the Archer of Fate, with the Divine Bow. This was the first vanguard of images that were exposed to the armies of the humans. He is the Father of the Prophets ﷺ and the origin of the pure *Awliya* ﷺ. The garland of excellence and glory was placed around his spectacular and handsome neck. The alphabets were written on the images; and a dot on the words of the tablet of existence. It is a preamble in the book of the secrets of existence; and on a curtain of the Door of *Allāh* ﷻ. It is a treasury from the treasuries of Divine Power, and a fountain of wisdom. It is a chest from the chests of nobility; and a lamp of the glorious sanctuaries. It is a tongue of the teeth of elevations; knowledge, and a pupil of the eye of the body of the universe. The reason as to why he was exalted was that to raise him from a tiny sandy abode to lofty stations of solidarity, which is above the leaping infuriated fire. Then the hand of the paralyzed clay of the lap of his pride, hung in paralysis; from his honourable garb bags of selected bonded soil.

Destiny decreed: 'Leave him alone because he is to fly with the arms of My Choice; and his dignity is worthy of the elegance of My Signs; which We had exalted and preferred. There is none besides him, who was privileged with this honour; whom We may consider. There is none besides him who is revered; and Nabī Mūsā ﷺ with the eyes of magnanimity observed the Eternal Lord ﷻ; which was generated with intensity on Mount of Tūr for him. Close, did we draw him to us in order to whisper to him; and from the Treasury of Favours, the Hand of Lord's Grace offered him a cup of the Drink, comprising Love. We called out to him towards Mount of Tūr and his exclusive ears heard the pleasant voice with his sacrosanct life, hence disclosing: *'Verily, I am Allāh ﷻ!' And then he drank the Pure Drink of Love from the Hands of the cupbearer seated on the chosen bedding. I have chosen you by My Divine Being with the Divine Drink of Love. And O Mūsā! What is on your hand?'*

Discussing Sayyiduna Nabī Mūsā ﷺ

The companions of the Sanctified Realm distributed the selected Drink of Pleasure in the cups, bearing the alphabets of Divine Speech [*O Mūsā!*] and a call, heralded from the tree of his intellect: إِنِّي أَنَا رَبُّكَ - *'Verily, I am your Lord ﷻ!'* [151] He was addressed in the Divine Presence of his Lord ﷻ; فَاخْلَعْ نَعْلَيْكَ - *'Remove both your shoes.'*[152] The authoritarians of honour, who were in a state of charisma informed him of the nobility of that station, as follows: إِنَّكَ بِالْوَادِ الْمُقَدَّسِ طُوًى - *'Indeed you are in the sacred valley.'*[153] When he consistently drank the sips of the Pure Drink of Speech; from the hands of the honourable cupbearers, the breeze of friendship and love perpetually blew and whooshed: *'When a revelation [waḥī] is sent to you, listen to it carefully.'* May there be permanence in this communication of love; in that: *'Worship Me!'* and this gentle breeze remains procured: *'O Mūsā! You have been given your question.'*

Having consumed the Pure Drink; his intoxication manifested on his cheeks. Owing to the Cup of Proximity, it drowned in the currents of the Euphoric Ocean. Its tradition of a cheerful disposition was obliterated by his armies of venture; for it was close to, in exceeding its limits. If his efforts did not come to his salvage, the sheet of his patience, would then have been removed; owing to a state of deep unconsciousness. The strong Drink of Secrets strengthened his eyes with fervour; and the hermite of his soul stood all night in tranquillity; attentive in the convent of Tūr.

He then placed his advancing feet onto the limits of the norms of the seekers. He intended to acquire that excellence, which the Messengers before him did not accomplish. Then he said in total inebriation; رَبِّ أَرِنِي *'O my Lord! Show me Your glory.'*[154]

[151] *Al-Qur'ān al-Karīm* Sura Tā-Ḥā verse 12
[152] *Al-Qur'ān al-Karīm* Sura Tā-Ḥā verse 12
[153] *Al-Qur'ān al-Karīm* Sura Tā-Ḥā verse 12
[154] *Al-Qur'ān al-Karīm* Sura Aʿrāf verse 143

It was said to him; *'O Kalīm! O you, who was made exclusive with honour! You are subjected to your Tūr and restricted to your desire. Sometimes you say: 'I am the master of my life,' and other times you say: 'I have killed one of them,' sometimes you say: 'I am dependent on the favours You have done on me,' sometimes you say: 'I have oppressed myself,' sometimes you say: 'O my Lord! Open my chest for me.' This path is for those whose excuses have weakened; when whispering to the beloved and ran to limits in obtaining your goal. O son of 'Imrān! O inebriated! Verily, the cure of intoxication of an addictive drink is not obtained without a bitter substance; and most the bitter thing is that you would never be able to see Me [in this world in wakefulness]'*

He then returned dejected and roamed about like a pauper. A fire ignited in his heart and melted it. He was awakened by the hands of ardour, and the breeze of love blew over him. On the contrary, he was summoned to look at the mountain; which rejuvenated the executioner of his desires; and his coffers of enthusiasm were removed. Thus, he pronounced to grab the hand of the one who was drowning; or onto the morning breeze; whilst conferring glad tidings to the zealous seeker.

Then eternal scribe summoned the messenger to admonish the question of the story of the lover; by surrendering it to the rocks of the mountain, for it to be thrown down. The excuses then constricted; and thereby caused more problems. Hope declined and hence, the confrontation ended. Disorder began emerging and there was no dry place on earth, which did not turn green. There was no branch, that did not bear leaves; and there was no darkness, that did not ignite. There was not an impaired person; whose vision was not restored, and there was not a sick individual, that was not cured. The entire dried up water flowed again, and Sayyiduna Mūsā عليه السلام fell to the ground in a state of unconsciousness. When he regained his consciousness, he affirmed: *'O Allāh جل جلاله! You are pure, and I seek repentance in Your Presence.'*

The Meʿrāj of the beloved Prophet ﷺ to the Heavens

The person with Muḥammadī ﷺ and Aḥmadī ﷺ image, i.e. the Hāshimite progeny, is praised by the Divine; signified by angelic signs; and ultimately, blessed with a distinctive degree of dignity and repute. He was exclusive to the *Jawāme'h al-Kilam.*[155] By virtue of his bestowed honour and eminence the pillars of the dwelling sites for existence were erected. Owing to his glory, the structures of the lower and upper worlds were arranged.

He is the secret words of the Imperative Book. He is the epistle of the actions of creation and the skies; and the pen for the composition of the scribe of new creation. He is the pupil of the eye of the universe who moulded the ring of existence. He drank the milk from the breast of *Waḥī*; thereby carrying the Secrets of Eternity; and moreover, the interpreter of Perpetual Speech; and bearer of the Flag of Honour. He is the owner of the Reins of Nobility and hierarchy of Prophethood; the Pearl of the Crown of Messengership; driver of the convoy of Prophets, and Commander of the army of Messengers. Invariably, being the leader of the courtiers in Divine Presence; he is first in reason [of creation] and the final in genealogy [last Prophet]. He was sent with a distinction of a superlative degree, in order to potently institute correct deportment; and in presenting an unwavering exposition to the veils of courage and morale. He reverted difficulty to ease, removed the doubts from the bosom; replenished the darkness of the heart with light; and transformed the indigent hearts into affluence in view of the fact that they would forsake their lusts. Eradicating distress, within the confines of its constriction; he entrenched the imminence of joy, coupled with love. Dispersing from the crowd, of those who were oblivious or unwary, he ushered in the rudiments of happiness. Prevalent predominance of hypocrisy was exterminated; the dead were raised to felicity; and furthermore, he eliminated the designated areas of rebellion.

He raised the banner of guidance; and supervised the ones intelligently inclined towards the Divine Communion. He originated inspiration from the treasuries of sadness; that ensued towards Divine Beauty; and stimulated the enthusiastic pursuit in meeting with the friends of *Allāh* ﷻ [*Awliya*]. He

[155] A person is brief in speech; but whose words unfold in to an ocean.

prompted the eye of love to the field of generosity and reminded the souls of their primordial pact with *Allāh* ﷻ [*Youme-Alast*]. Buds germinated on the branches of the tree of *Sharī'āh,* when he irrigated them. Owing to him, within the gardens of Knowledge, the garden of laws flourished, and through his establishment, the signs of *Allāh* ﷻ manifested and established itself. Through his appearance, the entities of mysterious miracles were exposed so that it may be directed to the elements of the eloquent; and its eloquence astounded their magniloquent expressions. His brief manifest expressions superseded their comprehensive languages; and henceforth, they fell into prostration in respect of his intellectual wisdom. All the congregates of rhetorics rallied around him, in order to procure a share of his eloquence, although in the presence of the rope of the banner, it was ascertained that: *'If the entire creation assembled, they will still not be able to produce a similitude of his eloquent words.'*

After listening to his comprehensive words, the light of the sun of their understanding thereby extinguished; and the full moon blemished; by the rays of his wisdom. The Sublime Lord ﷻ dispatched Sayyiduna Jibrā'īl ؑ along with the *Burāq* to fetch him, and authorized him without any reservations to visit the Beauty of Eternal Glory within the Proximity of Infinite and Ultimate Reverence; where the curtains of the seven heavens shall split open to cordially welcome him. The night will expand its black sheet; the epoch will be covered with veils [time will stop]; and the garden shall blossom with the fragrance of the morning breeze. The indistinctness of twilight shall be illuminated at the crack of dawn. The expanse of the sky shall be folded, with a firm conviction that: *'His special servant will be taken on a journey at night.'* The eye of destiny will focus on him; with the precise command: *'Bring him to Me as I have chosen him.'* Heavens, as well as Angelic Realm shall present themselves, dressed in a Reverential Garb; in assertion to the fact that he ﷺ shall be shown the Signs of his Lord ﷻ. The concealed secrets and transactions, pertinent to both the Worlds; the sciences of Humankind and Jinns shall be decorated in his Hall of Reception, proclaiming: *'He will certainly see the massive Signs of his Lord ﷻ.'*

The Sovereign of the Messengers shall come to Him ﷻ and greet Him. He ﷻ shall be in the Upper Transcendental Realm; Commanding His vicegerents to sit in readiness at the Doors of the Heavens, in order to await the arrival of the Honourable and Celebrated Guest ﷺ. The King of the angels [Jibrā'īl] ﷺ makes an effort to proceed to the curtain in front of him. *Sidrat al-Muntahā* [156] is furthest point of access to the arch Angel Sayyiduna Jibrā'īl ﷺ. Angels had requested to view this lofty station; taking into account, that their eyes could benefit from its splendour. As their hearts yearned, they endeavoured to see its glorious face.

Sidrat al-Muntahā, thereby covered their intellect with a luminous light that encompassed distinguished sciences of knowledge; thus extending to the doors of the heavens. Its splendour obscured them; and through the intensity of its glory, the eyes comprising the bodies of light, viz. the angels were astonished. The aura of an inspirational grandeur of resplendence, enthralled the residents of the upper heavens. Its powerful and exquisite magnetism, flattened the necks of the dwellers of the tall camps. In perceiving the status and exclusivity of *Sidrat al-Muntahā*, the heads of the worshippers bent in the heavens of radiant sanctuaries. The eyes of the elite administrative angels are locked and staring; owing to its excellence and honour.

The designated angels of confidant are assembled in rows and melodious voice in glorification; of the pure group of angels sweetened and amplified. The purity of the spirit of the angels in spiritual ecstasy arose in motion; and the *'Arsh* and *Kursī* observed them; thus swaying in contentment. For his ﷺ arrival, Paradise was embellished. Creation that overflowed with his happiness,

---

[156] '*Sidrat al-Muhtaha*', is the furthest frontier of creation. No creation can exceed this limit. This is the Super Transcendental Realm of Divine Jurisdiction; exclusive to the Sublime Lord of Power ﷻ. It is only, and it must be emphasized that only our Master, the most beloved of *Allāh* ﷻ, Sayyiduna wa Mawlāna Rasūlullāh ﷺ to whom *Allāh* ﷻ vested the authority and granted permission to enter. The world of the spirit ends at this point; therefore it is called the Lote Tree of the ultimate perimeter.

descended along with their families from greater heights to the lower realm; in order to celebrate his vision [*ziyārah*]. The palaces of the heavens were glittering with lights and planet Saturn, ascended with light. Curtains, for the chosen vision were raised and veils were removed for the luminary. *Rūḥ al-Amīn* [Jibrā'īl ﷺ] proceeded to his ﷺ circle; for there is none amongst us [angels] whose station is not determined; and hence prescribed to him: *'O beloved Ḥabīb! Prepare yourself to proceed alone to meet Almighty Allāh ﷻ.'* Sayyiduna Jibrā'īl ﷺ placed the beloved Ḥabīb ﷺ into the light, and thus positioned himself aside. During the phase of the ultimate bounds, the one who moves forward; becomes motionless. The illustrious Prophets ﷺ in their physique with dignity, stood up at the feet of servitude. The faces of the angels raised up with noble feet on the level of glory; and the faces of the lovers in the Station of Enthusiasm were astonished, with the hope that they shall be privileged to see him on his return, so that they may inhale the air of aspirations of his life.

The journey of the Beloved ﷺ subsequently reached such a juncture, which was of an apprehensive characteristic. The reverberation of the pen of *Waḥī* could be clearly perceived. He mounted onto the *Rafraf,* and proceeded to the Ultimate Transcendental Realm of the Divine. With the veils of ardour, sailed to the station of 'دَنَا فَتَدَلّٰى - *the Spectacle became closer, and came down in full view.'* The Scale of Divine Grace procured him to the Garden of قَابَ قَوْسَيْنِ - *only two arms' length,* and positioned the carpet of 'أَوْ أَدْنٰى - *or even less*' [157] The beloved Ḥabīb ﷺ heard the following salutation emerging from the Exalted Divine Court: 'اَلسَّلَامُ عَلَيْكَ اَيُّهَا النَّبِيُّ – *Peace be upon you O Prophet*'. The beloved Ḥabīb ﷺ met his Sublime Lord ﷻ with honour, and his Lord ﷻ hurried.[158]

[157] Refer to *Al-Qur'ān al-Karīm,* Surat al-Najm, Verses: 1-9 for details.

[158] Sayyiduna Ghawth al-Aʿzam ﷺ uses the term 'hurried' which cannot be fully understood. Since he is a beloved son of Sayyiduna Rasūlullāh ﷺ, he will know better, because he was blessed with Ocean of Divine Secrets. The little that we can understand about the word 'hurried' is: that the direct intensity of Divine Radiation at that close range demanded to hurry.

The salutation removed his fear and he experienced eternal bliss. Anxiety was replaced with love. He remembered the dictums: 'فَأَوْحَىٰ إِلَىٰ عَبْدِهِ مَا أَوْحَىٰ - *So Allāh divinely revealed to His servant, whatever He divinely revealed.*' He experienced this disclosure with the eyes of: 'وَلَقَدْ رَآهُ نَزْلَةً أُخْرَىٰ - *And indeed he did see the Spectacle again.*' The Ḥabīb ﷺ intended to greet his Lord ﷻ, as well as to answer to His ﷻ Lord's Sacred Salutation, but his Lord ﷻ surpassed him. Henceforth, he ﷺ opened his sanctimonious mouth; wherein a drop from the Ocean of Eternal Knowledge fell; and the Knowledge of the Past and Future [*Awwalīn wa Ākhirīn*] was entrenched in his heart. [159]

The position of his stately tongue, including his universal generosity acclaimed: *'There is hope in the Court of Blessings and Bounties; the Treasury of Mercy, Sanctuary of Grace, Bedding of Bravery and Fountain of Benevolence.'*

It is only and solely the beloved Ḥabīb of *Allāh* ﷺ in the entire universe who was bestowed with the courage and strength to withstand such intense Divine Radiation in close Divine Proximity. *Allāh* ﷻ and His *Rasūl* ﷺ know best. [Faqīr ʿAbd al-Hādī].

[159] *Suḥānallāh*! A very significant point to note here, is that in the 5th Century Sayyiduna Ghawth al-Aʿzam Shaykh ʿAbd al-Qādir al-Jilānī ﷺ clearly states with Direct Transcendental Knowledge: that Almighty *Allāh* ﷻ blessed Sayyiduna Rasūlullāh ﷺ with *ʿIlm al-Ghayb* – Knowledge of Unseen. Centuries before the birth of Wahabism, the pristine belief of the *Ahle Sunnah wa Jamāʿat* was accepted by the majority of the *Ummah* since its inception. But the notorious Wahabī/Deo-bandī renegades now, reject this Islāmic Belief and classifies it as *kufr* and *shirk*. How unfortunate is it that the *Muslim Ummah* is condemned as disbelievers by these erroneous individuals for subscribing to this corrected and agreed upon pristine beliefs. The great Mujaddid, Aʿlā-Ḥaḍrat Imām Aḥmad Riḍā al-Qādirī Muḥaddith Bareilwī ﷺ has written a detailed book in 1323 A.H. [1908 C.E.] in Makkah al-Mukarramah, refuting the blasphemy of the Wahabī/ Deo-bandī cult. He entitled this masterpiece and monumental work *Ad-Dowlat al-Makkiyyah bil Ma'dat al-Ghaybiyyah – Makkan Treasure on the Subject of the Unseen.* By the Grace of *Allāh* ﷻ this *magnum opus* was translated into English by Shaykh ʿAbd al-Hādī al-Qādirī Raḍawī and published by the Imam Ahmad Raza Academy. Copies of this book can be obtained online from sufipages.com and the Imam Aḥmad Raza Academy in Durban, South Africa.

With regard to the law of nobility, it is not recommended to introduce the practice specification amongst brothers; and in traits of faithfulness, it is not advised to ignore the hardship of friends.

The beloved Ḥabīb of *Allāh* ﷺ then diverted his attention to his favours; and focused his virtues towards them. The nobility of his status and blessings are indeed exceptional, which were specifically reserved for him. The compassionate Prophet ﷺ remembered his beloved *Ummah* in such a place of zenith; where the worshipper forgets himself in the secret communication with the Mighty Lord of Power ﷻ. Yet, he did not forget his beloved *Ummah* in this special and confidential dialogue with *Allāh* ﷻ and proclaimed: 'اَلسَّلَامُ عَلَيْنَا وَعَلٰى عِبَادِ اللهِ الصَّالِحِيْن – *Peace be upon us and on all the pious servants of Allāh* ﷻ.' *Allāh* ﷻ, then addressed his beloved Ḥabīb ﷺ, by conferring the glad tidings:

> 'O Master of Masters! O Leader of the pious! At the beginning and the end; externally and internally, there is excellence and glory bestowed upon you. Nobility and benevolence, generosity and purity are all endowed to you. Did We not open and expand your chest? Did We not raise and augment your praises? Did We not give you precedence over all Prophets in Eternity? Did We not send you as a universal Prophet to the black and red, i.e. to all creations? Did We not strengthen your nobility and status in the upper heavens? Did We not sent Nabī ʿĪsā عليه السلام as a Prophet to herald the glad tidings; that there will be a Prophet who will come after him; whose name shall be Aḥmad? Nabī Mūsā عليه السلام requested for his chest to be opened; but in your instance, We have opened your chest for you.

Nabī Mūsā عليه السلام requested for a vision of *Allāh* ﷻ and it was conveyed to you:

> 'Did you not see your Lord ﷻ? We have made you a witness to your *Ummah;* and in the Hereafter; that which you desire shall transpire. When you have concluded your duty of establishing, and correlating the administrative Laws of *Sharīʿah,* engage thereby in Spiritual Devotion and turn to Me regarding the matters of your *Ummah.*'

The message of love was then circulated amongst the friends. The breeze became subtle by this address to the beloved Ḥabīb ﷺ. The inebriated confidant, i.e. the Holy Prophet ﷺ subsequently conceded:

> 'O my Lord! I am a recipient of Your Blessings and I relinquish Your Sanctity. I am a child of the Cradle of Your Covenant and was nurtured by the milk of Your Favours. I was raised in the lap of Your Munificence and my tongue is locked by the cascade of Your Mercy. My eyes are astonished with the vision of the territories of Your Graciousness. Instantaneously, please undo the knot of my tongue; remove the veils of speech, and support the power of my heart.'

The glorious Lord ﷻ responded:

> 'Look! I have removed the veils of anger, and have duly supported your attributes of par excellence, to the range that you may see everything outside the Curtains of Magnificence; and as well as to observe the upper domains of reality without any heedlessness. Although I have formulated your heart into an abode of wisdom, I have also made your tongue a palace of expression. I have enjoined your elements into a treasury of eloquence; and have composed your praises to a fountain of wonderment. Upon your return journey from the *Me'rāj,* inform my servants thereof; and convey to them the tidings that I am very Merciful and Gracious. Reveal to them that I am very close to them; and whenever anyone calls upon Me, and I am willing to fulfil their requests.'

The Master of glorious Messengership ﷺ thereby praised *Allāh* ﷻ; and applied honorific terms of praiseworthiness; with a tongue of eloquence and professed: *'O Allāh! I cannot fulfil the rights of Your praises as it befits Your Status. You are as You praise Yourself.'*

Thereafter, Sayyiduna Rasūlullāh ﷺ returned with honour to the inhabitants of the world. The elite angels placed their foreheads onto his feet. Sayyiduna Jibrā'īl عليه السلام thereby hoisted a banner of Sublime Knowledge in front of him. Angels stood in rows with heads bent, in servitude to honour him. Sayyiduna

Nabī Ādam ﷺ held a Banner of his Glory, whilst Sayyiduna Nabī Ibrāhīm ﷺ spread out the Ḥabīb's ﷺ Paradigm of Veneration. Sayyiduna Nabī Mūsā ﷺ whispered out from pages of the face on the western side. He looked at the eyes of the Ḥabīb ﷺ which revealed that he saw his beloved *Allāh* ﷻ; and persistently requested him to return to the Divine Proximity. One vision became closer to the other. Thereafter, Divine Power exclaimed to him [Nabī Mūsā ﷺ] from the direction of Mount Ṭūr: *'I have fulfilled My Command.'* Sayyiduna Nabī ʿĪsā ﷺ avowed on Almighty *Allāh* ﷻ the oath that: *'I will certainly descend* [160] *to the dwellers of earth and confirm to them of the astonishing happenings above the horizons of the skies of the experiences of the Master of Qābā Qousayn ﷺ so that they remember it.'*

A messenger pronounced in the presence of Sayyiduna Ḥabībullāh ﷺ: *'These are my blessings,'* and recited the stanza that follows: *'This is the servant on whom We have blessed him with favours. On his head is the Crown of Excellence and he is Muḥammadur-Rasūlullāh ﷺ.'* His incomparable attire of distinction is such that; the vision is captivated by it, and does not slip away from it. The honourable messenger from the Curtains of Creation declared with a tongue from the Pages of Existence:

إِنَّ اللَّهَ وَمَلَائِكَتَهُ يُصَلُّونَ عَلَى النَّبِيِّ ۚ يَا أَيُّهَا الَّذِينَ آمَنُوا صَلُّوا عَلَيْهِ وَسَلِّمُوا تَسْلِيمًا

'Indeed Allāh and His angels send blessings on the Prophet; O People who believe! Send blessings and abundant salutations upon him. [Everlasting peace and unlimited blessings be upon the Holy Prophet Muḥammad ﷺ.][161]

Allāh ﷻ focuses special favours on His *Awliya*

I was informed by Shaykh Abu-Muḥammad Ḥasan ﷺ who states that he had heard from his father, who in turn had heard from his father articulating that

[160] This descent signs of Sayyiduna Nabī ʿĪsā's ﷺ re-advent in the Last Hour.

[161] *Al-Qur'ān al-Karīm,* al-Aḥzāb, Verse no: 56

he had heard the honourable Shaykh ʿĀrif ﷺ confess: I served Shaykh Abu-ʿAbdullāh Muḥammad b. Aḥmad al-Balkhī ﷺ for one year in Baghdād. I questioned him about his initial stages; but he did not expose them to me. In the following year, I questioned him once more about it; to which he asserted: *'Do you really want to know?' 'If you think it is appropriate,'* I replied that the Shaykh ﷺ confirmed: *'As long I am alive, do not mention this to anyone.' 'Very well,'* I replied. When Shaykh Balkhī ﷺ was satisfied that I will keep it a secret, he revealed:

> In my youth, I travelled from Balkh to Baghdād to visit Sayyiduna Shaykh ʿAbd al-Qādir al-Jilānī ﷺ. I met him in a state, when he was performing *salāh* in his *Madrassa*. I had not seen him before this; nor did he see me before. When he terminated with *salām*, people rushed to greet him. I also proceeded and shook his hand. The Shaykh ﷺ held my hand and smiled. He then looked at me and enunciated: *'O Balkhī! O Muḥammad! Glad tidings to you. Allāh ﷻ knows your status and your intention.'*

Shaykh Balkhī ﷺ alludes to fact that the words of Sayyiduna Shaykh ﷺ are a balm for the wound and a cure for the sick. When the Ghawth ﷺ uttered those words to me, my eyes were captivated with the fear of *Allāh* ﷻ; and the flesh of my shoulders began shaking with reverence. My intestines snapped owing to love and enthusiasm. My soul began getting stirred up with people. This condition progressed and eventually, developed into strength, as I fought against it. In the darkness of night, I got up to read my *wazāif*, and saw two persons emerge from my heart. One had a pure Drink of Love in his hand, and the other had a garb of stateliness. The one with the garb declared to me: *'I am ʿAlī ibn Abī-Tālib and the other person is a confidant angel. This is a pure Drink of Love and in my hand is a Garb of Contentment.'* Sayyiduna ʿAlī al-Murtuḍah ﷺ adorned me henceforth with that garb; whilst his companion handed to me that Drink of Love. The brilliance of its light lit up the east and west. When I drank that Drink, the secrets of the unseen, the stations of the *Awliya* and other astonishing wonders were exposed to me. Amongst these stations, was one specific station, where the feet of the intellect slipped onto its secrets; and the understanding of deliberations drowned in its glory. The neck of the brain bent through its esteem, which resulted in the secrets of disposition, to be forgotten by its dignity and values. The rays of its light awestruck the eyes of the heart.

The exalted administrative and confidant angels yearned to acquire this station with backs bent like those in *rukūʿ,* in honour of its grandeur. They glorified Almighty *Allāh* ﷻ with purity and welcomed those in this station. There is nothing else beyond this station, except the Sacred Throne [*ʿArsh*] of *Allāh* ﷻ. The onlookers gaze towards it; possessing the vision of realization. Therein is preserved the status of the connected; the condition of the inebriated; the secrets of the beloved; the knowledge of the Gnostics; the station of the approximate with every beginning and consequence of brevity; detailed with information of some of its beginning and end. All was created therein, emanated from it, and perfected by it.

I remained in this station for some time and I did not possess the courage to look at it, until I gained the strength to observe it. Thereafter, I remained there for a certain duration, but I did not possess the courage to ensure who was inside. After some time, I realized who was inside, and saw that it was Sayyiduna Muḥammad Rasūlullāh ﷺ. Located on his right side, were Sayyiduna Nabī Ādam عليه السلام, Sayyiduna Nabī Ibrāhīm عليه السلام and Sayyiduna Jibrā'īl عليه السلام and to his left side, were Sayyiduna Nabī Nūḥ عليه السلام, Sayyiduna Nabī Mūsā عليه السلام and Sayyiduna Nabī ʿĪsā عليه السلام. May peace and blessings be upon them.

Before the glorious Prophet of *Allāh* ﷺ, stood the senior *Sahābah* رضي الله عنهم; and *Awliya* رحمهم الله as servants in subservience. The Reverential supremacy of the august Ḥabīb of *Allāh* ﷺ thereby impeded to such an extent that they stood motionless; comparable the birds that were reclining on their heads. The *Saḥābah* whom I recognized were: Sayyiduna Abu-Bakr رضي الله عنه, Sayyiduna ʿUmar رضي الله عنه, Sayyiduna ʿUthmān رضي الله عنه, Sayyiduna ʿAlī رضي الله عنه, Sayyiduna Ḥamza رضي الله عنه and Sayyiduna ʿAbbās رضي الله عنه. Amongst the *Awliya*, I recognized: Sayyiduna Maʿrūf Karkhī رحمه الله, Sayyiduna Sirrī Saqatī رحمه الله, Sayyiduna Junaid Baghdādī رحمه الله, Sayyiduna Suhāil Tasturī رحمه الله, Tāj al-ʿĀrifīn Shaykh Abu al-Wafa رحمه الله, Sayyiduna

Shaykh ʿAbd al-Qādir al-Jilānī ؓ, Shaykh Aḥmad al-Rifāʿī ؓ and Shaykh ʿAdī b. Musāfir ؓ.

Amongst the *Saḥābah,* Sayyiduna Abu-Bakr ؓ was the closest to Sayyiduna Rasūlullāh ﷺ and amongst the *Awliya*, the adjoined was Sayyiduna Shaykh ʿAbd al-Qādir al-Jilānī ؓ.

Then I heard a messenger pronouncing: *'When the confidant Angels, Prophets and Messengers, Awliya and Lovers are ardent for the ziyārah of Sayyiduna Rasūlullāh ﷺ, then he ﷺ descends from the elevated Station in the Divine Proximity of Allāh ﷻ to this station. Then, the lustres of the observer, doubles in splendour by his ziyārah. His sacred vision purifies them and through his blessings, their status are elevated. Thereafter, the august Ḥabīb ﷺ returns to the lofty Station of Divine Proximity.'*

After this [announcement], I heard everyone, submitting:

﴿سَمِعْنَا وَأَطَعْنَا ۖ غُفْرَانَكَ رَبَّنَا وَإِلَيْكَ الْمَصِيرُ﴾

> *"We hear, and we obey; Your forgiveness be granted, O our Lord, and towards You is our return."* [162]

A flash appeared from the Lights of the Great Sanctity to me, which made me to disappear from every present entity. It grasped me from every existence and stripped me from the senses of understanding things. I remained in this state of euphoria for three years. I am oblivious of the fact as to how I started to talk suddenly; and Sayyiduna Shaykh ʿAbd al-Qādir ؓ had his hand gripping onto my chest. His one foot was at my side and his other foot was in Baghdād. My senses were restored, and I became the owner of my affairs. Sayyiduna Shaykh ؓ affirmed to me: *'O Balkhī! Verily I was ordered to return you, back to yourself and make you the owner of your condition. I was also commanded to confiscate all those things that are overpowering you.'*

[162] *Al-Qur'ān al-Karīm,* al-Baqarah, Verse no: 285

Sayyiduna Ghawth al-Aᶜzam ﷺ then began informing me about my condition, as well as my experiences in detail, from the beginning to the end. He was aware of every minute; inclusive of the details concerning me. Sayyiduna Shaykh ﷺ stipulated to me:

> 'Regarding yourself, I had requested Sayyiduna Rasūlullāh ﷺ seven times; and it is thereby, you were granted the strength to observe that station. Seven times thereafter, I requested for the courage of your entrance. Thus, you were able to get information about the inside of that station. I requested another seven times, then only could you hear the declaration of the messenger. Indeed! I requested to *Allāh* ﷻ over seven times, until you saw the flash of that light. Prior to this, I requested seventy times on your behalf, and hence, *Allāh* ﷻ provided the Drink of His Love; and adorned you with the Garb of His Pleasure. O my beloved Son! Now perform the *Qaḍa* of all the *Farāid* that you have missed.'[163]

Nubuwwah and Wilāyah [Prophethood and Sainthood]

Sayyiduna Shaykh ﷺ conversed about the *Awliya* ﷺ. He verified that *Wilāyah* is the shadow of *Nubuwwah* and *Nubuwwah* is the shadow[164] of *Allāh* ﷻ. *Nubuwwah* is nurtured and nourished by Divine Revelation [*waḥī*] issued from the Eternal and Unseen. *Wilāyah* is the contemplation and declaration of

[163] This is indicative of the fact that Shaykh Balkhī ﷺ remained in a state of spiritual euphoria for three years, and he was nonexistent in this physical world. Owing to this factor, Sayyiduna Ghawth al-Aᶜzam ﷺ commanded the Shaykh to perform his *Qaḍā Salāh* which he had missed for those three years. Such was the deep love and obedience of the great Ghawth ﷺ to the sacred *Sharīᶜah*. # Faqīr ᶜAbd al-Hādī al-Qādirī

[164] Here again we would like to caution the reader not to take the literal meaning of the word 'shadow'. Almighty *Allāh* ﷻ is pure and free of any body or shape that casts a shadow. The word 'shadow' here refers to the manifestation of the Divine Mercy of Almighty *Allāh* ﷻ. His Divne Power and Mercy manifests in *Nubuwwah* [Prophethood] whose reflected radiation reflects in *Wilāyah* [Sainthood]. # *Qādirī Faqīr ᶜAbd al-Hādī.*

manifestations by the soul; observed with such purity; in that it purifies all human impurities. This is such purification which cleanses the impurities of secrets. Thus, the Prophets ﷺ are the springs of Truth and the *Awliya* are the spectacles of Truth. A *Mo'jizah* [miracle] of a Prophet is a station; bearing the event of *waḥĩ*. The wisdom in claiming the meaning of secrets, is a marvel of Divine Power. It is an evidence of truth and a manner of command. The arguments and objections of those in refutation, are obliterated.

The Definition of Karãmat

The *karãmat* [miracle] of a *Walĩ* is steadfastness to the Sacred Laws of the verbatim expressions of Sayyiduna Rasũlullãh ﷺ. It is an offence to speak about the secrets of *Wilãyah;* whilst engaging in the valleys of its breeze is *karãmat.*

The terminology, *karãmat* is pertinent to the effects of the shadow of the *Nũr* of *Allãh* ﷻ, which falls into the heart of a *Walĩ*. By the Grace of *Allãh* ﷻ, this shadow extracts its light from the fountain of the Absolute [complete] Light. This occurs without the intent of a *Walĩ;* for it is Divinely Ordained and they are used as a medium by *Allãh* ﷻ to display His Divine Power and Authority; which is similar to a light bulb that has no intent in lighting up. However, the person can light it up by pressing the switch whenever he wishes to. The *Awliya Allãh* are exclusively linked, and strongly bonded to Prophetic Commands; absolute information; secrets of radiant sanctified souls; spiritual breaths and pure observations.

The *Awliya* are the representatives of the Prophets; and the receptacles of the left over secret drops of the rains of generosity of the elite. They are the embodiment and sanctuaries of secrets from the Eternal World. They are ones who sleep in spring; and sit in the dining halls of the kitchen, similar to, when the crescent takes its pieces and moves gracefully with the purity of its secrets, towards its resting place [sets]. They surpass their physical selves; as well as from the bondage of their selves [lust] with the purification of their faces; and the light of their souls [progress spiritually] towards the demarcation of their [spiritual] positions; and to their stations of renowned observations. They have established their truthful inner eyes in facing the exhibition of secrets of the Angelic Realm; and, as well as the Realm of Attributive Qualities. They immobilized themselves under the spectacle of the sunlight of the Prophets ﷺ and *Asfiya*[165] ﷺ. The reflection of the original light of the sun fell onto the sub-light of the clear mirror; then the effect of the light of the unseen was embedded on it. Images of the unseen, which manifested were printed on it. Various examples of the secrets of wisdom, inclusive of fate emerged. The King of *Jabarūt* [166] initiated the private gardens of assembly in the shelters of *Malakūt* [167] for the honourable and elite. They love Him and He loves them. For their reception, marques of affection were laid out in the gardens of truth, within the precincts of the Lord of Power ﷻ.

Eternity regulated the scribe of the Chamber of Destiny to write a Divine Decree for the Messenger of Eternity, whom *Allāh* ﷻ calls towards *Dār al-Salām* [The House of Peace]. The Divine Decree read as follows: *'Be obedient to Allāh ﷻ and He will befriend you and He has sent that transport that, 'Indeed towards you has come a light* from Allāh.... [* The Holy Prophet ﷺ is a light from Allāh ﷻ].* This was also heralded in the Cities of Secrets: *'Take provisions, because the best gift is piety.'* They mounted onto the horses of enthusiasm; and the carriers of burnt hearts, and advanced towards the jungles of astonishment. They displayed the banner of: *'O our Lord! We heard the announcer calling for Imān. We sang in melody that we heard and obeyed.'*

The nightingales [lovers] were engrossed in the poetry of love, and hence, with weeping faces, they were riding on beautiful mounts, whilst singing songs of love in the jungles: *'He who is obedient to the Messengers, is obedient to Allāh ﷻ.'* As for those who became concealed, in extinction of love under the banner of their pursuit; they are then called out, from under that banner: *'Which ever direction you turn your face, you will find the Being of Allāh ﷻ there.'*

[165] The elite, pious *Awliya*

[166] The Realm of the Majestic Attributive Qualities of *Allāh* ﷻ

[167] The Angelic Realm

The mode in which they come out of their condition; they thus pass through that abode, although the *ziyārah* of that abode had been designated for them; but the eyes of the heart removed the curtains of secrets from them. The companions of love, in the Palaces of Glory henceforth, served them cups of Pure Drink from *Allāh* ﷻ. This zeal strengthened their Vision. These cups rotate in their heads, which are served to their souls. Life functions delightfully as the Pure Sacred Drink has established its home in them. Tribes are stimulated by friends, and the intellect plunges into unconsciousness by the address [speech]. The messengers of glade-tidings appear from all directions. Entities are ecstatic; and separation perishes. Thirst disappears and the eye is perplexed by the opening of the veils. Divine Drink is permanent and its proximity is closer. Love looted the fabric of the curtains; displeasure transformed into pleasure; the fruit of the jungle ripened, and the *majlis* is augmented by illumination. The nightingales of poetry sang the song in the praises of His Name; and the heart was enchanted. Senses flew away; whilst thoughts were astonished. Patience dissipated and love remained. Ardour, the friend of desire and the associate of destruction, who was the doorkeeper, departed. O servant! When the ardent lover's heart looks at the beauty of the exalted beloved, then the Beauties of Meaning; and, the Meaning of Beauties are exposed to the mirror of his intellect.

When it is thereby polished, the beauty of its elegance is enhanced. The love of the beauty of its face is embedded onto the slate of his heart. The ray of its light has an impact on the heart, and the movement of its desires spreads. The spiritual power in which are the qualities of beauty of the beloved, are aroused. Its ruler walks besides the head, and the eyes engages itself towards the direction of contemplation. The brain is filled with intoxication; the soul gets close to love and returns to the heart; hands over restlessness; and returns it to his thoughts, and to the places of astonishment within himself. It is only then, the enthusiasm of seeing the beloved increases. The soul becomes happy with the excellence of the beauty of the beloved; and this happiness sinks into the organs of power within the body.

Every organ draws its required power from it, and all the senses become imprisoned in its Divine Beauty. Every tongue becomes speechless to verbalize about anyone, except about the beloved. The ears become deaf to hear about anyone else; and the eyes become blind to see others. In amazement, the eyes are sealed in his direction, and the heart rejects the palpitations of others. The skin objects to the touch of others; and patience makes it a dependant. Love becomes its ruler and intoxication looted it. Astonishment overpowers it; and ardent love [*'Ishq*] imprisons it. Love snatches the light of the eye of its intellect, with its potent rays; and his concentration on the beloved becomes the focal point.

The beloved transmutes into the soul of his life; and the objective of the glory of his face transforms into the garden of the eye of his intellect. Enhancing the union of his charismatic desires, enhances the rose of fragrance that is embedded in his heart. His closeness becomes the pinnacle of his desires; whilst aspiration yearns in desperation for his vision. His greatest longing is to be in conversation with the beloved; with the ultimate desire of being in his presence.

The branches of the trees of intellect then spread out, onto the hearts of the streams. This takes place in accordance to the protocol in the time zone of union with exhilaration within the veils of exquisiteness. Branches of love sing songs that convey love in the breeze; with a burning desirous heart of love in the Sacred Gardens. Souls in the plains of the images of lovers, ecstatically celebrated by smelling the sweet fragrance of the beloved. As the zeal of the morning breeze sang, it danced in joy. The intoxicated nightingale was enthralled in melancholy and sang melodious lyrics; adjacent to the cups of Pure Drink in the caves of music. Birds of love ascended the Pulpits of Praises and climbed onto the pegs of observance and began screaming, and chirping with happiness in the Palaces of Secrets. They were influencing their friends for enthusiasm. The Treasury of ardour is accumulated in the plains of

ʿAnadiya;[168] with the Trumpet of Sayyiduna Isrāfīl ﷺ in the images of concern; with Eternal Tongues in the closeness of true pavilions of Authoritative Sovereignty.

O servant! The station of closeness is where people are suspended with strangers. They do not descend [remain suspended] and nor are they the residents of the Station within Divine Proximity, although they are acquainted with its signs. Hence, as long as they are brothers of honour, they are enshrouded by the Sheets of Tranquillity. Until such time one does not hold steadfast onto the obedience of *Farḍ*, one shall not be a beloved of *Allāh* ﷻ.

O child! Beautify that allegiance [first Day of Covenant - *Alast*]; [169] which *Allāh* ﷻ had taken from you. Adopt the sustenance of that milk, and oblige it as a witness. Drink the milk of that breast; because He sanctions it. Where is the proof of the reality that He loves them? My heart's desire is to be informed by the: "*For me*". I need an invariable confirmation from my heart

I had heard from Shaykh Abu-ʿAbdullāh b. Muḥammad b. Kāmil Shaybānī ؒ who had heard from Shaykh ʿĀrif Abu-Muḥammad Shādar Sabtī Maḥal ؒ declaring:

> 'I went to Baghdād to meet my Shaykh, Sayyiduna Shaykh ʿAbd al-Qādir al-Jilānī ؓ. For a certain duration, I lived in his company. When I intended to return to Cairo alone, I sought his permission to leave. Sayyiduna Shaykh ؓ thereby advised me: *'Do not ask anyone for anything,'* and then he placed his two fingers on my lips and instructed me to suck onto them. I did as he had ordained, and left Baghdād for Cairo. My

[168] This is such an esoteric place, of which the masses do not have any information. It is only the elite *Awliya*, like Sayyiduna Sultān al-ʿĀrifīn Ghawth al-Aʿzam ؓ who are aware of such places. He knows better where this place is, and what it looks like as he speaks of it. No explanation can be rendered about it. # [Faqīr ʿAbd al-Hādī al-Qādirī]

[169] *Al-Qur'ān al-Karīm,* Al-Aʿrāf, Verse no. 172 أَلَسْتُ بِرَبِّكُمْ قَالُوا بَلَىٰ - *"Am I not your Lord?"; they all said, "Yes surely You are, why not?*

condition became such; that I did not eat nor drink anything all the way, and I felt very strong.'

Intellect, Sharaḥ and Prophethood

Sayyiduna Ghawth al-Aᶜzam ﷺ discoursed about the intellect, *Sharī'aḥ* [Divine Law] and the Divinely Ordained institution of Prophethood.

Intellect

He professed that the intellect is a bright shining light [*nūr*], which emanates from the sides of the boundaries of maximum limits of contemplation [*fikr*]. The rays of its presence polishes the Mirror of Guidance. It is at that juncture, that the people of intellect receive the light of intensity, in order to come out of the darkness of matters and; as well as out of the existence of entities; in so much so, that the bird of their success develops wings in order to fly; and their faces, through the dawn of realization, illumes. Intellect is an invisible bird that cannot be hunted without the support of the Eternal net. Intellect is a Stately guest, which is unable to fly through the Divine Grace of the Gracious Lord ﷻ. It has the Angelic attributes of the appraising and illuminant angels. It is classified as the life of your pure soul, and the Jibrā'īl of your heart. It takes the revelation from the heights of the heavens, and reveals it to the emissaries of the heart. It descends with the receiving of unseen gifts from your Lord ﷻ; and renews your imperceptible qualities with refined attributes. It converts the beads of knowledge to precious gems. It is justice, and a treasury of the tongue of virtue; comparable to the bounties of wisdom. It is a place of security with blessings; a pillar of contemplation; the secret proof of understanding, and the interpreter of the Sacred Law. By the testimony of the intellect, destiny has ordained to instruct the Commander of Information.

Its Imperial Honour is unparalled in the Kingdom, comprising the Perfection of Infinity. The Sovereigns of Authority patrol through its pastures, whilst the birds of eloquence, encircle it. The children of knowledge sip onto its milk;

i.e. the Gifts of Guidance. Praises in reference to the Wrath of Dominance, destroyed its opponents and enemies; as the stations of both worlds are linked to its rope of support.

Prophethood [Nubuwwah]

Nubuwwah is a lustre of the Lustres of Honour and it bears the stamp; i.e. the Seal of the Sanctified Soul [170]. Its powers execute immense duties of the Sublime Lord ﷻ. Its meaning is superbly extensive, and its external is a disciple [*murĩd*] of the Actions of *Allãh* ﷻ. It obliterates obsolete [incorrect] norms and practices; for its internal is close to *Waḥĩ* [Divine Revelation]. Prophethood is a secret of Eternity and the unseen [*ghayb*] of the Sayyiduna Jibrã'ĩl ﷺ [*Rũḥ al-Quds*] and the manifestation of Divine Ordinance. It is an exposure of the ornamental meaning of destiny; and the landing place of the perception of the Secrets of Authority. It is a virtuous place between infinite and finite.

Waḥĩ - Revelation

Waḥĩ is categorized as a radiant full moon; on the threshold of Prophethood [*Nubuwwah*], which rises on the firmament of Messengership [*Risãlah*], and it is received from Almighty *Allãh* ﷻ. Sayyiduna Jibrã'ĩl ﷺ [*Rũḥ al-Quds*] is imbued with it, and he extends issues that are complex to it. Concealed secrets emerge from its precincts, which exposes the Keys of Eternity. It is deduced from this, that information of the composition of elements of the transactions of the universe, in various sciences of knowledge; intellects; worlds; signs; proofs; customs; confederates; composites and duplicates are determined. Through the reality of *Waḥĩ*, the meanings of the Divine Unity of *Allãh* ﷻ are uncovered. Divine Secrets do not disclose, without the mode of direct *Waḥĩ*. It is a messenger of Eternity, which is linked to the arcane transactions of the treasury of Sempiternal Secrets in the Domains of the Unseen Eternal Secrets. It splits open, the secrets from the hands of the Trustee of the Kingdom; and

170 Sayyiduna Jibrã'ĩl ﷺ

remains ahead of the army of angels for those whom the Scribe of Destiny has recorded; in the Assembly of Eternity, to be relayed to the *Rusul* [Messengers]. Its light, thereby polishes the mirror of their hearts. *Waḥĩ* relays information about the details of the conditions of both the worlds; i.e. pertaining to the details of the Laws of people and secondly, information pertinent to both the worlds. Thus, the luminosity of its light has an effect on the purity of the jewels of the heart. Its eyes of kindness observe the Cumbersome Signs of its Lord ﷻ and thus, meets with the companions of the highest ranking in paradise. At this moment, the heart of the *Nabĩ* enhances further into a niche of light. In the niche is the Glass of Prophethood [*Nubuwwah*], and in the glass is a light of the Lamp of Messengership [*Risãlah*], which is suspended by the tail end of the wick of *Waḥĩ*. *Waḥĩ* is the mysterious secret of the disseminator of *Waḥĩ* [*Allãh* ﷻ].

The exalted Prophets عليهم السلام are ones who drink milk from the breasts of the mysterious Eternal Domicile; and sit next to Sayyiduna Jibrã'ĩl عليه السلام who is an embodiment of the secret of *Waḥĩ*. He is the Ambassador of Truth and the pillars of the canopies of the upper heavens cannot be firm without his power.

He is the pillar of the expanse of Nobility; and it is positioned owing to his esteem. No superb faced angel can remain in the exalted sanctuaries, unless his glory is present with them; and thus, does not take his shade, in engaging in lofty *tasbĩḥ*. His attribute of splendour is compassionate to them. No friend [Prophet] has ascended the heights of Divine Proximity without its support; being his ladder. There is no *Walĩ* on his journey who does not use this ladder on his path to *Allãh* ﷻ.

Without its excellence, the stability of pillars is not possible for the virtuosity of the *Karãmat* of any human and the strength of the foundation of the status of the servants is not achieved; without the foundation laid by Sayyiduna Ibrãhĩm عليه السلام.

Alcohol becomes Vinegar.

I was informed by Shaykh Abu al-Ḥasan b. Abu-Bakr Abharī ﷺ who narrates from Qāḍī al-Quḍāt Shaykh Abu-Sālih Nasar Jilānī ﷺ, that he had heard from his father, Sayyiduna Shaykh Tāj al-Dīn ʿAbd al-Razzāq Jilānī ﷺ, stating that his father, Sayyiduna Shaykh Muḥiyy al-Dīn ʿAbd al-Qādir al-Jilānī ﷺ, left one day for *Jumʿāh Salah*. My two brothers, Sayyid ʿAbd al-Wah'hāb, Sayyid ʿĪsā and myself were with him. On the way we saw the courtiers and other officials of the Sultan moving with three barrels of alcohol. Sayyiduna Shaykh ﷺ instructed them to stop by and they began hastening away; in fear. Sayyiduna Ghawth ﷺ then commanded the animals that carried the barrels to stop; and with immediate effect, they stopped their strides. The courtier consistently beated them, but they refused to even move a step ahead. All of them began to experience severe colic pains; and as a result, began rolling with pain on the ground. They began screaming, whilst reciting the *tasbīḥ* in repentance.

Their pain subsided and the alcohol miraculously turned into vinegar. They opened the barrels and discovered that all their alcohol had transformed into vinegar. This news reached the Sultān who wept in fear. Thereby, he visited Sayyiduna Shaykh ﷺ and sat in his presence with utmost respect and humility.

Discussion of Umm al-Moʿminīn Sayyidah ʿĀ'īeshah ﷺ

Haḍrate Ghawth ﷺ addressed about Umm al-Moʿminīn Sayyidah ʿĀ'īeshah ﷺ as follows: Once, Sayyiduna Rasūlullāh ﷺ intended to travel to some place. He took Sayyidah ʿĀ'īeshah ﷺ along with him. The beloved Prophet ﷺ issued a command to his servant, Sayyiduna Mastaḥ ﷺ to take charge of the camel that carried her veiled cradle [as was it the tradition of that time]. At a place of recess, the caravan stopped. Sayyiduna Mastaḥ ﷺ rested, since he was overpowered by sleep.

While they were asleep, Divine Ordinance compelled Sayyidah ʿĀ'īeshah Siddiqah ﷺ to leave her cradle owing to the call of nature, so she walked out alone. On her way, the chain of her necklace broke through the Divine Hand, and its beads scattered on the ground. She began gathering the beads. Destiny issued instructions to Sayyiduna Jibrā'īl ﷺ that one of beads from the necklace of Lady ʿĀ'īeshah ﷺ was lost; and that he should safeguard it. Sayyiduna Mastaḥ ﷺ awoke and prepared the camel to leave; devoid of the fact that Sayyidah Ā'īeshah Siddiqah ﷺ was not present therein. They left and upon reaching Madinah Munawwarah, he discovered her absence in the cradle. Hence, he set out to look for her. Destiny arouse the Treasury of Secrets; and the malicious ones promulgated false allegations against her.

When the news reached the one who drinks milk from the breast of *Waḥī*, the guardian of Secret Information [*ghayb*] as well as the carrier of the Banner of Glorification [Sayyiduna Rasūlullāh ﷺ], observed the eyes of the false allegations of the opponents; and simultaneously perceived their internal mischievous curtains of *shirk.* This aggrieved his sanctified heart and his intellect was wounded by the spear of dejection. The glass of his heart shattered, whilst his accumulated commands fell into pieces. Fundamental love and compassion for his beloved wife; signalled to her in secrecy to relocate to her father's home. He assured her that Sayyiduna Jibrā'īl ﷺ will soon bring down a revelation [*Waḥī*], pertinent to the issue in question.

The pious wife's eyes flowed with tears; the light of her day turned into night and the tranquillity of her night turned into turmoil. Her painful breaths increased, her patience diminished and she despondently cried out to the beloved Prophet ﷺ:*'Why are you abandoning me when I have not committed any sin? I have not transgressed. Is my beloved listening to the accusations of the antagonists and deserting me?'* It was said to her; *'O Siddiqah and O real Siddiqah! Acquittal comes according to the degree of love and victory is under the armpit of patience.'* When she was questioned about what had transpired, her anger and her patience had become apprehensive. Her breathing intensified; and the stars of her senses drowned. Tears of the fire of comprising her pain, began to flow; the upright beams of her chastity bent; and the period of separation from her beloved increased. The milk of the nurturing breast dried up, and she implored: *'O my Lord! It is from you that the destitute seek help and it is Your Honourable Court that the oppressed take shelter. Who is there besides You that removes the pain of the distressed and is there anyone besides You who will accept the duas of the perturbed? You are fully aware of my chastity and knows more about me that my plea.'*

She held onto the Yaʿqūbī dome and separation caused a Yūsufī condition[171]. Her dome became a prison of the sadness of Nabī Yūsuf ﷺ. The breeze of the Ḥabīb ﷺ propelled towards her and he questioned: '*What is your condition?*' She replied:

> 'I was raised within the veils of eloquence; and I dwell in it, which is more difficult than the pronunciation of the letter ḍaad [ض]. The ت is for the addressed [مخاطب]; and the ك is for the distant absent [غيب بعيد]. Where is the ت of انت, the ك of the ذالك, the ها of هذا and the ك of تيكم ? The grouping of م in each of the afore-mentioned, does not make one specific.
>
> O my Lord! I was the flower of love of the colour [black] of the eye of the one who is leaving me [the Ḥabīb ﷺ]; and the ulterior motives of the soiled hearts of enemies. The condition of time, changes constantly and the harvest is that; which is always victorious. 'O my Lord! The ocean of my worries has drowned me and the heat of my sadness has burnt me. The sadness of my heart has made me depressed.'

The angels of the heavens, thus screamed and the occupants of the glorious courts began reciting various *tasbīḥs*. The dervishes of the Luminous [*Nūrī*] Sanctuaries were petrified and the Spiritual souls declared: '*He is the Glorified Lord Who cements the broken hearts and makes the insignificant honourable. O my Lord! The clean heart of the pure bedding of Nubuwwah has been soiled and the atom of the intellect of the pearl of the ocean of excellence has cracked. The accusation of the hypocrites has withered the Prophetic Rose. The hypocrites have snatched away the milk of the breast of Waḥī from its suckling dependants.*' It was decreed to the

171 Sayyiduna Ghawth ﷺ is portraying the picture of the dejection of Sayyiduna Nabī Yaʿqūb ﷺ and distress of Sayyiduna Nabī Yūsuf ﷺ when he was imprisoned in Egypt.

Ambassador of the Divine Domain; the Commander and Chief of the angels: *'O Jibrā'īl! Take along with you from the Secret Tablet of Records, Slates with the acquittal of faults; a pure verse in the Undisclosed Language, because I have already ordained in Eternity and primordial Destiny that I have engraved [acquittal of purity] on the clothing of his wife, Lady ʿĀ'īeshah.'* The Messenger of Eternity thereby descended with the verses of *Sura Nūr,* and revealed it to the Incomparable Precious Creation, Sayyiduna Muḥammad ﷺ.

When Sayyidah ʿĀ'īeshah ﷺ heard the soft soothing sound of this glad-tiding, she articulated: *'Pure is His Being who comforts the broken heart and gives honour to the insignificant. He gives justice to the oppressed and removes grief. I take an oath in the name of Allāh! My exalted sanctified Lord* ﷻ *will reveal a verse of the Holy Qur'ān concerning me and shall mention me in a Waḥī to His beloved Prophet* ﷺ*. But I was certain that Sayyiduna Rasūlullāh* ﷺ *shall be informed of my acquittal in a dream.'* The oppressed must henceforth, not lose hope in the assistance of *Allāh* ﷻ. The suppressed always places his trust and hope in patience; for whatever is contained in the curtains of Destiny; is subjected to changes during the day and night.

Maʿārifah and inebriation

I was informed by Shaykh Abu al-Ḥasan ʿAlī b. Muḥammad b. Azūmar ؒ who states that had he heard from his Shaykh, Sayyiduna ʿAbd al-Qādir al-Jilānī ؓ and I was informed by Shaykh ʿAbdullāh b. Muḥammad b. ʿAlī Tawḥīdī ؒ who narrates from his maternal uncle Qāḍī al-Qudāt Sayyid Abu-Sāliḥ Nasar b. Al-Ḥāfiz Abu-Bakr ʿAbd al-Razzāq al-Jilānī ؒ. He confessed that he had heard Shaykh ʿĀrif ʿUthmān Sarīfīnī ؒ state: In the early stages; my condition was such that, one night: I was outside in Sarīfīn, lying on my back, I saw 5 pigeons flying over me. I heard one of them professing eloquently, similar to that of the speaking of a human:

سبحان من عنده خزائن كل شيء وما ينزله الا بقدر معلوم

Glorified is He who has the treasuries of everything.
And He brings it down according to a known method.

The second pigeon resonated:

سبحان من اعطی کل شیء خلقه ثمّ هدیٰ

Glorified is He who has created everything and then gave guidance.

The third one pronounced:

سبحان من بعث الانبیآء حجة علی الخلق و فضل علیهم محمد صلی الله علیه و سلم

Glorified is He who has sent the Prophets as proof to creation and gave excellence to Sayyiduna Muḥammad ﷺ above them all.

I heard the fourth one exclaim:

كُلُّ مَا كَانَ فِي الدُّنْيَا بَاطِلٌ اِلَّا مَا كَانَ لِلّٰهِ وَرَسُوْلِهٖ

All things in the world are useless beside what is with for Allāh and His Rasūl.

And I heard from the fifth, the confession:

یا اهل الغفلة عن مولاکم قوموا الیٰ ربّکم ربٌّ کریمٌ یعطی الجزیل و یغفر الذنب العظیم

O negligent of Allāh! Stand up in attention to your Lord Who is very compassionate and bestows you with abundance and He forgives major sins.

I heard this, and dropped unconscious. After regaining consciousness, the love for this world and everything therein, disappeared from my heart. In the morning I entered into a pact with *Allāh* ﷻ, that I shall bequeath my hands to the hands of such a Shaykh [*Murshid*] who will disclose the path to *Allāh* ﷻ to me. I set off from there; and I did not know, as to where I was going to. Unexpectedly, I then met an illustrious and remarkable personality who greeted me: *'As Salāmu 'Alaykum O 'Uthmān!'* I answered to him and exclaimed: *'I gave you an oath and ask who you are? How did you know my name? I have not met you before nor did you meet me.'* He informed: *'I am Khiḍar and was just now with Shaykh 'Abd al-Qādir. He declared to me: 'O Abu al-'Abbās! Tonight a person amongst the people of Sarīfīn whose name is 'Uthmān has been drawn. His concentration is towards Allāh ﷻ and he is accepted by Allāh ﷻ. He has been called from the seven skies; 'O my servant! You have come happily' He has made a pact with Allāh ﷻ that he will offer himself to such a person who will lead him to Allāh ﷻ.*

Hence, go to him and you will find him on the way and bring him to me.' Sayyiduna Khiḍar ﷺ then affirmed: *'O ʿUthmān! In this time and age, Shaykh ʿAbd al-Qādir is the leader of the ʿĀrifīn [Gnostics] and he is the Qibla [focal point] of those who come to him. You must present yourself to him and make it your earnest duty; and a compulsion to honour and revere him.'* Thereafter, I remembered nothing, except being present within a short space of time in Baghdād. Thereafter, Sayyiduna Khiḍar ﷺ disappeared.

I presented myself to Sayyiduna Shaykh ʿAbd al-Qādir ؓ who divulged to me: *'Congratulations to such a person who's Lord ﷻ had absorbed him with the tongues of birds and accumulated lots of virtues for him. O ʿUthmān! Soon Allāh ﷻ will give you a murīd whose name shall be ʿAbd al-Ghanī b. Nuqta. He will surpass a number of Awliya. Allāh ﷻ will express pride regarding him to the angels.'* Thereafter Sayyiduna Ghawth ؓ placed a hat on my head, and by virtue of it being placed on my head, I experienced a cold sensation in my palate which progressed to my heart. The condition of the Angelic Realm [*ʿĀlame-Malakūt*] was then exposed to me. I heard the entire universe with all its entities, glorifying [*tasbīḥ*] *Allāh* ﷻ in different languages. I was on the verge of losing my senses, when Sayyiduna Ghawth ؓ placed cotton wool onto me; which he had possessed in his hand. *Allāh* ﷻ, thereby stabilized my senses, and strengthened my courage.

Sayyiduna Ghawth ؓ confined me then, to sit in seclusion; wherein I spent many months. I swear an oath that I have not found anything in me externally or internally; of which Sayyiduna Shaykh ؓ did not inform me about; before I could express a single word. Furthermore, there was no station that I had reached, nor did I have an experience of any secret exposed to me; of which Sayyiduna Ghawth ؓ did not envisage its details in advance. He also solved its difficulties and explained its origins and branches [pros and cons]. Continuously, he conveyed me from one station to another, which was encompassed by *Allāh's* ﷻ Knowledge. He had also informed me about all experiences that I shall encounter. Thirty years later, all his predictions unfolded precisely, identical to that, of which he had previously informed me about. In estimation of the timespan, after wearing his Sacred Sūfī Garb [*khirqah*], and the Sūfī Garb that Shaykh Ibn Nuqta ﷺ wore from me, there was a difference of 25 years.

Wisāl – Divine Communion

Sayyiduna Ghawth al-Aʿzam ﷺ, conversed on *wisāl,* and highlighted the following:

> When the breeze of *wisāl* [communion] blows on the homes of the *mushrikīn*, then it cries out enthusiastically, and when the desolate ones reflect on the nights of communion, they burst out crying. When the strings of passion, perceive Eternal love; and their species stick onto the assembly of love; and when it mounts in the presence of the ones who drinks milk from the breasts of love; the trees of intellect then sway in the gardens of the hearts. The branches of the spirit advances into the containers of images. The jewels of the hearts rave with gratification in the palaces of images. The brilliance of unveiling [*kashf*] burns the liver with the sparks of love. The particles, comprising the components of people; are burnt by the lightning of wonderment. Existence, together with its subordinate becomes ecstatic. Arrows of the archers of love, wound the intimacy of the lovers. The foundation of the pillars of the heart is shaken, whilst the eyes, by the intoxication of its vision are in a state of astonishment. The souls are attentive to its question as follows: what phenomenon is this? Owing to the tears flowing from the eyes, its vision ceases; and the conditions of Ādam stands upright; on the feet of the confession of sin; appealing that: *'O Allāh! I have the desire of this behest, forgive my failure.'*
>
> The Mūsā of determination reached the peak of *Tūr* and dropped unconscious, revealing that: *'I turn to You.'* 'The Ayyūb of love exhibited signals with that hand; that: *'I received hardship.'* The Sulaymān of excitement on the bedding of happiness of his power of rule; glided with that air of declaration: *'The fragrance of the era of your days belong to you Lord ﷻ.'* Ants, within their hearts conformed to entertain the army of

the glorious king; and at the time of dominance of the armies of the kingdom of wonderment; it was asserted: *'O Ants! Enter your homes.'* The lights of juxtaposition were exposed, and its rays spread. The canopies for meeting were erected, and the angels of sanctum arranged the cushions of reception on the platforms. On the plains of observance; the secret meeting was convened; under the banner of the King. Between the decorative tents of glamour in their *Ḥaram*, the ropes of spectacular lustres were fortified; and hence, the condition of the lovers stabilized by meeting with their beloved. The drink of bliss was served; and that moment transformed, into an aroma of lucrative fortune. Malice disappeared and along the path of Eternal Attributes, the mysteries of permanence emerged. Indeed! This is indeed a very elusive path; and the presumption thereby was dumbfounded in understanding its reality. This is so delicate or complicated; that the thoughts of the mind are moreover, constricted in grasping the knowledge of its essence.

They flash like the lightning of Eternal clouds in front of the eyes of the heart; and increase like the sun, rising in the course of its location. By *Allāh* ﷻ! At this moment even the radiance of the sun is astonished; as it becomes ashamed at the time of that appearance, with its intensity of light.

When the hand of ordainment lifted the veils from the forehead of its effected magnificence, for the eyes of conversation; the Eternal decorators thus, adorned the thrones of splendour; and seated the seeking lovers on it; which was indicative of intimate exhilaration. The resplendent tablet exposed the intimate and reserved [i.e. the close and distant] concealed abodes to them; and the Unitarian Attribute furnished and exposition of the concepts of heights, as well as that of essences.

The eye of sparkle pointed out to the love of the ardent lovers; upon which their strong insight conversed with the astounding vision of the

Gnostics. When they had come to observe its brilliance, its splendour presented itself for observance. The crown of boon befell ecstatic within the assembly of excellence and thereby, it sacrificed the jewels of acceptance and pleasure for them. Thereafter, the veils of honour and magnificence concealed itself behind Divine Grandeur. Henceforth, the heart split into pieces, owing to ardour and the intensity of love; and the souls became perturbed with thirst, followed by a burning sensation. The branches of love began bending; and the air of heat commenced speaking. The leaves of patience initiated shedding, whilst complaining about the anxiety of separation [*firāq*].

O mounts of the soul! Engage diligently to attain these levels [*maqamāt*]. Oh pious mounts of the heart! Hasten towards procuring these ranks [*darajāt*]. Oh Beloved Nabī ﷺ! Tell them [*Ummah*] to engage in devotion.

Take what you desire

I narrate from Shaykh Abu al-Fataḥ ʿAbd al-Raḥmān b. Shaykh Sāliḥ Abu al-Faraj Tūba b. Ibrāhīm b. Sultān Bakrī Siddiqī al-Baghdādī who narrates from his father. He narrates from Shaykh Makārim an-Nahr Khālisī who said:

'One day I was sitting with Sayyiduna Ghawth at the door of the *Madrassa* in *Azj*.[172] I saw a partridge flying over, in front of me and a sensation entered my heart, to eat it with curd. *Allāh* is my witness; that I did not utter a single word in this regard.

Sayyiduna Ghawth looked at me. Smiling thereafter, he looked up into the sky, and that partridge then fell onto the floor of the *Madrassa*. It struggled to fly; whilst I had it positioned on my lap for over an hour.

[172] Azj is the locality where Sayyiduna Ghawth al-Aʿzam had lived. It was called *Bāb al-Azj*. Only the meaning for Azj could be detected, which refers to termitary or ant-hill. *Allāh* Knows best as to what it really means, in those golden epochs and the reason as to why that locality was attributed this name. # [*Faqīr ʿAbd al-Hādī*].

Sayyiduna Shaykh ﷺ then pronounced: *'O Makārim! Take what you desired or Allāh ﷻ remove the desire of partridge and curd from your heart.'*

Shaykh Makārim ﷺ admits to the fact that, as from that actual moment, I developed hatred for partridge and curd in my heart. If it is cooked or roasted and kept in front of me, then I do not have the strength to tolerate its smell for it displeases me. Prior to this, no one loved it more, than I did.

Shaykh Mahkārim ﷺ further articulated that once he was present in the *majlis* Ḥaḍrate-Ghawth ﷺ and he was discussing the stations of the *Wāsilīn*[173] and the observations of the *'Ārifīn* [174]. The impact of this discussion had intensely permeated the hearts of the audience; that every single person was imbued with the fervour about *Allāh* ﷻ. Within the sphere of my heart, I also contemplated on: what the path shall be to reach *Allāh* ﷻ in order to fulfil my goal. Subsequently, Sayyiduna Ghawth ﷺ stopped his discourse, looked at me and thereby professed: *'Oh Makārim! Between you and achieving your goal are two steps. With one step the duniya [the mundane world]; and with the other step, your nafs must be obliterated. Then it will be you and your Lord ﷻ.'*

Firāq – separation or absence of the Beloved

Sayyiduna Ghawth ﷺ states that the separation of the beloved is such a fire that is equated to the raging flames of Hell Fire, which the Lord of Constrictions [*Allāh* ﷻ] had kindled. The absence of the beloved is parallel to a thunderous sound, which is sent by the cloud of love to the debtor [lover]. The concealment of *Shuhūd* [175] is such a separation, that the branches of communion become fragile in the gardens adjacent to it.
The concealment of a radiant entity is such a sword, which the beloved draws with the hand of dejection from the sheath of elegance.

[173] *Wasīlīn* are those *Awliya* that have reached their destination in the Path of *Sulūk*.
[174] *'Ārifīn* are the senior *Awliya* blessed with the *Ma'rifah* [gnosis –realization] of Almighty *Allāh* ﷻ.
[175] The observance of the Divine Presence of the Sublime Lord ﷻ.

For the present to be absent is such a spark, whose flint of love it lit to burn the love of the heart.

Distance from the beloved is such a sip of bitter drink, which is given in hands of the lover comprising of a cup of restriction; with such a taste that is sweeter than honey. He drinks it in a state of suffocation.

The detachment from proximity is a severe punishment, which grips the heart with the fire of separation and perishes it.

To be imbibed in intoxication of the issues of admonition, is far more appealing than the desires of the soul.

The separation of a friend is a powerful dominance. It tramples the madness of love ruthlessly from the flanks of the soul; drags it to the barren plains of love and bashes it against the piles of veils of desires.

The brides of fortune are such jewels of intuition; which the administrator of Eternity has emphasised. The gardens of *Kashf* [unveilings] are such gardens of eloquence, which were germinated by wisdom.

Shouq [enthusiasm] are those veils that are hung on the faces of the brides of Prophets ﷤.

Love is that sun, whose rays of light falls onto the cities of the heart.

Mushāhidah [Spiritual Observation] is that pure Drink brought to the *'Ārifīn* [Gnostics], which are beyond their desires; and under the spring [bloom], in the assembly of union near the *Sidrat al-Muntaha* of hope; they are brought by the messengers of the cavalry of the lovers. Behind the pastures of the herders of the mounts of Divine Proximity, on the right of side of the exclusive beauty of *Allāh* ﷻ, the cupbearers [*sāqī*] of Eternity serve the cups of Divine Address to the associates of [pure] souls.

Oh lovers! All those who are ardent in the love with the notions of excellence of the Attributes of *Allāh* ﷻ, O Lovers! Stand up. O people! Those who are sincere in their ardent love of the confidant Ḥabīb ﷺ, stand up for the anthem of union, because every person listening to the sweet melody of the singer, is being entertained by it. The harmonious melody of the singer is enthralled with blessings of the tears of concern of the compassionate; who himself, is enchanted with the melodious euphony of the singers. These singers were inviting them to the honourable, uncovered and cordial gathering of the beloved.

Despondent, in the captivation of love, is indeed an incentive of Destiny. The soul is remembering the recitation; relevant to the spectacle of the gathering, when your Lord ﷻ blessed His special servant with the Divine Vision. All of them were ecstatic and focused on the exhibition of the treasures of secrets; which were remnants of the presence of the First Day of Covenant [*Youm Alast*]. At that time the souls were individual [separated] in the configuration of shapes; which were created separately in the *Nūrī* Realm.

Simultaneously, your soul gets the subtle breeze from the fragrance of Love and affection from the *dhikr* of Ḥabīb al-Aʿzam ﷺ in the gardens, during the season of the blessings of spring, which emanates from the Eternal Lord ﷻ. He reminds you of the initial fundamental conditions of *Bayʿāh,* including the excellent movements of Eternity. The flames of the fire of grief then raged in the heart of the desolate owing to the depression of separation. Disunion will be lit by the secretive fire of the yearning for the beloved; and they will be called by the thirsty voice of the burning ardour of the beloved:

.عَلىٰ مَثَلِ لَيلىٰ يَقتُلُ المُرُّ نَفسَهُ وَ يَحْلُوْلَهُ مُرُّ الْمَنَايَا وَ يَعْذِبُ

The men sacrifice their lives for a beloved like Layla,
Their bitter desires will become sweet and tasty.

The dried date tree comes to life

I was informed by Shaykh Abu-ʿAbdullāh al-Wāḥid b. Sālih b. Yaḥyah Qurashī al-Baghdādī ؓ and he narrates from Shaykh Abu al-Faraj Ḥasan b. Muḥammad b. Aḥmad Dera al-Basrī ؓ who narrates from Shaykh Abu al-ʿAbbās Aḥmad b. Mutīʿh b. Aḥmad Ba-Ḥayrānī ؓ. He stated that he had heard from Shaykh Sālih Abu al-Muzaffar Ismāʿīl b. ʿAlī b. Sinān Ḥumayrī al-Zarīrānī ؓ. He was a pious Shaykh and he lived in the company of Shaykh, the leader ʿAlī b. al-Hītī ؓ. Shaykh Sālih ؓ affirms that when the master, Shaykh ʿAlī b. al-Hītī ؓ fell sick; he sometimes visited my land in Zarīrān where he spent a substantial amount of time.

Once, when he was sick there, my master, Sayyiduna Shaykh Muḥiyy al-Dĩn ʿAbd al-Qãdir al-Jilãnĩ thereby came to visit him. Both were present on my land. I had two date trees in my land that had dried up for the last four years and bore no fruits. I intended to cut them. Sayyiduna Shaykh ʿAbd al-Qãdir then stood up and went under one of those dried trees and performed *wuḍũ*. He then performed two *rakʿãts nafil* under the other tree. Miraculously, they instantaneously became green and bore fruit the same week, when it was not during the season of dates. I took some of those dates and presented them to Sayyiduna Ghawth al-Aʿzam and he ate them. He then supplicated: *'May Allãh give barkãt in your land; your money, your weights and your milk [of your livestock].'*

Shaykh Sãliḥ confirms that after this *duʿã* of Sayyiduna Ghawth, from that year onwards, the harvest of my crops tripled. My state transformed to such a degree, that if I spent one *dirham*, the result was that, triple that amount came into my possession. I used to keep one hundred bags of wheat in a room, of which I used up fifty bags, and in the following instances, when I came into that room; I discovered that there were one hundred bags therein. My livestock increased through its offsprings to the extent, that I had lost count of them. This condition is prevalent up to this day, and undoubtedly, all this is attributed to *barkãt* of the *duʿãs* of Sayyiduna Ghawth al-Aʿzam Shaykh ʿAbd al-Qãdir al-Jilãnĩ.

The Secrets of the Divine Names of Allãh

Sayyiduna Ghawth al-Aʿzam briefly discussed the *meʿrãj*. He confirmed that the limit of every *meʿrãj* is up to the limit of each of the lofty Names [of *Allãh*]. Every step for ascension is to *Allãh's* Name. Elevation has acquired lustre [*tajallĩ*] through the Divine Names. This lustre is then manifested. His Actions and the entire existence is lit up with the radiance of this lustre. In both existences, detailed evidences were emitted. It shall manifest in the Domes of Justice and Command in both the worlds. Thereafter, the Names were revealed and the attribute separated. Different languages were created; actions completed, multiplicities were distributed and species were determined. Thus, all were in harmony by the power of justice. Each one of them began proclaiming *Allāh's* ﷻ *Tawḥīd,* because the lustres [*tajallī*] manifested in them.

The reason as to why it points to him is, because the secrets of the Names are concealed in him. It is for this reason that he is recognized. From Eternity to Eternity, His knowledge is linked to creation. Everyone in the world is in a state of astonishment. Had it not been for His Mercy, which was procured from His Exquisiteness of His *Ma'rifah* [cognizance], it would then not have been a favour. If astonishment did not have perception, and if His severe seizure in the lustres of His Divine Name was then exposed to the mountain, they would have halted. If they were exposed to the oceans, they would have become restless; and if exposed to fire, it would have begun blazing. As a result, entities which are static because of Him, shall also move owing to Him. As He exposed the lustres of His lofty Name on the *'Arsh* [Divine Throne], its angels were then created in accordance to the decree of that Divine Court. Thus, each one has a soul. For the soul, in their souls; there is then life. There is a soul for each of their *dhikr;* and in each of them, the magnificence of the lustre that is characterized by His Names, rendered them unconscious.

Each of its persons was thereby captivated by those Divine Names. They thought that they were unconscious, but were still the remembering ones [*dhākir*];[176] and were unconscious of remembrance [*dhikr*]. Their remembrance [*dhikr*] now, in so far as the Divine Names are concerned, is '*Anta Anta*' – *You You*, and owing to unconsciousness is '*Hu Hu Hu*' – *He, He, He*; concerning lustres is '*Ha Ha Ha*' – *self, self, self* -[177] and owing to

[176] A *dhākir* is one who engages in the *dhikr* of *Allāh* ﷻ

[177] *Hā* is a feminine pronoun of *Hu* in Arabic and it points out to the *nafs*. In Arabic the word *nafs* is femine and, henceforth the feminine is used. In *murāqiabah* and *dhikar* the *nafs* is focused

concealment is '*Subḥanaka Subḥānaka Subḥānaka – You are Pure, You are Pure, You and Pure.*' The *Karrubīn* [178] glorified *Allāh* ﷻ and were drawn into in a line. Hence, they were astonished. *Roḥāniyīn* [The spiritual servants] pleaded, the *Muqarribīn* [the confidant servants who achieve Divine Proximity] read the *tasbīḥ* and His light of radiance lit up existence in such a manner; that the secrets of their existence was disclosed by their appearance. Through this, *Allāh*'s ﷻ Divinity and Authority was confirmed. Thus, the carriers of the *dhikr* of the *dhakirīn*, the residents of the residence are drawn to such entities, which are safely enveloped in the glorious tents. Indeed! They are the remarkable Attributes of the Divine Names.

The secrets of the *ʿĀrifīn* circulates within the secretive sciences of these Divine Names. They manoeuvre in such a manner, that owing to these Glorious Names, their faces observe such things that the people in both existences, retain it as a trust. By virtue of this observance, they acquire the knowledge of the execution of the secrets of Destiny in the Angelic Realm. At this juncture, there is no information about knowledge left; except the secrets of moments drawn by the hands of *Nūr* [light] and excellence, with exposure. They functioned in their lives with the excitement of love. They dived into the ocean of the light of wonderment. When they surfaced, their faces were brilliant with the rays of wonderment, which dazzled the eyes of the human and jinn observers. Their internal and external was filled with the light of the Divine Names; in so much so, that all issues of doubts were obliterated.

It then, exposed the secrets of its existence to our existence, which was recorded by the Pen of Destiny, which was preserved in trust, in a designated domain of tranquillity. Thus, entities that were hidden were exposed; and the *ʿĀrifīn* observed themselves, with these secrets. They saw everything, except *Allāh* ﷻ; bearing their names. They observed the excellence of the Reality of

---

and trained to achieve purity and accountability. Since the *nafs* [feminine tense] is addressed, so the feminine pronoun was used that is *Hā*.

[178] The *Karrubīn* are an elite group of angels closest to the Sublime Lord ﷻ. Their leader is Sayyiduna Jibrīʾīl ؑ.

the Absolute ﷻ, within the Absolute Realm. They moved with those entities, which they had observed at the edge of the Angelic Realm. It opened the meanings of *Takwīn* [causing to create]; then to them, every existence was extremely influential; similar to the effects of the underlying Divine Command: *'O that Being! Who has exposed His grandeur and glory on the veils of the Divine ʿArsh [Throne]. O Allāh ﷻ! I plead to You ﷻ through those majestic Attributes in which no creation is victorious. I beg for such love; with which I can observe the secrets of Allāh ﷻ and wipe off the grief of thoughts until my time pleases You. Then I shall please You with my moments.'*

I was informed by Shaykh Abu al-Maʿālī ʿAbd al-Raḥīm b. Muzaffar Qurashī رحمه الله who narrates from Shaykh ʿAlī b. Sulaymān, the Baker رحمه الله in Baghdād who had heard that Shaykh Abu al-Ḥasan al-Jowsiqī رحمه الله assert that he was engulfed in an immense misfortune. This created difficulty in much of his work. He thereafter, came to his Master, Shaykh ʿAlī b. Hītī رحمه الله to enquire about his problem. He enunciated to me: *'O Abu al-Ḥasan! Your problem is an Act of Allāh ﷻ. This cannot be sorted out by words; for it requires an excellent spiritual condition for its solution. Go to Sayyiduna Shaykh ʿAbd al-Qādir رضي الله عنه in Baghdād, for presently, he is the king of the ʿUlama-e-ʿĀrifīn. He is the owner of the reins of segregated issues.'* I proceeded to Baghdād and presented myself to our Master, Sayyiduna Shaykh Muḥiyy al-Dīn ʿAbd al-Qādir رضي الله عنه. I observed him to be in a sitting position; whilst he was facing the direction of the *Qibla*. There were people sitting around him and I took my place in front of him. The honourable Ghawth رضي الله عنه looked at me and I was convinced that he had perceived my condition; as well as the reason for my visit to him.

He thereby took out a piece of string that was coiled into five strands from underneath his prayer mat. One end of the string was given to me to hold onto, and the end was held by his consecrated hand. He then opened one strand, which initiated my heart to understand one gigantic aspect of my misfortune; as I envisaged this as an enormous issue. As the great Ghawth رضي الله عنه uncoiled the strands, I predicted a huge and limitless issue; that was inspired to me. Concerning this, I saw the reality of two things; which I could not comprehend. Eventually, he opened all of the five strands. It was only then, that all the future occurrences were exposed to me.

The exposure of this issue emitted from in-between the concealed secrets. My insight was inaugurated by the *Nūrānī* [illuminant] powers, and the veils were ripped open. Sayyiduna Ghawth ﷺ then looked at me and commanded: *'Hold it tightly and order your people to take the virtuous things from it.'* I then took leave from his presence; and by *Allāh* ﷻ! I avow that I did not mention a single word to him; nor did those who were present, understand anything about my problem. I left Baghdād and came to Zirān to the presence of my Master, Shaykh ʿAlī b. al-Hītī ؓ. Before I could reveal anything to him, he self-confessed to me: *'Did I not tell you that Sayyiduna Shaykh Muḥiyy al-Dīn ʿAbd al-Qādir ؓ is the king of the ʿUlama-e-ʿĀrifīn and the owner of the reins of segregated issues? O Abu al-Ḥasan! You were unable to observe the issues of your future matters, but when the vision of Sayyiduna Shaykh ʿAbd al-Qādir ؓ fell on your future misfortunes, then only you were able to observe them. If it was not for his command to say, here take it and hold steadfast onto it, then you would have lost your senses and you would have then been in the category of the insane and Lovers. Ḥaḍrate Ghawth ؓ has informed you that you would be the leader of the people, because he commanded you to inform your people to adopt virtues.'*

Principals of the Stations of the ʿĀrifīn

Sayyiduna Ghawth al-Aʿzam ؓ confirmed that there are seven principles pertaining to the stations of the *ʿĀrifīn*.

1) *Ḥuḍūrī* – attendance. To learn the *Ādāb* [disciplines] of *Ḥuḍūrī* for devotion.
2) *Idrāq* – perception, through which one achieves humility and progress.
3) *Maʿārif* – wisdom, to concentrate on it for guidance.
4) *Wiṣāl* – communion, to remain hungry for it.
5) *Munajāt* – supplications, the separation of the soul when engaged in it.
6) *Waḍā* – conduct, must be such that it should be established with *Tawḥīd*.

7) *Surat al-Ikhlãs*, must be [constantly] read [*dhikr*] in the heart. When an *'Ãrif* accomplishes any of these stations, Almighty *Allãh* ﷻ, then at the end of each station, opens the Door of Favours for him. By perfecting them, the ethics of *Ḥuḍũrĩ* opens the doors for the comfortable following of the *Sharĩ'ah*.

Allãh ﷻ disposes an expanse of favours and subtleties upon him in this world, *Malakũt,*[179] and as well as in *Jabarũt*[180]. He then remains with knowledge; and bodily on the vastness of this world; whilst his conditions and heart are in *Jabarũt*. On the latitude of *Jabarũt,* he permeates with his soul and secrets. Henceforth, are the Truth of the secrets and conditions exposed to him; the negation of the hidden extinction of spiritual attention; and the address of the answer, with His address. The soul acquires the breeze of *Qurb* [proximity] and owing to this *nisbah* [relation], it achieves love. This is actually the secret of *'Irfãn* [intrinsic knowledge] which is inculcated by *Taqwã* [piety]. This is the first *Mushãhidah* [observance] of the *'Ãrifin,* i.e. their initial stage of the first reality. One of the ethics of the *Ḥudũrĩ* [attendance] of Sayyiduna Rasũlullãh ﷺ is that; when *Allãh* ﷻ conveyed *Salãm* to him on the Night of *Me'rãj* at the Station of *Qãbã Qousayn* in the following words: 'اَلسَّلَامُ عَلَيْكُمْ يَا اَيُّهَا النَّبِيُّ وَرَحْمَةُ اللهِ وَبَرَكَاتُهُ – *Peace be upon you O Nabĩ and mercy of Allãh, and blessings*. The beloved Ḥabĩb ﷺ did not reply then to this *Salãm* with a *Salãm,* owing to the magnificence of his *Ḥudũrĩ* [attendance], within the Proximity of the Divine. In fact, he accepted this Divine Gift and did not express recompense for it. The reality of the believers and followers [*Ummah*] was exposed to him; and he thereby expressed peace upon himself, as well as upon his *Ummah* in the following diction: 'اَلسَّلَامُ عَلَيْنَا وَعَلٰى عِبَادِ اللهِ الصَّالِحِيْنَ – *Peace*

179 The Angelic Realm

180 The Realm of Majestic Attributive Qualities

upon me and on the pious servants of Allãh ﷻ. *Raḥmah* and *Barakah* comprises three ranks, and except himself; there are three other ranks of supplementaries; viz. *Siddiqĩn, Shuhadah* and *Sãliḥĩn*. Consequently, peace [*Salãm*] was for the *Siddiqĩn*, Mercy [*Raḥmah*] for the *Shuhadah* and blessings [*Barakãt*] for the *Sãliḥĩn*. The experiences of the beloved Prophet ﷺ with the Actions of *Allãh* ﷻ are of three types; categorized into three incidents.

1) Firstly, that His ﷻ Mercy supersedes his anger, and hence, owing to this quality, peace [*Salãm*] becomes *Wãjib* [incumbent].
2) Secondly, on the one side is *Jannah*, and on the other side is *Jahannam*, and hence, owing to this quality of Mercy [*Raḥmah*] becomes *Wãjib* [incumbent].
3) Thirdly, '*for whom this Day is Kingdom?*' For the exposition, of this quality, blessings [*Barakãt*] are deemed as *Wãjib* [incumbent].

As for that person whose actions exceeds his mercy above that of his anger, and thereby, he becomes respectful in the first meeting; there is then peace [*Salãm*] for him. He is from those *Siddiqĩn,* who sit on the cushions of *Jabarũt*. He who places the pleasure of *Allãh* ﷻ before the desires of the self [*nafs*], and he then becomes respectful in the second meeting; hence, for him is mercy [*Raḥmah*] destined. Finally, he who does not fear anyone, except *Allãh* ﷻ, and thus, knows that besides *Allãh* ﷻ, there is no one who can give him any benefit, and as a result, he becomes respectful in the third meeting; henceforth, for him there are blessings [*Barakãt*]. He befits one of those *Sãliḥĩn,* who sits on the cushion of Kingdom. The descent from these three ranks of that person, who is inclined to the ethics of the Prophet of *Allãh* ﷺ, is in harmony with him; because he had achieved them from three sanctuaries. This is in perspective, because these ranks were created and exposed for the strong individuals of the *Ummah* with the blessings, by the indication of Sayyiduna Rasũlullãh ﷺ. To reach the perception of humility, is synonymous to climbing onto to the door of Dignity [*Tamkĩn*]. For this secret, *Allãh* ﷻ strengthens the lustres of *Ḥudũrĩ* [attendance] and the secrets of *Hudũrĩ*. Thus, they are with the secrets of *Allãh* ﷻ, in the Lustres of observation. In Sayyiduna

Rasulullāh ﷺ, the splendour of the observance of these secrets are encompassed at both levels, briefly and in detail; by the virtue of the Right Path [*Sirāt al-Mustaqīm*] and *Sunnah*. This is what is ordained for the real and absolute obedience; and as well as the following of the beloved Prophet ﷺ. When the devotee is present in devotion, as well as in absence, the signs of secrets transform into permanency. Thus, in absence; the signs of secrets, although they are of permanence; they are yet concealed by Eternity. When they are in extinction; they are also concealed by Eternity.

Their knowledge is of permanence [with knowledge]; and extinct from the 'known'. Concentration in *Ma ʿārif* [gnosis] unlocks guidance to the door of contemplation; and that, which is in the lustres of contemplation, is strengthened in the physical and spiritual realms [*Mulk* and *Malakūt*]; inclusive of its worlds. These are the people who confine themselves to Eternity, from the servitude of creation. They have understood the brevity and details of the secrets of subjugation and have accepted the Sacred Laws [*Sharī ʿāhs*] through the medium of *kashf* [spiritual perception]. They also understand the intricacies of the spiritual worlds and ponder over them. In the World of Souls, those entities are exposed to them by the gift of *Allah* ﷻ; Whose impact falls onto the souls of the believers; whereby their *Imān* is illuminated. Their spiritual stations progress towards them and withdraws from the world of constraints. They abandon the choice of creation because of *wisāl* [spiritual communion] and hunger opens the door of angelic powers; and real spirituality; coupled with the lustres of perpetuity which excels over their existence. Its lustrous beams remove the darkness from the physical body. Towards him the enemy of physical disposition returns; since the charity of the courtyard, after its calculation; is known to the verifiers. This is the initial condition of hunger of the nation; but in their final stages, their bodies, split open the veils of the unseen; and the springs of wisdom burst open in the treasuries of the heart. Their food is the Divine Speech of *Allāh* ﷻ and their drink is the *Sunnah* of the beloved Prophet ﷺ. Their sustenance is from the food of mercy from the sanctuary of serenity, and their thirst is quenched by the *Salsabīl* [sacred fountain] from the Precincts of the Divine; which is stamped by the Seal of Love. For him, at the time of the separation of the souls, during Divine Devotion, the doors of tranquillity are opened in a state of spirituality. This is interpreted as the self [being] and soul. Owing to the purity of the heart and its presence in union and, by the inhalation of the fragrance of *Qurb*, is a blissful moment. This is for the person whose *Salāh* is consistent and his *munajāt* [glorification] comprises permanent perpetual observation. There is *wisāl* [communion] and speech in the whispers of every moment from him. At every moment there is perpetual observation, and its every movement is serene. Almighty *Allāh* ﷻ has blessed him with this power in *ʿĀlam Arwāḥ;* that whenever he desires, he may detach himself for engrossment in the pursuit of the plains of excellence; and whenever he desires, he may associate himself to the world of consciousness and feelings. There are secrets of Power in the *ʿArsh* [Divine Throne] of *Allāh* ﷻ similar to the secrets of *Takwīn* [causing to be, creating] in His *Kursī* [Divine Seat], though His *Qālib* [form] as a metaphor of senses; the manifestation of His Light in a manner of application; and the observation of Truth, are all pure and void of a unification[181]. With His ﷻ *Tawḥīd* in a sense of establishing His uniqueness, opens the doors of Divine Favours.

Allāh ﷻ, then retains the *ʿĀrif* steadfast on his initial intentions, by virtue of the reality of his acceptance and his initial characteristics. With his knowledge, he thereby hears Almighty *Allāh* ﷻ; and through his actions, he presents himself in front of the Doer [*Allāh* ﷻ], whilst by his attributes, he speaks of that *Tawḥīd* about which *Allāh* ﷻ Himself speaks of. Indeed! He ﷻ has kept this in the trust of that Reality, which is attributed with excellence, entirely to His Divine Names.

Thus, this is that fact, which Sayyiduna Rasūlullāh ﷺ had brought, so that the human sphere is reminded of the initial characteristics of this matter. This is similar to the reason for teaching the reality of the human being to a foreign

[181] Unification. A reference to Truth without the Creation of any form or body. All these are merely metaphoric for explanatory purposes. *Allāh* ﷻ is pure and free of a body, shape or form.

specie. It is for this reason that the beloved Messenger of *Allāh* ﷺ possessed perfection and excellence. He is the giver of glad-tidings [*Bashīr*] to the people, who are steadfast to the right; and warner [*Nazīr*] to the people, who are steadfast to the left. In order to position the reality of understanding of *Tawḥīd*, it causes the eyes to be lethargic and blind; tears the veils; and breaks the dishes, whilst the exposure of lustres that are in the often repeated seven verses of *Surah Fātiḥa* [*Sab'ā Mathānī*]; opens the doors of the splendour to the recitation of *Surah Ikhlās*.

The reason as to why the lustres of *Allāh* ﷻ are beamed on creation, is that they are servants. Hence, the tongues of creation become speechless. By the movement of their tongues, they glorify *Allāh's* ﷻ *Tawḥīd* in accordance to the computation of those people who glorify His *Tawḥīd;* and in their silence, they glorify *Allāh's* ﷻ *Tawḥīd;* in accordance to the count of those people who do not glorify His *Tawḥīd*. Although all creation believes in the Oneness of *Allāh* ﷻ; but there is he, who glorifies the *Tawḥīd* of *Allāh* ﷻ; according to the coercion of that person who persuasively glorifies *Allāh's* ﷻ *Tawḥīd*. Moreover, there are those who do not acknowledge the Oneness of *Allāh* ﷻ; according to the secrets of that person who does not acknowledge the Oneness of *Allāh* ﷻ. He is the secret of *Qutb-e-Tawḥīd* [182], hidden *Tafrīd* [183]and *Latīfa-e-Tajrīd* [the Subtle Revealings][184]. These are classified as the elite servants who have perceived the nature of *Tawḥīd* of the lustres of Almighty *Allāh* ﷻ; the Beneficent.

The stones now benefit from this secret, they love and listen to this speech in the secret world. Henceforward, when they listen to the *kalām* of *Allāh* ﷻ, the

---

[182] *Qutbe-Tawḥīd* means a pivot or authority who understands the *Tawḥīd* of *Allāh* ﷻ.

[183] *Tafrīd* means that all praise or approbation is attributed to *Allāh* ﷻ and not to oneself. This is based on the concept that *Allāh* ﷻ is the Origin or Source of all things, and there is no originator or source of power other than *Allāh* ﷻ. This refutes the freedom of the will.

[184] *Tajrīd* means the abandonment of worldly life, i.e. desires and ambitions connected to the ego and subjective judgements, in favour of the spiritual life; i.e. obedience to *Allāh* ﷻ, and the objective of its principles.

lustres of reverence showers upon them; and following them, comes *Tawḥīd* in a comportment of love. The lustres of reverence fall upon them when they converse, and in view of this fact, it comes silently from the arrear, owing to *adab* [respect]. The lustres of reverence fall upon them when they move with speech; and stop at the back within their limits, owing to disgrace. When they are absorbed into a state of spiritual grandeur, on the lustres of reverence, and thereby precede it, they develop a defined mode of awareness to follow on the footsteps of the sacred *Sharī'āh*. Henceforth, owing to these disciplines, their Lord ﷻ shows them these realities in a present long period of time, which they will not be in a position to comprehend in the Hereafter. His *nūr* [light] spreads *Kashf* [*spiritual unveiling*] amidst the spheres of creation. He now becomes aware of the information of creation, which is recorded on the Sacred Tablet of Record [*Louḥ e Maḥfūz*] and he observes the places of creation in the Universe; through the secrets of Eternal Favours; and as well as those entities, which were prepared in accordance to the decree of his destiny. They also hear the caller of their hearts, which is enjoined to secrets of the addressed. Hence, the caller of their heart, who in both the worlds, speaks in their presence, with the reality of the souls. At that juncture, the reality of *Jannah* and *Jahannan* [heaven and hell] are exposed to them. These comprise two types:

1) One is for those individuals, who have perfected the stations and understood them through the faculty of *Kashf*.
2) The other is for those, who have not perfected the stations. Thus, these phenomena are alien to them; which are behind the veils of these signs.

That which now addresses their secrets is from the reality of the Sacred Law from Almighty *Allāh* ﷻ and thus, they speak with an assortment of understanding of *Tawḥīd,* which concurs with its manifestation of secret subtleties. When anyone of them looks at creation with the eye of *Tawḥīd*, for them then; the exposure of the power of the lustres of *Tawḥīd* strengthens their status. When they look at creation, with the eye of knowledge, they see thereby, from the innermost intent of Destiny, by the separation of knowledge and the merger of *Tawḥīd*. By the lustres, of this disclosure, it is by the fact that the innermost parts of creation tears; when those entities which are preserved in the disposal of secrets, are thereby exposed to him. The ascetic devotees reap the benefits thereof. Regarding the conditions of the reality of the people of friendship, it is weighed on the scale of the extensiveness of *Kashf*. Almighty *Allah* ﷻ assists the condition of the *Wãsilĩn*[185] by the Angelic Power; supervises the inner self of the *Salikĩn*[186]; perfects the imperfect; reveals Himself according to the conception of the observer; and at times, emerges in his thoughts. Because there is expertise in a *murĩd,* and He ﷻ; sometimes manifests the resplendence, for the power of *Sulũk;* and sometimes He ﷻ addresses the *murĩd* from the segments. The Masters of Spiritual State are now assisted with secret subtleties by the Lord of devotion with honorific invocations. The *ʿÃrif* is blessed with the power of authority and at times, he draws near to the intrinsic qualities of proximity; with his innermost self. At other times, by the modus operandi of *Qudrat* [authority], he falls far away from the analogy of the *kashf*; which is pertinent to the conditions.

The Book of Philosophy changed to the Excellence of the holy Qur'ãn

I was informed by Shaykh Abu al-Futũḥ Nasrullãh b. Abu al-Muḥãsin Yũsuf b. Khalĩl al-Azjĩ ﷺ who heard from Shaykh Abu al-ʿAbbãs Aḥmad b. Ismãʿĩl b. Ḥamza al-Azjĩ ﷺ , prominently known as Ibn Battãl, that he had heard from Shaykh Abu-Muzaffar Munsũr b. al-Mubãrak al-Wãstĩ Wãʿiz ﷺ, commonly known as Jarãdah who asserts:

> 'During my youth I was present in the gathering of Sayyiduna Shaykh ʿAbd al-Qãdir al-Jilãnĩ ﷺ. I had a book in my possession; relevant to philosophy, which encompassed the sciences of spiritualism. The *Jamãʿat* affirmed to me: '*You have not read the book, nor did you ask any question, as to what is contained in the book. O Mansũr! This book is your debauched companion. Go and delete it*' I decided to get up from the

[185] The *Wãsilĩn* are classified as those *Awliya,* who have reached their destination and have successfully completed their journey to the Lord of Power ﷻ

[186] The *Sãlikĩn* are in the category of the travellers, on the Path of *Sulũk*, who are on their way to their ultimate goal.

Shaykh's ﷺ presence, in order to go home; so that I may subsequently leave the book and not bring it again, hence taking into consideration, the fear of the great Ghawth ﷺ. My heart did not desire to delete its contents, because I had loved the subject matter of the book. Part of its contents had created a home in my heart. When I decided to get up, Sayyiduna Ghawth al-Aʿzam ﷺ thereafter, caste an awesome glance at me; and my condition became such that; as though I felt that I was a prisoner.

Sayyiduna Ghawth ﷺ issued an instruction to me: '*Give me your book*' When I opened it, the contents of its pages were cleared; indicative of its transformation to clear white paper; without a single letter being visible on them. I gave the book to Sayyiduna Shaykh ﷺ, who he flipped through its pages and ratified: '*This book is on the excellence of the Holy Qur'ān, written in beautiful calligraphy by Muḥammad b. Kharīs.*' Henceforward, Shaykh ﷺ advised me: '*Repent from those things which are not in your heart.*' In the affirmative, I declared with obedience: *yes my Master!* He then ordered me to stand up; to which I complied, and discovered that all those aspects, which I had memorized from book; pertaining to philosophy and spiritualism were washed away from my heart in totality. They disappeared from my chest, as though I had never ever remembered them.

A corrupt person claims excellence over Sayyiduna Nabī Yūnus b. Matī ﷺ and the Anger of the Ghawth ﷺ

Shaykh Mansūr ﷺ expresses that once he had visited Sayyiduna Ghawth al-Aʿzam ﷺ in a position; that he was seated and leaning onto a large pillow. It was declared to him that there was a certain person who was famed in spiritual devotion, asceticism and charismatic exploitations. The person professed that he had bypassed the status of the noble Prophet, Sayyiduna Nabī Yūnus b. Matī ﷺ. The face of Sayyiduna Shaykh ﷺ then raged with anger; whilst he sat in an upright manner, and he took the pillow with his hands and threw it in front of him. In a state of infuriation, he then articulated: *'I have grabbed hold of his heart.'*

Hastily, we then got up and went to examine this person. When we reached his home, we found him dead, although he had been a person who was of sound health. A certain period had elapsed, and I saw him in a splendid condition in my dream; and I questioned him as follows: *'Inform me as to what Allāh* ﷻ *did to you?'* He replied: *'He forgave me and the words I uttered about Sayyiduna Nabī Yūnus b. Matī* ﷺ *was returned to me. Sayyiduna Shaykh 'Abd al-Qādir* ﷺ *pleaded on by behalf to Allāh* ﷻ *and Sayyiduna Nabī Yūnus b. Matī* ﷺ *on my behalf also pleaded for forgiveness. Hence, I gained immense integrity from this.'*

Concerning Dhikr

The big sweet wharf to which the thirsty intellects comes, is to the wharf of *dhikr* and *Tawḥīd*. Blowing onto the heart and brain, with the most fragrant breeze, is that love for *Allāh* ﷻ. The pleasure, enjoyment and sweetness of *Allāh's* ﷻ glorification are achieved from the cups of pure Drinks of the souls. The *dhikr* of *Allāh* ﷻ is a pandemonium to the eyes of the brain; and the crown can only be attained by the arrangement of the pearls in the remembrance of *Allāh* ﷻ, which are on the path line of the separation of secrets. The scented gratitude of musk cannot be applied onto anything else, except onto the pockets of the clothing of the souls. Flowers of praise do not blossom, without the trees of the tongues' of the *mo'min* servants. When you are absorbed in the *dhikr* of your Lord ﷻ; with virtuosity of the tongue, Almighty *Allāh* ﷻ will henceforward, open the locks of your heart.

When you engage in *dhikr*, with the tongue of subtleties on the command of secrets, you shall thereby be a real *dhākir* [devotee]. If you generate His ﷻ *dhikr* from within your heart; henceforth, by virtue of His Status, embracing Mercy, He ﷻ will draw you close to Him ﷻ. Whilst you make His *dhikr* to Him, He will then indeed draw you ten steps closer to Him; and if you are sincere in His love, He will consequently raise you for His curtains of Mercy to the lofty Station of *Sidq* [Truth].

For that person who has not understood the majesty of *Allãh's* ﷻ Glory, and he who becomes lazy for a moment in the *dhikr* of *Allãh* ﷻ and His Eternal Unity; turns its focus to the negligent, is parallel to the one who looked at someone else other than Him ﷻ. The breeze of *dhikr* blows from the Mercy of His Divine Presence on the souls of the *Dhãkirĩn* [devotees of *dhikr*]. Its intoxication moves the edges of the souls that are mourning the separation of the bodies; and the intellect rises and dances in the gardens of images. The secrets come out of the jungles of ecstasy in amazement, and the nightingale sings with those melodies that are imbued in the depth of the heart. Whilst the lover burns in the fire of regret, the zeal regretfully, to a certain degree vanishes from itself. The tongues of the ecstatic lover dances with gladness, from the closeness of euphoria and express: *'Indeed I smell the fragrance of Yũsuf* عليه السلام*.'* Thus, the bridesmaids of the decorators of Eternity emerged to adorn the camps of secrets of the beloved. This embellishment of the skilled brides took place in the presence of the intelligent, in the palaces of denunciation. Thereafter, the temperamental veils of absence are burnt down from them; and they are covered with the veils of excellence. The eye of their intellect becomes infected with the heat and dryness of love; and their feet of enthusiasm gives up; owing to their long journey in the jungles of detachment. The ambassador of generosity; thereafter, sends the physician of destiny to them, who treats their infected eyes with the *kohl* of *'Bismillãhir Raḥmãnir Raḥĩm.'* When the glory of *Jabarũt* of this Name is raised, the movement under the banner of overwhelming heights spread out. The eyes of the intellect shall be dazzled; the eyes of understanding shall delve into unconsciousness, whilst the movement of the birds of contemplation shall stop. The pages of the universe shall be deleted; and the awe-inspiring tongue of Divine Unity shall elucidate: *'Voices will soften for the Beneficent Lord* ﷻ*.'*

The solid mountains shall then tremble, and the grounds of human characteristics shall burst into pieces, by the splendour of the rays of lustre.

The feet of the souls shall be cut off; and their flight in the Realm of *Tafrīd* shall cease. They become fervent about the zeal of love and secrets; and are thus, astonished at the ardour of its love.

Thereafter, contemplations are despondent, in the jungles of propinquity. His ﷻ Commands extends to every being. The Signs of the predisposition of His ﷻ Sovereignty glitters on every relic, and the marvels of His ﷻ creation are exposed to all creations. The evidence of His Unitarianism [*Waḥdaniyah*] is ascertained to every creation. The lustres of His ﷻ Divine Power are luminous in Commands, which engulfs every being. The lustres of His ﷻ Divine Power are exceptional in front of every eye of the intellect; and the tongue of the wonders of *Allah's* ﷻ creativity speaks with Divine Gesture to every single existence. The mirrors of the intellect are in front of the people in wonderment of His ﷻ Divine Speech. By the brides of the secrets of the unseen, the eyes of the hearts of His servants are enhanced. Your *Allāh* ﷻ is your Lord, who owns the Kingdom; whilst those deities [idols] that you call upon; do not own even the skin of a date.

I narrate in 670 *hijrī* on the plains of Cairo from Shaykh Abu-Ḥafs ʿUmar b. Muḥammad b. ʿAmar al-Nīrī رضي الله عنه, recognized as Ibn Mazāḥim who affirms: My Master, Shaykh Abu al-Ḥasan ʿAlī b. al-Hītī رضي الله عنه held my hand in 550 *hijrī* and took me to our Master, Sayyiduna Shaykh Muḥiyy al-Dīn ʿAbd al-Qādir رضي الله عنه. Shaykh ʿAlī b. al-Hītī رضي الله عنه declared to the Ghawth رضي الله عنه: *'This is my servant.'* Sayyiduna Ghawth رضي الله عنه removed his garb [*khirqah*] and put it on me and articulated: *'O ʿAlī! You have now donned the Garb of Comfort.'* I have worn this garb for 65 years and during this period; I have never experienced any pain, nor sickness, about which I could complain.' Once again in 560 *hijrī* Shaykh ʿAlī رضي الله عنه took me to Sayyiduna Ghawth al-Aʿzam رضي الله عنه and alluded to him: *'I also request a Spiritual Garb [Bātinī Khirqah] for him [Shaykh Abu-Ḥafs].'* Sayyiduna Ghawth رضي الله عنه bowed his head in mediation for a while; and I then saw a flash of light emanate from the Ghawth's chest; which drew close to me. At that instant, my condition became perceptible to such an extent, that I could see the dead, as well as their conditions; and I could also see the angels in their realms. In various dialects, I also heard their *tasbīḥ*. I could also see; and as well as read the writings on the foreheads of every human. Great entities and subjects were revealed to me through the medium of *kashf*.

The great Ghawth ﷺ assured me: *'Take this and do not be afraid.'* My Master Shaykh ʿAlī ﷺ thereby revealed to the Ghawth ﷺ: *'I fear that he will lose his senses.'* Sayyiduna Shaykh ﷺ thereafter, struck me on my chest and I felt that my inner self [*bātin*] had transformed, similar to an anvil[187]. From that juncture, whatever I saw or heard henceforth, did not terrify me. To date, I see light with that flash on the paths of *Malakūt*.

Shaykh Abu-Ḥafs ﷺ further elaborates: when I came to Baghdād for the first time I did not know anyone, nor did I know any locality. Hence, I ended up at a renowned *Madrassa*, which belonged to Sayyiduna Shaykh Muḥiyy al-Dīn ʿAbd al-Qādir ﷺ. I proceeded to the inside of the *Madrassa*, and discovered that there was no one therein. I then heard the voice of someone from the inside, pronouncing: *'O ʿAbd al-Razzāq! Come out and see who is there.'* He came out and saw me, and thereafter, returned and notified: *'There is a Habashī [African] child there.'* I heard a voice, stating with conviction, as follows: *'That child will have a high status [in the future].'* Sayyiduna Ghawth ﷺ thereby, came out holding onto some bread in his hand; and this was the first time that I had seen him. As a mark of respect, I stood up and the Shaykh ﷺ issued an instruction to me: *'O ʿAlī! You stay here,'* whilst he left the food in front of me. Furthermore, he beseeched: *'May Allāh ﷻ give you benefit; May Allāh ﷻ give you benefit, May Allāh ﷻ give you benefit. A time shall come when people will be dependent on you, and you shall reach an elevated status.'* Shaykh Abu-Ḥafs ﷺ concedes to the fact that: *I am the duʿā of Sayyiduna Shaykh ʿAbd al-Qādir* ﷺ.

Concerning the Sacred Sharīʿāh

Sayyiduna Ghawth ﷺ proclaimed that *Imān* is an unseen bird, which descends from the above. Almighty *Allāh* ﷻ, by His Mercy makes it exclusive for

[187] A heavy steel block on which metal is hammered.

whomsoever He destines. It comes and falls on the tree of the servant's heart; and it sings harmonious melodies into it. Its Lord ﷻ furnishes it with glad tidings, and it flies from the cage of its owners chest to the Domain of Truth, i.e. *Sharī ʿāt e Mutahhārah Muḥammadiyyah*. The fruit of the tree of the Nation of *Islām* is invariably such a sun whose light brightens the darkness of existence [creation]. Obedience to its *Sharī ʿāh* blesses one with the providence of both the worlds. One should avoid stepping out of its circle; and one should avoid abstaining from the people of consensus. There are incredible trusts [*amanāh*], entrenched in the heart of the owner [Sayyiduna Rasūlullāh ﷺ] of the Great *Sharī ʿāh*. It is the secrets of the treasury of the concealed secrets of the owner of Great Honour [The august *Ḥabīb* ﷺ]. Obedience to his commands has been decreed as the path towards Almighty *Allāh* ﷻ. The *Kā ʿabah* [focus] of your intellect was created as the landing zone of the words of its Laws. From the clouds of its axioms, the thirsty souls drink the water. In the springs of the lives of its words, the dangers of the intellect are made and the messenger of the souls that is obscured in the hearts that calls out.

The residents of high spirits fly in the plains of love; with the wings of the effects of love and subsequently, enduring pain; they fall onto the branches of fervour. During the time of *fajr*, the nightingales melodiously and passionately sing the hymn of the boon and reminiscence pertinent to: اَشْهَدُ اَنَّهُمْ – *I have made Him a witness.* The subtle breeze of love reminds them of the sweetness of the call of the First Day of Covenant اَلَسْتُ بِرَبِّكُمْ – *Am I not you Lord?*

Some birds come out of the cages of the chest and display their primeval locations of flight. The palace of speech inhales the fragrance of the air; and hence, remembering their lives under the thorny tree of union. They complain about the pain of love, after being separated from friends; and henceforth, they begin to hear the callers of *Allāh* ﷻ, in the voice of bona fide existence. The *du ʿā* of Sayyiduna Rasūlullāh ﷺ becomes engraved on the lines of the tablets of the souls. The *du ʿā* of the Holy Prophet ﷺ transmutes into such a breeze; that it shakes the branches of the hearts. Owing to this breeze, the mounts of the intellect, on the plains of images became ecstatic. The intellect remembered the delight of the treaty; and began moving by the hands of ecstasy; and its life transformed into a mystery from the mysteries of Eternity, and its excitement enhanced from a subtlety of the subtleties of destiny.

When the secret lustres radiate onto the independent souls, the secrets are then secured, and the external veils are lifted from the eyes of the heart. He observes the Divine Beauty of the Owner of Creation [Almighty *Allãh* ﷻ]; by the transparency of the mirror of secrets. The *Ka'ãbah* of an *'Ãrif* is the locale of his Eyes of Truth. Amongst all the paths, the closest path towards *Allãh* ﷻ is to hold steadfast to the Laws of Servitude, as well as to diligently hold onto the link of the *Islãmic Sharī'ãh,* and to remain steadfast on the path of piety.

Love for Allãh ﷻ

The extent of your love for *Allãh* ﷻ shall be in accordance to the extent of your detachment from other creation, other than Him ﷻ; and your reliance on the Will of *Allãh* ﷻ shall be in accordance to the extent of your understanding [*Ma'ãrifah*] of Him ﷻ. Impurity in actions is a type of deprivation. Engrossment in seeking this world, generates evasiveness of one's mind in seeking *Allãh* ﷻ. Hypocrisy in desires, is parallel to the eclipse of the sun of pursuit; and deceitfulness in goals [intentions], is a blemish on the face of intention. The absence of the desired [*Allãh* ﷻ] is punishment of the hearts; and detachment from friends is a chastisement of the brain. The regions of *zuhd* [asceticism] in this world are such a curtain; that they obstructs the path to the lofty Angelic Realm. Concentration in the worship of *Allãh* ﷻ in this world is a reason for the Mercy of *Allãh* ﷻ; in order to concentrate on you.

If the child of your intellect reaches the lap of *adab*, it shall then, not pay attention to this mundane world; but shall prepare itself in that cradle, in which his wealth and family had obliged him to.

The pure souls are the necklaces of the chandelier of the body, and unadulterated intellects are kings of the faces of the palaces. O servant! Open the eye of your intellect, in view of the fact that you may meet the brides of Eternity; and sense the air of the subtleties of Destiny; with the brain of your soul. Verily, *Allāh* ﷻ has placed the concept of existence, to test the eyes of the intelligent, consecutively at the shores of the oceans of this world. They are rescued from concentrating on the attractions of this world; for they are stationed in firm containers under the souls, and raised in the laps of virtues. They are enveloped with the curtains; which are relevant to the verses that encompass Commandments. Should these subtle curtains of destiny be removed; and perchance, the brides of the unseen are embellished on him; whilst the secrets of the brides of the *ʿĀrifīn* are returned to the caves of grace; the reflections of the *ʿĀrifīn* are thereby astonished. The strong mountain of the intellect is trembled to a level; and hence, it questions: what are these hidden secrets that are being exposed to me?

O souls of the Believers! Fly towards *Allāh* ﷻ with the enthusiastic wings of true love; and travel towards *Allāh* ﷻ with an intention focused on legitimacy; and hence, conclude by reaching the border of the long spiritual bedding. Transform the self into a driving force, similar to a moth and fly around the lamps in His ﷻ pursuit, so that you may fall in the vicinity of that light. Revolve around His ﷻ pastures with the wings of the feet of love. Appeal to *Allāh* ﷻ for that which Sayyiduna Nabī Ādam ﷺ had implored: *'O my Lord! We have oppressed our souls, and if You do not forgive us and be merciful unto us, then we will be the ones with great loss.'*

Disobedience of a Servant and its consciences.

I narrate in 699 *hijrī* in Cairo from the Shaykh of noble origin, Abu-ʿAbdullāh Muḥammad b. Shaykh Abu al-ʿAbbās Aḥmad b. Shaykh Abī-Isḥāq Ibrāhīm b. ʿAbdullāh b. ʿAlī Tabrī al-Asl al-Jawī ؓ who narrates in 615 *hijrī* in Jawī, from his father Shaykh Aḥmad ؓ; and he narrates from Shaykh Nūrudīn Abu-ʿAbdullāh al-Jīlī ؓ, originally a Qazwīnī, who had stated in 618 *hijrī*, in Qazwīn. Both of them confirmed that, when Sayyiduna Shaykh Muḥiyy al-Dīn

ʿAbd al-Qãdir ﷺ was deemed to be renowned in the cities, then three *Mashã'ikh*, thereafter set out from Jilãn to meet him. When they reached the *Madrassa* in Baghdãd, they sought permission and thereby entered. They observed that Haḍrate Ghawth ﷺ was seated with a book in his hand. They caught sight of his water container [*lota - jug*]; which was not facing in the direction of the *Qibla*; and the *Khãdim* was standing in front of him. Owing to the negligence of the *Khãdim*, the three *Mashã'ikh* looked at one another in amazement [because the container was not facing the *Qibla*]. Subsequent to the thoughts in their hearts, Sayyiduna Ghawth ﷺ placed the book down and stared at the three visiting *Mashã'ikh* and consequently, he stared at the *Khãdim*, who fell dead to the ground. Henceforth, he stared at the water container which revolved and had thereby stopped facing the *Qibla*.

The very same two narrators state that in 540 *hijrĩ*, in the *Madrassa* of Sayyiduna Ghawth ﷺ; Shaykh Baqã b. Bat'tũ ﷺ, Shaykh ʿAlĩ b. al-Hĩtĩ ﷺ, Sayyid Sharĩf Shaykh Abu-Saʿĩd al-Qaylawĩ ﷺ and Shaykh Mãjid al-Kurdĩ ﷺ were present. Sayyiduna Ghawth al-Aʿzam ﷺ instructed the *Khãdim* to lay out the table cloth with food. Whilst they were eating, Sayyiduna Ghawth ﷺ commanded the *Khãdim* to sit and eat as well. He informed that he was fasting. Shaykh ﷺ affirmed: *'Eat and you will get the thawãb of one fast.'* He repeated that he was fasting. Shaykh ﷺ asserted: *'Eat and you will get the thawãb of fasting for one week.'* He stated again that he was fasting. Shaykh ﷺ enunciated: *'Eat and you will get the thawãb of fasting for one month.'* Yet again he declared that he was fasting. Shaykh ﷺ issued the instruction: *'Eat and you will get the thawãb of fasting for one year.'* He insisted yet again that he was fasting. Shaykh ﷺ thereby commanded: *'Eat and you will get the thawãb of fasting for your entire life.'* He still persisted that he was fasting. The great Ghawth ﷺ then looked at him with anger; and as a result, he fell to the ground. His body began swelling, and pus emerged out of his body. The *Shuyũkh* pleaded on behalf of the *Khãdim* and when his temperament subsided; he forgave him. The *Khãdim* then returned to his original state as if nothing had happened to him.

Regarding Tanziyah – Purity

The points that have been accumulated of Sayyiduna Ghawth ﷺ regarding the Purity of *Allāh* ﷻ are listed as follows:

- Our Lord, Almighty *Allāh* ﷻ in His heights is Close.
- In His Proximity, He is High.
- In His *Qudrat* [power], He creates creation.
- In His Wisdom, He analyses Commands.
- His Knowledge encompasses everything.
- His words are absolutely perfect.
- His Mercy is universal; except for Him, there is no other deity, which can be assigned in comparison to Him.
- Anyone who claims partnership with Him or believes that anything is difficult for Him, is a liar.
- The enumeration of *Allāh's* ﷻ *tasbīḥ* are: the count of the creation; the weight of the *'Arsh*; the breaths of His Pleasure; the tone of His words, the infinite degree of His Knowledge; and according to everything that He Ordained to be created; and that which He has brought out of the ground.
- He is fully Aware of the hidden and exposed.
- He is *Raḥmān* [Beneficent], *Raḥīm* [Merciful], *Malik* [Sovereign], *Quddūs* [sanctified], *'Azīz* [Almighty], *Wāḥid* [One], *Fard* [Unique] and carefree.
- He has no children nor is He a child of anyone.
- He has no competitor and there is nothing like Him.
- He is all Seeing and all Hearing.
- He has no shape, no similarity, no assistant, no support, no partner, no minister, nor an adversary or advisor.
- He is pure from shape and form, which cannot be felt by touch.
- He is not an atom that can be perceived and He is not an *'Arḍ* [188] that fades.

[188] That which cannot exist on its own. Consistently dependent on its origin [*Johar*].

- He is not a *Murakkab* [combined] that can be split into pieces.
- He is not someone with an instrument that has a shape.
- He is not a configuration, which can be described.
- He is not a substance that can be perceived and whose limits can be explained.
- He is not of those with natural disposition.
- He is not of those who rises and sets like the sun.
- He is not darkness that is exposed and He is not light that needs to be ignited.
- He has encompassed things with His Divine Knowledge but they are not joined to Him.
- He is a witness to His information [Revelation] but He does not impede into them or review them.
- He is *Qãhir* [Victorious], *Ḥãkim* [Ruler], *Qãdir* [Powerful] and Merciful.
- The Concealer [of sins]; the Creator [of the Universe]; the Unique; the *Ma'bũd* [the worshipped]; Ever-Living and Eternal. [belief in the concept of: from Eternity to Eternity].
- He is Eternal and never dies and His Regime is permanent
- His *Jabarũt* [Realm of Power] is permanent
- He is *Qayyũm* [Self Subsisting] and He is *'Azĩz* [The Mighty]; and no one can oppress Him.
- He uproots, and none can replicate Him.
- His Names are exceptional and His Attributes are eulogised.
- His Being is lofty and His Nobility is sturdy.
- Suppositions cannot perceive him, and thoughts cannot comprehend Him.
- He cannot be understood through estimation and His Paradigm cannot be given to people.
- Intellect cannot explain His Essence, and the mind cannot constrain Him.
- He is far beyond comprehension; he can be conceived through His Attributes, or given the evidence of His Existence by that; which He

has created.

- He takes into account of every breath.
- He has knowledge of everything that is earned by His creation. He is ever existent and verily, He has a detailed account of everything, and is fully aware of all the occurrences and its consequences.
- Every creation will come to Him individually on the day of Judgement.
- He provides food and is not provided with food.
- He grants sustenance and is not granted sustenance.
- He ensures security, and does not have to be ensured of security.
- Whatever He created was not for the purpose of benefit; nor for the eradication of harm; and neither because of anyone's programme or thought that arose in their minds. In fact, He creates by His Will which is pure from the changes of new creation.
- He is Unique in His Power in creating; removal of harm and misfortune, changes in existence and amendments of conditions.
- Whatever He Ordains; He executes them at the stipulated moment.
- There is no one in His Domain that advises Him in His Ordainment.
- He is alive, and such a life, was not acquired and no one has surpassed Him in any matter.
- He is an *Ālim* [all-Knowing] with such infinite Knowledge that is neither created nor concealed behind curtains of isolation.
- He is Omnipotent, possessing such Power; which cannot be encompassed or limited.
- The administration and plan of His Will is flawless and prudent; hence, pure from any defect.
- He is a Protector who is devoid of error and forgetfulness.
- He introduces contraction and expansion and becomes pleased and angry
- He forgives, for He is merciful.
- He brings entities into existence, and takes away entities into non-existence.
- It befits His Divine Integrity; to be called the Most Powerful.
- He cures the sickness of creation and inflicts sickness.

- His Attributes are perfect and complete; and it is incumbent that He deserves to be called the Lord.
- He subjects the actions of creation in accordance to His Divine Will.
- He deserves to be called *Ma'būd* [the One to be worshipped].
- His Knowledge is not such that conflicts with Eternal Knowledge and therefore it apprises Him to be called the Real and Absolute *'Ālim*.
- There is nothing in similarity to His Divine Being; and Majestic Attribute and hence, it is obligatory to proclaim that there is nothing like Him.
- Everything that exists is, because of His eternal and permanent Divine Existence.
- The life of every living creature is subjected to Him and benefits from His Command.
- If intellect was His honour, then present an example; and if knowledge argues about His Glory; understand that, it will become unconscious and cease to function. Thoughts will tire and become senseless.
- There is no replacement which has been discovered for the splendid lustre comprising purity of His Glorious Honour. His *Tawḥīd* cannot be ignored.
- If the army of purity comes to the forefront, then speech will be humiliated, and despatched.
- It is impossible for the Intellect to grasp the reality of the Divine Being of *Allāh* ﷻ, because it is concealed behind the veils of His Magnificence.
- The vision of the eyes are unable to perceive the reality of the Light of His Permanence.
- If the limits of the knowledge of creation are lifted; and turn to information,

  or if the limits of the knowledge of kingdoms raise their eyes and see; for them, shall then a flash appear from the First Day [*Azal*]; that will take out a veil of excellence, which is pure from defects to the similarity of the veiled. No one has the power to see the Light of His Company, even though their power of perception is accumulated.

- The signs of their power in the contact with the qualities of Eternity are so close to the Attributes of the Last Day [*Abad*]; that separation is not always before it. They are not those who reach separation. Such an awe appears from the most distinguished and sacrosanct Honourable Presence that annihilates all defects.
- Solitude prevents enumeration; presence turns away limits; glory rejects Condition; perfection eliminates examples; merit obliges Oneness as being obligatory; Divine Power expands the kingdom and nobility; and thereby, annihilates praises.
- ʿIlm [knowledge] comprehends the following: whatever is on the earth, skies and in between them; and that which is under the earth and in the depths of the oceans; and whatever is in every tree and root of every hair; including the spot where ever leaf will fall; the weight of every grain; mountain and ocean with every action; inclusive of the signs and breaths of every servant.
- He is unlike His servants
- No place is void of His Knowledge
- Hence, all creatures revert; since there is no way out, except the acceptance and confirmation of His Unitarianism as there is no first before His Eternity, there is no last after His Permanence. There is no condition or example that can enter his superfluity [*Samadiyat*], and there is no knowledge that can use its qualities for creation to achieve the knowledge of *Allāh* ﷻ; in order that he may understand that *Allāh* ﷻ is one and establish His existence; and not use a similitude for *Allāh* ﷻ. Hence, *Imān* proves Him correct with *ʿIlm al-Yaqīn* [Direct or Certain Knowledge] so as to be enlightened with knowledge, whose reality is the *Ghayb* [unseen]. The intellect cannot venture to comprehend Him. That which the assumption imagines; or the understanding confers it brightness upon; or the intellect visualizes it, are all in contrast to the glory, magnificence and status of Almighty *Allāh* ﷻ, taking into consideration, that which the mind comprehends; can never ever be *Allāh* ﷻ.
- He is *Awwal* [Only the First], *Ākhir* [Only the First and Last], *Zāhir*

[Only the Evident] and *Bātin* [Only the Concealed].

➢ He is the *ʿĀlim* [Knower] of everything.

Amazing Incident of a Trader

I narrate in 669 *hijrī* in Cairo from Shaykh Faqih Abu al-Fatāḥ Nasrullāh b. al-Qāsim b. Yūsuf b. Khalīl b. Aḥmad al-Hāshimī al-Baghdādī al-Karkhī ﷺ, who narrates from two senior *Shuyūkh*, Qāḍī al-Quḍāt Abu-Sāliḥ Nasar b. Shaykh Sayyid Abu-Bakr ʿAbd al-Razzāq b. Sayyid Imām Muḥiyy al-Dīn Sayyid ʿAbd al-Qādir Jilī ؓ and Shaykh Abu al-Ḥasan ʿAlī b. Sulaymān ﷺ, the Baker in 631 *hijrī* in Baghdād, who narrates from Shaykh Abu-Sāliḥ ؓ, and he narrates in 591 *hijrī* from His father Sayyid ʿAbd al-Razzāq al-Jilānī ؓ and his uncle Sayyid ʿAbd al-Jabbār al-Jilānī ؓ. Shaykh Abu al-Ḥasan ﷺ narrates from Shaykh ʿImrān al-Kaymātī ﷺ and Shaykh Baz'zār ﷺ in 590 *hijrī*, and they narrate from Shaykh Abu-ʿAbdullāh b. ʿUbādah ʿAbdul Moḥsin b. Munzir Ansārī al-Jilī ﷺ in 673 *hijrī*, in Cairo. He narrates from two *Shuyūkh,* Shaykh, the leader Abu-Muḥammad ʿAbdullāh b. ʿUthmān al-Yunīnī ﷺ in 616 *hijrī*, in Damascus and Shaykh ʿĀrif Abu-Isḥāq Ibrāhīm b. Maḥmūd b. Jowhar al-Baʿalbakki al-ʿAqībī ﷺ in 623 *hijrī*. Both of them accentuate that they narrate from their Shaykh, Shaykh Abu-Muḥammad ʿAbdullāh al-Batā'iḥī ﷺ, who had said that in 553 *hijrī* Abu al-Maʿālī Muḥammad b. Aḥmad ﷺ, the trader attended the *majlis* at the *Madrassa* of Sayyiduna Shaykh Muḥiyy al-Dīn ʿAbd al-Qādir al-Jilānī ؓ. During the session, he felt extremely uncomfortable within his bowels, and needed to go to the toilet. He was in such discomfort that he could not stand, nor walk. He desperately looked in anguish at Sayyiduna Ghawth al-Aʿzam ؓ, and immediately the Ghawth ؓ intercepted for he perceived his plight whilst delivering his speech. He took one step down from his *mimbar* [pulpit]. On the first step, a face similar to that of the Ghawth ؓ appeared; and thereby, continued by articulating the similar words of Ḥaḍrate Ghawth ؓ and hence, continued with the lecture. Nobody, except the trader and those whom *Allāh* ﷻ had decreed could see the emergence of this figure.

Sayyiduna Ghawth ﷺ streaked through the people and stood in front of the trader, and covered his head with his sleeve. Sayyidi ʿAbd al-Razzāq al-Jilānī ﷺ states that his father covered him with a shawl. The trader affirmed that, at once he found himself in a huge jungle where there was a river flowing. There was a tree, where he took his bunch of keys and hung it onto one of the branches, and then went to relief himself. After he had finished, he performed *wuḍū* in the river and thereafter engaged in two *rakʿāts* of *salāh*. As soon as he terminated with *salām*, Sayyiduna Ghawth ﷺ removed his sleeve or shawl from him; and he was sitting fully relieved in the same *majlis*. His hands were still wet with his *wuḍū* water. Sayyiduna Ghawth ﷺ was sitting on his original spot, and delivering his speech, as though he had never retreated from there. The trader remained silent; and did not mention his experience to anyone. He discovered that his bunch of keys were missing.

Over a period of time, he prepared a caravan for trading purposes to a non-Arab country. He travelled for fifteen days and stopped to rest in a jungle; wherein there was a river. He went into the jungle to relieve himself and found the jungle and the river to be very familiar to the one he had visited long ago from the *majlis* of Sayyiduna Ghawth ﷺ. It reminded him of that astonishing day; and to his amazement, it was that very same spot, where he had relieved himself; the very same river, and the very same tree. He immediately remembered everything, and forgot nothing. Thereafter, he proceeded to that branch; where he had forgotten his bunch of keys, and found them hanging, where he had left them.

When he returned to Baghdād, he went straight to Sayyiduna Ghawth ﷺ to report on his remarkable experience. Before he could utter a single word, Sayyiduna Shaykh ﷺ held his ear and asserted: *'O Abu al-Maʿālī! Do not inform anyone about this in my life time.'* From that day Abu al-Maʿālī ﷺ remained in his service, until the demise of Sayyiduna Ghawth ﷺ.

Comments of Sayyiduna Ghawth al-Aʿzam ﷺ Concerning Shaykh Mansūr al-Ḥallāj ﷺ

Ḥaḍrat Sayyiduna Ghawth al-Aʿzam ﷺ expressed, with regard to Ḥaḍrat Mansūr al-Ḥallāj ﷺ. Their eyes are sewn with threads. The human was created weak. They had located nothing in the skies that could turn them away from hunting. A prey was then exposed to them; vocalizing that: *'I have seen Allāh* ﷻ*.'* Their astonishment intensified through the statement of the beloved: *'Whichever direction you turn, you will see the Divine Being of Allāh* ﷻ*.'* It then returned to earth, and desired for that particular bird from the cage of some *ʿĀrifīn*, which flies away from its tree of images from its homes, and tears open the lines of the angels in the skies and henceforth, settles there. It is a falcon of the falcons; which is more beloved than the fire beneath the ocean. It observed with the eye of intellect and attained nothing else, except its signs. Henceforward, it propelled its hunt yet again, and discovered nothing in both the worlds; except the beloved, Almighty *Allāh* ﷻ. At that moment, it rejoiced and pronounced, by the emotional tongue of its heart: *'I am Allāh.'* It sang this with such an intonation, which was contrary to the dialect of the human. It eulogised this in such an expressive voice, which in fact did not harmonize with the condition of the human beings.

It presented itself in front of death that its inner self shrieked: *'O Ḥallāj! You have believed that your strength is with you. Now announce to the representation of all the ʿĀrifīn that the Oneness of the One is sufficient. Say that O Muḥammad! You are the Sultān of Reality. You are the pupil of the eye of existence and the necks of the ʿĀrifīn are bowed at the threshold of your door. The foreheads of all creation are placed on your glorious protected pasture.'*

The Holy *Kāʿabah* in front of his eyes

I was informed in 671 *hijrī* in Cairo by Faqih Abu al-Ḥijjāj Yūsuf b. ʿAbd al-Raḥīm b. Ḥijjāj b. Yaʿla b. ʿĪsā al-Maghribī Fāsī al-Mālikī Muḥaddith ﷺ and he narrates from his grandfather Shaykh Ḥijjāj ﷺ in 623 *hijrī*, in Fās from Shaykh Bin Muḥammad b. Sāliḥ b. Dīrjān al-Wakālī ﷺ, whom he joined in 623 *hijrī*, during the *Ḥajj*. When they were in *ʿArafāt*, they met Shaykh Abu al-Qāsim ʿUmar b. Masʿūd al-Baghdādī ﷺ distinguished as Baz'zār. Whilst the two of them were sitting, they began recalling the glorious days of Sayyiduna Ghawth al-Aʿzam ﷺ. Shaykh Abu-Muḥammad ﷺ declared that his Shaykh, Shaykh Abu-Madyan ﷺ directed him as follows: *'Go to Baghdād to Sayyiduna Shaykh ʿAbd al-Qādir ﷺ so that he may teach you the Path of Faqr [Spiritual Culture].'* As a result I went to Baghdād.

When I saw Sayyiduna Shaykh ʿAbd al-Qādir ﷺ in Baghdād, I did not see anyone more august than him. He confined me to seclusion for 120 days. He came to me and issued the command: *'Look to this direction [Qibla]'*, and to his command, I replied: *'Yes I see'*. Thereafter, he questioned: *'What do you see?'* I confirmed that: *'I see the Kaʿābah.'* He then instructed me to look in the direction of east; and questioned: *'What do you see?'* To this effect, I replied: *'Yes I see'* He enquired further: *'What do you see?'* I thereby answered: *'I see my Shaykh Abu-Madyan.'* Sayyiduna Ghawth ﷺ henceforth, queried from me: *'What is your intention? Do you want to go to the Kaʿābah or to your Shaykh?'* I affirmed: *'To my Shaykh Abu-Madyan.'* Ḥaḍrate Ghawth ﷺ questioned: *'Do you want to return in one step, or as you came?'* I replied: *'As I came.'* He then pronounced: *'Very well.'* He thereby advised: *'O Abu-Sāliḥ! If you intend to achieve Faqr, you will never achieve it, if you do not climb onto its stairs. The steps of Tawḥīd and the king of Tawḥīd is that you evade every new creation that glitters in front of you.'*

I put forth an appeal: *'O my Master! I need your assistance in this matter.'* He cast a glance on me and all the excitement of my intentions disappeared; from within my heart, synonymous to the brightness of the day, that pushes away the darkness of the night. To date, I still utilize and benefit from his single glance of that day.

Shaykh Baz'zār ﷺ said that he too was once confined to seclusion in front of Sayyiduna Ghawth al-Aʿzam ﷺ and he exclaimed to me: *'O my beloved son! Guard my back so that a cat may not fall on it.'* I reflected within myself that; *'How will a cat fall from the ceiling, when there are no holes in it?'* Sayyiduna Ghawth ﷜ had not completed the words as to what he was saying, when a cat fell on his back. Thereafter, he placed his sacred hands on my chest; and a reflection, similar to the light of the sun shone into my heart; whereby I discovered *Allāh* ﷻ. Until this day, that specific light increases in my heart.

Sayyiduna Ghawth ﷜ then instructed:

> 'Step aside, you who worship *Allāh* ﷻ without knowledge. Such a person will cause more damage than the person who rectifies it. Procure from your Lord ﷻ the lamp of the Sacred Law. One who worships with knowledge, *Allāh* ﷻ shall make one an inheritor of such knowledge; about which one was oblivious of. Detach yourself from your possessions; depart from your brothers; and turn your back towards the transitory entities; and thus, prepare yourself for *zuhd* [Asceticism], because *Allāh* ﷻ has blessed you with profound ethics. Detach yourself from the foreign, as well as the worldly commodities.
>
> Fear! That your lamp may extinguish; and implement 40 days of *Ikhlās* [sincerity] for *Allāh* ﷻ, so that wisdom begins to flow from your lips. Your condition shall be such that, you shall precipitously see the fire of *Allāh* ﷻ; in comparison to how Sayyiduna Nabī Mūsā ﷺ saw the fire from the tree, within his heart. You shall declare to your *nafs*; your evil spirit; your disposition; and your belongings: wait! I have felt the fire! Within the heart, a voice shall be heard; cautioning: *'I am your Lord and worship me. Refrain from turning to the closeness of others. Do not have relationships with anyone; other than Me. Become ignorant of all, except Me. Meet with Me; and not with others. Seek from Me, and refrain from others. Come towards My Knowledge; My Proximity; My Divine Realm and My Lordship; until our meeting is complete, and whatever is thereby decreed to happen, will happen.'* Inspiration shall be given to His servants of what He Ordains; and all veils shall be lifted. All impurities shall disappear; and the soul shall experience tranquillity. Esteem shall be showered, and you shall be addressed as follows: *'O heart! Go to Pharaoh, O ego! Go to the*

devil and chain them and thereby bring them to Me. Guide them towards Me. Enlighten them to be obedient to Me; so that I may show them the path to Righteousness. Meet them, and thereby, followed by detachment, meet with them yet again.'

I was informed in 671 *hijrī* in Cairo by Shaykh Abu-Ghālib Faḍalullāh b. Ismāʿīl b. ʿAlī b. Aḥmad b. Ibrāhīm Misrī al-Baghdādī al-Azjī al-Ḥanbalī ﷺ who narrates from three *Shuyūkh*, Shaykh Abu-ʿAmar ʿUthmān b. Sulaymān ﷺ prominently recognized as Qas'sīr, in 629 *hijrī* in Baghdād and Shaykh Abu al-Ḥasan Khafāf al-Baghdādī ﷺ in 625 *hijrī* and Shaykh Abu al-Ḥasan ʿAlī b. Sulaymān ﷺ distinguished as the Baker, in 634 *hijrī* who related that Shaykh Khafāf ﷺ narrates from his Shaykh, Shaykh Abu-Saʿūd al-Ḥarīmī ﷺ in 579 *hijrī* in Baghdād and Shaykh Qas'sīr ﷺ narrates from his Shaykh, Shaykh Abu-Muḥammad ʿAbd al-Ghanī b. Nuqta Baghdādī ﷺ in Baghdād in 580 *hijrī* and he narrates from his Shaykh, Shaykh Abu-ʿAmar ʿUthmān al-Sarīfīnī ﷺ in 539 *hijrī*. Shaykh Abu al-Ḥasan the Baker ﷺ narrates from his Shaykh, Shaykh ʿUmar al-Kimyānī ﷺ and Shaykh ʿUmar Baz'zār in 591 *hijrī* in Baghdād.

The hand of Shaykh Ḥammād ﷺ is rectified

I narrate in 673 *hijrī* in Cairo from Shaykh Abu al-Ḥasan ʿAlī b. Azdamar Muḥammadī al-Baghdādī ﷺ who narrates in 629 *hijrī* in *Jāme'h Khalīfah* from Baqiyat al-Salf Abu al-Ḥasan ʿAlī b. ʿAlī b. Muḥammad b. Aḥmad b. Ḥusain ʿUmar Kimyamānī al-Baghdādī Sūfī ﷺ, prominently known as Saqā. He asserts that his Shaykh, Sayyiduna Shaykh ʿAbd al-Qādir ؓ visited the Shanūzī cemetery, on Wednesday 27th Dhil-Ḥijja 529 *hijrī*. Many *Fuqahah* and *Fuqarah* were present. He stood at the grave of Sayyiduna Shaykh Ḥammād b. Muslim al-Dabbās ؓ, [the juice merchant] for a long time, and it became very hot in the sun. Everyone were standing behind the Ghawth ؓ. He then left the grave; smiling and signs of happiness were noticed on his luminous face. He was questioned about the reason for his prolonged stay at the grave of Shaykh Ḥammād ؓ. Henceforward, he proclaimed:

'One day, on the 15th of *Sha'bān* 439 *hijrī* in Baghdād, I was with the group of Shaykh Ḥammād ﷺ to perform *Jum'āh* in *Jāme'h al-Ruḍāfah*. Shaykh Ḥammād ﷺ was with us. When we reached the river, Shaykh Ḥammād ﷺ pushed me into the river. It was a very cold day; and I recited: '*Bismillāh*' with the intention of the *Jumm'āh ghusal*; whilst I fell into the chilly river. I was wearing a *Sūf* [woollen] *jubba* [cloak] and I had pages from a book in my sleeve. I lifted my hand in order to avoid the pages from getting wet. The group left me and moved on. I got out of the water, squeezed my *jubba* and followed the group. Although it was a cold day, and the water was also cold; but this did not make me uncomfortable. I did not feel cold. The Shaykh's *murīds* began mocking me, and hence, the Shaykh ﷺ rebuked them and vociferously pronounced: *'I did this to test him, but I found him to be an unswerving mountain; which would not move from its spot.'* Sayyiduna Ghawth ﷺ proceeded further by stating that today, he had seen Shaykh Ḥammād ﷺ wearing a gem studded garb in his grave. He wore a crown on his head comprising rubies; and in addition there were gold bangles on his hands. The shoes that he wore were made of gold; but however, his right hand was paralyzed. I questioned him about the problem pertinent to his right hand. He admitted to the fact that: this is the same hand that I used to push you into the river. I appeal to you to pardon me for this. I earnestly declared: I forgive you; but he insisted that I should plead to *Allāh* ﷻ on his behalf to normalize his hand once more.

I then supplicated to *Allāh* ﷻ on his behalf and 500 *Awliya* in their graves, responded by the invocation of *Āmīn*, to my *du'ā* and pleaded to *Allāh* ﷻ to accept my *du'ā*. They were pleading on my behalf to *Allāh* ﷻ whilst I consistently made *du'ās*, until *Allāh* ﷻ transformed his hand to its normal state. Shaykh Ḥammād ﷺ thereby, shook my hands with that very same hand, and he was showered with bliss.

When this news spread in Baghdād, all the *murīds* and *Sūfis* of Shaykh Ḥammād ﷺ were summoned to an assembly by Sayyiduna Ghawth ﷺ in order to confirm this occurrence. Others also joined them. All of them came to the *Madrassa* of Sayyiduna Ghawth ﷺ, but not a single one of them could utter a word; because of his distinguished reverence. Henceforward, Ḥaḍrate Ghawth ﷺ addressed them about their desires and asserted: *'You select two Mashā'ikh of your choice to testify on what I said about Shaykh Ḥammād ﷺ.'* They appointed Shaykh Abu-Yaʿqūb Yūsuf b. Ayyūb b. Yūsuf al-Hamdānī ﷺ who had just arrived on that day in Baghdād, and Shaykh Abu-Muḥammad ʿAbd al-Raḥmān b. Shoʿayb b. Masʿūd al-Kurdī ﷺ. These two were the prominent *Asḥāb e Kashf* [people of unveiling]; the ones with charismatic qualities [*karāmat*], and who were perfect in their spiritual inclination.

The people stated that they would issue Sayyiduna Ghawth ﷺ with a mandate until Friday; for these *Shuyūkh* to testify to this incident. But Sayyiduna Ghawth al-Aʿzam ﷺ intervened and resonated: *'You will not get up from here before you are informed about this matter.'* He bowed his head in meditation and everyone also bowed their heads. All the *Fuqarah* outside the *Madrassa* began screaming. Spontaneously, Shaykh Abu-Yaʿqūb Yūsuf b. Ayyūb b. Yūsuf al-Hamdānī ﷺ hastened, and in a barefooted condition; he entered the *Madrassa* and declared: *'Just now Allāh ﷻ had revealed Shaykh Ḥammād to me and he said: 'O Yūsuf! Hasten to the Madrassa of Shaykh ʿAbd al-Qādir ﷺ and inform those Mashā'ikh assembled there that: Whatever Shaykh ʿAbd al-Qādir had said about me is the truth.'*

Before Shaykh Yūsuf ﷺ could complete his words, Shaykh ʿAbd al-Raḥmān ﷺ also arrived, and verbalized the same dictums of Shaykh Yūsuf ﷺ. Subsequently, all the *Mashā'ikh* sought pardon from Sayyiduna Ghawth al-Aʿzam ﷺ.

Advices for the Faqīr [Spiritual Pauper]

Ḥaḍrat Ghawth al-Aʿzam Muḥiyy al-Dīn ʿAbd al-Qādir al-Jilānī ﷺ instituted counselling and advice to the travellers on the Path of Spiritualism. It is advisable for the *Faqīr* to wear the garb of purity and adorn himself with contentment; so that he may reach *Allāh* ﷻ. Seek the Door of Proximity; with the feet of Sincerity. He must flee from the world and the *Ākhirah*, viz. creation and existence. He must be perceptive of the fact that he shall die a thousand times; and shall live a thousand times. The mercy; compassion; benediction and love of *Allāh* ﷻ shall be focused on him. His emotions; vision and honour should enjoin the alliance of the exalted Prophets عليهم السلام, *Siddiqīn* and souls of the angels. With these objectives and implementations, progress henceforth, towards *Allāh* ﷻ. His heart and the innermost being must be pure; and he should be aloof from every newly created entity. Get close to *Allāh* ﷻ, and carefully undertake an introspection of your past deeds from page to page; and stop thereby, to ponder over every word and letter. Stop at every paragraph; period; moment and second in contemplation. Only then, shall the reversion of the seeker, become easy to be sought. As fear captivates him to its side; on the same token, proximity attracts him to its side; and thereby he shall consistently adjust from one condition to another, until he reaches to its closest. He shall be unique and alone within the Divine Proximity; and secrets shall be disclosed to him. He will be given a robe, tray and a stately crown. Henceforth, he shall fervently proclaim the Sovereign Power [Almighty *Allāh* ﷻ] to be his Witness; and he shall not change his beliefs in Him. His companionship with *Allāh* ﷻ shall be unwavering, whilst his sainthood [*Wilāyah*] shall attain permanency. *Zuhd* will not remain with *Ma'rifah*. O men of the heart! Your seeking of *Jannah* is a chain from Almighty *Allāh* ﷻ.

I narrate in 670 *hijrī* in Cairo from Shaykh Abu-Muḥammad Rajab b. Mansūr al-Dārī رحمه الله who narrates from two *Shuyūkh*, Shaykh ʿĀrif Abu-Faḍal Isḥāq b. Aḥmad b. Khānam al-Ghansī رحمه الله and Shaykh Abu-Bakr Muḥammad b. ʿUmar b. Abī-Bakr Muqrī al-Baghdādī رحمه الله renowned as Ibn Khilāl in 667 *hijrī*, in Baghdād. Shaykh Abu-Faḍal رحمه الله affirms that he narrates in 592 *hijrī*, in Baghdād from Shaykh Abu-Muḥammad Talḥā b. Muzaffar b. Ghānim al-ʿAlshī رحمه الله and Shaykh Abu-Bakr رحمه الله, who narrates from two *Shuyūkh*, Shaykh Abu-Ḥafs ʿUmar b. Abī-Nasar b. ʿAlī al-Baghdādī رحمه الله distinguished as Ibn Ghazāl and Shaykh Abu al-Thanā Mahmūd b. ʿUthmān رحمه الله prominent as Baqqāl in Baghdād.

Reason the great Ghawth ﷺ is called Muḥiyy al-Dīn

I narrate in 659 *hijrī* in Cairo from Faqih Abu al-Faraj ʿAbd al-Samīʿh b. ʿAlī b. Aḥmad b. Muḥammad b. ʿAbdus Salām al-Baghdādī al-Basrī al-Ḥirmī ﷺ who narrates from two *Shuyūkh*, Shaykh Sharīf Abu al-Qāsim Haybatullāh b. ʿAbdullāh ﷺ, eminently known as Mudallal in Baghdad; and in 579 *hijrī*, in Baghdād from Shaykh Abu-ʿAbdullāh Muḥammad b. Qā'idūnī ﷺ. Shaykh Abu al-Ḥasan ﷺ narrates from two *Shuyūkh*, Shaykh ʿImrān al-Kaymātī ﷺ and Shaykh Baz'zār ﷺ in 591 *hijrī*, in Baghdād. Both of them confirm that their Shaykh, Sayyiduna Shaykh Muḥiyy al-Dīn ʿAbd al-Qādir ﷺ was questioned in our presence: *'What is the reason for your name being Muḥiyy al-Dīn?'* To this effect he replied:

> 'In 511 *hijrī*, I once came barefooted on a journey to Baghdād so that I could go for *Ḥajj*. On the way I passed by a weak, and pale faced sick person. He looked at me and thereafter, greeted: *'As Salāmu ʿalaykum O ʿAbd al-Qādir.'* I replied to his greeting and he requested me to come closer to him. I proceeded closer to him; and he further requested me to position him in sitting up mode. I placed him up, in a sitting position; and his body began growing, his face became magnificent and his complexion had cleared up. I became afraid; whilst he besought: *'Do you know who I am?'* I replied in the negative, and he revealed to me: *'I am the Religion [Dīn]. I was as you initially saw me in a dilapidated condition and verily, Allāh ﷻ gave me a new life because of you. You are Muḥiyy al-Dīn.'*
>
> I took leave of him, and came to the *Jām ʿeh Masjid*. There I met a person who gave me shoes to wear; and addressed me as: *'O my Master Muḥiyy al-Dīn!'* After I performed my *Salāh*, people rushed towards me, and began kissing my hand and thus, proclaiming: *'O Muḥiyy al-Dīn.'* Before this encounter, no one addressed me by this name.

The Reasons to Gain the Closeness of Allāh ﷻ

Sayyiduna Ghawth al-Aʿzam ﷺ discoursed the significant facts; that assists one to attain closeness to *Allãh* ﷻ. He deliberated as follows:

Oh servants of *Allãh* ﷻ; and His *murĩds*! Firstly, the *nisbah* [relation] with people [*Awliya*] is compulsory upon you for the gratification of *Allãh* ﷻ. They are your guides and your keys. It is by following them, that you shall be transported to the closeness of Almighty *Allãh* ﷻ. You heart, secrets and intrinsic qualities are directed to the Sublime Lord ﷻ. If you follow and be practically obedient to the Holy *Qur'ãn* and Sayyiduna Rasũlullãh ﷺ with sincerity; and possess purity of conviction in your actions, you shall invariably be assisted with mercy, favours and love. These attributes shall enter your heart and the Mercy of *Allãh* ﷻ shall precipitate into it. There shall be those favours in these mysteries, which will surpass you; whilst the Divine Knowledge of *Allãh* ﷻ is fully aware of your zeal for the attainment of His Divine Proximity. He will then allure you to Him, and admit you to His closeness. He will position you in front of Him; and allow you to observe those entities, which no eyes have seen, nor did any ear has heard.

When the servant reaches that phase, his heart will then receive sacred garbs, and the crown of kingship will be placed onto his head. The royal ring from the kingdom will be placed onto his finger. He wears the protective garb of piety and the servant's heart is protected. Thereafter, he disappears from creation; and is concealed by Him; i.e. by the One Who conceals [*Allãh* ﷻ]. He then returns him to creation for the purpose of their reformation. At that moment he returns to the beloved Messenger of *Allãh* ﷺ. Respectfully he expresses his allegiance to the Holy Prophet ﷺ: *'These are the favours that I was blessed with through your blessings.'*

At that juncture, the servant returns to creation in the company of Sayyiduna Rasũlullãh ﷺ; together with the legion of his illustrious *Saḥãbah* ﷡. He holds the Holy *Qur'ãn* in his right hand and the *Sunnah* in his left hand. The souls of the noble Prophets ﵈ surround him; and it is stipulated to him: *'Remember the blessings of Allãh ﷻ that are on you.'*

I narrate in 673 *hijrī* from Shaykh Abu al-Ḥasan ʿAlī b. Azūmar al-Muḥammadī ﷺ, who narrates from Shaykh Muḥiyy al-Dīn Abu-ʿAbdullah b. Aḥmad al-Tawḥīdī ﷺ in 639 *hijrī*, in Baghdād, whilst he narrates from his maternal uncle, Qāḍī al-Quḍāt Sayyiduna Shaykh Abu-Sāliḥ Nasar b. Sayyiduna Imām ʿAbd al-Razzāq al-Jilānī ﷺ b. Sayyiduna Shaykh Muḥiyy al-Dīn ʿAbd al-Qādir al-Jilānī ﷺ and Shaykh Sharīf Abu al-Qāsim Haybatullāh b. Aḥmad ﷺ; renowned as Ibn al-Mansūr, in 624 *hijrī*, in *Jāmeʿh Mansūr,* both of them narrate from Sayyiduna Ḥāfiz Abu-Bakr ʿAbd al-Razzāq al-Jilānī ﷺ b. Sayyiduna Shaykh Muḥiyy al-Dīn ʿAbd al-Qādir al-Jilānī ﷺ in 598 *hijrī*....

Adhān pronounced at Midnight

I narrate in 669 *hijrī* in Cairo from Shaykh Abu al-Ḥasan ʿAlī b. Abī-Bakr b ʿUmar b. Isḥāq al-Baghdādī ﷺ, who narrates from two *Shuyūkh* in 603 *hijrī,* in Baghdād. Shaykh Abu al-Ḥasan ʿAlī b. Sulaymān, the Baker ﷺ and Shaykh Abu-ʿUmar ʿUthmān b. Sulaymān, known as Qas'sīr ﷺ. Both of them confirmed that their Master, Sayyiduna Shaykh Muḥiyy al-Dīn ʿAbd al-Qādir al-Jilānī ﷺ called for the *Muazzin* of his *Masjid* on Thursday night, the night of 1st *Ramaḍān* 545 *hijrī;* and instructed him to climb onto the minaret and call out the *adhān;* to which, he adhered to. Thereafter, he commanded him to call out the *adhān* for the second time, during the third portion of the night. The third time that he issued the instruction for the *adhān* to be called out, was before the time of the *Fajr Salāh* and finally; after a certain duration, he instructed him to call out the fourth *adhān*, which was during the time of *Salāt al-Fajr*.

Just before midday, some *murīds* questioned the Ghawth ﷺ with regard to the reason for the pronouncements for those *adhāns*; and to which he replied:

> When I instructed him to call out the first *adhān,* the *ʿArsh,* then shuddered powerfully, and a messenger under the *ʿArsh* heralded that the confidant pious [*Akhyār*] should stand up in devotion. When I commanded him to call out the second *adhān*, it was similarly declared under the *ʿArsh,* that all the holy *Awliya* [*Abrār*] should stand up in

devotion. During the time of the third *adhān*, the *ʿArsh* trembled a little, and the proclamation was made for those who make *Istighfār* in the early hours of the morning, should stand up. Hence, in the first *adhān*, I pointed out to the ones of the first station; that their time had arrived for devotion. The second *adhān* was a reminder to the people of the second station; and the third *adhān* was a reminder to those of the third station.

Abstain from this *Duniya* and focus to the *Ākhirah*

Sayyiduna Ghawth al-Aʿzam enunciated that the *duniya* from *Ākhirah* and *Ākhirah* from the Lord of *duniya* and *Ākhirah,* is a chain. Thus, he will not take them, nor engage in them, but when he reaches there, he shall then reach there towards them, with the intrinsic qualities of his heart and intellect. Abstain from this material world and concentrate on the *Ākhirah,* and thereafter, abstain from *Ākhirah* and concentrate on *Allāh* . Both, [*duniya* and *Ākhirah*] shall then be obedient to you. Place both of them behind you; and henceforth the *duniya*, as well as your share in it; shall come to you; and shall seek for you in the *Ākhirah*. If it does not find you there, then it shall query from the *Ākhirah,* as to where it took you. *Ākhirah* will confess that it proceeded to search for him at the Door of the Mighty Sovereign Power [*Allāh*], but could not find him; and thus, is still on the lookout for him.

Both, *duniya* and *Ākhirah* shall stand up; rushing behind you, and shall reach you. You shall be located at the Door of the Mighty Sovereign Power; i.e. *Allāh* . The *duniya* will, henceforth complain to the Mighty Sovereign Power , and it shall be disclosed: how did you leave your *amānah* [trust]; as they were allotted to you in accordance to Divine Ordinance? Hence, you shall have the intercession in the Divine Court of *Allāh* in this regard; and in view of that fact, you may take your share. Certainly, remember His advice; that whilst taking from the *duniya*, concentrate on the *Ākhirah* as well. You shall then return with the angels and souls of the Prophets . Thereafter, you shall go to a shop, situated between *Jannah* and *Jahannam*; and between the *duniya* and *Ākhirah*; between Creator and creation; between the cause and causative;

between the exposed and hidden; between the sensible and insensible; between the strong and weak; between the comprehending and non-comprehending; and between the understood and the misunderstood.

You will thereby have four faces. With the first one, you will look at the *duniya*; with the second one, you will look at *Ākhirah*; with the third one you will look at creation, and with the fourth one you will look at the Almighty Creator ﷻ.

The first Ḥajj of Sayyiduna Ghawth al-Aᶜzam

I narrate in 673 *hijrī* in Cairo from Shaykh Sharīf Khalīl Abu al-ᶜAbbās Aḥmad b. Shaykh Abī-ᶜAbdullāh Muḥammad b. Abī al-Ghanā'im Muḥammad Azharī b. Abī al-Fākhir Muḥammad Mukhtār al-Ḥusainī al-Baghdādī , who narrates from his father in 629 *hijrī*, in Damascus; who stated that he had heard in 559 *hijrī* in Baghdād from his Shaykh and Master, Sayyiduna Muḥiyy al-Dīn ᶜAbd al-Qādir al-Jilānī who informed:

> 'The first Ḥajj that I performed was in 509 *hijrī* from Baghdād. I was young at that time [±39 years old] and undertook this journey alone on the steps of *Tajrīd* [189]. When I reached the sacred Minaret of *Umm al-Qorūn,* I met Shaykh ᶜAdī b. Musāfir who was also alone. He enquired as to where I was going, and I replied: *'Towards Makkah al-Mukarramah [for Ḥajj].'* He found out from me, whether I needed a companion, and I enlightened him that I was on the feet of *Tajrīd*. Shaykh ᶜAdī testified that he was also on the same mission and thus, both of us set out to *Makkah al-Mukarramah*. After travelling for a while, they suddenly saw a very feeble *Ḥabshī* [African] maidservant, fully covered in *ḥijāb*. She came in front of us; and looked at me with the side of her eyes and articulated: *'O young man! Where are you from?'* I replied: from ᶜ*Ajam* [Persia]. She confessed that: *'Today, you have put me in distress.'* I enquired as to why? She elucidated: *'Just now I was in Ḥabsha [Ethiopia]*

[189] *Tajrīd* means to remain aloof. *Tajrīd* also encompasses, remaining alone, even in the midst of a crowd.

and I testify that verily, Allãh ﷻ has beamed a Tajallĩ [lustre] onto your heart, and as far as I have knowledge, He has given you a share from His Communion to such an extent, that which He has not given to anyone. I then decided to meet with you.' She further declared: *'Today I will remain with you and make Iftãr with you tonight.'* She then began walking on the one side of the jungle, whilst we walked on the other side. When the evening appeared, we noticed that a tray descended from the sky, and halted in front of us. We saw that it had contained six breads, some gravy and vegetable.

She exclaimed: *'All praises are for Allãh ﷻ Who has honoured my guests. Every night I receive two breads.'* Each of us took two of the breads and ate them. Henceforward, three containers of water came down, and each of us drank from it. The water in this container was different to the taste and sweetness of the water of this world. She then departed from us during the same night; and eventually, we reached *Makkah al-Mukarramah*. While we were engaged in *Tawãf, Allãh* ﷻ emitted a *Tajallĩ* of the lustre of the dignity of Shaykh ʿAdĩ رضي الله عنه and he befell unconscious; so much so, that I heard a voice reverberating that he is dead.

Simultaneously, the same lady appeared at his head side, looked at him and implored:

'That *Allãh* ﷻ, Who has killed you shall make you alive. That *Allãh* ﷻ is pure, For the Light of His Glory to be perceived; it is not possible without the confirmation of occurrences. The universe cannot exist without the support of the manifestation of His Attributes. In fact, the ray of the intensity of His Glory snatches away the eyes of the intellect. Its splendour; co-opted with exquisiteness, engulfs the intellect of the hearts of great people.

Sayyiduna Ghawth رضي الله عنه verbalized as follows:

'All praises are from *Allãh* ﷻ who has bestowed upon me, the lustres of spiritual stations in *Tawãf*. I heard a voice within me pronouncing: 'O

ʿAbd al-Qādir! Leave external *Tajrīd* [190] and hold steadfast to *Tafrīd-e-Tawḥīd*[191] and *Tajrīd-e-Tafrīd* [192] because We will show you Our Mysterious Signs. Thus, do not merge My Will with your desires and position your feet steadfast in front of Me. Do not look towards any authority in creation; except that of Mine. You will always experience My *Shuhūd* [presence], when you embark on conferring benefit to others; because amongst My servants, there is My speciality. Sit in a manner, which people may benefit from you; because there is My speciality in my servants. Soon, I will take them to My Divine Presence, through your hands.'

The lady thereby revealed to me:

'O young man! Your status today is that verily, a tent will be erected for you and the angels have surrounded the skies. The eyes of the *Awliya* in their stations have raised their vision towards you. Hopes are moving towards what was bestowed upon you.' After saying this, she left.

Advices of the Ghawth ﷺ on Zuhd [Asceticism]

Sayyiduna Ghawth al-Aʿzam ﷺ discoursed as follows:

Zuhd, in this world is defined as a destitute, and an *ʿĀrif* is classified as one who is poor[193] in this world, and as well as in the *Ākhirah*. It is for this reason that a *Zāhid* adopts *Zuhd* which is in his hands. The love for this world is detached from his heart; and he sits patiently for *Allāh* ﷻ, on the floor of *Tawakkul* [reliance]; either on the hands of the commodities of creation; or *Takwīn* [cause to be by the Divine Command of *Kun*.] He certainly lives amongst the people of this world.

---

[190] *Tajrīd* means renounce this worldly life for solitude and worship.

[191] *Tafrīd* means that all praises and repute is attributed to *Allāh* ﷻ and not to oneself.

[192] To confine oneself in solitude for the remembrance of *Allāh* ﷻ solely.

[193] Poor in this context is in reference to that person, who does not possess any worldly, perishable commodities. He is wealthy by the Mercy, Blessings and Favours of *Allāh* ﷻ in abundance. One who desires *Allāh* ﷻ, every creation of *Allāh* ﷻ, automatically becomes his.

An ʿĀrif is a *Zāhid* in this world, and shall be a *Zāhid* in the *Ākhirah*. There is nothing in the world and *Ākhirah* that can divert him from *Allāh* ﷻ; and likewise, the hands of the *Ākhirah* and the face of this world cannot be concealed from him.

The Sublime Lord ﷻ covers this world [its commodities] from the *ʿĀrif*'s vision so that he remains protected from its *fitna* [discord]. The *Ākhirah* is also concealed from his vision so that he is not attracted to it. Other than *Allāh* ﷻ, every other face or image is also concealed from him; in order that his innermost being is not allured. He possesses the *Kashf* of every exposed and concealed entity, and he recognizes them. He observes these creations with his *Kashf*. The Doors of Divine Closeness are opened for him and he observes its Beauty and Glory. He glances at Destiny, the Realm of the Divine, as well as the Sovereign Power; and he observes the creation, imagination, and the consumable between the two words: كُنْ فَيَكُوْن - *"Be," and it is.'*

Seek with your heart from that Mighty and Gracious Lord ﷻ; and stand at His Door. Always beg from Him, whether He gives or not. Do not complain about anything, that He does to you; because His refusal to such a servant, who is a *Sālik Qāsid* [194] is similar to a net, that traps one and renders one useless; to the extent that he reaches *Allāh* ﷻ [195]. When he reaches *Allāh* ﷻ, he becomes encaged and thereafter, he shall never ever be rendered useless; and as a result, creation is denied access to him. He is called until he enters the Realm of Proximity and the doors are closed to others. His *nafs* and ego are then severed from greed and choice; intentions and uncouth behavioural patterns. These wings are cut off, and replaced by another two fresh wings, and he is thereby

[194] A messenger travelling on the Spiritual Path - *Sulūk*

[195] *Allāh's* ﷻ repudiation has wisdom in it, and this repudiation is better for the servant. What Sayyiduna Ghawth ﵁ is referring to in this context, is that if the servant is granted his desire, then he will be entrapped in a net, which will encage him and prevent him from reaching *Allāh* ﷻ. #[Faqīr ʿAbd al-Hādī]

returned to creation. Henceforward, he flies in the *duniya* and *Ākhirah,* i.e. between Creator and creation. He flies from the *'Arsh*; till the earth in between its plains. His *du'ās* are accepted instantly; and he is addressed as a representative. He is endowed with the inspiration of *du'ā*, until they are accepted. He is then stopped from *du'ās* and its acceptance; until he wishes, and he calls upon *Allāh* ﷻ; without any choice or restrictions.

How should the *'Ārif* make *du'ā* when *Allāh* ﷻ has given him his share of this *duniya* and has made him wealthy in His House of Hospitality. When His servant's gnosis is perfected; and develops the power of Divine Closeness, he is then returned to creation. Some people are granted salvation owing to him, whilst some are guided and others are led astray.

This is similar to the mercy and punishment which concerns the noble Prophets عليهم السلام and the *Awliya* who are their subservients. Whoever obeys and acknowledges them; that then becomes a mercy for them. But anyone who turns away and falsifies them, that then, warrants a torment for them. People who sincerely honour and love the *Awliya* are held by their hands and presented to *Allāh* ﷻ and are granted admittance into their Paradise; where the jewellers lead them to the Treasures of *Allāh* ﷻ; whilst those who reject, are led to the Fire of Hell. This method of the Prophets عليهم السلام and *Awliya* رحمهم الله will continue till the Day of *Qiyāmāh.*

The Prophets عليهم السلام are relocated forward; and *Allāh* ﷻ calls them towards Him. The aspirations of the Prophets عليهم السلام are stored in the hearts of the *Awliya, Abdāl* and *Siddiqīn.* When any one of them physically transcends this world, he is replaced by another. When an *'Ālim* practices upon his knowledge which is created [worldly knowledge], then verily, he does inherit from the estate; pertinent to the correct knowledge from the glorious Messenger of *Allāh* ﷺ. When he inherits the correct knowledge, his heart then rises to the Realm, within the Proximity of

Almighty *Allāh* ﷻ; and the angels surround this Realm, and his heart becomes an angel, which travels to the Closeness of the Absolute Sovereign Power, i.e. Almighty *Allāh* ﷻ. Accept whatever Sayyiduna Rasūlullāh ﷺ presents to you, and be obedient to his *Sunnah* [actions and commands]; so that they shall hold your hands in the *duniya* and *Ākhirah*. Dedicate yourself to him; and walk with every step in accordance to his footsteps; and become the speck under both these wings, i.e. the *Sunnah* of commands, followed by actions.

The mucus and spit of Shaykh Aḥmad رحمه الله stops by the Command of Sayyiduna Ghawth رضي الله عنه

I narrate in 670 *hijrī* in Cairo from Shaykh Abu-ʿAbdullāh Muḥammad b. Aḥmad b. Manzūr al-Kittānī رحمه الله; and he narrates from Shaykh ʿĀrif Abu-ʿAbdullāh Muḥammad b. Abī al-Fataḥ Hirwī Sayyāḥ رحمه الله in 623 *hijrī* in Cairo. He stated that he was standing beside his Master, Shaykh Muḥiyy al-Dīn ʿAbd al-Qādir al-Jilānī رضي الله عنه in 540 *hijrī*, in Baghdād. Suddenly his nose began leaking, with mucus emanating therefrom, and he cleaned it. He felt extremely embarrassed, that he had cleaned his nose in front of such an august personality like Sayyiduna Ghawth al-Aʿzam رضي الله عنه.

The Ghawth رضي الله عنه then professed to me: *'O Muḥammad! It does not matter, but from this day onwards, there will not be any mucus nor saliva.'* Shaykh Muḥammad رحمه الله affirms: *'Presently, I am 83 years old, and since the proclamation of the Ghawth* رضي الله عنه*, I did not spit, nor did the mucus flow out from my nose anymore.'* He states that Sayyiduna Shaykh رضي الله عنه named him '*Tawīl* – long; but he revealed to him; that I am short in height. Sayyiduna Ghawth رضي الله عنه confirmed that your age shall be extended. Thus, Shaykh Muḥammad lived for 137 years and travelled extensively, whilst seeing amazing things. He also went to *Kohe Qāf*. He was the first person to be in the service [*khidmat*] of Sayyiduna Shaykh Muḥiyy al-Dīn ʿAbd al-Qādir al-Jilānī رضي الله عنه.

Ḥaḍrat Ghawth ﷺ comments about Kashf [spiritual unveiling].

He revealed that *Kashf* [spiritual unveilings] is from the *Af'āl* [actions]; and *Mushāhidah* [observation] of *Allāh* ﷻ, which exposes those entities to the *Awliya* and *Abdāl* that astonishes their intellect. It provides proof for the opposite of habits and traditions. These are two types – *Jalāl* [splendid and temperamental] and *Jamāl* [gracious and tranquil]. The magnificence of *Jalāl* creates such fear; that one gets agitated and restless; and the heart suffers a severe disorder; which manifests in the organs of the body.

This is similar to the narration that Sayyiduna Rasūlullāh ﷺ; for the fear of *Salāh* people used to hear a sound from his consecrated chest, similar the sound of water that was boiling in a pot. This was possible, because he could see the *Jalāl* of Almighty *Allāh* ﷻ and its magnificence was manifested to him.

Similarly, there is a narration about Sayyiduna Khalīlullāh Nabī Ibrāhīm ﷺ and Amīr al-Mo'minīn Sayyiduna 'Umar al-Fārūq ﷺ. On the contrary, the observance of the lustres of *Jamāl* on the soft hearts are brilliant, with the *Nūr* and gladness. They are tender and graceful; appealing to the soothing speech of the beloved, which encompasses great gifts and dignity. This lustre is from the Divine Realm of Proximity, towards which he will revert, whilst the pen of his past destiny would dry up. This is a great favour and blessing from *Allāh* ﷻ upon him, and this gift in the *duniya* is his providence of steadfastness; at the time of death. This is because of the excessive fear of the enthusiasm for *Allāh* ﷻ, which is fanned by ardent love. It may result in the bursting and destruction of his veins, which may fail in the steady servitude, at the ascertained time of death. This immense Benediction and Mercy of *Allāh* ﷻ upon His beloved servants is for their consolement and hospitality. *Allāh* ﷻ is indeed *Ḥakīm* [The Wise], *'Alīm* [All-Knowing], *Latīf* [The Subtle One], *Raouf* [The Compassionate] and *Raḥīm* [The Merciful] to His servants. Therefore the beloved Prophet ﷺ used to request to the *Muazzin*, Sayyiduna Bilāl ﷺ: *'O Bilāl! Give me tranquility.'* i.e. call out the *Iqāmah* so that we may engage in *Salāh* and observe the *Jamāl* [Divine Glory] of *Allāh* ﷻ. This is what we had mentioned earlier. Therefore, Sayyiduna Rasūlullāh ﷺ had revealed: *'Salāh is the coolness of my eyes.'*

I narrate in 672 *hijrī* in Cairo from Shaykh Abu al-Ḥasan ʿAlī b. Abī-Bakr b. ʿUmar al-Azjī al-Muḥaddith رحمه الله and Shaykh Abu-Muḥammad Jāʿafar b. ʿAbdul Quddūs b. Aḥmad b. ʿAlī b. Muḥammad al-Hilālī al-Baghdādī Ḥarīmī رحمه الله. Both of them state that they narrate in 629 *hijrī* in Baghdād from two *Shuyūkh*, Ḥaḍrat Qāḍī al-Quḍāt Sayyiduna Abu-Sālih Nasar Jilānī رحمه الله and Shaykh Imām al-Faḍal Isḥāq b. Aḥmad al-ʿAlthī رحمه الله. Both affirm that on the morning of 5th Rajab 543 *hijrī* Shaykh Baqā b. But'tū رضي الله عنه came to the *Madrassa* of our father, Sayyiduna Muḥiyy al-Dīn رضي الله عنه. Shaykh Baqā رضي الله عنه elucidated to us follows:

> Why did you not question about my reason for coming very early this morning? He elaborated: Last night I saw a light that lit the edges of the skies and it spread commonly onto creation. I saw the secrets of the people of secrets; who were running towards this light. Some of them reached its closeness, whilst others were stopped by the closures.
>
> There was no secret affiliated to it, but the brilliance of it light intensified. Thereafter, I looked at the source of this light; and I suddenly observed that it was emanating from Sayyiduna Shaykh ʿAbd al-Qādir رضي الله عنه. I intended to open up to its reality; but then I observed that it was the light of His *Shuhūd* [Presence]; which was alongside his heart. The luminescence of both these lights flashed; and the glow of both these lustres reflected on the mirror of his dignity. The rays of this glitter merged owing to the multitude of his vision and reached the attributes within proximity. Owing to this proceeding, the entire existence illumined. There was not an angel on that night; which did not come down to earth; and proceed to Sayyiduna Shaykh ʿAbd al-Qādir رضي الله عنه; in order to shake his blessed hands. Amongst the angels he was known as *Shāhid* [witness]. The angels revealed that they came in the service [*khidmah*] Sayyiduna Ghawth al-Aʿzam رضي الله عنه; and they enquired from him: *'Did you perform Salāt al-Raghāib on this night?'* Ḥaḍrate Ghawth رضي الله عنه

thereby, read the lines as inscribed below:

إِذَا نَظَرَتْ عَيْنِيْ وَجُوْهَ حَبَائِبِيْ فَتِلْكَ صَلَاتِيْ فِيْ لَيَالِي الرَّغَائِبِ

When my eyes saw the faces of my friends, then this is my Salāh of the nights of Raghāib

وُجُوْهٌ اِذَا مَا اَسْفَرَتْ عَنْ جَمَالِهَا أَضَاءَتْ لَهَا الْاَكْوَانُ مِنْ كُلِّ جَانِبِ

They were such faces that if they exposed their beauty, then both the worlds would brighten up with their faces

حَرَمْتُ الرَّاضِيَ اَنْ لَمْ كُنْ بَادِلًا دَمِيْ أُزَاحِمُ شَجْعَانَ الْوَاغِيْ بِالْمَنَا كِبِ

I would be deprived of my happiness if do not spill my blood. I defend word by word with the brave soldiers of war

أَشُقُّ صُفُوْفَ الْعَارِفِيْنَ بِعِزْمَةٍ فَتَعْلُوْ بِمَجْدِيْ فَوْقَ تِلْكَ الْمَرَاتِبِ

I tear open the line of the ʿĀrifīn with my solid intentions, then due to my nobility they progress pass those stages

وَمَنْ لم يُوْفِ الْحُبَّ مَا يَسْتَحِقُّهُ فَذَاكَ الَّذِيْ لَمْ يَأْتِ قَطُّ بِوَاجِبِ

And the person who does not be faithful to the rights of his friend, then that person does not fulfil his obligatory duties

I narrate in 670 *hijrī* in the May'dān of Cairo from Shaykh Abu-Ḥafs ʿUmar b. Abu al-Majd Mubarak b. Nasībīnī al-Ḥanbalī ﷺ, who narrates from Shaykh Abu ʿAbd al-Raḥīm ʿAskar b. ʿAbd al-Raḥīm al-Nasībīnī ﷺ in 693 *hijrī*. in Nasībīn. He narrates in 593 *hijrī* in Baghdād from Shaykh Abu al-Qāsim ʿUmar b. Masʿūd Baz'zār ﷺ.........

I also narrate in 673 *hijrī* in Cairo from the exalted Jurist, Shaykh Abu al-Qāsim Muḥammad b. ʿUbādah al-Ansārī ﷺ, who narrates from the pious Shaykh ʿAlī b. Muqrī al-Qurashī ﷺ in Damascus; and both profess that in 554 *hijrī* they were present when Sayyiduna Shaykh Muḥiyy al-Dīn ʿAbd al-Qādir ﷺ was requested to inform them pertaining to his initial state of exemplification, which he received; so that they may follow on his footsteps. Then Sayyiduna Ghawth ﷺ recited the following lines of poetry:

اَنَا رَاغِبٌ فِيْمَنْ يَقْرُبُ نَفْسَهُ وَمُنَاسِبٌ لِفَتًى بِلَا طَغْلَطَفُهُ

I am drawn to that whose self-desires proximity and I am suitable for such a youth who is generous like Him.

وَمَفَاوِضُ الْعُشَّاقِ فِي اَسْرَارِهِمْ مِنْ كُلِّ مَعْنًى لَمْ يَسَعْنِيْ كَشْفُهُ

And I am the supplier of grace in those secrets of the lovers of each intrinsic quality whose Kashf does not give me scope.

قَدْ كَانَ بِسُكْرَتِيْ مِزَاجُ شَرَابِهِ وَالْيَوْمَ يُسْحِيْنِي لَدَيْهِ صَرْفُهُ

The drink of his spirit inebriates me and today His authority has kept me sober.

وَاَغِيْبُ مِنْ رُشْدِيْ بِاَوَّلِ نَظْرَةٍ وَالْيَوْمَ اَسْتَجْلِيْهِ ثُمَّ اَزِفُّهُ

At the first glance I disappeared from my senses and today I polish and beautify it.

People confessed to him: *'We keep fasts like you, worship like you and engage in spiritual struggles like you, but why is it that our conditions are not like yours?'* The great Ghawth ﷺ responded: *'In your actions, you have hindered me. Do you think that you can hinder the blessings of Allāh ﷻ? I do not eat until it is said me; I give you the oath of My Rights; eat. I do not drink until it is said me; I give you the oath of My Rights, drink and I do not do anything until it is said me to do it.'*

Shaykh Abu-Ḥafs al-Nasībīnī ﷺ states that Shaykh ʿAskar ﷺ often recited these couplets, but the concluding stanza differs slightly in diction. Sayyiduna Ghawth ﷺ pronounced: *On the first glance <u>I disappeared from my senses</u>*; and Shaykh ʿAskar ﷺ recited it in his words: *On the first glance <u>I lost my senses.</u>*

Then Sayyiduna Ghawth ﷺ confirmed: There is considerable wisdom in the following Injunction of *Allāh* ﷻ: *'Verily, in the creation of the skies and earth.....'* The eyes of the intelligent are astonished by it. This verse has disabled the eloquent tongues. There are bright stars of dangers; and since, this is such a new creation; it substantiates the firmness of Eternity. These are such brides, which manifest on the faces of the subjects of Certainty; and they are such witnesses; that demonstrate the authority of Command of the Creator of the Universe ﷻ. These are such signs; which are the rejection of the secrets of the nightingale. These are such mysteries; whose knots cannot be unbound by the intelligent. These are those signs that speak with the mysterious tongue; and the unseen has decorated the gardens of paradise with the flowers of the stars.

The garden of the sky is joined to the branches of the shooting stars; and the whiteness of the cheeks of the day is embellished by the blackness of the hair of the night. The sky is a flat surface, whose mirrors are studded with stars. It is such a picturesque garden that the flowers of the meteors, are its cheek. It is such a beloved that the infiltrator of its beauty is the night. This is the beauty of the beloved; and the splendour of its beauty is the day.

The sky is a chart of wisdom; and the composition of the scribe of Destiny. The stars are the dots of the book of existence. The sun is the king of the cities on the horizon; and the moon is the commander of the army of creation.

Creation of the Sky and Earth

When *Allãh* ﷻ created the sky and earth, there was darkness prevalent on the firmament of existence. In the Light of the edges, the lantern of the sun became lit; and the lamp of the stars lit up in the minarets of space. The chandelier of the moon was hung in the places of worship in the skies; and from the cheeks of the day the images of the entire existence were exposed. They were then painted with the flora of the night; and the petals of the roses were spread onto their cheeks. Lanterns of Light were lit in front of them; and the eyes of the lover, were then astonished at its splendour. The *Qãrĩ* [reader] of Warning spotted this line, which was written on the clear face of the tablet that: '*Almighty Allãh* ﷻ *is the light of the skies and earth.*' In the zenith of the night, the forehead of the night wore a veil; and the scarf of space fell off from the face of the sun. The water of light began flowing, in the streams of the day.

The *Khatĩb* [deliverer of the sermon] of the Command of Eternity began reciting the *Khutbah* [sermon] on the *mimbar* [pulpit] fashioned with certainty.

We have made the day for earning a livelihood; and then the Hand of Destiny turned around the issue of deliberation; and thereafter, Turks of Lights flee from the Negros of Darkness. The rosy cheeks of the sun transform into the colour of saffron; and the water of weakness begins to flow on the length of the ranges of day. The musk of darkness falls onto the locks of the cheeks of others; whilst the garden of the sky is adorned with the flowers of the stars. The army of darkness begins to walk at the edge of the plains; and the tents of darkness are erected in all the corners of the world. The approaching night covers the eyes of every living being; so much so; that the *Muazzin* of the mediator calls out the *adhān*; whereas the hand of destiny folds the sheets of darkness, when the ultimate part of the night is completed. At that juncture, the Isrāfīl of destiny blows into the horn of personas; so that the dead in the cradle of night would rise.

Suddenly, the pillars of the light of dawn then split. The vulture of the transport of the earth relays to the messenger of the *ʿĀrifīn* to become enthusiastic; and to proceed towards the home of Layla [beloved]; because they are raising her to life.

The Night is a Garden of the ʿĀrifīn

The night is that King, who is the owner of all the inhabitants of every nook and corner, inclusive of all the cities. The army of the night marches like every single drop of rain; that flows with the rain in flood. The flag of the sweet rain drops fall onto the heads of all; and the ropes of its tents are secured on all existence. The emissary of blessings, heralds its overwhelming assistance; that the night was created for you to rest. The night is a garden of the *ʿĀrifīn* in which they receive delightful blessings from *Allāh* ﷻ at night. The Master of Existence[196] [*Sayyid al-Wujūd* ﷺ] progressed to the Realm of *Qabā Qousayn* [197]at

[196] Reference to the beloved Messenger of *Allāh* ﷺ

[197] This is super transcendental Realm of Divine Proximity that is absolutely restricted to all creation. This is exclusive to the beloved Messenger of *Allāh*, Sayyiduna Rasūlullāh ﷺ who is allowed excess to this super arcane realm. He was welcomed by the Supreme Lord of Power ﷻ in the Night of *Meʿrāj* in this exclusive Realm.

night. The condition of some *'Ārifīn* is that, when the night approaches, they assert: *'Welcome to the beloved souls who are given glad-tidings.'* The sword of the morning is always hidden within the sheath of darkness; until the hand of the day draws it out; and thereby, spreads light for the eyes of those that envisage it.

O man! *Allāh* ﷻ did not create you to waste your time during the day, and to sleep at night. You have been assigned to spiritual duties [*wazāif*] and services [*kidmāh*], so that you may pursue for the closeness of the Creator ﷻ; with each of them and through its activation you may accomplish your understanding of the incumbent reason for creation.

The sky is a palace of personas; and as well as the freshness of the eyes of the sky. For the shooting star, there is pelting; and the stars are for adornment, whilst the sun is for the calculation of the ripening of the fruits; and as well as for the nurturing of the flora. The moon is subjected for time and period [months]; which is in accordance to the disposition of the human. Spring is compared to the freshness of the youth, and summer is in comparison to the maturity of youth [adulthood]. The season of autumn is equivalent to the strength of a seventy year old person; and winter depicts extreme feebleness; when the approach of death draws to a close. In reality, this is decreed by Divine Ordinance of the *'Azīz* [The Almighty - Honourable] and *'Alīm* [All-Knowing]. The mirror of Space is always free from the rust and grime of the clouds; in view of the fact that in this mirror, the existence of thoughts can be visible; and thereby the horizons of the sky turns into darkness, owing to the setting of the sun. The darkness of the cavities in the brides of the shooting stars; expands and the lions of the clouds roar in the rain forests. The sword of lightening is drawn out from the sheath; and the atmosphere amplifies the barren clouds in generating rain. The Isrāfīl of rain, drops in the shape of foliage and blows the trumpet; so that the seeds that are asleep in the beds of non-existence would stand up in readiness in order to germinate; so that their flowers are visible to the observers on the day of presentation. The interpreter of destiny scrutinizes the condition of all; in the following words: *'Thus, you observe the signs of the Mercy of Allāh* ﷻ.' There is a secret in every creation, which cannot be comprehended by the intellectuals.

There is a treasury in every creation; towards which the hands of danger cannot point a finger. One creation has a mouth that speaks of the *Tawḥīd* of *Allāh* ﷻ.

There are examples in every creation, which astonishes those who view them; and as a result, the intellect of the guided ones becomes senseless. The understanding of the people of proximity becomes staggered. The Sublime Lord ﷻ has informed His servants of His amazing creativity; and that, He is the Creator of the skies and earth.

The intense devotions of Sayyiduna Ghawth al-Aᶜzam ؓ

I narrate in 673 *hijrī* in Cairo from Shaykh Sharīf Abu al-ᶜAbbās Aḥmad b. Abī-ᶜAbdullāh Muḥammad b. Muḥammad Hazārwī al-Ḥusainī al-Baghdādī ؒ who narrates from his father in 629 *hijrī* in Damascus .....

I also narrate in 671 *hijrī* in Cairo from Shaykh Abu al-Faḍal Aḥmad b. Shaykh Abu al-Ḥasan ᶜAlī b. Ibrāhīm b. Ismāᶜīl al-Wāstī al-Baghdādī ؒ who narrates from his father in 673 *hijrī* in Baghdād. He narrates in 611 *hijrī* in Baghdād from Shaykh Abu al-ᶜAbbās Aḥmad b. Yaḥyah b. Barkat b. Maḥfūz al-Baghdādī ؒ renowned as al-Dabīqī who saw his Shaykh, Sayyiduna Muḥiyy al-Dīn ᶜAbd al-Qādir Jīlī ؓ in 558 *hijrī* whilst sitting on his chair; pronouncing:

> For twenty five years have I travelled in the jungles of Baghdād [in spiritual devotion], and for forty years I performed my *Fajr Salāh* with my *Esha wuḍū*. For fifteen years after the *Esha Salāh*, I stood on one leg and recited the Holy *Qur'ān*. I held an iron peg in my hand; fixed to the wall in fear of not falling off to sleep. I continued the recitation of the entire *Qur'ān* till the time of *Fajr*.'
>
> Once, I was climbing up the stairs and my *nafs* asserted to me: *'What harm is there if you slept for a few moments, and thereafter continued with your*

worship?' I stopped at that very spot; stood on one leg and recited the entire *Qur'ān*.

From three to forty days, I spent my life in such a condition; that I used to eat nothing. Sleep used to appear in amazing forms in front of me, and I screamed at it till it vanished. *Duniya* used to approach me with its pomp and glory, together with good and dreadful reflections; but I screamed at it till it disappeared.

I lived for eleven years in a tower which is now called *Burj al-Ajam* [*Ajamī* Tower]. This name was given to this tower, because of my extended dwelling therein. I entered into a pact with *Allāh* ﷻ; that I would not eat until I was fed and I will not drink until I was provided to drink. I remained for forty days without food and water. On the 40th day, thereafter, a person came to me with bread, and placed it front of me and thereby left. My *nafs* moved me close to the bread and owing to the pangs of hunger; I fell onto the bread.

I articulated to myself: *Wallāh*! I will not break the pact, which I had entered into with my Lord ﷻ. From my innermost self, I then heard yells of: *hunger! hunger!* However, I did not pay any attention to it. Shaykh Abu-Saʿīd Makhramī ﷺ[198] then passed by the tower, and heard the yelling; and henceforth, came to investigate. He queried from me: *'O ʿAbd al-Qādir! What is it?'* To this effect, I replied: *'It is the screams of agitation of my nafs but my soul is peaceful with Allāh ﷻ.'* My Shaykh ﷺ commanded me to come to the door of Azj, and left me in my original condition. I pronounced to myself, that I shall not leave this place

[198] Sayyiduna Shaykh Qāḍī Abu-Saʿīd Makhramī ﷺ is the *Murshid al-Kāmil* of Sayyiduna Shaykh ʿAbd al-Qādir al-Jilānī ﷺ. Some *Mashā'ikh* and, as well as the *Mashā'ikh* of the translator's *Silsila Āliya Qādiriyyah Raḍawiyyah* pronounce the word as *Makhzūmī* instead of *Makhramī*. In October 2000, during the first visit of the translator to the *Mazār al-Sharīf* of Sayyiduna Qāḍī Abu-Saʿīd ﷺ in Baghdād, he saw the inscription of his ﷺ name on a marble stone. It read Shaykh Qāḍī Abu-Saʿīd Makhramī ﷺ. *Allāh* ﷻ Knows best. *[Faqīr ʿAbd al-Hādī]*

without the consent of *Allāh* ﷻ. Sayyiduna Khiḍar ﷺ appeared and decreed: *'Get up and let us go to the door of Abu-Sa'īd.'* Henceforward, I stepped up and advanced towards *Bāb al-Azj* and discovered that my Shaykh was waiting at the door. He elucidated to me: *'Was my command not sufficient for you that Sayyiduna Khiḍar had to repeat my words?'* Thereafter, he took me to his home. There, I observed that the food was ready; and he began feeding me mouthfuls until my stomach was full. After the meal, he dressed me with a *khirqah* [*Sūfī* Garb]; and I thereby engaged in the *Shaghal* [199] *dhikr.*

Prior to this incident, I was on a journey and a stranger came to me. I had not seen him before. He questioned me as to whether I would prefer to remain with him; and I replied in the affirmative. He approved of my acceptance; but there was one condition attached to it; i.e. that I would not oppose him; and I acceded to his demands. He directed me to sit down, and to wait for him at that particular spot, until he returned and thereafter, he departed. He disappeared for a year; and when he returned, he located me at that very same spot. He sat with me for a while, and then stood up and commanded: *'Do not get up from this spot until I return.'* Thereby, he disappeared for another year. When he returned, he found me at that very same spot. He spent some time with me and before taking leave of me, he instructed me to wait there, until his return. After a year had elapsed, he then returned; carrying some milk and bread in his hand. He revealed to me: *'I am Khiḍar and Allāh ﷻ has commanded me to eat with you.'* Subsequently, both of us ate the bread. Thereafter, he instructed me to go to Baghdād; and both of us departed to Baghdād. Sayyiduna Shaykh ؓ was questioned as to what he ate in those years, whilst sitting and in await. He replied: *'Just whatever was lying*

---

[199] *Shaghal dhik*r is a silent *dhikr,* within the heart, whereby the person locks his tongue onto his palate and does not utter a single word. All the *dhik*r is done by the heart. This is the most excellent form of *dhik*r.

on the floor.' [200]

Advices of Sayyiduna Ghawth ﷺ for the ʿĀrifīn

O group of *ʿĀrifīn*! Listen to the words of *Allāh* ﷻ with the ears of your intellect; and listen to the words of the Creator ﷻ with the ears of understanding. Almighty *Allāh* ﷻ is Pure and therefore, reflect on the meanings of His ﷻ Divine Commandments with the perception of the heart. Procure the honey of His ﷻ Command with the bees of your souls, from the flowers of the trees of *Sharīʿat-e-Muḥammadī* ﷺ. Look at the Signs of His ﷻ Power [*Qudrat*] in the arrangement of the faculties of destiny, with the eyes of your heart. Purify the springs of knowledge; from the defilement of your *nafs*. Before the existence of creation, the flies of the souls flew from their nests; in the plains of the gardens of *Tawḥīd*, so that they could graze on the flowers of the trees of affection. Eat from the sources of *Maʿrifah*; and make their nests on the mountain tops of honour, in the cities of glory. Walk on the path of closeness towards your Creator and Sustainer ﷻ in the exalted Realm of Proximity; and receive the Drink of Divine Presence; with the hands of elevated spirits.

Henceforth, the hunter of Destiny hunted the prey with the net of difficulty; and locked them in the cage of adversity. With the images of its superb architecture, he then entertains them and begins to love the human homes; and hence, forgets his pure and honourable country. Then your Lord ﷻ forwards a revelation to the flies of the souls: *'Become humble and come towards the path of your Lord ﷻ by walking on the narrow paths of images. Eat from the fruits of the Sharīʿah and graze on the flowers of the lustres of Ḥaqīqah [Reality].'* When his bird flies away and grazes on the seeds of love, in the gardens of venture, he thereby gets entrapped in the net of humility; and observes the water of

[200] The translator has read in various other books of biography that this incident occurred when Sayyiduna Ghawth ﷺ came to Baghdād for the first time from his home town Jilān. He was 18 years old at that time. Before entering the city of Baghdād, he was met by Sayyiduna Khiḍar ﷺ when this incident took place.

misfortune in the pond of stability. He then verbalizes: *'How can he get freedom from this beautiful garden whose fruits are bitter, though the spring water is sweet but its edges are life threatening?'*

In a compassionate tone thereafter, the driver of the vehicles of the seekers of truth exclaimed: 'Oh excited one in the love of the souls! Oh walkers of the extreme desires of the *'Ārifīn*! There is nothing except me and your goals; in lifting the veils of images; and no one can stop you except the veils of images. Thus, you should fly towards Him ﷻ; with the wings of love, in order to seek the life of permanency. Expire from your egotism of aspirations so that He ﷻ shall grant you life in the Realm of Truth. Affliction is the flower of the soul of the *'Ārifīn*; and calamities are the gifts of the secrets of the *Wāsilīn*. Friendship are two stars; that rise on the sky of felicity and diligence; and love are two flowers, which shine on the branches of Proximity. The greatest adversity is the loss of the beloved; and greatest catastrophe is not to find him.'

O group of the *'Ārifīn*! Exemption from might and power cannot be achieved by anything; except by the reality of *Tawḥīd*. *Tafrīd*; [201] can only be achieved by the erasure of every glittering entity from the eyes of the intellect. The exclusion of every existence from the hand of greed denotes real *Tajrīd* [202]. Appeal to *Allāh* ﷻ to grant you the strength to refrain from them; whilst they; i.e. the *duniya* and its commodities, continue with their activities.

When the angels looked at the flies of souls, they were hidden in the curtains of secrets, and were relaxing on the beds of the low charitable earth; under the shade of the tree of union. The breeze of union then blew, and the flowers of the soul of friendship became fragrant in his gathering. For him the flash of lightning of the *Nūr* of *Ma'ārifah* [Gnosis] flashes; whilst the intoxication of the drink of *Mushāhidah* [observance]; shakes his shoulders, and the effective anecdotes become his companion. The fragrance of the lofty Spiritual Realm

[201] *Tafrīd* means that all praises and repute is specified for *Allāh* ﷻ and not for oneself.
[202] *Tajrīd* means the abandonment of this worldly life for solitude and worship.

perfumes his cheerful self and the eyes of the images of *Nũr*; and the heights of their brilliance become astonished with his conduct.

Then Destiny declared: 'Oh dwellers of the sanctuaries of *Nũr*! Oh birds that fly to the station of Dignity! Look at that bird that flies from its nest in the tree of Great Dignity, who is termed as Aḥmad ﷺ. His ﷺ place of flight is the *Qabã Qousayn* in the Absolute Plain of Eternity. He ﷺ flies with the wings of exaltation. It is towards this nest of eminence that people fly to. It is owing to the obedience and devotion of his ﷺ Law that these people land on the branches of the tree of excellence. Here, a *Nũr* flashes in the eye of their intellect. Thus, they reach this lofty station, because of the blessings of his ﷺ security. This is the hope of Bilqĩs that flies from the mysterious cities to the intellect of Sulaymãn; with certain information of such a book that has no false Injunctions, documented in and around it. When the occurrences of his beloved comes to it, it confesses: *'I am unlike you.'*

Sayyiduna Muḥammad ﷺ is unique and par-excellence amongst the Prophets عليهم السلام by the blessings of Almighty *Allãh* ﷻ. On the Night of *Me'rãj*, the bee of his soul grazed on the flowers of such a tree; i.e. 'فَأَوْحَىٰ إِلَىٰ عَبْدِهِ مَا أَوْحَىٰ - *So Allãh* ﷻ *divinely revealed to His bondsman, whatever He Divinely Revealed*. Pearls were sacrificed on his head of nobility and verily, he ﷺ saw the Great Signs of his Lord ﷻ in the assembly of فَكَانَ قَابَ قَوْسَيْنِ أَوْ أَدْنَىٰ - *So the distance between the Spectacle and the beloved was only two arms' length, or even less*. It is owing to him ﷺ, that the sheet of the exquisiteness of time is placed on the shoulders of the splendour of the abode.

Integrity of the servant is solely for the gratification of *Allãh* ﷻ. With his heart and ears, he listens to His ﷻ Words; without reducing his disposition to a veil through negligence. He follows these Commandments of *Allãh* ﷻ; hence, they are the ones who precipitously see.'

Blood from the Bags

I narrate from Shaykh Abu-ʿAbdullāh Muḥammad b. Shaykh Abu al-ʿAbbās Khiḍar b. ʿAbdullāh b. Yaḥyah Ḥasan al-Mosulī ﷺ who narrates from his father in 623 *hijrī* in Mosul who states that, one night he was with his Shaykh, Sayyiduna Shaykh Muḥiyy al-Dīn ʿAbd al-Qādir ﷺ in his *Madrassa*. The King, Mustanjid-Billāh Abu-Muzaffar Yūsuf visited Sayyiduna Ghawth al-Aʿzam ﷺ and greeted him. He requested for advice and left ten bags in front of Sayyiduna Shaykh ﷺ, which were carried by ten servants. Ḥaḍrate Ghawth ﷺ insisted that he had no need for it and therefore refused to accept it. Owing to his humble insistence, Sayyiduna Ghawth al-Aʿzam ﷺ then held one bag with one hand, and another with the other. He then squeezed them and blood began dripping from them. He then cautioned: *'O Abu-Muzaffar! Do you not fear Allāh that you take the blood of people and bring it to me?'* The king heard this and befell unconscious. Sayyiduna Ghawth ﷺ asserted: *'I take an oath of the honour of my Lord ﷻ! If I had no regard for your family ties*[203] *with the Messenger of Allāh ﷺ, then I would have left this blood to flow till your house.'*

The Mysterious Apple

The narrator states that one day, he saw the *Khalīfah* in the presence of Sayyiduna Ghawth al-Aʿzam ﷺ. He requested to him, that he would prefer to witness a *karāmat*; so that his heart would be appeased. Sayyiduna Shaykh ﷺ questioned him about what he would prefer to see; and he requested to see an apple from the unseen. This request was put forth in the season; when there not a single apple available. The great Ghawth ﷺ raised his hand towards the sky; and one apple appeared in his hand, whilst another one in the *Khalīfah's* hand. The *Khalīfah* was surprised and proclaimed: *'What is this?'* Ḥaḍrate Ghawth ﷺ cut the apple and it was absolutely white, and from which

[203] The ruler Mustanjid-Billāh Abu-Muzaffar Yūsuf belonged to the ʿAbbāsī Dynasty who are the descendants of Sayyiduna ʿAbbās ibn ʿAbdul Muttalib ﷺ; the noble uncle of Sayyiduna Rasūlullāh ﷺ. Therefore, Sayyiduna Ghawth ﷺ mentioned: *'If I had no regard for your family ties with the Messenger of Allāh ﷺ.'*

emanated a sweet fragrance of musk. Khalīfah Mustanjid, then cut his apple and there were worms in it. He was astonished and remarked: *'Why is it that your apple is pure and my apple has worms?'* Sayyiduna Shaykh ﷺ thereby replied: *'Abu-Muzaffar! Your apple touched the hands of oppression.'*

The Murīd [disciple] and Murād [desired]

Sayyiduna Shaykh Muḥiyy al-Dīn ﷺ confirmed that the intention of a *murīd* is *murād.* The real intention is to abandon whatever one has a tendency to desire. The reality of desire is for Almighty *Allāh* ﷻ and to exclude everything else; except Him ﷻ. When a servant discards the obsession of desiring the pleasures of the *duniya* and *Ākhirah*, he becomes sturdy in his desire. Thus, intention is the prelude of every matter, and thereafter, follows his goal. Action is the fundamental beginning of the path of a *Sālik* [spiritual traveller] and this is his initial station.
Almighty *Allāh* ﷻ declared to His beloved Messenger ﷺ; *'Do not eject those who call on their Lord ﷻ morning and evening and they desire His Divine Being. Do not turn away your vision from them. Do you [people] desire the beauty of the world?'*

Hence, it is apparent that *Allāh* ﷻ summoned His beloved Prophet ﷺ to exercise patience with them, live amongst them; and subject the *nafs* in their company. They were praised, that their intention is the desire of the Divine Being of *Allāh* ﷻ. Thus, it is deduced that the reality of intentions; is the intention for the desire of *Allāh* ﷻ, and not for the desire of the glamour of *duniya* and *Ākhirah*.

Concerning the *murīd* and *murād*; a *murīd* is he who has the qualities; as listed hereunder:

- ✓ He must be engrossed consistently in the obedience of his Lord ﷻ.
- ✓ He must refrain from others.
- ✓ He must unswervingly listen and obey *Allāh* ﷻ.
- ✓ His actions are implemented in accordance to the *Qur'ān* and *Sunnah*.
- ✓ He is deaf to anything else; other than the *Qur'ān* and *Sunnah*.

- ✓ He sees with the *Nūr* of *Allāh* ﷻ.
- ✓ In the entire creation he does know anything, except the Commandments of *Allāh* ﷻ.
- ✓ He becomes blind to see anything, except *Allāh* ﷻ, Who is the real Creator of events.
- ✓ He deems the actions of others as a reason; and as the medium of the actions of *Allāh* ﷻ.

The Sublime Lord ﷻ elucidates the words of Bilqīs [Queen Shiba]: *'When a king enters a new town, he destroys everything it and disgraces its honourable people.'*

There is a proverb, that an infection humiliates every fear. Its sleep is its dominating force; food is its starvation; its speech is necessary, its *nafs* shrieks, and it does not succumb to its beloved possessions. He is compassionate to the servants of *Allāh* ﷻ and remembers Him in solitude. *Allāh* ﷻ is patient with him with regard to his sins; and he is content with the Destiny of *Allāh* ﷻ. He embraces the Commandments of *Allāh* ﷻ and is self-conscious of the vision of *Allāh* ﷻ. He strives for the entities that is loved by *Allāh* ﷻ; and he is always attentive to the entities; which serves as a reason, in drawing him closer to *Allāh* ﷻ. Seclusion is his love; and he remains unidentified; and he does not adhere to praising creation. Excessive *Nawāfil* [optional] prayers is performed by him, which are solely for the pleasure of *Allāh* ﷻ so that he befriends his Lord ﷻ; so much so, that he reaches his ultimate destination of the Divine Domain. He is then admitted to the fraternity of the *Awliya*. With the institution of this initiation, he is characterized by the name Murādullāh, i.e. one who desires *Allāh;* whilst taking cognisance of the fact that, the difficulties and burdens of people who are striving on the Path of *Allāh* ﷻ are removed through him. He is purified with the water of the mercy and blessings of *Allāh* ﷻ; and hence, a home is constructed for him in the vicinity of the Sublime Lord ﷻ. Numerous types of garbs are received by him; and the *Ma'rifah* and friendship of *Allāh* ﷻ, becomes his tranquillity.

Thereafter, with the permission of exposition, he speaks of the Wisdom and

Concealments of the Almighty Lord ﷻ. In fact, he even discloses the secretive path to *Allāh* ﷻ. Thereby, he is attributed with such honorific titles, that he becomes unique amongst the *Awliya*. Henceforward, he is admitted to the special confidants of *Allāh* ﷻ; and he bears that name, which no one else is aware of. Although he is informed of such secrets that are exclusive to him; he does not expose them to creation. He hears from *Allāh* ﷻ; sees by the Power of *Allāh* ﷻ, grasps and speaks with the Power of *Allāh* ﷻ. He strives in the obedience of *Allāh* ﷻ and his serenity is with *Allāh* ﷻ. He sleeps in the servitude of *Allāh* ﷻ; and remembers Him ﷻ in his speech, through the Certainty of *Allāh* ﷻ. Consequently, he becomes a trustee and witness of *Allāh* ﷻ and an *Awtād*[204] and a friend of those steadfast servants [*Awliya*].

Excessive Performance of Nafil takes one Close to Allāh ﷻ

Sayyiduna Rasūlullāh ﷺ reveals from Almighty *Allāh* ﷻ Who declares: *'My believing servant always achieves My Closeness by performing Nawāfil until I admit him as My friend. When I accept him as my friend, then I become his ear; his eye, his tongue, his hand, his feet and his heart. Thus, he hears from Me; sees from Me, talks to Me, understands from Me and grasps from Me.'*

This is the servant whose intellect is dominant, and the movements of his ego ceases, because he in the custody of the All-Powerful Lord ﷻ and his heart transforms into a treasury of *Allāh's* ﷻ secrets.

Thus, he becomes the beloved of *Allāh* ﷻ. Thus, Oh servant of *Allāh*! Generate the intention of attaining His *Ma'ārifah*; because a *murīd* is a beginner, and *murād* [goal] is the limits. A *murīd* is he, who is the focus of the eye of *'Ibādah* and is subjected to this practice.

[204] The Pillars, the Pegs, the Mainstays. An expression used for four men, whose stations are the four corners of the world: East, West, North, and South. The place of each one of them is the place of the corresponding direction.

Murãd refers to that undertaking, which is accomplished without difficulties. The *murĩd* lies in pain and dejectment; whilst *murãd* is a Bounty from the Bounties of *Allãh* ﷻ. Thus, for the information of the beginner messengers, this is a concern for the *Sunnah* of *Allãh* ﷻ; which was executed and completed to the letter, by *Mujãhidah* [spiritual struggle] with the *Tawfĩq* of *Allãh* ﷻ. Thereafter, in order to draw his servant towards Himself ﷻ; He ﷻ lessens his burden; decreases the quantity of his performance of *Nawãfil*; abandons carnal desires, so that he would be steadfast on all forms of worship; and in strict compliance to performing the *Farã'id* and *Sunnah*, in order to protect the heart and that he does not violate limits and stations; and hence, keeps the heart pure from the thoughts of others; except that of *Allãh* ﷻ. The devout servant's external self is within creation; but his spiritual being is with *Allãh* ﷻ. His tongue reverberates the Command of *Allãh* ﷻ; and his heart is inclined to the knowledge of *Allãh* ﷻ. His speech is directed to the compassion of creation; and his secrets are levelled for the protection of the trust of *Allãh* ﷻ. As a result, the gifts of Peace, Blessings and the Mercy of *Allãh* ﷻ be upon them, as long as the sky and earth and the servants of *Allãh* ﷻ are upright in obeying and protecting His Rights and Directives.

The Difference between Murĩd and Murãd

The friend of the *murĩd* is physical principles and consideration; and the observance of Truth is the friend of *murãd*, because the *murĩd* walks and *murãd* flies. How can one who walks catch up with one who flies? This could be understood from the condition of Sayyiduna Mũsã عليه السلام and Sayyiduna wa Mawlãnã Rasũlullãh ﷺ.

Sayyiduna Nabĩ Mũsã عليه السلام was a *murĩd* and our beloved Prophet Sayyiduna Muḥammad ﷺ is the *murãd*. The extreme limits of the journey of Nabĩ Mũsã عليه السلام was to the Mount of Sinai; whilst the limits of the journey of our beloved Master, and beloved of *Allãh* ﷺ is extended to the Divine *'Arsh* and *Louḥe Maḥfũz* [to the ultimate Divine Presence].

- ✓ A *murĩd* is a seeker and a *murãd* is the sought.

- ✓ The *ʿIbādah* of a *murīd* is *Mujāhidah* and the worship of *murād* is generosity.
- ✓ A *murīd* is present and *murād* is transitory.
- ✓ The *murīd* makes *ʿamal* [practices] for reward and *murād* does not look at *ʿamal* but looks at *Tawfīq* and kindness.
- ✓ A *murīd* runs when he moves and *murād* stands at every crowd on the path.
- ✓ The *murīd* sees with the light of *Allāh* ﷻ and *murād* sees with *Allāh* ﷻ.
- ✓ A *murīd* exists by the Command of *Allāh* ﷻ, and the *murād* exists with the procedures of *Allāh* ﷻ.
- ✓ The *murīd* opposes his desires, whilst the *murād* is repelled by its desires.
- ✓ A *murīd* seeks proximity; whilst proximity is with *murād*
- ✓ A *murīd* protects, and *murād* guides. It is given food and gifts, and is sought.
- ✓ The *murīd* protects and *murād* is protected.
- ✓ A *murīd* progresses [travels], and *murād* is at the destination, and is stationed by its Sublime Lord ﷻ in the lofty palaces. It finds all goodness and entities of wonderment at its disposal.

Sayyiduna Ghawth al-Aʿzam رضي الله عنه Cured the born Blind with vision and raised the Dead

I narrate in 671 *hijrī* in Cairo from Shaykh Abu-Muḥammad Rajab b. Abī-Mansūr al-Dārī رحمه الله, Shaykh Abu-Zayd ʿAbd al-Raḥmān b. Sālim al-Qurashī رحمه الله and Shaykh Abu-ʿAbdullāh Muḥammad b. ʿUbādah al-Ansārī رحمه الله; and all three of them narrate in 618 *hijrī,* on Mount Qāsiyūn, Damascus from the pious Shaykh Abu al-Ḥasan al-Qurashī رحمه الله. He stated that in 549 *hijrī* he and Shaykh ʿAlī b. al-Hītī رحمه الله were present with Sayyiduna Shaykh Muḥiyy al-Dīn ʿAbd al-Qādir al-Jilānī رضي الله عنه in his *Madrassa* at the door of Azj. Abu-Ghālib Faḍlullāh b. Ismāʿīl al-Baghdādī al-Azjī, the trader visited Sayyiduna Ghawth رضي الله عنه and articulated: *'O my Master! Your honourable Grandfather ﷺ said that whoever is given an invitation; he should accept it and attend. I am present to invite you to my humble home for a meal and request that you bless us with your presence.'* Sayyiduna Shaykh ﷺ replied: *'If I am granted permission.'* He then bowed his head for a short while in meditation [*murāqibah*] and affirmed: *'Very well, I will attend.'* He then mounted on his mule and Shaykh ʿAlī b. al-Hītī ﷺ held onto the right stirrup, and I [Shaykh Qurashī ﷺ] held onto the left stirrup. When we reached there, we observed that the *Mashā'ikh* and *'Ulama* of Baghdād were present; and the table was laid, spread out with a variety of food. We entered and took our seats. A heavy basket was carried by two people and left on one side of the table; that was spread out with the variety of food. Abu-Ghālib recited: *Bismillāh* and requested the guests to start eating; but Sayyiduna Ghawth ﷺ had his head positioned in *murāqibah*. He did not eat, nor did he grant permission to eat; and nor did anyone else also eat. The entire *majlis* was illuminated by such a reverential aura of the great Ghawth ﷺ; that all of them were motionless, similar to the birds, which were sitting on their heads. Henceforth, Sayyiduna Ghawth ﷺ indicated to me and Shaykh ʿAlī to bring that basket. We picked it up and it was quite heavy; and we placed it front of Sayyiduna Ghawth ﷺ. He commanded that it should to be opened. Therein was the blind, paraplegic and leper son of Abu-Ghālib. This child was born in this condition.

Sayyiduna Ghawth al-Aʿzam ﷺ instructed the child to rise by the Command of *Allāh* ﷻ and he, immediately arose and began running around; as though he was never sick or paralyzed. People saw this and there was pandemonium. Ḥaḍrate Ghawth ﷺ arose in an astounding state, and left the house without eating anything.

Subsequent to this incident, I visited Sayyiduna Shaykh Abu-Saʿīd al-Qaylawī ﷺ and reported this incredible miracle. He declared to me that Sayyiduna Shaykh ʿAbd al-Qādir al-Jilānī ﷺ is the one who cures those who are born blind, and as well as the leper. By the permission of *Allāh* ﷻ, he ﷺ also resurrects the dead.

Shaykh Abu al Ḥasan al-Qurashī ﷺ further narrates; 'In 559 *hijrī,* I was present in the *majlis* of Sayyiduna Ghawth al-Aʿzam ﷺ and a group of *Rāfḍīs [Shiʿā]* brought two baskets with its cover sewn; and questioned the Ghawth ﷺ as follows: *'Tell us what is in these baskets?'* He withdrew from his chair, and placed his blessed hand on one basket and confirmed: *'There is a child in this basket who is paralysed with rheumatism.'* Sayyiduna Ghawth ﷺ issued a directive to his son, Sayyiduna ʿAbd al-Razzāq ﷺ to open the basket, and therein was a sick child as predicted by the Ghawth ﷺ. He commanded the child to stand up; and so it did; and the child began walking normally. He then proceeded to the second basket and placed his hand on it; and verified: *'In it is a normal healthy child without any sickness.'* He instructed his son to open it. When the basket was opened; a normal healthy child was therein. He stood up and started walking; and thereafter, Shaykh ﷺ held him by his hair and directed him to sit down. The child immediately became paralysed and could not get up. The group of *Rafḍīs* perceived this; and turned to repentance [*Toubah]* at the hands of the great Ghawth ﷺ. The atmosphere was indeed astonishing; whereby three people died in this session. I met earlier senior *Mashā'ikh* who stated that there were four such *Shuyūkh* that cured those who were born blind; and including the lepers. They are: Shaykh ʿAbd al-Qādir al-Jilānī ﷺ, Shaykh Baqā b. Bat'tū ﷺ, Shaykh Abu-Saʿīd Qaylawī ﷺ and Shaykh ʿAlī b. al-Hītī ﷺ.

To function in the Graves like the living

Shaykh Abu al-Ḥasan al-Qurashī ﷺ asserts that he knows of four *Mashā'ikh*[205] that functioned in their graves; similar to the living people. They are enumerated as follows:

1) Sayyiduna Shaykh Muḥiyy al-Dīn ʿAbd al-Qādir al-Jilānī ﷺ.
2) Sayyiduna Shaykh Maʿrūf Karkhī ﷺ.
3) Sayyiduna ʿAqīl Mambajī ﷺ.
4) Sayyiduna Shaykh Ḥayāt b. Qays Ḥarrānī ﷺ.

Verily, one day I visited Sayyiduna Shaykh ʿAbd al-Qādir al-Jilānī ﷺ and I

[205] These illustrious *Awliya* are known as *'Ahle Mutasarrif'* # Faqīr ʿAbd al-Hādī

desired to relieve myself. Thus, I rushed and relieved myself; and thereafter, I returned to the great Ghawth ﵁. He emphasized to me: *'Ask what you desire?'* I desired to be infused with certain spiritual matters; of which I made mention of.' He thereby commanded: *'Here, take the matters.'* Instantaneously, I received all those matters.

The Mutasawwif and the Sūfī

Sayyiduna Ghawth al-Aʿzam ﵁ discoursed on the *Mutasawwif* and the *Sūfī*. He revealed that the *Mutasawwif* is a beginner; and a *Sūfī* is the frontier of the furthest. A *Mutasawwif* begins on the path of Union; whilst the *Sūfī* has completed this journey and reaches the ultimate destination; which is the end of the Path of *Wasal* [union]. *Mutasawwif* is a title and a *Sūfī* is an attribute. A *Mutasawwif* carries light and heavy items; so much so that he melts, and he loses his senses. His intentions and desires become non-existent and thereby, he becomes a *Sūfī*.

He is then loaded with weight and hence, he befits an attribute to the office of Divine Ordinance; a recipient of nurturing by glory; a fountain of knowledge and wisdom; a house of commands; *Nūr*, a sanctuary for the *Awliya* and *Abdāl*, and a centre of peace and prosperity; because he becomes the eye for the tread of the pearl of the crown, which is a display for *Allāh* ﷻ and thus, he is highly praised. He carries the burden of grief of the *nafs*; ego and the cursed evil spirit; and the *duniya* and *Ākhirah*. He worships *Allāh* ﷻ; focussing with such concentration, that he ignores everything in six directions[206] of the world. He abandons all kinds of dedication, commitment or conformation; which is in agreement to them. He is devoted to internal spiritual purity and sincerely inclined to them. He opposes the stoned devil and this material world is abandoned by him. He leaves all the creation of *Allāh* ﷻ and his companions; in accordance to the Commandments of *Allāh* ﷻ, in order to engage in seeking for the *Ākhirah*.

---

[206] Reference is made to the East, West, South, North, up and down.

He makes *Mujãhidah* with his *nafs* and ego; moreover to fulfil the Commands of *Allãh* ﷻ; which *Allãh* ﷻ has reserved for the *Awliya* in the *Ãkhirah*, in *Jannah*. He leaves all these entities, owing to his deep inclination towards his beloved Creator ﷻ. In occurrences of both worlds, he does exist and transforms into a gem for *Allãh* ﷻ. All relationships, entities of this world, family and possessions cut off from him; and all the directions close. Within the self towards facets, a door of the doors opens. He is content with the Destiny of his Lord ﷻ; of all lords, and the Lord of creation ﷻ. Whatever, that which is concerned with the past and future is solely destined by Divine Cause. The *Sũfi* becomes aware of the exposed and the concealed aspects; inclusive of those traits that cause the limbs to move; and as well as those secrets, which are hidden within the heart and intentions.

Thereafter, at this door, another door opens, which is termed as the Door of Proximity of the Powerful Sovereign Power and Mighty Ruler ﷻ. They are lifted to the excellent *majlis* of friendship and seated on the Chair of *Tawḥĩd*. Eventually the veils are then lifted for them; and they enter into the home of *Fardaniyyat* [singularity] from which, honour and glory emanates. When he looks at this honour and glory, he thereby remains in extinction; and progresses to the extinction of his desires; *duniya* and *Ãkhirah*; intentions, which include power of movement, and as well as the qualities of his *nafs*. He transmutes, similar to that of a transparent container in which water is filled, and images are seen therein. Except the Ordinance of Destiny, no one else can command it. Apart from the Divine Commandment, no one can make him present; and he is extinct from his segment. He exists by the Command of his Lord ﷻ and does no desire privacy; because privacy is for the existent. He becomes like that child who does not eat, until it is fed; and if it is not dressed, it does not dress. He is left and handed over as it is revealed in the *Qur'ãn*: *'And We turn then to right or left.'*

Reason for the Name Sũfi

He is existent and separate. He is present with people with his body but separate as far as his actions, deeds, secrets and intentions are concerned. It is at this juncture that he is named *Sũfi*, because he is pure from the defects of creation. If you desire, you may name him an *Abdãl*; from one of the *Abdãls*. He is manifested in his self, and as an *'Ãrif* of *Allãh* ﷻ who raises the dead. He guides the *Awliya* towards the Station of Proximity; and removes the darkness from misconception, through the desire of his feelings and the self; with his *dhikr*, gnosis, knowledge, secrets and *Nũr*. *Allãh* ﷻ advances him thereby, towards His ﷻ Divine Light, as He ﷻ explicitly declares in the Holy *Qur'ãn*:

﴿اللَّهُ نُورُ السَّمَاوَاتِ وَالْأَرْضِ ۚ مَثَلُ نُورِهِ كَمِشْكَاةٍ فِيهَا مِصْبَاحٌ ۖ الْمِصْبَاحُ فِي زُجَاجَةٍ....... ﴾

Allãh is the Light of the heavens and the earth; the example of His light is like a niche in which is a lamp;...[207]

Allãh ﷻ is the friend of the *mo'minĩn* [true believers] and He ﷻ removes them from the darkness into light. Thus, *Allãh* ﷻ undertakes the responsibility upon His Divine Self to remove them from darkness to light. He informs them of those secrets that are concealed from the hearts of others and intentions that are dominant on them, because *Allãh* ﷻ makes them spies of the heart and a trustee of secret and hidden entities and intentions [thoughts]. Thus, his devil does not mislead him. There is no egotism which he follows, and there is no goading of the *nafs* [*Nafs e Ammãra* – satanic interference]; that shall draw him towards sins; and there are no carnal desires that shall call him to lust and destroy him; and that which would exclude him from the fold of the *Ahle Sunnah wa Jamã'at*. Almighty *Allãh* ﷻ stipulates in the Holy *Qur'ãn*;

﴿كَذَٰلِكَ لِنَصْرِفَ عَنْهُ السُّوءَ وَالْفَحْشَاءَ ۚ إِنَّهُ مِنْ عِبَادِنَا الْمُخْلَصِينَ﴾

This is what We did, to turn away evil and lewdness from him; indeed He is one of Our chosen bondmen.[208]

[207] Al-Qur'ãn al-Karĩm, Chapter 24, Surah Nũr, Verse no. 35
[208] *Al-Qur'ãn al-Karĩm*, Chapter 12, Surah Yũsuf, Verse no. 24

Our Sublime Lord ﷻ protects His Divine Angelic Realm from the arrogance and greed of their *nafs*. Therefore, He ﷻ maintained their station steadfast, and granted them the *Tawfīq* for their inner self to remain sincere to the truth; and to exercise patience in places of restlessness and separation; and to fulfil all the compulsory duties [*farāiḍ*]; and to protect the perimeters and laws; and to hold steadfast to their positions, until they are rectified. Behaviour becomes pure, clean and remains undefiled. He becomes pure; clean; elevated in spirituality and becomes regular in the execution of good deeds. Only then, will *Allāh* ﷻ complete and perfect his *Wilāyah* and trusteeship. Almighty *Allāh* ﷻ is a friend of the believers [*mo'minīn*] and hence, proclaims: *'He ﷻ is a friend of the pious.'* These pious servants travel to the Sovereign Power of Sovereignty. ﷻ with their status; which is depicted in their presence. They are frequently whispered to; and through this, they whisper in reply, with their hearts and secrets. It is then that these pious servants detach themselves from all creation and engage in the devotion of *Allāh* ﷻ. They also detach themselves from the self [*nafs*]; whilst everything else occupies them in worship. *Allāh* ﷻ is the Lord and Master ﷻ of everything; and reigns over everything under His ﷻ control. He imprisons their intellects and makes them a trustee. Thus, they are in His ﷻ Divine Custody and security. When the soul is not content with Proximity, then it lives on the plains of *Tawḥīd* and *Raḥmah* and avoids contact with everything else. When they are commanded to engage in devotions, and the time comes for the movement of their body to act, and they then, procure shelter in the fortified sanctuaries of worship in order to protect their actions. These actions do not entail the heart [which is constantly engaged in spiritual devotion]. This shelter is to safeguard them from the destruction of the interference of the cursed devil and egotism within the self.

They are protected from the negative attributes of the devil; which are embedded in their *nafs*; and which are the shoots that are linked to the power of boastfulness; greed; revenge; arrogance and rewards for their deeds. In fact, they observe all these facets as a creation of *Allāh* ﷻ; and by His ﷻ blessings and *Tawfīq*; they too endeavour likewise; so that in their beliefs, they would not stray away from the *Sunnah* of guidance. They are then returned to those stations, which they had made compulsory for themselves after completing and fulfilling their rights. They reconcile with this, and preserve it safely within their hearts. Verily, they are later designated as trustees, and disseminate to another state; and each one is individually addressed: *'Indeed, in My Court today you are a dignified trustee.'* Henceforth, they are not subjected to permission [to execute things] because they have become similar to those who are granted full authority to act wherever they go; and their authority accompanies with them.

Thereafter, the love; *Nũr*, knowledge and gnosis of *Allãh* ﷻ is filled in the hearts of His ﷻ; elite servants. He is no longer questioned about anything; and as well as anything pertaining to himself. Almighty *Allãh* ﷻ positions him on this lofty status; with a condition, that is obligatory. When the chosen servant fulfils all the conditions and protects them prudently; without moving an inch, or otherwise; or by violating it commands, he is thereby, transported from there to the Kingdom of *Jabarũt*. His egotism is constricted by the Sultãn of *Jabarũt* until it is humiliated and rendered useless.

From here, as promised, the beloved servant is taken to the Sovereign Realm of the Divine Being ﷻ to be fulfilled, with that, which his heart had anticipated. These are those principles of desires, which prove accountability. He is then transported to the Divine Domain of Glory and is taught *Adab* [ethics]; and therefrom, he is transported to the Power of Divine Sovereignty and purified, and henceforth, he is transported to the Divine Realm of Dignity. He exercises patience and therefrom, he is transported to the Divine Domain of Radiance; which comprises Excellency. He is then transported to the Realm of Splendour, where he becomes all-embracing. From here, he is transferred to the Divine Precincts of Wonderment; where he is nurtured and called to the Divine Realms of Mercy, where he is made strong and brave. Thereafter, he is moved to the Divine Sphere of *Fardaniyyat* [singularity], where he is familiarised. Providence and preferential here, treatment feeds him and tenderness bonds him so that he develops into a spiritual state. Love and enthusiasm draws him closer, and Esteemed Beneficence has accepted him;

and draws him even closer. He is then given time off; and an abode, where it is whispered to him; that therefrom, itself, abundant space shall be granted; and henceforth, it ceases him. Honour and beneficence; after this, becomes his companion; wherever and whenever the beloved servant goes to, it is at his disposal. The servant becomes a trustee of the trustees of the secrets; and whatever is sent from *Allāh* ﷻ to His ﷻ creation; is sent through his elite servant. When the servant reaches this stage, then all qualities, which includes speech and worship disappears.

Thus, this is the furthermost limits of the heart and intellect, and the uttermost limits of the condition of the *Awliya*; to which they return. Above this is the exclusive station of the exalted Prophets and Messengers of *Allāh* ﷺ. This is the case, because the end of a *Walī* is the beginning of a *Nabī*. May *Allāh* ﷻ shower His ﷻ peace and blessings upon all of them.

The Difference between Wilāyah and Nubuwwah

The difference between *Wilāyah* [Sainthood] and *Nubuwwah* [Prophethood] is that, *Nubuwwah* is a *kalām* [speech] which is revealed by *Allāh* ﷻ. With it, is the *rūḥ* [soul] of *Allāh* ﷻ. Then revelation [*waḥī*] is conveyed and concludes with the *rūḥ* of *Allāh* ﷻ; which is accepted and amalgamated. It is incumbent to accept, fortify and confirm this Divine *Kalām* [speech]. Anyone who rejects it, becomes an infidel [*kāfir*] because he has rejected the verbatim Divine words of Almighty *Allāh* ﷻ.

On the contrary, *Wilāyah* is in reference to a *Walī* of *Allāh* ﷻ [non-Prophet]; and this is his *Revelation* [tradition], categorized as *Ilhām* [inspiration], which is revealed to him. This is also classified as *Revelation,* which is totally different to the Speech of Truth of *Allāh* ﷻ; as compared to *Waḥī*. [*Ilhām* encompasses tranquillity and it is experienced in the heart of a *Walī*] The *Walī* accepts this *Ilhām* and receives tranquillity through the medium of it.

Thus, *Kalām* [Speech - *Waḥī*] is for the *Anbiya* [Prophets] and *Ilham* is for the

Walī. Hence, rejection of the *Kalām* of the Prophet ﷺ make one a disbeliever [*kāfir*], because he has rejected the Divine *Kalām*, *Waḥī* and *Rūḥ* of Almighty *Allāh* ﷻ. But if someone rejects the *Ilham*, then he will not become a disbeliever [*kāfir*], but will be deprived and deemed a failure. This rejection will result in a great tragedy and he will encounter problems. His heart will be looted because he has rejected the words of Truth; which were inspired into the heart of *Walī* by the Love and Knowledge of *Allāh* ﷻ. Thus, this was issued by the Truth; and conveyed to the heart. *Ilham* is the manifestation of that knowledge which emanates in accordance to the Divine Ordinance. In fact *Ilham;* by its nature [*Fi al-Nafs*] is similar to a secret. Indeed this *Ilham* is from *Allāh* ﷻ and increases love for His ﷻ servants which will then permeate his heart with truthfulness. The heart will peacefully accept it.

The Cooked Chicken becomes Alive

I narrate in 673 *hijrī* in Cairo from Shaykh Abu-Muḥammad ʿAbd al-Wāḥid b. Sāliḥ b. Yaḥyah b. Muḥammad al-Qurashī al-Baghdādī ؓ, who narrates in 641 *hijrī* in Baghdād from Shaykh Abu al-Ḥasan ʿAlī b. Sulaymān al-Baghdādī ؓ, distinguished as the Baker. He stated that Shaykh ʿImrān al-Kimyānī ؓ and Shaykh Baz'zāz ؓ narrate from Shaykh Abu al-Futūḥ Muḥammad b. ʿAbdullāh b. Abu al-Muḥāsin Ismāʿīl al-Qurashī al-Tamīmī al-Qatfanī ؓ in 669 *hijrī* in Cairo and Shaykh Abu al-Ḥasan b. al-Shaykh Abī al-Majd b. Mubārak b. Zāhirī al-Ḥarīmī ؓ in 615 *hijrī* in Cairo narrate from Shaykh Abu al-Ḥasan ؓ in Baghdād, renowned as the Sock Merchant, narrates in 620 *hijrī* in Baghdād. Both of them declare that they had heard from their Shaykh, Shaykh Abu-Saʿūd Mudallal ؓ in Baghdād........

I also narrate in 670 *hijrī* in Cairo from Shaykh Abu al-Ḥasan ʿAlī b. ʿAbdullāh b. Abī-Bakr Abharī al-Baghdādī ؓ, and both of them profess that they narrate in 630 *hijrī* in Cairo from Shaykh Abu-Tāhir Khalīl b. Shaykh Abu al-ʿAbbās Aḥmad b. ʿAlī al-Sarsarī ؓ, who narrates from his father ؓ and he narrates in 671 *hijrī* in Cairo from Shaykh Abu al-Ḥasan ʿAlī b. Zakariyah b. Yaḥyah b. Abī al-Qāsim al-Azjī ؓ. He narrates in Baghdād in 632 *hijrī* in Baghdād from two *Shuyūkh*, Shaykh Qāḍī al-Quḍāt Sayyid Abu-Sāliḥ Nasar b.

Ḥāfiz ʿAbd al-Razzāq al-Jilānī ﷺ and Shaykh Abu al-Faḍal Isḥāq b. Aḥmad al-ʿAlsī ﷺ. Both of them proclaim that they narrate in 601 *hijrī* in Baghdād from Sayyiduna Shaykh Ḥāfiz Abu-Bakr ʿAbd al-Razzāq al-Jilānī ﷺ......

I narrate in 674 *hijrī* in Cairo from Shaykh Imām Shamsudīn Abu-ʿAbdullāh Muḥammad b. Shaykh ʿAllama ʿImādudīn Abu-Isḥāq Ibrāhīm b. ʿAbd al-Wāḥid al-Maqdisī al-Ḥanbalī ﷺ, who narrates in 631 *hijrī* in Baghdād from Shaykh Sharīf Abu al-Qāsim Haybatullāh b. ʿAbdullāh ﷺ, prominent as Ibn-Mansūrī. He narrates in 538 *hijrī* in Baghdād from the exalted Shaykh Abu-ʿAbdullāh Muḥammad b. Abu al-Maʿālī b. Qā'id al-Awānī ﷺ. All of them concur that a lady brought her son to Sayyiduna Shaykh Muḥiyy al-Dīn ʿAbd al-Qādir ﷺ and proclaimed: *'I see that the heart of this child of mine is greatly attracted to you. I, for the sake of Allāh ﷻ and for your sake relinquish my rights over him,'* Sayyiduna Ghawth al-Aʿzam ﷺ accepted the boy and instructed him to engage in *Mujāhidah*, and to observe the Path of the *Salf* [predecessors]. After a certain duration, the lady came to visit her son, and saw him to be weak and pale faced owing to hunger, and staying awake at night. At that time she noticed her son eating a piece of barley bread. She took leave of him, and proceeded to the chamber of Sayyiduna Ghawth al-Aʿzam ﷺ, and found a plate with fresh chicken bones kept in front of him which he had just eaten. She exclaimed: *'O my Master! You are eating chicken and my son is eating barley bread?'* Sayyiduna Ghawth al-Aʿzam ﷺ heard this and placed his sacred hands over the bones and issued a command: *'Stand up by the Command of that Lord ﷻ Who will raise those bone which will be perished.'* Instantly that particular chicken resurrected, stood up and crowed. Sayyiduna Shaykh ﷺ asserted: *'When your son reach this status then he can eat whatever he desires.'*

The dead vulture is resurrected

The same narrators report that one day there was very strong wind and a vulture flew over Sayyiduna Ghawth al-Aʿzam's ﷺ *majlis*, making noises. This disturbed the concentration of the audience. Sayyiduna Ghawth ﷺ caught sight of this and commanded: *'O Wind! Grab hold of it [the vulture].'* As soon as the Ghawth ﷺ articulated these words, the vulture fell dead onto the ground;

with its head on one side and the body on the other. Sayyiduna Ghawth ﷺ thereby, held the vulture with one hand, whilst he stroke it with the other hand, and recited: *'Bismillāhir Raḥmānir Raḥīm.'* The vulture resurrected and flew away. Everyone watched this incredible miracle.

The Signs of Taqwa [Piety]

Sayyiduna Ghawth ﷺ pronounced that there are many types of *taqwa*.

- ✓The *taqwa* of the general people [*'Āam*] is to refrain from *shirk* [idolatry or polytheism].
- ✓The *taqwa* of the elite [*khās*] is to abandon the lust of egotism and sins and to oppose the *nafs* in all circumstances.
- ✓The *taqwa* of the super elite [*Khās al-Khawās*], who are the *Awliya-Allāh* is the omission all entities. Intentions, *nafil* worship should not be linked to reasons, and attraction to others; except for *Allāh* ﷻ. In fact, in state and status, they make special preparations in executing all laws of compulsion [*Farāiḍ*].
- ✓The *taqwa* of the Prophets ﷺ is that nothing in the unseen [*ghayb*] supersedes them. Thus, they are from *Allāh* ﷻ and go towards *Allāh* ﷻ. He ﷻ commands them, and forbids them. He ﷻ grants them *Tawfiq* and teaches them *adab*. He consistently preserves them clean and pure. He has conversations with them; retains them on the right Path; grants them *Hidāyah* and peace; gives them glad tidings and information, and assists them. Intellect does not dare interfere in these matters. The Prophets are unlike humans; and in fact supersede angels; in their external application; and those exposed laws, that are beneficial for the *Ummah* and the masses; because they are also included; pertinent to them. Otherwise, they are unique amongst creation; and occasionally the senior *Abdāls*, including the distinctive *Awliya* are granted these qualities. The tongue is exhausted to explain their worship. This is not exposed to creation nor can one hear about it or perceive it.

Taqwa is inferred by three things;

1) To inculcate effective reliance when one cannot get something.
2) To exercise appropriate submission when one gets something.
3) To exercise persistent patience when something is lost.

If there is no *taqwa* and the imperative of status between Creator and creation; one cannot henceforward, reach the station of *Kashf* [spiritual unveiling] and *Mushāhidah* [mystical observance]. Thus, a pious individual is he who is not attracted or affected by his external contradictions and his internal defects. He always stands up in attention at the time of meeting with *Allāh* ﷻ. His external is a vanguard of the boundaries; and his internal is the intention of fidelity. The first clause of the path to *taqwa* is in safeguarding oneself; and to refrain from all major and minor sins; and the oppression and the denial of the rights of others. Thus, the sins of the heart, which is classified as the mother of all sins, that embraces boastfulness; greed; temptations; fear of creation; and placing hope in them for status and rule; and in expressing pride in one's family members whose details are widespread. Opposition to rumours and exaggerations of these malicious characteristics strengthens its negation and credibility. Thereby, intend in engaging oneself in the worship of *Allāh* ﷻ, in such a condition that, one does not include anyone; other than *Allāh* ﷻ. The pious does not entangle his plans by the Ordainment of *Allāh* ﷻ. He is not attracted to or desires anything, except *Allāh* ﷻ. He does not look at or depend on anyone for his sustenance; and he does not object nor is he displeased with any Command of *Allāh* ﷻ on creation. He submits to, and fulfils all of them with enthusiasm and sincerity. He places himself on duty to fulfil them and he submits himself to the Power of *Allāh* ﷻ, similar to a suckling infant in the hands of its breastfeeding mother; or a corpse in the hands of its washer. Such a person has no authority, choice or power and his intentions cease. This is indeed salvation.

Method of Acquiring Piety

If anyone refutes that there is one way to reach this destination; it shall then be clarified to them to seek true refuge in Him ﷻ and to submit to Him ﷻ in totality. Live by His ﷻ Commands and refrain from all that, which He ﷻ forbids you from and make his obedience obligatory upon yourself. Accept His ﷻ Ordinance of Destiny, and protect your condition within His ﷻ prescribed limits. Anyone who does not observe these conditions will never acquire salvation. Observe faithfulness, be steadfast on modesty and adopt sole pleasure of *Allāh* ﷻ. Ensure a sincere detachment from this mundane world, as it is a huge veil. This world [*duniya*] is the criterion that determines between the pure and impure.

The Excellence of Sayyiduna Ghawth al-Aᶜzam

I narrate in 674 *hijrī* from Qāḍī al-Quḍāt Shamsudīn Abu-ᶜAbdullāh al-Maqdisī al-Ḥanbalī, who narrates from Shaykh Haybatullāh b. Mansūrī in 633 *hijrī* in Baghdād. He narrates from Shaykh Sāliḥ Abu al-ᶜAbbās Aḥmad b. Muḥammad al-Qurashī, who was a fellow-rider of Sayyiduna Shaykh Muḥiyy al-Dīn ᶜAbd al-Qādir al-Jilānī. He enunciated that Sayyiduna Ghawth saddled, and rode to *Jāmeʿh Mansūr* [for *salāh*]. When he returned to his *Madrassa,* he removed the covering from his face; and held a scorpion with his hand from his forehead and threw it onto the ground. I began spinning on the ground and Sayyiduna Ghawth commanded it to die, and it died. He then declared: '*O Aḥmad! From the Jāmeʿh Masjid to here, this scorpion stung me seventy times.*'

Shaykh Aḥmad states that he complained to Sayyiduna Ghawth about hunger, and many children to feed in the days, when there was a severe drought in Baghdād. Sayyiduna Ghawth then gave him a container of wheat and instructed: '*Place this in a clay container and close its opening and leave a small portion of the lid open. Whenever you need to use wheat, take out the grains from this opening and grind it for your use. Do not open the entire lid.*' Shaykh Aḥmad admits that we ate out of this container for five years; and my wife then opened the entire lid and found it as Sayyiduna Ghawth had initially given it to me. After my wife opened the lid, we ate out of it for seven days and the wheat was exhausted. I reported this to Sayyiduna Ghawth ﷺ and he asserted: *'Had you left that lid closed, you would have eaten from it till the day of your death.'*

What is Piety and Religiousness [Waraʿh]

The gesture of piety [*warã h*] points out to stopping at everything and abstain from it until the ruling of the sacred *Sharĩ ãh*. If there is permission from the *Sharĩ ãh*, use it then, otherwise refrain from it. Piety is the king of all actions. There are three categories of piety as follows:

1) Piety of the general public [*ʿÃam*]. They refrain from *Harãm* and doubtful things
2) Piety of the elite [*Khawãs*]. These individuals abandon the lust and desires of their egotism
3) Piety of the Super-elite [*Khãs al-Khawãs*]. This high ranking piety, which avoids every intention and thought.

Further, there are two types of piety as listed below:

1) The external piety. This means that every movement of the body is for *Allãh* ﷻ.
2) The internal piety. This is not to allow anything else in the heart, except *Allãh* ﷻ.

Anyone who does not pay attention to the details of piety will not qualify for the subtle entities of Divine Gifts. Piety in speech is extremely difficult and *zuhd* [Asceticism] in statesmanship is very difficult. *Zuhd* is the first stage to piety, similar to contented being on one side of acquiescence. In the rules of piety, food and clothing are inclusive as well. The food of the pious is that people do not follow him, and the sacred *Sharĩ ãh* does not demand justification from him. The food of a *Walĩ* is devoid of greed, which in fact is by the Command of *Allãh* ﷻ; whilst the food of the *Abdãl* is without intention; but by the grace of *Allãh* ﷻ. Hence, a person who does not have the first quality, he will not reach the following stations in accordance to its sequence. Absolute dejectment or grief results in the disobedience to *Allãh* ﷻ; and therefore, there should not be anything that is non-*Islãmic*, i.e. against the

Sharī'āh.

People possess three types of clothing;

1) The clothing of the pious which has been aforementioned. It may be woollen or cotton.
2) The clothing of the *Awliya* is that, which they are commanded to wear. It is very modest and sufficient enough to cover their *satar*[209] so that their *nafs* [ego] is supressed.
3) The clothing of the *Abdāls* is to protect the parameters, sufficient enough as prescribed by the Ordinance of Destiny; i.e. a *qamīs* [shirt – *kurta*] to the value of one *qirāt* [one carat] or one garb worth a 100 *dinārs*. They do not have any intentions in this matter; nor how to wear it; or desire it, to be woollen. All this is left to the Choice and Bounties of *Allāh* ﷻ. Piety cannot be perfected without engaging the self in the following ten characteristics:
    1. Protect the tongue from backbiting, because *Allāh* ﷻ commands us not to slander one another.
    2. Withdraw from doubts. *Allāh* ﷻ commands us to refrain from suspicion, because some suspicion is a sin. Sayyiduna Rasūlullāh ﷺ cautions to safeguard yourself from suspicion, because it is considered as a severe lie.
    3. Do not make a mockery of others, because *Allāh* ﷻ orders one nation not to mock the other, because it may be so, that they are better than the other.
    4. Protect your vision from the *meḥram* [foreign women]. *Allāh* ﷻ commands: *'Tell the believers to lower their gaze.'*
    5. Always speak the truth. *Allāh* ﷻ stipulates: *'When you talk, be just [talk the truth].'*
    6. Always remember that everything is a Bounty from *Allāh* ﷻ; so that the ego does not become proud and arrogant. *Allāh* ﷻ declares: *'It is Allāh's* ﷻ *favour upon you that He has guided you*

[209] A man's *Satar* or *'Awrah* is from the navel to below the knees.

with Imān.'

7. Spend your wealth on Truth and do not waste it on futile items. Almighty *Allāh* ﷻ elucidates: *'When these people [pious] spend their wealth, it is not on extravagance and waste i.e. it is not spent on sins or on things against the Sharīʿah.'*
8. Do not be boastful and arrogant [self-praise]. The Glorious Lord ﷻ issues a stern warning: *'I have created the House of Ākhirah for those who do not intend status on earth nor dissention.'*
9. Always protect your five times daily *salah* by performing their *rukūʿ* and *sajdah* correctly. They must be read within their prescribed time, because *Allāh* ﷻ stipulates: *'Guard all your prayers, and the middle prayer; and stand with reverence before Allah* ﷻ*.'*
10. Always be steadfast on the beliefs of the *Ahle Sunnat wa Jamāʿat, because Allāh* ﷻ proclaims: *'This Path of Mine is straight and you follow it. There are many other paths that you should not follow because they will turn you away from the Straight Path [Sirāt al-Mustaqīm].'*

Sayyiduna Ghawth al-Aʿzam ؓ offers Assistance to a Distant Place

I narrate in 633 *hijrī* in Cairo from Shaykh Abu al-ʿAfāf Mūsā b. Shaykh ʿĀrif Abu al-Maʿālī ʿUthmān b. Mūsā al-Baqāʿī ؒ, who narrates in 614 *hijrī* in Damascus from his father ؒ. He narrates in 569 *hijrī* in Baghdād from two *Shuyūkh*, Shaykh Abu-ʿAmar ʿUthmān al-Sarīfīnī ؒ and Shaykh ʿAbd al-Ḥaqq al-Ḥarīmī ؒ. Both of them state that on Sunday 3rd Safar 555 *hijrī* they were with Sayyiduna Ghawth al-Aʿzam ؓ in his *Madrassa*. He was standing and making *wuḍū*, whilst wearing a pair of wooden sandals. He then performed two *rakaʿats nafil salāh*. After the *salām* he screamed loudly, and threw one of his wooden sandals into the air; that disappeared from our vision. He then screamed again and threw the other sandal into the air, and this also disappeared from our vision. He then sat down and no one had the courage to question him as to why he did that. With the elapse of twenty three days, a caravan from a foreign land [Persian state] arrived, and the leader revealed: *'We have a gift for Sayyiduna Shaykh.'* We sought permission from the Sayyiduna Ghawth ﷺ and he permitted us to take the gift. They presented some reverain[210] and silk fabric, some gold and the two wooden sandals of the Ghawth ﷺ that he threw away on that day. We questioned them as to where they acquired those wooden sandals. They informed us that they were travelling on Sunday and coincidently an Arab caravan appeared with its leader in front of them. They began looting our belongings and killed some of our people. Henceforward, they set out to the jungle and began distributing the loot. We also stepped onto one side of the jungle and exclaimed to ourselves: *'We should have remembered Sayyiduna Shaykh ʿAbd al-Qãdir ﷺ when these bandits attacked us.'* Thereafter, we effected an intention, that should our lives be saved, we shall thereby gift Sayyiduna Shaykh ﷺ with something and thus, we began to remember him. Then we heard two loud, deafening sounds that filled the jungle; we then saw the bandits, who were absolutely terrified; whilst we were under the impression that another Arab caravan had attacked them. A few of them came to us and requested us to come and to take back all our belongings, and to witness the calamity that had befallen them. They took us to their leader and we found him lying dead on the ground; and one of these sandals that was wet with water, was lying next to him. The robbers returned all our goods and admitted to the fact that this incident was something enormous.

Concerning the Dangers of the Heart

Sultãn al-ʿÃrifin Sayyiduna Ghawth al-Aʿzam ﷺ states that there are six dangers within the heart:

---

[210] A type of aquatic fabric, similar to silk.

1) *Nafs* [the negative force - ego]
2) The cursed *shaytãn* [devil]
3) *Rũḥ* [the soul]
4) *Malak* [angel]
5) *'Aql* [intellect]
6) *Yaqĩn* [certainty]

❖ The danger of *nafs* is that, it draws and commands you to engage in lust and evil.

❖ The danger of the devil is that it drags you to *kufr*, *shirk* and creates doubts and comments in all that *Allãh* ﷻ has promised His servants. The stoned devil distracts the people from the seriousness of sinning and takes away the conscious of repentance, which is the reason for destruction of the *nafs* in this world and the *Ãkhirah*. Thus, both these dangers are of a very serious nature, which commands the soul to engage in sin. These dangers are prevalent amongst the general believers [*mo'minĩn*].

❖ The dangers of the soul and angel descends with Truth [*Ḥaqq*]; and with obedience to *Allãh* ﷻ and His Commandments by which the servant's consequences in this *duniya* and *Ãkhirah* remain safe and sound; in accordance to knowledge. Thus, both these matters are praiseworthy and the special servants do not exclude these issues.

❖ The dangers of the intellect, sometime issues the same command as the *nafs;* and the devil; and sometimes; that which the soul does. This is the Wisdom of *Allãh* ﷻ and the strength of His ﷻ creativity, so that the servant has the sense and ability of understanding the virtues and the vices of the reasons for existence within the company of witnesses. Therefore, the reason of the servant's conclusion will manifest; which will result in a worthy recompense or punishment; because Almighty *Allãh* ﷻ has created the body as a place to execute His ﷻ Divine Commandments, and as well as a centre for implementing the foundation of Wisdom of His ﷻ Divine Ordinance. Similarly, *Allãh* ﷻ has created the intellect as a vehicle of virtues and vices so that both, together with the components of the body are implemented. This is so; because this is a place of pains and praises, and a reason for praise. Thus, for the intelligent, there are Bounties from *Allāh* ﷻ or a painful punishment is meted out.

❖ But the dangers of *yaqīn*; which is the soul of belief, and the reason for the increase of knowledge. This returns to *Allāh* ﷻ, which is issued by *Allāh* ﷻ. This danger is exclusive to the super-elite *Awliya-Allāh*, which embraces the *Ahle-Yaqīn*[211], *Siddiqīn*[212], *Shuhadāh*[213] and *Abdāl*[214] and it only manifests with Truth [*Ḥaqq*]. These manifestations are very secretive, subtle and not exposed, because they are related to *'Ilme Ladunnī* and information of the *Ghayb* [unseen]. Thus, it is an empowerment from *Allāh* ﷻ; and objective of the beloved servants, which is hidden from the functions with it. They are hidden from their exposure, and their external [*zāhir*] worship; excluding their internal [*bātin*] worship is transformed into *Farāiḍ*[215] and *Sunan-e-Muak'kidah*[216]. They are consistently engrossed in internal *Murāqabah*[217] and *Allāh* ﷻ disciplines their external condition as He ﷻ specifies in the Holy *Qur'ān*:

﴿إِنَّ وَلِيِّيَ اللَّهُ الَّذِي نَزَّلَ الْكِتَابَ ۖ وَهُوَ يَتَوَلَّى الصَّالِحِينَ﴾

Indeed my Protector is Allah Who has sent down
the Book; and He befriends the righteous. [218]

---

[211] People with certainty [*Awliya*].
[212] The elite Truthful.
[213] The Martyrs
[214] These are forty senior *Awliya*. They are the ones occupied with carrying the weight of Creation, so that they are not free to act except on behalf of the other-than-*Allāh* (*Fi haqq al-ghayr*). According to Prophetic Tradition, they are based in Shām (Syria). They move around the globe daily in different direction on different dates. These *Sayrs* or visits are under the supervision of Sayyiduna Khiḍar عليه السلام and under the Spiritual Command of Sayyiduna Ghawth al-Aʿzam Shaykh ʿAbd al-Qādir Jilānī رضي الله عنه
[215] The Compulsions.
[216] The *sunnahs* not to be omitted.
[217] Spiritual contemplation
[218] *Al-Qur'ān al-Karīm,* Chapter 7, Surah Aʿrāf, Verse no. 196

Allāh ﷻ befriends these chosen servants; and this is sufficient for them. Their hearts are retained, busy in the concentration of the secrets of the unseen; and a lustre lights up near each of them. They are exalted for Divine Speech and made exclusive for *Allāh's* ﷻ Love and Glory, coupled with peace and tranquillity. They are in a stage within the Beloved Lord's ﷻ Proximity, where there is infinity, and the Divine Grace is such that, it does not terminate. Hence, every day their knowledge, *Ma'ārifah* and *Nūr* increases in profusion. This is an infinite realm of the Sublime Lord of Power ﷻ. When the book reaches its limits and destination in *Dār al-Fana* [Realm of Extinction]; where it's *Baqa* [existence] is destined, then it is transferred to a far better place; similar to the transference of a bride from a low abode to a prestigious and appropriate home. The *duniya* for them is *Jannah*, and *Ākhirah* is the coolness of their eyes. He makes the *ziyārah* of the Divine Vision [Beauty] of *Allāh* ﷻ without veils, doors and courtiers or restrictions; oppression; harm; interruption or end, as *Allāh* ﷻ elucidates:

﴿ نَّ الْمُتَّقِينَ فِي جَنَّاتٍ وَنَهَرٍ فِي مَقْعَدِ صِدْقٍ عِندَ مَلِيكٍ مُّقْتَدِرٍ ﴾

Indeed the pious are amidst Gardens and springs. Seated in an assembly of the Truth, in the presence of Allah, the Omnipotent King. [219]

The above stated Divine Command is for those who have engaged themselves in virtuous deeds and have exercised piety. They are the ones who shall undertake this sacred *ziyārah* to their Sublime Lord ﷻ.

There are two abodes in the inspiration of the *nafs* and *Rūḥ*, i.e. angel and devil. The angel will place *taqwa* into the heart, whilst the devil will mislead one towards transgression and sins. Thus, the heart desires the organs to be used for sins; and in the inauthenticity of both the abodes, the intellect and lust manoeuvre as the leaders. This is analysed as *Tawfīq* or pride. There are two *Nūrs* [lights] shining in the heart, which comprises of knowledge and *Imān*. These are all the components and speciality of the heart. Between them,

[219] *Al-Qur'ān al-Karīm,* Chapter 54 Surah Qamar, Verse no. 55

the heart is like an angel. This is the army of the heart that reaches him; or like a bright clear mirror reflecting the images of the components of the heart at its edges. He thereby sees them, illuminates and receives them. Henceforward, is the danger of the speech [address]; which addresses the heart. If the communication is from the angel, then it is *Ilhãm* [inspiration], but if it is from the devil, then it is *waswasa* [satanic whisperings]. When it is from the *nafs*, it is termed as *hãjis* [suspicion]. If it is from *Allãh* ﷻ and the words of His ﷻ address enters the heart [with tranquillity], then it is *Ḥaqq* [Truth].

The sign of *Ilhãm* is that it comes in accordance with *ʿIlm* [knowledge], thus, *Ilhãm* without any external proof is classified as *bãtil* [false]. The sign of *hawa* [lust] unfolds, when the desire of any one of the exclusive qualities of the *nafs* is persistent, tenacious and constant; even though it takes a long time to achieve its desire, and to achieve its goal. The sign of *waswasa* [satanic whisperings] is that if it tries to entice one to a sin and if it is opposed, it will then use its *waswasa* to try and attract one to a different sin; because as far as *waswasa* is concerned; all opposition to it is equal, as *Allãh* ﷻ stipulates: *'Indeed, he [satan] calls his army so that they become amongst the dweller of Hell Fire.'* The dangers of *Ḥaqq* [Truth] is that, it does not reach the stage of *Ḥayrah* [astonishment] or drags one into sins. In fact, it comes with the increase of knowledge and cognizance. Its praises are understood at the time of receiving it. When the heart experiences such dangers of *Ḥaqq* [Truth] which is followed by the danger of *Ḥaqq* [Truth], Shaykh Jayyid رحمه الله then pronounces: *'The first is very strong, because when it remains, it will then revert to meditation and this is a place of knowledge.'* Shaykh Ibn ʿÃtã رحمه الله declares: *'The second is more powerful, because its power increases with the first.'* Shaykh Ḥafif رحمه الله proclaims: *'Both are equal, because both are from Allãh ﷻ. One does not have excellence over the other, but only due to special probability. And when there is a variety of dangers, then recite the following excerpt:*

سُبْحَانَكَ الْمَلِكِ الْخَلَّاقِ إِنْ يَّشَاءِ يُذْهِبْكُمْ وَيَأْتِ بِخَلْقٍ جَدِيْد

Glorified is the King and the Creator. If He wills, He can take you away [exterminate you] and bring other

creatures [in your place]. [220]

The above mentioned Injunction is not difficult for *Allāh* ﷻ to implement. It is the consensus of everyone; that if anyone who eats *Ḥarām*, he will not have the power to differentiate between the dangers.

The devil is a Liar

I narrate in 639 *hijrī* from Shaykh Abu al-Fatāḥ Nasrullāh b. Qāsim b. Yūsuf al-Hashimī ﷺ who narrates in 630 *hijrī* in Baghdād from Shaykh Abu al-Ḥasan ʿAlī b. Sulaymān ﷺ, the Baker, who affirms that he had heard from his Shaykh, Shaykh Abu-Ḥafs ʿUmar al-Kimyānī ﷺ, who stated that, one night he was in seclusion and the wall split. A very ugly person emerged and came to me. I questioned him: '*Who are you?*' He replied: '*I am iblīs [the devil] and I have come to advice you.*' I asserted to him: '*Your advice is of no use to me.*' He articulated: '*I will teach you how to sit in Murāqabah.*' He then reclined on his back and raised both his knees, placed his head on them; and flipped over backwards. In the morning, I proceeded to my Master, Shaykh Muḥiyy al-Dīn ʿAbd al-Qādir al-Jilānī ﷺ to inform him about this incident. I shook his hand and before I could affirm anything, the Ghawth held my hands and enunciated: '*O ʿUmar! He spoke the truth, but he is a liar. After this do not regard any of his words as the truth in the future.*' Shaykh Abu al-Hasan b. Sulaymān ﷺ, the Baker, states that this sitting posture was that of Shaykh Abu-Ḥafs ʿUmar al-Kimyānī ﷺ.

Allāh ﷻ is the Manifestor of Wonders

Sultān al-ʿĀrifīn Sayyiduna Muḥiyy al-Dīn Shaykh ʿAbd al-Qādir al-Jilānī ﷺ discourses that the sacred word '*Allāh*' is the *Isme Aʿzam*. This will only be *Isme-Aʿzam* for you; until you call it out in a state; that your heart is devoid of everything, except *Allāh* ﷻ. The effect of '*Bismillāh*' on the lips of an *ʿĀrif* is like the Command of '*Kun*' of Almighty *Allāh* ﷻ. This Divine Word dispels 'I'

[220] Last portion of this *duʿā* is from Chapter 35, Surah Fātir, Verse no. 12

and 'you'; and destroys the effect of poison. Its *Nūr* [light] is for all [general] and dominant over every power. *Allāh* ﷻ is the Manifestor of Wonders. The Law of *Allāh* ﷻ is most lofty and His ﷻ Divine Being is most exalted. The Divine word '*Allāh*' ﷻ is the stepping stone [pulpit] to heights, and as well as the protector of the heart. *Allāh* ﷻ expresses anger on the oppressors and destroys tyrannical kings. *Allāh* ﷻ is the Knower of every secret and exposed entity. There is nothing concealed from Him ﷻ. Whoever submits in totality to *Allāh* ﷻ, he shall fall under His ﷻ Divine Protection. He, who loves *Allāh* ﷻ will not look at, nor depend on anyone. He, who walks on the Path of *Allāh* ﷻ, will reach *Allāh* ﷻ and when he reaches *Allāh* ﷻ; he shall spend his life in the protection of *Allāh* ﷻ. He, who is enthusiastic for *Allāh* ﷻ; loves *Allāh* ﷻ, and when he leaves others, he becomes pure with *Allāh* ﷻ. Knock at the Door of *Allāh* ﷻ, seek His ﷻ security and place your reliance on Him ﷻ. Oh those who turn away from Him ﷻ! Return to Him ﷻ. If this is the state of hearing My ﷻ Name in the House of *Shifa* [cure], what do you think; then will be your state when meeting with Me ﷻ? If this is the condition of the House of sorrows, what do you think will be the condition of the House of Graciousness? This is My ﷻ Name and you are standing at My ﷻ door; what do you think will be your situation; henceforward, when the veils are lifted? If this is the condition when I ﷻ Call upon you; what do you think thereby, will be the condition when I beam My lustres onto you? The nation is engaged in *Mushāhidah* [Divine Observance] and nobleness has reached them. The condition of the lover is synonymous to that animal that does sleep on trees. He whispers to His ﷻ beloved in the privacy of the morning; and the breeze of proximity blows onto them. Henceforth, they become enthusiastic for their Lord ﷻ. Remember Me ﷻ with submission and humility, I ﷻ shall cause you to be spoken of in a much better authoritative mode. Their statement is understood by the following Divine Command of *Allāh* ﷻ:

وَمَن يَتَوَكَّلْ عَلَى اللَّهِ فَهُوَ حَسْبُهُ

And he who has reliance on Allāh ﷻ*, He*
is sufficient for him.[221]

[221] *Al-Qur'ān al-Karīm,* Chapter 65, Surah Talāq Verse no. 3

The Sublime Lord ﷻ of Power stipulates:

- You remember Me ﷻ with ardour and love; I will cause you to be spoken of with communion and closeness.
- You remember Me ﷻ with praises and glorification; I will cause you to be spoken of with favours and recompense.
- You remember Me ﷻ with repentance; I will cause you to be spoken of with forgiveness of sins.
- You remember Me ﷻ without forgetfulness; I will cause you to be spoken of without intermissions.
- You remember Me ﷻ with remorse; I will cause you to be spoken of with favours and blessings.
- You remember Me ﷻ with excuses; I will cause you to be spoken of with pardon.
- You remember Me ﷻ with intent; I will cause you to be spoken of with esteem.
- You remember Me ﷻ with fidelity; I will cause you to be spoken of with fidelity.
- You remember Me ﷻ with your heart; I will cause you to be spoken of by removing your sorrows.
- You remember Me ﷻ with your tongue; I will cause you to be spoken of with protection.
- You remember Me ﷻ with poverty; I ﷻ will cause you to be spoken of with status.
- You remember Me ﷻ with apology and repentance; I ﷻ will cause you to be spoken of with mercy and forgiveness.
- You remember Me ﷻ with your heart; I ﷻ will cause you to be spoken of by removing the veil from you.
- You remember Me ﷻ with *fānī* [extinction]; I ﷻ will cause you to be spoken of with *bāqī* [permanence].
- You remember Me ﷻ with humility; I ﷻ will cause you to be spoken of with favours.
- You remember Me ﷻ with abasement; I ﷻ will cause you to be spoken of with forgiveness of sins.

- You remember Me ﷻ with confession; I ﷻ will cause you to be spoken of with washing away your sins.
- You remember Me ﷻ with a clean heart; I ﷻ will cause you to be spoken of with special virtues.
- You remember Me ﷻ with absolute sincerity; I ﷻ will cause you to be spoken of with compassion.
- You remember Me ﷻ with clarity; I ﷻ will cause you to be spoken of with significance.
- You remember Me ﷻ with reverence; I ﷻ will cause you to be spoken of with honour.
- You remember Me ﷻ with *Takbīr* [magnification]; I ﷻ will cause you to be spoken of by freedom from the Hell Fire.
- You remember Me ﷻ with abandoning oppression; I ﷻ will cause you to be spoken of with protection and loyalty.
- You remember Me ﷻ with sins; I ﷻ will cause you to be spoken of with various types of forgiveness and gifts.
- You remember Me ﷻ with sincere servitude; I ﷻ will cause you to be spoken of with the fulfilment of my blessings.
- You remember Me ﷻ with your status; I ﷻ will cause you to be spoken of with My Status.

Indeed! The *dhikr* of *Allāh* ﷻ is Great!

The Commands of Sultān al-Awliya Sayyiduna Ghawth al-Aʿzam رضي الله عنه regarding the ʿĀrifīn

Sayyiduna Shaykh Muḥiyy al-Dīn ʿAbd al-Qādir al-Jilānī رضي الله عنه testifies to the fact that a lightning flashed from the effervescence of Eternity onto the firmament of the hearts of the *ʿĀrifīn*. A breeze blew onto the intellect of the souls of the *Makāshifīn* [the *Awliya* with unveiling - *kashf*] from the garden of permanence. An assortment of fragrant flowers from the Sanctimonious Realm cherished the secret flowers of the *Mushahidīn* [observers]. The reason as to why these intellects travel into the ocean of *'Bismillāh'* is that, the foam of the ultimate perimeter reaches the plains on the shores of *'Ar-Raḥīm'*. Hence, the Unique and Incomparable Lord ﷻ is affluent with pearls, and He ﷻ is in prosperity and is in sole possession of the Mysterious Gifts of the Eternal Treasury. On that night, with the accomplishment at his behest, Sayyiduna Nabī Mūsā ﷺ insisted upon *Allāh* ﷻ as follows:

'Oh! Allāh ﷻ, Show me Your Beauty as far as the splendid Nūr of Your Tūr [mountain] of seeking, so that it gives Light to the pious group of the 'Ārifīn [Gnostics].'

The *'Ārifīn* are blessed, for they perceive the Divine Grandeur. To die in the war of Love is an all-embracing life; whilst being with others, even if it is just for a moment; portrays death in reality. If the eye of your intellect becomes blind to the vision of others, its recompense shall be assured in the Hereafter. To this effect, *Allāh* ﷻ confirms in the Holy *Qur'ān*:

﴿وُجُوهٌ يَوْمَئِذٍ نَّاضِرَةٌ ۝ إِلَىٰ رَبِّهَا نَاظِرَةٌ﴾

On that day, some faces will shine with freshness.
Looking towards their Lord.[222]

Swiftly with His ﷻ sword, if His ﷻ Love slays you, the blood will only then ooze after a delay, because the lover is preserved alive by His ﷻ Sustainer; and he is thereby, nourished with sustenance. The cup-bearers of Eternity stand with the Pure Drink of '*Alast*'[223] in front of the souls of some humans in the concealed chambers of their congregation. When your Lord ﷻ imposed a vow upon you, the cup-bearer [*sāqī*] rendered you unconscious, and not the Drink. The inebriation did not stop on the constituent parts of those entities; until the dawn of the sacred *Sharī'āh* of Sayyiduna Aḥmad ﷺ did not appear on the horizon of Messengership [*Risālah*] and the secret subtleties of the Sovereign Lord of Eternity ﷻ did not emanate. Henceforth, the intoxicated lovers were awakened to remind them of the allegiance that their Lord ﷻ had obtained from them in the concealment of the Night of *Alast*. They then flew with their wings towards Him ﷻ and promptly declared:

---

[222] *Al-Qur'ān al-Karīm,* Chapter 75, Surah Qiyāmah Verse no. 23

[223] First Day of Covenant.

'O my Lord! Towards You so that You be pleased.'

The above quoted statement substantiates that the souls observed that He is *Allāh* ﷻ. The hearts received tranquillity by the pronouncement of this statement that, there is none worthy of worship, except Him ﷻ. The secrets fear this statement, for owing to this, the knowledge of the unseen is exposed. By the words, *'Ar-Raḥman Al-Raḥīm,'* the intellect received acumen.

Huwiyyat [He-ness; the Divine Identity] is an ocean in which every swimmer drowns and every ship plunges down in search for it. If the intellect, mounts onto the vehicle of contemplation and reaches its shores with evidence of certainty; its waves shall then throw the gems of the secrets of Eternity at it, and it shall bestow upon it, the gifts of the perceptive secrets of the unseen. It illustrates the light of guidance of *Ḥaqq al-Yaqīn* [Real Certainty]. It takes on the splendid pedestals of benediction to the proximity of the Mountain of *Qāf.*[224] The Khiḍar of its head immerses in the Fountain of Life and its darkness transfers one towards light. Thus, one sees the *Sharīʿāh* of the Master of the Universe ﷺ. The lamps of the intellect of the *ʿĀrifīn*, with the splendour of the lightning of their Lights, shortly strips the eyes of the *Wāsilīn*[225]. The hands of its decorating followers embellish the faces of the brides of the Stations of Proximity. The persisting fragrance adorns the signs of knowledge of the *Mushāhidīn* [observers] of permanent spiritual state.

O humankind! Your heart is the station of the observance of Eternity. Tents of Divine Closeness are pitched onto the plains of your chest. Heaven and Hell was created for you in view of your sins. The pertinent Injunction was revealed as follows:

'Verily, I will surely forgive that person who repents and brings faith [Imān].'

The Appointment of an Abdāl

I narrate in 672 *hijrī* in Cairo from Shaykh Abu al-Ḥasan ʿAlī b. Abī-Zakariyyah

[224] The Mount of Qāf has been explained in detail in Footnote no. 137. Refer to it.
[225] Those *Awliya* who have reached their destination.

Yaḥyah b. Abī al-Qāsim al-Baghdādī al-Azjī ﷺ who narrates in 631 *hijrī* in Baghdād from Qāḍī al-Quḍāt Sayyiduna Abu-Sāliḥ Nasar al-Jilānī ؓ and Sayyiduna Shaykh Abu al-Muḥāsin Faḍlullāh al-Jilānī ؓ. Both of them are sons of Sayyiduna Shaykh Ḥāfiz Abu-Bakr ʿAbd al-Razzāq al-Jilānī ؓ s/o Shaykh al-Islām Sultān al-ʿĀrifīn Sayyiduna Muḥiyy al-Dīn ʿAbd al-Qādir al-Jilānī ؓ. Both state that they narrate in 601 *hijrī* from their father, Sayyiduna Abu-Bakr ʿAbd al-Razzāq al-Jilānī ؓ who narrates from Shaykh Abu al-Ḥasan b. Tantana al-Baghdādī ﷺ who confessed to me on the morning when we buried my father, Sayyiduna Ghawth al-Aʿzam ؓ:

> I was studying with Sayyiduna Ghawth ؓ and often stayed up during the nights in order to serve him, in case he needed anything. One night in the month of *Safar* 553 *hijrī;* Sayyiduna Ghawth al-Aʿzam ؓ came out of his room and I hastened with a container of water for his *wuḍū*. I presented it to him, but he did not accept it, and thereby he walked towards the door of the *Madrassa*. It opened on its own accord; and he then walked, until he reached to the door of the city. This door too, opened on its own accord and I followed him; in anticipation that he was unaware that I was following him. As we passed the door, it closed on its own. We walked for a short distance and then we reached such a city, which was beyond my recognition He entered into a guest house. There were six people therein, and all of them made *salām* to Sayyiduna Ghawth ؓ. As I was hiding behind a pillar, I watched, and I heard a weeping sound, emanating from one of the rooms. After a while the weeping sounds stopped and thereby, a man arrived and proceeded towards that room. He returned carrying a person on his shoulder from that room. Another person arrived bareheaded, with long hair and an enormous sized moustache and sat down in front of Sayyiduna Ghawth ؓ. Haḍrate Ghawth ؓ dictated to him to recite the *Shahādah,* and reverted him to a *Muslim*. His hair and moustache was trimmed and Sayyiduna Ghawth ؓ placed a hat on his head, named him Muḥammad and proclaimed: *'I was commanded to replace the marḥūm [departed] with this person.'* All of them answered in agreement.

When the Ghawth ؓ left, he also left, whilst the rest of them remained behind. We walked for a short distance and reached the entrance of the city of Baghdād. The entrance opened on its own accord and hence, we entered, and it thereby closed on its own. We then walked to the *Madrassa* and its door opened on its own. Ḥaḍrate Ghawth ﷺ proceeded to his room. The next morning I attended his class and I could not read a word owing to his powerful veneration. He verbalized to me: *'My son! Read, there is no harm.'*

Henceforward, I solemnly declared an oath to him in explaining the night's incident, to which he affirmed:

> *'That was the city of Nihawand and the six people whom you saw there were senior Abdāls. The soft weeping that you heard was of the seventh one, who was sick and he passed on. Abu al-ʿAbbās Khiḍar* ﷺ *was the person, whom you saw, that was carrying him out of the house in order to make arrangements for his ghusal and burial. The person to whom I prescribed to read the Shahādah, was a Christian from Qustuntuniya [Constantinople – present day Istanbul]. I was commanded to replace him with the deceased Abdāl. He was summoned there and he embraced Islām at my hands. Now he is one of them [Abdāls].'* Then Sayyiduna Ghawth ﷺ averred a vow from me; not to disclose this occurrence until he lived.

Sultān al-ʿĀrifīn Sayyiduna Ghawth al-Aʿzam ﷺ elucidated: A *khirqah* [a patched *Sūfī* Garb] is the name of the burning fervour of an *ʿĀrif* who does not deviate from the path and stood steadfast onto the foot of *Ikhlās* [fidelity]. The Throne of Secrets is positioned in the camp of *Ḥaqq al-Yaqīn* [Real Certainty] and *Ḥaqq al-Yaqīn* is a spot of the circle of *Tawḥīd*, and moreover, *Tawḥīd* is the rule of existence. *Huwwiyat Aḥadiyah* [Unity of Divine Identity] refers to an iron magnet within the hearts of the *ʿĀrifīn*. The Eternal Garden is the grazing pastures of the secrets of the *Makāshifīn* [226]. On the night of the First Covenant [*Alast*], the unveiling of the souls is extracted from the Secrets of Eternity. In view of the fact to their adherence to the vow of their speech, the intellect is also blessed. In the presence of the Domain of Eternity, the one

[226] The *Awliya* who possess powerful spiritual perception

who delights the mind with the gratification of 'وَاَشْهَدَهُمْ – *And I testify on them;*'[227] procures one to the closeness of the secrets, by the address of *Alast*, within the Precincts of Eternity. They were given Drinks from the Cups of His ﷻ Love by the hands of the cup-bearers from the Divine Presence. They returned to this world [*duniya*] in such a state; that their heads were inebriated with the effects of the Drink of Love, together with the relics of Divine Exquisiteness in the eyes of their intellect. The radiance of the Divine Presence is entrenched in the eyes of their hearts. Alas! How did you die with such a behaviour pattern; whereby you did not recognize your Lord ﷻ? Bravery is classified as a moment of patience.

O Ajamī! Work wisely and travel towards the Arabian country. O humankind of disposition! Travel to the *Hindī* [Indian] cities of guidance. Some *'Ārifīn* drank a drop of this Divine Drink; whilst the Eternal cup-bearer gave him a little to drink from that sacred Drink and his soul swayed in a blissful delight amongst his associates, and it thereby, stood up. At the time of the flash of the lustre, the mountain of Sayyiduna Mūsā عليه السلام shook enthusiastically. The head of the beloved observed and the overwhelming effects of the sacred Drink of love exclaimed: *'I am Allāh.'* His other associate asserted in the state of exhilaration: *'Subḥānī – Glorified am I.'* A group of the birds of the souls, gave up the birds of images. The birds of ardour flew in the plains of love. From the highlands of the burning desires of love, I intended for the jungle of the messenger of Eternity; for the desire of grazing in the pastures of the love of *Mushāhidah* [observance] on the Mount *Tūr* of Eternity. Henceforward, the falcon of honour pounced on the pigeons of pursuit and the inhabitants of the skies and earth befell unconscious, except for those; upon whom *Allāh* ﷻ Ordained permanence, for the flashes of invigorated glorious secrets of the worlds. From the niche of light of the unseen Eternity, the light of Divine Unity flashed for the eyes of the *'Ārifīn*; and the feathers of the feet of creation bonded with that jungle, because they did not appreciate *Allāh* ﷻ within the appropriate ambits, as they should have ensured. The sinners were discarded

227 Reference here is made to the *'Ārifīn* who were close to the secrets in the Presence of *Azal* at the time of the dialogue of *Alast* [the first Day of Covenant].

in that jungle, because they had become oblivious of the Sublime Lord ﷻ of Power.

O group of *Murīds*! A secret from the unseen was entrusted to the face of man, and a lofty treasure was buried in his sand. Thereafter, everyone dismissed an arrow [rushed] to achieve His ﷻ *Maʿrifah* and His ﷻ Treasure, but the guard of the souls impeded them. They could not find any way to reach *Salsabīl* [228]. O group of *ʿĀrifīn*! Fear the deceitfulness of the thieves of desires and expectations; because this is an extremely difficult mission. There is only the veil of Divine Identity between you and the beloved. Furthermore, the beloved is not absent from you. By *Allāh*! The desires of the self are the shackles for the intellect. The path of lust is invariably a slippery ground for the feet of understanding. O my Brothers! Inculcate elevated spirits; and travel towards the beloved; and take provisions from him, because the best provision is piety.

Incident of a Girl kidnapped by the Jinn

I narrate in 669 *hijrī* in Cairo from Shaykh Abu al-Fataḥ Nasrullāh b. Qāsim b. Yūsuf b. Khalīl al-Hāshimī al-Baghdādī ﷺ, and he narrates in 630 *hijrī* in Baghdād from Qāḍī al-Quḍāt Shaykh Abu-Sāliḥ Nasar al-Jilānī رضي الله عنه s/o Sayyiduna Ḥāfiz Tāj al-Dīn ʿAbd al-Razzāq al-Jilānī رضي الله عنه. Both of them narrate from their father Sayyiduna Shaykh ʿAbd al-Razzāq al-Jilānī رضي الله عنه and their uncle Sayyiduna Shaykh ʿAbd al-Wah'hāb al-Jilānī رضي الله عنه.....

I also narrate in 668 *hijrī* in Cairo from Shaykh Abu al-Futūḥ Muḥammad b. Abu al-Muḥāsin Yūsuf b. Ismāʿīl b. Aḥmad b. ʿAlī al-Qurashī Tamīmī Bakrī al-Baghdādī al-Qutfanī ﷺ who narrates in 630 *hijrī* in Baghdād from Sharīf Abu-Jāʿafar Muḥammad b. al-Qāsim Labīb b. Nafīs b. Yaḥyah al-ʿAlawī al-Ḥusainī ﷺ and he narrates in 594 *hijrī* in his house in *Bāb al-Azj* in Baghdād

[228] *Salsabīl* is a spring in *Jannah*. It also means the river or fountain in Paradise. The *Qur'ān* states: *'And there they will be given a cup whose mixture is of Zanjabīl [ginger]. A fountain 'there', called Salsabil.;' Al-Qur'an*, sura 76 [Al-Insān], *verse no:* 17-18

from Shaykh ʿĀrif Abu al-Khayr Bashīr b. Maḥfūz b. Ghanīmah ﷺ. All of them contend that they had heard in 554 *hijrī* in Baghdād from Abu-Sāʿad ʿAbdullāh b. Aḥmad b. ʿAlī b. Muḥammad al-Baghdādī al–Azjī who affirmed:

> In 530 *hijrī*, my daughter Fātimah climbed onto the roof of our house and someone kidnapped her from there. At that time, she was 16 years of age. I proceeded thereafter to Sayyiduna Shaykh Muḥiyy al-Dīn ʿAbd al-Qādir al-Jilānī ﷺ and reported this calamity to him. He advised me to go on the same night to the jungle of Karkh; and to sit on the 5th hillock, and thereby to draw a circle around myself, whilst reciting the following: بِاسْمِ اللهِ وَنِيَّةِ عَبْدُ الْقَادِر *[In the name of Allāh and intention of ʿAbd al-Qādir]*. After a short while, a group of *Jinns* would come to you, whose faces would be different. You must not be afraid of them. I then departed to Karkh and executed whatever Sayyiduna Shaykh ﷺ commanded me to do. Some very horrific faces encountered me; but they had no power in reaching close to the circle that I had drawn. Through the night, group after group accosted and departed. Eventually, towards the morning, their King came with an army and questioned me as what my problem was. I revealed to him that Shaykh ʿAbd al-Qādir had directed me to him. Immediately, he got off his horse and kissed the ground; and together with his associates sat down outside my circle. Thereafter, he enquired about my problem and I henceforth, related to him about my missing daughter. He questioned his associates as to who had committed this misdemeanour. They also replied in the negative. After a while they arrested a *jinn* and brought him along with my daughter. This *jinn* had hailed from China. The king queried from him as to what had tempted him to kidnap a girl from under the saddle of the *Qutb*. He replied: *'I saw her and fell in love with her.'* The King regimented for him to be beheaded; and my daughter was returned to me. I professed to the King: *'I have not seen anything so amazing like this in my life. You are so obedient to Sayyiduna Shaykh ʿAbd al-Qādir ﷺ.'*
>
> He asserted with conviction: *'Yes, indeed! He sits in his home and watches the Jinns even though they are in distant places. By his glance, the Jinns get*

terrified and flee. When Allãh ﷻ appoints a Qutb, He grants him control and authority over the humans and Jinns.'

Cured from Epilepsy

The above narrators state that once a person came to Sayyiduna Ghawth al-Aᶜzam ؓ and declared: *'I am a resident of Asbahãn and my wife often suffers from convulsions of epilepsy. The spiritual healer with litanies and duᶜãs have failed to cure her.'* Sayyiduna Ghawth ؓ said: *'This is a jinn from Sarandĩb [Sri Lanka] and his name is Ḥãnis. Now when your wife experiences an epilepsy attack, say this into her ears, 'O Ḥãnis! Shaykh ᶜAbd al-Qãdir of Baghdãd commands you not to come back anymore. But if you do not obey, you will then be destroyed.'* That person then left and was absent for ten years. When he returned, we enquired from him about his wife, and he confirmed: *'I did what Sayyiduna Ghawth ؓ commanded me to do, and ever since my wife has never experienced epilepsy anymore.'*

The Status of Sayyiduna Rasũlullãh ﷺ

Sultãn al-ᶜÃrifĩn Sayyiduna Ghawth al-Aᶜzam ؓ expressed about the consecrated body of the beloved Messenger of *Allãh* ﷺ. He pronounced that his sacred body is like a niche; and his holy soul is like a lamp in this niche. The brilliance of *Waḥĩ* [revelation] is the flame of this lamp. *Waḥĩ* that enters and exits is undoubtedly, Light upon Light. When the Light of *Nubuwwah* [Prophethood] is lit in the lamp of the niche of the heart, the mirror of his heart then becomes glorious. With this brilliance, he is in a position to perceive the most concealed entities in the universe. He is addressed by an eloquent tongue, and a sanctuary is opened towards the upper heaven for the eye of his intellect. In this, the secret subtleties of Eternity are presented, which is an interpreter between eternal and non-eternal. It is in accordance to the extent of the Light of *Maᶜãrifah,* that it is nurtured by *Allãh* ﷻ. *Maᶜãrifah* is in correlation to the power of the intellect. The extent of the intellect is according to what was stipulated in the *Dewãn* [Divine Court]; and *Allãh* ﷻ has distributed it.

Wilāyah and Nubuwwah

A *Walī* is he, who follows on the footsteps of a *Nabī*. *Nubuwwah* [Prophethood] and *Wilāyah* [Sainthood] signify the manifestations of *Allāh's* ﷻ exclusive Mercy. Sayyiduna Ghawth al-Aʿzam رضي الله عنه elaborates further, that *ʿAql* [intellect] and *Sharaʿh* [Sacred Law] are two *Nūrs* [lights] that enter the crevices of the *moʾmin's* heart owing to its luminosity. They merge with them in such a manner; in similarity to how water mixes with drinks, and the air that fuses with subtleties. The auras of *Nubuwwah* reflect on the clarity of the mirror of the intellect, parallel to the light of the soul which reflects onto the darkness of the body. The intellect is in a form, which is placed in the gardens of secrets at the spot, where the water of the souls releases, so that the hunter of *fikr* [reflection], hunts the birds of the realm of the *ghayb* [unseen]. *Nubuwwah* is a Divinely Ordained *Nūr* and it is situated within that eye of the intellect that is attributed to *yaqīn* [certainty]. It shines with intrinsic lustres from which the rays of glitter receives its power. Its light will shine; and by falling onto its head, the effects are such that; it reflects on the bodies of the souls during the darkness of the morning. What munificence does the internal insight receive from the generosity of the Sublime Lord ﷻ? The reflections of secrets are from the brilliance of grace; and the splendour of its light is its extensive mercy. This is acquired owing to incumbent knowledge; because of one body in two places, and the relationship of one *ʿArḍ*, [229] comprising two *Johars*; [230] with reference to both forms, i.e. righteousness and evil, both of which are impossible.

The beneficence of the light and the secrets of the guidance of the sun of *Nubuwwah* do not shine on anything, except onto the pebbles of the cities of the intellect for which; it was primed to undertake the work of heavenly laws. *Nubuwwah* is a mystical guidance that progresses on honourable carriers to some humans on the Path of the plan of Eternity; and that, which *Allāh* ﷻ

[229] That which cannot exist on its own. Always dependent on its origin [*Johar*].

[230] Origin or reality of matter.

prefers, He ﷻ creates.

The Walī who flies in the Air

I narrate in 674 *hijrī* in Cairo from Shaykh Sharīf Abu al-ʿAbbās Aḥmad b. Shaykh Abī ʿAbdullāh Muḥammad b. Abī al-Ghanāīm al-Ḥusainī al-Damishqī ﷺ, later al-Baghdādī, who narrates from his father in 674 *hijrī* in Damascus. He relates that one day Shaykh ʿAlī b. al-Hītī ﷺ visited the home of Sultān al-Awliya Sayyiduna Shaykh Muḥiyy al-Dīn ʿAbd al-Qādir ﷺ. I was with him and we located a young man, who was lying flat on his back on the floor of the veranda. He asserted to Shaykh ʿAlī ﷺ to ardently plead on his behalf to Sayyiduna Ghawth al-Aʿzam ﷺ. When we met Sayyiduna Ghawth ﷺ, Shaykh ʿAlī ﷺ pleaded on behalf of the young man and the Ghawth ﷺ reverberated: *'I forgive him for your sake.'* Thereafter, Shaykh ʿAlī ﷺ proceeded to the outside, and I accompanied him. He confirmed to the young man that Sayyiduna Ghawth ﷺ had accepted his plea and that, he had forgiven him. The young man thereby got up, left the veranda and flew away into the atmosphere, whilst we were observing him. Henceforth, we entered inside and enquired from the Ghawth ﷺ with regard to what had transpired. He replied: *'This young man was flying over Baghdād and formulated in his heart that there is no perfect man [Insān al-Kāmil] in this city, hence I stripped him of his powers. ʿAlī! If you were not here, I would not have returned his status.'*

The Greetings of the Rijāl al-Ghayb in Court of the great Ghawth ﷺ

Sayyiduna Shaykh ʿAlī b. Hītī ﷺ states that between *Maghrib* and *Esha* on the night of Saturday 9th *Rabi al-Ākhir* 552 *hijrī,* he was on the roof of the *Madrassa*. It was a hot summer's day and he was lying on his back. At the same time, Sayyid Shaykh Muḥiyy al-Dīn ʿAbd al-Qādir ﷺ was in front of him and was facing towards the direction of the *Qibla*. I saw a person flying like an arrow that had been fired into the sky. He wore a marvellous turban on his head; with both its ends, being suspended onto both his shoulders. He was wearing a white garb and a cloth was tied around his waist. When he reached above the Ghawth ﵁, he plunged down, similar to a falcon that was targeting for its prey. He came and sat in front of Sayyiduna Ghawth ﵁ and greeted him. Henceforth, he ascended to the sky; until he disappeared from my vision. I got up to approach Sayyiduna Ghawth ﵁, so that I could affirm from him as to who that person was; but consequently, he questioned me: *'Did you see him?'* I replied in the affirmative and subsequently, he ratified: *'He is from the Men of the Unseen [Rijāl al-Ghayb] who fly around. May Allāh's ﷻ salām be upon them.'*

The Roof Collapses

Shaykh ʿAlī b. al-Hītī ﵁ states that one day at a gathering, in the month of *Muḥarram* 559 *hijrī*; there were three hundred people who had assembled under the shelter. Sayyiduna Ghawth ﵁ hastened from his room and screamed and alerted the people: *'Get out from under the shelter, get out from under the shelter.'* When everyone ran out from under the shelter, the roof collapsed and the people were rescued. At that juncture, the great Ghawth ﵁ proclaimed: *'I was inside my room and it was said to me that the roof of the shelter will shortly collapse. Therefore, I rushed to caution you.'*

The Comments of Sayyiduna Ghawth ﵁ about Shaykh Mansūr al-Ḥallāj ﵀

One *ʿĀrif* flew onto the side of Claims, armed with the adages of '*Annal-Ḥaqq*'. He discovered that the Garden of *Hidāyah* [guidance] was barren of living creatures, and as well as companions. He blew the whistle to call for his death; without any of his own dialects. Thereafter, the Falcon of Sovereignty emerged for him from that veil; that indeed! Almighty *Allāh* ﷻ is carefree in the worlds. The Falcon of Sovereignty jabbed its claws into his flesh and issued forth a declaration: *'Every living creature has to taste death.'* The era of the *Sharīʿah* of Sulaymān verbalized to him: *'Why did you speak without your praise? Why did you sing in an unidentified voice which was not meant for you? Now enter into the cage of your existence and return from the honourable path of Infinity to the narrow paths of occurrences. Declare with your tongue of confession, so that the claimers may listen to your word that: 'It is sufficient for the receivers to declare that the One is Alone.'* The foundation to the protection of the Path, is to be steadfast, in adherence to the sacrament of the sacred *Sharī ʿah.*

It happened as the great Ghawth ﷺ predicted

I narrate in 671 *hijrī* in Kittān from Shaykh Abu-ʿAbdullah Muḥammad b. Aḥmad b. Manzūr al-Kittānī ﷺ and he narrates in 598 *hijrī* from his grandfather Shaykh Manzūr ﷺ and Shaykh Muwaffiq al-Dīn ʿAbd al-Raḥmān b. Abu al-Ḥaram al-Makkī b. Imām Abu-ʿAmar ʿUthmān Saʿādī al-Sharāʿī ﷺ. Both of them narrate in 598 *hijrī* in the main street of Cairo from Shaykh Abu-Ḥasan ʿAlī b. Abī-Zāhir Ibrāhīm b. Najā b. Ghanāim al-Ansārī al-Damishqī Faqīh al-Ḥanbalī ﷺ, who stated that once he performed *Ḥajj* and he and his friend came to Baghdād. This was their first trip to Baghdād, where they did not know anyone. All that they had in their possession was a knife, which they sold and bought some rice to eat. They disliked the taste of it and as a result, they did not fill their stomachs. They proceeded to the *majlis* of Shaykh ʿAbd al-Qādir al-Jilānī ﷺ and settled down. Upon their arrival, the Ghawth ﷺ discontinued with his discourse and elucidated as follows: *'The poor, destitute had come from Ḥejāz [Arabia] and all they had was a knife, which they sold and bought some rice. They disliked the taste of the rice, which did not fill their stomachs.'* When I heard his comments, I was amazed. After the Shaykh ﷺ expressed his words, the table spread was laid. I whispered to my friend: *'What would you like to eat?'* He requested for *kashak* [a dish made of barley water boiled with vinegar or milk] and partridge and I contended within my heart about honey. Henceforward, Sayyiduna Shaykh ﷺ directed the *khādim* to hasten and to bring the *kashak*, partridge and honey. He brought it and Sayyiduna Shaykh ﷺ commanded him to place it in front of them. The *Khādim* placed the honey in front of my friend and the *kashak* and partridge in front of me. Ḥaḍrate Ghawth ﷺ interjected with an assertion: *'Switch them around, otherwise there will be a problem.'* I viewed this and screamed; jumped over the people, and ran towards the Ghawth ﷺ.

Hence, he revealed to me: *'The orator of the country of Egypt came as well.'* I admitted to him: *'O my Master! I can't even read a Fātiḥa properly.'* He affirmed: *'This is how I was instructed to address you.'* The narrator concedes to the fact that he thereby joined Sayyiduna Shaykh's ﷺ classes and studied under his tutelage for a duration of one year. *Allāh* ﷻ instilled within my heart, a vast faculty of knowledge; which others would spend twenty years and would still not have achieved, that which I had achieved during the course of one year. I sought permission from Sayyiduna Ghawth ﷺ to relocate to Egypt, but he informed me: *'Soon you will go to Damascus. When you reach there, you will find the Turks preparing to conquer Egypt in order to seize it under their rule. You must inform them that they will never be victorious in this first attempt, therefore, they should abandon their mission. Tell them to go the next time, and they will be victorious and shall capture it under their rule.'*

The narrator confirms that when he arrived in Damascus, he saw the Turks preparing to go to Egypt; and he informed them of what Sayyiduna Ghawth ﷺ had envisaged. They did not pay heed to him and proceeded. When he arrived in Egypt, he saw the *Khalīfa* preparing for war. The *Khalīfa* was informed by the narrator that he needed not to worry; for he would be victorious, as the Turks would not be successful and would revert. When the Turks entered Egypt, they were overpowered and reverted. Being gratified with him, the *Khalīfah* designated him as his confidant, with whom he shared his secretive issues.

When the Turks returned for the second time, they were victorious and conquered Egypt. Because of what was revealed to them in Damascus, they expressed great respect for him and presented him with a gift to the value of 150,000 *dinārs*. This particular narrator, Shaykh Zain al-Dīn ﷺ[231] lived for a lengthy period in Egypt; and it is heralded about him, that apart from other sciences, he had memorized the subject matter of most of the books on *Tafsīr*,

[231] It cannot be understood as to why the author used the name Zain al-Dīn in this context, because in the chain of narrators the name Zain al-Dīn is not mentioned. However, it has been translated in accordance to the original text, owing to the reason, that it may be possible, that his other name is Zain al-Dīn. #*[Faqīr 'Abd al-Hādī]*

which deemed him as a celebrity there. He emerged as one of the prominent Masters of *Ḥadith* in Egypt, and delivered inspirational lectures from which the people benefitted tremendously. He passed away in the month of *Ramaḍān* 596 *hijrī*. He was born in Damascus in 508 *hijrī*.

The Three Conditions of the Path of Sulũk

Sultān al-ʿĀrifīn Sayyiduna Ghawth al-Aʿzam ﷺ alludes to the fact that solitude in the Path of *Sulũk* is a sign of true Love. If the eye of the heart looks only once at anything, except *Allāh* ﷻ, it is henceforward, a sign of remoteness or being distant from *Allāh* ﷻ. To speak of anything else, except the *dhikr* of *Allāh* ﷻ, is symbolic of that mirror of the heart which is tarnished. Anyone who engages or indulges in the *dhikr* of any other than *Allāh* ﷻ, is the one who has not tasted the sweetness of Divine Communion [*wasal*].

For a single moment, if anyone is attracted to anything else, other than *Allāh* ﷻ, one shall thereby not attain closeness to the Divine Presence. There are three conditions of *Sulũk*;

1) *Ḥaqq* – Truth
2) *Sidq* – Veracity or an Embodiment of Truth.
3) *ʿAdal* – Justice

ʿAdal is positioned onto the body, *Sidq* is embedded onto the intellect and *Ḥaqq* is entrenched into the heart. Anyone who seeks *Allāh* ﷻ with a heart of legitimacy, his truthfulness then becomes such a mirror within his heart that he begins to perceive the wonders of *duniya* and *Ākhirah*.

Safeguarding the laws of permanent life [*Ḥayāt e Abadī*] is far more superior than safeguarding the laws of the transitory world or mortal life [*Ḥayāt e fānī*]. Remaining in solitude, is the door to definite contemplation [*fikr*]; and often *fikr* is a sign of being in attendance. To be in the presence of *Allāh* ﷻ with a conscientious and submissive heart, with concentration in its entirety is a sign of *Tawfiq*. Invariably, the attainment of *Tawfiq* guides one to *Ḥaḍrate Quds*

[Blessed Precincts]. To consume a stomach full of food, soils the purity of the spring of servitude. To avert from the fulfilment of duties, pertinent to spiritual services; is the reason for aversion. Oh servant! Do not equate yourself to that nightingale, which is delighted with its melodious voice during spring; and thereby, stops with a sorrowful prolonged voice. It spends its time in rendering its melodious voice. This cannot be achieved, except by the complaints of the burning devotion of love. Become like the falcon that does not concern itself about the chanting of the nightingales in the gardens; whereby it does not become jovial with the sweetness of the unseen melodies, for it is dependent on the dominance of the intellect. Sayyiduna Nabī Mūsā ﷺ sought the real Water of Life [*Ãabe-Ḥayãt*] in the land where he implored: *'O my Lord! Show me Yourself.'* It was thereby revealed to him: *'He is behind that mountain and you will never be able to see Him.'*

Alexander the Great who sought this Water of Life [*Ãabe-Ḥayãt*] became dependant on the basis of that burning zeal, in order to disrupt the walls of *Yajũj* [Gog] and break down the walls of *Majũj* [Magog]. Rebuild it by strengthening it with the veracity of *Tawḥĩd,* so that it removes the brightness from the eyes of the intellect; and thus leads it in undertaking the journey from this world towards the *Ãkhirah*; because it will find itself under the shade of such a tree that is commanded, as enshrined below:

﴿وُجُوهٌ يَوْمَئِذٍ نَّاضِرَةٌ ○ إِلَىٰ رَبِّهَا نَاظِرَةٌ﴾

On that day, some faces will shine with freshness.
Looking toward their Lord. [232]

This tree is in the glorious Presence of the Sovereign Power ﷻ, which does not rise in the mystical heavens of the eastern borders. In fact, it rises in the East of the mystical heavens or the western heavens; within the ambits of the paradise of existence. Sayyiduna Nabī ʿĪsā ﷺ, essentially, pursued the fountain of Real Life on earth, within the western intrinsic qualities of the hearts. It was

[232] *Al-Qur'ãn al-Karĩm*, Chapter 50, Surah Qiyãmah, Verse no. 23

revealed to him at that juncture, that he will not find it, but only after adversity, as expressed in the following excerpt: *'I will take you altogether,'* in the shade of the planks under this station: *'I will be raising you to Me'*. Only the ultimate Beloved of all Beloveds, Sayyiduna Aḥmad[233] ﷺ discovered the Fountains of Life; during his *meʿrāj*. When His ﷻ exclusive servant was taken on a journey at night to that *majlis*, about which it is certainly confirmed that: *'The sight did not shift, nor did it cross the limits'*. [234] It was revealed to him to immerse in this water; as it is evident from the following extract: *'The heart did not deny, what it saw'*. [235] He was commanded to take a garland of pearls from it, which was crafted by the director of fervour; as threaded in the sequence of the subsequent Divine Injunction: *'Indeed he saw the supreme signs of his Lord'*. [236] This validates the reason that after this, his being shall not die; to which the forthcoming *Ḥadith* of the exalted Prophet ﷺ bears testimony to the fact that: *'The deeds of my Ummah are presented before me'*.

The Treasurer of Destiny

I narrate from Shaykh Abu ʿAbd al-Ghālib b. Aḥmad b. ʿAlī b. Ibrāhim b. ʿAbd al-Raḥmān al-Tamīmī al-Wāstī رضي الله عنه who was originally from Baghdād, and thereafter settled in Cairo. He narrates from Shaykh Abu-Muḥammad al-Latīf b. Shaykh Abī al-Najāt Sālim b. Aḥmad al-Baghdādī رضي الله عنه, who narrates in 630 *hijrī* in Baghdād from Maʿrūf Khitāb رضي الله عنه, the *Khādim* of Sayyiduna Ghawth al-Aʿzam Muḥiyy al-Dīn al-Jilānī رضي الله عنه. He narrates in 579 *hijrī* in Baghdād from his father, who disclosed that once his Master, Sayyiduna Muḥiyy al-Dīn ʿAbd al-Qādir al-Jilānī رضي الله عنه was in several debts, which amounted to 250 *dinārs*. A person came; whom I did not recognize and he entered the private apartment of Sayyiduna Ghawth al-Aʿzam رضي الله عنه without permission. He had a lengthy

[233] Sayyiduna Ghawth رضي الله عنه here addresses the beloved Prophet ﷺ as Aḥmad ﷺ because he is known as Aḥmad in the heavens and Muḥammad ﷺ on earth. Since the discussion is of the heavens, therefore the great Ghawth رضي الله عنه used the name Aḥmad ﷺ.

[234] *Al-Qur'ān al-Karīm*, Chapter 53, Surah Najam, Verse no. 17

[235] *Al-Qur'ān al-Karīm*, Chapter 53, Surah Najam 53, Verse no. 7

[236] *Al-Qur'ān al-Karīm*, Chapter 53, Surah Najam Verse no. 18

conversation with the Ghawth ﷺ; gave him some gold and elucidated: *'This is to pay all your debts.'* He declared this and took leave of the Ghawth ﷺ. Thereafter, Sayyiduna Ghawth ﷺ dictated to me to take the gold and to settle the debts owing to all the creditors. He then informed me about that the being who brought this gold is *'Sarrāf-e-Qadr – the Treasurer of Destiny.'* I questioned him as to who *Sarrāf-e-Qadr* was? He revealed that *Sarrāf-e-Qadr* is an angel that is assigned by *Allāh* ﷻ to pay off the debts of His ﷻ *Awliya.*

O Israelite, Listen to Muḥammadī ﷺ Words

The above mentioned narrator further conveys that one day Sayyiduna Ghawth ﷺ was delivering his discourse; when he spontaneously walked in the air and promulgated: *'Oh Israelite! Stop and listen to the words of Muḥammadi ﷺ.'* Upon completion of his declaration, he returned to his pulpit [*mimbar*]. When he was questioned about this occurrence, he vociferously asserted: *'Sayyiduna Abu al-ʿAbbās Khiḍar ﷺ flew; rushing over my majlis, and therefore, I flew up into the air and articulated to him; that which you had heard.'*

The Creation of the Human Being

Sayyiduna Ghawth al-Aʿzam ﷺ conversed about the creation of the human being; and how marvellous is the human creation; and in accordance to wisdom, how mysterious it is. The Creator, Almighty *Allāh* ﷻ has appointed an angel with the human intellect. If human nature did not have the inclination towards greed, lust and impurity, they would have thereby, been bestowed with the attributes of refinement.

The human being is categorized as a treasury in which the mysteries of the secrets of the unseen; and a compilation of various sciences are kept in trust. This is a vessel which is filled with *Nūr* [light]; amidst the darkness of the skin in which the brides of the souls are hidden within the veils of awe-inspiring faces from the eyes of the foreign. Destiny has illumined its gorgeousness in the eyes of the angels in a garb; as specified in the following extract: *'Indeed, I*

ﷻ *have blessed the human.'* In this gathering: *'I have given them excellence.'* Intellect highlights and leads one towards the fact that one is from the Realm of *Shahādah* [exposure - witness].

Sultān ʿAql and Sultān Hawa [ego]

The reason as to why, the shells of personas have gathered all the pearls of the Ocean of Existence in the vessels of knowledge, is that they could perfect their luminosity with the Light of Certainty. Thereafter, it took the lust of the soul to the islands of observance; where, in view of the fact that the king of intellect may stand in front of the king of lust. Henceforth, both of them engaged in a bloody encounter in the middle of the vast field. Ego is a special armament of the king of lust; whilst the soul is a special squadron of the king of intellect. Thus, the *Muazzins* [callers] of Command resonated: *'Oh caravans of the people of Allāh ﷻ! Mount up: Oh army of Truth! Come out, O army of Lust! Come forward.'* Each one intends to assist its group and each one wants to subdue its enemy. Thereby, *Tawfīq* pronounced to both of them in the words of the unseen past: *'He to whom I give assistance shall have the flag of victory secured to it.'* To whomsoever, that I provide aid to, shall be blissful in both the worlds. With whomsoever I shall be, I shall lead them to the true abode. *Tawfīq* is referred to that, upon whom *Allāh* ﷻ focuses His ﷻ gracious glance with a vision of felicity.

Obedience to the Intellect

Oh Servant! Be obedient to the intellect for verily, there is an expansive path of great providence awaiting you. Abandon your lust and egotism. I observe an incredible entity that the soul is celestial and concealed; whereas the *nafs* comprises of sand and earth. A subtle bird flew from a dense nest, with the wings of esteem to the tree of heights. It sang melodiously with the tongue of passion and the allies of love conversed with it. It gathered the jewels of reality from the vicinity of sciences. It became heavy; and hence, enclosed into the cage of the darkness of existence. When the body becomes extinct, henceforward, the secrets of the heart remain alive. If it casts a single glance at your heart, it shall position you onto the station of the Divine *ʿArsh*. The reality of sciences was bestowed onto the intellect, so that it augments into a treasury of the secrets of gnosis [*Maʿārifah*]. Thus, at this phase, the eye of intellect observes the sanctity of Eternity; and abandons everything else, which is attributed to the qualities of creation, that is subject to extinction. Here, in forefront of the insight of your heart, the world of the spiritual realm stands in front of the mirror of the heart. The brides that portray the signs of victory of reality in the assembly of unveiling are thus, adorned. Thereafter, all the shining traces of the effects of the brides would be erased from the slate of their courage and spirit [*himmah*].

Oh Man! The radiant intellect in the darkness, is in fact a lamp of the perfect man. Reflections of purity are the evidences of the *ʿĀrifīn*; inclusive of the preceding goodwill itself, which removes the veils of doubts from the frontage of certainty. When suspicion and intentions transform into a position rivalry, the evidence of falsehood hence, surfaces and is nullified and obliterated by virtue of being in the presence of truth.

No Rain on the Majlis, but it rained Elsewhere

I narrate in 671 *hijrī* in Cairo from Shaykh Abu-Sālim b. ʿAlī b. ʿAbdullāh al-Damyātī ﷺ who narrates in 624 *hijrī* in Baghdād from Shaykh Abu al-Ḥasan Khāfāf ﷺ. He narrates in 579 *hijrī* in Baghdād from Shaykh Abu-Saʿīd Mudallal al-Ḥarīmī ﷺ and he narrates in 670 *hijrī* in Cairo from Shaykh Abu al-Ḥasan ʿAlī b. Aḥmad b. Muḥammad b. Yūsuf b. ʿAbdullāh Qaṭāmī al-Zubaydī ﷺ, originally from Baghdād and he narrates in 643 *hijrī* in Baghdād from Shaykh Abu al-Ḥasan ʿAlī, the Baker ﷺ, who narrates in 591 *hijrī* in Baghdād from Shaykh ʿImrān al-Kamīmānī ﷺ and Shaykh Baz'zār ﷺ. I also narrate in 670 *hijrī* in Cairo from Shaykh Abu-ʿAlī Ḥasan b. Najīm al-Ḥowrānī ﷺ, Shaykh Abu al-Qāsim Muḥammad b. ʿUbādah b. Muḥammad al-Ansārī ﷺ. Shaykh Abu-ʿAlī ﷺ narrates in 617 *hijrī* in Cairo from Shaykh Abu-Muḥammad ʿAlī b. Idrīs al-Yaʿqūbī ﷺ and Shaykh Abu al-Qāsim ﷺ, who narrates in in 618 *hijrī* in Damascus from Shaykh Abu al-Ḥusain ʿAlī al-Qurashī ﷺ. I narrate in 672 *hijrī* in Cairo from Shaykh Abu-ʿAbdullāh Muḥammad b. Abu al-Ḥusain ʿAlī b. al-Ḥusain al-Damishqī, later Mosulī ﷺ and he narrates in 640 *hijrī* in Mosul from Shaykh ʿAdī ﷺ, who narrates from his father, Shaykh Abu al-Barkāt ﷺ, who narrates from his uncle, Shaykh ʿAdī b. Musāfir ﷺ. All of them concurred that one day it was raining; whilst Sayyiduna Ghawth al-Aʿzam Shaykh Muḥiyy al-Dīn ʿAbd al-Qādir al-Jilānī ﷺ was delivering his discourse. Owing to the rain, several people commenced to leave the *majlis*. Sayyiduna Shaykh ʿAbd al-Qādir ﷺ thereby raised his head towards the heavens and supplicated: *'O Allāh! I am gathering the people [for Your sake] and You are dispersing them.'* As soon as he expressed these words, henceforward, by the Dictates of *Allāh* ﷻ, the rain stopped on the scenario of the *majlis*; but it continued to rain around everywhere else, outside the zone of the *madrassa*. Not even a single drop of rain fell onto the audience of the *majlis*.

The Power of the ʿAsā [staff] of the Ghawth ﷺ

The narrators apprised that one year the flood waters of River Tigris rose to great heights that the city of Baghdād began flooding. People complained to Sayyiduna Ghawth ﷺ about the flood and he seized his *ʿAsa* and proceeded towards the banks of the river. Thereafter, he implanted it at the water's edge and disclosed to the river: *'Do not move past here.'* Instantaneously, upon his command, the water diminished.

The Rain Stopped

I was informed in 674 *hijrī* in Cairo by Qāḍī al-Quḍāt Shaykh Shams al-Dīn Abu-ʿAbdullāh Muḥammad b. Shaykh Imām ʿImād al-Dīn Ibrāhīm al-Maqdisī al-Ḥanbalī ﷺ who narrates from Shaykh Ḍiya al-Dīn Abu-ʿAbdullāh Muḥammad b. ʿAbd al-Wāḥid b. Aḥmad al-Maqdisī ﷺ, who had asserted that he had heard from Shaykh Abu-Bakr Aḥmad b. Muḥammad al-Kharāsī ﷺ who narrates from Shaykh Maʿmād ﷺ who proclaimed that Sayyiduna Shaykh Muḥiyy al-Dīn ʿAbd al-Qādir al-Jilānī ﷺ was once delivering his discourse in an open field, which was devoid of a shelter. It started to rain and Sayyiduna Ghawth ﷺ raised his head and looked towards the heavens and beseeched: *'I am assembling the people [for Your sake] and You are dispersing them.'* The narrators submit to the fact that by the Dictates of *Allāh* ﷻ, it stopped raining onto the *majlis*.

The aforementioned narrator says that once he left *Taḥūna* [a town or village] and was on his way, when it started to rain. He declared: *'O my Lord! Verily trustworthy narrators have narrated to me from other trustworthy narrators with regard to and such and such. By their honour, from Your Divine Domain, stop this rain.'* As soon as he rendered this supplication, the rain stopped until he reached his home. No sooner, he had entered his home, it began raining once more.

The Rain Clouds moved away from the Majlis of Sayyiduna Ghawth ﷺ

I narrate in 671 *hijrī* from Shaykh Abu-Zayd ʿAbd al-Raḥmān b. Aḥmad ﷺ who was present in 619 *hijrī* with Shaykh al-ʿĀlam Abu-Isḥāq Ibrāhīm b. Sumayd al-Dārī al-Thalabī ﷺ in Damascus. Together with him were Malik Muʿazzam, Malik Amjad, Malik Sāliḥ Ismāʿīl, Taqī al-Dīn and Mujīr al-Dīn, the sons of Ayyūb. It began raining and we were in an open field. Shaykh Ibrāhīm ﷺ pronounced to them: *'Once My Master, Shaykh Muḥiyy al-Dīn ʿAbd al-Qādir al-Jīlānī ﷺ was sitting on his chair and delivering his discourse and it began raining. Ḥaḍrate Ghawth ﷺ then elucidated: 'I am assembling the people and You are dispersing them.'* The rain clouds thereafter, drifted away from the *majlis;* and it began raining around the *majlis*. The narrator confirms: *'By the oath of Allāh* ﷻ*! Before Shaykh Ibrāhīm ﷺ completed his words, it stopped raining on us, but it continued raining around us.'*

Truth and Cleanliness

O Servant! Make truth and cleanliness binding upon you. Had it not been for these two characteristics, no human could have then reached the *Qurb* [closeness] of Almighty *Allāh* ﷻ.

O Servant! If your stone resembling heart was struck with the pure *'Asā* [staff] of Sayyiduna Nabī Mūsā ﷺ, then truth will flow from its darkness. Henceforth, an *'Ārif* flies with the veils of faithfulness towards the plains of sacred light from the darkness of the cages of existence. After this flight, he descends onto the station of the shade of the garden of truth.

O Servant! When the light of *Yaqīn* flashes into the heart of any servant, surely the illumination of this light, henceforward, manifests through the glory on his face. Indeed, this invariably gratifies the Sublime Lord ﷻ. The angels call upon him from the lofty Angelic Realm and he shall arrive in the companionship of the *Siddiqīn* on the Day of *Qiyāmah*. O Servant! *Tajrīd* [237] is to abandon the lust of the *nafs*. In fact, *Tawḥīd* itself is for the hearts of the *'Ārifīn* which is in purity and encapsulated with the lustres of the dedication of love, to the extent that they do not enjoy the pleasure of communion with someone else. In realism this illustrates the excitement and love of the hearts of the Lovers; that leads them to the jungles of love. Moreover, in the absence of the provision of truth, the journey to Almighty *Allāh* ﷻ is not possible. Divine Presence cannot be attained without the examination of the hearts. In the *Ākhirah*, the similarity of the *Iftār* of the sacred drink shall not be possible, without fasting with abstention from the world, and everything else that is contained in it. Your single vision in abstention from your own self should not be a burden upon you. In order to get out of existence is not an immense factor, for a small side view of the eye. When the physical nature of the humans is purified of all defilement; perfections of the laws are then accomplished. When the vision of the intellect of an *'Ārif* becomes vigorous, then Light of the Lord ﷻ is elevated in his heart. The illustrious *Awliya* are elite in the Sovereign Court, whilst the *'Ārifīn* are the companions in the Noble Gathering. The sweetness of the honey of love consistently calls out, and eradicates the bitterness of patience.

[237] *Tajrīd* means to renounce this worldly life, in lieu of solitude and worship.

O Servant! The eyes of the intellect of true men do not focus on this world. They are not intimidated, and nor are they deceived by the attraction of its pomp and glory. In fact, they understand the words of the beloved; who had warned them, that the life of this world is nothing; but a place of play and amusement.

O Servant! By the embracing of egotism, the cursed evil spirit enters your heart and reaches the bosom, through the path of lusts. It sows the seed of deceitfulness of the love of this world, with the inclusion of the hatred for the *Ākhirah*. Glad-tidings are for him, who awakens from the slumber of the unconsciousness of the intellect; whereby his condition becomes purified in his mission for the Proximity of his Lord ﷻ. He hastens towards this objective, which is imperative. He evaluates his *nafs* before anything else; and strives for the *Ākhirah*, because this transitory world is only a field for those who intend to progress. Good deeds are a sheet for the progressive success and a mode to cross the bridge [*pulsirāt*]. *Qiyāmah* is a calamity which shall be a very resentful event.

Descent of misfortune owing to the Anger of the Ghawth رضي الله عنه

I narrate in 671 *hijrī* in Cairo from Shaykh Abu al-Qāsim b. Shaykh Abu al-Qāsim Aḥmad b. ʿAbdullāh b. Aḥmad b. ʿAlī al-Qurashī al-Hāshimī al-Baghdādī Ḥarmī al-Ḥanbalī رحمه الله, who narrates in 638 *hijrī* in Baghdād from Shaykh Abu al-Ḥasan ʿAlī b. Sulaymān al-Baghdādī رحمه الله, notably recognized as the Baker. He narrates in 608 *hijrī* in Baghdād from Shaykh Abu al-Qāsim ʿUmar b. Saʿīd Baz'zār رحمه الله, who articulates that Shaykh Baqa b. Bat'tū Nahar-Malikī رضي الله عنه, a Shaykh and a youngster had visited Sayyiduna Ghawth al-Aʿzam رضي الله عنه. The Shaykh appealed to Ḥaḍrate Ghawth al-Aʿzam رضي الله عنه: *'Make du ʿā for him, he is my son.'* This was not true, because the youngster was not his son, but a person who was classified as a transgressor [*fāsiq*]. Sayyiduna Ghawth رضي الله عنه was enraged in this regard and questioned: *'Is my relation with you gone to such limits?'* He left them in a state of infuriation, and returned to his home. Instantly a fire, then broke out in the outskirts of Baghdād. When the fire was extinguished at one place, another place caught on fire. Shaykh Abu al-Qāsim Baz'zār ﷺ states: *'This fire of ruin in Baghdād was because of the infuriation of Sayyiduna Ghawth ﷺ. I proceeded quickly to the apartment of the Ghawth ﷺ and discovered him to be in a state of enragement; so I sat down in one corner and beseeched him: 'O my Master! Have mercy on the people. They shall all perish.' I repeated this plea, until his enragement subsided, and I thereby witnessed that the calamity had ended, with the extinguishing of all the fire.'*

The Hearts of the People are in my Hands

On the authority of the aforementioned chain of narrators, it is narrated by Shaykh ʿUmar Baz'zār ﷺ as follows:

> On Friday 15th *Jamādi al-Ākhir* 556 *hijrī* I accompanied Sayyiduna Shaykh Muḥiyy al-Dīn ʿAbd al-Qādir al-Jilānī ﷺ to the *Jāmeʿh Masjid* for *Jumʿāh*. On the way, no one greeted the great Ghawth ﷺ and this startled me, because every Friday when we proceeded for *Jumʿāh*, a massive crowd rallied around him, which caused difficulty in reaching the *Masjid*. As soon as this notion came to my mind, Sayyiduna Ghawth al-Aʿzam ﷺ glanced at me and smiled and thereby, everyone flocked to greet him. The crowd became so massive that I was separated from Ḥaḍrate Ghawth ﷺ. My inner being then revealed to me: *'The first situation was better and peaceful.'* Once more he intervened into my thoughts; and with a smile glanced at me, and confirmed: *'O ʿUmar! This was your intention. Do you not know that the hearts of the people are in my hands? I can turn them away from me or draw them towards me.'*

The Reality of Fana [extinction]

Sayyiduna Ghawth al-Aʿzam ﷺ dictated that one must become extinct [*fana*] by the Commandments of *Allāh* ﷻ; and also from one's desires, and as well as from the desires of the people. Become *fana* with your intentions in the prescriptive procedures of *Allāh* ﷻ. Only then you shall develop the power to transform into a container for the knowledge of *Allāh* ﷻ. The sign of being extinct from creation shall unfold, when you shall abstain from them; and have no confidence in whatever reclines in the hands of creation. The sign of being extinct from one's desires depicts that one shall withdraw from all desires viz. profits, losses and destruction in all undertakings. Thus, there should be no illusive movement made from one's side, or trust placed on oneself. Neither of these preceding calibres should defend anything from one's side nor seek assistance for oneself. In fact, all these endeavours are submitted to the beloved [*Allāh* ﷻ]; Who in turn, shall eventually befriend you. The sign of being extinct from one's intentions is that, one shall not intend or seek anything, except Almighty *Allāh* ﷻ. In fact, conceding to the Commandments of *Allāh* ﷻ means to permeate into a state, in totality within yourself, that your limbs shall become motionless with *Imān* that infiltrates your heart. Whilst your bosom expands, your inner self shall bloom and remain prosperous in the remembrance of *Allāh* ﷻ to the extent of being cut off from the contemplation of everything else. The Divine Hands of *Qudrat* controls your existence; and the tongue of Eternity calls upon you to educate you and clothe you with *Nūr*. You will be led to the first station of the people of knowledge and your heart will always remain enthusiastic in *Allāh* ﷻ and all intentions will be deleted from your heart, except the intentions of *Allāh* ﷻ. At this station, you will be attributed to *Takwīn* [238] and charismatic recompenses. Externally, your movement may seem to be your own actions, but in reality, these movements are the true movements of the *Qudrat* of the Sublime Lord of Power ﷻ. Thereby, *fana* is at the extremes and it is at a place of observation. In this Realm nothing exists, except Almighty *Allāh* ﷻ; initially as it was prior to the advent of creation when *Allāh* ﷻ existed alone. This phase is termed as *fana*.

When you shall die [become extinct - *fana*], it will be revealed to you: *'May Allāh ﷻ shower you with blessings, you have been killed by your desires.'* You will also be informed: *'May Allāh ﷻ have mercy on you. May you be killed; by your intentions and desires.'* When you shall be killed by your intentions, it shall be proclaimed to you: *'May Allāh ﷻ have mercy on you and keep you alive.'*

[238] The power of bringing about being.

Thereafter, you shall be granted a life of permanence; i.e. a life after which there shall be no death. You shall be such an affluent person that there would be no poverty anymore. Such infinite bounties shall be bestowed upon you, to which there shall be no further hindrance. You shall be granted such knowledge, that never shall ignorance be prevalent any longer. Such protection shall be afforded to you, whereby there shall be no more fear. Subsequently, you shall be so blessed that you shall never be inferior; for you shall be esteemed; to any extent whereby, there shall be no scope for disgrace to be cast upon you; for you shall be so close to the Precincts of *Allāh* ﷻ, where you shall never be distanced from. Integrity and dignity shall be showered upon you; and henceforth, you shall never be insignificant, for you shall be pure and shall never be subjected to any form of defilement any longer.

Oh Humankind! Live amidst *Allāh* ﷻ as though no creation exists; except *Allāh* ﷻ Alone. Live with creation as if though the *nafs* [egotism] is non-existent. When you live amidst *Allāh* ﷻ, it means that creation no longer exists in every other facet and hence, you are amidst *Allāh* ﷻ; aloof in extinction. When you are enjoined with creation, it must be as though the *nafs* does not exist; and as such you will exercise justice, where you shall remain unwavering. Leave all your components outside the door of seclusion and enter into solitude alone. You shall see your companion in solitude, with the eye of your heart; and apart from existence, you shall perceive the mysteries of the super-arcane. Your *nafs* shall be obliterated and replaced by the Commandments of *Allāh* ﷻ; within the parameters of Divine Proximity. In this realm, there shall be transition of your ignorance to knowledge; your distance with nearness; your silence with *dhikr,* and your fear with love shall come to fruition.

Oh Humankind! There is nothing at this juncture, except the Creator and creation. Henceforward, if you choose the Creator ﷻ, declare henceforward, that the rest are your enemies. Only *Allāh* ﷻ is your friend. Then Sayyiduna Ghawth رضي الله عنه discoursed: *'He who has tasted, has understood.'* When he was questioned: *'How can one taste sweetness when one is overcome by the bitterness of bile?'* To this effect he asserted: *'Diligently exterminate the egotism from the heart.'*

Oh Humankind! When a *mo'min* [true believer] executes virtuous deeds, his *nafs* converts to the heart, whereas his heart becomes the head. Thereafter, his head becomes *fana* [extinct] and eventually, the *fana* disappears; and then his existence also becomes extinct. Ḥaḍrate Ghawth ﷺ ordained: that every friend does not have the aptitude to enter every door.

Oh Humankind! *Fana* is defined as the transformation from the non-existence of creation to the disposition of the angels. Thereafter, *fana* from the disposition of angels enjoins with the first condition; when at this moment, your Lord ﷻ shall give you a drink, that which you shall have to consume. He ﷻ shall henceforth, implant into you that plant, which shall be destined by Him ﷻ. If this was your intention, reaffirm *Islām* with full conviction with the knowledge of *Allāh* ﷻ, and through His ﷻ *Ma'ārifah* hold steadfast to His Divine Existence. When your existence becomes extinct in Divine Existence, only then shall all of you become exclusive to *Allāh* ﷻ. *Zuhd* [Asceticism] is a moment of *Taqwa* [piety] and two moments of *Ma'ārifah* is a permanent division.

A Brilliant Light

I narrate in 672 *hijrī* from Faqih Abu-Muḥammad ʿAbd al-Raḥmān b. Aḥmad b. Muḥammad al-Qurashī ﷺ, who narrates 631 *hijrī* from Shaykh Abu-Muḥammad Mālik b. Shaykh Abī-ʿAbd al-Malik Zayāl ﷺ. He narrates in 623 *hijrī* from his father who stated that in 560 *hijrī*, he was in the Madrassa of Sayyiduna Ghawth al-Aʿzam Shaykh Muḥiyy al-Dīn ʿAbd al-Qādir al-Jilānī ﷺ. Sayyiduna Ghawth ﷺ exited his household with an *'Asā* [staff] in his hand. A thought emanated in my heart; that how delightful would it be, if the Ghawth ﷺ disclosed to me a *karāmat* [miracle] with his *'Asā*. He looked at me and smiled and pierced his *'Asā* into the ground. Lo! I saw a bright light originating from the *'Asā*, as though it was a resplendent torch. This light proceeded into the sky and its luminosity illuminated the entire universe. This light of brilliancy remained for one hour and thereafter, the great Ghawth ﷺ seized this, and it thereafter, restored into an *ʿAsã*. Thereby, Ḥaḍrate Ghawth ﷺ proclaimed to me: *'O Ziyãl! You desired to see this.'*

A Tranquil Discourse

Sayyiduna Ghawth al-Aʿzam ﷺ decrees: Firstly the Star of Command flashes into the heart of a *mo'min*; thereafter, the Sun of Knowledge, which is followed by the Sun of *Ma'ãrifah*. Such a *mo'min* views the *duniya* with the light of the star of Command; he perceives the *Ãkhirah* with the light of the moon of the heart; and he grasps *Allãh* ﷻ with the light of the sun of *Ma'ãrifah*. *Nafs-e-Mutma'inna* [the relaxed soul] is a star. The perfect heart is a moon, whereas the head is a devout sun. The station of the *nafs* is the door; the station of the heart is in the hall of a Noble audience, whilst the station of the head is within the veil; which stands in the presence of Almighty *Allãh* ﷻ. It teaches the heart, whilst the heart teaches the *Nafs-e-Mutma'inna*. Thereafter, the *nafs* dictates through the tongue. The tongue relates to creation; and the existence of the *nafs* is deemed to be a place of blameworthy. The existence of the heart is the place of doubt. At the time of the purification of the senses, astounding entities are visualized. Until such time you obey your *nafs*, and consume *ḥarãm* whilst remaining in the companionship of the straying heart, you shall be consuming doubtful provisions. When your senses undergo a process of purification and consume absolute *ḥalãl* food, your heart shall be close to the pleasure of ordainment, and it shall enter the abode of virtue.

This occurs owing to the consumption of wholesome food and the drink, comprising love and affection. Secrets are categorized as the nation of the tall mountains of the earth and the pegs of existence. The allies of Love whisper in such words, which is sweeter than *Munn*[239]. He professed to them that after this restriction, there shall be an expansion of comfort; followed thereafter, by

[239] A kind of sweet gum

separation; where there shall be communion, and after bitterness there shall be sweetness. In following this humility, there shall be honour and after this extinction, there shall existence. At this moment the owner of this station is present in front of the face of the proximity; and He ﷻ places a veil in front of creation. He combines Commandments and Knowledge into their hearts. *Qurb*, i.e. Divine Proximity, which is defined as *Nūr* [light]; and which is created by *Allāh* ﷻ, and this is indeed classified as a mystery. The hearts of the nation observes; other than *Allāh* ﷻ, with the light of *Allāh* ﷻ. He ﷻ admits them to the paradise in accordance to their surveillance. When they gaze towards existence, they exclaim: *'O proof of astonishments! Inform me about the shortest way of reaching you.'* Hence, remain astonished in this state and adhere to hear the sound of the reciter of *tasbīḥ* [glorification]. They do not pay any attention to their worlds. When the hands of love and kindness appear, henceforth, the hands of their heart grasp hold of it. He is placed in the lap of benevolence, in the companionship of love and within the delightfulness of proximity. His garb of travel is removed; and is taken to their stations, and is allocated a seat in the Divine Presence. Doors are made for his heart; where he observes the grandeur and power of his kingdom through every single door. There are semblances of concealments in their treasury of knowledge; and also within the parameters of the intentions of their hearts. As their secrets encircle the abode of the heart, knowledge and secrets descend into it. He then settles in that house and observes the treasures, and thereby reaps the benefits. Every segment of his expands and his wings are strengthened; and subsequently, he flies to the tents of that Realm, which is a return to his Lord ﷻ. Nevertheless, if they have to fall, it shall be a fall within the courtyard of that house. They supplicate in the presence of the Divine Precincts of *Allāh* ﷻ and their *du'ās* are accepted. They return as *Majzūbs* [240] and *Meḥbūbs* [241] and their hearts are under the jurisdiction of *Allāh* ﷻ; extinct in the mystery of mysterious. When their hearts are unsealed, they thereby perceive the Grandeur of *Allāh* ﷻ with the eye of mysteries, which removes all veils.

[240] Inebriated servants

[241] Beloved servants

Oh Humankind! The weighty treasury of the secrets of the Lord of the Worlds is implanted within the inner being of the *Siddiqīn*[242]. Within them dwells the stars and sun of Realities, from which the angels derive their light.

The Ḥanafī Walī

I narrate in 675 *hijrī* from Shaykh Abu al-Faḍal Mansūr b. Aḥmad b. Abu al-Faraj Irāqī al-Dourī ﷺ, who narrates in 631 *hijrī* in Baghdād from his Shaykh, Shaykh Kamāl al-Dīn Abu al-ʿAbbās Aḥmad b. Muḥammad b. Samdaya al-Sarīfinī ﷺ. He narrates from Shaykh Abu al-Taqā Muḥammad b. Azhar al-Sarīfinī ﷺ who asserts:

'I waited for a period of time to acquire consent from *Allāh* ﷻ to meet a Man of the Unseen [*Rijāl al-Ghayb*]. One night I dreamt that I was visiting the grave of Imām Aḥmad b. Ḥanbal ؓ, where I witnessed that a person was standing next to his grave. A thought entered into mind, which indicated that this person is from the *Rijāl al-Ghayb*. When I awoke, a strong sensation within my heart resonated that I shall meet with one of them. Immediately, I advanced to visit the grave of Imām Aḥmad b. Ḥanbal ؓ. Lo! I saw that it was the same person at the grave of the Imām ؓ. He made his *ziyārah* and departed. I followed him until we reached the banks of the River Tigris. Henceforward, the width of the river narrowed for him; until it became similar to a step to get across. He crossed the river and I pledged an allegiance in order to converse with me. He stopped, and I then questioned him about as to which *Madhab* [School of Jurisprudence] he had followed. He affirmed: *'I am a Ḥanafī Muslim and I am not of the mushriks.'* Immediately, I comprehended that he was a *Ḥanafī Muqallid* [follower of Sayyiduna Imām al-Aʿzam Abu-Ḥānīfah ؓ]. He then departed and I formulated within my heart that I shall enquire from Sayyiduna Ghawth al-Aʿzam Shaykh ʿAbd al-Qādir al-Jilānī ؓ with regard to what I had experienced. Thereafter, I proceeded to the *Madrassa* of the great Ghawth ؓ and

[242] The super-elite truthful servants

stood at the door. Sayyiduna Ghawth ﷺ verbalised to me from his apartment, whilst issuing a confirmation: *'O Muḥammad! From the east to the west, there is no Ḥanafī Walī besides this person.'* [243] The Ghawth ﷺ proclaimed this fact without opening the door for me.

Regal Glory and Excellence

Sayyiduna Ghawth ﷺ professed that if any person exercises sincerity and graciousness with his Lord ﷻ, he shall then consistently remain fearful[244] of *Allāh* ﷻ; instead of other than *Allāh* ﷻ. Oh nation! Do not claim that which is not within you. Be steadfast on *Tawḥīd* and abstain from *shirk*[245]. Become the targets of the arrows of destiny; whereby you shall only experience a graze from it, without causing your death. Any person who is annihilated in the cause of *Allāh* ﷻ, then *Allāh* ﷻ shall invariably recompense him with another in his place. Do understand that *Allāh* ﷻ shall be merciful upon you, and it is better for you to be content with the pre-destined Laws of *Allāh* ﷻ; otherwise, I[246] shall break your teeth. Moreover, until such time your *nafs* is not purified, it shall deem equivalent to the dog of *Aṣḥābe-Kahf* who sits at the door and waits to be addressed: *'O Nafs-e-Mutma'innah [The peaceful soul]! Go towards your Lord.'* It is only then, that the heart progresses towards the sanctuary of the Sublime Lord ﷻ; and enters it; and hence, transforming into a *Ka'ābah* as the spectacle of the Mighty Lord ﷻ. A glory of stateliness and excellence is exposed to him and his abode is formed in the Tents of Proximity. A tree is

243 This narration seems to be an addendum to the original text of the author, as it is difficult to understand this statement of Ḥaḍrate Ghawth ﷺ; because in that golden era, there were numerous senior *Ḥanafī Awliya* present such as Sayyiduna Khawaja ʿUthmān Hirwanī ﷺ, Sayyiduna Khawaja Gharib Nawāz ﷺ and a host of others. *Allāh* ﷻ and His beloved *Rasūl* ﷺ know best what Sayyiduna Ghawth al-Aʿzam ﷺ really meant! The translator confesses his remorse and repents to *Allāh* ﷻ in case he has unintentionally misconstrued or misunderstood this particular matter of concern. # *[Faqīr ʿAbd al-Hādī]*

244 The implication is that they may not mislead him or divert his attention from Almighty *Allāh* ﷻ.

245 The concept of Polytheism or Idolatory, i.e. Ascribing partners to *Allāh* ﷻ.

246 Sayyiduna Ghawth ﷺ elucidates this fact.

planted in the neighbourhood of Sovereignty and its nobility is manifested and sets out to meet him. Its standard [flag] is handed over to him and he hears a voice exclaiming from the above: *'O my servant! Live with Me. You are for Me and I am for you.'* When the servant spends a considerable amount of time in this secret realm, the Power of Sovereignty discloses the secrets from the Domain of Sovereignty to him; and entrusts him as a *Khalīfah* [vicegerent] of the Divine Realm and a trustee of the Divine Concealments. He is despatched to the oceans; in order that he may save those who are drowning and sent to the jungles; whereby he may show the flowers the path. When he then bypasses a dead person, he resurrects him; whereas if he bypasses the sinners, he counsels them to repent and to engage in virtuous deeds. If he bypasses those who are distanced, he draws them closer and he transforms the wretched into the pious. The *Walī* is a servant of the *Badal*[247] and the *Badal* is a servant of the *Nabī*. The *Nabī* is a servant of Sayyiduna Rasūlullāh ﷺ. Similar to *Wilāyah,* there is a dialogue with the Divine Being and the unfolding of secrets in His Divine Presence. This beloved servant also remains close to the Divine Being, but as for him, in concealment is the canopy of love reserved at night; and the rostrum of his Divine Being in the day, within the Divine Proximity. Oh my beloved Son! As a result do not reveal your dreams in the presence of your brothers.

The Miracle of the Hand of Sayyiduna Ghawth رضي الله عنه

I narrate in 670 *hijrī* from Shaykh Abu-ʿAbdullāh Muḥammad b. Khiḍrī al-Ḥusainī al-Mosulī رحمه الله, who narrates from his father in 623 *hijrī* who stated that he had served Sayyiduna Shaykh Muḥiyy al-Dīn ʿAbd al-Qādir al-Jilānī رضي الله عنه for 13 years and during this period he had witnessed numerous *Karāmāt* [miracles]. From amongst them was a case where all the physicians had failed to cure an ailing person, who was brought to Sayyiduna Ghawth رضي الله عنه. He

[247] These are senior *Awliya* appointed the *Wilayat* [control] over the seven continents of this earth. They are seven selected ones and blessed with immense duty by *Allāh* جل جلاله. They protect these seven regions with great prudence. They are from the senior *Abdāl* group and also known as the seven *Abrār*.

supplicated [*du ʿās*] for the ailing person whilst he simultaneously, rubbed his noble hands over the ailing body. Instantaneously, the ailing person could stand up and by the Command of *Allāh* ﷻ, he was entirely cured and resumed to be healthy. Whenever an ailing person visited Ḥaḍrate Ghawth ﷺ, the ailing person would depart healthy and cured. Once a close relative of the *Khalīfah* of Baghdād, Mustanjid Billāh was brought to Sayyiduna Ghawth al-Aʿzam ؓ. He was suffering from dropsy[248] and stomach ailments. Sayyiduna Ghawth ؓ rubbed his blessed hand over his weak stomach. Despite having a weak stomach; he spontaneously rose up fully cured; as though he was never sick.

Deliverance from Sickness

Abu al-Maʿālī Aḥmad Muzaffar b. Yūsuf al-Baghdādī al-Ḥanbalī proceeded to Sayyiduna Ghawth ؓ and petitioned: *'It is for the past fifteen months that fever has not left my son, Muḥammad.'* Ḥaḍrate Ghawth ؓ commanded: *'Go back and disclose this into the ears of your son; O Umm-Maldam! Shaykh ʿAbd al-Qādir instructs you to get out of my son and go away towards Ḥilla.'* Pertinent to this miracle, we enquired from Abu-Maʿālī and he affirmed that he had repeated the expressions as Sayyiduna Shaykh ؓ had advised him to do so into the ear of his son. From that day onwards, he was cured. After a year we enquired from Abu-Maʿālī once more, and he confirmed that since that day, his son never experienced fever any more. They received the news that the people of Ḥilla had experienced proportions of fever.

The speed of a weak Camel

Abu-Ḥafs ʿUmar b. Sālih al-Ḥaddāwī brought his weak camel to Sayyiduna Ghawth al-Aʿzam ؓ and appealed: *'I intend to go for Ḥajj but my camel is very weak and cannot walk. I do not have another camel to ride for Ḥajj.'* Ḥaḍrate Ghawth ؓ struck the camel with his sacred heel and rubbed his blessed hand on its

[248] A disease in which water fluid collects in cavities or tissues of the body.

forehead. Thereafter, the condition of this camel transformed healthy to such an extent that it became faster than all the camels and left them far behind.

The Dove recites the Tasbīḥ of Allāh ﷻ and the powerful kashf of Sayyiduna Ghawth ﷺ.

Shaykh Abu al-Ḥasan ʿAlī b. Aḥmad b. Muhazzab al-Azjī ﷺ became sick and Ḥaḍrate Ghawth ﷺ visited him. He possessed a dove and a pigeon within his home. Shaykh Abu al-Ḥasan ﷺ revealed to the Ghawth ﷺ that this pigeon does not lay eggs; and furthermore, it has been nine months, since this dove had spoken. Sayyiduna Shaykh ﷺ advanced towards the pigeon and stood in front of it and thus, elucidated: *'Give benefit to your owner.'* Thereafter, he approached the dove and decreed to it: *'Recite the Tasbīḥ of your Creator ﷻ.'* Shaykh Abu al-Ḥasan ﷺ testifies that the dove immediately, began talking excessively, so much so, that the people of Baghdād began gathering around it to listen to its *Tasbīḥ*. The pigeon continued to lay eggs till its death.

Sayyiduna Shaykh ﷺ conversed with me in 560 *hijrī*:

> 'Oh Khiḍar! Go to the city of Mosul, because there are [sperms of the unborn] children in your back which you will expose [will be born]. The first child shall be a son and his name shall be Muḥammad. A visual impaired *Ḥāfiz* [of the *Qur'ān*] from Baghdād, named ʿAlī shall teach him the *Qur'ān*. He shall memorize the *Qur'ān* at the age of seven, within a time span of 7 months. You shall be alive for 92 years, I month and 7 days and shall die in the city of Irbil. Your ear [hearing] and your eye [vision] shall remain in perfect health.'

Abu-ʿAbdullāh Muḥammad relates that his grandfather settled in Mosul; and that he was born in the early month of Safar 601 *hijrī*. A visually impaired *Ḥāfiz* was brought to teach him the *Qur'ān* and he memorized it in less than a duration of 7 months. My father asked the *Ḥāfiz* his name, and from which city he had hailed from. He replied: *'My name is ʿAlī and I am from Baghdād.'* Henceforth my father mentioned the prudent words Sayyiduna Ghawth al-

Aʿzam ﷺ and as he had predicted. He passed away in 625 *hijrī* in Irbil at an exact age of 92 years, 1 month and 7 days. In this old age, *Allāh* ﷻ protected his senses and its strength till his death as foretold by the great Ghawth ﷺ.

The Stations of Maʿārifah

Sayyiduna Ghawth al-Aʿzam ﷺ affirms that there are three stations of *Maʿārifah*:

1) The first is the *Maʿārifah* of the attributes [*sifāt*] and pride [*nakhwat*]; whose name appears with communication. Its proof then appears with the expertise and the best splendour in the life of the intellect; with the vision of light; which is permanently established in the head of existence. The permanence of the elation of the heart is between reverence and pleasant trust with a sound vision. This *Maʿārifah* prevails amongst the people general, which cannot be established without the condition of trust. Its ground is a pillar. The affirmation of qualities with one's name without similarity is to be removed without abandonment. Its comprehension and search for its interpretation are unproductive.
2) The *Maʿārifah* of the Divine Being and distinguishing between the Being and the Divine Attributes is the knowledge that stays firm with communion and is pure of defect, in the field of purity. Its excellence is with permanence and glances into the Fountain of Communion. It has three pillars, viz. to send qualities on proof; to send means on ranks; and to send markings of composition. This is the speciality of *Maʿārifah* that it is linked with the boundaries of *Ḥaqīqah*.
3) The third *Maʿārifah* is that which gains momentum merely by praises and cannot be reached by inference, nor can any proof be applied to it or fit into any medium [*wasīla*]. This encompasses 3 pillars.
    a) Presence of closeness;
    b) Progression in knowledge;
    c) Observation of unification from the horizon of *Azal* [Eternity] is categorized as the *Maʿārifah* of the super-elite

[*khās al-khawās*].

Maʿārifah by the virtue of *Tawḥīd* means to progress from the controversy of the intellectuals and to supersede the relation of evidences. This stipulates that *Tawḥīd* does not depend on any proof to be established, and that *Tawakkul* [reliance] does not require any reason to be understood. Thereby, one should be an observer of the superiority of Truth based on the laws and knowledge. Entities must be placed in their proper perspective and customs must be confined to concealment. Knowledge can be rectified by research and realization; and further purified by the absolute observation of the Truth. It hauls one towards the *Tawḥīd* of the Masters of Unification. This is such *Tawḥīd* which the Sublime Lord ﷻ has characterized exclusively for Himself ﷻ, and by the virtue of His *Qudrat* [power], He ﷻ makes His ﷻ beloved servants recipients in order to qualify for it. *Allāh* ﷻ has cast His lustres upon the leaders of the exalted group; and has transformed them into sinners [incompetent] through His ﷻ praises, and as well as the inadequacy to spread this special lustre. It is from Him ﷻ that the *Qutb* of signs emanate; inclusive of the leader that nullifies occurrences [*Ḥudūth*] and establishes Eternity [*Qidam*]. Apart from this, the sign of this *Tawḥīd* is also a defect; for without its examination and realization, it shall not be appropriate to invalidate it. This *Tawḥīd* is other than *Allāh* ﷻ; towards which presence points out in giving it permanence or diminution.

This location is not precise for any servant, until such time he transmutes into a corpse in the hands of the bather, whereby he resumes absolutely extinct in the love of *Allāh* ﷻ. The Sublime Lord ﷻ flashes His ﷻ lustres upon the representative authority of ordained Laws on the beloved servant in the currents of the oceans of Eternity. This esteem is bestowed owing to the sincere intentions and constant plea of the self; and the existence of the servant in the Divine Realm of *Allāh* ﷻ; and in the pursuit of the establishment of Truth. This representation of authority is issued only after extinction [*fana*] of the servant. The mode in which this occurs, is that the last state of the servant returns to the first state. His state resumes similar to that of which he was initially assumed to be. The Permanence of Almighty *Allāh* ﷻ remains; as He ﷻ is infinitely with His ﷻ Divine Knowledge. There is nothing that can be compared to or parallel to the Sublime Lord ﷻ, and neither can His Majestic Attributes be negated.

The stability of the heart is accomplished by the refutation of similarity, and the omission of deactivation. These factors are for the truthful existence of the Real Absolute ﷻ, which embraces *Ma'ārifah* on the path in conjunction with freedom from all defects. To be independent, pertaining to inference and evidence, incorporates the removal of various concealments, through the deep deliberation on the ocean of absolute existence. Through this, no qualities or measure can be determined. The *Ma'ārifah* on the path of excellence is to distance the presence of the dignified wonderment; and to be jubilant with the sweetness of the address of the heart. The vision of the beloved also makes the soul ecstatic; and as such he discusses obscure subjects with the beloved on the firmament of light; within the assembly of proximity. This is a simple issue; similar to the awe-inspiring, which is far more excellent than spiritual depression. Affection denotes wisdom and fear depicts absence. Thus, every person who exercises affection is wise, and moreover, every fearful person is regarded as being in absence.

When the servants are placed in the nest of love; they are then positioned, as though they are addressed in *Jannah* by the tongue of light. When they are placed into the ocean of fear, it is as though they are addressed by the Fire of Hell. According to the stages of opposition for fear and reverence, they are hence, different. In zeal, according to one's opposition, it is separate from one's affection.

Henceforth, the dust-storm of fear blows on them; and they fly, but when the breeze of love blows on them, they remain alive. These are now the hearts of the lovers and the secrets of the *Siddiqīn*; which live in the Vicinity of the breeze of His ﷻ love, and in the gardens of His ﷻ Sanctified Domain. They call upon *Allāh* ﷻ with the voices of their status.

Ma ʿārifah on the path of *Wilāyah* refers to that condition, prevalent to the identity of solitary extinction of love; and the presence of truth with due consideration to the management of *Wilāyah.* Then the lustres of their Lord ﷻ continuously descends upon them. When these lustres continuously descend upon them, *Allāh* ﷻ befriends them and elevates them. When they are elevated; they are purified. When they are purified, they are whispered to that; which assists their souls in their Spiritual endeavors. They are clothed with the garb of love in adversity, and the doors of closeness are opened for them. Thereafter, they are raised to the assembly of victory and assigned to the chair of *Tawḥīd.* The veils are then removed for them, and the glory and honour are disclosed, where they exist without air. Invariably, a *Walī* is a flower of *Allāh* ﷻ; and the *Siddiqīn* senses their fragrance, which reaches their hearts. Therefore, except *Allāh* ﷻ, they become fervent in accordance to their status. Thus, the *Awliya* are the confidants of Almighty *Allāh* ﷻ and no one sees them, except the confidant. They remain concealed within the veil of modesty; and nobody is aware of them, except the beloved.

Ma ʿārifah on the path of *Tajrīd*[249] is that Sovereign Presence by which, the impurities of the qualities by occurrence are observed, which in turn cleanses self-pride and also relocates the heart to solidarity. As a result of this being present within you, there is no need to look further. Here, one shall conceive those mysteries that are present. You shall witness those concealed entities which were alluded to you, and that, which comprises three pillars:

1) To be secluded from the unveiling in acquiring certainty.
2) To be secluded from the unification, in the acquisition of knowledge.
3) To be secluded within the absolute presence of *Tajrīd*; whilst this presence is separate from that presence.

Ma ʿārifah on the path of *Tafrīd* [250] entails removing the word *Muḥ'dath* [created], and in combining it to solitary confinement with Eternity. It

[249] *Tajrīd* means to renounce worldly life for the perseverance of solitude and worship.
[250] Individualism, isolation. Being in solitary confinement, and be with the Truth within you.

establishes the pearls of the realities of individuality; making special reference to *Ḥaqq* [truth]; and is inclusive of being with the truth. With the truth, one thereby, enhances into a unique individual, which encompasses 3 pillars:

1) *Tafrīd* intended on the basis of thirst.
2) *Tafrīd* of love by the manner of loss.
3) *Tafrīd* of presence in the mode of communion.

These 3 contain 3 signs:

1) *Tafrīd* with signs and honour.
2) *Tafrīd* with signs and peace.
3) *Tafrīd* with signs and spiritual constriction [*qabḍ*].

The aforementioned evidence rejects all in spiritual expansion [*bast*]; and includes pure spiritual constriction [*qabḍ*] by the process of salvation of the truth.

On the path of *Jamᶜ* [communion], there is also *Maᶜārifah* [gnosis] and *Tafraqāh* [separation]. Separation is to observe other entities, rather than *Allāh* ﷻ and communion portrays the observation of others with *Allāh* ﷻ. *Jamᶜ al-Jamaᶜ*[251] is a super esoteric moment of the exposure of the Realities [*Ḥaqā'iq*]; whereby the *ᶜĀrif* seeks absolute extinction. These are classified into three categories:

1) *Jamᶜ al-ᶜIlm* – This pure *ᶜIlm Ladunnī* which deems the Knowledge of Observation extinct.
2) *Jamᶜ al-Wujūd* – This makes the essential existence extinct in a true

[251] *Jamᶜ al-Jamaᶜ* - Gathering of the gatherings. *Jamᶜ al-jamᶜ* is the experience of communion which is devoid of all distinctions, even of the philosophy of being one with *Allāh* ﷻ. This is the station of 'Two Bows Length', the station of Perfection which is attained only by the greatest Independent Perfect Man, Sayyiduna wa Mawlana Rasūlullāh ﷺ. The Gathering of the gatherings is also termed as 'The Station of Great Glory'. This is also Unity in Multiplicity. Annihilation in totality for *Allāh* ﷻ – in the Presence of the Divine Grandeur. This is the opposite of *farq* [separation]. This is Unity without separation. To gather that which belongs to *Allāh* ﷻ within you, and to surrender all of it in totality to Him, is indicative of real surrender. In the cosmos, there is nothing but *Allāh* ﷻ, His Names and His attributes. Briefly, this is designated as *jamaᶜ*. When we say *jamᶜ*, it implies the center of multiplicity.

sense of absolute union.

3) *Jamʿ al-ʿAyn* – It makes all those entities extinct, that grasp those stations towards the presence of *Allāh* ﷻ. It duplicates it; and leads one towards that mode of true present observation of praises of impediments of the victorious Real Sovereign Power. This is signified by the secrets of speech of the present heart, together with the attributes of unveilings, i.e. without the confrontation of the Realities of Signs; where there is no wavering for the need of evidences. Furthermore, it is instituted without the converser of the Law of the exposure of the opposite [other]. In fact, a conversation with him is undertaken with apparent speech and information. Words are undisclosed upon insistence. Hence, the blockade is substantiated with proof and the observance of Realities; in which are the observation of lustres, whilst the conversation is in secrecy.

Maʿārifah, is in reference to the path of *Baqa* [permanence], which expresses extinction in entirety, until one becomes unyielding with *Allāh* ﷻ; which in fact is a manifestation of the Mighty Lord of Power ﷻ. Thereafter, *Ḥaqā'iq* [realities] are exposed to him from *Allāh* ﷻ and owing to the presence and observance of *Allāh* ﷻ through his state of *Baqa* [permanence], his *Fana* [extinction] is replaced with *Baqa*. When this happens, the realities of the veneration and glory of the Supreme Sovereign Being ﷻ are disclosed to him. Through the observation of *Baqa,* his knowledge of the observance of *Fana* becomes extinct. Thereafter, the realities of realization are exposed to him; although at that juncture there are no realities. These realities are such, that they obliterate the signs of the observation of knowledge. With *Fana* they thereby, develop into *Fana* from *Fana* to such an extent, that they do not perceive *Fana* nor *Baqa*. Thereafter, Almighty *Allāh* ﷻ protects them in such a modus; similar to the protection of a new-born child. This encompasses three pillars:

1) *Baqa Maʿlūm Bāʿad suqūt al-ʿIlm* – Knowledge declines from the vision, but not from the memory

2) *Baqa Mash'hūd bā'ad suqūt al-shuhūd* – Observation plunges from existence, but not from the mind.
3) *Baqa ma lam Yazil Ḥaqqan bī Isqāt ma lam yakun Meḥwan* – Existence of those entities that have always existed in a realm of Truth; which were not obliterated. These factors are not applicable to anyone whose *nafs* [egotism] has not withdrawn itself from all desirable components.

One has to be strict on the ethics of servitude and steadfast in upholding the laws of the sacred *Sharī'āh*. In spiritual principles, every *Jamaᶜ* [communion], without *Tafraqah* [detachment from all, other than *Allāh* ﷻ] is evaluated as a spiritual sacrilege, and every *Tafrīd* [seclusion], without *Jamaᶜ* [communion], views one as ineffectual. Anyone who does receive the symbol of isolation, he is then rejected from the station of *Baqa*.

He who has perceived the Divine Secrets, which are not overwhelmed, and are subject to purity from changes; and neither encompassed nor comprehended; he has then indeed perceived the Eternal Attributes. Otherwise, these are merely conceivable inferences and not inbound Glory. The attributes of an *'Ārif* are that he understands Almighty *Allāh* ﷻ through monotheism, Divine Majestic Attributes and acknowledges its status and furthermore he is unwavering and sincere in adhering permanently to its laws. Be a stranger to outsiders [other than *Allāh* ﷻ] and free and aloof from the detractions and interferences of the *nafs*. The heart is to be pure of defects and the encounters of physicality. Refrain from looking at creation with one's secrets.

The Definition of Qutb

I narrate in 670 *hijrī* in Cairo from Shaykh Faqī Abu al-Ḥasan ᶜAlī b. Shaykh Abu al- ᶜAbbās Aḥmad b. al-Mubarak b. Asbāt al-Baghdādī al-Ḥarmī al-Shāfaᶜī ﷺ; and he narrates in 643 *hijrī* in Baghdād from Shaykh Abu-Jaᶜāfar Muḥammad b. Shaykh Abī-ᶜAbdullāh ᶜUmar b. Muḥammad b. ᶜAbdullāh b.

ʿUmrawiyah al-Sohrowardī al-Sūfī ﷺ; who narrates in 611 *hijrī* in Baghdād from Shaykh Abu al-ʿAbbās Aḥmad b. Yaḥyah b. Barkat al-Baghdādī Baz'zār, prominently known as Ibn Zayqī ﷺ. He narrates in 571 *hijrī* in Baghdād from Shaykh Abu al-Raḍī Muḥammad b. Aḥmad b. Dāʿūd al-Baghdādī Muad'dab Ḥisāb ﷺ, distinguished as Mufīd, states that he had searched for the person from whom he could enquire about the attributes of a *Qutb*. Once, in 548 *hijrī*, Shaykh Abu al-Khalīl Aḥmad b. Asʿad b. Wahb b. ʿAlī Muqrī al-Baghdādī, later Hirwī ﷺ and I departed to *Jāʿmeh Rusāfah*. There we met Shaykh Abu-Saʿīd al-Qaylawī ﷺ and Shaykh Abu al-Ḥasan ʿAlī b. al-Hītī ﷺ. I enquired from Shaykh Abu-Saʿīd ﷺ about the attributes of a *Qutb* and he pronounced that a *Qutb* in his era is bestowed with a Sovereignty of Commands. He is treasured with such a glorious status that the control of the affairs of the entire creation is handed over to him [by the Grace of Almighty *Allāh* ﷻ]. Thereafter, I queried from him as to who was the present *Qutb*. Hence, he replied: Shaykh Muḥiyy al-Dīn ʿAbd al-Qādir al-Jilānī ﷺ. When we heard this, we immediately progressed to join the *majlis* of Sayyiduna Shaykh ʿAbd al-Qādir al-Jilānī ﷺ. Amongst us there was no trace of anyone who had reached first or remained behind. We remained together, listening in order to derive more on this subject from the great *Qutb* ﷺ. When we reached the *majlis,* we discovered that the *Qutb* ﷺ was delivering his speech. As soon as we took to our seats, Sayyiduna Shaykh ʿAbd al-Qādir al-Jilānī ﷺ discontinued with his speech and asserted: Now, I shall praise that person who has accomplished the status of a *Qutb*.

- ✓ There is no such path in *Ḥaqīqah* [Reality]; whereby a strong source is not for him.
- ✓ There is no station in *Wilāyah*, where an abode is not established for him.
- ✓ There is no dignity within the extreme limits; onto which his foot is not secure.
- ✓ There is no stage in *Mushāhidah* [spiritual observance] in which he does not have a pleasant pavilion.
- ✓ There is no elevated step of the ladder of proximity, on which he does not have a lofty journey.

- ✓ There is no affair in this world and in the heavens; wherein he does not have a spiritual unveiling [*kashf*] and charismatic attributes [*karamāt*].
- ✓ There is no secret in *Ālame Shahādah* [the visible world] and *Ālame Ghayb* [the hidden world], of which he does not know the details of.
- ✓ There is no manifestation in existence, with which he does not have an association with.
- ✓ There is no action of power that he does not have an input to.
- ✓ There is no such light in which he does not have a spark in it.
- ✓ There is no phase of the progress of any person; in which he does triumph over that extreme limit.
- ✓ There is no destination of those who had reached [in *Sulūk*], that which he has not reached.
- ✓ There is no eminence which was not bestowed upon him.
- ✓ There is no status, to which he was not drawn towards.
- ✓ There is no breath in which he is not a beloved.
- ✓ He is a possessor of honour.
- ✓ He draws the sword of *Qudrat* from its sheath.
- ✓ He is the ruler of the Throne of Time.
- ✓ He is the Authority of the Army of Love.
- ✓ He is entrusted with the authority of appointment and dismissal.
- ✓ Any person who sits in his company shall not be wretched.
- ✓ His presence is never absent from him.
- ✓ He is never stripped of his status.
- ✓ No one has a vaster swimming area in the ocean of love than him.
- ✓ He has the largest landing strip.
- ✓ He is unique in existence.
- ✓ No appearance is more distinct than him.
- ✓ There is no one more strict in obedience to the sacred *Sharī'āh* than him.
- ✓ He is such an existence that he is extraordinary, close, favoured, earthly, celestial, sanctified, concealed, a medium, pure, humane

and benevolent.

- ✓ He has a limit that ends with him
- ✓ He is imbued with a virtue, which is far too concise for his status
- ✓ There are etiquettes which are obligatory upon him, but owing to its being in conjunction, at that time with its communion, during the occasion of the observation of Eternity; it is concealed from the eye of separation of fear and affection. In the Valleys of Observation, owing to its excellence at the time of separation, between the excessive glory and fervor of exquisiteness; and owing to the disagreement of characteristics; and although, through the indispensable merit of location, the exposure of the decline of its partial condition still prevails.

His caretaker of individuality, calls out aloud with signs within the communion of secrecy of the issues of command; together with secrets on the exposure of dominance. Therefore, people with such secrets are concealed within veils. Their esteemed appearance is addressed with concealed signs as commanded. Had this not been the case, then the grasp of the movement of time would not have the ability and strength to manifest them at the Station of Expansion [*bast*]. It is for this reason, pertaining to the reign and wisdom; that nothing from the realm of the unseen and power is exposed from the layer of the veils with reference to the signs of the secrets, restrictions and limitations. Hence, every existence would be able to conceive these mysteries. This is apparent, because its brevity and detailed features are concealed at the beginning and at the end of the power of the chosen and beloved Messenger Sayyiduna Muḥammad ﷺ. His pure drink is mixed with the flavours of the heavenly drink of *Tasnīm* [sacred Drink of *Jannah*]. The virtue of its great fortunes and misfortunes, union and disunion are under the control of this ideal. Thus, the arrow of Destiny rips through the wall of command. Pertaining to this issue, reference is made by the translator to the effect that, which creates a tongue, you would then have heard and witnessed the mysteries. Thereafter, the great Ghawth رضي الله عنه recited the following verses without any rhythm:

مَا فِي الصَّبَابَةِ مَتَهَلٍّ مُسْتَعْذَبٍ   آلاَوْلَى فِي آلأَلَذِّ آلاَطْيَبِ

There is no sweet fountain in Love in which, for me, there is more sweetness and excellence.

اَوْ فِى الْوِصَالِ مَكَانَةٌ وَخُصُوصَةٌ   اِلَّا مَنْزِلَتِى اَعَزُّ وَاَقْرَبُ

Or there is no special place for communion that is better, and beloved than my station [place].

وَهَبَتْ لِىَ الْاَيَّامُ رَوْنَقَ صَفْوِهَا   فَحَلَّتْ مَنَاهِلُهَا اَوْ طَابَ الْمَشْرَبُ

Time has given me its purity and brilliance, thus, its fountains are sweet and its shores are outstanding

وَغَدَوْتُ مَخْطُوْبًا لِكُلِّ كَرِيْمَةٍ   لَا يُهْتَدَى فِيْهَا اللَّبِيْبُ وَيَخْطُبُ

I was addressed with every excellence by which understanding did not achieve salvation nor addressed

اَنَا مِنَ الرِّجَالِ لَا يُخَافُ جَلِيْسُهُمْ   رَيْبُ الزَّمَانِ وَلَا يَرَى مَا يَرْهَبُ

I am of those men whose associates do not fear the difficulties of time and do not see those things that makes them fearful.

قَوْمٌ لَهُمْ فِىْ كُلِّ مَجْدٍ رُتْبَةٌ   عَلَوِيَّةٌ وَبِكُلِّ جَيْشٍ مَرْكَبُ

There is one nation for whom there is every elevated status of nobility and its rider is in every battlion.

اَنَا بُلْبُلُ الْاَفْرَاحِ اُمْلِىْ رَوْحَهَا   طَرَبٌ وَفِى الْعَلْيَاءِ بَازٌ اَشْهَبُ

I am a nightingale of happiness and sings joyously on the tree tops and I am a white falcon of heights.

اَضْحَتْ جُيُوْشُ الْحُبِّ تَحْتَ مَشِيَّتِىْ   طَوْعًا وَمَهْمَا رَمَيْتُهُ لَا يَغْرِبُ

Under my ordinance, the army is happy and when I intend, they do not fly away.

اَصْبَحْتُ لَا اَمَلًا وَلَا اُمْنِيَّةً   اَرْجُوْ وَلَا مَوْعُوْدَةً اَتَرَقَّبُ

When I begin the morning, I have no hopes nor desires for which I should have hoped. I do not have any promises for which I should wait.

مَا زِلْتُ اَرْتَعُ فِىْ مَيَادِيْنِ الرِّضَا   حَتّٰى وَهَبْتُ مَكَانَةً لَا تَرْهَبُ

I constantly climb the plains of Riḍã [pleasure] until I am blessed with such a lofty status that was not given to others.

اَضْحَى الزَّمَانُ كُحُلَّةً مَرْقُوْمَةً　　تَزْهُوْ نَحْنُ لَهَا الطِّرَازُ الْمَذْهَّبُ

Time is like such an excuse that is brilliant and colourful, but I am at its golden edging

اَفَلَتْ شُمُوْسُ الْاَوَّلِيْنَ وَ شَمْسُنَا　　اَبَدًا عَلٰى اُفُقِ الْعُلٰى لَا تَغْرِبُ

The early people's sun has set, but my sun is on the heights of the heavens that never sets.

Sayyiduna Ghawth al-Aʿzam ﷺ then professed: *'You are an animal that speaks and does nothing. The falcon does things but does not speak therefore, its threshold is the hand of Sovereigns.'* Thereafter, Shaykh Abu al-Muzaffar Mansũr b. Mubãrak Wãʿiz ﷺ, distinguished as Jarãdah, stood up and recited the following verses:

بِكَ الشُّهُوْرُ تَهْنَاءُ الْمَوَاقِيْتُ　　يَا مَنْ بِاَلْفَاظِهٖ تَغْلُو الْيَوَاقِيْتُ

O you [the Ghawth ﷺ] whose words are treaded with pearls! It is through you, that the months and time are cheerful.

اَلْبَازُ اَنْتَ فَاِنْ تَفْخَرُ فَلَا عَجَبٌ　　وَسَائِرُ النَّاسِ فِيْ عَيْنِيْ فَوَاخِيْتُ

You are a falcon, and it is not surprising if you are delightful and the rest of the people in my vision, are doves.

اَشُمُّ قَدَمَيْكَ الصِّدْقَ مُجْتَهِداً　　لِاَنَّهُ قَدَمٌ فِيْ فِعْلِهِ الصَّيْتُ

I sense the fragrance of diligent truth from both your sacred feet, because your feet are those from whose sandals is a voice.

Thereafter, Shaykh ʿAlĩ b. al-Hĩtĩ ﷺ stood up and kissed the feet of Sayyiduna Shaykh ʿAbd al-Qãdir ﷺ. He confirms that he took note of everything that occurred in this *majlis*, and retained it safely in his custody. Shaykh Ibn al-Abĩqĩ ﷺ states that he visited Shaykh Abu al-Khalĩl al-Hirwĩ ﷺ and questioned him about this issue and he relayed the very same information with preciseness.

Instructions of Sayyiduna Ghawth al-Aʿzam ﷺ

Sayyiduna Ghawth ﷺ states that Almighty *Allãh* ﷻ does not manifest within a servant with two Qualities; or with one Quality on two servants, until graciousness exists; and time is present; whilst communion is noted and disposition is familiar, with the establishment of limit. It is not exposed nor is there any fixed limit of a servant. Every limit has a merit, whilst every merit has a mode, and every mode has a lustre, whereby every lustre has a status. Every status contains a secret; every secret encompasses a *me'rāj* [elevation], and every *me'rāj* has an objective, and every objective in the Presence of *Allāh* ﷻ has a precinct that is entrusted with Divine Knowledge. When the servant is within his limits or on its side, his vision thus, is fixed to the final confines. He then becomes an attendant of the veils; because he is designated as a witness. This is a realm where the manifestation, for the permissibility of Eternal Quality denotes the example of its opposite; because the place within the bounds and extent of serenity is *Durūd* [*Salawāt 'alan Nabī* ﷺ]. Its extent of litenies is best for its perimeters. Limits do not have the power to comprehend the Existence of the Absolute Being ﷻ nor can extent carry His ﷻ Reality; on which His *Qudrat* [power] is established. When a servant departs from within his limitations and boundaries, perception of the attributes of the Absolute Existence, which is self-established, discernibly becomes absolute. This is so because it is based on the merit of perception [*Shuhūd*] and this is an attribute; for which there exists no similitude. There is no power attached to it for it to be steady, but except its reality. It does not reveal a manifestation in entity. When *Shuhūd* is *Shuhūd,* as it deems necessary, that there is a meaning to it. From its meaning, it must be indicative that it stands by its existence and is concealed. Absolute *Shuhūd* is only inclusive of accuracy, when *Shuhūd* is secluded from *Shuhūd* and when there is detachment from combinations and compilations; because of such opposing features, which become a reason for extraction or borrowing. There are conflicts between the very two scribes, whereby this leads to misconception and error. Within pure *Tawḥīd* and *Jam' al-Jama'*, which comprises of one characteristic, during the time of its stability; henceforward, there is an amalgamation of the external and internal *Shuhūd.*

Stripped of Status and Spiritual Conditions.

I narrate in 671 *hijrī* from Shaykh Abu al-Ḥasan ʿAlī b. Yaḥyah b. Abu al-Qāsim al-Azjī ﷺ, who narrates in 629 *hijrī* from *Qāḍī al-Quḍāt* Sayyiduna Shaykh Abu-Sāliḥ Nasar al-Jilānī ﷺ. He narrates in 591 *hijrī* from his illustrious father, Sayyiduna Shaykh Tāj al-Dīn ʿAbd al-Razzāq al-Jilānī ﷺ and his uncle Sayyiduna ʿAbd al-Wah'hāb al-Jilānī ﷺ.

I also narrate in 702 *hijrī* from Shaykh Abu al-Ḥasan ʿAlī b. ʿAbdullāh al-Abharī al-Baghdādī ﷺ, who articulates that he narrates in 631 *hijrī* in Baghdād from two *Shuyūkh*, Shaykh Abu-Tāhir Khalīl b. Shaykh Abī al-ʿAbbās Aḥmad al-Sarsarī ﷺ and Shaykh Abu al-Ḥasan b. Sulaymān, the Baker ﷺ. Shaykh Abī al-ʿAbbās al-Sarsarī ﷺ narrates from his father ﷺ and Shaykh Abu al-Ḥasan, the baker ﷺ narrates from Shaykh ʿImrān al-Kamīmānī ﷺ and Shaykh Baz'zār ﷺ in 592 *hijrī*.

I also narrate in 671 *hijrī* from Shaykh Abu-Muḥammad Rajab al-Dārī ﷺ, who narrates from two *Shuyūkh* in 617 *hijrī*, in Baghdād, viz. Shaykh Abu al-Ḥasan, the sock merchant ﷺ and Shaykh Abu al-Badr b. Saʿīd ﷺ. Both of them narrate in 580 *hijrī* from their Shaykh, Shaykh Abu-Saʿūd al-Ḥarīmī ﷺ, who is well recognized as Mudallal. He narrates in 674 *hijrī* from Shaykh Abu al-Ḥasan b. Najīm al- al-Ḥowrānī ﷺ, who narrates in 651 *hijrī* there, from Shaykh Abu al-Ḥasan ʿAlī b. Idrīs al-Yaʿqūbī ﷺ and he narrates in 673 *hijrī* from Shaykh Abu-Muḥammad Sālīm b. ʿAlī al-Damyātī Sūfī ﷺ. He narrates in 625 *hijrī* in Baghdād from Imām Shahāb al-Dīn Abu-Ḥafs b. Muḥammad al-Sohrowardī ﷺ who stipulates that Shaykh ʿIbād ﷺ and Shaykh Abu-Bakr al-Ḥamāmī ﷺ were both of perfect spiritual ranking. Sayyiduna Shaykh ʿAbd al-Qādir al-Jilānī ﷺ used to resonate to Shaykh Abu-Bakr al-Ḥamāmī ﷺ that the sacred *Sharīʿāh* is complaining to Sayyiduna Shaykh ʿAbd al-Qādir al-Jilānī ﷺ about Shaykh Abu-Bakr al-Ḥamāmī ﷺ. Sayyiduna Ghawth ﷺ forbade him from various facets, but he did not pay any heed to them. Ḥaḍrate Ghawth ﷺ proceeded to *Jāmeʿh Rusāfa* and located Shaykh Abu-Bakr ﷺ there. The great Ghawth ﷺ caressed his chest with his sacred hand and instructed: *'Abu-Bakr! Get out of*

Baghdād.' As soon as Sayyiduna Ghawth ﷺ issued this instruction, Shaykh Abu-Bakr was stripped of all his spiritual status and abilities and was reduced to a state of zilch [zero]. He was totally devoid, as he plunged into distress and detachment. His condition became such that, whenever he intended to enter Baghdād, he used to fall flat on his face, onto the ground. If anyone assisted him or attempted to bring him into the city of Baghdād, both would fall onto the ground. His mother reached out, crying to Sayyiduna Ghawth al-Aʿzam ﷺ and expressed her desire and love for her son. She complained that she was unable to move physically in order to see her son. Sayyiduna Ghawth ﷺ listened to her plea and thereby, bowed his head for a while in meditation and affirmed: *'I have granted him permission to travel from Farq; a place of exile which is underground, and shall talk to you from your well at home.'* It is documented that once a week, he would come out from underground to meet his mother.

Allāh ﷻ is pleased with Shaykh Abu-Bakr Ḥamāmī ﷺ

Sayyiduna Shaykh ʿAdī b. Musāfir ﷺ directed Shaykh Qāḍīb al-Baan Mosulī ﷺ to plead to Sayyiduna Ghawth al-Aʿzam ﷺ on behalf of Shaykh Abu-Bakr al-Ḥamāmī ﷺ. Ḥaḍrate Ghawth ﷺ effected a promise in this regard. There was a mutual relationship, encompassing love and respect between Shaykh Muzaffar Jamāl ﷺ and Shaykh Abu-Bakr ﷺ. Shaykh Muzaffar ﷺ perceived Almighty *Allāh* ﷻ in a dream and it was asserted to him: *'O my servant! Desire something.'* He beseeched: *'O my Lord! Rectify the condition of my brother Abu-Bakr.' Allāh* ﷻ elucidated: *'The solution to this is in the hands of the guardian of this world and the Ākhirah. Go to him and inform him that his Lord delegates, by the virtue of that command that I ordained to send bala [calamity] on the people, thereby, you intercede on their behalf and I accept you as an intercessor. Furthermore, it is for the reason of that matter, which you have requested Me that I should be merciful on that moʾmin who has perceived Me. Thus, I have done just that and verily, I am pleased with Abu-Bakr. Now you also must be pleased with him.* Suddenly Sayyiduna Rasūlullāh ﷺ appeared and enunciated: *'O Muzaffar! Go and inform my deputy and inheritor of the earth, Shaykh ʿAbd al-Qādir al-Jilānī ﷺ that his grandfather, the Messenger of Allāh ﷺ commands that he should reinstate the condition of Abu-*

Bakr, because he is angry with him for the sake of my Sharī ͨāh. Now I have forgiven him.' When Shaykh Muzaffar ﷺ resumed to his physical state, he delightfully proceeded to convey the glad tidings to Shaykh Abu-Bakr. He was aware of the entire episode; although he was stripped of all his spiritual powers, whilst previously he was obscure regarding all matters. I encountered him half way on the street and took him along to meet Sayyiduna Ghawth al-Aͨzam ﷺ. The Ghawth ﷺ observed us and decreed: *'O Muzaffar! Relay your message.'* He then relayed his message, but he had forgotten a part of it. Henceforth, Sayyiduna Ghawth ﷺ reminded him of his forgotten message. Thereafter, the great Ghawth ﷺ dictated to Shaykh Abu-Bakr ﷺ to repent for all his erroneous deeds, with which the Ghawth ﷺ was displeased. Thereafter, the great Ghawth ﷺ embraced him with a chest to chest genre. Instantaneously, all the integrity and status, which he had lost, were restored. In fact, his integrity and status heightened.

It is stated that Shaykh Muzaffar ﷺ relayed all his experiences pertaining to this matter. We enquired from Shaykh Abu-Bakr ﷺ as to how he met his mother during the days of his exile. He professed that whenever he intended to meet his mother, someone would carry him to the underground and thus, leading him to the well of his mother. He used to meet her there, and subsequent to their meeting, he would once more be carried back, to where he initially started and left from.

All these narrators declare that once, ͨIbād had proclaimed that he shall be alive after the demise of Shaykh ͨAbd al-Qādir al-Jilānī ﷺ and shall become the heir of his spiritual ranking. Thereafter, Sayyiduna Shaykh ͨAbd al-Qādir ﷺ seized him by his hand and cautioned him: *'O ͨIbād! I shall fire an arrow between you and your pride, and release my horses of separation so that the purity of your pastures shall swiftly be wiped out.'* The Ghawth ﷺ grasped onto his hand, until he was stripped of all his spiritual dimensions. All his matters were deleted and his status had declined where he remained in this desolate condition for a considerable period of time. One night Shaykh Jamāl Badawī ﷺ was in seclusion and coincidently an unknown person accosted him and removed his gown that he was wearing. He felt a subtle light which was exceptionally white. He was in a position to view, hear and understand. Thereby, he was carried to the Angelic Realm and transported to such a gathering where a group of *Mashā'ikh* had congregated. There were some whom he had recognised, whilst others were beyond his recognition. A breeze then blew onto him and he befell unconscious. Thereafter, everyone exclaimed that this is the fragrance from the station of Shaykh ʿAbd al-Qādir al-Jilānī ﵁. It was conversed to him in his ears; that this is such knowledge which is not discovered with a concealed attribute. This is classified as meritorious, which cannot be praised with undisclosed knowledge. In reference to it, a speaker implored: *'O Allāh! I plead to you to rectify the condition of brother ʿIbād.'* Henceforward, an answer was released into his ears: *'His condition can only be returned by him who had stripped it from him.'* Shaykh Jamāl then reverted to his normal physical senses and arrived at Sayyiduna Ghawth ﵁, who questioned him: *'O Jamāl! Did you plead on behalf of ʿIbād?'* He replied in the affirmative and Ḥaḍrate Ghawth ﵁ decreed to him to bring ʿIbād to him. When he arrived, Sayyiduna Shaykh ﵁ commanded him to join a *Ḥājī* in the capacity of a security scout. He thereby agreed as it was the season of *Ḥajj*. Many caravans were set to leave for *Ḥajj* from Irāq. ʿIbād joined one of them, and departed. On the way he caught sight of a tree and transmuted into a deep state of euphoria [*wajd*] and as a result, he began screaming and whirling. This occurrence continued until he annihilated from his existence. His nostrils swelled and began bleeding till the blood reached his feet. Thereafter, he regained consciousness and all his spiritual characteristics were reverted to him, with the inclusion of a more exalted status.

Upon returning to Baghdād, Sayyiduna Shaykh ʿAbd al-Qādir al-Jilānī ﵁ at that specific moment proclaimed to Shaykh Jamāl: *'Almighty Allāh ﷻ has returned the condition of ʿIbād to him and also so much more. I have pledged an oath on Allāh ﷻ that his condition shall not be returned, until he does not dive into the blood of separation [hijr]; and today he has dived into it.'*

It is noted that *ʿIbād* travelled with the *Ḥujjāj* up to a place called *Qaid*, where the Arab bandits attacked them. When ʿIbād intended anything, he screamed and his work would come to fruition. During the attack he also screamed to defeat the bandits but his scream was returned to him and he died. Hence, his death occurred in *Qaid*, where he was buried and moreover, he became legendary amongst the *Ḥujjāj*. Sayyiduna Ghawth al-Aʿzam ﷺ conveyed the message of his death on the day he died to Shaykh Jamāl ﷺ.

It is acclaimed that whenever Shaykh Jamāl ﷺ related this incident as he witnessed and heard it as well, he would then recite the following verses about the light that emerged to him:

صَفَيْتَنِي وَوَحَدْتَنِي أَنْتَ وَاحَدْنِي　　وَإِنْ تَعَدَّدَتْ فِي مَنْ أَكْثَرَ الْعَدَوَا

You purified me and secluded me. You are one who secludes me. Even though you are multiple amongst those who are mostly numbers.

لَكَ اِصْطَفَيْتُ لِمَعْنَى فِيكَ أَعْرِفُهُ　　وَإِنْ عَرَفْتُ عَرَفْتُ الْوَاحِدَ الصَّمَدَا

For you, I am pure for such a meaning that which I recognize and if I recognize, I recognize a Samad [The Eternal and Independent].

فَأَنْتَ مِشْكَوٰةُ نُورٍ فِي غَبَاهِبِهِ　　وَ كَوْكَبٌ فِي دَيَاجِي الْغَرْقَدِ وَقَدَا

You are a recess of light and a star in darkness that lights up in the darkness of honour.

فَاسْتَوْقِفِي الرَّكْبَ رَكْبَ الْحُبِّ إِنَّهُمْ　　تَحْتَ اللِّوَاءِ الَّذِي بِالْمَلِكِ قَدْ عَقَدَا

Stop the caravan of love because it is under the flag that is erected for a King.

وَ عَاهَدْتَنِي أَنْ لَا تَهْجُرِي وَصْلِي　　حَتَّى يُرِيْنِي بِكُلِّ الْكُلِّ مُنْفَرِدَا

Make me a promise that you will not leave my communion so much so that you will see me in a crowd alone with you.

تَشَعَّشِي فِي الرِّيَاضِ الْقُدْسِ وَ ابْتَهِجِي　　مِنْ بَعْدِ عِزِّ مَدَى الْأَحْيَانِ وَ الْأَمَدَا

May there be tents and brilliance in the garden of Quds, till the extreme limits of time and moments after honour.

It is revealed that Sayyiduna Shaykh Muḥiyy al-Dīn ʿAbd al-Qādir al-Jilānī ﷺ

used to comment after these two incidents: '*There were two people who fought over my state and both their heads were chopped off in front of Allāh* ﷻ.'

I narrate all these chapters from the comments, explanations and instructions of Sayyiduna Muḥiyy al-Dīn ʿAbd al-Qādir ؓ from two *Shuyūkh*, Shaykh Faqih ʿĀlim ʿĀbid Jamāludīn Abu-ʿAbdullāh Muḥammad b. ʿAbd al-Karīm b. ʿAlī b. Jaʿāfar b. Jarādah al-Qurashī ؒ and the senior Shaykh, Abu-Muḥammad Ḥasan b. Abī al-Qāsim Dalaf b. Aḥmad b. Muḥammad al-Baghdādī al-Ḥarīrī ؒ prominently known as Ibn-Qūqah. I heard these narrations from these two personalities. Shaykh al-Qurashī ؒ states that he narrates from Shaykh Abu al-ʿAbbās Aḥmad b. Abī al-Fataḥ Maghraj b. ʿAlī b. ʿAbd al-ʿAzīz b. Maghraj b. Salma al-Damishqī ؒ, who sent his book to me in 648 *hijrī* from Damascus. I narrate from Shaykh Qūqah ؒ, who narrates from Shaykh Sharīf Abu al-Qāsim Haybatullāh b. ʿAbdullāh b. Aḥmad b. Haybatullāh b. ʿAbd al-Qādir b. Ḥusain al-Khatīb ؒ well renowned as Ibn Mansūrī. Both of them affirm that they narrate from *Shaykh al-Islām Muftī al-Anām* Muḥiyy al-Dīn Abu-Muḥammad ʿAbd al-Qādir b. Abī-Sāliḥ al-Jīlī ؓ as an *ijāzah* [certificate].

The Method of Sayyiduna Ghawth al-Aʿzam's ؓ Dhikr

I narrate from Shaykh Abu al-Fataḥ Muḥammad b. Muḥammad b. ʿAlī Hilālī al-Azjī ؒ who narrates from Shaykh Abu-Muḥammad b. ʿAlī b. Idrīs al-Yaʿqūbī ؒ, who stated that he queried from his Master, Shaykh Abu al-Ḥasan ʿAlī b. al-Hītī ؒ, as to what the method of *dhikr* was of Sayyiduna Shaykh Muḥiyy al-Dīn ʿAbd al-Qādir al-Jīlānī ؓ. He replied:

> 'He abhorred and abstained from whirling and screaming; and as well as from the application of pressure. His *dhikr* was authoritative and included submission. His subordination was firm, and had a devout heart that was present in the Station of Servitude with *Tajrīd Tawḥīd*[252] and *Tafrīd Tawḥīd*[253]. This was devoid of everything; and not just for anything,

[252] This means to renounce this worldly life for the sole purpose of solitude and worship of *Tauḥīd*

[253] This means to be consistent in solitary confinement with Truth [*Allāh* ﷻ] in *Tawḥīd*.

but absolutely for *Allāh* ﷻ and only for *Allāh* ﷻ. His servitude was appropriate and perfect, which was duly assisted by the eye of Absolute Divine Sovereignty. He was such a servant who remained aloof from the companionship that prompted separation. With steadfastness on the Laws of the sacred *Sharīʿah*, he had reached the Domain of Divine Communion through the Real Absolute Lord of Power ﷻ.

I narrate from Shaykh Abu-Muḥammad ʿAbd al-Ghālib b. ʿAbd al-Bāqī b. ʿAbd al-Samad al-Qurashī al-Mosulī ﵀, who narrates from Shaykh Abu al-Mafākhir ʿAdī ﵀. He narrates from Shaykh Abu al-Barkāt b. Sakhr ﵀, who asserted that he had requested his uncle, Shaykh ʿAdī b. Musāfir ﵀, with particular reference to the method of worship of Sayyiduna Shaykh ʿAbd al-Qādir al-Jilānī ﵁. He affirmed that Sayyiduna Ghawth al-Aʿzam ﵁ created harmony between the heart and soul; and as well as the external and inner self, within the principled passages of *Sulūk*. Strenuously, he personally laboured, and paid no heed to the regulations of the attributes of the *nafs* for its benefits and losses; and inclusive of the nearness and distance, that ensued through the spiritual stations.

I narrate from Shaykh Abu al-Ḥasan ʿAlī b. ʿAbdullāh b. Abī-Bakr al-Abharī ﵀, who narrates from Shaykh Abu-Tāhir Khalīlī b. Aḥmad al-Sarsarī ﵀, who stated that he had heard from the honourable Shaykh Baqa b. Bat'tū ﵀, who affirmed that there existed a mutual agreement and a harmonious precedent in the path, words and deeds of Sayyiduna Shaykh ʿAbd al-Qādir ﵁ was similar to his *nafs*, heart, *ikhlās* [fidelity] and *taslīm* [submission]. At every given moment and condition, Ḥaḍrate Ghawth ﵁ adhered strictly and decisively to the Holy *Qur'ān* and *Sunnah*. The senior exalted *Mashā'ikh* concur that Ḥaḍrate Ghawth ﵁ was to a superlative degree, perfect in his spiritual principles, and remained unwavering when interacting with *Allāh* ﷻ, pertaining to any issue. All of them conceded to the status and steadfastness of Ḥaḍrate Ghawth ﵁. I also heard that Sayyiduna Shaykh Abu-Saʿīd al-Qaylawī ﵀ asserted that the power of Ḥaḍrat Shaykh ʿAbd al-Qādir al-Jilānī ﵁ embraced the love in communion; i.e. for *Allāh* ﷻ, in *Allāh* ﷻ and with *Allāh* ﷻ. During that era, the power of the senior *Mashā'ikh* was invariably delicate as compared to the mystic power of Ḥaḍrate Ghawth ﷺ, in view of the ascertained fact of his powerful path and relationship of permanency, with *Allāh* ﷻ. He had surpassed the status of many *Mashā'ikh* who were his predecessors. In realism [*Ḥaqīqah*], owing to his profound vision, Almighty *Allāh* ﷻ had augmented him to a lofty and esteemed status, which is beyond the comprehension of the ordinary human mind.

I narrate from Shaykh Abu-ʿAbdullāh Muḥammad b. Kāmil b. Abu al-Muʿālī al-Ḥusainī al-Nisānī ﷺ, who narrates from Shaykh ʿĀrif Najmudīn Abu al-ʿAbbās Aḥmad b. the pious Shaykh Abu al-Ḥasan ʿAlī Batā'īhī al-Rifāʿī ﷺ, who confessed that he had heard his uncle Shaykh Abu al-Faraj ʿAbd al-Raḥīm ﷺ conversing that he came to Baghdād and visited Sayyiduna Shaykh ʿAbd al-Qādir al-Jilānī ﷺ. When he witnessed the condition, affluent heart and the secrets of seclusion of Sayyiduna Shaykh ʿAbd al-Qādir al-Jilānī ﷺ, it beguiled his mind. When I came to Umm ʿUbaydah, I mentioned this to my uncle, that Sayyiduna Shaykh Aḥmad al-Rīfāʿī ﷺ, had reported as follows: *'O son! Who can be equated to his power and who can reach the lofty stage that he has reached. No one can be compared to him.'* I narrate from Shaykh Faqih Sāliḥ Abu-Muḥammad Ḥasan b. Qāḍī Abī-ʿImrān Mūsā b. Aḥmad al-Qurashī Sūfī ﷺ, who had heard Shaykh ʿĀrif Abu al-Ḥasan al-Qurashī ﷺ relaying to a person, that if he would have seen Shaykh Muḥiyy al-Dīn ʿAbd al-Qādir al-Jilānī ﷺ, he would have henceforth, seen someone whose power of his path is focused in its entirety to Almighty *Allāh* ﷻ. His strength was far and wide more powerful than the power of all the *Mashā'ikh* of *Tarīqah*.

His path, characteristics, commands and conditions were based on *Tawḥīd*. The sacred *Sharīʿāh* depicted his internal and external realization. His disposition was that of a content and tranquil heart, within a pure soul which embraced an impeccable spirituality. He is imbued with such secrets that strangers had never opposed. He possessed such an attuned heart, which influence could not convince nor attract it. Hence, with his unique disposition and spiritual state, he retreated from the Angelic Realm and advanced in order to secure a great realm under his sacred feet.

For forty years he performed Fajr Salāh with his ʿEsha Wuḍū

I narrate from Shaykh Abu-ʿAbdullāh Muḥammad b. Aḥmad b. Manzūr al-Kinānī ﷺ, who had heard Shaykh ʿĀrif Abu-ʿAbdullāh Muḥammad b. Abu al-Fataḥ al-Hirwī ﷺ declare that for a duration of 40 years, he had served Sayyiduna Shaykh Muḥiyy al-Dīn ʿAbd al-Qādir al-Jilānī ؓ. During this period he observed the great Ghawth ؓ performing his *Fajr Salāh* with the same *wuḍū* as that of the *ʿEsha Salāh*. Whenever his *wuḍū* was nullified, he immediately effected a fresh *wuḍū* and performed two *rakʿāts salāh [Taḥiyyat al-Wuḍū*].

His condition was such, that after the termination of his *ʿEsha salāh*, he would proceed to his apartment of seclusion [*khalwa*] alone. Nobody entered with him. He only departed from his room at the time of *Fajr salāh*. Shaykh al-Hirwī ﷺ informs that he had slept for a few nights, whilst engaged in the service of his *khalwa*. His routine entailed the performance of some *nafil salāh* during the first portion of the night; followed by the engagement in *dhikr*, until the end of the first third of the night. Thereafter, he recited the following *tasbiḥ*:

اَلْمُحِيْطُ الرَّبُّ الشَّهِيْدُ الْحَسِيْبُ الْفَعَّالُ الْخَالِقُ الْبَارِئُ الْمُصَوِّرُ

Oh Lord who encompasses the entire creation, the Witness, the Sufficient, One who takes account and Doer of things, the Creator, the Evolver and the Fashioner.

Spiritual Seclusion

Whilst being in seclusion, his body would sometime become small and weak; and sometimes it would emerge to be huge. At times he will float in the air and disappear from my sight. Furthermore, he would stand up until the second portion of the night and recite the Holy *Qur'ān*. He would thereby undertake lengthy *sujūd* [prostrations] and would rub his face onto the ground. Thereafter, he would engage in *Murāqibah* and *Mushāhidah*, until just before the time of *fajr*. During this time he would sit up in concentration and thereafter, he would be engrossed in *du'ā* with a sense of humility and submission; whereby such a light would envelope him that shall overpower your eye. Henceforward, he would disappear and I would hear a voice, reverberating: *As salām 'alaykum*; to which' Sayyiduna Shaykh ﷺ would respond. This sacred procedure would continue until he would depart from his *khalwa* for the *fajr salāh*.

Twenty Five years in the Jungles

I narrate from Shaykh Abu-Muḥammad Rajab b. Abī al-Mansūr al-Radārī ﷺ, who narrates from Shaykh Abu-Bakr Muḥammad b. ʿUmar Nakhāl al-Muqrī ﷺ and he accentuates that he had heard the pious Shaykh Abu al-Masʿūd Aḥmad b. Abī-Bakr al-Ḥarīmī ﷺ state that he had heard Sayyiduna Shaykh Muḥiyy al-Dīn ʿAbd al-Qādir ﷺ promulgate, as documented below:

> I wandered alone for twenty five years in the jungles of Irāq. I did not know the people, nor did they know me. *Rijāl al-Ghayb* and *Jinns* visited me and I used to teach them the path towards *Allāh* ﷻ. Sayyiduna Khiḍar ﷺ met me during inception; when I entered Baghdād. Before this meeting, I did not know him. He furnished a condition to me that I should not oppose him, nor should I institute any rejection to him. He commanded me to sit at a designated a spot, and as well as not to depart from there. Henceforward, he undertook his departure. For three years, I sat at that designated spot. Every year, he would come to me and issue me with an ultimatum to remain seated there until he returns. The gorgeousness of the world appeared to me in marvelous forms, in attracting me, but my Lord ﷻ protected me in deviating from my focus onto my Sublime Lord ﷻ. The cursed devil appeared to me in terrifying imageries and initiated in fighting with me. However, my Lord ﷻ granted me the power and victory over them. My *nafs* [negative forces] appeared in an image in front of me; and pleaded that it would follow me in accordance to my dictates. As aforementioned, it sometimes fought with me. *Allāh* ﷻ consistently granted to me the victory over it.

His Condition of Mujãhidah

Sayyiduna Ghawth ﷺ reports:

During my early life, when I initially adopted any genre of *Mujãhidah*, I remained steadfast onto it, and thereby embraced it. I used to absorb it with my hands and lived in the ruins and jungles of Madãyan for long periods of time, engaged in the *Mujãhidah* of the *nafs*. For a year I only consumed components of vegetation, which I discovered scattered around, and moreover, I did not drink any water. Within the following year, I did not drink any water, nor did I consume anything else. During the third year I did not drink water, nor did I consume anything, and furthermore, nor did I sleep. One night it was extremely cold and thus, I proceeded to the ruins of the palace of *kisra*, and thereby I fell asleep. When I experienced a nocturnal emission, I woke up and advanced towards the Euphrates River, where I took a bath. I proceeded to sleep and yet again, I experienced a nocturnal emission. Once more, I took a bath and continued to sleep. This occurred forty times, and whereby I took a bath forty times. Owing to the fear of falling asleep, I climbed onto the gigantic pavilion, which kept me awake, owing to the fear of falling down.

People regarded the Ghawth ﷺ as insane

Sayyiduna Ghawth ﷺ further elucidates:

I lived in *Karkh* for years and except herbs, I consumed nothing else. Every year a person would bring a *Sũf* [course woollen cloak] for me, which I wore. I mastered a thousand skills and in the process, I also derived benefits from this world. Nobody recognized me, and every individual characterized me as a dumb, imprudent and an insane person. I wandered around barefoot in the midst of those bushes, which were infested with thorns. I did not encounter any fearful feature that I was not in a position to confront. My *nafs* could not subjugate me; nor could the pomp and glory of the *duniya* attract or enthral me. Unwaveringly, my deportment remained the same, as it was during the phases of my youth.

Challenging the cursed devil

I narrate from Shaykh Abu al-ʿAfāf Mūsā b. Shaykh Abu al-Muʿālī ʿUthmān b. Mūsā al-Baqāʿī ﷺ who narrates from his father, who asserts that he was informed by Shaykh ʿĀrif Abu-Muḥammad ʿUthmān al-Sarifīnī ﷺ in Sarifīn that he had heard from Sayyiduna Shaykh Muḥiyy al-Dīn ʿAbd al-Qādir al-Jilānī ﷺ who accentuated:

I had lived day and night in the jungles and did not ever travel into the city of Baghdād. The devils would approach me with an army, mounted, and as well as on foot. They had huge faces which were alarming, and they were equipped with various types of weapons. They threw fire balls at me, but I remained steady at heart, about which I could not expound upon. I used to listen to a voice originating from my hand, which simultaneously substantiated: *'O ʿAbd al-Qādir! Stand up to them, for I have made your feet firm and have assisted you.'* Thereafter, I used to chase them away by running towards them, whilst they would disperse onto either sides; and eventually flee to wherever they arose from.

Henceforth, one of them came alone to me and dictated to me to leave that place, and issued threats of inflicting harm to me. He attempted various strategies in order to scare me, but when I slapped him on the face, he sprinted away. I commenced by reciting: *La ḥowla wa la quwwata illāh Billāhil ʿaliyyil ʿAzīm*, which would thereby burn him, whilst I remained in observation.

Once, he appeared to me in a very disgusting form and he possessed a dreadful stench. He revealed to me: *'I am iblīs and the reason I have come to you is to serve you, because you have tired me and my associates.'* I commanded him to leave but he was obstinate and refused to leave. Thereafter, a hand appeared from the above and struck him on his head and as a result he sunk into the ground. He then returned to me holding a fire ball, and began hostilities with me. A person then came to me, riding on a white horse and handed over to me a sword. When the cursed devil viewed this, he began walking backwards and retreated. Later, he appeared at a distance; and he was crying, and whilst rubbing sand onto his head he began confessing: *'O ʿAbd al-Qādir! Indeed! I have lost hope with you.'* I said to him: *'O cursed! Keep away from me, because I always fear you of misleading me.'* He affirmed: *'Of this, what you have proclaimed, is even more difficult on me.'* Several nets and traps were then placed around me by him, and about which I questioned him. He deliberated that it is the traps of *duniya*, which he aligns for people of a similar nature to you to be trapped. At that juncture I engaged in devotion, for a complete year and broke all those traps and nets. Thereafter, several features emerged close to me and I questioned the devil with regard to them. The cursed devil thereby responded by stating that they were the entities from creation that were linked to you. In repetition, I engaged in devotion for yet another year, until all these entities aligned to the cursed devil broke and were destroyed; hence leaving me alone to myself, in order to engage in devotion without interference.

Becoming aware of the Hidden Things

Sayyiduna Ghawth ﵁ affirmed:

The condition of my inner being was exposed to me, and I discovered that the inner self was linked to many components. My intentions and authority were revealed to me. For the duration of one year, I contemplated on these dynamics, until I became detached from them, and which resulted in the purification of my heart. Henceforward, the condition of my *nafs* was exposed to me, and I perceived that there were still defects and illnesses therein, and its desires were still prevalent. The influence of the devil deemed mischievous. I endeavoured in eradicating this defect for yet another year, until my *nafs* was cured of all illnesses, whilst its desires were obliterated. My devil embraced *Islām* and reverted to a *Muslim*. All matters enhanced solely for the gratification of *Allāh* ﷻ; as I remained alone without any interference in order to worship my Sublime Lord ﷻ, whilst the rest of creation remained behind me. Reference here is made to the time, when I had not yet reached my specific objective. I was then elicited towards the Door of Reliance [*Tawakkul*] so that by its inspiration, I could reach my objective. Apparently, I experienced difficulties [*zahmah*] with it; and I surpassed through it, whereby I was elicited towards the Door of Submission [*Taslīm*]; in order to accomplish my objective. Here, I detected that there were also difficulties [*zahmah*] in vogue. I also surpassed through this phase and was drawn to the Door of Proximity [*Qurb*], so that I could attain my objective. Here too, I experienced difficulties [*zahmah*] and I also surpassed it, and I was hauled to the Door of Spiritual renunciation [*faqar*]. Here, I discovered that it was void and hence, I entered therein. As I surpassed through it, I discovered the unravelling of great treasures. Through these treasures, I was blessed with great esteem, permanent wealth and absolute freedom. My preceding condition and characteristics were deleted and substituted with another existence.

Triumph over Conditions

I narrate from Shaykh Abu-Ḥafs ʿUmar b. Muḥammad b. Mazāḥim al-Dinsarī ﷺ, who narrates from the leader, Shaykh Abu - ʿAbd al-Raḥīm al-Nasībī ﷺ. He asserts that he narrates from Shaykh Abu al-Qāsim ʿUmar b. Masʿūd Baz'zār ﷺ, who stated that he had heard Sayyiduna Shaykh Muḥiyy al-Dīn ʿAbd al-Qādir al-Jilānī ﷺ affirming:

'During my initial stages and days of worship, I was confronted with various challenges and I fought against them; until I overpowered them with my existence. When the morning dawned, and subsequent to the experience, I regained my consciousness and discovered myself in a remote place. I discovered myself in a place, where I was originally present.

Once I experienced spiritual ecstasy in the jungles of Baghdãd which persisted for an hour. I was oblivious to everything, and had no consciousness of anything. When I resumed to my physical state, I located myself to be in Sharshastar [another town]. The duration of travel between this town and Baghdãd was twelve days. When I developed apprehension about my condition, a woman then exclaimed as follows: *'You are Shaykh ʿAbd al-Qãdir and you are amazed?'*

I am a Beggar of my Lord ﷻ

I narrate from Shaykh Abu-ʿAbdullãh Muḥammad b. Khiḍar b. ʿAbdullãh al-Ḥusainī al-Mosulī ﷺ, who had heard his father disclosing:

I served Sayyiduna Muḥiyy al-Dīn ʿAbd al-Qãdir al-Jilãnī ؓ for thirteen years. During this period I did not witness the Ghawth ؓ cleaning his nose nor spitting. Neither did a fly ever sit on him. He never rose up in respect for the wealthy, and nor did he proceed to the door of a king. He never sat on their mats, and nor did he consume their food. There was one incident when he sat with the king or people of such calibre; and he conceived this as a punishment that shall swiftly be meted out.

Whenever a *Khalīfah* or minister visited Sayyiduna Muḥiyy al-Dīn ʿAbd al-Qãdir al-Jilãnī ؓ, whilst he was seated, he would rise and proceed to his apartment. He would emerge from his apartment, whilst the dignitary was still standing. In this way, the application of his standing would not denote the respect for the politician. Whilst rendering advice to the kings and ministers, he would speak to them in a harsh tone. On the contrary, the politician would kiss his hands and exercise great humility and reverence to the Ghawth ؓ.

Whenever Sayyiduna Muḥiyy al-Dīn ʿAbd al-Qãdir al-Jilãnī ؓ wrote a letter to the *Khalīfah*, he would verify: *'ʿAbd al-Qãdir commands you, and my command is binding upon you. It is compulsory upon you to obey me as I am your leader, and a proof for you.'* Upon receipt and acknowledgment of his letter, the *Khalīfah* would always kiss it and would absolutely confirm:

'*ʿAbd al-Qādir speaks the truth,*'

The Speech of a Bull and blessings of Truth

I narrate from the Shaykh of all creatures, the erudite scholar Najam al-Dīn ﷺ, who narrates from *Qāḍī al-Quḍāt Shaykh al-Shuyūkh* Shams al-Dīn Abu-ʿAbdullāh Muḥammad al-Maqdisī ﷺ. He narrates from Shaykh Sharīf Abu al-Qāsim Haybatullāh b. ʿAbdullāh b. Manthūrī ﷺ, who had heard Shaykh, the leader, Abu-ʿAbdullāh Muḥammad b. Qā'id al-Awānī ﷺ affirm that he was in the presence of Sayyiduna Shaykh Muḥiyy al-Dīn ʿAbd al-Qādir al-Jīlānī ﷺ. Some person questioned him: '*What are your etiquettes based on?*' The Ghawth ﷺ certified:

> Truthfulness! I have never spoken a lie; even when I was studying at the elementary *madrassa*.' The Ghawth ﷺ further confirmed: 'When I was a child, from my town [Jilān - Iran], I proceeded into the jungles on the Day of ʿ*Arafah*. When I saw a bull, I followed it. It turned around, glared at me and conversed: '*Oh ʿAbd al-Qādir! You were not created for this nor were you commanded to do this.*' Its speech terrified me, whereby I returned home and climbed onto the roof. Thereafter, I saw the *Ḥujjāj* who had assembled on the Plains of *ʿArafāt*. I approached my mother, and requested her to surrender me for the cause of *Allāh* ﷻ and to allow me to go to Baghdād in order to seek knowledge, where I would and sit in the company of the pious. She questioned me with regard to the reasoning behind this; and thereby, I related my experiences to her. When she heard about my reasons, she cried and brought forth eighty *dinārs* to me, which my father had bequeathed before his demise. My mother had kept forty *dinārs* for my brother; and sewed the other forty *dinārs* below the armpit of my cloak. Henceforth, my mother granted me the permission to relocate to Baghdād. Before my departure, my mother procured an allegiance from me and a promise, that under any circumstances, I would never tell lies. She then came out in order to bid farewell to me, and affirmed: '*Now, I am allowing you to go for the gratification of Almighty Allāh* ﷻ. *From now onwards I shall not see your face*

until Qiyāmah.' I joined a small caravan and departed to Baghdād. When we passed through Hamdān and reached a narrow wet path, sixty robbers from the jungle launched an attack on us. They surrounded the caravan and one of the robbers intimidated me: *'O pauper! Do you have anything?' I replied: 'Yes I have 40 dinārs.'* He enquired from me as to where it was. I revealed that it was sewn below the armpit of my cloak. He thought that I was jesting with him and he thus, retreated.

Another robber accosted me and posed the same question as the first robber. I provided him with the same answer, and he also departed. Both these robbers proceeded to their leader and reported my answer to him. He instructed them to bring me to him, to which they conceded. I viewed the leader and his associates who were sitting on a hilltop, whilst distributing the possessions from our caravan which they had looted. The leader questioned me about as to what I had in my possession, and I thereby, declared that I had forty *dinārs*. He queried about where it was, and I informed him that it was sewn in my cloak. He issued a directive to tear my cloak and located the forty *dinārs*. Furthermore, he enquired as to what had obliged him to disclose his money; and I revealed to him that my mother had procured an allegiance and a promise from me, that never would I tell lies. Therefore, I shall never discard my allegiance nor break that promise. When I pronounced this, the leader began crying with assertion: *'You did not break the promise of your mother; and I have been breaking the promise of Allāh* ﷻ *for so many years.'* He then repented at my hands and his associates proclaimed: *'You were our leader in robbery, and now you are also our leader in repentance.'* All of the sixty robbers repented for their sins at my hands. They returned all the belongings that they looted from our caravan. These were the first people who had sought *toubah* of their sins at my hands.

The Snake spoke to Ḥaḍrate Ghawth رضي الله عنه

I narrate from Shaykh Abu-Muḥammad al-Ḥasan رحمه الله whose grandfather, Ibn Qouqah رحمه الله was very illustrious. He narrates from Shaykh Imām Abu-

Hurayrah Muḥammad b. Layth ﷺ, renowned as Ibn al-Wastānī who had heard Shaykh, the Jurist [Faqih] Abu al-Faḍal Aḥmad b. Sāliḥ b. Shāfʿaī al-Jilī ﷺ proclaim that he was with Sayyiduna Shaykh Muḥiyy al-Dīn ʿAbd al-Qādir ﷺ in *Jāmeʿh Nizāmiyah*. Many *Foqahā* [Jurists] and *Fuqara* [*Sūfis*] were present together with him. They were discussing about pre-destination with the Ghawth ﷺ, who was explaining to them. Immediately, a large snake fell onto the lap of the Ghawth ﷺ from the roof. Everyone departed with fear, and left the Ghawth ﷺ alone. The snake entered through his clothing and moved within his body, and came emerged through his neck and thereafter, coiled around it. Although this was in vogue, Sayyiduna Ghawth al-Aʿzam ﷺ continued with his speech, paid no attention to the snake, and nor did he move from his position. The snake then moved out from his body and stood up on its tail in front of the Ghawth ﷺ. It conversed with him, whilst Sayyiduna Shaykh ﷺ replied to it; but none of us could comprehend the conversation. The snake thereafter, departed and the people returned to their seats. They queried from the Ghawth ﷺ about what the snake had conversed, and as well as that, which he had replied to. Sayyiduna Ghawth al-Aʿzam ﷺ asserted: *'The snake declared to me that it had tested several Awliya-Allāh, but it had not seen anyone as firm and steadfast as I was.'* I replied to it as follows: *'You fell on me, when I was speaking about Qaḍa and Qadar [Fate and Destiny].*[254] *Hence, I intended that my deeds should not be in contradiction to my words.'*

Sayyiduna Ghawth ﷺ was Steadfast both Externally and Internally

I narrate from Shaykh Abu al-Ḥasan ʿAlī b. Azdamar al-Muḥammadī ﷺ, who narrates from Shaykh Muḥiyy al-Dīn Abu-ʿAbdullāh Muḥammad b. ʿAlī al-Tawḥīdī ﷺ. He narrates from his maternal uncle, *Qāḍī al-Quḍāt* Sayyiduna

[254] What the Ghawth ﷺ refers to in this context is that: Oh snake! What are you? You are merely a reptile that *Qaḍa* [fate] shakes and *Qadar* [destiny] makes it motionless. This snake was in reality the cursed devil in disguise. # [Faqīr ʿAbd al-Hādī]

Shaykh Abu-Sāliḥ Nasar al-Jilānī and he narrates from his father, Sayyiduna Shaykh Tāj al-Dīn ʿAbd al-Razzāq al-Jilānī. He had heard from his illustrious father, Sayyiduna Ghawth al-Aʿzam Muḥiyy al-Dīn ʿAbd al-Qādir al-Jilānī who affirmed:

> One night I was performing *salāh* in *Jāmeʿh al-Mansūr* and perceived movements of something onto the pillars, whilst I heard a voice. A huge snake appeared and opened its gigantic mouth on the spot of my *sajdah*. When I advanced into *sajdah*, I removed it out of my way and continued my *salāh*. When I sat in *Attahiyyāt*, it slithered up my thighs and then coiled around it. After pronouncing my *salām*, i.e. upon the termination of *salāh*, I could not see it anymore. On the next day I proceeded out of the *masjid*; into the fields, and I observed a person who was tall in stature, and whose eyes resembled that of a cat. I realised that he was a *jinn*. He disclosed to me that he was a *jinn*, and moreover, he was the very same snake, which I had seen on the previous day. He thereby accentuated: '*I had tested many Awliya-Allāh in this mode and had never discovered anyone more firm and steadfast than you. There were some who were petrified externally and internally; whilst some became uncomfortable internally but remained steadfast externally, and there were others that were stirred up externally, but remained steadfast internally. On the contrary, I discovered you to be fearless and steadfast, both externally and internally.*' He then requested for the extension of my hand to him in order to repent; and henceforth, I extended my hand to him and accepted his repentance.

He is one who will Die

I narrate from Shaykh Abu al-Maʿālī ʿAbd al-Raḥīm b. Muzaffar al-Qurashī, who narrates from Ḥāfiz Abu-ʿAbdullāh Muḥammad b. al-Najjār al-Baghdādī, who reveals that there was a correspondence between Shaykh ʿAbdullāh b. Ḥusain and myself. I hereby quote from his letter, wherein he alludes to the fact that whenever a child of Sayyiduna Shaykh Muḥiyy al-Dīn ʿAbd al-Qādir al-Jilānī was born, he would place the child into his hands and elucidate: '*You will shortly die,*' and thus, detach his love from his heart. The narrator exposes that when that child, whether it was a male or female passed away during the *majlis* of the Ghawth ؓ, he would never terminate his discourse; but continue whilst confined to his chair. The bathers would bathe the child, prepare it for burial and hence, bring it to the *meḥfil* where Sayyiduna Ghawth al-Aʿzam ؓ would perform the *Janaza salāh*.

He would sweat in extreme winter

By the same chain of narrators, reaching up to Shaykh al-Najjār ؒ, who states that he had heard from Ḥāfiz Akhḍar ؒ, who had articulated that he was present during winter with Sayyiduna Shaykh ʿAbd al-Qādir al-Jilānī ؓ. The weather was extremely cold and the Ghawth ؓ wore only a single *qamīs* [upper garb] and a hat covering his head. He would be sweating and the people around him would be fanning him with fans similar to those fans utilized during extreme heat.

Life and Death

I narrate from Shaykh Abu-Muḥammad Ḥasan b. Zarrād ؒ, who narrates from Shaykh Abu-Bakr Muḥammad b. Naḥāl al-Misrī ؒ and he narrates from Shaykh Abu- Bakr ʿAbdullāh al-Siddiqī ؒ. He verifies that one day Sayyiduna Muḥiyy al-Dīn ʿAbdul Qādir Jilānī ؓ expressed:

> 'My condition became quite constricted and owing to adversity, my *nafs* reacted by demanding rest and peace. I was then summoned, pertaining to my desire and I affirmed as follows: 'Death is in which there is no life; and life is in which there is no death.' Furthermore, I was questioned: 'What is that death in which there is no life; and what is that life in which there is no death?' To this effect, I replied: 'Death, is my death in which there is no life; which is similar to that of my fellow human beings, in which I do not view the prerequisites of profit and loss. May my death be emancipated from the desire, intention and lust of my *nafs* of *duniya* and the *Ākhirah* and may I not be alive or in existence in all these matters. However, that life in which there is no death, and be it also my life; is solely by the Will of my Lord ﷻ in which I am non-existent. My death

is conceived as my existence with my Lord ﷻ. From time immemorial, during my youth I began to perceive and understand that this was my most excellent aspiration.'

I narrate from Shaykh Abu al-Ḥasan b. Zarrād ﷺ and he narrates from Shaykh ʿĀrif Nāsirudīn b. Qā'id al-Awānī ﷺ that Sayyiduna Ghawth al-Aʿzam ﷺ was requested to motivate his view with regard to his comment: *'This was my most excellent desired matter'* and he replied:

This excellent intention of mine remained, until it was attributed to me as His [*Allāh's*] ﷻ Intent. Otherwise, the prescription granted to the option of my *nafs*, by virtue of the merit of its intention would have been eliminated. Its stipulation by Almighty *Allāh* ﷻ encompassed the abandonment of choice and the negation of intentions.'

[May *Allāh* ﷻ be pleased with him]

The progeny and attributes of Sayyiduna Ghawth al-Aʿzam ﷺ

I narrate from Shaykh Faqih ʿĀlim Abu al-Maʿālī Aḥmad b. Shaykh Muḥaqqiq Abu al-Ḥasan ʿAlī b. Aḥmad b. ʿAbd al-Razzāq b. ʿĪsā al-Hilālī al-Baghdādī ﷺ and he narrates from Qāḍī al-Quḍāt Sayyiduna Shaykh Abu-Sāliḥ Nasar al-Jilānī ﷺ, who narrates from his esteemed father, Sayyiduna Tāj al-Dīn ʿAbd al-Razzāq al-Jilānī ﷺ. He resonates: 'My illustrious father, Sayyiduna Ghawth al-Aʿzam Muḥiyy al-Dīn ʿAbd al-Qādir al-Jilānī ﷺ was questioned about his progeny, to which he replied: *'ʿAbd al-Qādir b. Abī-Sāliḥ Mūsā Jangi Dost b. Abī ʿAbdullāh b. Yaḥyah Zāhid b. Muḥammad b. Dāʾūd b. Mūsā b. ʿAbdullāh b. Mūsā al-Joon b. ʿAbdullāh al-Maḥaz [his title is also Majal] b. Ḥasan Muthannah b. Ḥasan b. ʿAlī ibn Abī-Tālib ﷺ.'*

The great Ghawth ﷺ is the grandson of Sayyiduna Abu-ʿAbdullāh al-Soumaʿī Zāhid ﷺ. When he was in Jilān, he became renowned with the designation of Jilānī. When the Ghawth ﷺ was questioned about his birth, he informed: *'In reality I do not know, but the year I came to Baghdād is the year in which Shaykh Tamīmī ﷺ passed on and I was then 18 years old.'* The narrator states that Tamīmī was Abu-Muḥammad Rizqullāh b. ᶜAbd al-Wah'hāb b. ᶜAbd al-ᶜAzīz b. Ḥārith b. Asad ﷺ, who passed away in 488 *hijrī*. According to this date, it is established that Sayyiduna Ghawth al-Aᶜzam ﷺ was born in 470 *hijrī*.

I narrate from Shaykh Abu-ᶜAbdullāh Muḥammad b. Shaykh Abu al-ᶜAbbās Aḥmad b. ᶜAbd al-Wāseᶜh b. Amīr Kāh b. Shāfeᶜh al-Jilī al-Ḥanbalī ﷺ, who narrates from his grandfather Shaykh ᶜAbd al-Wāseᶜh ﷺ and he narrates from Shaykh Abu al-Faḍal Aḥmad b. Sāliḥ b. Shāfeᶜh al-Jilī al-Ḥanbalī ﷺ, who affirmed that Sayyiduna Shaykh Muḥiyy al-Dīn ᶜAbd al-Qādir al-Jilānī ﷺ was born in Jilān in 471 *hijrī* and he arrived in 488 *hijrī* in Baghdād. At that time he was 18 years of age. I confirm that he is attributed to Jeel with a *kasra* under the *jeem* with the letter *ya* being silent. This was one of the cities in Tabristān. He was born in the village of Neef, which is also called Jilān, Gilān and Geel. Geel is also a village on the banks of the River Euphrates. This would have been the duration of a day's journey from Baghdād, which is on the way to Wāsit.[255] It is also called Jeel with a *jeem*, because of Geel *ᶜAjam* and Geel ᶜIrāq and as well as Jeel *ᶜAjam* and Jeel ᶜIrāq.

Some information about his Grandfather, Sayyiduna ᶜAbdullāh Somaᶜī ﷺ

Abu al-ᶜEer Thābit b. al-Kaylī ﷺ was from ᶜIrāq. Jeel is also a village that falls under the jurisdiction of Madāyan. According to one narration, it is professed that Jilān is attributed to his grandfather. Sayyiduna ᶜAbdullāh Somaᶜī ﷺ hailed from the senior wealthy, *Zāhid* and *Mashā'ikh* of Jilān. He was a *Walī* with perfect spiritual characteristics and charismatic attributes [*karamāt*]. Numerous senior *Mashā'ikh* from *ᶜAjam*[256] met with him.

[255] The former, the locality of Neef in the city of Jilān [Irān] is the concenses of the *Mashā'ikh* and correct while the latter view, Geel on the banks of the River Euphrates is a supposition and incorrect. This is so because the great Ghawth ﷺ himself had mentioned that he is an *ᶜAjamī* and *ᶜAjam* at that time referred to Persia which is todays Iran. # Translator *[Qādirī Faqīr ᶜAbd al-Hādī Raḍawī]*

[256] A non-Arab territory referring to Persia.

I narrate from Shaykh Faqih Abu-Sāʿad ʿAbdullāh b. ʿAlī b. Aḥmad b. Ibrāhīm al-Qurashī ﷺ, who narrates from Shaykh Abu al-ʿAbbās Aḥmad b. Isḥāq b. ʿAlī b. ʿAbd al-Raḥmān al-Hāshmī al-Qazwīnī ﷺ. He narrates from Shaykh the leader, Nūrudīn Abu-ʿAbdullāh Muḥammad al-Jilī ﷺ and he narrates from Shaykh ʿĀrif Abu-Muḥammad al-Dārbānī al-Qazwīnī ﷺ, who declared that Sayyiduna Shaykh ʿAbdullāh al-Somaʿī ﷺ was one of those *Mashā'ikh* that he discovered in *ʿAjam* to be one; whose *du ʿās* were always accepted [*Maqbūl al-Du ʿā*]. When he was infuriated with anyone, Almighty *Allāh* ﷻ would promptly inflict vengeance upon him. On the same token, whenever he was pleased with anyone, the Sublime Lord ﷻ would bestow bounties in accordance to his wishes.

Although he experienced old age and was curtailed to physical weakness, he would perform excessive *nafil* [optional] *salāh* and would consistently engage in *dhikrullāh*. He exercised great patience and submissiveness in his worship and was very punctual in his times. He predicted matters before they occurred, and the occurrence was in exactitude to his prediction.

The narrator confesses that some of his associates informed him that once, they departed with a caravan on a trading mission, and henceforward, mounted robbers launched an attack on them in the jungles of Samarqand. They screamed out to Sayyiduna ʿAbdullāh al-Somaʿī ﷺ for help. Lo! We saw him present in front of us, and whereby he audibly pronounced: سُبُّوْحٌ قُدُّوْسٌ رَبُّنَا الله and implored: *'O army of Allāh! Separate yourself from us.'* Through *Allāh* ﷻ, we observed that the mounted robbers did not have the strength to control their horses, and they bolted towards the jungle together with their riders. None of them were together, and all of them were individually scattered throughout the jungle, and *Allāh* ﷻ thereby saved us from their attack. We searched for the Shaykh ﷺ, but could not find him anywhere. It was beyond our understanding as to where he had disappeared. Upon returning from our trading mission to Jilān, we informed the people of our ordeal, whilst they confirmed that: *'By Allāh! Our Shaykh never left Jilān nor was he out of our sight.'*

His Chaste Mother

His pious and honourable mother is Sayyidah Sharīfah Umm al-Khayr Amat al-Jabbār Fātimah bint Abī-ʿAbdullāh Somaʿī ﷺ. She was a lady adorned with piety, virtues and excellent morals. I was informed by Faqih Abu-ʿAlī Isḥāq b. ʿAlī b. ʿAbdullāh al-Hamdānī Sūfī ﷺ, who had heard from the Shaykh of noble origin Abu-ʿAbdullāh Muḥammad b. ʿAbd al-Latīf b. Shaykh the leader, Abu al-Najīb ʿAbd al-Qāhir al-Sohrowardī ﷺ and he had heard from Shaykh Abu-Khalīl b. Aḥmad b. Asad b. Wahb b. ʿAlī Muqrī al-Baghdādī ﷺ, then distinguished as Hirwī, who asserts that he had heard from two pious individuals, the pious Imām, Abu-Sāʿad ʿAbdullāh b. Sulaymān b. Jaʿrān al-Hashimī al-Jilī ﷺ and the mother of Aḥmad Jiliyah ﷺ in Jeel. Both of them proclaim that the mother of Sayyiduna Shaykh ʿAbd al-Qādir ﷺ, Sayyidah Umm al-Khayr Amat al-Jabbār Fātimah ﷺ had firmly stepped in the path of *sulūk*. We had heard her relate on many occasions: *'When I gave birth to my son ʿAbd al-Qādir, he would not consume milk during the day in Ramaḍān. The people could not see the crescent of Ramaḍān owing to a hazy horizon, and as a result they came to enquire from me, whether my son had consumed milk. I informed them that my son did not consume milk in the day. Hence, they realized it was the first day of Ramaḍān and thereby they observed the fast. It became legendary in our city that a certain child is born in the family of the Sharīf,* [257] *who does not consume milk during the day in Ramaḍān.*

Shaykh Abu-ʿAlī al-Hamdānī ﷺ states that he had heard Qāḍī al-Quḍāt Sayyiduna Shaykh Abu-Sāliḥ Nasar al-Jilānī ﷺ, who had verified in Baghdād, that he had heard from his uncle Sayyiduna Shaykh ʿAbd al-Wah'hāb al-Jilānī ﷺ, who had confirmed: *'When I went to Baghdād, the Mashā'ikh of ʿAjam narrated from their seniors that he did not consume milk during the days of Ramaḍān; i.e. his father, Shaykh Muḥiyy al-Dīn ʿAbd al-Qādir Jilī ﷺ.'*

Sayyiduna Ghawth al-Aʿzam ﷺ had a brother whose name was Sayyiduna

---

257 The Arabs usually classified the *Sayyids as: Ahl al-Bayt Sharīf.* # [*Faqīr ʿAbd al-Hādī*]

Shaykh Abu-Aḥmad ᶜAbdullāh ﷺ. He was younger than Sayyiduna Ghawth al-Aᶜzam ﷺ, and he was well tutored in knowledge, and also groomed with spiritual characteristics. At a tender age, he passed away in Jilān.[258]

His paternal aunt was Umm-Muḥammad [mother of Muḥammad] Sayyidah ᶜĀ'īeshah bint ᶜAbdullāh ﷺ, who was very pious. Moreover, she was bestowed with apparent charismas [*karamāt*].

It Rained by the Duᶜā of his Aunt

I narrate from Shaykh Abu-Sāliḥ ᶜAbdullāh b. ᶜAbdullāh al-Tabqī al-Naḥwī ﷺ, who affirmed that two *Shuyūkh* [259] came to him in 564 *hijrī* and informed that once there a drought in Jilān and people performed *Salāt al-Istsiqā*, but it was in vain. Henceforth, these two *Shuyūkh* proceeded to Sayyidah Umm Muḥammad ᶜĀ'īeshah ﷺ, the aunt of Sayyiduna Ghawth al-Aᶜzam ﷺ and appealed to her to engage in *duᶜā* for rain. She advanced into her courtyard and began sweeping. Thereafter, she supplicated as follows: *'O Allāh! I have swept the yard, now, You sprinkle it with water.'* Within a short while of her supplication, it began raining heavily, as though someone had opened the mouth of a water bag. People returned to their homes drenched, dripping with water, and once more Jilān became lush. In Jilān was the demise of this pious lady ﷺ.

Generally, the word Joon is the title of Sayyiduna Mūsā ﷺ and this is derived from the paradoxical names. It is used most of the time with reference to black and white. Reference here is made, because Sayyiduna Mūsā Joon ﷺ was brown in complexion. Hind bint Abī-ᶜUbaydah ﷺ used to verbalize to him:

---

[258] No reference could be detected of the actual date when he physically transcended from this mundane world.

[259] The author of *Al-Qalāid wa al-Jawāhir* records that these two *Shuyūkh* were Shaykh Abu al-ᶜAbbās Aḥmad ﷺ and Shaykh Abu-Sāliḥ al-Mutbaqī ﷺ. Both of these *Shuyūkh* requested to Sayyidah ᶜĀ'īeshah ﷺ to make *duᶜā* for rain. *Allāh* ﷻ and His beloved Rasūl ﷺ knows best. *#[Faqīr ᶜAbd al-Hādī]*

أَنْتَ اِنْ تَكُوْنُ جُوْنًا أَنْدَعَا أَحْذِرُ اَنْ تَضُرَّهُمْ اَوْ تَنْفَعَا

Verily you're dark in complexion that has been drawn,
You fear that it harms you or benefit you.

Sayyidah Umm al-Khayr Ammat al-Jabbār Fātimah ﷺ was 60 years old, when she conceived a child; and it is thereby, believed that no other woman would fall pregnant at such an elderly age except a woman who hails from the *Quraysh.*[260]With the exception of an Arab woman, no other woman would fall pregnant at the age of fifty.

Her maternal grandmother was, mother of ʿAbdullāh, is Umm Salma bint Muḥammad b. Talḥa b. ʿAbdullāh b. ʿAbd al-Raḥmān b. Sayyiduna Abu-Bakr as-Siddīq ﷺ. The word *Maḥaḍ* which is prefixed to his name includes the designation of ʿAbdullāh. This is used for an entity that is pure from defects, in all facets and thus, this is the designation of Sayyiduna ʿAbdullāh ﷺ, because his father is Ḥasan b. Imām Ḥasan b. ʿAlī al-Murtuḍah ﷺ. His mother is Fātimah bint Imām Ḥusain b. ʿAlī al-Murtuḍah ﷺ. Hence, his lineage from both the maternal and paternal fraternity is virtuous, because it is chaste and free from any slave or a lady slave; and its culmination is Sayyiduna ʿAlī al-Murtuḍah ﷺ.

His designation is *Mujil* [pre-eminent] which reveals the meaning of *Ijlāl* [reverence]. This feature is extracted from the *Ism Mafʿūl* [Passive Participle] and *Ajalahī* [praise for him]; which denotes that Fātimah married ʿAbdullāh Mutrif b. ʿAmr b. ʿUthmān ﷺ and gave birth to Muḥammad Dībā; after the marriage of Ḥasan and Ḥusain. His designation was *Dībā* owing to his splendour, whilst the designation of his father was *Mutrif* [handsome] owing to his exquisiteness. When ʿAbdullāh b. ʿAmr was born, the people then remarked that after Sayyiduna ʿAbdullāh ibn Zubair ﷺ, he was the most handsome. The mother of Mutrifa ﷺ was Sayyidah Ḥafsa bint ʿAbdullāh b. Sayyiduna ʿUmar b. al-Khattāb ﷺ. Included in the word *Mutrif* [مطرف], the

[260] A woman who belongs to or hails from the Quraysh tribe.

letter '*Meem* - م' shall be read with a '*Ḍamma*', whilst the letter '*Raa* – ر' with a '*Fatḥā*' and the word shall be an '*Ism Maf'ūl* - Passive Participle.' This is derived from اطرفه بكذا – meaning: *I have decorated this with that.*

Physical Description of Sayyiduna Ghawth al-Aᶜzam ﷺ

I narrate from *Qāḍī al-Quḍāt* Shamsudīn Abu-ᶜAbdullāh Muḥammad b. Imām ᶜImādudīn Abu-Isḥāq Ibrāhīm b. ᶜAbd al-Wāḥid al-Maqdisī ﷺ, who clarifies that he was informed by his Shaykh, Imām ᶜĀlim-e-Rabbānī Muwaffiq al-Dīn Abu-Muḥammad ᶜAbdullāh b. Aḥmad b. Muḥammad b. Qudāma al-Maqdisī ﷺ, who proclaims that their Shaykh, Shaykh al-Islām Muḥiyy al-Dīn Abu-Muḥammad ᶜAbd al-Qādir al-Jilānī ﷺ was of slender built; medium height, broad chest, wide and had long beard, with a clearly exposed complexion, black eyes, a clear and audible voice, very handsome, awe-inspiring, and with a disposition, that encompassed complete knowledge in all facets.

The Discourses of Sayyiduna Ghawth al-Aᶜzam ﷺ

I narrate from Shaykh Abu-Ḥafs ᶜUmar b. Mazāḥim al-Danīrī ﷺ and he narrates from Shaykh Abu al-Ḥasan and prominently known as the sock merchant. He narrates from Shaykh Abu al-Saᶜūd Aḥmad b. Abu-Bakr al-Ḥarīmī ﷺ, who had informed us about the discourses of Sayyiduna Muḥiyy al-Dīn ᶜAbd al-Qādir al-Jilānī ﷺ. He implored as follows: Realize! May *Allāh* ﷻ record your name amongst the people of felicity, and make you one of them, who were successful in piety and thus, elevate your status. When Shaykh al-Islām Muḥiyy al-Dīn ᶜAbd al-Qādir al-Jilānī ﷺ was exemplified with the garb of the sciences of *Sharīᶜah* and acquired its subtleties, he was inaugurated with an exclusive crown of stateliness. His merits and excellence were enjoined, and he ascended to the Sublime Lord of Power ﷻ, thereby, leaving creation behind. The journey to his Sublime Lord ﷻ adorned him with the profound gifts of spiritual etiquettes [*adab*] and imbued within him the most exceptional realisms. A flag of *Wilāyah* was hoisted for him, whose tassels were flying high in the heavens. His status was elevated and his stars of providence glittered within the heavens of Divine Proximity. His sanctified heart perceived the valleys of the signs of success, unveilings and secrets. Its secrets carefully observed the Suns of Realities with lustres; and his insight witnessed the Brides of Reality in their secret palaces. Its soul received peace and tranquillity from the lover and, as well as from the beloved in the concealment of the sanctified Domain. The observation of its secrets, nobility and excellence depicting the signs of honour and glory were raised in the perpetuity of Divine Presence. Here, the impenetrable secrets were exposed to the great Ghawth رضي الله عنه; including the reality of concealed Truth was disclosed to him. He was informed of the intrinsic characteristics of the concealed secrets of existence.

He commenced by observing the places of destiny with the authority of intentions. Moreover, he extracted the commands of substances; and unveiled the gifts from their locations. All impurities, doubts and fallacies were eradicated and an authentic and pure authority was arranged; whenever the illustrious Ghawth رضي الله عنه reclined on his chair to deliver his discourses. His first *majlis*, when he delivered his discourse was in *Shawwāl* 521 *hijrī* in Baraniyyah. Indeed! It was an august gathering which was permeated with awe-inspiring and splendour. This *majlis* was inundated by angels and the *Awliya*. Sayyiduna Ghawth al-Aʿzam رضي الله عنه stood up in supremacy and addressed the gathering on the subject matter of the Holy *Qur'ān* and the *Sunnah*. He invited the people towards *Allāh* جل جلاله and everyone hastened and subscribed to his call with submission.

The Awliya رضي الله عنهم used to resonate:

> Oh caller whose words were accepted by the souls of the enthusiastic! Oh emissary on whose call the *ʿĀrifīn* [Gnostics] responded! Oh melodious caller whose mounts are roaming zealously in the jungles of ardour! Oh you guide who has led the honourable carriers towards the pastures of reunion! Oh you bearers of the vessels who has quenched the thirst of the intellects with the drink of love!

He removed the veils of doubts from the faces of reality, i.e. the secret sciences and the unfolding of the veils of clouds from the vision of the prestigious subtleties. Through the praises of the serenity of Eternity, there are motions around the hearts. The personas of the souls swayed upon hearing the praises of the meritorious deeds of generosity. Melodiously, the birds of secrets tweeted the elegant melodies of love from their glorious sanctuaries. Thereafter, from their surrounding nests, the birds flew out to investigate this awe-inspiring light. The brides of discourses were embellished, and owing to their charisma, the lovers enhanced into an ecstatic state. The maidens of the secret Harem, who were gifted by the Lord were adorned. Every zealous person fell in love with its awe-inspiring exquisiteness. In the gardens of love, which comprised dense pastures, he verbalized with precious wisdom. These pearls of *Tawḥīd* originate from the oceans of knowledge; whose waves are pounding. It depicts the meaning, that as though it is exposing pearls and rubies. It discovers its medication from the pearls, and derives nourishment and decorum from the splendid garden of realities from the rubies. On this path, there is no width or evidence to progress to *Allāh* ﷻ. The pearls of success are scattered onto the forums of understanding, whereby the intellects and pens were first to hasten for its acquisition. The pearls of guidance were henceforth, studded onto the necks of the high-spirited ones whom Almighty *Allāh* ﷻ leads to the glorious stations. Their souls expressed such velocity, similar to the movements of breaths within the chest. There was such fragrance in their hearts, parallel to the sweet sensation in the garden after a rainfall. The souls were cured from their ailments, whilst their disposition was absolved from doubts. Thus, that person who had heard this being exposed, his darkness remained with repentance, whilst his eyelashes were reluctant to cry. How meticulously he directed the sinners towards *Allāh* ﷻ; and how many travellers were imbibed with steadfastness because of him. How much drinks were to their avail; and how many of them were inebriated with the drinks. Many offenders were freed from their shackles. Owing to his tenderness and graciousness, many individuals were transformed into *Abdāls*[261] and *Awtāds*[262]

[261] The Nobles. There are forty of them, and they are the ones who have been designated in

by *Allāh* ﷻ. Several servants were blessed with spiritual esteem and stations by the *Abdāls* and *Awtāds*.

عَبْدٌ لَهُ فُسُوقَ الْمَعَالِي رُتْبَةٌ وَلَهُ الْمَجْدُ وَالْفِخَارُ الْاَفْخَرُ

He is such a servant that his loftiness has stages. For him is felicity and honour.

وَلَهُ الْحَقَائِقُ وَالطَّرَائِقُ فِي الْهُدٰى وَلَهُ الْمَعَارِفُ كَالْكَوَاكِبِ تَزْهَرُ

In guidance, he possesses realities and ethics. His sciences are illuminated like the stars.

وَلَهُ الْفَضَائِلُ وَالْمَكَارِمُ وَالنَّدٰى وَلَهُ الْمَنَاقِبُ فِي الْمَحَافِلِ تُنْشَرُ

He has excellence, honourable disposition and favours. He has praises which are mentioned in gatherings.

وَلَهُ التَّقَدُّمُ وَالتَّعَالِي فِي الْعُلٰى وَلَهُ الْمَرَاتِبُ فِي النِّهَايَةِ تُكْبَرُ

He is elevated above heights and he has stations which are very lofty.

غَوْثُ الْوَرٰى اَغْيَثُ النَّدٰى نُوْرُ الْهُدٰى بَدْرُ الدُّجٰى شَمْسُ الضُّحٰى بَلْ اَنْوَرُ

He is the Ghawth [helper] of the people, the generous rain and the light of guidance. He is the Sun of the forenoon and the brilliant full Moon, but in fact even more illumined than that.

قَطَعَ الْعُلُوْمَ مَعَ الْعُقُوْلِ فَاَصْبَحَتْ اَطْوَارُهَا مِنْ دُوْنِهِ تَتَحَيَّرُ

He has disseminated sciences with intellect. Then, its condition became such that initially it was enthralled.

مَا فِي عُلَاهُ مَقَالَةُ الْمُخَالِفِ فَمَسَائِلُ الْاِجْمَاعِ فِيْهِ تَسْطُرُ

---

carrying the weight of Creation, so that they are not free to act except on behalf of other-than-*Allāh* ﷻ [*Fi haqq al-ghayr*]. According to the *Ḥadith*, they are based in *Shām* [Syria] and circulate around the globe daily on different dates and in different directions for administrative duties. These *Sayrs* or visits are under Spiritual Command and Supervision of none other than, Sayyiduna Ghawth al-Aʿzam Shaykh ʿAbd al-Qādir al-Jilānī رضي الله عنه

[262]The Pegs, the Mainstays. An expression for four men whose locations are the four corners of the world: East, West, South, and North. The location of each one of them is the location in accordance to the former mentioned corresponding direction.

No antagonist has objections about his loftiness, because the issues of consensus are documented in them.

The Secret of the Heart is Exposed

I narrate from Shaykh Abu-Muḥammad Ḥasan b. Shaykh Abī-Muḥammad ʿAbd al-Raḥmān b. Zarda ﷺ, who narrates from Shaykh Abu-Bakr Muḥammad b. ʿUmar b. Niḥāl al-Muqrī ﷺ. He narrates from Shaykh Abu-Bakr ʿAbdullāh b. Nasar al-Bakrī ﷺ, who narrates from Shaykh Sharīf Abu al-Fatḥāh Masʿūd b. ʿUmar al-Hāshmī al-Aḥmadī ﷺ. He stipulates that one day the Deputy Minister, ʿĪzzudīn Abu-ʿAbdullāh Muḥammad b. Wazīr ʿOunudīn Abī al-Muzaffar b. Hubayra and the educator of the palace, ʿIzzudīn Abu al-Futūḥ ʿAbdullāh b. Haybatullāh and a courtier, Majudīn Abu al-Q̱āsim ʿAlī b. Muḥammad and Amīnudīn Abu al-Q̱āsim ʿAlī b. Thābit b. Musajjal [may *Allāh* ﷻ have mercy on them] and others were present in the *majlis* of Sayyiduna Ghawth al-Aʿzam Shaykh ʿAbd al-Q̱ādir al-Jilānī ﷺ. Sayyiduna Shaykh ﷺ began revealing that which was entrenched within their hearts. He exposed their inner secrets by virtue of his transcendental, mysterious insight [*mukāshifa*]. They were overwhelmed by terror. Owing to their silence and status, Almighty *Allāh* ﷻ detached their fear to the extent that they began weeping. They bowed their heads with reverential allegiance, as though they were being summoned for justice on the Day of *Qiyāmah* in order to account, and answer for their past deeds. They exhibited their fearfulness in answering for them. Sayyiduna Shaykh ﷺ was aware of their deep habituated indulgence in drinking liquor; and he pounced upon them, similar to a lion would.

The narrators concur that when Sayyiduna Ghawth ﷺ arose from his chair, he would not pay any attention to anyone, nor looked around. Shaykh Sharīf Abu al-Fatḥa ﷺ commented: *'O Master! There is no worship here that is softer than this worship, and you have killed them with fear.'* Ḥaḍrate Ghawth ﷺ replied: *'O son of the Masters! When the palm is not hard, it does not release the grime. For me to kill them today; is a reason for their life in the Hereafter.'*

Removal of Darkness with a single Flame

I was informed by Shaykh Abu al-Ḥasan ʿAlī b. Khabbāz ﷺ, who was informed by Shaykh Abu al-Futūḥ Nasrullāh b. Abu al-Muḥāsin Yūsuf b. Khalīl al-Azjī ﷺ, who asserts that he was informed by Shaykh ʿUmar al-Kamīmānī ﷺ; that one day Naqīb al-Nuqā b. al-Atqā visited Sayyiduna Ghawth al-Aʿzam ﷺ. This was his first visit to Sayyiduna Shaykh ﷺ who pointed at him and said:

> Alas! How nice it would it have been if you were never born and perhaps, if you were born, you would then have known the reason for your birth. Oh people in slumber, awake from your sleep! Open your eyes and look at that which is in front of you. The legion of punishment has arrived. Oh traveller! Oh degenerator! Oh the one who shall die: Lest you should travel for a thousand years and listen to one word from me. Let someone relay my message that how many worldly people; similar to you and your temporary pomp have been deceived by this world. Victims of the deceitfulness of this world have murdered them. My state is such that, when the concealment and sincerity of my disposition emanates in full steam, I do not even tread two steps, but I lead creation and their souls to the Sublime Lord ﷻ.
>
> O my *Murīd*! It is only two steps; whereby you shall reach the *duniya* and *Ākhirah*. Look towards *Allāh* ﷻ and you shall revert towards all dictates.

When Sayyiduna Shaykh ﷺ arose from his chair, some of his students articulated to him: *'O our Master! You have given him excessive advice.'* He responded: *'This was a light that removed his darkness.'*

The narrator confirms that after this congregation, with the exception of the *majlis* congregation, the Deputy Minister visited the great Ghawth ﷺ regularly and sat in his presence with absolute humility.

Advice to those who came to Repent and become Murīds

Whenever anyone came to repent in his august presence, he would assert [the Words of *Allāh* ﷻ]:

> 'Oh individual! You would not stand up to repent; until you were not elevated; and you would not come, until your repentance was not acceptable. You did not come, until you were brought here from the journey of oppression. Oh individual! When you had abandoned Me ﷻ, I ﷻ did not leave you. When you departed from Me ﷻ, I ﷻ did not detach Myself ﷻ from you. When you had forgotten Me ﷻ, I ﷻ did not cause you to be disremembered. You were busy in your matters, whilst My ﷻ Concession protected you. You were immersed in oppression and thereby, My ﷻ Benediction considered you. I ﷻ, henceforward, instituted a tremble within you for the aspiration of My ﷻ closeness, and called upon you for a communion. I ﷻ have brought you close for the cause of My ﷻ love; and have addressed you with My ﷻ signs.

NB: The above is an address from Almighty *Allāh* ﷻ to His ﷻ creation, which was reiterated by His ﷻ senior vicegerent, Sayyiduna Ghawth al-Aʿzam Shaykh ʿAbd al-Qādir al-Jīlānī رضي الله عنه to awaken the people from their slumber.

Mischief upon Mischief

When an old man would come and stand in front of him, in order to initiate himself as a *murīd*, Sayyiduna Ghawth al-Aʿzam Shaykh ʿAbd al-Qādir al-Jīlānī رضي الله عنه would resonate [the Commands of *Allāh* ﷻ]:

> 'Oh individual! You have sinned, and have delayed to repent. You have advocated evil and you have forgotten about it. Whereas, when I gave you grace, you have prolonged the period of repentance, and continued to sin. As your age advanced, your jinn [devil] became more malicious. During your childhood, you had abandoned Me ﷻ and I ﷻ had granted clemency to you. You fought with Me ﷻ in your youth and I gave you

grace. When you abandoned Me ﷻ in your old age, I ﷻ thereby, inflicted you with a severe punishment; as though you would experience on the Day of *Qiyãmah*. You would be like a strand of white hair; whilst holding a black book of records.

NB: The above is also an address from Almighty *Allãh* ﷻ to His ﷻ creation, which was reiterated by His ﷻ senior vicegerent, Sayyiduna Ghawth al-Aᶜzam Shaykh ᶜAbd al-Qãdir al-Jilãnĩ رضي الله عنه to awaken the people from their slumber.

70 thousand people in the Majlis of the Ghawth رضي الله عنه

I narrate from Shaykh Abu al-Maᶜãlĩ ᶜAbd al-Raḥĩm b. Muzaffar al-Qurayshĩ رحمه الله, who narrates from Shaykh Ḥãfiz Abu-ᶜAbdullãh Muḥammad b. Najjãr al-Baghdãdĩ رحمه الله, who asserted that Shaykh ᶜAbdullãh al-Jabã'ĩ رحمه الله wrote to him, and he quotes him as follows:

> Sayyiduna Shaykh Muḥiyy al-Dĩn ᶜAbd al-Qãdir al-Jilãnĩ رضي الله عنه proclaims: 'I was commanded in person and in my dream regarding the Laws of the *Sharĩᶜãh*, and I was overwhelmed by these *Nasĩḥa* [advices]. My heart was inundated by it, but when I tried to speak, I felt as though I was being choked, and was unable to speak. Initially, a few people attended my discourses and thereafter, many people began listening to me; to the extent that I was flooded with people, who sat at the door of my *majlis*. The seating place became restricted for the people. As a result, my chair was taken to the outside of the city and was placed in the field of the *ᶜEid-Gah*. People flocked in great numbers mounted on horses, mules and camels and lined up, depicting the similarity of walls in the gathering. There were about seventy thousand people, who were in attendance at my discourses.

His Valuable Advices

I heard from Shaykh Abu al-Khayr Saᶜãdullãh b. Abĩ-Ghãlib Aḥmad b. ᶜAlĩ al-Azjĩ رحمه الله, who had heard from the pious Shaykh, Abu-ᶜAbdullãh Muḥammad b.

Ismāʿīl b. Ḥamza Atfāl al-Azjī ﷺ, who affirmed that he had heard from the pious Shaykh Sayyiduna Abu-Faraj ʿAbd al-Jabbār al-Jīlānī ﷺ s/o Sayyiduna Shaykh ʿAbd al-Qādir al-Jīlānī ﷺ advocate: *'I heard my father often say, 'By the honour of my Lord! I have not spoken or glorified Allāh ﷻ without the inspiration of my Lord ﷻ"*

The Khutbah of his Majlis and Discourse

It is stipulated that the great Ghawth ﷺ would begin his discourse with the pre-amble, الحمد لله رب العالمين and thereafter, would remain silent. Once more he would recite الحمد لله رب العالمين and would stop for a while and thereby again recite الحمد لله رب العالمين, and use to remain silent, after which he would then recite the *Khutbah* as documented below:

اَلْحَمْدُ لِلّٰهِ رَبِّ الْعَالَمِيْنَ عَدَدَ خَلْقِهٖ وَ زِيْنَةَ عَرْشِهٖ وَ مِدَادَ كَلِمَاتِهٖ وَ مُنْتَهٰى عِلْمِهٖ وَ جَمِيْعِ مَا شَآءَ وَ خَلَقَ وَ ذَرَاءَ وَ بَرَأَ عَالِمِ الْغَيْبِ وَ الشَّهَادَةِ اَلرَّحْمٰنِ الرَّحِيْمِ الْمَلِكِ الْقُدُّوْسِ الْعَزِيْزِ الْحَكِيْمِ وَ اَشْهَدُ اَنْ لَّا اِلٰهَ اِلَّا اللّٰهُ وَحْدَهٗ لَا شَرِيْكَ لَهُ الْمُلْكُ وَ لَهُ الْحَمْدُ يُحْيِى وَ يُمِيْتُ بِيَدِهِ الْخَيْرُ وَ هُوَ عَلٰى كُلِّ شَيْءٍ قَدِيْرٌ وَ اَشْهَدُ اَنَّ مُحَمَّداً عَبْدُهٗ وَ رَسُوْلُهٗ اَرْسَلَهٗ بِالْهُدٰى وَ دِيْنِ الْحَقِّ لِيُظْهِرَهٗ عَلَى الدِّيْنِ كُلِّهٖ وَ لَوْ كَرِهَ الْمُشْرِكُوْنَ اَللّٰهُمَّ اَصْلِحِ الْاُمَّ وَ الْاُمَّةَ وَ الرَّاعِى وَ الرَّعِيَّةَ وَ اَلِّفْ بَيْنَ قُلُوْبِهِمْ فِي الْخَيْرَاتِ وَ ارْفَعْ شَرَّ بَعْضِهِمْ عَنْ بَعْضٍ اَللّٰهُمَّ اَنْتَ الْعَالِمُ بِسَرَائِرِ فَاَنْ صَلَحَا وَ اَنْتَ الْعَالِمُ بِذُنُوْبِنَا فَاغْفِرْهَا وَ اَنْتَ الْعَالِمُ بِعُيُوْبِنَا فَاسْتُرْهَا وَ اَنْتَ الْعَالِمُ بِحَوَائِجِنَا فَاقْضِهَا لَا تَأْذَنَّا حَيْثُ نَهَيْتَنَا وَ لَا تَفْقِدْنَا مِنْ حَيْثُ اَمَرْتَنَا لَا تَفَّا ذِكْرَكَ وَ شُكْرَكَ وَ حُسْنَ عِبَادَتِكَ

He would then turn to his right and recite:

لَا اِلٰهَ اِلَّا اللّٰهُ مَا شَآءَ اللّٰهُ كَانَ لَا حَوْلَ وَ لَا قُوَّةَ اِلَّا بِاللّٰهِ الْعَلِيِّ الْعَظِيْمِ

Then he would turn to his left and pronounce the same, and would thus, continue:

لَا تُبِدْ اَخْبَارَنَا وَ لَا تَهْتِكْ اَسْتَارَنَا وَ لَا تُوَاخِذْنَا بِسُوْءِ اَعْمَالِنَا وَ لَا تُحِيْنَا فِي غَفْلَةٍ وَ لَا تَأْخُذْنَا عَلٰى عِزَّةٍ رَبَّنَا لَا تُؤَاخِذْنَا اِنْ نَّسِيْنَا اَوْ اَخْطَأْنَا رَبَّنَا وَ لَا تَحْمِلْ عَلَيْنَا اِصْراً كَمَا حَمَلْتَهٗ عَلَى الَّذِيْنَ مِنْ قَبْلِنَا رَبَّنَا وَ لَا تُحَمِّلْنَا مَا

لَا طَاقَةَ لَنَا بِهٖ وَاعْفُ عَنَّا وَ غْفِرْ لَنَا وَارْحَمْنَا اَنْتَ مَوْلَانَا فَانْصُرْنَا عَلَى الْقَوْمِ الْكَافِرِيْنَ

Thereafter, he would commence with his discourse.

The Address of Sayyiduna Ghawth ﷺ to those with imperfect Imãn and Taubah

When anyone with imperfect *Imãn* and *Taubah* stood up in his *majlis*, he would repeatedly express the following dictates of the Compassionate Lord ﷻ:

> Oh individual! When We ﷻ called upon you, you did not respond. Were We ﷻ not compassionate to you, whilst you were inattentive? We hastened, but you did not. We ﷻ rebuked you, but you were shameless. We ﷻ cared for you of which you were aware of; that We ﷻ had cared for you, and granted you respite for a few days and months. We ﷻ concealed your shortcomings for years, but you remained adamant without responding. You did not progress, but averted to transgressions, and you had severed in many promises and pacts. Thereafter, you returned, and thus, Our ﷻ link would always be attached to the *majlis*. We ﷻ had alarmed you, so that you may stand up to repent; whereas had We ﷻ only rejected you; what would then have been your situation? We ﷻ did not intend to disregard you. Had We ﷻ not returned to you, We ﷻ would have then destroyed your homes. Had We ﷻ not accepted your return; were you aware that you would have then come begging to Us ﷻ and had culminated with humility at Our ﷻ door? Instead, you turned and walked away. I ﷻ am astounded at that individual who claims to love Me ﷻ, but yet, does not prudently accomplish his claim of love. I ﷻ am astonished at that individual who received the breeze of My ﷻ closeness; drank the sips of My ﷻ love; but why did he yet run away from My ﷻ group? If you were truthful, you would have certainly complied accordingly. If you possessed true love, you would have not opposed it. If you were amongst My ﷻ friends, you would have not been deprived of the taste of the Drink of My ﷻ Love.

Oh you who were moulded with hands! Oh you who were fashioned by Divine Esteems! Oh you who have received the nourishment of Divine Blessings! Oh you who were nurtured by generosity! How should I ﷻ meet with you, when you oppress? How much do you tear apart the garb of alliance, and how much do I ﷻ have to restore it? How much do you lie to Me ﷻ, whilst I keep on forgiving you?

The Rain of Mercy on the Majlis of the Ghawth ﷺ

I was informed by Shaykh Abu-Mũsã ʿĪsã b. Yaḥyah b. Isḥãq al-Maqdisĩ al-Awãnĩ ﷺ, who was informed by The Shaykh of noble origin ʿAbd al-Raḥmãn b. ʿAbdullãh b. Shaykh al-Islãm Muḥiyy al-Dĩn ʿAbd al-Q̲ãdir al-Jilãnĩ ﷺ who reveals that he was informed by his uncle, Sayyiduna Imãm Abu-Bakr ʿAbd al-Razzãq al-Jilãnĩ ﷺ, who had heard from Shaykh the leader, ʿAlĩ b. al-Hĩtĩ ﷺ, that when his father ﷺ reclined to his chair, he would chant '*Alḥamdulillãh*' and all the *Awliya-Allãh* on the earth would observe silence and present themselves in his *majlis*; or if they were absent, he would repeat the chanting of '*Alḥamdulillãh*' and thereby, observe silence. The *majlis* would then be imbued with *Awliya* and Angels. Furthermore, there would be more of them who could not be seen;[263] than those who could be seen,[264] and mercy would rain onto the *majlis*.

The Duʿã of the Ghawth ﷺ in his Majlis

I was informed by Shaykh Abu-Sãʿad ʿAbd al-Ghãlib b. Aḥmad b. ʿAlĩ al-Hãshmĩ ﷺ, who was informed by Shaykh Muḥiyy al-Dĩn Abu-ʿAbdullãh Muḥammad ﷺ and he states that his father, Sayyiduna Shaykh Abu-Sãliḥ Nasar al-Jilãnĩ ﷺ confirmed that his illustrious father, Sayyiduna Shaykh Abu-Bakr ʿAbd al-Razzãq al-Jilãnĩ ﷺ informed him that the *du ʿã* of his august father, Sayyiduna Ghawth al-Aʿzam ﷺ at his *majlis* read as follows:

---

[263] In this context, unseen refers to the Angels, *Rijãl al-Ghayb* and *Jinns*.

[264] Reference made to the human beings

اَللّٰهُمَّ اِنَّا نَسْئَلُكَ اِيْمَاناً يَصْلِحُ لِلْعَرْضِ عَلَيْكَ وَ اِيْقَاناً نَقِفُ بِهٖ يَوْمَ الْقِيَامَةِ بَيْنَ يَدَيْكَ وَ عِصْمَةً تُنْقِذُنَا بِهَا وَ مِنْ لَطَفِ الذُّنُوبِ وَ رَحْمَةً تُطَهِّرُنَا بِهَا مِنْ دَنَسِ الْعُيُوْبِ وَ عِلْماً نَفْقَهُ بِهٖ اَمْرَكَ وَ نَوَاهِيْكَ وَ فَهْماً نَعْلَمُ بِهٖ كَيْفَ نُنَاجِيْكَ وَ اجْعَلْنَا فِي الدُّنْيَا وَ الْاٰخِرَةِ مِنْ اَهْلِ وِلَايَتِكَ وَ امْلَا قُلُوْبَنَا بِنُوْرِ مَعْرِفَتِكَ وَ كَحِّلْ عُيُوْنِ عُقُوْلِنَا بِاِثْمِدِ هَدَايَتِكَ وَ احْرِسْ اَقْدَامِ اَفْكَارِنَا مِنْ مَزَائِقِ مَوَاطِي الشُّبْهَاتِ وَ امْنَعْ طُيُوْرِ نُفُوْسِنَا مِنَ الْوُقُوْعِ فِيْ شُبَّاكِ مُوْلِقَاتِ الشَّهْوَاتِ وَ اَعِنَّا فِيْ اِقَامِ الصَّلٰوةِ وَ عَلٰى تَرْكِ الشَّهْوَاتِ وَ امْحُ سُطُوْرَ نَسِيْأٰتِنَا مِنْ جَرَائِدَ اَعْمَالِنَا بِاَيْدِي الْحَسَنَاتِ كُنْ لَنَا حَيْثُ يَنْقَطِعُ الرَّجَاءِ مِنَّا اِذَا اَعْرَضَ اَهْلِ الْوُجُوْدِ بِوُجُوْهِهِمْ عَنَّا حَتّٰى تَحْصُلَ فِيْ ظُلَمِ اللَّحْوِ وَ رَهَائِنِ اَعْمَالِنَا اِلَى الْيَوْمِ الْمَشْهُوْدِ اِجْبِرْ عَبْدِكَ الضَّعِيْفَ عَلٰى مَا اَلَّفَ مِنَ الْعِصْمَةِ مِنَ الزَّالِ وَ وَقِفْهُ وَ الْحَاضِرِيْنَ لِصَالِحِ الْقَوْلِ وَ الْعَمَلِ وَ اَجْرِ عَلٰى لِسَانِهٖ مَا يَنْتَفِعُ بِهِ السَّامِعُ وَ قَلْنَا رَقَّ بِهِ الْمَدَامِعُ وَ يَلِيْنُ لَهُ الْقَلْبُ الْخَاشِعُ وَ اغْفِرْلَهُ وَ الِلْحَاضِرِيْنَ وَ لِجَمِيْعِ الْمُسْلِمِيْنَ

Sayyiduna Shaykh ʿAbd al-Razzāq al-Jilānī ﵁ states that the following had been included in one of his *du ʿās* which was recited in his *majlis*:

اللهم انا نعوذ بوصلك مِنْ صَدِّكَ وَ بقربك مِنْ طَرْدِكَ وَ بِقَبُوْلِكَ مِنْ رَدِّكَ وَ اجْعَلْنَا مِنْ اهل طاعتك وَ وُدِّكَ وَ اَهِّلْنَا لشكرك و حمدك

Sayyidī ʿAbd al-Razzāq al-Jilānī ﵁ states that his noble father would conclude his *du ʿā* with the following words:

جعلنا اللهُ وَ اِيَّاكُمْ مِمَّنْ تَنَبَّهَ لِخَلَاصِهٖ وَ تَنَزَّهَ عَنِ الدُّنْيَا وَ تَذَكَّرَهُ يومَ حَشْرِهٖ وَ اقْتَفٰى آثَارَ الصَّالِحِيْنَ اَنَّهٗ وَلِيُّ ذٰلِكَ وَ الْقَادِرُ عَلَيْهِ

I narrate from Shaykh Abu al-Fataḥ Aḥmad b. ʿAlī b. Ḥasan b. Aḥmad b. Muḥammad al-Hāshimī al-Qatfanī ﵀, who narrates from Shaykh Abu-Sulaymān Dāʿūd ﵀. He narrates from his father Shaykh Al-Fatḥa Sulaymān ﵀, who affirmed that he narrates from Sayyiduna Shaykh Abu-ʿAbdullāh ʿAbd al-Wah'hāb al-Jilānī ﵁, who confirmed that his noble father used to recline on his chair in the *majlis* and engage in the following recitation:

وَ رَضِيَ اللهُ عَنِ الرَّفِيْعِ الْعِمَّاءِ الطَّوِيلِ الْفَحَادِّ الْمُؤَيَّدِ بِالتَّحقيقِ الْمُكَنّٰى بِالْعَتِيْقِ الْخَلِيفَةِ الشَّفَقِ الْمُسْتَخْرَجِ مِنْ اَظْهَرِ اَصْلِ عَرِيْقِ الَّذِيْ اِسْمُهٗ مَعَ اِسْمِهٖ مَقْرُوْنٌ وَ جِسْمُهٗ مَعَ جِسْمِهٖ مَدْفُوْنٌ اَلَّذِيْ قَالَ فِيْ حَقِّهٖ

سَيِّدُ كُلِّ فَرِيْقٍ لَوْ كُنْتُ مُتَّخِذاً خَلِيْلاً غَيْرَ رَبِّيْ لَاتَّخَذْتُ اَبَابَكْرٍ اَلصِّدِّيْقِ رضى الله عنه وعَنِ الْقَصِيْرِ الْاَمَلِ
اَلْكَثِيْرِ الْعَمَلِ الَّذِيْ لَا يَتَدَاخَلُ اَفْعَالُهُ زَالُ الْمُؤَيَّدِ بِالصَّوَابِ اللّٰهم فَصْلُ الْخِطَابِ الْمَنْصُوْرِ يَوْمَ الْاَحْزَابِ
عُمَرَ بْنِ الْخَطَّابِ رضى الله عنه وعن مُشَيِّدِ الْاِيْمَانِ وَمُرَتِّلِ الْقرآنِ وَمُشَتِّتِ الْفُرْسَانِ وَمُضَعْضِعِ الطُّغْيَانِ
عثمانَ ابْنِ عَفَّانٍ رضى الله عنه اَفضلُ الشُّهَدَاءِ وَاَكْرَمُ الْكُرَمَاءِ ذِى النُّوْرَيْنِ رضى الله عنه وعَنِ الْبَطَلِ
الْمُهَوِّمِ وَزَوْجِ الْبَتُوْلِ وَسَيْفُ اللهِ الْمَسْلُوْلِ وَابْنِ عَمِّ الرَّسُوْلِ مَظْهَرِ الْعَجَائِبِ لَيْثُ بَنِيْ غَالِبٍ عَلِيٍّ بِنِ اَبِيْ
طَالِبٌ رضى الله عنه وعَنِ السِّبْطَيْنِ السَّيِّدَيْنِ الشَّهِيْدَيْنِ ابى محمدٍ الْحَسَنِ وَاَبِيْ عَبْدِ اللهِ الْحُسَيْنِ رضى الله
عنهما وعَنِ الْعَمَّيْنِ الشَّرِيْفَيْنِ حَمْزَةَ وَالْعَبَّاسِ وَعَنِ الْاَنْصَارِ وَالْمُهَاجِرِيْنَ وَالتَّابِعِيْنَ لَهُمْ بِاَحْسَانٍ اِلَى
يَوْمِ الدِّيْنِ آمين

The Majālis of Sayyiduna Ghawth al-Aᶜzam ﵁

The Jinns listened to his Discourses

I was informed by Shaykh Abu-Ḥasan ᶜAlī b. ᶜAbdullāh al-Abharī ﵀, who was informed by Shaykh Abu-Zakariyyah Yaḥyah b. Abī-Nasar b. ᶜUmar al-Baghdādī ﵀. He informed that he had heard from him his father, who stated that once he summoned the *Jinns* to an invocation, whereby they abnormally delayed in their coming. They then came and dictated to me: *'Do not call us when Sayyiduna Shaykh ᶜAbd al-Qādir ﵁ is delivering a lecture.'* I queried about their reason, and hence, to which they replied: *'We are present in his lectures.' 'Do you also go to his majlis?'* I questioned them further, and they affirmed: *'Yes! We are more in number than the humans who are present. There are many groups amongst us that embraced Islām and repented at his hands.'*

Garbs of Honour descends in the Majlis of the Ghawth ﵁

I narrate from Shaykh Abu-Muḥammad Ḥasan b. Zardād ﵀, who narrates from Shaykh Abu-Bakr Muḥammad b. al-Nuḥāl al-Muqrī ﵀ and he narrates from Shaykh Abu-Ḥafs ᶜUmar b. Ḥasīn b. Khalīl Tībī ﵀. He states that one day

Sayyiduna Ghawth al-Aʿzam Shaykh Muḥiyy al-Dīn al-Jilānī ﷺ asserted to him: *'Never be absent from my majlis, because garbs of honour are distributed therein. How unfortunate is he who misses out.'* Shaykh Abu-Ḥafs ﷺ affirmed: *'A long time had passed, and once I was present in the majlis and overcome by sleep. As I closed my eyes, I saw red and yellow garbs descending from the heavens and dropped onto the people who were present in the majlis. In excitement, I got up from my sleep and jumped up to inform the people in majlis about this occurrence.* Sayyiduna Ghawth al-Aʿzam ﷺ shouted at me and cautioned: *'O son! Observe silence. To be informed is different from that of witnessing.'*

I narrate from Shaykh Abu al-Maʿālī ʿAbd al-Raḥīm al-Qurashī ﷺ, who narrates from Shaykh Ḥāfiz Abu-ʿAbdullāh Muḥammad b. Najjār ﷺ. He narrates from Shaykh Muḥammad b. Abu al-Maʿālī b. Tībī ﷺ, who narrates from Sayyiduna Imām Abu-ʿAbdullāh Shaykh ʿAbd al-Wah'hāb ibn Shaykh al-Islām Muḥiyy al-Dīn al-Jilānī ﷺ. He states that he narrates from Shaykh Abu-Ḥafs ʿUmar b. Ḥusain b. Khalīl al-Tībī ﷺ.

I also narrate from an elevated chain, from Shaykh Abu-Muḥammad Ḥasan b. Zarrād ﷺ, who narrates from Shaykh Abu-Bakr Muḥammad b. Naḥāl ﷺ and he narrates from Shaykh Abu-Bakr ʿAbdullāh al-Tamīmī ﷺ. He narrates from Shaykh Abu-Ḥafs ʿUmar b. Ḥusain b. Khalīl al-Tībī ﷺ, who had pronounced that he attended the *majlis* of Sayyiduna Ghawth al-Aʿzam Muḥiyy al-Dīn al-Jilānī ﷺ and sat before him. I saw something, shaped like a crystal lantern; descending from the sky, until it reached the sacred mouth of Sayyiduna Ghawth ﷺ. It then quickly arose. This occurred three times. Hysterically, I stood up in order to inform the people of this astonishing occurrence that I had witnessed. Sayyiduna Ghawth ﷺ cautioned me hastily to sit down, because a *majlis* is governed by *amānah* [trust]. I quietly sat down and I refrained from disclosing this occurrence, until the demise of the great Ghawth ﷺ.

The Opening of the Knots

In the first chain which reaches out to Shaykh Najjār ﷺ; it is narrated from Shaykh Abu al-Taqā Ḥusain al-Ḥanbalī al-ʿĀqīrī ﷺ and he narrates from

Shaykh Yaḥyah b. Najāḥ Adīb ﷺ, who articulated that he formulated within his heart to witness how many poetic stanzas Sayyiduna Shaykh Muḥiyy al-Dīn ᶜAbd al-Qādir ؓ shall recite during his lecture. Hence, I took a piece of string and proceeded to the *majlis* of his lecture. I obscured the string under my clothes; and whenever the Ghawth ؓ recited a verse, I would make a knot as I was seated right at the back of the *majlis*. Instantaneously, I heard him revealing: *'I am opening the knots and you are tying them.'*

Spiritual Rapture [ḥāl] in his Majlis

I was informed by Shaykh Abu-ᶜAbdullāh Muḥammad b. Khiḍar al-Ḥusainī al-Mosulī ﷺ, who had proclaimed that he had heard his father testify that initially the Ghawth ؓ would speak on various sciences of knowledge and whatever he expressed, he would memorize it. As soon as Sayyiduna Ghawth al-Aᶜzam ؓ reclined to his chair, the entire *majlis* would be ensured with a reverential aura; where no one had the courage to cough, clean their noses or spit. The great Ghawth ؓ would then reinforce: *'Enough with words, now I shall address you in a state of ḥāl [spiritual state].'* As soon as he emphasized this, an awe-inspirational state of euphoria engulfed the audience, and they would transform into a state of spiritual ecstasy.

The Audience heard him equally from Near and Far

One of his charisma [*karāmat*] revealed that those who were sitting in his *majlis* faraway within the huge gathering heard him distinctly; similar to those who had sat close to him. He lectured in accordance to the condition of the hearts of the people, and focused on them with *kashf*. When he stood on his chair, everyone stood up owing to his resplendence. In the event, if he commanded them to be silent, they would consequently become so silent owing to his veneration. Apart from their breathing, nothing else would be noticed or heard. When anyone placed his hand on someone, he would only know that it is a hand by touching it, and not by viewing it, because all visions, comprising undivided attention were focused onto the Ghawth ؓ.

During the lecture, screams would be heard from the heavens. At times, voices were heard and a cloak would descend upon the *majlis* from the heavens. These would emanate from the *Rijāl al-Ghayb* and other unseen entities.

Being Aware of the condition of the Hearts

I narrate from Shaykh Abu al-Qāsim ʿUmar Baz'zār ﷺ, who narrates from Shaykh ʿĀlim Zāhid Abu al-Ḥasan Saʿād al-Khayr b. Muḥammad b. Sahl b. Saʿād al-Ansārī al-Andalūsī ﷺ, who had declared: 'I was present in 529 *hijrī* at the *majlis* of Sayyiduna Muḥiyy al-Dīn ʿAbd al-Qādir al-Jilānī ﷺ, and I was seated right at the back of the gathering. The Ghawth ﷺ was speaking on *zuhd* [asceticism], but my heart desired that he should speak on *Maʿārifah* [gnosis]. Immediately, he terminated speaking on *zuhd* and began with an address on *Maʿārifah*. I had never heard such an inspirational lecture before from anyone, pertaining to the topic of *Maʿārifah*. Henceforth, my heart desired that he should speak on *Shouq* [enthusiasm - zeal], and the Ghawth ﷺ terminated his discourse on *Maʿārifah* and began speaking about *shouq*. Never before had I heard any valid information presented to this effect on *shouq*. Thereafter, my heart desired that he should ensue with a discussion on *fana* [spiritual extinction] and *baqa* [permanence]. The Ghawth ﷺ diverted from the subject of *shouq* and spoke on the topic of *fana* and *baqa*. It was such an awe-inspirational speech, which I had not listened to before. Thereby, my heart desired that he should have spoken on *ghabat* [absence] and *ḥudūrī* [presence]. Astonishingly, the great Ghawth ﷺ deviated to this particular subject and rendered a stimulating explanation. Thereafter, he turned towards me and exclaimed: *'O Abu al-Ḥasan! Is this enough for you?'* When he posed this question, I became overwhelmed and uncontrollable, to the extent that I began tearing my clothes.

Everyone used be Present in the Majlis of the Ghawth ﷺ

I narrate from Shaykh Sāliḥ Abu-Muḥammad Aḥmad b. ʿAlī b. Yūsuf b. Ghassān al-Tamīmī al-Baghdādī ﷺ and he narrates from Shaykh Sharīf Abu-Hāshim

Akmal b. Masʿũd b. ʿUmar al-Hãshimĩ ﷺ. He narrates from the pious Shaykh Abu-Muḥammad ʿAfĩf b. Mubãrak Ḥusain b. Maḥmũd al-Jilĩ ﷺ, who stated that he had heard from Sayyiduna Ghawth al-Aʿzam Shaykh Muḥiyy al-Dĩn ʿAbd al-Qãdir al-Jilãnĩ ﷺ, whilst he was reclining onto his chair, and advocated: *'O my sons! When I ascend onto the Mimbar, do not delay your presence in the attendance of my majlis, because you shall achieve the following in my presence*:

- *Wilãyah* [Sainthood].
- High stations of excellence.
- Seekers of repentance must recite *'Bismillãh'* and attend my presence for forgiveness.
- Seekers of sincerity must recite *'Bismillãh'* and attend my presence at least once a week if they desire purity.
- If once a week attendance is not possible, then at least once a month.
- If once a month attendance is not possible, then at least once a year.
- If attendance once a year is not possible, then at least once in your lifetime. You will achieve numerous benefits in my presence.
- O *ʿUlama*! Undertake a thousand months of journey to be in my presence and listen to my words. When you come to my presence, empty yourself of all knowledge, excellence and status and honour so that you may take from me your share of status.
- Angels, *Awliya* and Men of the Unseen [*Rijãl al-Ghayb*] attend my gatherings for the sole purpose of learning the ethics of reverence in the Divine Presence of the Almighty *Allãh* ﷻ.
- Prophets of *Allãh* ﷻ bless my gatherings with their honourable presence.[265]

---

[265] The distorted belief system of the *Salafi Wahabi/Deo-Bandi* cults object to the spiritual presence of Prophets ﷺ and misconstrue this fact, and hence condemn the *Ahle-Sunnah* for elevating a non-Prophet above a Prophet. This inappropriate interpretation is out of sheer ignorance and mischief-making. The presence of Prophets in the *majlis* of the great Ghawth ﷺ does not imply that the Prophets ﷺ attended to learn from the Ghawth ﷺ, but they graced the *majlis* with blessings and render their support to the Ghawth ﷺ, similar to a father that provides support to his son in a gathering or event. Least do they realize that a non-Prophet is always dependant on a Prophet and will remain his subservient at all times.

There is no *Walĩ* on earth who does not attend my gathering. If he is alive, then he comes physically, but if he has transcended this transitory world physically; his soul thereby, certainly attends my *majlis*.[266]

The Garbs Burn

I narrate from Shaykh Faqĩh Sãliḥ Abu-Muḥammad Ḥasan b. Aḥmad b. ʿAlĩ al-Qurashĩ al-Waqũfĩ ﷺ and he narrates from the pious Shaykh Abu-Bakr Muḥammad b. ʿUmar b. Abĩ-Bakr b. Niḥãl al-Baghdãdĩ al-Muqrĩ ﷺ and he narrates from Ḥãfiz Abu-Zarʿã Tãhir b. Muḥammad b. Tãhir al-Maqdisĩ al-Dãrãnĩ ﷺ, who confessed: 'In 550 *hijrĩ*, I attended the *majlis* of Sayyiduna Shaykh Muḥiyy al-Dĩn ʿAbd al-Qãdir al-Jilãnĩ ﷺ, and had heard him declare:

> 'My words have the ears of those who attended my *majlis* from *Kohe Qãf*. Their feet are in the air, and their hearts are present within the Divine Presence. Soon their hats and mantles shall burn in the fervour of Almighty *Allãh* ﷻ.' When Shaykh ʿAbd al-Qãdir al-Jilãnĩ ﷺ issued this declaration in his *majlis*, his son, *Tãj al-ʿÃrifin*, Sayyid ʿAbd al-Razzãq al-Jilãnĩ ﷺ, was seated at the feet of his father, besides the *mimbar*. He lifted up his head and for a few moments, became awe-stricken and he befell unconscious onto the floor. When he fell, his clothes and turban burst into flames. The Ghawth ﷺ immediately descended from the *Mimbar* and extinguished the flames and enunciated:

---

[266] This also provides evidence that the bodies of beloved servants of *Allãh* ﷻ are preserved in their graves and they are alive as the *Ḥadith al-Sharĩf* propounds:

- الانبياء والاولياء احياء يصلون فى قبورهم كما يصلون فى بيوتهم

Prophets and the Awliya are alive and perform worship in their graves as they performed it in their homes.

[refer: *Sirr al-Asrãr fi ma yaḥtãj ilayhir Abrãr* also *Musnad al-Baz'zãr* vol. 2 page 283 narrated by Sayyiduna Anas ﷺ]

This nullifies the corrupt belief system of the *Salafi Wahabi/Deo-Bandi* that Prophets turn to dust after death in their graves. [Refer *Taqwiyat al-Imãm,* pg. 53, line no. 3, Publishers: Rasheed Company, Printers: Muhammadi Printing Press, Deoband. This book was written by the father of *Wahabism* in the Indo-Pak Sub-continent Molvĩ Ismãʿil Dehlawi and is published and promoted by the *Deo-Bandies*. They classify this as an authentic book which they use to promote their corrupt version of *Islãm*.

'ʿAbd al-Razzāq! You are also one of them.'

The narrator proclaims that upon the termination of the session, he inquired from Sayyiduna ʿAbdur-ʿRazzāq about his experience. He affirmed: *'When my illustrious father made that declaration, I looked up into the sky and saw a huge gathering of the Men of the Unseen [Rijāl al-Ghayb] standing patterned in absolute attention, as though they were enraptured by Divine Wonderment. Their clothes were on fire. Some of them were screaming, whilst others were in a state of spiritual euphoric delight; pinned to their places. Some were trembling in fear. There were some who were so overcome with the veneration of my father that they fell to the ground.'* Further, he deliberated that during the lecture of my father, we would hear screams from the ground and cloaks would fall onto the *majlis* from the heavens.

Order to be Obedient

I was informed by Shaykh Abu-Muḥammad ʿAbd al-Moḥsin b. ʿAbd al-Majīd b. ʿAbd al-Jabbār al-Ḥusainī al-Irbilī, who was informed by Shaykh Asal Abu al-Falāḥ Sanj b. Shaykh Khalīl Abu al-Khayr Karam b. Shaykh the leader, Abu-Muḥammad Mutir al-Bādrānī. He affirms that he was present, when his father Shaykh Mutir al-Bādrānī had passed on. I asked my father to advise me and he elucidated: *'Be obedient to Sayyiduna Shaykh ʿAbd al-Qādir al-Jilānī.'* I thought that he said this due to the pangs of sickness, then I remained silent for a while. Again I asked him to give me some advice as to who should we follow after him, he elucidated: *'Be obedient to Sayyiduna Shaykh ʿAbd al-Qādir al-Jilānī.'* Thereby, I remained silent for a while, and once more I requested my father for advice, and he repeated the same words and expounded: *'Oh son! In the era in which Shaykh ʿAbd al-Qādir is present, do not follow anyone else, except him.'*

When I arrived in Baghdād and attended the *majlis* of Sayyiduna Shaykh ʿAbd al-Qādir al-Jilānī, I observed that Shaykh Baqa b. Bat'tū, Shaykh Abu-Saʿīd al-Qaylawī Shaykh ʿAlī b. al-Hītī and other most senior *Mashā'ikh* were present. Thereafter, I heard the Ghawth assert: *'I am not like your lecturers. I am with you by the Command of Allāh ﷻ. My lectures are for those who are in the air.'* He then raised his head and looked up towards the heavens; and I also looked up, and saw rows of luminous men who were mounted onto illuminated horses. They were so many of them, that I could not see towards the heavens. All of them had their heads bowed in submission. Some of them were crying, whilst others were trembling. The clothes of some of them were in flames. After this observation, I experienced dizziness, and stood up and ripped my way through the people and reached the chair of the Ghawth ؓ. He seized me by my ear and exclaimed: *'O Karam! Was the first advice of your father to you not adequate for you?'* Consequently, I became terrified of him, that henceforth, I bowed my head onto the ground.

The Presence of Angels and Prophets ؑ in the Majlis

I narrate from Shaykh Abu-Saᶜād ᶜAbd al-Ghālib Aḥmad b. al-Hāshimī ؓ, who narrates from Shaykh Abu al-Ḥasan ᶜAlī b. Sulaymān ؓ the baker, and he verifies that he narrates from two persons, Shaykh ᶜImrān al-Kamyānī ؓ and Shaykh Abu al-Qāsim ᶜUmar b. Saᶜīd al-Baz'zār ؓ. Both of them revealed that they had heard Shaykh Abu-Saᶜīd al-Qaylawī ؓ relate as follows:

> I saw Sayyiduna wa Mawlāna Rasūlullāh ﷺ and the souls of other Prophets ؑ several times in the *majlis* of Sayyiduna Ghawth al-Aᶜzam ؓ. Verily, the Master peeps at the servant and indeed, the souls of Prophets ؑ encircle the earth, parallel to the air of its time. I have seen *Jinns* and the *Rijāl al-Ghayb* rushing for preference in the *majlis* of the Ghawth ؓ. I saw Sayyiduna Abu al-ᶜAbbās Nabī Khiḍar ؑ often visiting his *majlis*. I enquired from Sayyiduna Khiḍar ؑ, and he elucidated: *'Anyone who seeks success should become a servant at the majlis of the Ghawth,'*

Four Hundred ᶜUlama record the Lectures of the Ghawth ؓ

I was informed by Shaykh Abu al-Fataḥ Muḥammad b. Wahb b. Isḥāq b. Ibrāhīm Rabᶜī al-Basrī ؓ, and he was informed by Shaykh Abu-Sulaymān Dāᶜūd ؓ. He states that he had heard from his father, Shaykh Abu al-Fataḥ

Sulaymān ﷺ, who had heard his father Sayyiduna Shaykh Abu-ʿAbdullāh ʿAbd al-Wah'hāb al-Jilānī b. Sayyiduna Ghawth al-Aʿzam ﷺ proclaiming: *'My father delivered lectures 3 times a week, i.e. on a Friday morning, at his madrassa, in the evening of Tuesday, and on Sunday morning, on the outskirts [field or 'Eid-Gah].Continuously, there were Ulama and Mashā'ikh and others present during his lectures.'* The Ghawth ﷺ delivered lectures for 40 years and his first lecture started in 521 *hijrī* and concluded in 561 *hijrī.* He taught at his *madrassa* and had issued *fatwas* for 33 years, starting from 527 *hijrī* to 561 *hijrī.* A *Qārī* would always recite the Holy *Qur'ān*, before he commenced with a lecture. His recitation would be without melodious tunes, but with *tartīl*[267] and *tajwīd*[268]. One of the *Qārīs* from his *majlis* was Shaykh Sharīf Abu al-Fataḥ Masʿūd b. ʿUmar al-Hāshmī al-Qārī ﷺ. Owing to the intensity of his spiritual radiation, two or three people used to pass on during his lectures. Four hundred erudite ʿ*Ulama* would record his lectures and at times, he would take steps in the air and thereafter, he would return to his seat.

The Ghawth ﷺ would weep when listening to the holy Qur'ān

I was informed by Shaykh Abu-Muḥammad Ḥasan b. ʿAbd al-Raḥmān b. Zardād ﷺ, who had heard from Shaykh Abu-Bakr Muḥammad b. Naḥāl ﷺ and he had heard from Shaykh Abu-Bakr ʿAbdullāh Nasar al-Tamīmī ﷺ. He asserted that he had heard from Shaykh Sharīf Abu al-Fataḥ al-Hāshmī al-Muqrī ﷺ, affirming that Sayyiduna Ghawth al-Aʿzam ﷺ summoned him to recite the *Qur'ān*. 'When I began reciting, he began weeping and articulated to me: *'By Allāh! I will certainly request you [for myself] from Almighty Allāh ﷻ.'*

The Door of Jannah opens

The same narrator testifies that a *Walī* of *Allāh* ﷻ stood up and pronounced: *'Oh Master! I saw Allāh ﷻ in my dream and the doors of Jannah were opened. A*

[267] Recitation in a slow measured rhythmic tone.
[268] The laws of reciting the holy *Qur'ān* correctly.

chair was positioned for you, and there was a command for you to lecture. You declared that you shall lecture, when Sharīf Muqrī [Sharīf Abu al-Fataḥ al-Hāshmī *Muqrī] shall come. It was then decreed to you, that he has come; and you stated that now I shall lecture.'*

One Hundred Thousand Sinners and Vagabonds repent

I narrate from Shaykh Abu al-Maʿālī ʿAbd al-Raḥīm b. Muzaffar al-Qurashī ﷺ, who narrates from Shaykh Ḥāfiz Abu-ʿAbdullāh b. Najjār ﷺ, stating that Shaykh ʿAbdullāh al-Jānī ﷺ wrote a letter to him from which he quoted. He writes that he had heard Sayyiduna Shaykh Muḥiyy al-Dīn ʿAbd al-Qādir ﷺ declare:

> My heart's desire is that I should remain, similar to my initial state, when I was alone in the jungles, engaged in worship so that no one sees me, and nor do I see them. But *Allāh* ﷻ ordained that people should benefit from me. More than five hundred Christians and Jews embraced *Islām* at my hands, and one hundred thousand evil, uncouth and loafers repented at my hands. Indeed! This is a great virtue.

The Rafḍī [Shiʿā] repent

I was informed by Shaykh Abu-Muḥammad Aḥmad b. Sāliḥ b. Ḥasan al-Tamīmī al-Bādrānī ﷺ and he had heard from Shaykh Abu al-Ḥasan al-Baghdādī ﷺ, who was well known as the sock merchant. He had heard from Shaykh ʿUmar al-Kamimānī ﷺ, who had confirmed that the *majlis* was never devoid of Christians and Jews, who were embracing *Islām*. Robbers were repenting, and *Rafḍīs* were repenting by retracting their inappropriate beliefs.

The Monk of Yemen embraces Islām

A monk appeared in the *majlis* of the Ghawth ﷺ, and embraced *Islām* at his hands. Thereafter, he informed the people that he was a resident of Yemen, and since *Islām* took roots into his heart, it henceforth, became firm. As a result he made up his mind to embrace *Islām* at the hands of that person, who was the best from the people of Yemen. He sat and, whilst contemplating upon his intention thus, fell asleep. He dreamt of Sayyiduna Nabī ʿĪsā ﷺ, who revealed to him: *'Oh Sinān! Go to Baghdād and embrace Islām at the hands of Shaykh ʿAbd al-Qādir Jilī, because he is presently the best person on this earth.'*

A Voice from the Unseen

It is stated that once 13 Christians arrived at the *majlis* and embraced *Islām* at his hands. They deliberated: *'We are Christians from the East and we had intended to revert to Islām, but there were some reservations about where we should proceed to, in order to embrace Islām. An unknown voice then called out to us and we could not see the caller. It dictated: 'Oh successful group! Go to Baghdād and become a Muslim at the hands of Shaykh ʿAbd al-Qādir, because you shall entrench Imān into your hearts through his blessings, which you shall not find elsewhere.'*

Pandemonium in the Majlis

I narrate from Shaykh Sāliḥ Abu-ʿAbdullāh Muḥammad b. Kāmil b. Abu al-Maʿālī b. Muḥammad Ḥusain al-Bayānī, who narrates from Shaykh ʿĀrif Abu-Muḥammad Mafraj b. Binhān b. Rakāf al-Shaybānī al-Bayānī ﷺ, who asserted that when Sayyiduna Shaykh Muḥiyy al-Dīn ʿAbd al-Qādir al-Jilānī ﷺ was pronounced as renowned; one hundred distinguished *Faqih* [jurists] and erudite scholars met in Baghdād with the intention of questioning the Ghawth ﷺ on matters pertaining to various sciences. Each one's question was different from the others. They intended to defeat and curb the Ghawth ﷺ. At a collective level, they came to the *majlis* during his lecture. I was also present there on that day. When the *majlis* convened, Sayyiduna Ghawth ﷺ had immersed into *murāqabah* and a light flashed out from his chest. Only those people could perceive this light, whom *Allāh* ﷻ had ordained to perceive. This light conceded the chests of the hundred *Faqihs* and as it conceded them, they became overwhelmed and nervous. All of them thereby, began screaming, whilst tearing their clothes, and threw away their hats, thus, becoming bare-headed. They proceeded to the chair of the Ghawth ﷺ and placed their heads at his feet. This caused an enormous turmoil within the *majlis*. The noise developed into intensive loudness, that I thought that the whole city of Baghdād would hear it. Thereafter, Sayyiduna Shaykh ﷺ embraced each one of them, till the last one and stipulated to them: *'This was your question and this is your answer.'* He relayed each of the hundred person's questions and answered every one of them.

When the *majlis* terminated, I approached those *Faqihs* and enquired from them about their condition. They affirmed: *'When we entered the majlis and sat down, we forgot all the knowledge we possessed, and felt as if we never knew anything. Afterwards, when Sayyiduna Shaykh ﷺ embraced us, all our deleted knowledge was returned to our chests. He answered all those questions, which we came with to put forth to him in such a modus that we did not even have the knowledge of.'*

The State of Engrossment [istighrāq] on his Seat

I narrate from Shaykh Sharīf Abu-ʿAbdullāh Muḥammad b. Khiḍar b. ʿAbdullāh al-Ḥusainī al-Mosulī ﷺ, who states that he had heard that Shaykh ʿĀrif Abu al-Qāsim Muḥammad b. Aḥmad b. ʿAlī al-Joh'nī ﷺ, asserting that he used to sit at the bottom of the pulpit [*mimbar*] of Sayyiduna Shaykh ﷺ. He had *naqībs* [escorts - guards] and two of them sat on two steps of his pulpit. Similarly, only those persons could sit close to him who were either *Awliya* or people with perfect spiritual ranking. The ones, who sat below his *mimbar* were the glorious *Awliya*; who possessed a powerful veneration, similar to a lion. Once the great Ghawth ﷺ immersed into a state of engrossment; whilst reclining on his chair, to the extent that one end of his *ʿamāmah* [turban] opened up, of which he payed no attention to. Upon witnessing this, the entire audience took off their turbans and hats and threw it under his chair. When he terminated his lecture, he instructed me: *'O Abu al-Qāsim! Return the turbans and hats to the people.'* I returned it to them. However, one head gear remained behind of which I had no knowledge, as to whom it belonged. Yet, all of them in the *majlis* received their hats or turbans. Sayyiduna Ghawth ﷺ requested for the head gear and placed it on his shoulder and thereafter, it vanished. I was astonished at this scenario, and when he descended from his seat, he placed his hand on my shoulder, and elucidated: *'A prop was placed on my hand.'* Furthermore, he continued in declaring: *'O Abu al-Qāsim! When the audience removed their turbans, one of my sisters in Asfahān also removed her head gear and threw it away. When I returned the turbans and hats to the audience, and placed her head gear on my shoulder, she stretched out her hand from Asfahān and procured it.'*

The ᶜUlama and Mashā'ikh attended the Majlis

I narrate from Shaykh Sharīf Abu al-ᶜAbbās Aḥmad b. Shaykh Abu-ᶜAbdullāh Muḥammad b. Azharī al-Ḥusainī ﷺ, who had heard his father, proclaiming that the senior *Mashā'ikh* of Irāq, the illustrious *'Ulama* and the chief *Muftī* attended the *majlis*. Amongst them were the following:

- ✓ Shaykh Baqa b. Bat'tū ﷺ
- ✓ Shaykh Abu-Saᶜīd al-Qaylawī ﷺ
- ✓ Shaykh ᶜAlī b. al-Hītī ﷺ
- ✓ Shaykh Najīb al-Dīn ᶜAbd al-Qāhir al-Sohrowardī ﷺ
- ✓ Shaykh Mājid al-Kurdī ﷺ
- ✓ Shaykh Abī-Ḥakīm b. Dinār ﷺ
- ✓ Shaykh Mutir al-Bāzrānī ﷺ
- ✓ Qāḍī Abu-Yaᶜhlā b. Farā ﷺ
- ✓ Qāḍī Abu al-Ḥasan ᶜAlī b. Dāmghānī ﷺ
- ✓ Imām Abu al-Fataḥ b. Muntahā ﷺ etc....

In Baghdād, there was no illustrious Shaykh, who did not attend his *majlis*. I have never witnessed Shaykh ᶜAbd al-Raḥmān al-Tafsunjī ﷺ enter Baghdād; but I observed him many a time in Tafsunj, seated for quite long periods and used to verbalize that he was seated quietly, because he had only desired to listen clearly to the words of Shaykh ᶜAbd al-Qādir ﷺ. I have also observed Shaykh ᶜAdī b. Musāfir ﷺ many a time in Lalish,[269] who used to come out of his room and proceed towards the mountain. He would then sketch a circle onto the ground and would herald: *'Anyone who wishes to hear the words of*

[269] This city is in the North of Irāq, approximately 550 km from Baghdād.

Shaykh ʿAbd al-Qādir, should come inside this circle.' Thus, his senior *murīds* would enter into that circle, and would listen to the lecture of the Ghawth ﷺ; whilst documenting it with its current date. When they arrived in Baghdād, they would meet with those, who had documented the speech on that day, and would compare it to their notes. It used to be identical. When Shaykh ʿAdī b. Musāfir ﷺ entered the circle on the mountains of Lalish and viewed the *majlis* of Sayyiduna Ghawth al-Aʿzam ﷺ in Baghdād, Sayyiduna Ghawth ﷺ would inform the audience at his *majlis* that Shaykh ʿAdī b. Musāfir's eyes are amongst them. The author, Imām Shatnūfī ﷺ elaborates at the beginning of the book, whereby Sayyiduna Ghawth al-Aʿzam ﷺ declared: *'My foot is on the neck of all the Awliya.'* A conscientious consideration of this declaration is sufficient. Almighty *Allāh* ﷻ is the Master ﷻ of guidance.

Green Birds in the Lecture

I narrate from Shaykh Abu-ʿAbdullāh Muḥammad b. Aḥmad b. Manzūr ﷺ, who had heard Shaykh Abu-ʿAbdullāh Muḥammad b. Abī al-Fataḥ al-Hirwī ﷺ affirm that he was present with Sayyiduna Ghawth al-Aʿzam ﷺ, whilst he was delivering a lecture. He was deeply engrossed in the discourse and said: *'If Allāh ﷻ Wills, He can send green birds to listen to my words, and for Him this is possible.'* Before he could complete his words, a charming green bird approached, and entered his sleeve, and hence, did not come out.

One day, whilst he was delivering a lecture, some of the people resumed to be lazy. He observed this and confirmed: *'If Allāh ﷻ Wills, He can send green birds to listen to my words, and this is possible for Him.'* Before he could complete his words, masses of green birds filled up the *majlis* and everyone who were present, witnessed this occurrence.

A Bird falls in Pieces

The narrator states that one day the Ghawth ﷺ was speaking on the *Qudrat* [power] of Almighty *Allāh* ﷻ and an aura of reverence engulfed the audience.

An amazing bird then flew over the *majlis*. Some people in the *majlis* were distracted from the discourse of Sayyiduna Shaykh ﷺ in order to view this amazing bird. He then asserted: *'By the honour of my Lord ﷻ! If I desire and dictate to this bird to die and shred into pieces, it will instantly die.'* Sayyiduna Ghawth ﷺ did not complete his words, and that bird tore into pieces and fell onto the ground.

The Audience began Screaming

I narrate from Shaykh Abu al-Ḥasan ʿAlī b. Yaḥyah b. Abu al-Qāsim al-Azjī ﷺ, who narrates from Qāḍī al-Quḍāt Sayyiduna Shaykh Abu-Sāliḥ Nasar al-Jilānī ﷺ. He states that he had heard his uncle Sayyiduna Shaykh Abu-ʿAbdullāh ʿAbd al-Wah'hāb al-Jilānī ﷺ reveal:

> I travelled to the non-Arab cities and acquired various sciences of knowledge. When I returned to Baghdād, I suggested to my father ﷺ that I would like to lecture to the people. He consented, and I sat on the chair [*mimbar*] and lectured to the people in sciences to the degree which *Allāh* ﷻ had ordained for me. My illustrious father ﷺ also listened to my lecture, but it did not have an impact on a single person. Nor did my lecture soften their hearts or brought tears to their eyes. Henceforward, the audience requested my father to deliver a lecture. I descended from the chair and my father reclined on it, and pronounced: '*Yesterday I was fasting, and Yaḥyah's mother fried some eggs and put them into a bowl and placed the bowl into a clay container. A cat came and dropped the container onto the floor, and it broke.*' After he verbalized this, the audience began screaming. I questioned my noble father about the reason for their screaming and he professed: '*O my son! You were proud of your journey that you travelled here and there [pointing his finger towards the heavens in different directions]. O my son! When I sat on the chair to speak, then a lustre from Almighty Allāh ﷻ beamed onto my heart, which expanded my heart with knowledge. It is then that I articulated those words, which you had heard that was clear, and dominated by esteem. That, then happened which you had noticed.*'

I descended from my father's chair and he reclined onto it and enunciated: *'Oh seekers of bravery! Observe patience for a moment.'* Upon hearing these words, everyone present in the *majlis* began screaming. I enquired from my honourable father with regard to this demeanour and he replied: *'You speak from within yourself, and I speak from the inner of the heart of the people.'*

When anyone posed a question to the great Ghawth ﷺ within the *majlis*, he often replied: *'I will first seek permission from Allāh ﷻ and then exercise fidelity.'* He would then bow his sacred head in *murāqabah*, and his reverential awe would manifest in his dignity. He would then speak on that subject which *Allāh* ﷻ had ordained.

The narrator states that Sayyiduna Ghawth ﷺ would also confess: *'I procure an oath by the honour of my Lord ﷻ, that until it is not dictated to me: 'I dedicate to you the allegiance of My Rights! Lecture to the people. I have protected you from rejection.'* I would not lecture until this is not delegated to me. It is also declared to me: *'O ʿAbd al-Qādir! Deliver the lecture for you would be given a listening.'*

The Manifestation of Lordly Lustres

I narrate from Shaykh Abu al-Ḥasan ʿAlī b. Azmard ﷺ, who narrates from Shaykh Sāliḥ Baqiyat al-Salf Abu al-ʿAbbās Aḥmad b. Yūsuf ʿAlī al-Takhmī Nahar-Malikī ﷺ and he states that he had heard from Shaykh Baqa b. Bat'tū ﷺ as follows:

> 'Once I attended the *majlis* of Sayyiduna Shaykh ʿAbd al-Qādir al-Jilānī ﷺ who was seated on the second step of the mimbar, whilst delivering a lecture. I noticed that the first step on the upper had expanded in size, to a great extent that which the eye could perceive, and it was covered with exquisite green silk. I observed that Sayyiduna wa Mawlāna Rasūlullāh ﷺ, Sayyiduna Abu-Bakr as-Siddīq ﷺ, Sayyiduna ʿUmar al-Fārūq ﷺ and Sayyiduna ʿUthmān al-Ghanī ﷺ were seated on it. *Allāh's* ﷻ *Tajallī* [lustre] beamed onto the heart of Sayyiduna Ghawth ﷺ. He bowed so low that he was about to fall; and Sayyiduna Rasūlullāh ﷺ

clasped him in his sacred arms. Had the Messenger of *Allāh* ﷺ not clasped him, he would have fallen. Thereafter, he began to decrease in size, until he shrunk to the size of a little bird. Henceforth, he swelled up, being huge and frightening in size, and thereafter, everything was concealed from my vision.

It is believed that Shaykh Baqa b. Bat'tū ﵀ was questioned about the vision of Sayyiduna Rasūlullāh ﷺ and the *Saḥābah*, to which he replied: *'Their consecrated souls were in the form of humans and Allāh ﷻ grants them the power by which they manifest in this image. Almighty Allāh ﷻ observes them with His Divine Power and their images appear in the physical form, which can be perceived with the eye. The Ḥadith, pertaining to the Meʿrāj is a proof of this.'* He was questioned further about the decrease and increase of Sayyiduna Ghawth ﵁ in size, to which he replied: *'The first lustre that beamed upon the Ghawth ﵁ was of that quality on which, initially no work is stable without Prophetic acknowledgement and support. Therefore, if Sayyiduna Rasūlullāh ﷺ had not mediated and held Sayyiduna Ghawth ﵁, he would have fallen down. The beloved Prophet ﷺ aiding him is proof of his Prophetic support and acknowledgement. The second lustre was of the quality of Jalāl [glory - temperamental] by the virtue of close connection. Therefore he shrunk in size. The third lustre was of the quality of Jamāl [beauty, love] by the virtue of mushāhidah [observance], therefore, he swelled in size [in happiness]. This is the Mercy of Allāh ﷻ which He ﷻ bestows upon whom He ﷻ ordains. Almighty Allāh ﷻ is most Bounteous.'*

An Iron Spike sinks in the Foot

I narrate from Shaykh Abu al-Makārim Khalīfa b. Muḥammad b. ʿAlī al-Ḥarrānī ﵀, who narrates from Shaykh Abu-Tālib ʿAbd al-Latīf b. Muḥammad al-Qutbī al-Ḥarrānī ﵀. He narrates from Abu al-Faḍal Aḥmad b. Qāsim b. ʿAbdān al-Qurashī al-Baghdādī Baz'zār ﵀ who professed:

Sayyiduna Ghawth al-Aʿzam Shaykh ʿAbd al-Qādir al-Jilānī ﵁ wore a *chadar* [mantle] and the garb of the *ʿUlama*. He wore expensive clothing.

In 558 *hijrī*, his *Khādim* approached me with some gold sovereigns and requested for material that would not cost less than one *dinār* for a yard. The cost must not be more or less than this stipulated price. I supplied it to him and queried about who this fabric was for? He affirmed that it was for his master Sayyiduna Muḥiyy al-Dīn Shaykh ʿAbd al-Qādir al-Jilānī ﷺ. I contemplated within my heart, that the Shaykh had not left any fabric behind for the *Khalīfah*. My contemplation was not complete within my heart; when I discovered that a spike pierced into my foot from nowhere. Owing to the severe pain, it could perceive death. People rushed and tried to pull the spike out of my foot, but failed. I appealed to them to carry me to Sayyiduna Ghawth al-Aʿzam ﷺ. As soon as they placed me in the presence of Sayyiduna Shaykh ﷺ, he asserted to me: *'Why do you criticise me within your heart? I procure an oath by the honour of my Lord ﷻ that I do not wear any clothes, until I am commanded: 'I procure to you the oath of My Rights! Dawn that garb whose fabric is not less than one dinār.' O Abu al-Faḍal! This fabric is kafan [shroud] and the kafan of a deceased is to be seemly. This is after a thousand deaths.'* Sayyiduna Ghawth ﷺ then caressed my foot with his sacred hand and the spike disappeared, together with the tormenting pain. Thereafter, I could not recall where that spike had come from, and where it had disappeared to. I began walking normally. Sayyiduna Shaykh ﷺ declared to me: *'Your comment on me appeared as a spike.'*

Answer to his Sneeze

I narrate from Shaykh Abu-Muḥammad Rajab b. Abī al-Mansūr al-Rāzī ﷺ and Shaykh Abu-Zayd ʿAbd al-Raḥmān b. Sālim b. Aḥmad al-Qurashī ﷺ. They state that they were informed by two *Shuyūkh*, Qāḍī al-Quḍāt Sayyiduna Shaykh Abu-Sāliḥ Nasar al-Jilānī ﷺ and Shaykh Abu al-Ḥasan ʿAlī ﷺ the baker. Sayyidī Abu-Sāliḥ ﷺ confesses that he had heard from his father, Sayyiduna Shaykh ʿAbd al-Razzāq al-Jilānī ﷺ and Shaykh Abu al-Ḥasan ﷺ affirms that he had heard from Shaykh ʿUmar Baz'zār ﷺ and he had heard from Shaykh, the ʿĀlim Abu-Isḥāq Ibrāhīm b. Saʿīd al-Daldī al-Thalabī al-Ḥanbalī ﷺ in

Damascus. All of them verify that Sayyiduna Shaykh Muḥiyy al-Dīn ʿAbd al-Qādir ﷺ wore the clothes of the *Ulama* and a mantle [*chadar*]. He rode on a mule and a standard was raised in front of him when he rode. He sat on a large chair [*mimbar* - pulpit] when he delivered his lectures. His words were authoritative, clear and precise. Everyone was attentive to his speech, and when he spoke, there prevailed absolute silence. When he issued any command, people would hasten to comply with his command. In the event of a hard-hearted person who perceived him, his heart would melt. If you had observed his astonishing personality, it would have been as though you had viewed everyone else. When he walked to the *Jāmeʿh Masjid*, people in the market place would stand up in his honour, and make *duʿās* to *Allāh* ﷻ on his behalf for their desires to come to fruition. His voice was soothing, authoritative, clear and silencing. He sneezed one *Jumʿāh* in the *masjid* and everyone replied to his sneeze. The reply from the voices of the people echoed in the *masjid – may Allāh* ﷻ *have mercy on you and owing to you, have mercy on us.* The ruler of Baghdād, Khalīfah Mustanjid Billāh was in a room attached to the *masjid* and he enquired as to what the uproar was all about. He was informed that Sayyiduna Shaykh Muḥiyy al-Dīn ʿAbd al-Qādir ﷺ sneezed and the people responded to his sneeze.

The Awe of the great Ghawth ﷺ

I was informed by Shaykh Abu al-Ḥasan ʿAlī b. Azdamar al-Muḥammadī ﷺ, who had heard from Shaykh Abu al-Ḥasan ʿAlī b. Muḥammad b. Aḥmad al-Baghdādī Sūfī ﷺ prominently known as Saqqa, who alluded to the fact that Sayyiduna Shaykh ʿAbd al-Qādir ﷺ was an extremely awe-inspiring and impressive person. When Sayyiduna Shaykh ʿAbd al-Qādir ﷺ gazed at anyone, he would tremble with fear owing to his charismatic personality. When he reclined to his seat, people would gaze at him with the side of their eye, as though they were peeping at a lion. These were the people, who would hasten in obedience to his commands.

The Excellence of his Companions and their Glad-tidings

I was informed by Shaykh Abu-Muḥammad Sālim b. ʿAlī b. ʿAbdullāh al-Dimyātī Sūfī ﷺ, who was informed in Baghdād by Shaykh Sāliḥ Abu al-Ḥasan ʿAlī b. Muḥammad b. Aḥmad al-Baghdādī ﷺ, distinguished as Ibn Ḥamāmī. Shaykh Abu al-Ḥasan ʿAlī the baker ﷺ and Shaykh Abu-ʿAmar ʿUthmān ﷺ, prominently known as *Qas'sīr.*[270] Both were present and listening to Shaykh Ibn Ḥamāmī who affirmed that in 558 *hijrī*, he had dreamt about the river of Damascus. In those days, when I was a child, I observed that all the water had transformed into blood and puss. Its fishes had transformed into snakes and worms, and they had expanded in size. I became fearful that they may not harm me and rushed home. Eventually, I reached home safely. When I entered my home, I caught sight of a person, who had presented to me a hand fan, and had requested me to hold onto it tightly. I stated to him that the fan would not be able to raise me, and he replied: '*Your Imān shall raise you.*' I held onto one corner of the fan; and I observed that I was with that person on a platform at my home and thus, my fear had disappeared. I issued a confession to that person: '*I procure to you the oath of that Lord ﷻ who granted His favour upon me through you! Who are you?*' He replied: '*I am your Prophet Muḥammad ﷺ.*'

I trembled in view of the Holy Prophet's ﷺ luminosity and henceforth, pleaded to him: '*Oh Messenger of Allāh ﷺ! Please supplicate to Allāh ﷻ for me, to be steadfast on the Holy Qur'ān and your Sunnah, and I shall die for and with it.*' The Messenger of *Allāh* ﷺ assured: '*Yes [you would] and your Shaykh is Shaykh ʿAbd al-Qādir.*' Thrice, He ﷺ repeated this declaration.

When I awoke from my sleep, I informed my father about my dream. We departed to meet with Sayyiduna Ghawth al-Aʿzam ﷺ. It was on that particular day, that he had delivered his lecture on the field. We reached his *majlis*, whilst he was delivering his speech. We could not proceed close to him, owing to the massive crowd; and as a result we occupied the seats at the back of the

---

[270] *Qasīr* denotes being very short in height.

majlis. No sooner we had sat down, the great Ghawth ﷺ discontinued with his lecture and whilst pointing towards us, he dictated: *'Bring these two people to me.'* Actually, my father and I climbed over the shoulders of the people, and were brought to the chair of the Ghawth ﷺ.

Sayyiduna Shaykh ﷺ called for my father and he presented himself, whilst I stood behind him. He asserted to my father: *'O fool! You did not come to me without proof.'* Thereafter, he grasped his *kurta* [upper long shirt like garb] and placed it onto my father, and thereby, placed his mantle which he had been wearing on his head, onto me. My father noticed that the *kurta*, which was placed onto him, was upside down. When he intended to straighten it, he was advised to exercise patience, until the people had departed.

Upon the termination the *majlis*, Sayyiduna Ghawth ﷺ ascended from his chair. My father intended to wear the *kurta* appropriately, within the tumult of the departing people; but was astonished when he perceived that the *kurta* was already positioned appropriately onto his body. By witnessing this miraculous occurrence, my father had fainted, and the people were perturbed. Sayyiduna Ghawth ﷺ commanded that my father should be brought to him. When we proceeded to Sayyiduna Ghawth ﷺ, we were alarmed to find him seated on the *Qubba* [dome] of the *Awliya*. There was a dome in one portion of the guest house, which became well-known as *Qubba-e-Awliya*; because very often *Awliya* and *Rijāl al-Ghayb* were housed there, whenever they arrived in order to visit Sayyiduna Ghawth al-Aʿzam ﷺ.

Sayyiduna Ghawth ﷺ proclaimed to my father: *'He whose guide is Sayyiduna Rasūlullāh ﷺ and his Shaykh is ʿAbd al-Qādir, then why would there be no charisms [karāmat] in such a person? And this is your karāmat [charism].'* Thereafter, he requested for a pen and inkpot and wrote out the certificates of the *khirqah* [*khilāfah*] for us.

I was informed by Shaykh Sharīf Abu-ʿAbdullāh Muḥammad b. Shaykh Abu al-ʿAbbās Ḥāḍar b. ʿAbdullāh al-Ḥusainī al-Mosulī ﷺ and he was informed by his father who had heard in 551 *hijrī* in Baghdād from the leader, Shaykh Abu an-Najīb ʿAbd al-Qāhir b. ʿAbdullāh al-Sohrowardī ﷺ. He had heard from The Shaykh of noble descent Abu-Muḥammad ʿAbd al-Latīf b. Shaykh Abu an-Najīb ʿAbd al-Qāhir b. ʿAbdullāh al-Sohrowardī Faqih Sūfī ﷺ, who stated that his father had informed him that every night, a buzzing sound similar to that of a honey bee was heard emanating from Sayyiduna Shaykh Ḥammād b. Muslim al-Dabbās ﷺ. In 580 *hijrī* his *murīds* requested Sayyiduna Shaykh ʿAbd al-Qādir al-Jilānī ﷺ to enquire from Shaykh Ḥammād ﷺ about that sound, which they had heard emanating from him. In those days, Sayyiduna Shaykh ʿAbd al-Qādir ﷺ was living with Shaykh Ḥammād ﷺ. He queried from him and Shaykh Ḥammād ﷺ replied: *'I have twelve thousand murīds and every night I take into account, each one's name. If anyone of them needs anything from Allāh ﷻ, I plead for it on their behalf. If any of my murīd commits a sin, then a month does not pass by; either he dies or repents for his sins. I do this out of fear, in order that he does not become a habitual sinner, and nor does his sins increase.'*

Then Sayyiduna Shaykh ʿAbd al-Qādir al-Jilānī ﷺ said: *'If Almighty Allāh ﷻ gives me this status, I shall then enter into a pact with the Glorified Lord ﷻ that till Qiyāmah, my murīds shall not die, unless they have repented; and that I shall be present during this event of theirs.'* Henceforward, Shaykh Ḥammād ﷺ asserted: *'Allāh ﷻ has made me a witness to this, that soon you shall be given this status, and the shade of your status shall be covering them [your murīds].'*

Jannah for up till Seven Generations

I narrate from Shaykh Abu-Muḥammad ʿAbd al-Wāḥid b. Sāliḥ b. Yaḥyah al-Qurashī al-Baghdādī ﷺ, who narrates from Shaykh Muḥiyy al-Dīn Abu-ʿAbdullāh Muḥammad b. ʿAlī ﷺ well recognized as Tawḥīdī, who stated in Baghdād that he had heard from his maternal uncle, *Qāḍī al-Quḍāt* Sayyiduna Shaykh Abu-Sāliḥ Nasar al-Jilānī ﷺ, who narrates from his illustrious father Sayyiduna Tāj al-Dīn Shaykh ʿAbd al-Razzāq al-Jilānī ﷺ and Shaykh Abu al-Qāsim Haybatullāh ﷺ distinguished as Ibn al-Mansūrī. His maternal uncle affirmed that he had heard from his father, Sayyiduna ʿAbd al-Razzāq al-Jilānī and his other uncle, Sayyiduna ʿAbd al-Wah'hāb al-Jilānī concur that they had heard Shaykh Qāsim assert that the three *Shuyūkh* had informed him, Shaykh Abu al-Saʿūd al-Ḥarīmī, Shaykh Abu-ʿAbdullāh Muḥammad b. Qā'id al-Awānī and Shaykh Abu al-Qāsim ʿUmar Baz'zār. The three of them declared that Sayyiduna Shaykh Muḥiyy al-Dīn ʿAbd al-Qādir al-Jilānī is a guarantee for his *murīds* till *Qiyāmah*. None of them shall die without making *toubah* [repenting] for their sins. Sayyiduna Ghawth was accorded a promise, that for the duration of seven generations, his *murīds* shall die in a state of repentance, and shall enter *Jannah*.

Concealing the Faults of the Murīd

Sayyiduna Ghawth al-Aʿzam confirmed:

> I am responsible for every single matter pertaining to my *murīd* as well as the *murīd* of my *murīd* for the duration of seven generations. In the event that, clothes of my *murīd* falls off in the east and I am in the west, I shall cover him. I am commanded according to conditions and destiny, and I protect my *murīds* from destructions with my courage. Glad-tidings and fortune for those who saw me, or saw those who saw me. I grieve for those who did not see me.

Representation in the Divine Court of Allāh

I narrate from Shaykh Abu al-ʿAqāf Mūsā b. Abu al-Maʿālī ʿUthmān b. Mūsā al-Baqāʿī al-Damishqī, who asserts that his father states in Damascus that he narrates in Baghdād from Shaykh Sāliḥ Abu-Muḥammad Dāʿūd b. ʿAlī b. Aḥmad al-Baghdādī popularly known as Ba-Fanda. He testifies that in 548 *hijrī* he had dreamt of Sayyiduna Shaykh Maʿrūf al-Karkhī, and people were presenting their requests to him and he was forwarding them to the Divine Precincts of *Allāh*. Shaykh Maʿrūf then expressed to me: *'Request your desire so that I may present it to Allāh.'* I questioned: *'Is my Shaykh, [Shaykh ʿAbd al-Qādir al-Jilānī] demoted or dismissed?'* He verified: *'No, never, by Allāh*

ﷻ, *he is not dismissed.'* In the morning when I arose, I advanced to the *madrassa* of Sayyiduna Ghawth al-Aᶜzam ﷺ, and sat down at the door so that I could inform him about my dream. Before I could catch sight of him or speak to him, he disclosed to me from the inside of his room: *'O Dāᶜūd! Your Shaykh is not dismissed, and nor shall he be dismissed. Forward your request to me, so that I may present it to Allāh ﷻ. I procure an oath on Allāh ﷻ that there was never a time, that I presented a request of my murīd or anyone else that the request was rejected.'*

The Blessings of his Duᶜā and Garb

I narrate from Shaykh Abu al-Futūḥ Nasrullāh b. Abu al-Muḥās Yūsuf b. Khalīl b. ᶜAlī al-Baghdādī al-Azjī ﷺ, and he narrates in Baghdād from Shaykh Abu al-ᶜAbbās Aḥmad b. Ismāᶜīl b. Ḥamza al-Azjī ﷺ well-known as Ibn Tabāl. He narrates from Imām Ḥāfiz Tāj al-Dīn ᶜAbd al-Razzāq al-Jilānī ﷺ s/o Sayyiduna Ghawth al-Aᶜzam ᶜAbd al-Qādir al-Jilānī ﷺ, who declared that on Wednesday, the 9th night *of Shāᶜbān,* 550 *hijrī*: His father requested his mother to prepare some rice. She acceded to the request, and prepared some rice for him. The table spread was laid, comprising other dishes and as well as the rice. Thereafter, he moved on, in order to sleep. When midnight had passed, the wall split up, and an individual emerged from the wall. He consumed all the food; and as he was departing, Sayyiduna Ghawth ﷺ commissioned me: *'Meet him and request him to make duᶜās for you.'* I met with him on the other side of the wall, whereby he exited through the wall, which he had come through. He enunciated to me: *'This occurrence, which you have witnessed, is nothing but the duᶜās of your father and blessings of his khirqah [blessed sūfī garb], that has led me to this excellence.'*

The next morning I enquired from Shaykh ᶜAlī b. al-Hītī ﷺ about this matter; to which he replied:

> 'I have not witnessed such rapid effects of spiritual accomplishment and the blessings of any garb [*khirqah*], which was placed on the head of anyone, except that, which I have witnessed by the sacred hands of your father. Collectively, Almighty *Allāh* ﷻ blessed 70 men with spiritual

bliss on the night Sayyiduna Ghawth ﷺ positioned the garb onto them, whilst placing his sacred hands on their heads. It was owing to this factor, that they were bestowed with such immense providence. From the day I observed your illustrious father, I have not perceived another day, which was more virtuous and blessed.'

Contact with the Ghawth ﷺ is a reason for Salvation

I was informed by Shaykh Abu-ʿAbdullāh Muḥammad b. Aḥmad b. Manzūr al-Kittānī ﷺ, who had heard in Damascus from Shaykh Abu-ʿAbdullāh Muḥammad b. Abu al-Fataḥ al-Hirwī ﷺ. He had heard in Baghdād from Shaykh, the leader Abu al-Ḥasan ʿAlī b. al-Hītī ﷺ professing that there is no *murīd* of any Shaykh; who is not so blessed and devout as the *murīd* of Sayyiduna Shaykh ʿAbd al-Qādir al-Jilānī ﷺ. The relationship between Sayyiduna Shaykh Muḥiyy al-Dīn ʿAbd al-Qādir al-Jilānī ﷺ and his *murīds* is unique and certainly, incomparable to other *Shuyūkh* and *murīds.*

Shaykh ʿAlī b. al-Hītī ﷺ testified that he had heard in Baghdād from the Shaykh and leader, Abu-Saʿīd al-Qaylawī ﷺ, who affirmed that Sayyiduna Shaykh ʿAbd al-Qādir al-Jilānī ﷺ returned from the upper heavens with the proposition that; should there be anyone who cultivates a relationship with him, shall attain salvation.

Shaykh Abu-Saʿīd al-Qaylawī ﷺ stated that he had heard Shaykh, the leader Baqa b. Bat'tū ﷺ confessing: *'I have seen all the murīds of Sayyiduna Shaykh ʿAbd al-Qādir al-Jilānī ﷺ in the legion of the virtuous and prosperous, with shining foreheads, hands and feet.'*

Diving in the Ocean of Mercy

I was informed by Shaykh Abu al-Barkāt Yūnus b. Sālim b. ʿAlī b. Muḥammad al- Tamīmī Bakrī al-Mosulī Muqrī ﷺ and Shaykh Abu-ʿAbdullāh Muḥammad b. ʿAlī b. Ḥusain b. Muḥammad al-Damishqī ﷺ. Both of them said that they were informed in Mosul by their Shaykh, Shaykh Abu al-Mafākhir ʿAdī b. Shaykh Abu al-Barkāt ﷺ, who had heard from his father, who stated that he had heard in 554 *hijrī* from his uncle, Shaykh ʿAdī b. Musāfir ﷺ in his room on the mountains,[271] pronouncing that when the *murīd* of any *Mashā'ikh* requests from me for a *khirqah* [*sūfī* garb], I shall definitely adorn him with one. However, I shall not position one onto the *murīds* of Sayyiduna Shaykh ʿAbd al-Qādir al-Jilānī ﷺ; for indeed they are submerging into the ocean of mercy. Why should one abandon an ocean and proceed to a stream?

Love and Affiliation to the Ghawth ﷺ is a Reason for Forgiveness

I narrate from Shaykh Abu al-Ḥasan ʿAlī b. Shaykh Abu al-Jadd Mubārak b. Yūsuf al-Batā'iḥī Ḥaddādī al-Shafaʿī ﷺ, who narrates in Baghdād from Qāḍī al-Quḍāt Sayyiduna Shaykh Abu-Sāliḥ Nasar al-Jilānī ﷺ. He narrates from his father Sayyiduna Tāj al-Dīn ʿAbd al-Razzāq al-Jilānī ﷺ who asserted that he had heard from two senior *Shuyūkh*, Shaykh Abu-Muḥammad Ḥasan b. Abī ʿImrān Mūsā b. Aḥmad al-Qurashī al-Khālidī ﷺ and Shaykh Abu al-Qāsim Muḥammad b. ʿUbādah al-Ansārī al-Ḥalabī ﷺ. Both of them concur that they had heard in Damascus from Shaykh, the leader, Abu al-Ḥasan ʿAlī al-Qurashī ﷺ, who had heard Sayyiduna Ghawth al-Aʿzam ﷺ, who had stipulated that:

> A sheet was awarded to me, which was elongated as far as the eyes could perceive. Recorded on it were the names of my *murīds* and companions who shall appear till *Qiyāmah*. It was revealed to me that all those, whose names appear on the list, shall be forgiven, owing to my high ranking spiritual designation. I enquired from the caretaker of Hell, as to whether he had the name of any of my *murīds* on his list and thereby, he replied in the negative. By the Honour and Glory of my Lord ﷻ! My hand extends over my *murīds*, similar to the extension of the sky, which is above the earth. In the event that my *murīd* is not excellent, I yet am excellent. By the Dictates and Glory of my Lord ﷻ! My foot shall be firm in the presence of my Lord ﷻ, until such time I grant admission to

[271] Mountainous Region located in Lalish, within the vicinity of Northern Iraq.

all of you into *Jannah*.

Taking a Bath 70 times

I was informed by Shaykh Sharīf Abu al-ʿAbbās Aḥmad b. Shaykh Abu-ʿAbdullāh Muḥammad b. Abu al-Ghanā'im Muḥammad al-Ḥusainī al-Damishqī, and he had heard from his father in Damascus who enunciated that a *murīd* of Sayyiduna Shaykh Muḥiyy al-Dīn ʿAbd al-Qādir al-Jilānī had experienced 70 nocturnal emissions in one night. Each time he perceived a different woman in his dream; whom he had not perceived before. He had recognized some of those women, whilst he had no knowledge of the others.

In the morning he proceeded to Sayyiduna Ghawth in order to complain about his experience. Before he could utter a word, the Ghawth assured as follows: *'Do not be despondent about your experience, because I have viewed your name on the Louḥe Maḥfūz, and it was documented that you shall commit adultery with certain women. [Sayyiduna Ghawth revealed the names, and strategies of those women]. I pleaded to Allāh on your behalf, and Allāh transformed those 70 conscientious physical adulteries into a dream.'*

The Promise of my Lord

I was informed in Baghdād by Shaykh Abu al-Faḍal Mansūr b. Aḥmad b. ʿAtāullāh b. ʿAbd al-Jabbār, who had heard in 592 *hijrī* in Baghdād from Shaykh ʿImrān al-Kamīmānī and Shaykh Baz'zār. Both of them propounded that it was asserted to Sayyiduna Ghawth, that a person who calls out his name, but had not pledged an allegiance at his hands [*bayʿāh*], nor wore a *khirqah* presented by him; then is such a person eligible to be categorized as your *murīd*?

Sayyiduna Ghawth issued a vociferous assurance: *'Anyone who attributes himself to me and takes my name, Allāh shall accept him and cherish him, even though he is a sinner. Such a person is included amongst my murīds. Indeed! My Lord*

ﷻ *has promised me that He* ﷻ *shall admit into Jannah, all of my murīds, friends and all those who subscribed to the same belief as mine.*

The Status of those attributed to the Ghawth ؓ.

I narrate from Shaykh Abu-Muḥammad Rajab b. Mansūr al-Dārī ؓ and he narrates from two *Shuyūkh*, Shaykh the leader, Abu-ʿAbd al-Raḥīm ʿAskar b. ʿAbd al-Raḥīm al-Nasībīnī ؓ in Nasībīn and Shaykh Abu al-Ḥasan ؓ prominently known as the sock merchant affirmed that Shaykh ʿAbd al-Raḥīm ؓ declared that he had heard from three *Shuyūkh*, Shaykh Ḥāfiz Taqī al-Dīn Abu-Muḥammad ʿAbd al-Ghanī b. ʿAbd al-Wāḥid al-Maqdisī ؓ, Shaykh Imām Muwaffiq al-Dīn Abu-Muḥammad ʿAbdullāh b. Qudāmah al-Maqdisī ؓ in Damascus and Shaykh Sāliḥ Abu-ʿAbd al-Malik Ziyāl b. Abī al-Maʿālī b. Rāshid al-Irāqī ؓ in *Baith al-Maqaddis* [*al-Quds* –Jerusalem]. The three of them exposed that they had heard in Baghdād from our Shaykh, Sayyiduna Muḥiyy al-Dīn ʿAbd al-Qādir al-Jīlī ؓ, whilst he was reclining on his chair, decreed that he was posed with the following question in the months of 561 *hijrī*: What is the status and excellence of those who shall be attributed to you? He replied: *'My one egg*[272] *is equivalent to a thousand eggs, and no price can be attached to the chicks.'*

Punishment reduced due to the Ghawth ؓ

I narrate from Shaykh Abu-ʿAbdullāh Muḥammad b. ʿĪsā b. ʿAbdullāh Qaymān b. ʿAlī Azrafī Rūmī al-Ḥanafī ؓ and he narrates in 629 *hijrī* from Shaykh Khalīl b. Shaykh Abu al-ʿAbbās Aḥmad b. ʿAlī al-Sarsarī ؓ. He narrates from his father who stated he had heard Sayyiduna Shaykh Muḥiyy al-Dīn ʿAbd al-Qādir al-Jilānī ؓ declaring: *'Anyone who passes at the door of my madrassa, the punishment of Qiyāmah shall then be reduced for him.'*

A youth came to the Ghawth ؓ and enunciated to him: *'My father passed on,*

[272] A *murīd*; devotee, lover

and today I dreamt that he was being punished in his grave. My father instructed me to approach Shaykh ʿAbd al-Qādir ﷺ, and forward a request to him in order to make duʿā for him.'

Sayyiduna Ghawth ﷺ enquired as to whether his father had passed at the door of his *madrassa*; and he replied in the affirmative. Sayyiduna Shaykh ﷺ remained silent. On the following day, the youth returned and revealed that he had dreamt about his father, and had found him to be extremely jubilant and relaxed, whilst wearing a green garb. He confessed to me: *'The punishment was revoked from me, and the garb that you had viewed on me was adorned on to me, with the blessings of Sayyiduna Shaykh ʿAbd al-Qādir al-Jilānī ﷺ. Thus, O Son! It is incumbent upon you to be subservient to him.'* Sayyiduna Shaykh ﷺ, thereby confirmed: *'My Lord ﷻ has promised me to relieve the punishment of a Muslim, who passes at the door of Madrassat al-Muslimīn.'*

The youth bears testimony to the fact that, one day he proceeded to Sayyiduna Ghawth ﷺ and somebody had disclosed to him: *'I heard sounds coming out of the grave of a person, who was buried a few days ago in the Bāb Nawāj cemetery.'* Ḥaḍrate Ghawth ﷺ queried from that person whether he had worn his *khirqah* or not. The people responded that they were unaware. He stipulated: *'One who transgresses, shall incur more losses.'* He then bowed his consecrated head in *murāqabah* and reverential wonderment covered him, and the manifestation of dignity was evident in him. Thereafter, he articulated: *'Angels informed me that this person had observed my face, and had possessed noble views about me. Owing to you, Almighty Allāh ﷻ has favoured him.'*

The youth affirmed that from that day onwards, the people visited his grave several times, but they did not hear any sounds emanating from his grave.

Every World has a Powerful Representative of the great Ghawth ﷺ

I was informed by Shaykh Abu al-Ḥasan ʿAlī b. Aḥmad b. Muḥammad b. Yūsuf b. ʿAbdullāh Qatāʿī al-Zubaydī al-Baghdādī ﷺ and he had heard from Shaykh

Abu al-Ḥasan ʿAlī b. Sulaymān al-Baghdādī ﷺ the baker. He proclaims that he had heard from Shaykh the leader, Abu al-Ḥasan al-Jowsiqī ﷺ, who professed that he was present at the *majlis* of Sayyiduna Shaykh ʿAbd al-Qādir al-Jilānī ﷺ, and Shaykh ʿAlī b. al-Hītī ﷺ and Shaykh Baqā b. Bat'tū ﷺ were also present. Sayyiduna Ghawth al-Aʿzam ﷺ thereby revealed to me: *'I have a female animal in every stable, which have greater power and strength than others. I have a horse on every earth, and that no horse can be compared to it. I have a Sultān [commander] in every army, whom no one can challenge. I have such a Khalīfah in every location who shall not be dismissed.'*

Ḥaḍarte Ghawth ﷺ has the most Companions and Murīds

I narrate from Shaykh Abu-Muḥammad Qāsim b. Shaykh Abī-Aḥmad ʿAbdullāh b. Aḥmad b. ʿAlī al-Hāshimī al-Baghdādī Ḥaramī al-Ḥanbalī ﷺ and he narrates from the pious *Shuyūkh*, Shaykh Abu-Muḥammad ʿAbd al-Karīm b. Mansūr b. Abī-Bakr al-Baghdādī Muḥaddith ﷺ eminently known as Atharī and Shaykh Kamāl al-Dīn Abu al-Ḥasan ʿAlī b. Muḥammad b. Waḍāḥ al-Sheharbānī ﷺ narrated in *Jāmʿeh Mansūr* in Baghdād. These *Shuyūkh* state that in 620 *hijrī* they were in the presence of Shaykh the leader, Abu-Muḥammad Sālih b. Idrīs al-Yaʿqūbī ﷺ. Thereafter, Shaykh Sāliḥ Abu-Ḥafs ʿUmar al-Tharīdah ﷺ appeared, and Shaykh ʿAlī ﷺ dictated to him: *'Relate your dream within the presence of all these people.'* He commenced in relating his dream and asserted:

> 'I dreamt that *Qiyāmah* had been ordained and all the Prophets ﷺ together with their respective *Ummah* were advancing towards the plains of *Qiyāmah*. Following some of the Prophets, there were two individuals, whilst other Prophets had the following of only one individual. Sayyiduna Rasūlullāh ﷺ arrived and behind him followed his *Ummah,* comparable to torrential rain. Amongst them were also *Mashā'ikh* and each one was followed by their *murīds*, in varying degrees of numbers. There was one Shaykh whose *murīds* were in masses, which outnumbered every other Shaykh; and I enquired as to who this Shaykh was. I was informed that he was Shaykh ʿAbd al-Qādir al-Jilānī ﷺ, together with his companions and *murīds*. I proceeded forward and

expounded: 'Oh my Master! I have not discovered amongst the *Mashā'ikh* anyone more resplendent than thou, nor did I discover that their *murīds* were more esteemed than your *murīds*.'

Then Sayyiduna Ghawth ؓ recited the following verses:

إِذْ كَانَ مِنَّا سَيِّدٌ فِي عَشِيْرَةً   عَلَاهَا وَإِنْ ضَاقَ الْخَنَاقُ حَمَاهَا

Whenever our Master is in any tribe then he is exalted amongst them,
Even though strangulation narrows its protection

وَمَا اِخْتَبَرْتُ إِلَّا وَأَصْبَحَ شَيْخُهَا   وَمَا اِفْتَخَرْتُ الْأَ دُكَانَ فَتَاهَا

When I was put to test, then I was their Shaykh, and
I am proud that I am their youth.

وَمَا ضَرَبْتُ بِالْأَبْرَقَيْنِ خَيَامُنَا   فَأَصْبَحَ مَأْوَى الطَّارِقِيْنَ سِوَاهَا

Our tents were not just pitched on any ground
where the abode of those who come, be in some other place.

Shaykh Sālih Abu-Ḥafs ؒ states that when he awoke, he remembered the afore-mentioned verses. On that day Shaykh Muḥammad Wāʿiz al-Darzī ؒ was present and Shaykh ʿAlī b. Idrīs ؒ alluded to him: *'O Muḥammad! Adhere to the concept of Sayyiduna Shaykh ʿAbd al-Qādir* ؓ *in the syntax of your words.'* Hence, he recited the following verses:

هَنِيْئاً لِصَحْبِي إِنِّي قَائِدُ الرَّكْبِ   أَسِيْرُ بِهِمْ قَصْداً إِلَى لِأَنْزَلَ الْجَبَبِ

Glad-tiding to my friends and murīds that I am the leader of this caravan.
I am leading them to a spacious domain

وَأَكْنِفُهُمْ وَاكِلُ فِي شُغْلِ أَمْرِهِ   وَأَنْزِلُهُمْ فِي حَضْرَةِ الْقُدْسِ مِنْ قُرْبِ

I am taking them under security in such a condition, that
everyone shall be engrossed in their own state. I shall lead them to
the Divine Proximity.

وَلِيْ مَعْهَدُ كُلِّ الطَّوَائِفِ دُوْنَهُ   وَلِيْ مَنْهَلٌ عَذْبِ الْمَشَارِبِ وَالشُّرْبِ

And there is a promise for every group of mine, and apart from this, there
exists a huge spring whose bathing place and water is sweet.

وَأَهْلُ الصَّفَا يَسْعَوْنَ خَلْفِيْ وَكُلُّهُمْ   لَهُ هِمَّةٌ أَمْضَى مِنَ الصَّارِمِ الْغَضَبِ

The people of purity are marching behind me,
and the bravery of each one of them functions like a sharp sword.

Thereafter, Sayyiduna Shaykh ʿAlī ﷺ complimented him: *'You have rendered it meticulously, and whatever you exclaimed is the truth.'*

A Sacred Light

I was informed by Shaykh Abu-Ḥafs ʿUmar b. Shaykh Abu al-Majd Mubārak b. Aḥmad ʿAlī al-Nasībīnī ﷺ, who had heard from Shaykh Abu-ʿAbd al-Raḥīm ʿAskar al-Nasībīnī ﷺ in Nasībīn, who informed that he had heard from Shaykh Abu-Muḥammad ʿAbd al-Jabbār b. Shaykh al-Islām Muḥiyy al-Dīn ʿAbd al-Qādir al-Jīlānī ﷺ in Baghdād. He confirmed that whenever his mother entered a dark room, a lamp would thereby emerge, and brighten up the room.

Once, my father [Sayyiduna Ghawth ﷺ] entered into the room, and discovered this lamp. When he looked at it, it extinguished. He confessed to my mother: *'This light which you perceive is the devil, who is aiding you. I have now cast it away from you, and have replaced it with a sacred Light. It is a similar process to those who link themselves to me. This is my benediction upon them.'*

Sayyiduna Shaykh ʿAbd al-Jabbār al-Jīlānī ﷺ states that whenever his mother would enter into a dark room, it would then light up, identical to the moon; and its light would spread out to the surroundings.

I am a Guarantee for all my Murīds till Qiyāmah

I narrate from Shaykh Abu al-Ḥasan ʿAlī b. ʿAbdullāh b. Abu-Bakr al-Abharī later recognized as al-Baghdādī ﷺ, and he narrates from Shaykh Abu al-Ḥasan ﷺ, the baker, who narrates in Baghdād from Shaykh Abu al-Qāsim ʿUmar Baz'zār ﷺ. He asserts that several times he had heard from his Master, Sayyiduna Shaykh Muḥiyy al-Dīn ʿAbd al-Qādir al-Jīlānī ﷺ who had rendered the following exposition:

My brother Ḥusain Ḥallāj slipped with both his feet, and at that time, there was no one to lend support in clasping his hand. Had I been present in that time, I would have grasped onto his hand and would have rescued him. I have been designated as a surety for all my companions, friends and *murīds* till *Qiyāmah*. Indeed! I am designated as a surety for anyone; whose mount slips, and I shall thereby grasp hold of their hand.

Sayyiduna Ghawth al-Aᶜzam ﷺ assists all who call on him.

I narrate from Shaykh Abu al-Maᶜālī ᶜAbd al-Raḥīm b. Muzaffar b. Muhazzab al- Qurashī ﷺ, and he narrates from Ḥāfiz Abu-ᶜAbdullāh Muḥammad b, Maḥmūd b. Najjār al-Baghdādī ﷺ, who had mentioned in his presence in Baghdād: He said that Shaykh ᶜAbdullāh al-Jabāᶜī ﷺ wrote to him and he quoted from the contents of his letter as follows:

I met a man, by the name of Zarīf in Hamdān who hailed from Damascus. He said that he had met with Bash'sha Qarzī who was on the way to Nishapūr or perhaps on the way to Khawarzim. In his possession there were 14 camels which were loaded with sugar. He revealed that they had entered such a fear-provoking jungle; to the extent that a brother was fearful of being with another brother. During the early hours of the night, when they moved their camels, they discovered that four of the camels which were loaded with sugar were missing. I searched for them but could not locate them. The caravan moved ahead; whereas I detached myself from them in search of my camels. A camel charioteer assisted by linking up with me in search of the lost camels, but we were unable to locate them. In the morning, I recalled the assurance of my Shaykh, Shaykh Muḥiyy al-Dīn ᶜAbd al-Qādir al-Jilānī ﷺ who had proclaimed that, should you call upon me in the event of calamity, you shall henceforth, be certainly be relieved.

Henceforward, I called upon him by expressing: 'Oh Shaykh ᶜAbd al-Qādir! My camels are lost. Oh Shaykh ᶜAbd al-Qādir! My camels are lost. Thereafter, I gazed towards the horizon, when the day had dawned. As the horizon brightened, I perceived a person dressed in white clothes; standing on a hill, whilst summoning me to him by waving his sleeves. As soon as I climbed the hill, the person had disappeared, and I observed that the four camels were seated at the bottom of the hill in the jungle. We retrieved the camels; and thereby, joined the caravan once more.

Shaykh Abu al-Maʿālī states that he came to Shaykh Abu al-Ḥasan, the baker, and revealed this incident to him. He clarified that he had heard from Shaykh Abu al-Qāsim ʿUmar Baz'zār, articulating that Sayyiduna Shaykh Muḥiyy al-Dīn ʿAbd al-Qādir al-Jilānī asserted: *'Anyone who calls upon me in times of adversity, his adversity shall be eradicated [or I shall eliminate his adversity] and if anyone calls upon me during calamity, his calamity shall be eliminated [or I shall liberate him].'*

Salāt al-Ghawthiyah

Sayyiduna Ghawth al-Aʿzam expounded that: 'Anyone who has an aspiration and institutes my *tawassul* [medium], within the Divine Precincts of *Allāh*, his aspirations shall then be accomplished. This applies to anyone, who performs two *rakʿats nafil salāh*, with the recitation of *Sura Fātiḥa* and thereafter, followed by *Sura Ikhlās*, eleven times in each *rakʿat* and eventually, with the termination of with *salām*. Thereafter, recite *Salawāt* [*Durūd Sharīf*] upon the Sayyiduna Rasūlullāh; and remember me when embarking on eleven steps, towards the direction of Baghdād. Whilst expressing my name on every step, and by the grace of *Allāh*; his aspirations shall be conformed to.

Translator's Adendum

Method of performing Salāt al-Ghawthiyah

The great *Mujaddid*[273] and *ʿĀrif* of *Allāh*, Ala-Ḥaḍrat Imām al-Akbar Imām Aḥmad Riḍā al-Qādirī Muḥaqqiq Bareillwī in his book, *'Azhār al-Anwār fī*

[273] A Mujaddid is a chosen servant of *Allāh* who brings "revival" (تجديد - *tajdid*) to the

Saba Salāt al-Asrār,' documents the correct method of performing *salah* which are as follows: Following the performance of *Salāt al-Maghrib*, perform two [2] *rak'at nafil*, and recite in both *rak'ats*, after *Sura Fātiḥa,* 11 times *Sura Ikhlās*. Upon completion, glorify *Allāh* ﷻ with any *Tasbīḥ* and then recite 11 times *Salawāt 'alan Nabī* ﷺ [*Durūd Sharīf*], and 11 times the following *Du'ā*, whilst seated:

يَارَسُوْلَ اللهِ يَانَبِيَّ اللهِ أَغِثْنِيْ وَ أَمْدُدْنِيْ فِيْ قَضَاءِ حَاجَتِيْ يَاقَاضِيَ الْحَاجَاتِ

Ya Rasūlalāh Ya Nabiyallāh Aghithnī wa amdudnī fi qaḍa'ī ḥājatī Ya Qāḍīyal-Ḥajāt

Thereafter, stand up and take 11 steps towards the direction of Iraq, and recite the following *Du'ā* once on every step:

يَاغَوْثَ الثَّقَلَيْنِ يَا كَرِيْمَ الطَّرَفَيْنِ أَغِثْنِيْ وَ أَمْدُدْنِيْ فِيْ قَضَاءِ حَاجَتِيْ يَاقَاضِيَ الْحَاجَات

Ya Ghawth al-Thaqalayn Ya Karīm al-Tarafayn aghthnī wa amdudnī fi qaḍa'ī Ḥājatī Ya Qāḍī al-Ḥajāt

After the 11th step, raise your hands and sincerely engage in *Du'ā* to Almighty *Allāh* ﷻ, that through the *Wasīla* of *Sayyiduna Ghawth al-A'zam* رضي الله عنه, *In shā Allāh,* your aspirations shall be will be compensated.

---

religion. According to the *Ḥadith al-Sharīf,* it refers to a person who appears at the turn of every century of the *Islāmic* calendar to revive *Islām*, cleansing it of extraneous elements and restoring it to its pristine purity. The concept is reported in a famous *Ḥadith* recorded by Imām Abu Dā'ūd رضي الله عنه: narrated by Sayyiduna Abu-Hurayrah رضي الله عنه who heard the beloved Messenger of *Allāh* ﷺ state:

إنّ الله تعالى يَبْعَثُ لِهذِهِ الأُمَّةِ على رَأْسِ كلِّ مائَةِ سَنَةٍ مَنْ يُجَدِّدُ لها دِينَها

Allah will raise for this community at the end of every hundred years the one who will renovate its religion for it.
Reported in Sunan Abu Dā'ūd, *Book 37: Kitab al-Malahim [Battles], Ḥadith Number 4278* and many other Ḥadith Manuals.

His Excellent conduct

I narrate from Shaykh Abu al-Futūḥ Nasrullāh b. Abu al-Muḥāsin Yūsuf b. Khalīl b. ʿAlī al-Baghdādī al-Azjī ﷺ, and he narrates in Baghdād from Shaykh Abu al-ʿAbbās Aḥmad b. Ismāʿīl Ḥamza al-Baghdādī al-Azjī ﷺ, prominently known as Ibn Battāl. He narrates from Shaykh Abu al-Maʿmar Muzaffar Mansūr b. al-Mubārak b. al-Faḍal al-Wāstī Wāʿiz ﷺ, distinguished as Jarādah who professed:

> My eyes did not perceive anyone more renowned than Sayyiduna Shaykh Muḥiyy al-Dīn ʿAbd al-Qādir al-Jilānī ؓ, with a gracious disposition of a *Ḥāfiz,* who was exceptional in conduct; possessed an expansive bosom of wisdom; kind hearted, affectionate and promptly honoured all promises.
>
> Although he was the most exalted and elite, he was yet very kind and compassionate towards the young and held them in high esteem. He was always the first one to extend greetings. His company comprised the weak, and he exercised humility with the poor. He never stood up out of respect for any person who was inclined to the world; and never did he proceed to the court or door of any statesman, king or minister.

Sand falls from the Ceiling

The narrator enunciates that once he was in the sanctified room of the great Ghawth ؓ and he was busy with the writing of something. Some sand dropped from the ceiling onto his writing. This occurred three times, and each time he brushed it off. When the sand dropped for the fourth time, he gazed at the ceiling and discovered that a rat that was moving around. He then asserted: *'May your head fly off.'* As soon as he pronounced this, its body flew to one side and the head to the other.

Sayyiduna Ghawth ؓ discontinued with his writing and commenced with weeping. I enquired from him: *'O my Master! Why are you weeping?* He affirmed:

'I fear that, should I become aggravated with any Muslim; his condition would also be similar to the plight of this rat.'

A Bird dies and falls to the ground

I narrate from Shaykh Abu al-Rajā Yaʿqūb b. Ayyūb b. Aḥmad b. ʿAlī al-Hāshmī al-Farūqī ﷺ, who narrates from Shaykh Abu al-Ḥasan b. ʿAlī b. Sulaymān ﷺ, distinctly known as the baker, who states that he narrates from Shaykh Abu al-Qāsim ʿUmar b. Masʿūd Baz'zār ﷺ, who reports that:

> One day my Master Sayyiduna Shaykh Muḥiyy al-Dīn ʿAbd al-Qādir al-Jilānī ﷺ was performing *wuḍū* in his *madrassa* and a bird; which flew above messed his clothes. He gazed upwards and observed that the bird was flying away. Thereafter, the bird tumbled dead onto the ground. Henceforth, he washed the soiled part of the clothes, took them off and thereby handed it over to me. He assigned to me the task to sell them, and to distribute the proceeds from the sale of the clothes to charity. He further elaborated: *'There shall be a recompense for it; i.e. in respect of what had occurred.'*

Ya Allāh ﷻ Everything belongs to You

I narrate from Shaykh Abu al-ʿAfāf Mūsa b. Shaykh Abu al-Muʿālī ʿUthmān b. Mūsā al-Baqāʿī ﷺ and he narrates in Damascus in 614 *hijrī* from his father. He narrates from two *Shuyūkh* in Baghdād, Shaykh Abu-ʿAmr ʿUthmān al-Sarīfīnī ﷺ and Shaykh Abu-Muḥammad ʿAbd al-Ḥaqq al-Ḥarīmīnī ﷺ. Both said that their Shaykh, Sayyiduna Muḥiyy al-Dīn ʿAbd al-Qādir al-Jilānī ﷺ cried and said: *'O my Lord! How can I sacrifice my life for You because it is proven by decisive proof that everything belongs to You.'* He often recited this couplet:

وَمَا يَنْفَعُ الْأَعْرَابُ لَمْ يَكُنْ تَقِيٌّ وَمَا ضَرَّ ذَا تَقْوَى لِسَانٌ مُعْجَمُ

If there is no piety, then there is no benefit in speaking clear correct words;
And a non-eloquent tongue is not harmful to a pious person.

A Pauper becomes Wealthy

I narrate from Shaykh Abu al-Ḥasan ʿAlĩ b. Yaḥyah b. Abu al-Qãsim al-Azjĩ ﷺ and he narrates from *Qãḍĩ al-Quḍãt*, Sayyiduna Shaykh Abu-Sãliḥ Nasar al-Jilãnĩ ﷺ, who narrates from his illustrious father, Sayyiduna Tãj al-Dĩn ʿAbd al-Razzãq al-Jilãnĩ ﷺ, who had conveyed the following:

'When my father became well recognized, he performed *Ḥajj* once. Throughout his travel, I accompanied him, whilst I held onto the reins of his mount all continuously. When we reached Hilla [a town in southern Iraq], he instructed us to locate the most underprivileged person from the village. Within the ruins, which included a dilapidated house, we discovered that an old man, woman and a child had lived there. My father approached them and requested for permission to be housed with them. Gladly, they consented, and we were accommodated by them. The *Mashã'ikh* and wealthy people of Hilla had requested Sayyiduna Shaykh ﷺ to live with them but he refused their request. The villagers brought goats, cows and horses, gold and expensive clothing and presented them to him as gifts. People rallied to my father from all the surrounding areas. Sayyiduna Ghawth ﷺ declared that he would present all his gifts to the people of that house; whereby all of them were unanimous about his decision. Hence, all the goods and money, inclusive of the livestock were handed over to them. They spent the night there, and departed in the morning.

Several years had passed and I proceeded to Hilla; and discovered that the same old man was the wealthiest person of the village. He affirmed to me: *'All that you observe is the barakãt of that single night. The entire of this livestock was multiplied in abundance, in comparison to which I received on that night.'*

All the Gold pieces were distributed to Seventy Awliya-Allãh

I had heard from Shaykh Faqih Abu-ʿAlĩ Isḥãq b. ʿAlĩ b. ʿAbdullãh al-Hamdãnĩ

ﷺ, and he had heard from Shaykh Khalīl Abu al-Faḍal Isḥāq b. Aḥmad al-Althī ﷺ. He had heard from Shaykh Abu-Sāliḥ Talḥā b. Muzaffar ﷺ, who stated that his Shaykh, Sayyiduna Muḥiyy al-Dīn ʿAbd al-Q̱ādir al-Jilānī ﷺ had professed:

> During my early days in Baghdād, for a period of twenty days, I could not find anything to eat. I could not even find any *mubaḥ* [274] to eat. Thereafter, I set out to the ruins of Kisra's palace [in Madāyan], in search of any *mubaḥ* commodity to eat. There, I perceived seventy *Awliya-Allāh* who were in search of the same commodity, which I was in search of. I decided within myself that it was unethical to impede into their matters; and as a result, I returned to Baghdād. I met a family member, whom I had recognized and he handed to me a few pieces of gold [or silver] and relayed that my mother had sent them for me.
>
> I retained some of pieces for myself, and hastened with the rest to the palace of Kisra and distributed them amongst the seventy *Awliya-Allāh*. They asked me what that was and I said, my mother had sent this for me. I decided not to spend it exclusively on myself, and thus, decided not to exclude all of you, with a view to sharing.
>
> Upon returning to Baghdād, I purchased some food with the remaining pieces of gold or silver, and extended an invitation the poor in order to feed them. When the night had arrived I had nothing left from those pieces of gold or silver.

Serving the Foqaha and guests

I was informed by Shaykh Abu-Futūḥ Nasrullāh b. Yūsuf b. ʿAlī al-Azjī ﷺ, who had heard from Shaykh Abu al-ʿAbbās Aḥmad b. Sulaymān b. Ḥamza al-Azjī ﷺ, notably eminent as Ibn Battāl, and he was informed by

[274] Reference is made to a commodity, that is neither forbidden nor recommended, and at a religious decree, it remains neutral. In Islamic Jurisprudence, it is one of the degrees of approval [*aḥkām*].This terminology is often used as a synonym for the word *halāl*.

Abu-Muḥammad ʿAbdullāh b. Ḥusain b. Abu al-Faḍal ﷺ, who confirmed that whenever gold was presented to his Shaykh, Sayyiduna Muḥiyy al-Dīn Shaykh ʿAbd al-Qādir al-Jilānī ﷺ, he would delegate that it should be placed under his prayer mat [*musallah*], which he would not touch. When his *Khādim* would arrive, he would instruct him to seize whatever was under the prayer mat; and to hand it over to the baker.

His servant, Muzaffar ﷺ would come and stand at the door of the Shaykh ﷺ with a full tray comprising bread. Whenever, the *Khalīfah* forwarded any gift [money], he would dictate: '*Give this to Abu al-Fataḥ Ḥarsa.*' Sayyiduna Shaykh ﷺ used to purchase flour from him on credit, and used to feed the *Foqaha* and guests. He paid off his debt with these offerings.

The reason for his wheat being *ḥalāl* was that, every year some of his friends would cultivate it on their farms, whilst the other friends would grind them. At the time of *ʿAsr*, on a daily basis, four or five bread would be baked and would be brought to him. Sayyiduna Ghawth ﷺ would prepare the bread into pieces, and distribute it to those present and used to keep some of it for himself.

Whenever any gift was offered to him, he would distribute it to those who were present. He accepted gifts and he would reciprocate them with a gift. He accepted presents, and he also consumed from it.

He took off his Qamīs and gave it to a Faqīr

I was informed by Sayyiduna Sharīf Abu-ʿAbdullāh Muḥammad b. Ḥaḍar al-Ḥusainī ﷺ, and he had heard from his father, who had confessed:

I arrived the *Jumʿāh Masjid* with Sayyidī Muḥiyy al-Dīn ʿAbd al-Qādir al-Jilānī ﷺ. A trader advanced towards him and declared that he had some goods and had intended to distribute them to the poor and needy. These were not goods that were classified as the *Zakāt* category. I did not find anyone, who was a deserving recipient, and as such, I would prefer you to direct me to hand it over to whom you decide. Sayyiduna Ghawth ﷺ regulated: *'Give it to both, the deserving and non-deserving.'* [275]

The narrator expressed that Ḥaḍrate Ghawth ﷺ saw a dejected pauper and queried from him about his condition. He whined: *'Today I proceeded to the river bank and requested to the boatman to row me across. He refused, because I did not have any money. This refusal caused dejection within my heart.'*

No sooner, the poor man could complete lodging his complaint, an individual appeared; grasping onto a bag, containing 30 *dinārs,* which he presented to the Ghawth ﷺ. Sayyiduna Shaykh ﷺ alluded to the poor man: *'Here take this bag and hand it over to the boatman, and inform him, that he is never to decline a poor man anymore.'* Henceforward, he removed his garb [*qamīs*], and presented it to the poor man, and thereafter, he once more bought it from him for 20 *dinārs.*

Great Restlessness in the Audience

I had heard from Shaykh Abu-ʿAbdullāh Ḥasan b. Badrān b. ʿAlī al-Baghdādī ﷺ, who had heard from Faqih Abu-Muḥammad ʿAbd al-Qādir ʿUthmān al-Tamīmī al-Bardānī ﷺ. He had heard from Shaykh Abu-Muḥammad ʿAbd al-Laṭīf b. Aḥmad al-Qurashī ﷺ, who stated that one day his Shaykh, Sayyiduna Muḥiyy al-Dīn Shaykh ʿAbd al-Qādir al-Jilānī ﷺ was engaged in delivering a discourse, and the people became prone to laziness. He thereby gazed towards the sky, and recited the following couplets:

لَا تَسْقِنِيْ وَحْدِيْ فَمَا عَوَّدْتَنِيْ أَنِّيْ أَشُحُّ بِهَا عَلَى جُلَّاسِيْ

Do not give me to drink alone, because You did not make me habitual of this, So that I may exercise stinginess in the audience.

---

275 The *Mashā'ikh* have revealed that this command of Sayyiduna Ghawth ﷺ encompassed in-depth wisdom, and they concurred that wisdom of Ḥaḍrate Ghawth ﷺ portrayed: *'Give it to the deserving and non-deserving, so that Allāh ﷻ shall grant you what you deserve, and as well as that which you do not deserve.' Subḥānallāh*! # [Qadirī Faqīr ʿAbd al-Hādī]

اَنْتَ الْكَرِيْمُ وَهَلْ يَلِيْقُ تَكَرُّماً   اَنْ يَّعْبُرَ النُّدَمَاءُ دَوْرَ الْكَاسِيْ

You are generous and this does not compliment generosity
that an associate passes by like a cup passing by.

The narrator affirmed that the entire audience befell into a state of deep restlessness, and something huge entered into them. From amongst the audience one or two people had passed on. [The narrator, Tamīmī, is uncertain of the number of individuals that passed on].

His stunning Qualities

I was informed by Shaykh Abu-Ghālib Faḍlullāh b. Aḥmad b. Bayān Murtuḍah b. Shukrullāh al-Hāshimī al-Baghdādī ﷺ, and he had heard from Shaykh Abu al-Ḥasan ʿAlī b. Sulaymān ﷺ the baker. He stated that he had heard Shaykh al-Islām ʿUmar Baz'zār ﷺ, who asserted that: During the time, that we were seated in the company of Sayyiduna Ghawth al-Aʿzam ﷺ, it seemed as though it was a dream. When we awoke from that dream, we disremembered him. His conduct was of par-excellence and his characteristics were pure. His being had annulled evil; whilst his hands possessed the attributes of generosity. Every night he would emphasize that the table spread should be laid, and he would partake of the meals with the visitors. He would sit with the weak, and furthermore used to visit the sick. He exercised patience with the students. Those who were seated with him, never felt as though others were more eminent than him.

He consistently cared, and enquired about the condition of his companions in their absence. He always protected their friendship, and forgave them for their shortcomings. If anyone procured an oath, he would acknowledge it; and would conceal the knowledge about them. I have not discovered anyone more modest than him. The narrator revealed that when Shaykh ʿUmar ﷺ verbalized about Sayyiduna Ghawth ﷺ, he would recite the following verses:

اَلْحَمْدُ لِلّٰهِ اِنِّيْ فِيْ جَوَارِ فَتًى   حَامِي الْحَقِيْقَةِ نَفَّاعٌ وَضَرَّارُ

All praise are for Allāh that I am in the security of such a youth
Who is the carrier of Reality and the provider of benevolence and loss.

لَا يَرْفَعُ الطَّرْفَ إِلَّا عِنْدَ مَكْرُمَةً مِنَ الْحَيَاءِ وَلَا يَخْفِى عَلَيَّ عَارُ

Besides generosity the eyes do not lift up with the exception of
modesty; and on reproach he does not conceal.

I narrate from Shaykh Abu-Muḥammad Ḥasan b. Abī-ʿImrān Mūsā b. Aḥmad b. Ḥusain al-Maḥzūmī Khālidī al-Shafaʿī, who had affirmed that he was with Shaykh Abu al-Ḥasan ʿAlī al-Qurashī on Mount Qāsiyūn. He was questioned about Sayyiduna Shaykh ʿAbd al-Qādir al-Jilānī and he furnished the following information:

> He was an individual with multi-faceted external excellence; continually possessing an open countenance, exquisitely handsome, easily conspicuous within a wide stately federation, kind natured, with the emanation of a fragrant perspiration, benevolent, affectionate and esteemed to his companions. Whenever he observed them to be despondent, he would applaud them and thereby eliminate their despondency. I have not seen anyone with a more pure tongue coupled with pure words evolving, except from him.

I narrate from Shaykh Abu al-Ḥasan ʿAlī b. Azdamar al-Muḥammadī, and he narrates from Shaykh Imām Muftī of Irāq Muḥiyy al-Dīn Abu-ʿAbdullāh Muḥammad b. ʿAlī b. Muḥammad b. Jāmid al-Baghdādī al-Tawḥīdī ,who wrote in his letter in 626 *hijrī*. He penned down the following:

> Sayyiduna Shaykh Muḥiyy al-Dīn ʿAbd al-Qādir al-Jilānī was soft hearted, and cried instantly; for he was very fearful of *Allāh*. Being a personality classified as sacrosanct, his *duʿās* were promptly accepted. He was kind by nature. From amongst all the people, he was blessed with the perspiration of fragrance. He distanced himself from sins, and remained closest amongst the people of truth. He reacted aptly in instituting justice to anyone who defamed or insulted the beloved servants of *Allāh*. For personal reasons, he would never be infuriated, nor resort to vengeance, without the decree of his Lord. No beggar was turned down by him. The *Tawfīq* of *Allāh* engulfed him,

supported and assisted him. Knowledge granted him spiritual bliss within the Divine Proximity, which taught him *adab* [etiquette]. Presence was his treasure and *Ma ʿārifah* was his security, whilst his speech was his stateliness. The edge of his eye was his ambassador and love was his associate. His expansive heart was his soothing breeze, whilst truth was his standard. Victory was the wealth of his wisdom, and *dhikr* was his minister. Spiritual unveiling was his sustenance, whereas spiritual observance was his cure. The ethics of *Sharī ʿāh* were distinct on the exterior, and his characteristics revealed the reality of his inner self. He used to recite the following couplets:

لِلّٰهِ اَنْتَ لَقَدْ رَحِبْتَ جَنَاباً وَشَرَّفْتَ اَصْلاً طَاهِراً وَنِصَابَا

Lo! The extent of Your Court,
You have blessed original purity with dignity

وَ عَظَّمْتَ قَدْراً شَامِخاً حَتّٰى اِغْتَدٰى قَوْسَ الْغَمَامِ لِأَخْمَصِيكَ رِكَابَا

You have blessed lofty status with excellence,
That the bow of the clouds gave sustenance to the saddle of your feet

وَبَنَيْتَ بَيْتاً فِي الْمَعَالِي اَصْبَحَتْ زَهَرُ الْكَوٰكَبِ حَوْلَهُ اَطْنَابَا

You have made your home in heights
That the stars around them became of pearls

يَا مُلْبَسَ الدُّنْيَا بِرَوْنَقِ مَجْدِهِ بَعْدَ الْمَشِيْبِ فَضَارَةً وَشَبَابَا

O that person who after old age donned the splendid clothing
of your nobleness and made you a young person

طَلَبَتْكَ اَبْكَارُ الْعُلٰى نَجْمَ الْهُدٰى وَهِيَ الَّتِي قَدْ اَعْيَتِ الطُّلَّابَا

The virgins of lofty height asked you for the stars of guidance
And they are such who tire those who ask

لَمَّا رَأَتْكَ حَسَلُهَا كُفُواً لَهَا خَطَبَتْ اِلَيْكَ وَرَدَّتِ الْخُطَّابَا

When their beauty observed your compatibility,
then they proposed to marry you and rejected the others

وَاَتَتْكَ مَسْمَحَةُ الْقِيَادِ مَنَاقِبُ كَانَتْ عَلٰى مَنْ اَمْهَنَ صِعَابَا

And came to you the praises with youth

This is for him who easily understands in difficulties

رَجُلٌ يَرُوْقُكَ مَنْظَراً وَ جَلَالَةً وَمَكَارِماً وَ خَلَائِقاً وَ خِطَابَا

He is such that would cheer you with his vision; nobleness, glory, conduct and address

وَ يَرىٰ عَلَيْهِ مِنَ الْمَحَاسِنِ مَلْبَساً وَمِنَ الْمَهَابَةِ وَ الْعُلىٰ جِلْبَابَا

The garb of elegance is seen on him and on him is a mantle of Awe and loftiness

Names of some of his Mashā'ikh

Be cautious and may *Allāh* ﷻ sustain you with His ﷻ succour. May He ﷻ include you amongst His ﷻ legion. Indeed, the Hands of *Qudrat* [Power] have extracted a pearl from the Ocean of Prophethood; whose link is an orphan. The uniqueness of its nobility was created by *Tawḥīd*; which is incomparable in singularity. Its owner [*Allāh* ﷻ] has created it exclusively for Himself ﷻ, and purified it with the neighbourhood of glory. *Allāh* ﷻ illuminated it with the splendour of His ﷻ relationship, and purified it with His ﷻ love. He ﷻ has sanctified it for His closeness and absorption of His ﷻ mercy. He ﷻ called out to it with His ﷻ grace and communion, which deemed it to be extinct. He ﷻ entrusted it with the Treasury of His ﷻ Knowledge and Secrets; and adorned it with the exquisiteness of splendour and excellence; and henceforth, exposed it to the heights of inception; together with the legion of honour. This unique pearl emanated in the origin [dawn of his appearance in Baghdād] of the forehead of Sayyiduna Shaykh ʿAbd al-Qādir al-Jilānī رضي الله عنه; and thereby merged with honour, leading ahead, whilst followed behind by *Tawfiq*. He was raised and nurtured in the lap of bounties; and fed with the milk of munificence. He was covered with remission, protected by Divine Providence and was viewed with affection.

In 488 *hijrī*, Sayyiduna Ghawth al-Aʿzam رضي الله عنه, with his luminous appearance, combined with graciousness and felicity set foot in Baghdād. He settled in Baghdād and within its surrounding cities. Simultaneously the clouds rained with blessings. Hence, new and old entities were manifested.

The sparks of salvation doubled over him. Thereafter, the *Abdãls* and *Awtãd* were brightened, and the messengers of glad-tidings frequented him. Every moment an *'Eid* came to him together with his confederates, and henceforth, the signs of the paths became distinct. His students and people were accorded superiority. Heights brought him down to a condition, whereby garlands depicting the status of felicity were around his neck. Brilliance created room for him to such a state, that the crown on his head, symbolic of his status was studded with a unique pearl. The heart of Irãq was ecstatically whirled by his extensive bosom. The tongue with his teeth, and with the appearance of his resplendent face sang the praises of *Allãh* ﷻ as follows:

بِمَقْدَمِهٖ اِنْهَلَّ السَّحَابُ وَ اَعْشَبَ الْعِرَاقُ وَ زَالَ الْغَيُّ وَ اتَّضَحَ الرُّشْدُ

By your arrival the clouds rained and Irãq became lush;
Deviation from religion dispersed and guidance emerged

فَعِيْدَانُهُ رَنْدٌ وَ صَحْرَاءُ حِمًى وَ حَصْبَاؤُهُ دُرٌّ وَ اَمْوَاهُهُ شَهِدُ

Its wood is Agar wood and its jungles are safe pastures
Its pebbles are pearls and its water is honey

يَمِيْسُ بِهٖ صَدْرُ الْعِرَاقِ صَبَابَةً وَ فِيْ قَلْبِ نَجْدٍ مِنْ مَحَاسِنِهٖ وَجْدُ

The headquarter of Irãq [Baghdãd] is lush due to love and
the heart of the highlands is ecstatic due to its beauty

وَ فِي الشَّرْقِ بَرْقٌ مِنْ مَّحَاسِنِ نُوْرِهٖ وَ فِي الْغَرْبِ مِنْ ذِكْرٰى جَلَالَتِهٖ رَعْدُ

The east is the lightening of the beauty of light
And the west is trembling with the glory of its dhikr

Sayyiduna Ghawth ﷺ studied under these illustrious ʿUlama

Sayyiduna Ghawth ﷺ realized that knowledge is a security for life, the cure for the sick and the most appropriate path to piety. By the virtue of reasoning, it is most perfect. As far as proofs are concerned, it is most evident similar to a raised ladder. It is from the lofty stations of the pious and an extensive mission of *Dĩn*. Knowledge is from the dignified stations of the guided; and it is a ladder that conveys one to the gnosis within Divine Proximity of Almighty *Allãh* ﷻ. It is the medium of attaining the trusteeship of lofty noble stations. Thus, Sayyiduna Ghawth ؓ engaged in ardent perusal in order to attain this knowledge. He endeavoured to master the principles and branches of all sciences of knowledge; whilst seated in the company of such erudite Masters, who were the banners of guidance for *Imãms* and *ʿUlama* of the *Ummah*. He engaged himself in the studies of the *Qur'ãn*; until he perfected the understanding of its external and intrinsic meanings. He studied Islãmic Jurisprudence [*Fiqah*] under the tutelage following Masters:

- Shaykh Abu al-Wafa ʿAlĩ b. ʿAqĩl ؓ
- Shaykh Abu al-Khattãb Maḥfũz b. Aḥmad al-Kalũwafĩ ؓ
- Shaykh Abu al-Ḥasan Muḥammad b. al-Fãḍĩ b. Ḥusain b Ḥusain b. Muḥammad al-Farã ؓ
- Sayyiduna Shaykh Abu-Saʿĩd Mubãrak b. ʿAlĩ al-Makhzũmĩ ؓ

He extensively studied Religious Sciences and principles; which included branches of *Osũl o Furũʿh* [roots and branches]. He studied *Ḥadith* under the tutelage of following *Ḥadith* Masters:

- ✓ Shaykh Abu-Ghãlib Muḥammad b. al-Ḥasan b. Aḥmad b. Ḥasan al-Bãqalãnĩ ؓ
- ✓ Shaykh Abu-Sãʿad Muḥammad b. ʿAbd al-Karĩm b. Khãnĩsh ؓ
- ✓ Shaykh Abu al-Ghanãim Muḥammad b. ʿAlĩ b. Maymũn al-Rasĩ ؓ
- ✓ Shaykh Abu-Bakr Aḥmad b. al-Muzaffar b. Masũs ؓ date merchant
- ✓ Shaykh Abu-Muḥammad Jaʿãfar b. Aḥmad b. Ḥusain al-Qãrĩ Sirãj ؓ
- ✓ Shaykh Abu al-Qãsim ʿAlĩ b. Aḥmad b. Bayãn al-Karkhĩ ؓ
- ✓ Shaykh Abu-Uthmãn Ismãʿĩl b. Muḥammad b. Aḥmad b. Jaʿãfar b. Millat al-Asbahãnĩ ؓ
- ✓ Shaykh Abu-Tãlib ʿAbd al-Qãdir b. Muḥammad b. ʿAbd al-Qãdir b. Muḥammad b. Yũsuf ؓ and the son of his uncle,
- ✓ Shaykh Abu-Tãhir ʿAbd al-Raḥmãn b. Aḥmad b. ʿAbd al-Qãdir b. Muḥammad Yũsuf ؓ
- ✓ Shaykh Abu al-Barkãt Haybatullãh b. Mubãrak b. Mũsa al-Saqtĩ ؓ

- ✓ Shaykh Abu al-ʿIzz Muḥammad b. Mukhtār al-Hāshimī ﷺ
- ✓ Shaykh Abu al-Farr Muḥammad Abu-Ghālib Aḥmad Abu-ʿAbdullāh Yaḥyah s/o Imām Abu-ʿAlī Ḥasan b. Naba Abu al-Ḥusain al-Mubārak b. ʿAbd al-Jabbār b. Aḥmad b. Abu al-Qāsim al-Sairfī ﷺ well-known as Ibn al-Taywarī
- ✓ Shaykh Abu-Mansūr ʿAbd al-Raḥmān b. Abī-Ghālib Muḥammad b. ʿAbd al-Wāḥid b. Ḥasan al-Qizāz ﷺ
- ✓ Shaykh Abu al-Barkāt Talḥa b. Aḥmad al-ʿĀqūlī ﷺ

Acquiring ʿIlm al-Tarīqah

Sayyiduna Ghawth al-Aʿzam ﷺ inherited spiritual characteristics [*adab*] from Shaykh Abu-Zakariyah Yaḥyah b. ʿAlī al-Tabrīzī ﷺ. He sat in the company of those, and studied *ʿIlm al-Tasawwuf*; and thereby derived *tarbiyah* from Shaykh ʿĀrif, Leader of the Realizers, Ḥaḍrat Abu al-Khayr Ḥammād b. Muslim al-Dabbās ﷺ, the juice merchant. He pledged *bayʿah* and received the sacred *khirqah* [Spiritual *Sūfī* Garb] from *Qāḍī al-Quḍāt* Sayyiduna Abu-Saʿīd Mubārak al-Makhzūmī ﷺ.

He met with the most senior leaders, *Mashā'ikh, ʿĀrifīn* and *Zāhids* of Irāq and ʿAjam [Persia] and derived blessings from them, whose *barakāt* manifested in his later years that enhanced his impeccable status. Thus, he was a promoter, supporter and a medication for the sacred *Sharīʿah*; classified as a beacon and flag of *Islām*. He was a sword and shield for the Truth.

He diligently stood up to acquire the Sciences of the *Sharīʿah* from these illustrious personalities. He was steadfast on his studies, until he surpassed his contemporaries and excelled supreme with a lofty status.

Thereafter, Almighty *Allāh* ﷻ exposed him for the benefit of people and blessed him with popularity amongst the masses, and as well as the elite. He possessed astonishing awe-inspirational attributes amongst the *ʿUlama*; and within his heart *Allāh* ﷻ disclosed the sacred Law, whereas through his lips, the signs of *Allāh's* ﷻ Powers were visible. The manifestation of his sainthood [*Wilāyah*] is the evidence of his exclusivity. His feet were steadfast in his spiritual struggle [*Mujāhidah*]; and he detached himself from carnal desires. He exercised seclusion from creation, whilst engrossed in Divine Worship of his Sublime Lord ﷻ. Although he encountered great hardship and pain, yet he was fervent in his devotion. He exercised profound patience during adversity and prudently executed all his duties.

Henceforth, he was entrusted with the *madressa* of his honourable *Ustāz*, Shaykh Abu-Saʿīd Mubārak al-Makhzūmī ﷺ. The school was extended, for he built more classrooms around it for the influx of students. The wealthy contributed their wealth whole-heartedly in the cause of this construction; whilst the labour was provided by the devout poor. It was in 527 *hijrī* that this *madressa* was completed, and attributed to him. The great Ghawth ﷺ designated his seat therein; taught and issued Islāmic Rulings [*fatāwa*]. He delivered his discourses therein, and people flocked to attend and derive knowledge from him. Eventually, a massive crowd, comprising *ʿUlama*, *Mashā'ikh, Foqaha* and *Sāliḥīn* assembled to derive knowledge and spiritual benefits from him. Students from far and wide flocked to study under his supervision and would listen to his discourses. The training of the *murīds* of Irāq was completed under his able and vigorous supervision. He was entrusted with the Keys of Reality and the reins of the Gnostics [*ʿĀrifīn*]. Spiritual sciences were dispensed to him.

Taking his seat on the Station of Qutbiyat

Eventually, he reclined to his seat on the lofty throne of *Qutbiyat*[276], where he began issuing *fatāwas* and imparting Islāmic knowledge. He explained the laws at a rational and traditional level. Verbally and actively, he reinforced truth. He authored books at a prolific level, which were informative and beneficial.

[276] The designation of the Cardinal Pole of noble Saints (*Qutb*). The one person who forms the focus of *Allah*'s ﷻ supervision of the world in every age.

His companions promoted his discourses, and his prominence reached far and wide. People bowed their necks in submission to him. The eyes were purified by the gorgeousness of his gardens. He articulated in languages with extraordinary attributes. Whilst praising him, some opine that he was a person, possessing two languages and two speeches – *Dhu al-Bayanain*. Others praise him as *'Karĩm al-Jaddain wa al-Tarafain,* which means Noble, by virtue of the two Grandfathers [*Ḥasanĩ* and *Ḥusainĩ*].' Thus, from the both sides of the family and others attributed to him the title 'Holder of the Two Proofs and the Two Mandates - *Saḥib al-Burhanain wa al-Sultanain*,' whilst other individuals addressed him as 'The Imãm of the Two Parties and the Two Paths - *Imãm al-Farĩqain wa al-Tarĩqain.*' He was also named 'Master of the Two Lamps and the Two Routes - *Dhu al-Sirãjain wa al-Minhãjain*'. Hence, the Paths of time became illuminated and the Paths of Religion were sanctified owing to him. The stations of knowledge were elevated through him; and the legion of the Sacred Law [*Sharĩ'ãh*] was victorious owing to him. It is for this reason that a large group of *'Ulama* were aligned to him, and erudite senior Jurists [*Foqaha*] became his students.

As per information, those *'Ulama* who linked themselves to the great Ghawth ﵁, studied the science of *Sharĩ'ãh* with him and had heard the narrations of *Aḥãdith* from him. NB: It is apparent that, when a certain Shaykh took or wore a *khirqah* from Sayyiduna Ghawth ﵁, it meant that he pledged *Bay'ãh* at his hands. In other words, he became the *murĩd* of the great Ghawth ﵁. They are as follows:

1) Shaykh Imãm and leader Abu-ʿAmar ʿUthmãn b. Marzũq b. Ḥamĩd b. Salãmat al-Qurashĩ ﵁ hailed from Cairo, and was elegant amongst the *Mashã'ikh* and the exemplar of the *'Ulama.*

I narrate from Shaykh Abu- Saʿãd ʿAbd al-Ghãlib b. Aḥmad b. ʿAlĩ al-Hãshimĩ ﵁, and he narrates from Sayyiduna Shaykh Muḥiyy al-Dĩn Abu-ʿAbdullãh Muḥammad al-Jilãnĩ ﵁. He narrates from his father, Qãḍĩ al-Quḍãt Sayyiduna Shaykh Abu-Sãliḥ Nasar al-Jilãnĩ ﵁ that he had heard from his illustrious father, Sayyiduna Shaykh Tãj al-Dĩn ʿAbd al-Razzãq al-Jilãnĩ ﵁ s/o Sayyiduna Ghawth al-Aʿzam ﵁ pronouncing that the year in which his illustrious father performed *Ḥajj*, he accompanied him. Shaykh Abu-ʿAmar ʿUthmãn b. Marzũq ﷺ and Shaykh Abu-Madyan ﷺ met him at *ʿArafãt*. Both of them wore a *khirqah* from his father ﷺ; and he had heard a narration from Shaykh Abu-ʿAmar ʿUthmãn b. Marzũq ﷺ. Both of them were seated in front his father; with the same chain up till Shaykh Abu-Sãliḥ ﷺ. He exclaimed that he was informed by Shaykh Abu al-Khayr Saʿãd b. Shaykh Abu-ʿAmar ʿUthmãn b. Marzũq ﷺ, who stated that he was informed by his father ﷺ, who informed that his Shaykh ʿAbd al-Qãdir ﷺ said so and so.... I saw my Master Shaykh Muḥiyy al-Dĩn ʿAbd al-Qãdir ﷺ and proclaimed certain issues.....

2) Qãḍĩ Abu-Yaʿhlã Muḥammad Abu-Muḥammad b. Farã, who is the brilliance of *Islãm* [*Jamãl al-Islãm*] and the pride of the Jurists [*Fakhr al-Foqaha*].

I narrate from Shaykh Abu-Muḥammad Saʿãdullãh b. ʿAlĩ b. Aḥmad Rabʿĩ al-Fãrũqĩ ﷺ, who narrates from Shaykh Abu-Mansũr ʿAbdullãh b. Walĩd Ḥãfiz ﷺ and he narrates from Shaykh Abu-Muḥammad ʿAbd al-ʿAzĩz b. Akhḍar Ḥãfiz ﷺ, who stated that he had heard from Qãḍĩ Abu-Yaʿhlã Muḥammad b. Farã ﷺ, declaring that he had heard a proportion from Sayyiduna Shaykh Muḥiyy al-Dĩn ʿAbd al-Qãdir al-Jilãnĩ ﷺ, and he has narrated in accordance to his intentions.

3) Shaykh Faqih Abu al-Fataḥ Nasar b. Fatyãn b. Matar Muthnã ﷺ was a symbol of the Ascetics and unique amongst the *Foqahã*.

I narrate from Shaykh Abu-Bakr b. Shaykh ʿAbd al-Ḥaqq b. Makkĩ Sãliḥ al-Qurashĩ Misrĩ ﷺ, who narrates from his father, and he narrates from Shaykh Wajũhudĩn Dãʿũd b. Sãliḥ al-Mukrĩ ﷺ, who was visually impaired. He conversed that he used to visit Shaykh Imãm Zãhid Abu al-Fataḥ b. al- Muthnã ﷺ in Baghdãd. Indeed! I have heard him mention that Sayyiduna Shaykh ʿAbd al-Qãdir al-Jilãnĩ ﷺ was his Shaykh and *Shaykh al-Islãm*; categorized as our blessings, our leader, and that they had benefitted from him.

4) Shaykh Imãm Abu-Muḥammad Maḥmũd b. ʿUthmãn ﷺ [shoe merchant], was the enhancement of the *Ḥadith* Masters and Ascetics.

I narrate from Shaykh Abu-Ghālib Muḥammad b. al-Ḥasan b. ʿAlī al-Lakhmī al-Baghdādī ﷺ, who narrates from the Shaykh of noble origin Abu-Sulaymān Dāʾūd b. Abu al-Fataḥ Sulaymān b. Shaykh Abu-ʿAbdullāh ʿAbd al- Wah'hāb ﷺ. He enunciated that he had heard from his father, Shaykh ʿAbd al-Wah'hāb al-Jilānī ﷺ, who proclaimed that he had heard from Shaykh Maḥmūd ﷺ [shoe merchant]; Shaykh ʿUmar al-Fazāl ﷺ, Shaykh Abu al-Ḥasan Fārsī ﷺ, Shaykh ʿAbd al-Karīm al-Fārsī ﷺ and Shaykh Abu al-Faḍal Aḥmad b. Sāliḥ b. Shāfeʿh al-Jilī Ḥāfiz ﷺ. All of them were the *murīds* of my august father and had acquired knowledge from him; narrated *Ḥadith* from him, and reported on his charisms [*karamāt*].

5) Shaykh Abu-Muḥammad ʿAbdullāh b. Aḥmad b. Khashāb was an unparalleled grammarian and linguist.

I narrate in Muqayyid from Shaykh Abu-Ghālib Aḥmad b. Abī-Jaʿāfar b. Abī ar-Riḍā Muḥammad b. Aḥmad ﷺ distinguished as Jadda, who narrates from his father, and he had heard from his father, who affirmed that Shaykh Abu-Muḥammad Khashāb ﷺ was a student of Sayyiduna Shaykh ʿAbd al-Q̱ādir al-Jilānī ﷺ, and he had narrated from him.

6) Ḥāfiz Abu al-Khayr ʿAbdul Mughīth b. Zahar b. Zadād b. ʿAlawī al-Ḥarīmī ﷺ, who in his time was prominently known as Ḥāfiz al-Irāq

I narrate from Shaykh Abu al-Razād ﷺ, and he narrates from Shaykh Faqih Fāḍil Muḥiyy al-Dīn Yūsuf b. Imām Abu al-Faraḥ b. Jowzī ﷺ. He narrates from Shaykh Abu-Hurayra Muḥammad b. Layth al-Dīnārī ﷺ, who asserted that Ḥāfiz Abu al-Khayr ʿAbdul Mughīth ﷺ was a student of Sayyiduna Shaykh ʿAbd al-Q̱ādir ﷺ, and he was very zealous when speaking about him.

7) The unique Imām Abu-ʿAmar ʿUthmān b. Ismāʿīl b. Ibrāhīm al-Saʿādī ﷺ was classified as the Imām Shafaʿī ﷺ of his time.

I narrate from the Shaykh of noble origin Abu-ʿAbdullāh Muḥammad ﷺ, who narrates from Shaykh Abu-ʿAmar ʿUthmān ﷺ, and he narrates from his father, Shaykh Abu al-Ḥarīm al-Makkī ﷺ, who confirmed that his father wore a *khirqah* from Sayyiduna Shaykh Muḥiyy al-Dīn ʿAbd al-Q̱ādir al-Jilānī ﷺ, studied with him and was one who would call upon him on his behalf.

8) The pious Shaykh Abu-ʿAbdullāh Muḥammad b. Ibrāhīm b. Thābit ﷺ, distinctly identified as Ibn al-Kayrānī was the elegance of the *Qāris* [reciters] and *Zāhids* [Ascetics].

9) Shaykh Faqī Abu-Muḥammad Raslān b. ʿAbdullāh b. Shaʿbān ﷺ was the elegance of the *Foqahā* [Jurists], *Qāris* [reciters] and *Zāhids* [Ascetics].

I narrate from Shaykh Abu-Tālib ʿAbd al-ʿAzīz b. Sālim b. Khalaf al-Misrī Muqrī ﷺ, and he narrates from the pious Shaykh Abu-Muḥammad ʿAbd al-ʿAzīz b. Ibrāhīm b. ʿAbdullāh ﷺ, the date trader and *Muḥaddith,* categorically known as Ḥikmah. He narrates from two *Shuyūkh*, Shaykh Abu al-Fuḍayl ʿUmar b. ʿAbd al-ʿAzīz b. Haybatullāh al-ʿAsqalānī ʿĀdil ﷺ and Shaykh Abu al-Mansūr Zāfir b. Tarkhān b. Ḥawāb al-Ghassānī ﷺ. Both of them revealed in Cairo that Shaykh Abu-ʿAbdullāh b. Kayzānī ﷺ and Faqih Raslān ﷺ had received the *Sūfī khirqah* of *Tasarruf* [277] from Sayyiduna Shaykh Muḥiyy al-Dīn ʿAbd al-Qādir al-Jilānī ﷺ and reported his charismatic attributes [*karamāt*]. Whenever they gave a *khirqah* to anyone, they would emphasize: *'Your and our Shaykh is Shaykh ʿAbd al-Qādir al-Jilānī ﷺ.'*

10) Shaykh the leader, Abu al-Saʿūd Aḥmad b. Abī-Bakr al-Ḥarīmī ʿAttār ﷺ is the *Sirāj al-Awliya* [Sun of the *Awliya*]. He sat in the company of Sayyiduna Ghawth ﷺ narrated *Ḥadith* and studied with him. The most important thing is that he also narrated what he heard from Sayyiduna Ghawth ﷺ.

11) Shaykh the leader, Abu- ʿAbdullāh Muḥammad b. Abī-Maʿālī al-Adānī Shahīd ﷺ is the pride of the *ʿUlama* and *Mashā'ikh* who carry the martyrs, and the esteem of the theologians [*Fakhr al-Mutakallimīn*].

[277] *Tasarruf.* Free disposal or dispensation of spirituality. The Perfect Man governs the affairs of the world and controls them through the Divinely Ordained powers. He exercises spiritual dispensation throughout the world. This blessed spiritual authority [*tasarruf*] is the knower's power of bringing events to fruition, whilst directing his spiritual energy towards the sphere of all possibilities.

His bond with Sayyiduna Ghawth al-Aʿzam ﷺ is well recognized and which does not require any proof. At a later stage in the book, it shall be *in sha Allāh* mentioned about him.

12) Shaykh Abu ʿAbdullāh b. Sinān ﷺ, prominently known as Radīnī was the Shaykh of the *Foqahā* [Jurists] and *Zāhids* [Ascetics].

I narrate from the Jurist [*Faqih*] Abu-Muḥammad ʿAbd al-Jabbār b. Muḥammad ʿAlī al-Qurashī al-Misrī Muaddib ﷺ, and he narrates from Shaykh Abu al-Rabīʿh Sulaymān b. Aḥmad b. ʿAlī al-Saʿādī ﷺ, distinguished as Ibn al-Maghrīl who stated that their Shaykh, Radīnī ﷺ is attributed to Sayyiduna Shaykh ʿAbd al-Qādir al-Jilānī ﷺ. He exalted and revered him and when speaking of his excellence, he recited the following couplet:

حُسْنُكَ لَا تَنْقَضِي عَجَائِبُهُ   كَالْبَحْرِ حَدِّثْ عَنْهُ لَا حَرَجُ

The wonders of your beauty never ends, its example is like
the ocean that you speak about, and there is no harm in this.

13) The pious Shaykh Abu-ʿAlī Ḥasan b. ʿAbdullāh b. Rāfeʿh al-Ansārī al-Damyātī ﷺ, notably known as Qas'sār [the launderer], and he was the *Muftī* of the frontier and Master of the Teachers and *Awliya* [*Sayyid al-Mudarrisīn wa al-Awliya*].

I narrate from Shaykh Abu-Muḥammad Talḥā b. Wazīrayn ʿAbd al-Raḥīm al-Jazrī al-Misrī ﷺ, who narrates from Shaykh Abu-Muḥammad ʿAbdul Azīm b. Shaykh ʿAbd al-Karīm b. Muqrī ﷺ, prominently known as Ibn Alya al-Yemenī, who revealed that Shaykh Abu-ʿAlī Qas'sār ﷺ was a student of Sayyiduna Muḥiyy al-Dīn Shaykh ʿAbd al-Qādir al-Jilānī ﷺ and encouraged the people to be linked to him. I had heard several times from him that the praises of *Allāh* ﷻ is *Imān* and *Islām*, which are based on *Kitāb* [*Qur'ān*] and *Sunnah* it is through that belief; that we are the friends of Sayyiduna Muḥiyy al-Dīn Shaykh ʿAbd al-Qādir ﷺ.

14) Shaykh Muḥammad Abu-Talḥā b. Muzaffar b. Ghānim al-ʿAlthī ﷺ was the Shaykh of the *Foqahā, Muḥaddithīn* and *Zāhids* and a pillar of *Imān*.

I had heard from Shaykh Abu-ʿAlī Ḥusain b. Sulaymān al-Tamīmī al-Ḥarīmī ﷺ,

and he had heard from Shaykh Abu-Muḥammad Yūsuf b. Ḥasan al-ʿAlthī al-Muqrī ﷺ, who declared that Shaykh Talḥā al-ʿAlthī ﷺ was a student of Sayyiduna Shaykh ʿAbd al-Qādir al-Jilānī ﷺ and gave preference to him, over the *Mashā'ikh* of that era.

15) Shaykh Abu al-Khalīl Aḥmad b. Asad b. Wahb b. ʿAlī al-Baghdād al-Hirwī ﷺ was the brilliance of the *Qārīs*. He is attributed to the great Ghawth ﷺ and had studied under him.

I had heard from Faqih Abu al-Faḍal Aḥmad b. Yūsuf b. Muḥammad al-Azjī ﷺ, who had heard from his uncle, Shaykh Abu al-Ghanāim Rizqullāh b. Muḥammad b. Aḥmad b. ʿAlī ﷺ who elucidated that he had heard from Sayyiduna Shaykh Abu-ʿAbdullāh al-Jilānī b. Sayyiduna Shaykh ʿAbd al-Wah'hāb al-Jilānī ﷺ who pronounced that the senior Shaykh Aḥmad b. Asad ﷺ articulated to me that *Allāh* ﷻ has blessed him with providence, owing to the attachment with his honourable grandfather; and by virtue of wearing a *khirqah* and acquiring knowledge from him, and as well as the affection portrayed towards him ﷺ.

16) Shaykh Fāḍil Abu al-Baqa Muḥammad al-Azharī al-Sarīfīnī ﷺ is the Crown of the ʿ*Ulama* [*Tāj al-Ulama*], and a senior Shaykh Abu-Muḥammad Yaḥyah b. Barkat Maḥfūz al-Dabīqī Ba-Basrī ﷺ is the grandeur of Irāq. Both of these *Shuyūkh* are students and narrated *Ḥadith* from the great Ghawth ﷺ. They informed him about this. Faqih Abu-Nasar Ghānim b. Fataḥ b. Yūsuf al-Hāshimī al-Karkhī ﷺ states that he was informed about this by Shaykh Sharīf Abu al-Qāsim Haybatullāh b. Mansūrī al-Khatīb ﷺ.

17) Shaykh Abu al-Ḥasan ʿAlī b. Aḥmad b. Wahb al-Azjī ﷺ was the chief companion of Sayyiduna Ghawth ﷺ and had studied under him. He also narrated *Ḥadith* from the Ghawth ﷺ.

I was informed of this by Shaykh Abu al-Muḥāsin Yūsuf b. Shaʿbān b. Muḍir b. ʿAlī al-Hilālī al-Mārdīnī ﷺ, and he had heard *Qāḍī al-Quḍāt* Sayyiduna Shaykh Abu-Sāliḥ Nasar al-Jilānī ﷺ mentioning this.

18) *Qāḍī al-Quḍāt* Abu al-Ḥasan ʿAlī ﷺ and his brother the pious Qāḍī Abu-Muḥammad Ḥasan ﷺ were the sons of Qāḍī Abu al-Ḥasan ʿAlī b. Qāḍī al-Quḍāt Abu-ʿAbdullāh Muḥammad b. ʿAlī Dāmghānī Tāj al-A'imma Sirāj al-Aḥkām wa al-ʿUlama ﷺ.

I narrate from Shaykh Abu-Aḥmad ʿAbd al-Malik b. Fatyān b. ʿĪsā al-Azjī ﷺ, and he narrates from Shaykh Abu al-Ḥasan ʿAlī b. al-Nafīs b. Nūr al-Dīn Yūrūmar al-Māmūtī ﷺ, who informed that both Qaḍī Abu al-Ḥasan ﷺ and his brother were from the progeny of Shaykh Abu-Muḥammad Ḥasan al-Dāmghānī ﷺ. All of them refer to the name of Sayyiduna Shaykh ʿAbd al-Qādir al-Jilānī ﷺ, and also declare their relationship with him.

Qāḍī al-Quḍāt Abu al-Qāsim ʿAbdul Mālik b. ʿĪsā b. Idrīs al-Mārdīnī al-Shāfaʿī ﷺ, who was the glory of Qāsiyūn and the brilliance of *Islām*, whilst his brother Imām Abu-ʿAmar ʿUthmān Sharf al-Islām Fakhr al-ʿUlama ﷺ and his son the senior Qāḍī Abu-Tālib ʿAbd al-Raḥmān ﷺ were the chief *Muftī* of Irāq and the leader of the *ʿUlama*.

I narrate from Shaykh Abu-Tālib ʿAbd al-ʿAzīz b. Sālim al-Misrī al-Muqrī ﷺ, and he narrates from Shaykh Abu-Muḥammad ʿAbd al-ʿAzīz b. Ibrāhīm Muḥaddith ﷺ, the date merchant. He narrates in Cairo from Shaykh Abu al-Faḍal Aḥmad b. ʿAbd al-ʿAzīz al-ʿAsqalānī al-ʿĀdil ﷺ, who stated that Qāḍī Abu al-Qāsim b. Darbās and his son were linked to Shaykh ʿAbd al-Qādir al-Jilānī ﷺ. Both of them had recorded his charismatic attributes [*karamāt*].

19) Shaykh Imām Abu-Isḥāq Ibrāhīm b. Marbīl b. Nasar al-Makhzūmī ﷺ, the visually impaired was the crown of the Qārīs, Foqahā and Zāhids and their chief teacher. His son, Shaykh Abu-Muḥammad ʿAbdullāh ﷺ was the Shaykh of the Just and Jurists.

20) Shaykh Abu-ʿAbdullāh Muḥammad b. Shaykh Imām Raslān b. ʿAbdullāh Faqih al-Shafaʿī ﷺ was the pride of the *Qārīs* and pious. He was allied to the great Ghawth ﷺ and had received the *khirqah* from him. I was informed of this by Shaykh Sāliḥ Abu-Muḥammad Ismāʿil b.

ʿAlī b. Yūsuf b. Shabīb al-Kharzamī al-Misrī ﷺ Shaykh Muwaddab ﷺ, who affirmed that he was informed by Faqih Maqrī Abu al-Muhannad Sārim b. Khalaf b. ʿAlī al-Ansārī ﷺ, who asserted that he had heard from Shaykh Abu al-Thanā Aḥmad b. Mirah b. Aḥmad al-Misrī ﷺ, who had mentioned this.

21) The profound ʿĀlim, Shaykh ʿAbdullāh b. Nasar b. Ḥamza al-Tamīmī al-Bakrī Siddiqī al-Baghdādī ﷺ was the *Muftī* of Irāq and the leader of the *Salikīn* [travellers on the spiritual Path]. He studied the *Ḥadith*, and narrated them, and moreover, he procured a *khirqah* from Sayyiduna Ghawth ﷺ. I read this in his book, entitled '*Anwār al-Nāzir fī Maʿārifat Akhbār al-Shaykh ʿAbd al-Qādir.*'

22) Shaykh Abu-Muḥammad ʿAbd al-Jabbār b. Abī al-Faḍal b. Faraḥ b. Ḥamza al-Azjī al-Taqfī al-Hasrī Shahīd ﷺ is the grandeur of the *Qārīs* and *Foqahā*. He acquired knowledge, narrated *Ḥadith* and linked up with Sayyiduna Ghawth al-Aʿzam ﷺ. This is the mode in which our Shaykh Abu al-Abbās Aḥmad b. Muḥammad b. Samdawiyah al-Sarīfīnī ﷺ provided the information.

23) Shaykh, the erudite Jurist [*Fāḍil Faqih*] Abu al-Ḥasan ʿAlī b. Abī-Tālib b. Ibrāhīm b. Najār al-Ansārī ﷺ was a *Wāʿiz* [orator], *Mufassir* [Exegesist] and Pride of the *Foqahā* [jurists]. Ḥāfiz Abu-Tāhir al-Salfī ﷺ narrates from him, who was from the *ʿUlama* fraternity of *ʿAjam* and the grandson of Imām Abu al-Faraj ʿAbd al-Wāḥid b. Muḥammad al-Shirāzī ﷺ in Baghdād. Shaykh Abu al-Ḥasan al-Ansārī ﷺ wore a *khirqah* and narrated *Ḥadith* from Sayyiduna Ghawth al-Aʿzam ﷺ. Earlier, mention was made about him acquiring a *khirqah* from Sayyiduna Ghawth al-Aʿzam ﷺ.

24) Shaykh Imām Abu-ʿAbdullāh ʿAbdul-Ghanī b. ʿAbd al-Wāḥid al-Maqdisī ﷺ was called an *Amīr al-Moʾminīn* of *Ḥadith* [Leader of the *Ḥadith* Masters]. He was the bliss of the *Ḥuffāz* [*Ḥadith* Masters]; chief

of the ʿUlama, incomparable amongst the *Mashā'ikh* and the luminary of the *Zāhids* [Ascetics].

25) Shaykh Imām Abu-Amar Muḥammad b. Aḥmad b. Muḥammad Qudāmah al-Maqdisī ﷺ was unique amongst the ʿ*Ulama*; glory of the *Foqahā* and a symbol of the *Zāhids*.

26) Shaykh Imām Abu-Isḥāq Ibrāhīm b. ʿAbd al-Wāḥid al-Maqdisī ﷺ was the master of the *Qurra; Foqahā, Muḥaddithīn* and *Zāhids*.

27) Shaykh Imām Muwaffiq al-Dīn Muḥammad ʿAbdullāh b. Aḥmad b. Muḥammad b. Qudāmā al-Maqdisī ﷺ was unparalleled amongst the *Imāms*, the leader of the *Qurra*; and the lamp of *ʿUlama, Muḥaddithīn* and unique amongst the *Awliya*.

I narrate from Shaykh Qāḍī al-Qudāt Shams al-Dīn Abu-ʿAbdullāh Muḥammad al-Maqdisī ﷺ, who affirmed that he had heard from his Shaykh ʿĀlim Rabbānī Muwaffiq al-Dīn b. Qudāmā al-Maqdisī ﷺ; that both, he and Shaykh Ḥāfiz ʿAbd al-Ghanī ﷺ wore a *khirqah* at the same time from Shaykh al-Islām Muḥiyy al-Dīn ʿAbd al-Qādir al-Jilānī ﷺ. We studied *Fiqah* and narrated *Ḥadith* from him. We derived great benefits in his august companionship and spent 50 of the best nights of our lives in his companionship. Qāḍī al-Quḍāt ﷺ reveals to the best of his knowledge that, his father and Shaykh Abu-ʿAmar ﷺ sat in the companionship of the great Ghawth ﷺ.

28) The senior Shaykh, Qāḍī Abu al-Fataḥ Muḥammad was the pious Qāḍī Abu al-ʿAbbās Aḥmad b. Bakhtiyār b. ʿAlī al-Wāstī ﷺ, distinguished as Ibn al-Muhannad Baqiyat al-Salf Shaykh al-Quḍāt. He was the brilliance of the *ʿUlama* and the leader of the *Zāhids*.

I narrate from Shaykh Abu al-Jāʿad Nasar b. Miftāḥ b. Sakhar b. Musaddad al-ʿAlawī al-Karkhī ﷺ, who narrates from Shaykh Abu-Tālib ʿAbd al-Raḥmān b. Abu al-Fataḥ Muḥammad b. ʿAbd al-Samīʿh al-Hāshimī al-Wāstī ﷺ, who articulated to Shaykh ʿĀdil ﷺ that he had heard from Qāḍī Abu al-Fataḥ b. Mundāʿī ﷺ, who pronounced that Sayyiduna Shaykh Muḥiyy al-Dīn ʿAbd al-

Qādir ﷺ is our Master and the Shaykh of those who had acquired knowledge from him in that era; and henceforth, narrate from him.

29) Shaykh Khalīl Abu-Muḥammad ʿAbdullāh b. Ḥusain b. Abī al-Faḍal al-Jabāʿī ﷺ was the Shaykh of the *Musnads* and *Foqahā*. He sat in the company of Sayyiduna Ghawth al-Aʿzam ﷺ and studied *Fiqah*, and narrated *Ḥadith* from him. Faqih Abu al-Faraj ʿAbd al-Samad b. Aḥmad ʿAlī al-Qatfanī Baz'zār ﷺ reported this to me

I narrate from Shaykh Abu al-Fataḥ Nasar b. Riḍwān b. Tharwān al-Darānī al-Muqrī ﷺ, who reported about this.

30) Shaykh Faqih Abu al-Qāsim Khalf b. Ayyāsh b. ʿAbd al-ʿAzīz al-Misrī ﷺ was the pride of the *Foqahā, Qurrā* and *Muḥaddithīn* and *Baqiyat al-Salf* [pious ancestors]. He studied under the great Ghawth ﷺ and acquired a *khirqah* from him. Reference to his *khirqah* has been made earlier in the book.

31) Shaykh Imām Najam al-Dīn Abu al-Faraj ʿAbdul Munʿīm b. ʿAlī b. Nasīr Saiqal al-Ḥarrānī ﷺ was incomparable amongst the *ʿUlama* and was a pride amongst the erudite theologians. He linked up with, and accepted Sayyiduna Ghawth ﷺ as his Shaykh. His son, our Shaykh Najīb al-Dīn Abu al-Futūḥ ʿAbd al-Latīf ﷺ reported, and had recorded this.

32) Shaykh the leader, Abu al-Ḥasan ʿAlī b. Ibrāhīm b. Ḥaddād al-Yemenī ﷺ was the teacher of the *Mashā'ikh* of Yemen, and was the dignity of the *Foqahā* and *Muḥaddithīn*.

33) Shaykh Jalīl Abu-Muḥammad ʿAbdullāh al-Asadī ﷺ was the light of the *Baqiyat al-Salf* [pious ancestors] of Yemen and the Shaykh of the *Foqahā* and *Muḥaddithīn*.

I narrate from the Jurist [*Faqih*] Abu al-Yemen Barkāt b. Shaykh ʿĀrif Abu-Muḥammad ʿAtīf b. Ziyād al-Muqrī al-Yemenī ﷺ, who narrates from his father, and he had heard from Shaykh ʿAbdullāh al-Asadī ﷺ, who informed that when the eminence of my Master Sayyiduna Shaykh ʿAbd al-Qādir ﷺ spread in Yemen, I acquired the *khirqah* from Shaykh ʿAlī b. Ḥaddād ﷺ, whilst he wore a *khirqah* from Sayyiduna Ghawth al-Aʿzam ﷺ and had studied under him. He invited the people towards linking themselves with Sayyiduna Ghawth al-Aʿzam ﷺ. Thereafter, news reached Yemen that Sayyiduna Ghawth ﷺ would be performing *Ḥajj* in that year, and hence, I decided to proceed for *Ḥajj* so that I might be able to see him. I met with him at *ʿArafāt* and he blessed me with a *khirqah*; and I heard the *Ḥadith al-Nabawī* ﷺ from him. This was the reason as to why I declared this day to be commemorative.

34) Shaykh Abu-Ḥafs ʿUmar b. Aḥmad al-Yemenī ﷺ was distinguished as *Baḥr al-ʿUlūm* [ocean of various sciences], and the glory of the *ʿUlama* and pious.

35) Shaykh Abu-Muḥammad Mudāfeʿh b. Aḥmad ﷺ was the bliss of the *Foqahā* and ascetics.

36) Shaykh Abu-Isḥāq Ibrāhīm b. Bishārat b. Yuʿqūb al-ʿAdnī al-Muqrī Muḥaddith ﷺ was from the *Baqiyat al-Salf* [pious ancestors]. He was an associate, and had acquired a *khirqah* from Sayyiduna Ghawth al-Aʿzam ﷺ.

I was informed of this by Shaykh Faqih Abu-ʿAlī Ḥasan b. Gharfa b. Ḥusain al-Zubaydī ﷺ. He states that he was informed by Shaykh ʿĀrif Abu-Muḥammad ʿAbdullāh b. Mubārak al-Kirmānī ﷺ, who had heard from Shaykh Faqih Sāliḥ Abu-ʿAbdullāh Muḥammad b. Ismāʿīl b. Abī al-Sayf ﷺ and thus, had related it.

37) Shaykh the leader, Abu al-Qāsim ʿUmar b. Masʿūd b. Abu al-ʿIzz al-Baghdādī ﷺ renowned as Baz'zār was the leader of the *Awliya*, and prolific amongst the *Foqahā*. He narrated *Ḥadith* and studied *Fiqah* under Sayyiduna Ghawth al-Aʿzam ﷺ.

I narrate from Shaykh Imām Shams al-Dīn Abu-ʿAbdullāh al-Maqdisī ﷺ, who saw the *Fatāwa* of Shaykh ʿUmar Baz'zār ﷺ in Baghdād; whereby no evidence was needed for his staunch relationship with Sayyiduna Shaykh ʿAbd al-Q̲ādir al-Jilānī ﷺ.

38) Shaykh Sāliḥ Abu-ʿAbdullāh Shah Mīr b. Muḥammad b. Noʿmān al-Jilānī ﷺ. He was a *Faqih* and *Zāhid*. He was in the companionship of Sayyiduna Ghawth al-Aʿzam ﷺ and studied *Fiqah* and, other sciences under his tutelage. This was reported by Shaykh Abu-Mūsā ʿĪsā b. Yaḥyah b. Isḥāq al-Q̲urashī b. Q̲āid al-Duwānī ﷺ, and he was informed by Shaykh Abu-Muḥammad ʿAbdullāh b. Muḥammad b. Ḥasan al-Bādrānī Q̲āḍī al-Q̲uḍāt ﷺ, who had revealed this.

39) The Leader, Shaykh Abu-ʿAbdullāh al-Batāʾiḥī ﷺ a resident of Baʿalbak and the luminary of the *Mashā'ikh*, leader of the *Awliya* was the revered one amongst the *Foqahā*. He studied and obtained a *khirqah* from Sayyiduna Ghawth ﷺ. He also bestowed the *khirqah* onto the *Mashā'ikh* of *Shām* [Syria]. He was the *Shaykh* of the lions of Syria, viz. *Sultān al-ʿĀrifin* Abu-Muḥammad ʿAbdullāh b. ʿUthmān al-Yūyilnī ﷺ.

40) *Shaykh al-Shuyūkh* Imām Abu-Muḥammad Ibrāhīm b. Maḥmūd al-Baʿalbakī ﷺ, distinguished as Batāʾiḥī who was a Shaykh of Q̲arār and the venerated one amongst the *Foqahā* and *Muḥaddithīn*. His relationship with Sayyiduna Shaykh Muḥiyy al-Dīn ʿAbd al-Q̲ādir al-Jilānī ﷺ is distinctly recognized; that there is no need for its veracity or even in mentioning it.

41) Shaykh Imām Abu al-Ḥaram al-Makkī b. Imām Abu-ʿAmar ʿUthmān b. Ismāʿīl b. Ibrāhīm al-Saʿādī ﷺ was within the exquisiteness of the *ʿUlama, Muḥaddithīn* and *Zāhids*. His son, Shaykh Muwaffiq al-Dīn Abu al-Q̲āsim ʿAbd al-Raḥmān ﷺ was the chief of the *ʿUlama* and *Awliya* and has written numerous books, comprising prose and poetry.

42) Shaykh Abu al-Baqa Sāliḥ Bahā al-Dīn ﷺ was the light of *Islām*, and gem amongst the *ʿUlama*.

I narrate from Shaykh Abu-ʿAbdullāh Muḥammad b. Aḥmad b. Manzūr al-Kittānī ﷺ, who proclaims that the state of Shaykh Abu al-Ḥaram ﷺ, and his son was such that; when they pledged *bayʿah* of allegiance to be initiated as *murīd* by anyone, they would declare that their leader and Master; and as well as your leader and Master is Sayyiduna Shaykh ʿAbd al-Qādir al-Jilānī ﷺ.

It is stated that letters from both were viewed on two occasions; wherein both had written about their relationship, and their acquisition of the *khirqah* from Sayyiduna Ghawth al-Aʿzam ﷺ.

43) Shaykh, the unique Imām, Abu-Baqa ʿAbdullāh b. Ḥusain b. ʿAbdullāh al-ʿAkbarī al-Basrī ﷺ, who was visually impaired, was the *Imām* and Master of the *Foqahā*, linguist, theologians, grammarians and realistics. He was an *Imām* in possession of various sciences and had written prolific and beneficial books.

I narrate from Shaykh Abu al-Faḍal b. Mansūr b. Aḥmad al-Dūrī ﷺ, who narrates from his Shaykh Faqih Abu al-ʿAbbās Aḥmad b. Muḥammad b. Samdawiyah al-Sarīfīnī ﷺ and Shaykh Abu al-Ḥasan ʿAlī b. Azdamar ﷺ, who narrates from Shaykh Zayn al-Dīn ʿAbdullāh al-Baghdādī ﷺ, prominently identified as Ibn al-Maʿālij. Both of them concur that they had heard from their Shaykh Abu al-Baqa al-ʿAkbarī ﷺ affirming:

'One day, I advanced towards the *majlis* of Sayyiduna Shaykh Muḥiyy al-Dīn ʿAbd al-Qādir al-Jilānī ﷺ. I had not visited him before, and nor had I listened to his discourses. This was my first visit to him. I contemplated within my heart, that I would proceed to the *majlis* in order to listen to this *ʿAjamī* [non-Arab]. I entered the *madrassa* and heard him delivering a lecture. As I entered, he terminated his lecture and remarked: *'O blind with the eye and heart! What are you going to listen from this ʿAjamī?'* When I heard this, I could not encompass myself; and immediately proceeded to his chair, and removed my head gear, and whilst being bare-headed; I appealed to him: *'Position a khirqah onto me!'* He adorned a *khirqah* onto me and pronounced: *'Had Allāh ﷻ not informed me of your consequences, then you would have certainly been doomed.'*

44) The pious Shaykh Abu-Muḥammad ʿAbd al-Raḥmān b. Imām Abu-Ḥafs ʿUmar b. Ghazāl ﷺ was an orator, and the bliss of the *Awliya* and *Muḥaddithīn*.

45) Shaykh Abu-ʿAbdullāh Muḥammad b. Shaykh Imām Abu-Muḥammad Maḥmūd ﷺ [shoe merchant] was the luminary of the *Foqahā* and *Muḥaddithīn*.

46) Shaykh Abu al-Qāsim b. Abī-Bakr Aḥmad b. Abu al-Saʿādat Aḥmad b. Karam b. Ghālib ﷺ was the brilliance of *Islām* and blessed amongst the *Muḥaddithīn*.

47) His brother Shaykh Abu al-ʿAbbās Aḥmad b. Shaykh Abu-Bakr Aḥmad ﷺ was a renowned *Ḥāfiz* [*Ḥadith* Master].

48) Shaykh Abu-Bakr ʿAtīq ﷺ, prominently recognized as Maʿtūq b. Abu al-Faḍal was the leader of the *ʿUlama* and *Foqahā*. He was a companion of Sayyiduna Shaykh Muḥiyy al-Dīn ʿAbd al-Qādir al-Jilānī ﷺ and had narrated *Ḥadith* from him.

I narrate from Shaykh Abu al-Khayr Saʿādullāh b. Abī-Ghālib Aḥmad b. ʿAlī al-Azjī ﷺ, who narrates from Shaykh Muḥiyy al-Dīn Abu-ʿAbdullāh Muḥammad b. ʿAlī al-Tawḥīdī ﷺ, and he narrates from Shaykh Ḥāfiz Abu al-ʿAbbās Aḥmad b. Abī-Bakr al-Mundalījī ﷺ who had mentioned this.

49) Imām Ḥāfiz Abu-Muḥammad ʿAbdullāh b. Abī-Nasar Maḥmūd b. Mubārak al-Khabāndī ﷺ, distinctly identified as Ibn Khafā was the marvelous crown of the *Ḥuffāz* [*Ḥadith* Masters], who taught *Ḥadith* for 60 years and authored many profound books. His classes were conducted at *Jāʿmeh Misr*. During his time, he lived in Irāq.

I narrate from Faqih Abu al-Ḥasan ʿAlī b. Thābit b. Qāsim al-Misrī Muwaddab ﷺ ,who narrates from Shaykh Abu-Muḥammad ʿAbd al-ʿAzīz b. ʿAlī b. Ibrāhīm b. Zardād al-Baghdādī ﷺ, the nephew of Ḥafiz Abu-Bakr Muḥammad b. Qudwat al-ʿĀrifīn Abu-Muḥammad ʿAbd al-Ghanī b. Abī-Bakr Sujāʿh ibn

Nuqtã ﷺ, who states that he narrates from his maternal uncle, Shaykh Abu-Bakr ﷺ who testified that he had heard from Ḥãfiz Abu-Muḥammad b. Akhḍar ﷺ, promulgating that Sayyiduna Shaykh Muḥiyy al-Dĩn ʿAbd al-Qãdir al-Jilãnĩ ﷺ was categorized as a high-ranking *Imãm*, whereby he was the *Sultãn* of the *ʿÃrifin* [Gnostics] and Master of the *Zuh'hãd* [Ascetics]. During his time, Almighty *Allãh* ﷻ had embellished him with the sciences of the sacred *Sharĩʿãh* and the proficiency in *Fatãwa* [Islãmic Jurisprudence]. We realized his merit and *barakãt*, and gained tremendously from him.

50) Shaykh Abu-ʿAbdullãh Muḥammad b. Abu al-Makãrim Faḍal b. Bakhtiyãr b. Abĩ al-Nasar al-Yaʿqũbĩ Ḥãfiz Wãʿiz Khatĩb ﷺ, renowned as the Shaykh of the *Muḥaddithĩn* and moreover, the proof of the verbatim word of the Theologians. He was a companion of Sayyiduna Ghawth ﷺ and had narrated *Ḥadith* from him.

I was informed about this from Shaykh Abu-Jãʿad Nasar b. Miftãḥ b. Sakhr al-ʿAlawĩ al-Karkhĩ ﷺ, and he was informed by Shaykh Abu-Jaʿãfar Muḥammad b. Shaykh Abu-ʿAbdullãh ʿUmar b. Muḥammad b. ʿAbdullãh al-Sohrowardĩ ﷺ.

51) Shaykh ʿÃrif Fãḍil Abu-Malik Ziyãl b. Abu al-Maʿãlĩ b. Rãshid b. Bihãn al-Irãqĩ ﷺ, was visiting the Holy Land. He was the illumined amongst the *Mashã'ikh* and *Zuh'hãd*. His son, Shaykh Abu al-Faraj ʿAbd al-Malik ﷺ was the leader of the *Foqahã, Muḥaddithĩn* and *Zuh'hãd*.

52) Shaykh al-Islãm Abu-Aḥmad ﷺ, distinctly recognized as Faḍĩlah was an author and a pious *Shaykh*. He was an erudite scholar in *Islãmic* sciences.

All these *Shuyũkh* were the companions and students of the great Ghawth ﷺ, and they described his excellence. Shaykh Ziyãl ﷺ proceeded to Baghdãd and personally witnessed his charismatic attributes [*karamãt*].

I narrate from Shaykh Abu al-Qãsim Muḥammad b. ʿUbãdah b. Muḥammad al-Ansãrĩ ﷺ, who narrates from Shaykh ʿAbd al-Malik b Shaykh Ziyãl ﷺ. He affirmed that both, his father and Shaykh Abu-Muḥammad ﷺ, prominently known as Faḍĩlah highly revered Sayyiduna Shaykh Muḥiyy al-Dĩn ʿAbd al-

Qādir al-Jilānī ﷺ, and they documented that they were his followers, and as such were obedient to him. They invited people towards him and I was their adherent.

53) Shaykh Imām Abu al-Faraj ʿAbd al-Raḥmān b. Shaykh Abu al-ʿAlī Najam b. Sharf al-Islām Abu al-Barkāt ʿAbd al-Wah'hāb b. Imām Abu al-Faraj ʿAbd al-Wāḥid b. Muḥammad b. ʿAlī al-Ansārī al-Khazrajī al-Saʿādī ﷺ, who was renowned as Ibn Ḥanbalī was the exquisiteness of *Islām*; Pride of the Teachers, Master of the *Foqahā, Muḥaddithīn* and Theologians. He was the articulate tongue of the pious. His father, Shaykh Abu-ʿAlī ﷺ was the *Muftī* of the people and the light and elegance for the *ʿUlama* of the *Ummah*

I narrate from the pious Faqih Abu-Muḥammad Ḥasan b. ʿImrān Mūsā b. Aḥmad al-Qurashī al-Khālidī ﷺ, who asserted that he was present in Ḥalab in the *majlis* of his Shaykh Abu al-Faraj al-Ḥanbalī ﷺ in Ḥalab. On that day the *ʿUlama* were also present. Amongst them were Shaykh ash-Suyūkh ʿĀlim Rabbānī Shaykh Shahāb al-Dīn Abu-ʿAbdullāh ʿUmar al-Sohrowardī ﷺ, and our Shaykh Qāḍī al-Quḍāt Jamāl al-Ḥukkām Bahā al-Dīn Abu al-Ḥasan Yūsuf b. Rāfeʿh b. Tamīm ﷺ etc. Shaykh Abu al-Faraj al-Ḥanbalī ﷺ delegated: *'Call on the Mashā'ikh! My father advised me to be steadfast and firm on the path and the practices of Sayyiduna Shaykh Muḥiyy al-Dīn ʿAbd al-Qādir al-Jilānī ﷺ, whereas I was also steadfast on his path.'*

54) Shaykh Abu al-Majd ʿĪsā b. Imām Muwaffiq al-Dīn Abu-Muḥammad ʿAbdullāh b. Aḥmad b. Muḥammad b. Qudāmā al-Maqdisī ﷺ was the Shaykh of the *Muḥaddithīn*.

55) Shaykh Abu-Mūsā Abdullāh b. Ḥāfiz Abu-Muḥammad ʿAbd al-Ghanī b. ʿAbd al-Wāḥid al-Maqdisī ﷺ was the luminary of the *Ḥuffāz*.

56) Ḥāfiz Abu-ʿAbdullāh Muḥammad b. ʿAbd al-Wāḥid b. ʿAbd al-Raḥmān Maqdisī ﷺ was the pride of the *Ḥuffāz*, unique in his time, and a celebrity amongst the *ʿUlama*.

I inquired from Qāḍī al-Quḍāt Shaykh ash-Shuyūkh Shams al-Dīn Abu-ʿAbdullāh al-Maqdisī ﷺ, who had relayed to me that his father Shaykh ʿImād al-Dīn ﷺ and that his uncle, Ḥāfiz ﷺ, his Shaykh Muwaffiq ﷺ and Shaykh Abu-ʿAmar ﷺ his children, family and offspring and our Shaykh Ḍiya al-Dīn Muḥammad ﷺ and Shaykh Ḍiya al-Dīn Muḥāsin ﷺ and Qāḍī Najam al-Dīn Abu al-ʿAbbās Aḥmad b. Muḥammad b. Khalaf al-Maqdisī ﷺ [the author of books] and his father, Imām Shahāb al-Dīn ﷺ and Shaykh Abu al-Faraj ʿAbd al-Raḥmān b. ʿAbd al-Munʿim b. Baʿmar b. Sultān b. Surūr al-Maqdisī ﷺ and his brother, Shaykh al-ʿĀlam Abu-Muḥammad ʿAbdul Ḥamīd b. Shaykh Abu-Aḥmad ʿAbd al-Hādī b. Yūsuf b. Muḥammad b. Qudāma al-Maqdisī ﷺ and his brother, Shaykh ʿĀlim Musnad Abu-ʿAbdullāh Muḥammad ﷺ, all of whom are linked to him; and he is linked to Sayyiduna Shaykh Muḥiyy al-Dīn ʿAbd al-Qādir al-Jilānī ﷺ. He adopted the etiquettes [*adab*] from Sayyiduna Ghawth al-Aʿzam ﷺ, revered him and had cherished his affection within his heart. In *Tarīqah*, he followed his advices. Hence, amongst them, if there was anyone blessed to meet the great Ghawth ﷺ and to attend his *majlis*, has certainly acquired knowledge from him. As for those who did not meet with him, they acquired knowledge from those who had met him. This chain of narration proceeds from father to son.

57) Shaykh Abu al-Futūḥ Yaḥyah b. Shaykh Abu as-Saʿādāt Saʿādullāh b. Ḥusain b. Muḥammad b. Yaḥyah b. Sarī al-Tikrīnī ﷺ was the provident of the *Muḥaddithīn*. He was linked to the Ghawth ﷺ, and thereby, narrated *Ḥadith* from him, derived benefits and wrote about him.

I narrate from Shaykh Abu-Muḥammad ʿAbd al-Malik b. Sāliḥ b. Abī-Bakr al-Tikrīnī ﷺ, and he narrates from his uncle, Shaykh Faqih Abu al-Fataḥ Muḥammad b. Abī-Bakr b. ʿAlī b. Aḥmad al-Tikrīnī ﷺ, who brought this information to surface.

58) Shaykh Abu al-Futūḥ Nasar b, Abī al-Faraj Muḥammad b. ʿAlī al-Baghdādī ﷺ, distinguished as Ibn Ḥisrī was the pride of the *Awliya* and adornment of the *ʿUlama*. He perfected the 7 dialects [*qir'ats*] of the recitation of the Holy *Qur'ān* and also authored many books. He would

often listen to the *Ḥadith* narrations of Ḥaḍrate Ghawth ﷺ and benefitted from him; until he turned to be very old. He is an associate of Sayyiduna Ghawth al-Aᶜzam ﷺ, narrated from him and was engrossed in studying under him.

I was informed about this by Shaykh Abu al-Maᶜālī Bilāl b. Faqih al-Jalīl Abu al-Ulā Umayyah b. Nabghā b. Asad al-Hilālī ᶜAdal ﷺ. He confirmed that his father had narrated the same.

59) Shaykh Abu-Muḥammad Yūsuf b. al-Muzaffar b. Shujāᶜh al-ᶜĀqūlī al-Azjī Sihār ﷺ is of the senior elder *Mashā'ikh* and the veneration of the *Foqahā*. He was associated with, narrated from and derived blessing from Ḥaḍrat Ghawth al-Aᶜzam ﷺ. He was held in high esteem by the *Awliya* of *Ḥaqīqah* [Reality].

I was informed of these facts by Shaykh Abu al-Ḥasan ᶜAlī b. Thābit b. Abu al-Qāsim Muaddab ﷺ, who was informed by Shaykh Abu-Muḥammad ᶜAbd al-Raḥmān b. ᶜAlī b. Zarrād b. Aḥat al-Ḥuffāz Abu-Bakr Muḥammad b. Shaykh Abu-Muḥammad ᶜAbd al-Ghanī b. Nuqtā ﷺ, who pronounced that his maternal Uncle, Shaykh Abu-Bakr ﷺ had narrated this.

60) Shaykh Abu al-ᶜAbbās Aḥmad b. Ismāᶜīl b. Abu al-Barkāt Mubārak b. Ḥamza b. ᶜUthmān b. Ḥusain al-Azjī ﷺ, prominently known as Ibn Tabāl was the Shaykh of the *Foqahā* and *Muḥaddithīn*. His son, Shaykh Faqih Muḥaddith Sāliḥ Abu ar-Riḍā Ḥamza ﷺ and his brother Shaykh Abu-ᶜAbdullāh b. Ismāᶜīl b. Ḥamza ﷺ are from the origin of *Baqiyat al-Salf* and *Zayn al-Asḥāb*. All of them were the companions [*Asḥāb*] of Sayyiduna Ghawth al-Aᶜzam ﷺ and had narrated *Ḥadith* from him. They belonged to the home of *Fiqah,* and *Ḥadith* where there was an existence of piety.

I was informed about this by Shaykh Abu-Mūsā b. Yaḥyah b. Isḥāq al-Maqdisī Ibn al-Dūnī ﷺ, and he was informed by Shaykh Abu-ᶜAbdullāh Muḥammad b. Ismāᶜīl b. Ḥamza b. Mubārak al-Azjī ﷺ, prominently recognized as Ibn Tabāl; and this is the mode in which he narrated this.

61) Shaykh Faqih ʿĀlim Abu al-Faḍal Isḥāq b. Aḥmad b. Ghānim al-ʿAlsī ﷺ was a supportive pillar of *Islām;* a luminary of the *Mashā'ikh* and leader of the *ʿUlama* and *Muḥaddithīn.*

62) Shaykh Imām Abu al-Qāsim Haybatullāh b. Aḥmad b. Haybatullāh b. ʿAbd al-Qādir b. Ḥusain ﷺ, distinguished as Ibn al-Mansūr was the glory of the *ʿUlama*, and honour of the orators, *Muḥaddithīn* and *Noqaba* [The Examiners, a group of *Awliya*].

63) The erudite [*Fāḍil*] Shaykh Abu-ʿAbdullāh Muḥammad b. Samdawiyah al-Sarīfīnī ﷺ were the luminaries and the Muftīs of Irāq; whilst his son Shaykh Abu al-ʿAbbās Aḥmad ﷺ was the crown of the *Foqahā, Muḥaddithīn* and *Zuh'hād.*

I was informed by Qāḍī al-Quḍāt Shams al-Dīn al-Maqdisī ﷺ, who had heard from Shaykh Isḥāq al-ʿAlsī ﷺ, stating that he would assert his relationship, which he had with Sayyiduna Shaykh Muḥiyy al-Dīn ʿAbd al-Qādir al-Jilānī ﷺ. I had heard from Shaykh Abu al-Qāsim al-Mansūrī ﷺ, who had confessed: *'I was a year old, when I was brought to Sayyiduna Ghawth al-Aʿzam ﷺ. He placed a khirqah onto me. He also awarded me with a certificate to narrate all his books, and his anecdotes.'*

I had also heard from Shaykh Kamāl al-Dīn Aḥmad b. Samdawiyah ﷺ, who had mentioned about his and his father's relationship with Sayyiduna Shaykh Muḥiyy al-Dīn ʿAbd al-Qādir al-Jilānī ﷺ.

Shaykh Imām Shams al-Dīn ﷺ related that Shaykh Faqih Fāḍil Abu-ʿAmar ʿUthmān al-Bāsarī ﷺ; Shaykh Imām ʿĀlim Zāhid Abu al-Faraj ʿAbd al-Raḥmān b. Baqa ﷺ, prominently recognized as Ibn Sakāf, Shaykh Imām Faqih Musnad Abu-ʿAbdullāh Muḥammad b. Tālib al-Baghdādī Wāʿiz ﷺ, Shaykh Imām Sāliḥ Abu-ʿAbdullāh Muḥammad Wāʿiz al-Darzī ﷺ, Shaykh Jalīl Tāj al-Dīn al-Baghdādī ﷺ, and Shaykh Fāḍil ʿĀlim Nabīl Rukn al-Dīn al-Marātibī al-Baghdādī al-Ḥanbalī ﷺ were all *Qārīs* and had respected the lofty status of Sayyiduna Shaykh Muḥiyy al-Dīn ʿAbd al-Qādir al-Jilānī ﷺ and ascribed themselves to him.

64)Shaykh ʿĀlim Fāḍil Isḥāq b. Ibrāhīm b. Sāʿad al-Dārī ʿAlthī al-Ḥanbalī ﷺ was the tongue of the *Foqahā* [Jurists], *Fusaḥā* [eloquent] *and pride* of the *Muḥaddithīn* [*Ḥadith* Masters].

I was informed by Shaykh Abu-Zayd ʿAbd al-Raḥmān b. Sālim al-Qurashī ﷺ, who had heard Shaykh Ibrāhīm ﷺ declaring that he wore a *khirqah* from the blessed hands of Sayyiduna Shaykh Muḥiyy al-Dīn ʿAbd al-Qādir al-Jilānī ﷺ on the wooden *mimbar*. At that time, he was 7 years of age.

65) Shaykh Jalīl Abu-Tāhir b. Shaykh the leader, Abu al-ʿAbbās Aḥmad b. Alī b. Khalīl b. Ibrāhim b. Khalīl al-Jowsaqī al-Sarsarī ﷺ was the *Khatīb* and exquisiteness of the *Mashā'ikh*. He was classified as the gratification of the *Qurrā* [Reciters] and lamp of the *Awliya*. He acquired the *khirqah* from the great Ghawth ﷺ, studied spiritual principles under him, and he narrated them from him.

I had heard from Shaykh Abu al-Ḥasan ʿAlī b. Abu-Bakr al-Abharī ﷺ and Shaykh Abu-Muḥammad Sālim b. ʿAlī al-Damyātī ﷺ, and both of them had concurred that they had heard Shaykh Khalīl ﷺ proclaiming that he had studied, narrated *Ḥadith* and had imbued spiritual characteristics from Sayyiduna Shaykh Muḥiyy al-Dīn ʿAbd al-Qādir al-Jilānī ﷺ.

I was informed by Shaykh Abu al-Ḥasan ʿAlī b. Abu-Bakr al-Abharī ﷺ and Shaykh Abu-Muḥammad Sālim al-Azjī ﷺ, distinguished as Ibn al-Nuḥāl was the Shaykh of the *Qurra* and *Zuh'hād* who had acquired the *khirqah* from him; and this was often heard about from him.

I had heard from Shaykh Abu-Muḥammad Rajab b. Abu al-Mansūr al-Dārī ﷺ, who affirmed that he had heard Shaykh Abu-Bakr Muḥammad Naḥāl ﷺ, declaring that he wore a *khirqah* from Sayyiduna Shaykh Muḥiyy al-Dīn ʿAbd al-Qādir al-Jilānī ﷺ, when he was 7 years of age.

66) Shaykh Ra'īs Abu-Muḥammad ʿAbd al-Qādir b. ʿUthmān b. Abu al-Barkāt b. ʿAlī b. Abī-Muḥammad Rizqullāh b. ʿAbd al-Wah'hāb b. ʿAbd al-ʿAzīz al-Tamīmī al-Bardānī ﷺ was a *Baqiyat al-Salf*, and a luminous personality of the *Foqahā* and *Muḥaddithīn*. He was a companion, of the

great Ghawth ﷺ, studied *Fiqah* and other sciences with him, narrated *Ḥadith* from him and narrated numerous charisms [*karamāt*] of him.

I was informed of all these facts by Shaykh Abu-Muḥammad b. Ḥasan b. Badrān b. ʿAlī al-Azjī ﷺ, who had heard Shaykh Faqih Imām Abu-Muḥammad ʿAbd al-Qādir al-Tamīmī ﷺ articulating this fact.

67) Shaykh Nabīl Abu-Muḥammad ʿAbd al-ʿAzīz b. Dalaf b. Abī-Tālib al-Baghdādī ʿAdal Nāsikh ﷺ was the bliss of the *Muḥaddithīn* and leader of the *ʿUlama* and *Zuh'hād*. He studied a great apportion from Sayyiduna Shaykh Muḥiyy al-Dīn ʿAbd al-Qādir al-Jilānī ﷺ, and had written a vast amount. He reaped a lot of benefits, whereby he also narrated from him.

I was informed by Shaykh Abu-ʿAlī Ḥasan b. Aḥmad b. Sulaymān al-Tamīmī al-Ḥirzī ﷺ, who stated that Shaykh ʿAbd al-ʿAzīz Nāsikh ﷺ had invited people towards Sayyiduna Shaykh Muḥiyy al-Dīn ʿAbd al-Qādir ﷺ.

68) Shaykh Fāḍil Abu-Muḥammad ʿAbd al-ʿAzīm b. Shaykh Abu-Muḥammad ʿAbd al-Karīm b. Muḥammad al-Misrī ﷺ, popularly identified as Ibn Ilyāsmanī was the magnificence of the *Qurrā*. He belonged to the home of the *Mashā'ikh*, where knowledge and righteousness were prevalent; and his father was a student of Sayyiduna Ghawth al-Aʿzam ﷺ.

I was informed by Shaykh Abu al-Faraj ʿAbd al-Raḥīm b. Wazīr b. Ḥasan b. Qāsim al-Qurashī al-Misrī Muaddab ﷺ, who had narrated this.

69) Shaykh Imām Ḥāfiz Abu-Mansūr ʿAbdullāh b. Muḥammad b. Walīd al-Baghdādī ﷺ is the honour of the *Ḥuffāz* and the splendour of Irāq.

70) Shaykh Jalīl Abu al-Faraj ʿAbd al-Muḥsin ﷺ also called Ḥusain b. Muḥammad b. Aḥmad b. Wadīrah al-Basrī ﷺ was the pride of the *Qurrā, Foqahā, Zuhhād* and *Muḥaddithīn*. Both of them were attributed to Sayyiduna Ghawth al-Aʿzam ﷺ; and they had invited people towards

him, and had documented his virtues, and moreover, had narrated *Ḥadith* from him.

I was informed about this by Shaykh Faqih Sāliḥ Abu al-Thanā Ḥāmid b. Aḥmad b. Muḥammad b. ʿAlī al-Thaqafī al-Azjī Muqrī ﷺ. Thereafter, he mentioned about the both of them to me.

71) Shaykh Imām Muḥammad Ibrāhīm b. Maḥmūd b. Jowhar al-Baʿalbakī ﷺ, prominently known as Batāʾihī was the honour of the *Foqahā* and *Qurrā* and the symbol of the *Awliya*.

I was informed by Shaykh Faqih Abu al-Qāsim Muḥammad b. ʿUbādah b. Muḥammad al-Ansārī ﷺ, who had heard from Shaykh ʿĀlim, the leader Muḥammad Abu-Muḥammad Ibrāhīm al-Baʿalbakī ﷺ, who enunciated that subsequent to Sayyiduna Rasūlullāh ﷺ and his *As'ḥāb* ﷺ, my Shaykh and leader in the Precincts of *Allāh* ﷻ is Shaykh Muḥiyy al-Dīn ʿAbd al-Qādir al-Jilānī ﷺ. His relationship with Sayyiduna Ghawth ﷺ was well recognized.

72) Shaykh Fāḍil Faqih Abu-ʿAbdullāh b. Ḥusain b. ʿAbdullāh b. ʿĪsā b. Abī al-Rijāl al-Yunīnī al-Baʿalbakī ﷺ was the dignitary amongst the *Ḥuffāz* and Shaykh of the *ʿUlama* and *Foqahā*.

I was informed by Faqih Abu-Muḥammad Ḥusain b. Faqih Fāḍil Abu-ʿImrān Mūsā al-Khālidī ﷺ, and he was informed by Shaykh Faqih Taqī al-Dīn Muḥammad al-Yunīnī Ḥāfiz ﷺ, who enthusiastically and ardently conversed about, and wrote about Shaykh ʿAbd al-Qādir al-Jilānī ﷺ. He invited people towards him, and revered him greatly.

73) Shaykh Jalīl Abu-Abdullāh Muḥammad b. ʿAbd al-Samad b. Abī-ʿAbdullāh b. Ḥamā'il b. Khalīl b. Rāshīd al-Ansārī al-Saʿadī Sūfī ﷺ presently in Cairo. He was the pride and honour of the *Foqahā, Muḥaddithīn* and *Zuh'hād*. He is attributed to the great Ghawth ﷺ; and subsequent to *Allāh* ﷻ and His Messenger ﷺ, he trusted in adopting the path of Sayyiduna Ghawth al-Aʿzam ﷺ.

I was informed about this by his son, Shaykh Jalīl Nabīl Muḥammad b. ʿAbd al-Samad b. Abī-ʿAbdullāh b. Ḥamā'il b. Khalīl b. Rāshid al-Ansārī al-Saʿādī Sūfī

ﷺ, who is presently visiting in Cairo. He was a blessing to the *Foqahā*, *Muḥaddithīn* and *Zuh'hād*. He was attributed to Sayyiduna Ghawth al-Aʿzam ﷺ. Subsequent to *Allāh* ﷻ and His beloved Messenger ﷺ, he trusted and followed the path of Sayyiduna Ghawth ﷺ.

This information was provided to me by his son, Shaykh Jalīl Nabīl Abu-ʿAbdullāh Muḥammad ﷺ. He was amongst those who had heard the *Ḥadith* from the Sayyiduna Ghawth al-Aʿzam ﷺ. The following are also amongst the graduates of Sayyiduna Ghawth al-Aʿzam ﷺ:

- Shaykh Abu al-Qāsim Dalaf b. Aḥmad b. Muḥammad al-Baghdādī al-Ḥarīmī ﷺ, distinguished as Ibn Qūqā.
- Shaykh Abu-Yaʿqūb Yūsuf b. Ibrāhīm Haybatullāh b. Maḥmūd b. Tufayl al-Damishqī Sūfī al-Ḥirḍī ﷺ.
- Shaykh Abu ar-Riḍā Muḥammad b. Aḥmad b. Dāʿūd Muaddab Ḥāsib ﷺ, prominently known as Mufīd.
- Shaykh Abu-Tālib ʿAbd al-Raḥmān b. Abu al-Faraj Abu al-ʿAbbās Aḥmad b. Mutīʿh Ba-Jasrādī ﷺ.
- Shaykh Ḥāfiz Abu al-Ḥasan ʿAlī b. Nafīs b. Abu-Zaydān b. Ḥaam al-Baghdādī al-Mamūnī ﷺ, who also had studied *Fiqah* from the great Ghawth ﷺ.
- Shaykh Abu-Hurayrah Muḥammad b. Abu-Fatāḥ Layth b. Sujāʿah b. Masʿūd al-Baghdādī al-Azjī al-Dīnārī ﷺ, visually impaired and well recognized as Ibn al-Wastānī.
- Shaykh Sharīf Abu al-Qāsim Akmal b. Masʿūd b. ʿUmar ʿAmmār al-Hāshmī ﷺ.
- Shaykh, the leader Abu-Muḥammad ʿAlī b. Abī-Bakr b. Idrīs al-Idrīsī al-Rūḥānī al-Yaʿqūbī ﷺ.
- Shaykh Abu-Bakr b. Muḥammad b. Nasar b. Nisār b. Mansūr al-Baghdādī al-Azjī Muqrī ﷺ.
- Shaykh Fāḍil Abu-Tālib ʿAbd al-Latīf b. Shaykh Abu al-Faraj Muḥammad b, Shaykh Abu al-Ḥasan ʿAlī b. Ḥamzā Fāris b. Muḥammad al-Ḥarrānī, and later Baghdādī ﷺ the jeweler, popularly known as Ibn Saqtī.

As far as our knowledge is concerned, Shaykh Abu-ʿAbdullāh al-Ansārī ﷺ was the last amongst these *Mashā'ikh*, who had narrated from Sayyiduna Shaykh Muḥiyy al-Dīn ʿAbd al-Qādir al-Jilānī ﷺ.

Those who studied *Fiqah* under the tutelage Sayyiduna Ghawth ﷺ, narrated *Ḥadith* from him and his *Awlād* [offspring] ﷺ was Shaykh Ibn Saqtī ﷺ, an erudite *ʿĀlim*, pious, awe-inspiring; and an intelligent individual of a refined disposition. Amongst the other offsprings was Sayyiduna Shaykh Imām Sayf al-Dīn Abu-ʿAbdullāh ʿAbd al-Wah'hāb al-Jilānī ﷺ who is the light of *Islām*; leader of the *ʿUlama* and a blessing to the theologians who studied *Fiqah* under his illustrious father ﷺ, and thus, narrated *Ḥadith* from him and from others. Amongst them were, Shaykh Abu-Ghālib Aḥmad b. Ḥusain b. Nabā ﷺ, Shaykh Abī-Mansūr ʿAbd al-Raḥmān b. Muḥammad b. Muḥammad b. ʿAbd al-Wāḥid ﷺ, Shaykh Abu-Ḥasan Muḥammad b. Aḥmad al-Sarmī ﷺ, Shaykh Abu al-Faḍal Muḥammad b. ʿUmar al-Amawī ﷺ, Shaykh Abu al-Waqt ʿAbd al-Dawl b. ʿĪsā al-Shajrī ﷺ and so forth.

He travelled to non-Arab lands in pursuit of knowledge and after the demise of his noble father ﷺ, he began teaching at his *madrassa*. He narrated *Ḥadith*, delivered lectures and issued *Fatwas*. Many *ʿUlama* studied under him and had narrated from him. Amongst them were Shaykh Sharīf Abu-Jaʿāfar b. Abu al-Qāsim, Labīb b. al-Nafīs b. Abu al-Karam Yaḥyah al-Ḥusainī al-Baghdādī ﷺ and Shaykh Sāliḥ Abu al-ʿAbbās Aḥmad b. ʿAbd al-Wāseʿh b. Amīr b. Shāfeʿh al-Jilī ﷺ.

His demise was on the 25th night of *Shawwāl*, 593 *hijrī* in Baghdād; and he was laid to rest the next day in the cemetery of *Maqbarah Ḥalba [Racetrack]*. He was born in *Shāʿbān* 522 *hijrī*.

74) Shaykh Imām Awḥad Sharīf al-Dīn Abu-Muḥammad al-Jilānī ﷺ whose patronym was ʿAbu-ʿAbd al-Raḥmān ʿĪsā, was the honour of the *Islām*, grandeur of the *ʿUlama* and lamp of Irāq and Egypt. He was eloquent in two languages and delivered lectures in both. He studied *Fiqah* under his noble father and narrated *Ḥadith* from him. He also narrated *Ḥadith* from Shaykh Abu al-Waqt ʿAbd al-Dawl b. ʿĪsā al-Shajrī ﷺ. He

taught Islāmic sciences; narrated *Ḥadith*, lectured and issued *Fatwas*. He was also an author and wrote '*Jawāhir al-Asrār wa Latāif al-Anwār*' which dealt with the sciences of Sūfism. Its contents are indeed eloquent and clearly explained. In it he logically unveiled the concealments of esoteric spiritual reality. He arrived in Egypt, where he narrated *Ḥadith* and delivered discourses. The Egyptian scholars narrate *Ḥadith* from him. Some of the ʿ*Ulama* and *Mashā'ikh* who had narrated from him are as follows:

- ✓ Shaykh Abu-Tarār Rabīʿāh b. Ḥasan b. ʿAlī b. ʿAbdullāh al-Ḥaḍramī al-Sanʿānī al-Shafaʿī Ḥāfiz ﷺ.
- ✓ Shaykh Abu al-Ghanā'im Musāfir b. Yaʿmar b. Musāfir al-Misrī al-Mutalfī al-Ḥannī Muaddab ﷺ.
- ✓ Shaykh Abu al-Thana Aḥmad b. Mabsarah b. Aḥmad b. Mūsā b. Ghanā'im ʿAdwānī, the then Misrī Khalāl al-Ḥanbalī ﷺ.
- ✓ Shaykh Abu al-Thana Ḥāmid b. Shaykh Abu al-ʿAbbās Aḥmad b. Aḥmad b. Ḥāmid b. Mafraj b. Ghayāth Artājī al-Misrī Faqih al-Muqrī ﷺ and his uncle.
- ✓ Shaykh Shaykh Abu-ʿAbdullāh Muḥammad b. Aḥmad Faqih al-Muḥaddith ﷺ.
- ✓ Shaykh Abu al-Mansūr Zāfir b. Tarkhān b. Jawāb Ghasānī al-Shafaʿī Muqrī al-Naḥwī al-Loghwī ﷺ and a host of others.

Shaykh Imām Sharīf al-Dīn Abu-Muḥammad al-Jilānī ﷺ had a sharp intellect and was an eloquent person. His demise was in 573 *hijrī*, in Cairo and was laid to rest there. He was an erudite ʿ*Ālim* and a virtuous man; possessing a sound intellect and humility; but yet a man of great stature and lofty status. He consistently focused on the Hereafter.

75) A pious *Walī*, Imām Shams al-Dīn Abu-Muḥammad al-Jilānī ﷺ whose *kunniya* was Abu-Bakr ʿAbd al-ʿAzīz. He was the honour of Irāq and the bliss of the ʿ*Ulama*. He studied *Fiqah* under his noble father ﷺ, and narrated *Ḥadith* from the following *Ḥadith* Masters:

- ❖ Shaykh Abu-Mansūr ʿAbd al-Raḥmān b. ʿAbd al-Wāḥid Fazār ﷺ.

- Shaykh Abu al-Faḍal Aḥmad b. Tãhir al-Mahnĩ ﷺ.
- Shaykh Muḥammad b. Nãsir al-Salãmĩ ﷺ.
- Shaykh Abu al-Waqt ʿAbd al-Dawl b. ʿĪsã al-Shajrĩ ﷺ.

He narrated *Ḥadith*, delivered lectures and taught *Islãmic* sciences. A large group of people benefitted from him and narrated from him. He was an articulate, and also a trustworthy narrator; generous; seeking with an extensive intellect, an ocean of knowledge; humble and possessed a praiseworthy disposition. He relocated to Jiyãl, a village in Sanjãr, and settled there permanently.

76) Shaykh Imãm Jamãl al-Dĩn Abu-ʿAbd al-Raḥmãn al-Jilãnĩ ﷺ, whose *kunniyah* was Abu al-Faraj. He was the servant of the Compeller ﷻ and the lamp of the *ʿUlama*. He was the chief *Muftĩ* of Irãq. He studied *Fiqah* under his honourable father ﷺ and narrated *Ḥadith* from the following *Ḥadith* Masters:

- Shaykh Abu-Mansũr ʿAbd al-Raḥmãn Fazãr ﷺ.
- Shaykh Abu al-Ḥasan Muḥammad b. Muḥammad b. Aḥmad al-Sarĩ ﷺ.
- Shaykh Abu-Bakr Muḥammad b. ʿAbdullãh b. Zaʿafrãnĩ ﷺ.
- Shaykh Abu al-Waqt ʿAbd al-Dawl b. ʿĪsã al-Shajrĩ ﷺ.

He was a Shaykh with excellent spiritual characteristics, and rich with a broad bosom; profound with knowledge and an enhanced intellect. He hastened in obedience and was steadfast in spiritual traditions. He was affectionate to the *Awliya* and knowledge was illuminant at his hands.

77) Sayyiduna Shaykh the unrivalled Imãm Ḥãfiz Tãj al-Dĩn Abu-Bakr ʿAbd al-Razzãq al-Jilãnĩ b. Ghawth al-Aʿzam ﷺ was the Lamp of Irãq; dignitary of the *Imãms*, glory of the *Ḥuffãz*, wonderment of *Islãm* and leader of the *Awliya*. He studied *Fiqah* under his illustrious father ﷺ. Some of the *Mashã'ikh* from whom he narrated *Ḥadith* are as follows:

- Shaykh Abu-Muḥammad Ḥasan b. Aḥmad b. Muḥammad b. Sarmĩ ﷺ.
- Shaykh Abu al-Faḍal Muḥammad b. ʿUmar al-Amawĩ ﷺ.

- Shaykh Aḥmad b. Tāhir al-Mahnī ﷺ.
- Shaykh Muḥammad b. Nāsir al-Salāmī ﷺ.
- Shaykh Abu-Bakr Muḥammad b. ʿAbdullāh b. Zaʿafrānī ﷺ.
- Shaykh Abu al-Waqt ʿAbd al-Dawl b. ʿĪsā al-Shajrī ﷺ.
- Shaykh Sharīf Abu-Jaʿāfar Aḥmad b. Muḥammad b. ʿAbd al-ʿAzīz al-ʿAbbāsī ﷺ.
- Shaykh Abu al-Qāsim Saʿīd b. Aḥmad b. al-Nabā ﷺ.

With the exception of the above mentioned *Mashā'ikh*, he also narrated *Ḥadith* from a large group of *ʿUlama* and *Mashā'ikh*. He narrated and taught *Ḥadith*. *Fatwas* were issued by him. Moreover, he conducted research from *Ḥadith* and many *ʿUlama* and *Masha'ikh* narrated from him. Some of them are:

- Shaykh, the illustrious Imām Muhazzab al-Dīn Abu al-Faḍal Isḥāq b. Aḥmad b. Ghānim al-ʿAlthī ﷺ.
- The erudite Shaykh and Gnostic, Taqī al-Dīn Abu-Muḥammad b. Jamīl al-Baghdādī ﷺ.
- The erudite Shaykh, Gnostic and Ascetic, Abu al-Ḥasan ʿAlī b. Aḥmad ﷺ well-known as Muammim.
- The erudite Shaykh and Ascetic, Abu al-Ḥasan ʿAlī b. Aḥmad al-Roya ﷺ and so forth.

Amongst the people he was an individual of excellent deportment. He was very firm; far-sighted; an ocean of knowledge; possessed an extensive intellect, and engaged in permanent contemplation. He was quite reserved, and proper in spirituality and worship; and he focused on knowledge. He had great respect for people of knowledge. Being just in his actions and words, he continually and thoroughly investigated, before he narrated *Ḥadith*. It is narrated about him that he never lifted up his head for a duration of 30 years towards the heavens, owing to his modesty for the Sublime Lord ﷻ.

This information was given to me by Shaykh Abu al-Faraj Aḥmad b. Muḥammad b. Sāliḥ al-Azjī ﷺ and Shaykh Abu-Muḥammad ʿAbdullāh b. Ismāʿīl b. Yūsuf b. Qāsim al-Ḥanbalī ﷺ. Both of them state that they were informed by Shaykh Imām Muḥiyy al-Dīn Abu-ʿAbdullāh Muḥammad al-Jilānī

ﷺ and his brother Shaykh Sayf al-Dĩn Abu-Zakariyyah Yaḥyah al-Jilãnĩ ﷺ. Both brothers assert that they were informed by their august father, Qãḍĩ al-Quḍãt Sayyiduna Shaykh Abu-Sãliḥ Nasar al-Jilãnĩ ﷺ in Baghdãd in *Madrassat al-Muslimĩn* [278].

The demise of Sayyiduna Shaykh ʿAbd al-Razzãq al-Jilãnĩ ﷺ was on 6th *Shawwãl*, 603 *hijrĩ* in Baghdãd; and on the next day, he was laid to rest in Bãb al-Ḥarb. He was born in *Dhil-Qãdah* 528 *hijrĩ.*

78) The pious, Shaykh Sayyiduna Abu-Isḥãq Ibrãhĩm al-Jilãnĩ Zayn al-Foqahã Jamãl al-Musnadĩn ﷺ studied *Fiqah* under his noble father ﷺ and had narrated *Ḥadith* from him. He also narrated *Ḥadith* from Shaykh Abu al-Qãsim Saʿĩd b. Abĩ-Ghãlib Aḥmad b. al-Ḥasan b. al-Nabã ﷺ and Shaykh Abu al-Waqt ʿAbd al-Dawl b. ʿĨsã al-Shajrĩ ﷺ and also narrated *Ḥadith* from those, who were in the league of these two giants. He was a trustworthy narrator, modest and possessed a kind disposition. He respected the people of knowledge. In 592 *hijrĩ,* he relocated to Wãsit, where his demise was destined.

79) The pious erudite Shaykh, Sayyiduna Abu al-Faḍal Muḥammad b. Raees al-As'ḥãb Jamãl al-Musnadĩn al-Jilãnĩ ﷺ studied *Fiqah* under his illustrious father ﷺ, and narrated *Ḥadith* from him. He also narrated *Ḥadith* from Shaykh Abu-Qãsim Saʿĩd b. Aḥmad b. al-Nabã ﷺ and Shaykh Abu al-Waqt ʿAbd al-Dawl b. ʿĨsã al-Shajrĩ ﷺ. He narrated *Ḥadith* and was a trustworthy and pious narrator. His demise was on 25th *Dhul-Qaʿãdah* 600 *hijrĩ* in Baghdãd and he was buried on the same day in *Maqbarah Ḥalba [Racetrack].*

80) Sayyiduna, the Shaykh of noble origin Abu-ʿAbdullãh ʿAbd al-Raḥmãn al-Jilãnĩ ﷺ was a *Baqiyat al-Salf*, who narrated *Ḥadith* from his noble father ﷺ, and acquired knowledge from him at a very tender age. He also narrated *Ḥadith* from Shaykh Abu al-Qãsim b. Ḥusain Abu-Ghãlib

[278] This was the name of the famous *madrassa* of Sayyiduna Ghawth al-Aʿzam ﷺ

Aḥmad b. al-Ḥasan al-Nabā ﷺ. He was born in 508 *hijrī*. His demise was on 27th *Safar* 627 *hijrī* in Baghdād. He and his *awlād* [offsprings] experienced an extended lifespan.

81) Sayyiduna Shaykh Fāḍil Faqih ʿĀlim Jalīl Abu-Zakariyyah Yaḥyah al-Jilānī ﷺ who studied *Fiqah* under his illustrious father ﷺ, and had narrated *Ḥadith* from him. He also narrated *Ḥadith* from Shaykh Abu al-Fataḥ Muḥammad b. ʿAbd al-Bāqī ﷺ and others. He acquired knowledge and narrated *Ḥadith* from them. Thereafter, he arrived in Cairo. The Shaykh ﷺ was a prolific *Faqih* and an erudite *ʿĀlim* of an excellent disposition. He always had ardour for knowledge, and loved the people of knowledge. His demise was in mid *Shaʿbān* in 600 *hijrī* in Baghdād, and he was buried next to his elder brother, Sayyiduna Shaykh ʿAbd al-Wah'hāb al-Jilānī ﷺ. He was born on 6th *Rabīʿ al-Awwal* 550 *hijrī*, and was the youngest son of Sayyiduna Ghawth al-Aʿzam ﷺ.

82) Sayyiduna Shaykh Ḍiyā al-Dīn Abu-Nasar Mūsā al-Jilānī ﷺ was the brilliance of the *Foqahā* and honour of the *Muḥaddithīn*. He was *Baqiyat al-Salf*, who had studied *Fiqah* under his august father ﷺ, and had narrated *Ḥadith* from him. He also narrated *Ḥadith* from:
   - Shaykh Abu-Qāsim Saʿīd b. Aḥmad b. al-Nabā ﷺ.
   - Shaykh Abu al-Waqt ʿAbd al-Dawl b. ʿĪsā al-Shajrī ﷺ.
   - Shaykh Abu al-Fataḥ Muḥammad b. ʿAbd al-Bāqī ﷺ.
   - Shaykh Abu al-Faḍal Muḥammad b. Nāsir ﷺ and a host of others.

He narrated *Ḥadith* in Damascus and permanently settled there. He also visited Egypt. He was an erudite linguist, with a pious and flawless disposition. He also acquired *Fiqah* in ʿAqiyya and was a *Baqiyat al-Salf.* He settled in Damascus. On the night of 1st *Jamādil Ākhirah* 618 *hijrī*, it was the time of his demise and he was laid to rest at the bottom of *Mount Qāsiyūn*. He was born at the end of *Rabīʿ al-Awwal* 539 *hijrī*; and it is stated that he was the last son of

Sayyiduna Ghawth al-Aᶜzam ﷺ; who had physically transcended from this transitory world.

83) Sayyiduna Shaykh Imãm ᶜAfif al-Dĩn b. Mubãrak al-Jilãnĩ al-Baghdãdĩ ﷺ and he was the descendant [*awlãd*] of Jamãl al-Foqahã wa Fakhr al-Muḥaddithĩn ﷺ. He studied *Fiqah* and had narrated *Ḥadith* from his esteemed grandfather ﷺ and others such as the following:

- ✓ Shaykh Abu-Wazraᶜh Zãhir b. Ḥusain Zaradarãzĩ ﷺ
- ✓ Shaykh Abu-Bakr Aḥmad b. al-Muqarrab b. Ḥusain Faqĩh al-Karkhĩ ﷺ
- ✓ Shaykh Abu al-Qãsim Yaḥyah b. Thãbit b, Badrãn b. Ibrãhĩm al-Dĩnawarĩ ﷺ
- ✓ Qãḍĩ Abu-ᶜAbdullãh Muḥammad b. ᶜAbdullãh b. Muḥammad Bayḍãwĩ ﷺ
- ✓ Shaykh Abu al-Waqt ᶜAbd al-Dowl b. ᶜĨsã al-Shajrĩ ﷺ and others.

He was a trustworthy, pious and erudite *Faqĩh*. Indeed! He was very intelligent, a lover of knowledge and pondered over matters of religion. He was also a versatile calligrapher, and became famous for his calligraphy.

84) Sayyiduna Shaykh Imãm Mansũr ᶜAbdus Salãm b. Imãm Sayf al-Dĩn Abu-ᶜAbdullãh ᶜAbd al-Wah'hãb al-Jilãnĩ ﷺ was the luminary of the *Foqahã* and honour of the *ᶜUlama* and *Muḥaddithĩn*. He studied *Fiqah* and narrated *Ḥadith* from his august grandfather ﷺ and honourable father ﷺ. He also narrated *Ḥadith* from the following *Ḥadith* Masters: Shaykh Abu al-Ḥasan Muḥammad b. Isḥãq b. Sãbĩ ﷺ and Shaykh Abu al-Fataḥ Muḥammad b. ᶜAbd al-Bãqĩ b. Aḥmad ﷺ and a host of others. He also undertook intensive studies in Sciences of *Ḥadith,* and had recorded his research. He taught, issued *Fatãwas* and narrated *Ḥadith* at the *madrassa* of his august grandfather ﷺ. He became the owner of a few villages. A group of *ᶜUlama* in Baghdãd narrated from him. He was of a pleasant disposition and an ocean of knowledge and wisdom.

He had great reverence for the *ʿUlama* and held them in high esteem. He was trustworthy in his words and actions. His demise was during the month of *Rajab*, 611 *hijrī* in Baghdād and he was laid to rest on the same day at *Maqbarah Ḥalba [Racetrack]*. His brother is Sayyiduna Shaykh Faqih Abu al-Fataḥ Sulaymān al-Jilānī *Baqiyat al-Salf Zayn al-Irāq* ﷺ. He possessed profound knowledge and wisdom; and was altruistic in his generosity.

85) Sayyiduna Shaykh Imām Qāḍī al-Quḍāt ʿImād al-Dīn Abu-Sāliḥ Nasar b. Imām Ḥāfiz Tāj al-Dīn Abu-Bakr ʿAbd al-Razzāq al-Jilānī ﷺ is the brilliance of the *ʿUlama*; pride of the *Foqahā*, and the leader of the erudite scholars and *Muftī* of Irāq. He studied *Fiqah* under his illustrious father, Sayyiduna Tāj al-Dīn ʿAbd al-Razzāq al-Jilānī ﷺ; and he had narrated *Ḥadith* from his beloved uncle, Sayyiduna Shaykh ʿAbd al-Wah'hāb al-Jilānī ﷺ. On the advice of his noble father, he narrated *Ḥadith* from the following *Ḥadith* Masters:

- Shaykh Abu-Hāshim ʿĪsā b. Aḥmad al-Rūshānī ﷺ.
- Shaykh Abu-Shujaʿh Saʿīd b. Sāmī b. ʿAbdullāh al-Jamālī ﷺ.
- Shaykh Abu-Aḥmad Saʿād b. Baldāk al-Ḥabūbalī ﷺ.
- Shaykh Abu al-ʿAbbās Aḥmad b. al-Mubārak al-Marfaghānī ﷺ.
- Shaykh Abu al-Ḥusain ʿAbd al-Ḥaqq b. ʿAbd al-Khāliq b. Aḥmad b. Yūsuf ﷺ.
- Shaykh Abu-ʿAbdullāh Muslim b. Thābit b. Nuḥās ﷺ.
- Shaykh Abu al-Faḍal ʿAbd al-Muḥsin b. Barmak ﷺ.
- Shaykha Kātibah Shahdah bint Abu-Nasar al-Abrī ﷺ.
- Shaykha Fakhr al-Zamān Khadijah bint Aḥmad al-Hazdānī ﷺ and a host of others.

Two *Ḥadith* Masters, Shaykh Abu al-ʿUla Ḥasan b. Aḥmad al-Hamdānī ﷺ and Shaykh Abu-Tāhir Aḥmad b. Muḥammad al-Asfahānī ﷺ granted him permission to narrate *Ḥadith*, and he visited Qāḍī al-Quḍāt Abu al-Qāsim ʿAbdullāh b. Ḥusain al-Dāmghānī ﷺ and others. He taught at his grandfather's *madrassa*, where he narrated and dictated *Ḥadith*, delivered lectures and issued

Fatãwas. He was designated to the position of *Qãḍĩ al-Quḍãt* [Chief Justice] at *Madarsat al-Muslimĩn*. Numerous *ʿUlama* graduated under him. In Egypt, I met many of those who had studied under him. He was an erudite *Faqih; ʿÃlim, Fãḍil ʿÃrif* and *Zãhid*. He was very virtuous, possessing an intellect of perfection, with a broad bosom of knowledge. His blessed disposition gave priority to matters pertaining to religion. He loved knowledge and honoured the people of knowledge. He was humble and a trustworthy narrator, and as a result he always contemplated on his narrations. His impeccable spiritual characteristics needs no lengthy introduction. His demise was on 7th *Rabĩʿ al-Awwal* 633 *hijrĩ* in Baghdãd, and he was laid to rest in the *Bãb al-Ḥarb* cemetery. He was born on 24th *Rabĩʿ al-Ãkhir* 534 *hijrĩ*.

His chaste mother is Umm al-Karam Tãj an-Nisã bint Faḍãil b. ʿAlĩ al-Tikrĩnĩ ﷺ, who narrated *Ḥadith* from her husband Ḥãfiz Tãj al-Dĩn ʿAbd al-Razzãq al-Jilãnĩ ﷺ, Sayyiduna Ghawth al-Aʿzam ﷺ and Shaykh Abu al-Fataḥ Muḥammad b. ʿAbd al-Bãqĩ b. Aḥmad ﷺ. She was bestowed with a great share of graciousness and virtues. The 12th *Rajab* 613 *hijrĩ* marked her demise in Baghdad and she was laid to rest in the *Bãb al-Ḥarb* cemetery. Her brother, the pious Shaykh Abu al-Qãsim ʿAbd al-Raḥĩm b. ʿAbd al-Razzãq ﷺ, a glorious personality was the maestro of the theologians, and narrated *Ḥadith* from Shaykh Abu al-Fataḥ Muḥammad b. ʿAbd al-Bãqĩ b. Aḥmad ﷺ, Sayyidah Khadĩja bint Aḥmad al-Abrĩ ﷺ and a host of others. He also narrated *Ḥadith* and was an erudite, pious, and an individual of stateliness and humility. The 7th *Rabĩʿ al-Awwal* 606 *hijrĩ* marked his demise in Baghdãd, and he was laid to rest in the *Bãb al-Ḥarb* cemetery.

86) Shaykh Faqih Abu-Muḥammad Ismãʿĩl al-Jilãnĩ ﷺ was the honour of the elite and elegance of the learned scholars. He narrated *Ḥadith* from numerous *ʿUlama* and had studied *Fiqah*. He was pious, and a person of cool disposition, who portrayed a commendable character. His demise was on 13th *Muḥarram* 600 *hijrĩ* in Baghdãd, and he was laid to rest at the *Maqbarah* [mausoleum] of Imãm Aḥmad b. Ḥanbal ﷺ.

87) Shaykh the erudite *Faqīh* Abu al-Muhāsin Faḍlullāh al-Jilānī ﷺ was *Zayn al-Musnadīn* [the grace and honour of the *Shuyūkh*] and *Baqiyat al-Salf.* He studied *Fiqah* and narrated *Ḥadith* from his illustrious father Sayyiduna ʿAbd al-Razzāq al-Jilānī ﷺ and from the following *Ḥadith* Masters;

- ✓ His uncle Sayyiduna Imām Abu-ʿAbdullāh ʿAbd al-Wah'hāb al-Jilānī ﷺ.
- ✓ Shaykh Abu al-Fataḥ ʿUbaydullāh b. Muḥammad b. Naja b. Shanīl ﷺ juice merchant.
- ✓ Shaykh Abu al-Faḍal Masʿūd ʿAlī b. Aḥmad b. al-Ḥasan b. Abu-ʿAlī ʿUbaydah b. Nāsir Safā ﷺ.
- ✓ Shaykh ʿĀdil b. Yūnus ﷺ.
- ✓ Shaykh ibn Kulayb ﷺ.
- ✓ Shaykh Haybatullāh b. Ramaḍān ﷺ.
- ✓ Shaykh ʿAbdullāh b. Ḥamīd b. Yūsuf al-ʿĀqūlī ﷺ.
- ✓ Shaykh Abu al-Saʿādāt Mubārak ﷺ, who was also renowned as Nasrullāh b. ʿAbd al-Raḥmān b. Muḥammad b. ʿAbd al-Wāḥid Fazāz and prominently known as Ibn Ruzaiq.

Shaykh ʿAbd al-Ḥaqq b. Yūsuf b. Muḥammad b. Jaʿāfar b. ʿAqīl ﷺ and Shaykh Abu-Mūsā al-Asbahānī ﷺ granted him permission to narrate *Ḥadith.* He narrated *Ḥadith* and he was a kind person, who possessed a superb character, subtle qualities and was trustworthy. On 17th *Jamādi al-Ākhir* 622 *hijrī*, it was the day of his demise in Baghdād. The *Salāt al-Janāza* was performed by his eminent brother Qāḍī al-Quḍāt Sayyiduna Shaykh Abu-Sāliḥ Nasar al-Jilānī ﷺ.

88) Shaykha Sayyidah Umm-Muḥammad ʿĀ'īeshah al-Jilānī ﷺ [sister of Qāḍī al-Quḍāt Sayyiduna Abu-Sāliḥ Nasar al-Jilānī ﷺ] had narrated *Ḥadith* from Shaykh Abu al-Ḥusain ʿAbd al-Ḥaqq b. ʿAbd al-Khāliq b. Aḥmad ﷺ and from others. Personally, she had narrated *Ḥadith* and was a commendable, pious and devout lady. On the night of 13th *Rabīʿ al-Awwal* 628 *hijrī,* destiny had ordained her demise in Baghdād. On the next day, she was laid to rest in the *Bāb al-Ḥarb* cemetery.

89) The erudite Shaykh Abu-Muḥammad ʿAbd al-Raḥmān b. Shaykh ʿAbdullāh al-Jilānī ﷺ was the adornment of the *Mashā'ikh,* Shaykh of the Jurists and *Zuh'hād*. He narrated *Ḥadith* from his august grandfather Sayyiduna Ghawth al-Aʿzam ﷺ and also from Shaykh Qāsim b. Nasar b. ʿAkbarī ﷺ, Shaykh Saʿīd b. Aḥmad b. Ḥasan b. al-Nabā ﷺ and Shaykh Abu-Muzaffar Haybatullāh b. Aḥmad b. Shabnakī ﷺ. He was trustworthy, humble and compassionate. He transcended from this mundane world physically on 26th *Muḥarram* 614 *hijrī* in Baghdād. His brother, Shaykh al-Asīl Abu-Muḥammad ʿAbd al-Qādir al-Jilānī ﷺ was renowned and was the luminary of Jurists and *Baqiyat al-Salf.* He studied *Fiqah* under the tutelage of his illustrious uncle, Sayyiduna Tāj al-Dīn ʿAbd al-Razzāq al-Jilānī ﷺ and narrated *Ḥadith* from him. He also narrated *Ḥadith* from Shaykh Abu al-Ḥusain ʿAbd al-Ḥaqq b. ʿAbd al-Khāliq b. Aḥmad ﷺ. He was extensively knowledgeable, an intellectual, reserved and an individual with a glorious designation. *Rabīʿ al-Awwal*, 634 *hijrī* marked the date of his demise in one the villages of Baghdād, where he was laid to rest.

90) The pious Shaykh, the leader, Imām Abu-Muḥammad ʿAbdullāh b. Shaykh Abu-Muḥammad ʿAbd al-ʿAzīz al-Jilānī ﷺ was the exquisiteness of the *Awliya* and the eminence of the *Mashā'ikh*. He narrated from numerous *Shuyūkh*, and it is presumed that he had also narrated *Ḥadith*. He was very prominent and exalted in his time, and possessed powerful *kashf* [spiritual insight]. He was quite a reserved individual. Numerous *karamāt* were attributed to him and *in sha Allāh* ﷻ; some of them shall be mentioned later in this publication.

91) His sister, Sayyidah Shaykha Umm-Aḥmad Zah'rā ﷺ was granted the permission [*ijāzah*] to narrate *Ḥadith* from the sons of Shaykh Abu al-Ḥusain ʿAbd al-Ḥaqq b. ʿAbd al-Khāliq b. Aḥmad ﷺ and Shaykh Abu-Nasar ʿAbd al-Raḥīm ʿAbd al-Khāliq b. Aḥmad b. Yūsuf ﷺ. She also narrated *Ḥadith* from Shaykh Asʿad b. Baldarak ﷺ and a host of others. She also narrated *Ḥadith* and was of the *Baqiyat al-Salf.* A very pious;

chaste, recipient of excellent virtues and an exalted lady. Her demise was in 632 *hijrĩ*, in Baghdãd. May *Allãh* ﷻ shower His ﷻ Mercy upon her.

92) The prudent Shaykh Abu-Sulaymãn Dã'ũd b. Shaykh al-Jalĩl Abu al-Fataḥ Sulaymãn 'Abd al-Wah'hãb al-Jilãnĩ was the grandeur of *Islãm*. He studied *Fiqah* and he had heard *Ḥadith*, and he had narrated *Ḥadith*. He is from the *Baqiyat al-Salf* and the Shaykh of *murĩds*. It was his demise on 18th *Rabĩ 'al-Awwal,* 648 *hijrĩ* in Baghdãd, and was laid to rest on the next day in *Maqbarah Ḥalba [Racetrack]* cemetery; besides his father and grandfather.

93) Shaykh Faqih 'Ãlim Muḥiyy al-Dĩn Abu-'Abdullah Muḥammad b. Qãḍĩ al-Quḍãt Abu-Sãliḥ Nasar al-Jilãnĩ is the lamp of the *'Ulama* and *Muftĩ* of Irãq. He studied *Fiqah* from his illustrious father and many others. He had heard *Ḥadith* from his noble father and numerous *Mashã'ikh*, amongst whom were Shaykh Abu-Isḥãq Yũsuf b. Abĩ-Ḥãmid b. Shaykh Abu al-Faḍal Muḥammad b. 'Umar al-Amawĩ . He narrated *Ḥadith*, taught Islãmic sciences and issued *fatwas*. He had an excellent character, and highly educated, and blessed with a sharp intellect. He was a trustworthy narrator and always in the pursuit of knowledge. All his work proved ardent efforts. It was narrated to me that he resembled the grandfather of his father, *Shaykh al-Islãm* Muḥiyy al-Dĩn 'Abd al-Qãdir al-Jilãnĩ . His demise was in 656 *hijrĩ* in Baghdãd. His brother. *Shaykh al-Islãm* Sayyiduna Sayf al-Dĩn Abu-Zakariyyah Yaḥyah al-Jilãnĩ was the glory of Irãq, wonderment of the *'Ulama* and the esteem of the theologians. He studied *Fiqah* under his illustrious father and narrated *Ḥadith* from him and other *Ḥadith* Masters. Amongst them was Shaykh Abu al-'Abbãs Aḥmad b. Abu al-Fataḥ Yũsuf b. Abu al-Ḥasan b. Abĩ al-Ghanãim al-Daqqãq . He narrated *Ḥadith* and delivered lectures. He was a prolific *'Ãlim; Faqih*, linguist, intelligent, humble and had a par-excellence conduct. His speech on *Ahle-Ḥaqĩqah* [the Gnostics] was inspirational. He was a poet of instant calibre, and

composed clear and fine poetry. *Faqih*, the pious Imām ʿAfīf al-Dīn ﷺ read some of its verses to me.

I narrate from Shaykh Abu al-Ḥasan ʿAlī b. Azdamar al-Baghdādī ﷺ, who affirmed that he was in the companionship of Shaykh Sayf al-Dīn Qāḍī al-Quḍāt Abu-Sāliḥ ؓ in Baghdād and questioned him about *Tamkīm* [279] and he instantly recited the following verses:

يَسْقِيْ وَيَشْرَبُ لَا تَلْهِيْهِ سُكْرَتُهُ عَنِ النَّدِيْمِ وَلَا يَلْهُوْ عَنِ الْكَاسِ

He gives drinks of love and drinks himself whose inebriation does not makes him unconscious of his associates nor does he get unaware of the cup

اَطَاعَهُ سُكْرُهُ حَتّٰى تَحَكَّمَ فِيْهِ حَالِ الصِّحَاةِ وَذَا مِنْ اَعْجَبِ النَّاسِ

His inebriation is obedient to him until he dictates to the healthy; and he is an amazing person amongst people.

Thereafter, he made some changes to the verses and recited:

وَيَشْرَبُ ثُمَّ يَسْقِيْهَا النَّدَامٰى وَلَا تَلْهِيْهِ كَاْسٌ عَنْ نَدِيْمِ

He drinks the drink of love and gives it to his friends. The cup does not make him unconscious of his friends

لَهُ مَعَ سُكْرِهِ تَأْيِيْدُ مُبَاحٌ وَنَشْوَةُ شَارِبٍ وَنَدْمٰى كَرِيْمُ

He has the support of consciousness with his rapture and his bliss is of the consumers of the drink of love and honourable associates

Later, he was martyred in *Safar* 656 *hijrī* by the treacherous Tatars, in Baghdād. May *Allāh* ﷻ destroy those treacherous Tatars.

94) Shaykh Faqih, the pious ʿĀlim Muḥiyy al-Dīn Abu-ʿAbdullāh Muḥammad b. ʿAlī b. Muḥammad b. Ḥāmid al-Baghdādī al-Jilānī ﷺ well recognized as Tawḥīdī was the descendant of Sayyiduna Shaykh

[279] Stability. Refers to stabilization in *Talwīn* [traveller on the Path who has not yet reached his destination]. It is termed as the state of those, who have arrived within the Divine Presence [*Ahl al-Wusūl*].

Ḥāfiz Tāj al-Dīn ʿAbd al-Razzāq al-Jilānī ﷺ. He was the exquisiteness of Irāq; bliss of the *Foqahā, ʿUlama, Qurrā, Muḥaddithīn* and the honour of the *Awliya*. He studied *Fiqah* under his maternal uncle Qāḍī al-Quḍāt Abu-Sāliḥ al-Jilānī ﷺ and graduated. He also narrated *Ḥadith* from Shaykh Abu-Muḥammad ʿAlī b. Abī-Bakr b. Idrīs al-Yaʿqūbī ﷺ.

95) Shaykh, the leader Shahāb al-Dīn Abu-Ḥafs ʿUmar b. Muḥammad b. ʿAbdullāh al-Sohrowardī ﷺ and Shaykh Abu al-Faḍal Isḥāq b. Aḥmad al-ʿAlthī ﷺ and Shaykh Abu al-Qāsim Haybatullāh b. ʿAbdullāh b. Aḥmad b. al-Mansūr Khatīb ﷺ and a host of others narrated *Ḥadith* and lectured to the people. Many scholars of Baghdād graduated under them. Their speech was thought provoking and they composed eloquent poetry which have been documented by the translator. However, some of it shall be mentioned later, in sha *Allāh* ﷻ. In the event of short biographies of all those *Mashā'ikh* be undertaken, who were aligned to, studied and derived blessings from Sayyiduna Shaykh Muḥiyy al-Dīn ʿAbd al-Qādir al-Jilānī ﷺ; and inclusive of those, who had studied under their offsprings, the hand would then be a microcosm, whilst the field would be a macrocosm, which certainly would not encompass their detailed biographies. A lengthy period of time shall be required to provide a detailed account, pertinent to their biographies. Hence, whatever was intended, has been briefly noted in this book. Almighty *Allāh* ﷻ is the One ﷻ who grants *Tawfīq* and guidance, and it is He ﷻ who is worthy of all praises.

Forty Meanings of one Verse of the Qur'ān

I narrate from Shaykh Faqih Abu al-Ḥasan Muḥammad b. Abu al-Fataḥ Dāʿūd b. Aḥmad al-Qurashī ﷺ, who narrates from the eminent Shaykh Muḥiyy al-Dīn Abu-Muḥammad Yūsuf b. Imām Abu al-Faraj ʿAbd al-Raḥmān b. ʿAlī al-Jowzī ﷺ, who stated that he was informed by Shaykh Ḥāfiz Abu al-ʿAbbās Aḥmad b. Aḥmad al-Baghdādī al-Bandlajī ﷺ who proclaimed:

'One day, your father and I attended the *majlis* of Sayyiduna Shaykh Muḥiyy al-Dīn ʿAbd al-Qādir al-Jīlānī ﷺ. The *Qārī* recited one verse and the Ghawth ﷺ embarked on just one commentary on it. I queried from your father as to whether he had knowledge of this commentary, and he replied in the affirmative. Thereafter, Sayyiduna Ghawth ﷺ delved into a second commentary and I queried from your father, as to whether he had knowledge of this commentary, and he once more replied in the affirmative. Henceforth, the third commentary followed, and I queried from your father, as to whether he had knowledge of this commentary, and he thereby replied in the affirmative. Sayyiduna Ghawth al-Aʿzam ﷺ then discussed a further eleven commentaries of the same verse, and I questioned your father, as to whether he had knowledge of these commentaries, and he thereby replied in the affirmative. When Sayyiduna Shaykh ﷺ, dealt with the twelfth commentary, I thereby verified from your father, as to whether he had knowledge of this commentary, and he replied in the negative. The Ghawth ﷺ continued, and pursued with forty inspirational and valid commentaries of the same verse and attributed its meaning to its commentator. Your father admitted that he did not know the meaning of these commentaries. His admiration had been enhanced by the extensive astonishing knowledge bestowed upon the illustrious Walī, Sayyiduna Ghawth al-Aʿzam ﷺ.

Henceforward, the Ghawth ﷺ stipulated: *'Now I leave words [qaal], and turn to conditions [ḥaal].'* لااله الا الله محمد رسول الله, whereby the audience transformed into a state of intense restlessness and anxiety; whilst your father tore his clothes.

The Ghawth ﷺ spoke in 13 Sciences

I narrate from Shaykh Sharīf Abu-ʿAbdullāh Muḥammad b. Khiḍar al-Ḥusainī al-Mosulī ﷺ, who had heard his father conversing: *'My Master Shaykh Muḥiyy al-Din ʿAbd al-Qādir al-Jīlānī ﷺ spoke in 13 sciences and taught Tafsīr, Ḥadith,*

Fiqah and morals at his madrassa. He taught Tafsīr, Ḥadith, Fiqah, morals and principles of syntax in the morning and evening; and seven Qir'ats after Zuhr.'

He issued Fatwa in accordance to the Shafaʿī and Ḥanbalī Schools

I narrate from Shaykh Abu-Muḥammad Ḥasan b. Aḥmad b. ʿAlī b. Hāshim al-Baghdādī ﷺ, who narrates from three *Shuyūkh*; Shaykh Muḥiyy al-Dīn Muḥammad al-Jilānī ﷺ, Shaykh Sayf al-Dīn Yaḥyah al-Jilānī ﷺ; and from the both sons of Qāḍī al-Quḍāt Sayyiduna Abu-Sāliḥ Nasar al-Jilānī ﷺ and Shaykh Abu al-Ḥasan ʿAlī ﷺ, the baker. Shaykh Sayf al-Dīn ﷺ and Shaykh Muḥiyy al-Dīn ﷺ asserted that they had heard from their father ﷺ and he had heard from his father, Sayyiduna Shaykh ʿAbd al-Razzāq al-Jilānī ﷺ and his uncle, Sayyiduna Shaykh ʿAbd al-Wah'hāb al-Jilānī ﷺ who had revealed, and Shaykh Abu al-Ḥasan ﷺ had pronounced that he had heard from Shaykh Abu al-Qāsim Baz'zār ﷺ. All of them concurred that *Fatāwa* [*Islāmic* inference] developed from all over Irāq and other places and was forwarded to Sayyiduna Muḥiyy al-Dīn Shaykh ʿAbd al-Qādir al-Jilānī ﷺ. We have not witnessed any question that was forwarded; and an answer being delayed for the night, to contemplate upon or to refer to any book by Sayyiduna Muḥiyy al-Dīn Shaykh ʿAbd - al Qādir al-Jilānī ﷺ. In fact he read the question, and answered it instantly. He issued *fatwa* in accordance to the *Shafaʿī* and *Ḥanbalī* Schools. His rulings were presented to the *ʿUlama* of Irāq, who were not so alarmed by the correct answer, but were more astonished by his instantaneous reply.

When a student studied any sciences from the great Ghawth ﷺ, he emerged so proficient, that the great scholars of his era became subservient to him.

I narrate from the pious Shaykh, Faqih Abu-Muḥammad al-Ḥasan b. Faqih Jalīl Abu-ʿImrān Mūsā b. Aḥmad al-Khālidī ﷺ, who narrates from his Shaykh, Imām Abu al-Faraḥ ʿAbd al-Raḥmān b. Imām Abu-Yaʿla Najmudīn b. Ḥanbalī ﷺ who had heard his father professing that in Irāq, that Sayyiduna Muḥiyy al-Dīn Shaykh ʿAbd al-Qādir al-Jilānī ﷺ was amongst those, to whom the control of the knowledge of *Fatāwa* [*Islāmic* Inference] was handed over.

I narrate from Qāḍī al-Quḍāt Shaykh ash-Shuyūkh Shams al-Dīn Abu-ʿAbdullāh al-Maqdisī ﷺ, who asserted that he had heard from his Shaykh, Imām Muwaffiq al-Dīn b. Qudāma ﷺ, articulate that he had arrived in 561 *hijrī* in Baghdād and had observed Sayyiduna Muḥiyy al-Dīn Shaykh ʿAbd al-Qādir al-Jilānī ﷺ amongst those who were yielded to the kingdom of knowledge, devotions and issuing of *Fatāwas* [religious inference]. Students never thought of going anywhere else, for the acquisition of knowledge, because he was an embodiment of all fields of knowledge. The great Ghawth ﷺ dedicated himself and exercised patience in imparting knowledge to all his students. He had a broad chest, and a perfect insight into knowledge. The Sublime Lord ﷻ combined excellent characteristics and powerful conditions within him. I have not seen anyone, any who succeeded him, with such an astonishing disposition, and a remarkable authority.

An Amazing Question and Answer

I narrate from Shaykh Faqih ʿĀlim ʿĀbid ʿAfif al-Dīn Abu-Muḥammad ʿAbd al-Salām b. Muḥammad b. Mazrūʿh Misrī al-Basrī ﷺ, who narrates from Shaykh Sayf al-Dīn Abu-Zakariyyah Yaḥyah b. Qāḍī al-Quḍāt Abu-Sāliḥ Nasar al-Jilānī ﷺ, who stated that his father narrates from his illustrious father, Sayyiduna Shaykh ʿAbd al-Razzāq al-Jilānī ﷺ who professed that a question had been forwarded from *ʿAjam* [Persia] to Baghdād. Initially, this question was circulated amongst all the *ʿUlama* of Baghdād, but a satisfactory answer was not furnished. The question read: *'What is the ruling of the eminent ʿUlama with regard to a person, who has procured an oath for the application of three Talāqs from his wife; on condition, that he alone performs such worship on earth, which no one else shall perform at that time? What is this form of worship?'* This question was presented to my illustrious father ﷺ, who instantaneously replied: *'That person must proceed to Makkah Mukarramah and empty the matāf, i.e. to stop all Muslims from performing the Tawāf and then, he alone should undertake seven Tawāf of the*

Holy Ka ͑ābah. Through this strict compliance, his oath shall be conformed to, and his marriage shall be salvaged.' When this astonishing answer was conveyed, the man immediately departed on the same night to Makkah Mukarramah, and honoured his oath.

The Ghawth ﷺ visits the Grave of Imām Aḥmad b. Ḥanbal ﷺ and he meets and speaks to him.

I narrate from Shaykh Sharīf Abu al-ʿAbbās Aḥmad b. Shaykh Abu-ʿAbdullāh Muḥammad b. Abī al-Ghanā'im Muḥammad Azhārī al-Ḥusainī ﷺ, who narrates from his father and Shaykh Sālih Baqiyat al-Salf Abu-Thanā Maḥmūd al-Jilānī ﷺ, who testifies that he had heard the leader Shaykh Abu al-Ḥasan ʿAlī b. al-Hītī ﷺ, who revealed that he had proceeded to the *Rowḍah* [sacred grave] of Imām Aḥmad ibn Ḥanbal ﷺ, together with Sayyiduna Muḥiyy al-Dīn Shaykh ʿAbd al-Qādir al-Jilānī ﷺ, and Sayyiduna Shaykh Baqa b. Bat'tū ﷺ. I witnessed that Imām Aḥmad ibn Ḥanbal ﷺ arose from his grave, and embraced Sayyiduna Shaykh ʿAbd al-Qādir al-Jilānī ﷺ, and adorned him with an honourable robe [*khil ͑at*], and thereby confirmed: *'O ʿAbd al-Qādir! Verily I am dependent on your knowledge of the Sharī ͑ah, i.e. Ḥaqīqah, Ḥāl [spiritual state] and Fe ͑le Ḥāl [accomplishment of spiritual state].'*

Furthermore, I was informed by Shaykh Baqā Abu al-Fataḥ Muḥammad Aḥmad b. Aḥmad b. ʿAlī al-Sarīfīnī ﷺ, who was informed by Shaykh Abu al-Ḥasan ʿAlī al-Baghdādī ﷺ the baker, and he was informed by Shaykh Abu al-Qāsim ʿUmar Baz'zār ﷺ. He stated that he had heard from Shaykh Baqā b. Bat'tū ﷺ, who had reported on the afore-mentioned incident.

Sayyiduna Ghawth al-Aʿzam ﷺ and the Awliya-Allāh

I heard from Shaykh Sharīf Abu-ʿAbdullāh Muḥammad b. Khiḍar al-Ḥusainī al-Mosulī ﷺ, who had heard his father, relaying:

> 'In 591 *hijrī*, I had dreamt in Baghdād, that I was in the *madrassa* of My Master Shaykh Muḥiyy al-Din ʿAbd al-Qādir al-Jilānī ﷺ, who was

present in a spacious hall. The *Mashā'ikh* of the jungles and oceans also presented themselves, where Sayyiduna Ghawth al-Aʿzam ﷺ was their chair person. There were some *Mashā'ikh* who had been adorned with an *ʿAmāmah* [turban], bearing one ornamental tassel. Others had two ornamental tassels attached to their turbans, but Sayyiduna Ghawth al-Aʿzam ﷺ had three ornamental tassels affixed to his turban. I was extremely startled at these tassels. When I arose, I discovered that Sayyiduna Ghawth ﷺ was standing alongside me, and whereby, he elucidated: *'O Khiḍar! One tassel represents the honour of ʿIlm al-Sharīʿāh, the second represents the honour of ʿIlm al-Ḥaqīqah and the third represents the honour of dignity.'*

Steadfast on the Science of Esoteric Spiritual Reality

Previously, a detailed account pertaining to this subject matter, has been furnished, hence, there is no need for its repetition within this context.

I narrate from Shaykh Sāliḥ Abu al-Fataḥ Muḥammad b. Aḥmad b. ʿAlī al-Sarīfīnī ﷺ, and he narrates from Shaykh ʿĀrif Abu al-Ḥasan ʿAlī b. Sulaymān ﷺ the baker, who stated that he narrates from Shaykh, the leader, Abu al-Qāsim ʿUmar b. Masʿūd Baz'zār ﷺ. He declares that his eyes did not perceive anyone with more knowledge pertinent to the mysterious Spiritual Realism [*ʿUlūm al-Ḥaqāiq*] than Sayyiduna Shaykh Muḥiyy al-Dīn ʿAbd al-Qādir al-Jilānī ﷺ.

Seeing the Divine Light of Beauty

I narrate from Shaykh Abu al-ʿĀfāf Mūsā b. Shaykh Khalīl Abu-ʿAmar ʿUthmān b. Mūsā al-Baqāʿī ﷺ, who narrates from his father. He narrates from two *Shuyūkh*; Shaykh Abu-ʿAmar ʿUthmān al-Sarīfīnī ﷺ and Shaykh Abu-Muḥammad ʿAbd al-Khāliq al-Ḥarīmīnī ﷺ. They narrate from Shaykh Abu al-Ḥasan b. ʿAlī ﷺ, whose grandfather is the distinguished as Shaykh Abu-Qūqah ﷺ. He narrates in Baghdād from Shaykh Abu al-Qāsim Haybatullāh b.

ʿAbdullāh Naqīb al-Hāshimī ﷺ, who asserted that he narrates from Shaykh Abu-Talḥā b. Muzaffar b. Ghānim al-ʿAlthī ﷺ. He narrates from Shaykh Abu al-Qāsim ʿUmar al-Baz'zār ﷺ, and all of them were unanimous that Sayyiduna Muḥiyy al-Dīn Shaykh ʿAbd al-Qādir al-Jilānī ﷺ was informed about a certain individual and his *murīd* and revealed his name, who confessed that he had seen *Allāh* ﷻ with his physical eye. That individual was summoned and questioned about this confession; to which he replied in the affirmative. Sayyiduna Ghawth ﷺ rebuked him and forbade him from pronouncing such a statement, and procured a vow from him, that he would never repeat, the issuing of such a statement anymore. Sayyiduna Ghawth ﷺ was questioned as to whether the individual had been truthful or not? Henceforward, he replied:

> He is truthful, but he is doubtful, because he had conceived the light of *Allāh's* ﷻ Divine Grandeur with the eye of his heart. From his spiritual eye, a window opened to the physical eye, through which he observed this phenomenon with an insight [*basīrat*] of radiance. The rays of this light adjoined this observation and his presumption was that his physical eye had perceived it; whilst in fact, it was his spiritual insight which had observed it. He is oblivious of the fact that the insight of his vision had in fact, perceived this. Almighty *Allāh* ﷻ stipulates:
>
> ﴿مَرَجَ الْبَحْرَيْنِ يَلْتَقِيَانِ ۝ بَيْنَهُمَا بَرْزَخٌ لَّا يَبْغِيَانِ﴾
>
> *'He released the two seas, meeting [side by side]; between them is a barrier [so] neither of them transgresses.'* [280]
>
> According to Divine Ordinance, Almighty *Allāh* ﷻ directs with the Hands of His ﷻ Benediction [*Qudrat*]; the Light of Radiance and Glory towards the hearts of His ﷻ servants. Thus, one derives that concept, which is similar to that which an artist extracts from an image. This is not detrimental to anything. His ﷻ veil is one curtain of His ﷻ Eminence, which does nor tear.

[280] *Al-Qur'ān al-Karīm*, Chapter Ar-Raḥmān Verses no: 19-20

The narrator concedes to the fact that there was a group of *ʿUlama* and *Mashā'ikh* present during this session, where the words and explanation of Sayyiduna Ghawth ﷺ motivated them to such an extent that it captivated their sentiments. Some of them tore off their clothes, and had run off into the jungles.

O cursed! Go away

I narrate from Shaykh Abu-Muḥammad Rajab b. Abī al-Mansūr al-Dārī ﷺ, who had heard in 616 *hijrī* from the exalted Shaykh, Sayyiduna Ḍiya al-Dīn Abu-Nasar Mūsā b. Shaykh Muḥiyy al-Dīn ʿAbd al-Qādir al-Jilānī ﷺ had articulated that his illustrious father ﷺ had related:

> 'I was on a journey, travelling in the jungles. For a few days, I stayed there and could not locate any water. I was extremely thirsty, and observed that a cloud had appeared, which had shaded me. Thereafter, something fell onto me, which was similar to rain, and hence, I quenched my thirst with it. Henceforth, I saw a light that had penetrated the edges of the horizon, and thereby an image appeared. I heard a voice which declared: *'O ʿAbd al-Qādir! I am your lord and I have legalized Ḥarām entities for you, or probably the voice asserted: I have made Ḥalāl all those entities which are Ḥarām for others,'* I immediately read: اعوذ باللہ من الشیطان الرجیم – *I seek refuge in Allāh from the cursed devil, and asserted: 'O cursed! Go away.'* No sooner as I pronounced this, the light disappeared and darkness became prevalent. That image turned into to smoke and it conversed with me: *'O ʿAbd al-Qādir! You have protected yourself from me with your knowledge, by the Command of Allāh ﷻ and with your lofty rank of your Fiqah. I have misled seventy Mashā'ikh of this path with this method.'* I responded to the cursed devil: *'This is nothing, except the Mercy and Grace of my Lord ﷻ.'*

The narrator confirmed that he had inquired from Sayyiduna Ghawth ﷺ, as to how he had recognized that it was the cursed devil. To this effect, Muḥiyy al-Dīn ʿAbd al-Qādir al-Jilānī ﷺ replied: *'By his claim that, indeed I am your Lord, and I have made Ḥarãm entities Ḥalãl for you was quite evident in identifying the cursed devil.'*

The Difference between the Presence of the Divine Being and Presence of Divine Attributes

Sayyiduna Ghawth ﷺ was questioned about the difference between the presence of the Divine Being and the presence of the Divine Attributes and henceforth, he expounded:

> When the inner self observes an entity that is existent with its opposite; and concealed within the veil of its contrary; whilst hidden in its meaning and existence; and manifests with that existence which is other than itself. Therefore, that is indicative of the presence of Attributes. This is so; because its existence is with its origin [*mousũf* – the described noun][281], so it is necessary by its appearance that it hides along one side around it; because in the presence of such quality, existence is absorbent to the necessity of its opposite. The presence of the being is absent and is within the veil of its contradiction; because, when one who observes the Divine Resplendence, then the appearance of glory is not strong. He who desires excellence and splendour, does not remain firm owing to its magnificence and grandeur. An Attribute is in fact, not concealed in reality at the time of the exposure of the contradictory [object]. In fact, it is concealed by the presence of the present [object]. The reason is that the presence of the external attribute overpowers the concealed attribute and evolves into concealment in the essential attribute. This is because the meaning of every attribute is that it exists, together with its object. Thus, when the relevant meaning of its strong accomplishments manifests in the eye of Eternity of its object, the signs of its presence are thereby concealed within the meanings of its accomplishment. This is

[281] Origin refers to the product [*mousũf* - noun] such as a rose. Fragrance or beauty is the descriptive quality [*sifat* - adjective] of the rose [noun] and this quality cannot exist without its origin. Quality depends on its origin.

because *Waḥdat* [Divine Unity] is far beyond the neighbourhood of occurrences in number[282]. It is at this juncture that the surroundings are folded away from the attributes of the meanings of plurality of numbers. It manifests without these attributes in existence, because the undisclosed has observed the attributes with traditional physicality. It enters courageously into the ship of its ocean, which draws the corner of the eye and time; together with its controversies. There are three signs within this sphere:

1) The presence of insight which contains such power, that it is existent before its presence.
2) To reason after the disappearance of presence pertinent to its reality, with the prudence of presence.
3) For two separate presences to be confined to one attribute of presence.

When the present concealment, on its own, is adjoined to absolute existence, it refers to the *Shuhūd* [observation] of the Being. In such a manifestation, it is necessary that; the termination of both observances nullifies time. The proof of joining and separation for the corner of the eye; eliminates nearness, distance and the existence. *Shuhūd* remains isolated with the attribute of presence. In the Eye of Eternity, it remains permanently powerful against its contradiction. This manifests during the time, when its novelty is stripped. By its meaning, and in accordance to its attribute; command, condition and essence; it is void. Hence, at this location, the beginning of every single existence reverts to the end, because the characteristics of its beginning is obliterated in the non-existence [*ʿadam*]; and the characteristic of distance is annihilated in the Last Day [*abad*]. Everything that becomes exposed, becomes concealed by the constant wonderment in non-existence [*ʿadam*]. The sign of this *Shuhūd* [observation] is that it is a characteristic which is not accomplished before existence; and its application does not remain, subsequent to its being,

[282] Almighty *Allāh* ﷻ is not the mathematical one that is divisible e.g. two halves is one or four quarters is equal to one. The Divine Unity of the Sublime Lord ﷻ is the unique and indivisible ONE.

which becomes non-existent. Its reality cannot be thereby established by anything that emanates from it. No proof is to be produced of its reality on the basis of detachment from such characteristics; and subsequent to its limits of union of observance. This station is for none, except the dignified *Anbiya* ﷺ [Prophets]; the status of none, except the *Siddiqīn* [elite Truthful] and the designation of none, except the *Awliya*. All such realities cannot be accomplished by diligence and struggle, but is dependent on the blessings of the Sublime Lord ﷻ. It is not blessed by powers of reasoning, but by Eternal Divine Ordinance.

Sayyiduna Shaykh ʿAbd al-Qādir al-Jilānī رضي الله عنه was questioned about *Mawārid Ilāhiyyah* [spiritual Divine inspirations] and *Tawāriq Shaytāniyyah* [satanic whispers into the heart]. The illustrious Ghawth رضي الله عنه replied: *'Mawārid Ilāhiyyah is not attained by seeking it, and it does no disappear for any reason. It does not approach on a set pattern, nor at a specific moment. Tawāriq Shaytāniyyah is apparently the opposite.'*

The Meaning of Love

Sayyiduna Ghawth al-Aʿzam رضي الله عنه was asked about love and he resonated:

> Love is a state of confusion within the heart of the beloved. The world that confronts him then, becomes similar to a stone in a ring or a gathering of mourning. Love is intoxication without consciousness; it is a *dhikr* without deletion; it is uneasiness without, internal and external peace in all facets. It is the sincere powerlessness for the beloved; and not by the experiences of human nature nor formalities. Love is to become blind and overwhelming of everything, except the beloved. Hence, the lover becomes totally blind. The lovers are so inebriated that they do not possess any sensations, except that of the beloved. They befall so sick that they do not get cured, except by the vision of the beloved. They are engrossed in such amazement, and therefore, they do not experience love without their birth. Hence, nothing excites them, except the dialogue of the beloved. They do not answer to anyone,

except the beloved. As a result, they recite the following couplets from the poems of Majnu and Layla:

لَقَدْ لَامَنِيْ فِيْ حُبِّ لَيْلٰى أَقَارِبِيْ أَبِي وَابنُ عَمِّي وَابنُ خَالِي وَخَالِيَا

In the love of Layla, my close family met with me; my brother, my paternal brother, my maternal brother and my maternal uncle reprimanded me.

فَلَوْ كُنْتُ أَعْمَى أَخْبِطُ الأَرْضَ بِالْعَصَا أَصَمَّ فَنَادَتْنِي أُجِيبُ الْمُنَادِيَا

If I was blind, I would have searched the floor with a stick to answer; and if I was deaf, and I was called; then too, I would have answered.

وَأَخْرُجُ مِنْ بَيْنِ الْبُيُوتِ لَعَلَّنِي أُحَدِّثُ عَنْكِ النَّفْسَ بِاللَّيْلِ خَالِيَا

And at night, I pass by between the houses in the hope, that I have a moment alone in the night to talk to you.

وَإِنِّي لَا أَسْتَغْشِي وَمَا بِيْ غَشِيَّةٌ لَعَلَّ خَيَالاً مِنْكِ يَلْقَى خَيَالِيَا

I am not overcome by unconsciousness nor am I a patient of unconsciousness, but this engrossment is because, maybe your thoughts will engage me.

مُعَذِّبَتِي لَولَاكِ مَا كُنْتُ هَائِماً أَدُوْرُ عَلَى الأَطْلَالِ فِي الْبَيْدِ عَارِيَا

O oppressor! If you did not exist, I would not have become insane in your love; I would have not roamed barefooted on the hillocks.

فَإِنْ تَمْنَعُوا لَيْلَى وَحُسْنَ حَدِيْثِهَا فَلَمْ تَمْنَعُوا عَنِّي الْبُكَا وَالقَوَافِيَا

O my relatives! If you forbid me from speaking of Layla; then do not forbid me from lamenting and reciting poetry of the beloved.

وَأَشْهَدُ عِنْدَ اللهِ أَنِّي أُحِبُّهَا فَهَذَا لَهَا عِنْدِيْ فَمَا عِنْدَهَا لِيَا

And I testify in the Court of Allāh ﷻ that I love her; this is the status of Layla in my heart, but what is my status in her heart?

أُحِبُّ مِنَ الأَسْمَاءِ مَا وَافَقَ اِسْمَهَا وَأَشْبَهَهُ أَوْ كَانَ مِنْهُ مُدَانِيَا

I select that name from amongst names that is equivalent to her name; or a name that is similar to or anyway close to her name.

يَقُوْلُ أُنَاسٌ عَلَّ مَجْنُوْنُ عَامِرٍ يَرُوْمُ سُلُوّاً قُلْتُ أَنِّي طَابِيَا

People say that the Majnū of Banī ʿĀmir has returned again; he is torn apart with sorrow, but I say, I am intoxicated with love.

إِذَا مَا طَوَاكَ الدَّهْرُ يَا أُمَّ مالِكٍ! فَشَأْنُ الْمَنَايَا الْقَاضِيَاتِ وَشَانِيَا

O Umm Mālik! When the time is lengthened; then death will decide my fate [of my love].

The Meaning of Tawḥīd

When Sayyiduna Ghawth ﷺ was questioned about *Tawḥīd*, he resonated:

> This is a sign of concealing the undisclosed attribute of the *Sābir* [the patient] from both sides, during such instances, when they are with the Divine Presence; whereby the heart has surpassed the limits of the stations of thoughts. He has ascended the concealed lofty honourable stations of Divine Union and has reached the Divine Proximity with the feet of *Tajrīd*.[283]
>
> They ascend the heights of proximity with perseverance in *Tafrīd,*[284] which results in both the worlds becoming extinct and only the Reality of the Absolute *Allāh* ﷻ exists. By being detached from the characteristics of existence and creation, they are freed from both the worlds. Under this circumstances, they observe those entities, through which *Allāh* ﷻ inspires their hearts. They seek true *Tafrīd* and are sincere in the pursuit of attributes and as well as the deliberation [*talab*] of truth. This heralds forth, because the characteristic of individuality demands singularity. Henceforth, they proceed to the Divine Being with the connotation of the attribute of individuality. When the servant is

[283] Detachment. Withdrawing from other than *Allāh* ﷻ and the Universe, within one's heart and concealed Being [*Sirr*]. Reference is made to absolute devotion to *Allāh* ﷻ, the Supreme Being.

[284] *Tafrīd* means that all praise and accreditation is attributed to *Allāh* ﷻ, and not to oneself. This is based on the belief that *Allāh* ﷻ is the Source of all entities, and there is no originator or source of power other than *Allāh* ﷻ. This annuls the concept of free will.

defiled by reasons owing to other factors of refutations and impurities, he is then rejected from this privilege; and deprived of this communion. He thereby transforms into the physical human condition of reversion; where he is veiled within the characteristics of physicality and is totally oblivious of the lofty stations of spiritual lustres and elevation.

The Meaning of Tajrīd

Sayyiduna Ghawth al-Aʿzam ﷺ was asked about *Tajrīd* and this is what he professed:

Tajrīd means to separate secrets from deliberation in such a manner that one attains tranquil steadfastness in seeking the beloved and one dons the garb of serenity and detaches oneself from limitations [of creation]. One reverts from creation to Absolute Truth [*Allāh* ﷻ, the Creator].

The Meaning of Maʿārifah

Sayyiduna Shaykh Muḥiyy al-Dīn ʿAbd al-Qādir al-Jilānī ﷺ was posed with a question about *Maʿārifah*. Henceforth, he elucidated:

Maʿārifah is to become aware of those undisclosed realities that are screened behind the curtains of Concealment. As a result, information of all those meanings, pertaining to the Singularity of the Divine Being are brought to surface. Adjacent to this, the information of the testimony of the truth of all entities with their signs are inevitable. Thereafter, follows the acquisition of the knowledge of the restoration of every single perishable; and the reality of its mortality at such a time, when permanence is pointed out to it. To such an effect, when the lustre of the wonderment of Divinity beams, the effect of permanence is contained in it; and in conjunction to the signs of permanence. In this modus, the Brilliance and Grandeur of Divinity, which are linked to the eye of the heart are focused towards *Allāh* ﷻ.

The difference between the statements of Shaykh Manthūr al-Ḥallāj ﷺ and Shaykh Abu-Yazīd Bustāmī ﷺ

When Sayyiduna Ghawth ﷺ was probed about the difference between the statements of Shaykh Ḥallāj ﷺ and Shaykh Abu-Yazīd ﷺ, who expressed the word '*Subhḥanī*'. He elaborated:

Ḥallāj ﷺ treaded the path of Love, and attained the gems of the secrets of Love. In accordance to his personal experience, he kept these secrets in trust within the inner treasuries of his heart. Whereas, when the light of magnificence appeared in front of the eye of his perception, his vision deemed impaired from seeing existence. He then assumed that the place was devoid of existence. Henceforth, he refused to take it; and his hands were cut off; and moreover, he was subjected to prosecution. By the oath of your life! Any person who is the owner of this gem; shall not be content, except by the possession of a high degree of love, i.e. *fana* [annihilation].

Shaykh Abu-Yazīd ﷺ did not clearly express his love nor did he provide information about his love. It so happened that after the confirmation in the uttermost limits, the tiredness of the dust of the path fell on him. He exclaimed '*Subḥānī – Glorified am I,*' in thanksgiving to his acquisition. It is also documented that when Ḥallāj ﷺ reached the door and knocked; and a voice called out: *'O Ḥallāj! Only that person may enter this door who is purified from human attributes; has become extinct from physicalities, and dies owing to love and melts in ardent love. He sacrifices his life at the door and surrenders the self at the veils, and stands with the feet of reverence at the station of wonderment.'* When *fana* makes him speechless, *sukar* [inebriation] gives him speech and thus, he exclaims: '*Annal-Ḥaqq*'. Thereafter, the courtier replied: *'Today you shall be cut to pieces and killed; and tomorrow you shall be privileged with Divine Communion.'* Further, the condition of his tongue spoke [it was then that a single glance in comparison to the flow of his blood was not painful]. Abu-Yazīd ﷺ passed through the door; and his stature became praiseworthy; and his pastures became lush with greenery. His drums of *fana* were reverberated by the Divine Hands[285] of *Qudrat* within proximity.

The tents of *Mushāhidah* [observance] were erected with the first benediction in the pastures. It had two tongues with which it spoke; and two lights that shone. One tongue was that which spoke with the happiness of *Tamjīd* [glorification of *Allāh* ﷻ]; whilst the other tongue spoke the truth of *Tawḥīd* [Monotheism]. The tongue of the happiness of *Tamjīd* began singing: *'I saw Allāh ﷻ before whatever I saw,'* and the tongue of *Tawḥīd* sang: *'Subḥānī –glorified am I.'* Thereby, the light of *wajdān* [ecstasy] screamed: *'Proximity made me extinct and then made me alive.'* The light of communion screamed: *'Anal-Ḥaqq – I am truth, it has kept me bāqī [permanent] and raised me and I am purified for my beneficial and Just Lord ﷻ.*

فَيَادَارَهَا بِالْحُزْنِ اِنَّ مَزَارَهَا قَرِيْبٌ وَلٰكِنْ دَوْنَ ذَالِكَ اَهْوَالُ

Thus, O the house of His sorrows! Verily, His house is though near,
but the activities of its vicinity is very awesome and frightening.

It is also that the nightingale of Ḥaḍrat Ḥallāj ﷺ became ecstatic, and its screams became uncontrollable and requested for Divine Communion. It then retired on the carpet of tests and professed: *'O son of Manthūr! If you are a true lover, and an enthusiastic sales devotee, sell then yourself and your soul in fana so that you may reach Me.'* He was thus, obedient to the command and exclaimed: '*Annal-Ḥaqq*' so that he may be accepted. Similarly, *Allāh* ﷻ stipulates:

﴿وَلَا تَقُولُوا لِمَنْ يُقْتَلُ فِي سَبِيلِ اللَّهِ أَمْوَاتٌ ۚ بَلْ أَحْيَاءٌ وَلَٰكِن لَّا تَشْعُرُونَ﴾

And do not utter regarding those who are slain; in Allah's cause as
'dead'; in fact they are alive, but it is you who cannot perceive.[286]

[285] This refers to the Divine Power of *Allāh* ﷻ.
[286] Al-Qur'ān al-Karīm, Chapter 2, Surah al-Baqarah Verse no. 154

The statement of the cursed devil: '*Ana – me*', was owing to disobedience and objection. He was commanded to make *sajdah*, [prostrate] but replied that he was more excellent [than Nabī Ādam ﷺ] and hence, he was rejected and subjected to distance. Is *Allāh* ﷻ, not the Creator, and aware of this?

It is also that the army of love besieged the core of Ḥaḍrat Ḥallāj's ﷺ heart and the Sovereign of Love had overpowered his inconceivable concealments. It is only then that he exclaimed in zealous astonishment: '*Anal-Ḥaqq – I am truth*;' whilst the haughtiness of the pride of the cursed devil entered the core of his spirit and thus, he pronounced: '*Ana – me*.' The treasury of secrets stimulated the breath of his egotism, and he claimed that he is far superior to the human [Nabī Adam ﷺ]. He, who excels in the zeal of love; is worthy of being granted closeness to communion. Hence, when he who looked with the eye of pride at his *nafs*, it warranted the eligibility of the head to be crushed, and to be cut off by the sword.

Sayyiduna Ghawth ﷺ was further questioned about the secrets between the statements of '*Anal-Ḥaqq*' and '*Subḥānī*.' He enunciated as follows:

I cannot identify anyone who is qualified enough to understand my explanation of this reality; nor anyone to trust with the disclosure of its concealments.

The meaning of Himmah [High Spirits]

Sayyiduna Ghawth al-Aʿzam ﷺ was questioned, concerning the definition of elevated spirits, and thus, he expounded:

It is to divorce oneself and one's soul from the Hereafter. Furthermore, one must subjugate one's heart desires and intentions in accordance to the ordainment [prescription] of Almighty *Allāh* ﷻ. This means that one's intentions do not exist, and as such one ought to be content with whatever *Allāh* ﷻ has ordained for one. For a single moment, one must not even focus, nor direct one's head, i.e. intentions or desires, and nor blink the eye towards creation.

The meaning of Haqīqah [Reality]

Our Master, Sayyiduna Ghawth al-Aʿzam ﷜ was questioned with regard to *Ḥaqīqah*, and he expressed:

> *Ḥaqīqah* is that which refers to the opposition, which does not oppose its real meaning, and nor does it have an opposing interpretation. In fact, when reference is made to it, the opposite remains intact; and during the phases of comparison, the opposition is nullified.

The meaning of Dhikr

When people queried from Ḥaḍrate Ghawth ﷜ about the eminent stations of *dhikr*, he thereby pronounced:

> It is a sign of Truth [*Ḥaqq*] within the heart that which is adopted, when an effect of the past benediction is once more initiated. Hence, this *dhikr*, is termed as permanent and constant *dhikr*, wherein there is no interference of forgetfulness, injury or guilt. Forgetfulness does not defile him; even though he remains silent, breathes, walks or moves around. He shall consistently be in the concentration of *dhikr*, which indeed is a superior station of *dhikr*. It is about this particular *dhikr* that Almighty *Allāh* ﷻ has emphatically stipulated in His ﷻ glorious *Qur'ān*. The exceptional *dhikr* is that, which inculcates zeal in times of dangers and adversity, which approaches from the Majestic Almighty Lord ﷻ. Such *dhikr* is concealed within the Palace of Secrets.

The meaning of Shouq [zeal]

Sayyiduna Ghawth al-Aʿzam ﷜ was questioned about *shouq* and he reverberated:

The best *shouq* [zeal] is attained by *Mushãhidah* [observation]; and not by resuming lethargy, when meeting or becoming motionless by observance, or by departing from the proximity of communion, or by exhibiting deficiency in love. In fact, whilst the meeting with the beloved intensifies; the *shouq* also intensifies. *Shouq* does not reach the degree of perfection; unless it does not isolate itself from the intellect. It is in conformity to the soul or is in agreement to the morale or delight of the *nafs*. Hence, *shouq* is isolated from reason. The reason that appropriates *shouq* to be obligatory is that, one shall not be aware of *Mushãhidah* [being observed] and moreover, *mushãhidah* is only accomplished by the *shouq* of *mushãhidah*.

The meaning of Tawakkul [reliance]

When Sayyiduna Ghawth ﷺ was questioned about *Tawakkul*, and he thereby apprised:

It is to be engrossed in the Lord ﷻ with the heart and to be detached from everything else, except *Allãh* ﷻ. To forget everything else, except the one on whom you rely, and owing to this reliance, you shall attain carefreeness from everyone else. With this *Tawakkul,* the pomp of wealth diminishes. *Tawakkul* is to bow the head in submission towards the concealed matters of the unseen and to observe destiny with the eyes of *Ma ̔ãrifah*. This is classified as possessing trust and belief on the certainty of the reality of the heart pertaining to the principles of *Ma ̔ãrifah*. Hence, it is necessary that there should be no defect, and neither refutation therein.

The meaning of Inãbah [repentance]

Sayyiduna Shaykh ̔Abd al-Qãdir al-Jilãnĩ ﷺ was questioned about *Inãbah* and he elucidated:

Inãbah includes the seeking of those matters which have passed by; viz. fear of stopping at stations, to be frustrated with concealed matters, and to possess trust with an elated disposition on the heads of the courts of the gatherings. Thereafter, it is to revert to *Ḥaqq* [truth] after all presence, and observance of the gathering. *Inābah* also refers to the return to *Allāh* ﷻ with fear, i.e. the fear of turning to other, than *Allāh* ﷻ, and as well as the fear of concentration on every other site.

The difference between the 'Ana' of Shaykh Manthūr ﷺ and the cursed devil

Ḥaḍrate Ghawth ﷺ was questioned about the stoned devil who had confessed '*Ana*' and was rejected and Shaykh Manthūr ﷺ, who asserted '*Ana*' and attained Divine Communion. Sayyiduna Shaykh ﷺ elaborated as follows:

> Shaykh Manthūr ﷺ intended *fana* [spiritual extinction] in his statement so that he would be elevated with permanence and thus, he reached the *majlis* of communion, and was blessed with the garb of *baqa* [permanence].
>
> The cursed devil intended for *baqa* [permanence] in his statement of '*Ana*' therefore, he was stripped of his *wilāyah* of *fana* and benediction. His status was degraded; whilst the benedictions were elevated.

The Meaning of Taubah

People queried from Sayyiduna Ghawth ﷺ about the meaning of *taubah* and he stipulated:

> *Taubah* is when *Allāh* ﷻ looks at His ﷻ servant with His ﷻ primordial benevolence and focuses those benevolences onto his heart. He ﷻ draws His ﷻ servant by this encompassing benedictions with a special affection. When this occurs, the heart is then drawn away from all defective spirits, and is henceforward, attracted to the Real Absolute Lord of Power ﷻ. The soul and the intellect correlates in accordance to the heart. Indeed! It is evident that all matters are focused towards Almighty *Allāh* ﷻ.

The Meaning of Ikhlās [sincerity in faith]

Sayyiduna Shaykh ﷺ was questioned with regard to *Ikhlās* and he elaborated:

The reality of *Ikhlās* is similar to the reality of *Tawakkul*. The reality of *Ikhlās* is not to seek recompense for one's good deeds and have elevated spirits pertinent to this matter. This is similar to *Tawakkul* which departs from trials and tribulations and peacefully focuses on the Lord ﷻ of all. Sayyiduna Ghawth ﷺ further asserted: 'Oh servant! How many times was it relayed to you? Do you not hear and how much would you hear? Would you not understand; and how much would you understand? Would you not act; and how much would you act? Would you not exercise *Ikhlās* and how much of *Ikhlās* do you practice? Would you not annihilate your existence with your *Ikhlās*?'

Weeping

Sayyiduna Shaykh ﷺ was questioned with regard to weeping and he decreed:

Cry for Him ﷻ, and cry on Him ﷻ.

Duniya [this mundane world]

When enquired about the *duniya,* he resonated:

Remove it from your hearts and arms [possessions] so that it shall not harm you.

The meaning of Tasawwuf

Ḥaḍrate Ghawth ﷺ was questioned about *Tasawwuf* and he expounded:

A *Sūfi* is he who does not seek his lost entities from *Allāh* ﷻ and leaves the *duniya* behind him [detaches himself from it]. It is only then, that it shall serve him and grant him a share thereof. Before the *Ākhirah,* he shall achieve his goal in this *duniya*. Hence, upon him shall be the peace [*salāms*] of his Lord ﷻ.

Taʿazzaz and Takabbur [Reinforcement and Pride]

Ḥaḍrate Ghawth ﷺ was questioned about the difference between *Taʿazzaz* and *Takabbur*, and he articulated:

> *Taʿazzaz* is for *Allāh* ﷻ and be focused on *Allāh* ﷻ. This is very beneficial for the humiliation of the *nafs* and the enhancing of the elevated spirits towards *Allāh* ﷻ.
>
> *Takabbur* is for the *nafs* and its desires.[287] Its benefits are to create a zeal in one's disposition towards *Allāh* ﷻ. Natural pride in comparison to acquiring [self] pride is much easier.

The meaning of Shukar [Thankfulness]

Regarding *shukar* Sayyiduna Ghawth al-Aʿzam ﷺ was questioned, and he elaborated:

> The reality of *shukar* is to acknowledge and be grateful for the gifts of the Bestower in such a manner, whereby humility is demonstrated. The observance of the favour in the protection of its honour be in such a manner that every thankfulness is unable to fulfil the rights of its benevolence. There are many varieties in this. One is the thankfulness of the tongue, through which the blessings of peace are acknowledged as a blessing. The second, *shukar* is known as *Shukar bil Arkān* – thankfulness with its pillars. This means to express thankfulness by obedience and fulfilling one's duties. The third, *shukar* is that of the heart, and this is by permanently retreating with protection and honour in solitary confinement, and with the bedding of observance. Thereafter, be engrossed in witnessing the Bestower in the presence of that observance until His disappearance. Progress is focusing on the Bestower and not the favours.

[287] Here Sayyiduna Ghawth ﷺ refers to exercising haughtiness with egotism and its desires; combatting it with opposition rather than following its lust.

A *Shākir* [thankful] person is he who is thankful in the present and a *Shukūr* [extremely thankful] is he who is thankful in the absence of the favours. *Ḥāmid* is he who categorizes rejection as acceptance and harm as benefit. Thus, according to him both characteristics are equal. *Ḥamd* is that on which the praiser is to be seated; privileged on the bedding of proximity.

Sayyiduna Shaykh ﷺ was questioned as to why, in the Command of Almighty *Allāh* ﷻ, He ﷻ mentions the remembrance of the servant first and thereafter, followed by *Allāh* ﷻ, as enunciated in the following Qur'ānic extract:

﴿فَاذْكُرُونِي أَذْكُرْكُمْ﴾

Remember Me, I will cause you to be spoken of. [288]

The question is why were we are mentioned first and then *Allāh* ﷻ? And further, in the verse:

﴿يُحِبُّهُمْ وَيُحِبُّونَهُ﴾

.....who are His beloved ones and Allah is their beloved....[289]

In this verse, why did *Allāh* ﷻ place His love before ours? He expounded:

Dhikr is a station of intent and quest [*talab*]; and quest is the pre-amble of a gift or present. Therefore, our mention was made first. But on the contrary, love is solely a Lordly gift from destiny. The actions of the servant does not have forbearance in this matter and its existence within the servant cannot be perfect without it; because its manifestation emerged in the Hands of Ordinance, from the direction of the unseen. It is there that, the servant distances from self-requisition [*kasb*] and obliterates reasons [*sabab*]. It is for this reason that *Allāh* ﷻ placed first His ﷻ love first that He ﷻ has for us, before the love that we portray for Him ﷻ.

---

[288] *Al-Qur'ān al-Karīm*, Chapter 2, Surah al-Baqarah Verse no. 152

[289] *Al-Qur'ān al-Karīm*, Chapter 5, Surah al-Mā'idah Verse no. 54

Henceforward, he was questioned about the following command of *Allāh* ﷻ:

﴿ثُمَّ تَابَ عَلَيْهِمْ لِيَتُوبُوا﴾

He then accepted their repentance in order that they remain repentant [290]

What is the reason that *Allāh* ﷻ placed his repentance and reversion, which are upon us before our *toubah* and reversion towards Him ﷻ, when this is also parallel to self-requisition [*kasb*] similar to *dhikr*? Sayyiduna Shaykh رضي الله عنه replied: 'The reason for this is that *toubah* is the initial station of *talab* [quest] and the beginning of the essence of stations. Thus, He ﷻ has placed His ﷻ action before our action; for except Him ﷻ, no one else can open the door [of repentance], and no one has the strength to incline to it with ease, except by His ﷻ *Tawfiq*. It is certainly *Allāh* ﷻ who alerts the heedless and awakens the slumber of creation. It is He ﷻ who guides the wanderers to the path of the consciousness. It is solely and only *Allāh* ﷻ who turns people towards the remembrance of the beloved.

The Meaning of Sabar [patience]

When Sayyiduna Ghawth رضي الله عنه was questioned about *Sabar*, he articulated:

Sabar is the exercise of utmost respect, virtuous attributes and steadfastness during the times of adversity and prosperity. All bitter verdicts are wholeheartedly and happily accepted by the virtue of the Holy *Qur'ān* and *Sunnah*, since there are numerous laws that are to be accepted from the Divine Code. To exercise *sabar* with *Allāh* ﷻ is to be obedient and to execute all His ﷻ Commands and to abstain from all that *Allāh* ﷻ forbids. Another *sabar* is with *Allāh* ﷻ, which is pertinent to His ﷻ predestination, whereby one must always be jubilant and

290 *Al-Qur'ān al-Karīm*, Chapter 9, Surah Toubah Verse no. 118

content with one's application; and no comments of degradation are to be pronounced during poverty with regard to the desire of wealth. The other *sabar* is on *Allāh* ﷻ, which means to be attracted to His ﷻ promises, and for the true believer [*mo'min*], the path in both, this world and the hereafter shall be easy to walk upon. It is more difficult to abandon creation in comparison to abandoning *Allāh* ﷻ, and it is very difficult for the *nafs* to align itself to Almighty *Allāh* ﷻ. *Sabar* with *Allāh* ﷻ is indeed very difficult and therefore, a patient individual, who is poor is more outstanding, than someone who is thankful and wealthy. A thankful poor is more superb than both these two; and a poor who is patient and thankful is better than all of them. It is only an *'Ārif* that extends an invitation to hardship and misery.

The meaning of Fana [annihilation]

Sayyiduna Ghawth رضي الله عنه was questioned about *fana* and he professed:

> Almighty *Allāh* ﷻ examines the concealments of His ﷻ *Walī* and henceforth, existence becomes non-existent. A *Walī* should become *fana* [extinct] in the signs of *Allāh* ﷻ and his *fana* becomes *baqa*, but he becomes *fana* under the signs of *baqa*. When the signs of *Allāh* ﷻ heralds, it thereby makes him *fana* because His ﷻ lustres retains the servant existent as though he is prohibited from it. Thereafter, he is preserved in permanence with Him.

The meaning of Baqa [permanence]

When Sayyiduna Shaykh رضي الله عنه was questioned about *baqa*, he apprised:

> *Baqa*[291] cannot be accomplished without *liqa*, [292] because the *baqa* which does not comprise *fana* is with the same *baqa* that has no discontinuity; and this occurrence is similar to the blink of the eye or even quicker.

---

[291] Refers to Permanence.

[292] Union – meeting with the Beloved.

The signs of the people of *baqa* [*Ahle-Baqa*] is that, in the characteristics of their *baqa*, there is no *fana* of entities, because both these entities are the opposites of one another.

The meaning of Wafa [fidelity]

Ḥaḍrate Ghawth ﷺ was questioned about *wafa* and he pronounced:

Wafa is to consider the rights of the prohibitions of the Sublime Lord ﷻ in such a manner that it should not be deliberated upon with the heart or vision. Always safeguard the limitations of *Allāh* ﷻ, both verbally and in action. Hasten towards His ﷻ pleasure, both externally and internally.

The meaning of Riḍā [pleasure]

Sayyiduna Shaykh ﷺ was questioned about *riḍā* and he resonated:

Riḍā is to eradicate hesitation and wavering and to be satisfied with the ordinance of the Eternal Knowledge of Almighty *Allāh* ﷻ. *Riḍā* is also not to turn away from or to seek an alternative to the destiny of the Mighty Lord ﷻ. When any fate of *Allāh* ﷻ descends, one must not turn one's face away from it. Similarly, when any destiny of *Allāh* ﷻ is experienced, one must not permeate into its misery.

The meaning of Irādah [will - intention]

When Sayyiduna Ghawth ﷺ was questioned about *Irādah*, he elucidated:

Irādah is to engage in *dhikr* with the spiritual essence of eagerness, whereby the continuity of contemplation is within the heart.

The meaning of ʿInāyah [favour]

Ḥaḍrate Ghawth ﷺ was questioned about *ʿInāyah* and he professed:

ʿInāyah is eternal and it is derived from the attributes of *Allāh* ﷻ. He ﷻ has not disclosed this to anyone, and as such none can reach it without a medium. There are no reasons furnished, which may harm anyone; nor can anyone cause damage to it, and nor can anything soil it. This is a mystery of *Allāh* ﷻ of which no one is aware. From time immemorial it is a benediction, towards which creation has no access. It is not subjected to a specific time. In fact, *Allāh* ﷻ chooses from His ﷻ creation to whom He ﷻ ordains it and hence, qualifies him for it. *Allāh* ﷻ grants the people of *Ma ͨārifah* [*Ahle-Ma ͨārifah*] the authority of *Ināyah* and vests into them the power to function with creation. Thereafter, the allowance of opinion, and gifting them follows, whereby *Tawfiq* for the opinion of gifting is then rewarded on the opinion of speech. The signs of such a beloved servant, who is bestowed with *Ināyah* is under arrest; dragged, and absolutely imprisoned. He is drawn away from creation, when Sayyiduna Rasūlullāh ﷺ imprisons him. Moreover, he is further imprisoned by reverence, which remains with him.

The meaning of Wajd [spiritual ecstasy]

When Sayyiduna Shaykh رضي الله عنه was questioned about *wajd*, he articulated:

Wajd is when the soul engages in the sweetness of *dhik*r, and detaches itself from the rivalry of the beloved; and focuses on the Truth, and discharges itself from everything for the purpose of Truth. *Wajd* is a drink, which the Lord ﷻ provides His ﷻ servant with in order to drink on the pulpit of nobility. When the servant drinks this, he becomes light in weight, and when he becomes light in weight, his heart then flies with the wings of love to the sanctified gardens and falls into the ocean of reverence; where he is detached, because a person in *wajd* invariably experiences unconsciousness.

The meaning of Khauf [fear]

Sayyiduna Ghawth al-Aͨzam رضي الله عنه was questioned about fear, to which he apprised:

There numerous types of fear. *Khauf* [fear] is experienced by sinners; whereas, *rah'bah* [veneration] by the *ʿĀbidīn* [worshippers], *khashyah* [anxiety] by the *ʿUlama* [erudite scholars], *wajd* [rapturous delight] by the *ʿĀshiqīn* [lovers] and *haybah* [awe] by the *ʿĀrifīn* [Gnostics]. The fear of the sinners is owing to the fear of punishment; the fear of the *ʿĀbidīn* is owing to the elapse of the *thawāb* of worship, the fear of the *ʿUlama* is owing to hidden *shirk* [polytheism], the fear of the *ʿĀshiqīn* is owing to the loss of union, and the fear of the *ʿĀrifīn* is owing to wonderment and reverence; which is the greatest fear, because it is never terminated. When all these fears are faced by mercy and benevolence, they then receive tranquillity.

The meaning of Raja [hope]

When Sayyiduna Ghawth ﷺ was questioned about *raja,* he articulated:

> With regard to *raja* of the *Awliya*, the reality of their *raja* is to have a meritorious premise with *Allāh* ﷻ, because *raja* is a zeal. This is to yearn for that, which *Allāh* ﷻ has destined for His ﷻ servant. The yearning of the *Ahle-Safa* [people of purity] does not matter, whether it is profitable or the dispelling of evil; because the *Awliya* are certainly conscious of the fact that that Almighty *Allāh* ﷻ has fully endowed their affairs. Hence, in order to insistently delve into these matters, is unrestricted from the assertion of love. In such a situation, virtuous presumption is par-excellence than the hope of insistence. *Raja* actually originates owing to fear because, when an individual has the hope of accomplishing his goal; he shall certainly have fear, in view of the fact that he may not be deprived of it. Exceptional premise with *Allāh* ﷻ means to possess the gnosis [*Maʿārifah*] of all the Attributive Qualities of *Allāh* ﷻ, and to reach Him ﷻ through them; and not in the capacity of a servant, because He ﷻ knows that His ﷻ Attributes are *Muḥsin* [benefactor], *Karīm* [generous], *Latīf* [gracious] *and Raḥmān* [Merciful].

Virtuous presumption with *Allāh* ﷻ is to have courage on the first vision of bliss; whereby the heart is focused on the Creator ﷻ, i.e. a yearning heart, a desirous soul, coupled with spirits of hope in generality. When most of the requirements are satisfied, the concept of *raja* [hope] shall then be appropriately applicable to them. But when most of these entities are deranged, the word *tamʿāh* [greed] shall then be more appropriate than *raja*. Hope without fear depicts peace; and fear without hope denotes hopelessness.

ʿIlm al-Yaqīn [knowledge of certainty]

Sayyiduna Ghawth al-Aʿzam ﷺ was questioned about *ʿIlm al-Yaqīn* and he expounded:

ʿIlm al-Yaqīn is to adjoin *khabar* [news] and *maʿārifah* [gnosis] as though it is been observed. When this is comprehended and the decision and certainty of the heart accepts it with *maʿārifah* [gnosis]; and also understands it by observance, it then transforms into *ʿIlm al-Yaqīn* - knowledge of certainty.

The meaning of Muwāfiqat [conformity]

Sayyiduna Shaykh ﷺ was questioned about *muwāfiqat* and he resonated as follows:

Muwāfiqat is in conformity to the destiny of *Allāh* ﷻ, without any human intervention and thus, will or intent becomes singular; i.e. conformity of the human by the destiny of *Allāh* ﷻ.

Duʿā [supplication]

Ḥaḍrate Ghawth ﷺ was questioned about *dʿuā* and he expressed:

Duʿā comprises three stages:

- *Tasrīḥ* [making clear].
- *Taʿrīḍ* [ambiguity].
- *Ishārah* [sign or indication].

- ✓ *Tasrĩḥ* is discovered in the following statement of Sayyiduna Nabĩ Mũsã ﷺ:

﴿رَبِّ أَرِنِي أَنظُرْ إِلَيْكَ﴾

My Lord! Show me Your Self, so that I may see You. [293]

This points out to the vision of *Allãh* ﷻ.

- ✓ *Ta'rĩḍ* is understood by the statement of our beloved Nabĩ Sayyiduna Rasũlullãh ﷺ; *'O Allãh! Do not commit me for a moment to my nafs.'*
- ✓ *Ishãrah* is understood by the statement of Sayyiduna Nabĩ Ibrã'hĩm ﷺ:

﴿رَبِّ أَرِنِي كَيْفَ تُحْيِي الْمَوْتَىٰ﴾

My Lord! Show me how You will give life to the dead [294]

This refers to *roh'yah* [vision].

Ḥaya [modesty]

When Sayyiduna Ghawth ﷺ was questioned about *ḥaya,* he articulated:

Ḥaya is indicative, that the servant should be modest, when *Allãh* ﷻ stipulates something and His rights are disregarded or rejected. Furthermore, it is to communicate with *Allãh* ﷻ in a state of pride, when the servant is not aware that he is not qualified for it.

Moreover, it is to have desires from *Allãh* ﷻ of such entities, when the servant is aware that he does not deserve it. Modesty is to abstain from sins owing to *ḥaya* and not because of fear. Modesty is to think within lines of explanation and to worship *Allãh* ﷻ. Modesty denotes repute for *Allãh* ﷻ in totality of the intentions of your heart, and to be

[293] *Al-Qur'ãn al-Karĩm,* Chapter 7, Surah Ah'rãf, Verse no. 143

[294] *Al-Qur'ãn al-Karĩm,* Chapter 2, Surah Baqarah Verse no. 260

conscious of Him ﷻ. Sometimes *ḥaya* is generated, when the veil between the heart and esteem is lifted.

Mushāhidah [observance]

Sayyiduna Ghawth al-Aʿzam رضي الله عنه was questioned about *Mushāhidah* and he expounded:

Mushāhidah is when the eyes of the heart becomes blind to see both the worlds; whilst he sees with the eye of *ma ʿārifah*. Hence, he shall not have the slightest notion, nor a collection of visions within comprehension; and neither an emotional condition. *Mushāhidah* occurs when the heart receives information with the purity and certainty from *Allāh* ﷻ, which is relevant to a matter in informing him of undisclosed entities.

Qurb [Divine Proximity]

Sayyiduna Ghawth al-Aʿzam رضي الله عنه was questioned about *Qurb* and he affirmed:

Qurb is to travel the path with the elegance of *Qurb* [to the Divine Proximity].

Sukar [inebriation]

Sayyiduna Ghawth al-Aʿzam رضي الله عنه was questioned about *sukar* and he elucidated:

Sukar is when the lovers remember the beloved and their hearts are imbued with delight; whereas the restlessness within their hearts are, when the knowledge of the overwhelming fear of the beloved is experienced.

Yaqīn [certainty] is to investigate the concealment of the laws of the unseen. *Wasal* is union with the beloved and to be cut off from everything else, except from the beloved.

Farāgh-dili [open-heartedness] is the disappearance of pomp and dignity at the time of rectification of the self. Attachment emanates from solitude and grief.

Dhikr – In *dhikr* it is scandal to observe oneself, and then to suddenly disappear from it. Scandal is *Ḥarām* [forbidden].

Mushāhidah – In *Mushāhidah,* there is a spiritual euphoria on the condition of the abandonment of the dignity of appearance; because spiritual euphoria is situated on the carpet of *baqa* and *Mushāhidah*, is positioned onto the carpet of *qurb* [Divine Proximity]; and therefore, its abandonment is *Ḥarām.*

Sukr [inebriation] that is experienced at the time of *mushāhidah*, overpowers the intellect and imagination. In the presence of love, absence cannot be imagined; and when the will is strong and associated with *dhikr,* the goal of intention increases and it inculcates love. When the intention overwhelms the entire heart, it then possesses it. When it possesses the heart, its concentration on everything else henceforth, ceases and the fall of that king becomes a reality. This is pure companionship, whereby you have engaged in the *dhikr* of Him ﷻ, and you are a lover. When you hear Him ﷻ remembering you; you are then a beloved, and creation becomes your veil with your *nafs*; and your *nafs* becomes a veil from your Lord ﷻ. As long as you perceive creation you shall not perceive your *nafs*; and as long as you perceive your *nafs,* you shall not perceive your Lord ﷻ. Thus, *faqar* [spiritual poverty] implies death, which these people seek, and they are alive therein.

The general public follow *qāl* [speech], whilst the elite follow *ḥāl* [spiritual condition]. When you are given prosperity, then you become prosperous and your leave is transformed into obligation. There is the evidence of your obligation. Hence, leave is for those with incomplete *Imān* and obligation is for those with perfect *Imān*, whilst kingdom is for those who perish.

Henceforward, the *Qārī* recited the following verse in the presence of Sayyiduna Ghawth ﷺ:

﴿لِّمَنِ الْمُلْكُ الْيَوْمَ﴾

For whom is the kingship this day? [295]

Thereafter, Sayyiduna Ghawth al-Aʿzam ﷺ stood up and owing to his veneration, everyone stood up. He signalled to them to remain in their condition and he then continuously repeated: *'Who says that it is his kingship? Who says that it is his kingship?'* Thereafter, a pious individual stood up who was renowned as Shaykh Aḥmad. He was a great *ʿĀbid* and *Mujāhid* and began pronouncing: *'I proclaim it is my kingship, because it is for me, and as for this there is none like me.'* Sayyiduna Ghawth al-Aʿzam ﷺ audibly cautioned: *'O fool! When were you qualified for this that which, you claim is yours? When did you see misfortunes that encircled you, and that you knocked it towards you?'* Shaykh Aḥmad shrieked, took off his black woollen robe and ran off into the jungles.

On another day Sharīf Masʿūd b. ʿUmar Hāshimī al-Muqrī ﷺ recited the following verse:

﴿وَنَحْنُ نُسَبِّحُ بِحَمْدِكَ وَنُقَدِّسُ لَكَ﴾

Whereas we glorify You with praise and proclaim Your Sanctity [296]

Upon listening to the former mentioned verse, Sayyiduna Shaykh ﷺ asserted: *'O servant! Keep quiet.'* He then shrieked and declared: *'How long would you state you were reading tasbīḥ? How long would you proclaim that we are the ones who read the tasbīḥ? You have exposed your secrets, and we have concealed them. Thus, Divine Proximity makes us extinct; and vision kills us, and who will interpret for us?'* He then raised his head and articulated: *'O Angels of my Lord! You are present and most of our group are more perfect than your group.'*

[295] *Al-Qur'ān al-Karīm,* Chapter Surah Ghāfir Verse no. 16
[296] *Al-Qur'ān al-Karīm,* Chapter 2, Surah Baqarah Verse no. 30

Chains of Narrations concerning Dhikr

I was informed by Shaykh al-Jalīl Musnad Zayn al-Dīn Abu-Bakr Muḥammad b. Imām Taqī al-Dīn Abu al-Tāhir Ismāʿīl b. ʿAbdullāh b. Abu al-Moḥsin al-Anbātī ﷺ, and I have read this many times in front of him. I queried from him whether Shaykh Imām ʿĀlim Mawaffaq al-Dīn Abu-Muḥammad ʿAbdullāh b. Muḥammad b. Aḥmad b. Muḥammad b. Qudāmah al-Maqdasī ﷺ narrates in a state that it was read in his presence which he had heard. In *Zil-Qaʿdah* 610 *hijrī* in the *Jāmeʿh Masjid* of Damascus he acknowledged that he had heard from Imām Tāj al-ʿĀrifīn Muḥiyy al-Dīn Abu-Muḥammad ʿAbd al-Qādir b. Abī-Sālih al-Jilī ﷺ, who had read in his presence and which I had heard. I was informed in *Rabīʿ al-Awwal* 561 *hijrī* in Baghdād by Shaykh Abu-Ghālib Muḥammad b. Abu al-Ḥasan b. Aḥmad b. al-Ḥusain Bāqalānī ﷺ in *Jāmeʿh al-Qasr* that he had heard from Shaykh Abu-ʿAlī al-Ḥasan b. Aḥmad b. Ibrāhīm b. al-Ḥasan b. Muḥammad b. Shazran Baz'zār ﷺ, who had heard from Shaykh ʿUthmān b. Aḥmad Maymūn b. Isḥāq Abu-Sahl b. Ziyād ﷺ. All of them state that they had heard from Shaykh Aḥmad b. ʿAbd al-Jabbār ﷺ, who had heard from Shaykh Ibn Idrīs ﷺ, who narrates from Shaykh Ibn Jarīj ﷺ, who narrates from Shaykh Ibn ʿAmmār ﷺ; and he narrates from Shaykh ʿAbdullāh b. Tāsā ﷺ, he narrates from Shaykh Yaʿlah b. Omayyah ﷺ who affirmed: I declared to Sayyiduna ʿUmar b. al-Khattāb ﷺ that in the following verse: '*There is no objection on you if you fear and perform qasr salāh.*' Now people have become foolish. Sayyiduna ʿUmar ﷺ reacted: '*I am also surprised as you are in this matter and enquired from Sayyiduna Rasūlullāh ﷺ regarding this and he ﷺ confirmed: 'This is a gift that Allāh ﷻ has given you, so accept this gift.*' Imām Muslim ﷺ has narrated this *Ḥadith* in his *Saḥīḥ* regarding *salāh* from Sayyiduna Abu-Bakr b. Abī-Shaybah ﷺ, Sayyiduna Abu-Kurayb Muḥammad b. al-ʿUlā ﷺ and Sayyiduna Abu-Ḥathīmah Zuhair b. Ḥarb Isḥāq b. Ibrāhīm ﷺ. These four narrate from Shaykh ʿAbdullāh b. Idrīs ﷺ and Shaykh Muḥammad al-Maqdasī ﷺ, who narrate from Shaykh Yaḥyah b. Saʿīd ﷺ; and these two narrate from Shaykh Ibn Jarīj ﷺ; as I have referenced. Hence for us an exchange had occurred.

In the narration of Sayyiduna Ibn Shāzān ﷺ he states that he narrates from Shaykh Aḥmad b. Sulaymān ﷺ, who narrates this *Ḥadith* from Shaykh Ḥasan b. Mukarram ﷺ, who narrates from Shaykh ʿUthmān b. ʿUmar b. Yunūs b. Yazīd ﷺ, and he narrates from Imām Zuhrī ﷺ, and he narrates from Sayyiduna ʿAbdullāh b. ʿAbd al-Raḥmān b. Kāʿab b. Mālik ﷺ. He narrates from his father, who had heard from Sayyiduna Rasūlullāh ﷺ who states: *'The soul of a Muslim will be a bird which will hang on the door of Jannah until Allāh* ﷻ *will return it to its body on that day when he will be resurrected.'* This *Ḥadith* is reported by three *Imāms*; Imām Tirmidī ﷺ in his *Jāme'h* and Imām Nisā'ī ﷺ and Imām Ibn Māja ﷺ in their *Sunan*. *Tirmidī* in the chapter of *Jihād* narrates from Sayyiduna Muḥammad b. Yaḥyah b. Abī ʿUmar al-ʿAdnī ﷺ, and he narrates from Sayyiduna Sufyān b, ʿAyniyah ﷺ, and he narrates from Sayyiduna ʿAmar b. Dinār ﷺ. *Ibn Māja* narrates this in the chapter of *Janā'iz* from Sayyiduna Qutaybah b. Sāʿad ﷺ, who narrates from Sayyiduna Mālik ﷺ. *Ibn Māja* also narrates this *Ḥadith* from Sayyiduna Suwayd b. Sāʿad ﷺ, and he narrates from Sayyiduna Imām Mālik ﷺ. In the Chapter of *Janā'iz* Sayyiduna Muḥammad b. Yaḥyah al-Zahlī ﷺ narrates from Sayyiduna Yazīd b. Harūn ﷺ and Sayyiduna Muḥammad b. Ismāʿīl al-Aḥmasnī ﷺ, and he narrates from Sayyiduna Maḥāribī ﷺ; and both of them narrate from Sayyiduna Muḥammad b. Isḥāq ﷺ, and he narrates from Ḥarth b. Fudail ﷺ; and all three of them narrate from Sayyiduna Imām al-Zuhrī ﷺ. Thus, in the chain of *Ibn Māja* the narration of Sayyiduna Ibn Isḥāq ﷺ according to calculation, we achieve two outstanding degrees. And all praises are for *Allāh* ﷻ and it is His ﷻ Bounties.

The Excellence of Sawm [Fasts]

Imām Tirmidī ﷺ states that this *Ḥadith* is *Ḥasan Saḥīḥ*[297] and with the same chain up till Sayyiduna Ibn Shazān ﷺ, who asserts that he narrates from Aḥmad ﷺ, and he narrates from Ḥasan b. al-Mukarram ﷺ, and he narrates from Yazīd b. Hārūn ﷺ, who narrates from Shaʿabah ﷺ, and he narrates from Muḥammad

297 This term is known and has been accepted by the memorizers of *Ḥadith* [*Muḥaddithīn*] well before Imam at-Tirmidī ﷺ and after him. A tradition whose chain or partial narration is disputed, most scholars view it as *Ḥasan* [good] but some as *Saḥīḥ* [sound].

b. Ziyād, who narrates from Sayyiduna Abu-Hurayrah ؓ; and he reports from Sayyiduna Rasūlullāh ﷺ, who narrates from Almighty *Allāh* ﷻ Who stipulates: *'Every action has a compensation and fast is for Me and I will compensate for it.' 'The odour of the mouth of the one who is fasting in the presence of Allāh ﷻ is better than the fragrance of musk.'* This *Ḥadith* is reported by *Bukhārī* in his *Saḥīḥ* in the chapter with reference to *Tawḥīd* by the narration of Sayyiduna Ādam b. Abī-Yās ؓ, who narrates from Sayyiduna Abu as-Sitām b. al-Ḥāj b. Darū al-ʿAtqī ؓ as we have cited. Thus, for us the dividend is the same chain till Shaykh Ibn Shāzān ؒ, who states that he narrates from Shaykh ʿUthmān b. Aḥmad ʿAbdullāh b. Barya Aḥmad b. Yaḥyah Ādamī ؒ and Shaykh Maymūn b. Isḥāq ؒ. all of them concurred that they narrate from Sayyiduna Abu-Muʿāwiyah ؒ, who narrates from Sayyiduna Aʿmash ؒ, and he narrates from Sayyiduna Abu-Sāliḥ ؓ, and he from Sayyiduna Abu-Hurayrah ؓ, who reports that the Messenger of *Allāh* ﷺ states: *'Certainly! I say that the following words to me is more beloved to me than all those things on which the sun has risen:*

سُبْحَانَ اللهِ وَ الْحَمْدُ لِلّٰهِ وَ لَا اِلٰهَ اِلَّا اللهُ وَ اللهُ اَكْبَرُ

The Status of the Saḥābah

This *Ḥadith al-Sharīf* is reported by Imām Muslim ؓ in his *Saḥīḥ* in the Chapter of *Duʿās*, and narrated by Sayyiduna Abu-Bakr b. Abī-Shaybah Abu-Kurayb Muḥammad b. ʿUlā ؒ, and both of them narrate from Sayyiduna Abu-Muʿāwiyah ؒ as we have cited. Thus, we have received our reward, because with the same chain it reaches Sayyiduna Ibn Shāzān ؒ. I was informed by Shaykh ʿUthmān b. Samāk ؒ, and he narrates from Shaykh Aḥmad b. Al-Jabbār ؒ, and he narrates from Shaykh Abu-Muʿāwiyah ؒ, who narrates from Sayyiduna Aʿmash ؒ, and he narrates from Sayyiduna Abu-Sāliḥ ؓ, and he narrates from Sayyiduna Abu-Saʿīd al-Khudrī ؓ, who states that the beloved Prophet of *Allāh* ﷺ enunciates: *'Do not be vulgar to my Saḥābah, because I take an oath on that Being in whose control is my life that if any of you [non-Saḥābah] give charity of gold in the path of Allāh ﷻ to the equivalent of the Mountain of Uhud it will not even be equal to a kilogram of charity [of grain] to them [Saḥābah] or even half of it.'* This *Ḥadith al-Sharīf* is *Saḥīḥ* [sound] and there is agreement on its authenticity. The *Aimmah* of the *Siḥāh Sitta*, Imām al-Bukhārī ﷺ and Imām Muslim ﷺ in their *Saḥīḥ*, Imām Tirmidī ﷺ in his *Jāme'h*, Imām Abu-Dā'ūd ﷺ and Imām Ibn Māja ﷺ in their *Sunan* and Imām Nisāī ﷺ in his *Manāqib*; all narrate it. Imām Bukhārī ﷺ in the *Faḍāil* of Sayyiduna Abu-Bakr ﷺ narrates from Sayyiduna Ādam b. Abī Yās ﷺ, who narrates from Sayyiduna Sha'abah ﷺ, and he narrates from Sayyiduna A'mash ﷺ and proclaimed that he supports this narration. Imām Muslim ﷺ in the Chapter of *Faḍāil* narrates from Shaykh Ḥarīr ﷺ, and he narrates from Shaykh 'Abdullāh b. Dā'ūd ﷺ, and he narrates from Shaykh Abu-Mu'āwiyah ﷺ, and he narrates from Sayyiduna Mujāhid ﷺ, and he narrates from Sayyiduna A'mash ﷺ. *Saḥīḥ Muslim* has narrated this in a few ways from Sayyiduna A'mash ﷺ.

Imām Abu-Dā'ūḍ ﷺ in his *Sunan* narrates from Shaykh Musdac b. Musrahad ﷺ, and he narrates from Sayyiduna Abu-Mu'āwiyah ﷺ and Imām Tirmidī ﷺ in the Chapter of *Manāqib* narrates from Shaykh Ḥasan b. 'Alī Khalāl ﷺ, and he narrates from Sayyiduna Abu-Mu'āwiyah ﷺ, and he narrates from Sayyiduna Shou'bah ﷺ, and he narrates from Sayyiduna A'mash ﷺ. Imām Ibn Māja ﷺ in his *Sunan* in many ways, some of which some he narrates from Shaykh Abu-Kurayb ﷺ, and he narrates from Sayyiduna Abu-Mu'āwiyah ﷺ, and he narrates from Sayyiduna A'mash ﷺ. Imām Nisāī ﷺ in his *Manāqib* narrates from Shaykh Muḥammad b. Hishām ﷺ and he narrates from Shaykh Khālid b. Ḥarth ﷺ, and he narrates from Sayyiduna Sha'abah ﷺ, and he narrates from Sayyiduna A'mash ﷺ. Hence, our benefit is that all three Imāms; Imām Abu-Dā'ūd ﷺ, Imām Tirmidī ﷺ and Imām Ibn Māja ﷺ are two stages higher than Imām Nisāī ﷺ. This is the Bounty and Compassion of the Sublime Lord ﷻ.

To Sit on Burning Fire

With the same chain of transmission until Sayyiduna Ibn Shāzān ﷺ; who professed that he narrates the *Ḥadith* from Shaykh Aḥmad ﷺ, and he narrates from Shaykh Ḥasan b. Mukarram ﷺ, and he narrates from Shaykh 'Alī b. 'Āsim ﷺ, and he narrates from Sayyiduna Sahl b. Abī-Sāliḥ ﷺ, and he narrates from his father, and he narrates from Sayyiduna Abu-Hurayrah ﷺ, who reports that the beloved Messenger of *Allāh* ﷺ pronounces: *'For anyone of you to sit on the burning fire, which will burn your clothes and reach your skin surely is better than sitting on the grave of your brother.'* Imām Muslim ﷺ cites this *Hadith* in his *Sahīh* in the Chapter of *Al-Janā'iz* by the narration of Shaykh Zubayr b. Ḥarb ﷺ; he narrates from Shaykh Jarīr ﷺ; and Shaykh Qutaybah b. Saʿīd ﷺ; he from Shaykh Darāwardī ﷺ; he from Shaykh ʿUmar Nāfiz ﷺ; he from Shaykh Abu-Aḥmad Zuhayrī ﷺ; he from Sayyiduna Sufyān al-Thawrī ﷺ; and all of the three narrate from Sayyiduna Suhl ﷺ. He stated: *'Reach the skin,'* and not *'Until it [the fire] reaches the skin.'* The rest of the narration is similar. On the basis of count, the chain of Sayyiduna Sufyān al-Thawrī ﷺ warrants our chain to be further elevated by two stages. All praises are for *Allāh* ﷻ and His ﷻ Compassion.

The Fasts of the beloved Prophet ﷺ in Ramaḍān

I was informed by Shaykh Imām Qāḍī al-Quḍāt Shaykh al-Suyūkh Shams al-Dīn Abu-ʿAbdullāh Muḥammad b. Imām ʿĀlim ʿImād al-Dīn Abu-Isḥāq Ibrāhim b. ʿAbd al-Wāḥid ﷺ, and recited this in his presence. He states that he narrates from Shaykh Imām Abu al-Qāsim Haybatullāh b. Mansūrī Naqīb al-Hāshimī ﷺ, who narrates from Shaykh al-Islām Muḥiyy al-Dīn ʿAbd al-Qādir b. Abī-Sāliḥ al-Jilānī ﷺ. As per permission [*sanad*] of narration, Sayyiduna Ghawth ﷺ declared: he narrates from Shaykh Nasar Abu-Muḥammad b. Naba ﷺ, who narrates from his father, Shaykh Abu-ʿAlī al-Ḥasan b. Aḥmad b. ʿUmar b. Ḥafs Muqrī ﷺ and he follows Shaykh Abu al-Fataḥ Ḥāfiz ﷺ, and narrates from Shaykh Abu-Bakr Muḥammad b. ʿAbdullāh Shafāʿī ﷺ, who narrates from Shaykh Isḥāq b. al-Ḥasan ﷺ and he narrates from Shaykh ʿAbdullāh b. Muslimah ﷺ, and he narrates from Sayyiduna Mālik b. Anas ﷺ he narrates from Sayyiduna Abu-Nafar ﷺ, the servant of Sayyiduna ʿUmar b. ʿUbaydullāh ﷺ, and he narrates from Sayyiduna Abu-Salmah b. ʿAbd al-Raḥmān ﷺ, and he narrates from Umm al-Moʿminīn Sayyidah ʿĀ'īesha Siddiqah ﷺ; the beloved wife of the Holy Prophet ﷺ who reported: *'The beloved Messenger of Allāh ﷺ kept fasts to the extent that we said he ﷺ would not make Iftār and he made Iftār. Then we said he would not fast; and I have not seen Sayyiduna Rasūlullāh ﷺ keep the full month's fast, except in the month of Ramaḍān; but he ﷺ would fast in the whole month of Sha ʿbān. I have not seen him fast like this during any other month.'*

I narrate from an elevated chain, from the pious Shaykh Shahāb al-Dīn Abu-ʿAbdullāh Muḥammad b. ʿAbd al-Munʿim b. Muḥammad al-Ansārī, and I have read this *Ḥadith* in his presence; and he narrates from Shaykh Mawaffaq al-Dīn Abu-Ḥafs ʿUmar b. Muḥammad b. Maʿmar b. Tabarzad al-Baghdādī; who narrates from Shaykh Abu-Bakr Muḥammad b. ʿAbd al-Bāqī b. Muḥammad b. ʿAbdullāh al-Ansārī; who used to read, whilst we listened. I heard in 526 *hijrī* from Shaykh Abu-Muḥammad Ḥasan b. ʿAlī b. Muḥammad al-Jowharī, who dictated after *salāh* on the day of *Jum ʿāh* in *Jāme ʿh al-Mansūr* on 3rd *Shā ʿbān* 447 *hijrī*. He narrates from Shaykh Abu al-Ḥasan Muḥammad b. Muzaffar b. Mūsā al-Ḥāfiz; who narrates from Shaykh Aḥmad b. Muḥammad Taḥāwī; and he narrates from Shaykh Farnī; and he narrates from Sayyiduna Imām al-Shāfaʿī. He narrates from Imām Mālik; and he narrates from Sayyiduna Abu-Nasar, the servant of Sayyiduna ʿUmar b. ʿAbdullāh b. Abī-Salmah b. ʿAbd al-Raḥmān; and he narrates from Umm al-Moʿminīn Sayyidah ʿĀ'īesha Siddiqah, who affirmed: *'The beloved Messenger of Allāh ﷺ kept fasts to the extent that we said he ﷺ would not make Iftār; but he made Iftār. Then we said he would not fast and I have not seen Sayyiduna Rasūlullāh ﷺ keep the full month's fast, except in the month of Ramaḍān; but he ﷺ would fast during the whole month of Sha ʿbān. I have not seen him fast like this during any other month.'*

This *Ḥadith al-Sharīf* is *Saḥīḥ* [sound]; and consensus have been reached pertinent to it. *Bukhārī* and *Muslim* narrate this in their *Saḥīḥ*. *Bukhārī* narrates from Sayyiduna ʿAbdullāh b. Yūsuf, and *Muslim* narrates from Sayyiduna Yaḥyah, and both of them narrate from Sayyiduna Imām Mālik. Thus, we have deduced that this *Ḥadith* is in place of others.

Shaking Hands with the Angels and the structure of Jannah

I was informed by Shaykh Mufīd Sharfudīn Abu-Muḥammad al-Ḥasan b, ʿAlī

ʿĪsā b. al-Ḥasan b. ʿAlī al-Lakhmī ﷺ; and I read this in his presence. He narrates from Shaykh Abu al-ʿAbbās Aḥmad b. Abu al-Fataḥ al-Mafraj b. Abu al-Ḥasan ʿAlī al-Damishqī ﷺ; and he narrates from Shaykh Imām ʿĀrif Sultān al-ʿĀrifīn Abu-Muḥammad Muḥiyy al-Dīn ʿAbd al-Qādir b. Abī-Sālih al-Jilī ﷺ. I also narrate from a sound chain of illustrious *Shuyūkh*, Shaykh Imām ʿĀlim Safī al-Dīn Abu as-Safa Khalīl b. Abī-Bakr b. Maḥmūd Mirāʿī ﷺ and Shaykh Sāliḥ Baqiyat as-Salf Abu-Muḥammad ʿAbd al-Wāḥid b. ʿAlī b. Aḥmad al-Qurashī ﷺ; and Shaykh Musnad Abu-Bakr b, Imām Ḥāfiz Abu-Tahir Ismāʿīl b, ʿAbdullāh al-Anmātī ﷺ, who read and I listened. All of them concurred that they narrate from Shaykh Imām Abu-Nasar Mūsā b. Imām Jamāl al-Islām Awḥad al-Anām, Leader of the ʿĀrifīn Muḥiyy al-Dīn Abu-Muḥammad ʿAbd al-Qādir al-Jilī ﷺ, who narrates from Abu al-Waqt ʿAbd al-Dowl b. ʿĪsā al-Hirwī ﷺ; and it was read in his presence and thereby we used to listen. He narrates in 553 *hijrī* from Shaykh Abu-ʿAbd al-Raḥmān b. Muḥammad Muzaffar al-Dāʿūdī ﷺ; which was read in his presence, and I used to listen, and he narrates from Shaykh Abu-Muḥammad ʿAbdullāh b. Aḥmad Ḥamawiyah al-Ḥasanī ﷺ; which was read in his presence, and I used to listen, and he narrates from Shaykh Ibrāhīm b, Ḥarīm al-Shamnatī ﷺ, who narrates from Shaykh ʿAbd b. Ḥamīd b. Nasar ﷺ; and he narrates from Shaykh Sulaymān b. Dāʿūd ﷺ; and he narrates from Shaykh Zubayr b. Muʿāwiyah ﷺ; and he narrates from Shaykh Sāʿad Abu-Mujāhid Tāʿī ﷺ; and he narrates from Sayyiduna Abu al-Madlah ﷺ; the servant of Umm al-Moʿminīn Sayyidah ʿĀ'īeshah Siddiqah ﷺ, and he had heard Sayyiduna Abu-Hurayrah ﷺ articulate to the Holy Prophet ﷺ:

> *'Ya Rasūlallāh ﷺ! When we are in your presence, our hearts are soft, and we are from the people of the Ākhirah; but when we return to our wives and children, then the world seems nice to us.'* The Messenger of *Allāh* ﷺ replied: *'I take an oath of His Divine Being ﷻ in whose control is my life! If you remain in that condition that you experience in my presence, then the Angels will come and shake your hands [musāfaḥa]; and they will come to your homes and meet with you. If you do not commit sins; then Allāh ﷻ will replace you with such a nation who will commit sins and seek forgiveness from Him ﷻ and Allāh ﷻ will forgive them.'*

Then Sayyiduna Abu-Hurayrah ﷺ inquired: *'O Messenger of Allāh ﷺ! Inform us of the structure of Jannah.'* The Prophet of *Allāh* ﷺ confirmed: *'Its one brick is made of gold and the other of silver. Its pebbles are of pearls and rubies. Its cement is of musk and the sand is of saffron. Any person who enters it, will be fresh, energetic and young. He will reside in it for ever, and will never die, nor will his clothes get dirty or his youth will diminish. There are three persons whose du'ās will not be rejected: one who fasts, and at the time of iftār, he breaks his fast [iftār], the second is a just Imām and the third is the du'ā of the oppressed. Their du'ās will be raised to the clouds and the doors of the skies will be opened for them. Almighty Allāh ﷻ testifies: 'By the oath of My Majesty and Honour! I will give you victory even after a period [delay].'* This *Ḥadith* is *Ḥasan* [sound]. *Bukhārī* and *Muslim* have established proof from the *Ḥadith* of Sayyiduna Abu-Haythamah Zuhayr b. Abī-Muʿāwiyah ﷺ in agreement of Sayyiduna Abu-Mujāhid Sāʿad al-Tāʿī ﷺ. He was trustworthy, and narrates from Sayyiduna Abu al-Madlah ﷺ; the servant of Umm al-Moʿminīn Sayyidah ʿĀ'īeshah Siddiqah ﷺ; who, in accordance to the narration of Sayyiduna Abu-Hurayrah ﷺ is trustworthy. *Tirmidī* cites this in his *Jāmeʿh* and Ibn Māja in his *Sunan. Tirmidī* briefly cites from Shaykh Muḥammad b. ʿUlā al-Hamdānī ﷺ, and he cites from Shaykh ʿAbdullāh b. Numayr ﷺ; and *Ibn Māja* also cites in brevity from Shaykh ʿAlī b. Muḥammad ﷺ; and he cites from Sayyiduna Imām Wakīʿh b. al-Jarrāḥ ﷺ[298]; and both of them narrate from Sayyiduna Sāʿad b. Bishr ﷺ, and he narrates from Sayyiduna Sāʿad al-Tāʿī ﷺ. *Tirmidī* evaluates this *Ḥadith* as *Ḥasan* [sound]; and recognises it as it is narrated by Sayyiduna Abu al-Madlah ﷺ, the servant of Umm al-Moʿminīn Sayyidah ʿĀ'īeshah Siddiqah ﷺ; and from him; although this *Ḥadith* being lengthy; was also narrated. Henceforth, *Tirmidī* narrates the entire *Ḥadith* of Sayyiduna Zuhayr b. Abī- Muʿāwiyah ﷺ with appendages. Verily, *Muslim* cites this *Ḥadith* in his *Saḥīḥ* with a segment from Sayyiduna Ḥanzalah b. Rabīʿ al-Asadī ﷺ, and this *Ḥadith* has reached us with an elevated chain from another source. All praises are for *Allāh* ﷻ.

[298] Sayyiduna Imām Wakīʿh b. al-Jarrāḥ ﷺ is the *Ustāz* of Imām Shafaʿī ﷺ and student of Imām al-Aʿzam Abu-Ḥanīfa ﷺ who granted him permission to narrate *Ḥadith*.

The Day of ʿEid

I narrate with the endorsement from Shaykh ʿAbdullāh b. Ḥamīd ﷺ, who narrates from Shaykh Jaʿāfar b. ʿOun ﷺ, and he narrates from Shaykh Abu-ʿAmīs b. Muslim ﷺ; and he narrates from Sayyiduna Tāriq b. Shihāb ﷺ; who affirms that a jew came to Sayyiduna ʿUmar al-Fārūq ﷺ and revealed: *'O Amīr al-Moʿminīn! There is a verse in your book, i.e. Qur'ān, which you recite. The Jews affirm that if this verse was revealed to them, they would observe ʿEid on that day,'* Amīr al-Moʿminīn ﷺ enquired: *'Which verse is that?'* He stated:

﴿الْيَوْمَ أَكْمَلْتُ لَكُمْ دِينَكُمْ وَأَتْمَمْتُ عَلَيْكُمْ نِعْمَتِي...﴾

This day have I perfected your religion for you
and completed My favour upon you ....[299]

Sayyiduna ʿUmar al-Fārūq ﷺ elucidated: *'Indeed, I know very well that day on which this verse was revealed and the place where it was revealed. It was revealed in ʿArafāt on Friday,* i.e. it was revealed on the Day of *Ḥajj,* which was on a Friday, meaning that two ʿ*Eids* were combined on one day. This *Ḥadith* is *Saḥīḥ* and agreed upon. This *Ḥadith* is reported by three *Imāms*, Imām Bukhārī ﷺ and Imām Muslim ﷺ in their *Saḥīḥ* and Imām Nisāʾī ﷺ in his *Sunan. Bukhārī* and *Muslim* narrate it through various chains; amongst which *Bukhārī* in its Book of *Imān,* narrates from Sayyiduna Abu-ʿAlī al-Ḥasan b. Muḥammad b. Sabaḥ al-Baghdādī al-Zaʿfarānī ﷺ, and *Muslim* narrates from Sayyiduna Sulaymān b. Yūsuf al-Ḥarrānī ﷺ; and all three of them narrate from Sayyiduna Jaʿāfar b. ʿOun ﷺ as we have cited. Thus, we are in agreement with *Saḥīḥ Muslim*; and as an alternative to *Bukhārī* and *Nisāʾī.*

The Miracle of the Splitting of the Moon

By the chain of the same narration, I narrate from Sayyiduna ʿAbd b. Ḥamīd ﷺ, who narrates from Sayyiduna ʿAbd al-Razzāq ﷺ; and he narrates from

[299] *Al-Qur'ān al-Karīm,* Chapter 5, Surah Mā'idah Verse no. 3

Sayyiduna Maʿmar ﷺ; and he narrates from Sayyiduna Qatādah ﷺ; who narrates from Sayyiduna Anas b. Mālik ﷺ that the people of *Makkah al-Mukarramah* demanded a miracle from the beloved Messenger of *Allāh* ﷺ. Thus, the moon was split twice in *Makkah al-Mukarramah* and the following verse was revealed:

﴿اقْتَرَبَتِ السَّاعَةُ وَانشَقَّ الْقَمَرُ﴾

The Last Day came near, and the moon split apart.[300]

Sayyiduna Thābit ﷺ states that this is cited by three *Imāms*: Imām Muslim ﷺ in his *Saḥīḥ,* Imām Tirmidī ﷺ in his *Jāmeʿh* and Imām Nisāʿī ﷺ in his *Sunan* narrates from Sayyiduna Isḥāq b. Ibrāhīm ﷺ. All three of them narrate from Sayyiduna ʿAbd al-Razzāq ﷺ as we have formerly cited. Thus, we are in agreement with *Tirmidī*; and as an alternative to *Bukhārī* and *Nisāʿī*.

I narrate from Shaykh Imām Ḥāfiz Sharf al-Dīn Abu-Muḥammad ʿAbd al-Moʿmin b. Khalaf b. Abu al-Ḥasan al-Damyātī ﷺ in whose presence I read this *Ḥadith*. He asserts that he read the *Ḥadith* in Damascus in the presence of Shaykh Abu al-ʿAbbās Aḥmad b. Abu al-Fataḥ al-Mafraj b. ʿAlī al-Damishqī ﷺ. He narrates from Sayyiduna *Imām al-Awliya* Shaykh ʿAbd al-Qādir b. Sayyiduna Abu-Sāliḥ al-Jilī ﷺ. He narrates from Shaykh Abu-Bar Aḥmad b. Muzaffar b. Ḥusain b. Sosan ﷺ the date trader; who narrates from Shaykh Abu-ʿAlī al-Ḥasan b. Aḥmad b. Ibrāhīm b. al-Ḥasan b. Muḥammad b. Shazān Baz'zāz ﷺ; and he narrates from Shaykh Abu-Bakr Muḥammad b. al-ʿAbbās b. Najīʿh ﷺ; and he narrates from Shaykh Jaʿāfar b. Muḥammad b. Shākir ﷺ; and he confessed to Shaykh ʿAffān ﷺ, that he narrates from Shaykh Ḥammād b. Zayd ﷺ; he narrates from Sayyiduna ʿAtā b. Sā'ib ﷺ; and he narrates from his father ﷺ, who narrates from Sayyiduna ʿAmmār b. Yāsir ﷺ. He performed *salāh* and was brief about it. Upon completion of his *salāh*, I professed to him that I supplicated; that *dūʿā* which I had heard from Sayyiduna Rasūlullāh ﷺ. Thereafter, Sayyiduna ʿAmmār ﷺ left; and an individual stood up, and followed him. He reveals that, that individual was his father, who had

[300] *Al-Qur'ān al-Karīm,* Chapter 54, Surah Qamar, Verse no. 1

questioned him with regard to that *dũ ʿā*. Sayyiduna ʿAmmãr states that it was the following *dũ ʿā*:

اَللّٰهُمَّ بِعِلْمِكَ الْغَيْبِ وَ بِقُدْرَتِكَ عَلَى الْخَلْقِ أَحْيِنِىْ مَا كَانَتِ الْحَيَاةُ خَيْرًا لِىْ وَ تَوَفَّنِىْ إِذَا كَانَتِ الْوَفَاةُ خَيْرًا لِىْ وَ أَسْأَلُكَ خَشْيَتَكَ فِى الْغَيْبِ وَ الشَّهَادَةِ وَ أَسْأَلُكَ كَلِمَةَ الْحِكْمَةِ فِى الرِّضَاء وَ الْغَضَبِ وَ أَسْأَلُكَ قُرَّةَ عَيْنٍ لَا تَنْقَطِعُ وَ أَسْأَلُكَ الرِّضَاء عِنْدَ الْقَضَاءِ وَ أَسْأَلُكَ بَرْدَ الْعَيْشِ بَعْدَ الْمَوْتِ وَ أَسْأَلُكَ النَّظَرَ إِلىٰ وَجْهِكَ وَ الشَّوْقَ إِلىٰ لِقَائِكَ فِىْ غَيْرِ ضَرَّاءِ مُضِرَّةٍ وَ لَا فِتْنَةٍ مُضِلَّةٍ اَللّٰهُمَّ زَيِّنَا بِزِيْنَةِ الْإِيْمَانِ وَ اجْعَلْنَا هُدَاةً مُهْتَدِيْنَ

The recompense of Good Deeds

This *Ḥadith* is narrated by *Nisãʾī* from Shaykh Yaḥyah b. Ḥabīb b. ʿArabī; and he narrates from Sayyiduna Ḥammãd b. Yazīd; and he narrates from Sayyiduna ʿAtã b. Sã'ib as we have formerly cited. Thus, all praises are from *Allãh*.

I narrate from Shaykh Fãḍil Sharf al-Dīn Abu al-Faḍal al-Ḥasan b. ʿAlī b. ʿĪsã b. al-Ḥasan, and I read this *Ḥadith* in his presence. He narrates from Shaykh Abu al-ʿAbbãs Aḥmad b. Abī al-Fataḥ al-Faraj b. Abī al-Ḥasan ʿAlī al-Damishqī; and he narrates from Sayyiduna Tãj al-ʿĀrifīn Jamãl al-Dīn Imãm al-Sãlikīn Muḥiyy al-Dīn Abu-Muḥammad ʿAbd al-Qãdir b. Abī-Sãliḥ al-Jilī. May *Allãh* bestow benefit upon us with his love. He narrates from Shaykh Abu-Mansūr ʿAbd al-Raḥmãn b. Muḥammad b. ʿAbd al-Wãḥid Farãz; and he narrates from Shaykh Ḥãfiz Abu al-ʿUlã Ḥasan b. Aḥmad b. Ḥasan b. ʿAtã al-Hamdãnī; as was narrated by him in his presence and I listened to it. He states that he had heard in *Jamãdi al-Ākhir* 531 *hijrī* in *Bãb al-Azj* [Baghdãd] from Shaykh Imãm Ḥãfiz Abu-Bakr Aḥmad b. Abī-Thãlith al-Baghdãdī. It was read out in his presence, whereby I listened to it. He proclaims that he narrates in 463 *hijrī* from Shaykh Aḥmad b. Muḥammad b. Ghãlib; who narrates from Shaykh Abu-Bakr al-Ismãʿīlī; and he narrates from Shaykh Abu-Jaʿãfar Muḥammad b. Ibrãhīm b. ʿAbdullãh al-Jurjãnī. He narrates from Shaykh Muḥammad b. ʿAlī b. Zuhãyr; and he narrates from Sayyiduna

ʿUthmān b. Muslim ﷺ; and he narrates from Sayyiduna Ḥammād b. Salmah ﷺ; and he narrates from Sayyiduna Thābit ﷺ; who narrates from Sayyiduna ʿAbd al-Raḥmān b. Abī-Laylah ﷺ; and he narrates from Sayyiduna Suhaib al-Rūmī ﷺ. He affirms that the Prophet of *Allāh* ﷺ propounded on the following verse:

﴿لِّلَّذِينَ أَحْسَنُوا الْحُسْنَىٰ وَزِيَادَةٌ﴾

For the people of virtue, is goodness and more than that...[301]

Sayyiduna Rasūlullāh ﷺ reinforced: *'When the people of Jannah will be admitted into Jannah and people of Hell into the Hell Fire, then a messenger will call out; 'O dwellers of Jannah! There is an excess for you from Allāh ﷻ which He ﷻ ordains to accomplish for you.' The dwellers of Jannah will question: 'What is that? Has He ﷻ not illuminated our faces and not raised our measures? What can be more beloved than this; that which will make us happier than His ﷻ Divine Vision?'*

The Vision of Allāh ﷻ in Jannah

I narrate on the authority of three elevated chains from Shaykh Musnad Abu al-Faḍal ʿAbd al-Raḥīm b. Yūsuf b. Yaḥyah al-Damishqī ﷺ, which was read out in his presence and I had listened to it. He verbalizes that he narrates from Shaykh Abu-Ḥafs ʿUmar b. Muḥammad b. Maʿmar Tabarzadār al-Qaḍī ﷺ; which was read out in his presence; whilst I was present; and he narrates from Shaykh Abu al-Qāsim Haybatullāh Muḥammad b. ʿAbd al-Wāḥid b. Aḥmad b. Ḥusain al-Shaybānī ﷺ; which was read out in his presence and we had listened to it. He asserts that he narrates from Shaykh Abu-Tālib Muḥammad b. Muḥammad b. Ibrāhīm b. Ghaybalān Baz'zāz ﷺ; who narrates from Shaykh Abu-Bakr Muḥammad b. ʿAbdullāh b. Ibrāhim Shafaʿī ﷺ; and he narrates from Shaykh Muḥammad b. Muslim Wāstī ﷺ; and he narrates from Shaykh Yazīd b. Hardan ﷺ; and he narrates from Sayyiduna Ḥammād b. Salmah ﷺ; and he narrates from Sayyiduna Thābit ﷺ; and he narrates from Sayyiduna ʿAbd al-Raḥmān b. Abī-Layla ﷺ; and he narrates from Sayyiduna Suhaib ﷺ; and he

[301] *Al-Qur'ān al-Karīm,* Chapter 10, Surah Yūnus, Verse no. 26

reports from Sayyiduna Rasũlullãh ﷺ who expounded: "*When the people of Jannah will be admitted into Jannah and the people of Hell into the Hell Fire, then a messenger will call out: 'O dwellers of Jannah! There is a promise from Allãh ﷻ, which you have not seen.' The dwellers of Jannah will query: 'What is that? Has He ﷻ not raised our measures and not illuminated our faces? Has He ﷻ not admitted us into Paradise and saved us from the Fire of Hell?* Henceforth, the beloved Prophet ﷺ will respond: '*Almighty Allãh ﷻ will raise the veils, and they will look towards Almighty Allãh ﷻ. Thus, by the oath of Allãh ﷻ! There will be nothing given to them that will be more exceptional and appealing than the Vision of Almighty Allãh ﷻ.'* Thereafter, the Messenger of *Allãh* ﷺ recited the above mentioned verse.

This *Ḥadith* is *Saḥīḥ* on the authority of *Saḥīḥ Muslim* and the pious Imãm Aḥmad b. Muḥammad b. Ḥanbal ؒ; who cites it in his *Musnad* on the authority of Sayyiduna Abu-Bakr b. Abĩ-Shaybah ؒ; who narrates from Sayyiduna Yazĩd b. Ḥarũn ؒ as we have formerly cited. Thus, we are in complete agreement with Sayyiduna Imãm Aḥmad ؒ; and with an elevated status within the parameters of *Muslim*. In the preceding chains, by virtue of its numbers in the narrations, I had heard from Sayyiduna Abu-Mansũr ʿAbd al-Raḥmãn b. Muḥammad al-Qazãr ؒ by virtue of its numbers in the narrations. All praises are for *Allãh* ﷻ and it is His ﷻ Benediction.

With this chain, that was previously mentioned till Shaykh Abu-Manthũr al-Qazãna ؒ; who stated that he narrates from Shaykh Abu-Bakr al-Khatĩb ؒ; and he narrates from Shaykh Qãḍĩ Abu al-ʿUlã Muḥammad b. ʿAlĩ ؒ; and he narrates in Baghdãd from Shaykh Abu al-Ḥasan Muḥammad b. Ibrãhĩm al-Ḥaḍramĩ ؒ; who narrates from Shaykh Abu-Ḥãmid b. Qudãma Balkhĩ al-Darrãq ؒ in 698 *hijrĩ* from Shaykh Qutaybah b. Saʿĩd ؒ; and he narrates from Sayyiduna Imãm Mãlik ؒ; and he narrates from Sayyiduna Ibn Shihãb ؒ; and he narrates from Sayyiduna Anas ibn Mãlik ؓ who narrates: '*Verily, the Messenger of Allãh ﷺ entered Makkah al-Mukarramah wearing a helmet and he saw Ibn Khatal wrapped in the covering of the Kaʿabah. The Prophet ﷺ commanded that he should be killed.*'

I narrate from two elevated chains beyond this; i.e. from Shaykh Musnad Abu-Bakr Muḥammad b. Imām Ḥāfiz Abu-Tāhir Ismāʿīl b. ʿAbdullāh al-Anmātī ﷺ; in whose presence I read out this *Ḥadith*, and he narrates from Shaykh Qāḍī al-Quḍāt Abu al-Qāsim ʿAbd al-Samad b. Muḥammad b. Abī al-Faḍal al-Ansārī ﷺ; in whose presence this *Ḥadith* was read out and I had listened to it. He was informed as per permission to narrate by Shaykh Abu-Muḥammad ʿAbd al-Karīm b. Ḥamza b. Khiḍar al-Salmī ﷺ; and he narrates from Shaykh Abu al-Qāsim Ḥusain b. Muḥammad b. Ibrāhim al-Ḥayānī ﷺ; and he narrates from Shaykh Abu al-Ḥasan ʿAbd al-Wah'hāb b. Ḥasan b. Walīd al-Kilābī ﷺ; and he narrates from Shaykh Abu-Bakr Muḥammad b. Ḥarīm b. Muḥammad al-ʿAqīlī ﷺ; and he narrates from Sayyiduna Hishām b. ʿAmmār b. Nasar b. Mirāh al-Salmī ؓ; and he narrates from Sayyiduna Anas b. Mālik ؓ; who asserts: '*Verily, the Messenger of Allāh ﷺ entered Makkah al-Mukarramah wearing a helmet.*'

This *Ḥadith* is *Saḥīḥ* and there is a consensus pertinent to its authenticity; and the evidence of the *Ḥadith* is from Imām Dār al-Hijra Sayyiduna Imām Mālik b. Anas al-Asjī ؓ, who narrates from Sayyiduna Abu-Bakr Muḥammad b. Hisām al-Zuhrī ؓ. No one else is more trustworthy than Sayyiduna Zuhrī ؓ, who has narrated this *Ḥadith;* and except for Imām Mālik ؓ, no one has narrated this *Ḥadith* more accurately. An immense group of contemporary *Muḥaddithīn, Imāms* and allies of Sayyiduna Imām Mālik ؓ narrate this *Ḥadith* from him. Included amongst them are the following: Sayyiduna Imām Ibn Jarīj ؓ, Imām Maʿmar b. ʿAyniyah ؓ and a host of others. The *Muḥaddithīn* collaborate their methods and it is declared that approximately 200 narrators narrate this *Ḥadith* from Sayyiduna Imām Mālik ؓ. Imām Tirmidī ؓ stipulates that he is unaware of anyone, except Imām Mālik ؓ who has narrated this *Ḥadith*. This *Ḥadith* is cited by the Imāms of *Siḥa Sitta* and Imām al-Bukhārī ؓ and Imām Muslim ؓ cite this *Ḥadith* in their *Saḥīḥayn*; Imām Tirmidī ؓ in his *Jāmeʿh*, Imām Abu-Dāʿūd ؓ and Imām al-Nisāʿī ؓ and Imam Ibn Māja ؓ in their *Sunan*. Imām al-Bukhārī ؓ has narrated this *Ḥadith* in the Chapter of *Ḥajj* from Imām ʿAbdullāh b. Yūsuf ؓ, from the Chapter of *Jihād* from Imām Ismāʿīl b. Owaīs ؓ; and in the Chapter of Wars from Imām Yaḥyah b. Qazʿā ؓ; and in the Chapter of Clothing from Imām Abu-Walīd al-Tabāsī ؓ. Imām Muslim ؓ has narrated this *Ḥadith* in the Chapter of Rites of *Ḥajj*; whilst Imām Tirmidī ﷺ has narrated it in the Chapter of *Jihād;* and Imām al-Nisāʿī ﷺ has narrated it in the Chapter of *Ḥajj*. All of them narrate from Imām Qutaybah b. Saʿīd ﷺ. This is also narrated by Sayyiduna Yaḥyah ﷺ and Sayyiduna ʿUqbah ﷺ in the Chapter of Rites of *Ḥajj*. Imām Abu-Dāʿūd ﷺ narrates this in the Chapter of *Jihād* from Sayyiduna ʿUqbah ﷺ and Imām Māja ﷺ narrates with brevity from Sayyiduna Hishām b. ʿAmmār and Sayyiduna Suwayd b. Saʿīd ﷺ; and Sayyiduna Nawārdī ﷺ narrates it from Imām Mālik ﷺ. Hence, we are in agreement with the first chain of Imāms, viz. Muslim ﷺ, Tirmidī ﷺ and Nisāʿī ﷺ who narrate from Sayyiduna Qutaybah b. Saʿīd ﷺ and that which is a substitute of *Bukhārī*. In another chain, we adopt the eminent narration of Imām Ibn Māja ﷺ, who narrates from Sayyiduna Hishām b. ʿAmmār ﷺ and it is an esteemed substitute from all five narrations. Imām Tirmidī ﷺ, in his *Shamā'il* also narrates from Sayyiduna Aḥmad b. ʿĪsā ﷺ; and he narrates from Sayyiduna Ibn Wahb ﷺ. It is also narrated by Imām Nisāʿī ﷺ in his *Siyar* from Sayyiduna Muḥammad b. Muslim ﷺ; and he narrates from Sayyiduna Abu al-Qāsim ﷺ; whereas in the Chapter *Ḥajj,* he briefly cites from Shaykh ʿAbdullāh b. Fuḍālah ﷺ; and he cites from Shaykh Ḥamīdī ﷺ; and he cites from Sayyiduna Sufyān b. ʿAyniyah ﷺ, and all three of them narrate from Imām Mālik ﷺ. Thus, we received these three chains of narrations, and by virtue of computation [numbers], they are superior. All praises are for Almighty *Allāh* ﷻ; and it is His Mercy and Benevolence.

In this *Ḥadith,* I have received lengthy and brief chains of narrations which are not necessary at this juncture to discuss them details, and I have opted to maintain it brief as it is the discussed in the past chains of narrations up till Shaykh Abu-Mansūr al-Qazāz ﷺ. Shaykh Abu-Bakr al-Khatīb ﷺ pronounces that he narrates from Shaykh Aḥmad b. ʿAlī b. Ḥusain al-Nūrī ﷺ; and he narrates from Shaykh ʿUmar b. al-Qāsim b. Muḥammad al-Muqrī ﷺ; and he narrates from Shaykh Abu-ʿAbdullāh Muḥammad b. Isḥāq Maʿdal al-Marīnī ﷺ; and he narrates from Shaykh ʿAkbar ﷺ; and he narrates from Shaykh Zakariyyah b. Yaḥyah al-Marūzī ﷺ; and he narrates from Shaykh Qāḍī Abu-Bakr Aḥmad b. al-Ḥasan b. Aḥmad al-Ḥirsī ﷺ; and he narrates from Shaykh

Abu-Yaḥyah al-Marūzī ,who states that Shaykh Abu al-ʿAbbās Aḥmad b. Yaʿqūb al-Asam asserted to him that Shaykh Abu-Yaḥyah al-Marūzī narrates this *Ḥadith* to him and he had heard from Sayyiduna Sufyān ; who informed us with an exalted chain that he narrates from Sayyiduna Abu-Muḥammad al-Ḥasan b. ʿAlī b. ʿĪsā b. Ḥasan al-Lakhmī ; who read out this *Ḥadith* in his presence. I was informed by senior illustrious *Shuyūkh*, Shaykh Imām *ʿĀlim* the *Muftī* of the *Muslimīn*, Bahā al-Dīn Abu al-Ḥasan ʿAlī Abī al-Faḍal Haybah b. Salāmah b. Muslim who is a very senior *Shāfaʿī Imām*. This *Ḥadith* used to be read out in his presence and I used to listen to it. Shaykh Musnad Abu-Muḥammad ʿAbd al-Wah'hāb b. Zāfir b. ʿAlī and Shaykh Abu al-Qāsim ʿAbd al-Raḥmān b. Makkī Ḥāsib al-Kayyān used to inform everyone that they narrate from Imām Jamāl al-Islām Awḥad al-Anām Ḥāfiz Abu-Tāhir Aḥmad b. Muḥammad b. Aḥmad Salma al-Asbahānī ; and it used to be read out in his presence and we had listened to it. He narrates from Shaykh Ustāz Ra'īs Jamāl al-ʿIrāq Abu al-Ḥasan al-Makkī b. Mansūr b. Muḥammad b. ʿAlān al-Karkhī , who came in 491 *hijrī* to Asbahān; and his demise was also destined there. May *Allāh*'s Mercy shower upon him.

When will Qiyāmah come?

I had heard in Nishapūr from Shaykh Qāḍī Abu-Bakr Muḥammad b. al-Ḥasan b. Aḥmad Ḥirsī al-Ḥasrī ; and he had heard from Shaykh Abu al-ʿAbbās Aḥmad b. Yaʿqūb Asam ; and he had heard in Baghdād from Shaykh Abu-Yaḥyah Zakariyyah b. Yaḥyah b. Asad al-Marūzī ; and he had heard from Sayyiduna Sufyān ; and he had heard from Sayyiduna Imām Zuhrī ; and he had heard from Sayyiduna Anas b. Mālik ; who voiced that once a person [*Saḥābī*] came to the noble Prophet of *Allāh* and enquired: *'When will Qiyāmah come?'* The beloved Nabī promulgated: *'What preparations have you made for it? He said: 'I have prepared nothing, but all I know is that I love Allāh and His Rasūl .'* The compassionate Nabī affirmed: *'You will be with those whom you love.'* This is a *Saḥīḥ* [authentic] and distinguished *Ḥadith*. The *Hadith* of Shaykh Abu-Bakr Muḥammad b. Muslim b. ʿUbaydullāh b. ʿAbdullāh b. Shihāb al-Zuhrī is narrated from Sayyiduna Abu-Ḥamza ; and he narrates from Sayyiduna Anas b. Mālik al-Ansārī ; and he narrates from Sayyiduna

Rasũlullãh ﷺ. Imãm Muslim ؒ cites this in its *Saḥĩḥ* and narrates it in *Adab* from Shaykh Abu-Bakr b. Abĩ-Shaybah ؒ; and Shaykh ʿUmar b. Muḥammad b. Nãqid ؒ; and Shaykh Zuhayr b. Ḥarb ؒ, Shaykh Muḥammad b. ʿAbdullãh b. Numayr ؒ and Shaykh Muḥammad b. Yaḥyah b. Abĩ-ʿUmar ؒ; all five narrate from Sayyiduna Sufyãn b. ʿAyniyah ؒ. Thus, our chain is elevated and we received as a substitute for a substitute. Imãm Muslim ؒ also narrates from Shaykh Muḥammad b. Nãfeʿh b. Ḥamĩd ؒ; and all of them narrate from Sayyiduna Imãm ʿAbd al-Razzãq ؒ; and he narrates from Sayyiduna ʿUmar ؒ and the other two narrate from Imãm Zuhrĩ ؒ. *Bukhãrĩ* and *Muslim* both agreed upon this *Ḥadith* and reported it in their *Saḥĩḥayn* by the narration of Sayyiduna Sãlim b. Abĩ al-Jaʿad ؒ; and he narrates from Sayyiduna Anas b. Mãlik ؓ. Thus, we narrate this from the *Ḥadith* of Sayyiduna Jarĩr ؒ; and he narrates from Sayyiduna Mansũr ؒ; and *Bukhãrĩ* has reported this in the Chapter of *Adab* from Shaykh ʿAbdãn ؒ; he narrates from his father and he narrates from Sayyiduna Shũʿbah ؒ; and he narrates from Sayyiduna ʿAmar b. ʿAmar ؒ. Imãm Muslim ؒ also reports this from Shaykh Muḥammad b. Yaḥyah al-Lashkarĩ ؒ; and he reports from Sayyiduna ʿAbdãn ؒ, and he reports from his father and he reports from Sayyiduna Shũʿbah ؒ; and he narrates from Sayyiduna ʿAmar b. Marrah ؒ. These two narrate from Sayyiduna Sãlim ؒ. Thus, according to count; this reaches Sayyiduna Anas b, Mãlik al-Ansãrĩ ؓ. For us, the distinguished narration is the second chain. My Shaykh ؒ narrates this *Ḥadith* from the Faqih Zãhid Abu-Isḥãq Ibrãhim b. Muḥammad b. Sufyãn Nishapũrĩ ؒ, and he narrates from Imãm Muslim ؒ, the compiler of *Saḥĩḥ Muslim* who passed away on a Monday in the month of *Rajab* 300 *hijrĩ.* All praises are for Almighty *Allãh* ﷻ and it is His ﷻ Mercy and Bounties.

The fresh Dates - and fall into the well and come out

From the first chain, until Shaykh Abu-Mansũr al-Qazãz ؒ; it is narrated from Shaykh Abu-Bakr al-Khatĩb ؒ; and he narrates from Shaykh Abu-Bakr Muḥammad b. Muḥammad b. Zãhirĩ ؒ, who verifies that he had heard from Shaykh Abu-Khayr b. Samʿũn ؒ, who he had departed from *Madinatur-Rasũl* ﷺ for *Bayt al-Muqaddas*. He carried along with him some dates and other food.

He left this food at a place, where he stopped, which was not his actual destination. He proceeded further; and he desired to eat wet [fresh] dates and hence, began looking for them. Thereafter, he arrived in *Lāima* [a village] and thought that he would not acquire wet dates there? When the time of *iftār* arrived, he intended to break his fast with dates, and he found wet dates from *Siḥānī* [a place]. Therefore, he ate some from it. The next afternoon he returned to the first stop, where he had left his provisions, and found it in the same condition, and thereby, he ate from it.

With the first chain of narrators till Shaykh Abu-Mansūr Qazāz ﷺ, who affirms that he narrates from Shaykh Khatīb Abu-Bakr ﷺ; and he narrates from Shaykh Abu-Na'īm Ḥāfiz ﷺ; who narrates from Shaykh Aḥmad b. Muḥammad b. Muqsim ﷺ; and he narrates from Shaykh Abu-Bakr Khayyāt Sūfī ﷺ; and he states that he had heard from Shaykh Abu-Ḥamza ﷺ relating that he undertook a journey on *Tawakkul* [reliance on *Allāh* ﷻ]. One night, during this journey, his eyes were filled with sleep; and suddenly, he fell into a well. It was so deep that there was no way he could come out of it; and as a result he sat down. Whilst seated, he suddenly witnessed two men at its opening. One conversed with his companion: *'We should leave this well as it is, and go away.'* His companion reacted: *'We cannot do this, in fact we should close its opening.'* Shaykh Abu-Ḥamza ﷺ testifies: '*My nafs coaxed to me to pronounce: 'Why don't you tell them that you are inside?'* A voice from my inner self cautioned me: *'You have vouched to have Tawakkul on Me and now you complain about my affliction?'* I immediately observed silence and both those men departed. A short while had elapsed, when those two men returned with something, which they positioned onto the opening of the well and shut its opening. My *nafs* once more, persuaded me to: *'You are now safe inside the well, but you are also imprisoned in it.'* I sat there for one day and a night. The next day someone called out to me, whom I could not see. He instructed: *'Hold onto me tightly.'* I stretched out my hand and felt something solid; and I held tightly onto it. It lifted me to the top and threw me outside the well. I carefully looked at the device that threw me out; and discovered that it was a beast. Naturally, I panicked by looking at it. Thereafter, an unknown voice called out once more: *'O Abu-Ḥamza! I freed you from your awful situation with an awful entity; and the entity of which you are fearful. We shall suffice for that [protect you].'* Along with this chain of narrators till Shaykh Khatīb Abu-Bakr ﷺ, he narrates from Shaykh Abu al-Qāsim Riḍwān b. Muḥammad b. al-Ḥasan al-Dīnawarī ﷺ; who declared that he had heard from Shaykh Aḥmad b. Muḥammad b. ʿAbdullāh Nishapūrī ﷺ; who had heard from Shaykh Abu-Bakr Muḥammad b. Aḥmad b. ʿAbd al-Wah'hāb Ḥāfiz ﷺ; who had heard from Shaykh Abu-ʿAbdullāh Muḥammad b. Seem ﷺ; who had heard Shaykh Abu-Ḥamza al-Damishqī ﷺ state that when he was cast out from the well, he read the following verses:

نَهَانِي حَيَائِيْ مِنْكَ اَنْ اَكْشِفَ الْهَوىٰ   وَ اَغْنَيْتَنِيْ بِالْقُرْبِ مِنْكَ عَنِ الْكَشْفِ

Modesty forbade me to expose Your love and due to closeness, You have made me careless of exposing love.

تَرَا أَيتَ لِيْ بِالْغَيْبِ حَتّٰى كَاَنَّمَا   تُبَشِّرُنِيْ بِالْغَيْبِ اِنَّكَ فِي الْكَفِّ

I saw myself until as if You were giving me glad tidings in the unseen that You are in the palm [close].

اَرَاكَ وَبِيْ مِنْ هَيْبَتِيْ مِنْكَ وَحْشَةٌ   فَتُوْنِسُنِيْ بِالْعَطْفِ مِنْكَ وَبِاللُّطْفِ

I see You in such a condition that I am fearful of Your awe and then You are kind and compassionate on me.

وَيُحْيِيْ مُحِبٌّ اَنْتَ فِي الْحُبِّ حَتْفُهُ   وَذَا عَجَبٌ كَوْنُ الْحَيَاةِ مَعَ الْحَتْفِ

That lover is alive in love whom You gave death and it is surprising that life and death are together.

Along with the same chain of narrators, till Shaykh Khatīb ﷺ; he narrates in Rayy from Shaykh Abu-ʿAlī ʿAbd al-Raḥmān b. Muḥammad b. Aḥmad b. Fiḍālah al-Nishapūrī ﷺ; who proclaims that he had heard in Simnān from Shaykh Abu-Jaʿāfar b. Aḥmad b. al-Ḥasan b. Azdī al-Khatīb ﷺ; and he had heard from Shaykh Jaʿāfar b. Muḥammad al-Khaldī ﷺ, who affirmed that a group of *Mashā'ikh* departed from their homes to welcome Shaykh Abu-Ḥamza ﷺ. When he came from Makkah al-Mukarramah, his complexion changed, Shaykh Ḥarīrī ﷺ then commented: *'O my son! When qualities change, do secrets also change?'* He replied: *'Allāh ﷻ forbid! When secrets change the qualities change, but when the qualities change, the world will perish; but the secrets will remain tranquil. It protects it, and turns away from qualities and makes it non-existent.'* The Shaykh ﷺ then took leave of us; shrieking, whilst he recited the following couplets:

كَمَا تَرىٰ صَيَّرَنِي قَطعُ قِفَارِ الزَّمَنِ   شَرَّدَنِي عَنْ وَطَنِي كَأَنَّنِي لَمْ أكُنْ

As you see He has made me, the field of the era detached me from my country as if I did not exist.

إِذَا تَغَيَّبْتَ بُدّاً وَإِنْ بَدَا غَيَّبْنِي   يَقُولُ لَاتَشْهَدْ مَا تَشْهَدُ أَوْ تُشْهِدُنِي

When I disappeared, I became exposed and if I was exposed then I would have been made non-existent. He says, do not observe me who does or observe me.

End of Volume One

Notes

ـشِرٌ رَشِیدٌ مَشْهُودٌ بَشِیرٌ نَذِیرٌ

نَاهٍ رَسُوْلٌ نَبِیٌّ اُمِّیٌّ تِهَامِیٌّ

ـہٗ مُجْتَبٰی طٰسٓ مُرْتَضٰی حٰمٓ مُصْطَفٰی

ـعَزِیْزٌ عَلَیْهِ مَا عَنِتُّمْ
ـرَءُوْفٌ رَّحِیْمٌ

مُدَّثِّرٌ مَتِیْنٌ مُصَدِّقٌ طَیِّبٌ

اٰمِرٌ حِجَازِیٌّ نِزَارِیٌّ

ـالْكَوْنَیْنِ صَلَّی اللّٰهُ عَلَیْهِ وَاٰلِهٖ وَسَلَّمَ

حَافِظٌ كَامِلٌ صَادِقٌ

حَبِیْبُ اللّٰهِ نَجِیُّ اللّٰهِ صَفِیُّ اللّٰهِ

حَامِدٌ مُقْتَصِدٌ رَسُوْلُ الرَّحْمَةِ قَوِیٌّ حَفِیٌّ

ـلٌ اٰخِرٌ ظَاهِرٌ بَاطِنٌ نَبِیُّ الرَّحْمَةِ یَتِیْمٌ

مُحَرَّمٌ مُكَرَّمٌ مُبَشِّرٌ مُذَكِّرٌ مُطَهَّرٌ

ـلٌ شَهِیْرٌ شَهِیْدٌ رَسُوْلُ الْمَلَاحِمِ صَدَقَ اللّٰهُ الْعَظِیْمُ

مَحۡمُوۡدٌ قَاسِمٌ عَاقِبٌ فَاتِحٌ شَا

دَاعٍ شَافٍ هَادٍ مَهۡدٍ مَاحٍ

هَاشِمِيٌّ اَبۡطَحِيٌّ عَزِيۡزٌ حَرِيۡصٌ عَلَيۡكُمۡ رَءُوۡفٌ رَحِ

يٰسٓ اَوۡلٰى مُزَّمِّلٌ وَلِيٌّ

لَقَدۡ جَآءَكُمۡ رَسُوۡلٌ مِّ
حَرِيۡصٌ عَلَيۡكُ

نَاصِرٌ مَنۡصُوۡرٌ مِصۡبَاحٌ

قَرَشِيٌّ مُضَرِيٌّ نَبِيُّ التَّوۡبَةِ

اَسۡمَاءُ سَ

اَمِيۡنٌ عَبۡدُاللّٰهِ كَلِيۡمُ اللّٰهِ

مُحَمَّدٌ

خَاتَمُ الۡاَنۡبِيَآءِ حَسِيۡبٌ مُجِيۡبٌ شَكُوۡرٌ

مَأۡمُوۡنٌ مَعۡلُوۡمٌ حَقٌّ مُبِيۡنٌ مُطِيۡعٌ رَسُ الرَّ

كَرِيۡمٌ حَكِيۡمٌ خَاتَمُ الرُّسُلِ سَيِّدٌ سِرَاجٌ

قَرِيۡبٌ خَلِيۡلٌ مَدۡعُوٌّ جَوَّادٌ خَا

لا إله إلا الله محمد رسول الله